PEARSON

ALWAYS LEARNING

R. Glenn Hubbard • Anthony Patrick O'Brien

Macroeconomics
for Professor Paul Graf's ECON 202

Seventh Custom Edition for Indiana University

Taken from:
Macroeconomics, Sixth Edition
by R. Glenn Hubbard and Anthony Patrick O'Brien

Cover Art: Courtesy of Pearson Learning Solutions.

Taken from:

Macroeconomics, Sixth Edition
by R. Glenn Hubbard and Anthony Patrick O'Brien
Copyright © 2017 by Pearson Education, Inc.
New York, NY 10013

This special edition published in cooperation with Pearson Education, Inc.

All trademarks, service marks, registered trademarks, and registered service marks are the property of their respective owners and are used herein for identification purposes only.

Pearson Education, Inc., 330 Hudson Street, New York, New York 10013
A Pearson Education Company
www.pearsoned.com

Printed in the United States of America

1 16

000200010272048696

NH

ISBN 10: 1-323-46038-1
ISBN 13: 978-1-323-46038-2

CONTENTS

Glenn Hubbard, policymaker, professor, and researcher.
R. Glenn Hubbard is the dean and Russell L. Carson Professor
of Finance and Economics in the Graduate School of Business at
Columbia University and professor of economics in Columbia's
Faculty of Arts and Sciences. He is also a research associate of the
National Bureau of Economic Research and a director of Automatic
Data Processing, Black Rock Closed-End Funds, and MetLife.
He received his Ph.D. in economics from Harvard University in
1983. From 2001 to 2003, he served as chairman of the White
House Council of Economic Advisers and chairman of the OECD

Economic Policy Committee, and from 1991 to 1993, he was deputy assistant secretary of
the U.S. Treasury Department. He currently serves as co-chair of the nonpartisan Committee
on Capital Markets Regulation. Hubbard's fields of specialization are public economics,
financial markets and institutions, corporate finance, macroeconomics, industrial
organization, and public policy. He is the author of more than 100 articles in leading journals,
including *American Economic Review, Brookings Papers on Economic Activity, Journal of Finance,
Journal of Financial Economics, Journal of Money, Credit, and Banking, Journal of Political Economy,
Journal of Public Economics, Quarterly Journal of Economics, RAND Journal of Economics*, and *Review of
Economics and Statistics*. His research has been supported by grants from the National Science
Foundation, the National Bureau of Economic Research, and numerous private foundations.

Tony O'Brien, award-winning professor and researcher.
Anthony Patrick O'Brien is a professor of economics at Lehigh
University. He received his Ph.D. from the University of California,
Berkeley, in 1987. He has taught principles of economics for more
than 20 years, in both large sections and small honors classes. He
received the Lehigh University Award for Distinguished Teaching.
He was formerly the director of the Diamond Center for Economic
Education and was named a Dana Foundation Faculty Fellow
and Lehigh Class of 1961 Professor of Economics. He has been a
visiting professor at the University of California, Santa Barbara,
and the Graduate School of Industrial Administration at Carnegie

Mellon University. O'Brien's research has dealt with issues such as the evolution of the U.S.
automobile industry, the sources of U.S. economic competitiveness, the development of
U.S. trade policy, the causes of the Great Depression, and the causes of black–white income
differences. His research has been published in leading journals, including *American Economic
Review, Quarterly Journal of Economics, Journal of Money, Credit, and Banking, Industrial Relations,
Journal of Economic History*, and *Explorations in Economic History*. His research has been supported
by grants from government agencies and private foundations.

Unemployment

Module Outline and Learning Objectives

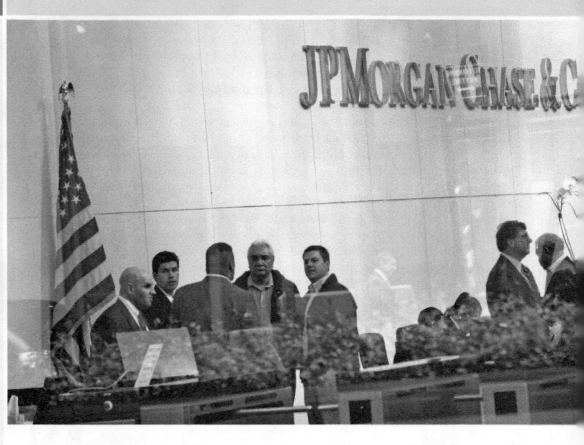

Why Is JPMorgan Chase Laying Off Workers?

When we study macroeconomics, we are looking at the big picture: total production, total employment, and the price level. But the big picture is made up of millions of individual consumers, workers, and firms. Many workers lost their jobs during the severe 2007–2009 recession, and many firms suffered sharp declines in sales. The banking industry was hit particularly hard by the recession. JPMorgan Chase, headquartered in New York City, is the largest bank in the United States and employs more than 240,000 people. The bank was founded in the early twentieth century by legendary financier J.P. Morgan. The bank saw its profit decline by two-thirds from 2007 to 2008 as the U.S. financial system experienced its worst crisis since the Great Depression of the 1930s. By 2009, the U.S. unemployment rate had risen to 10 percent for only the second time since the 1930s.

By 2015, both the U.S. economy and JPMorgan were well into a recovery from the recession. But banks were still struggling for three key reasons: First, interest rates throughout the economy remained at very low levels, reducing banks' profits by narrowing the difference between the interest rates banks paid customers on checking and saving deposits and the interest rates that banks were able to charge on loans to households and firms. Second, large banks were also dealing with increased federal regulation that caused some to stop certain activities, which in the case of JPMorgan included making student loans. Finally, banks were dealing with technological change as more banking activity, including depositing checks and applying for loans, was taking place online. In May 2015, JPMorgan announced that it would lay off 5,000 employees, with each bank branch losing an average of two tellers. The three other largest U.S. banks—Bank of America, Citigroup, and Wells Fargo—were also laying off workers for similar reasons.

The national unemployment rate, which had remained stubbornly high for several years after the 2007–2009 recession ended, had finally reached more normal levels by 2015. Many economists, though, were concerned that wages were increasing only slowly and that the fraction of people who either had jobs or were actively looking for them was at the lowest level in many years.

In this module, we will focus on measuring changes in unemployment as well as changes in the price level, or inflation. Because both unemployment and inflation are major macroeconomic problems, it is important to understand how these variables are measured.

Sources: Emily Glazer, "J.P. Morgan Aims to Cut 5,000 Jobs," *Wall Street Journal*, May 28, 2015; Ryan Tracy, Victoria McGrane, and Justin Baer, "Fed Lifts Capital Requirements for Banks," *Wall Street Journal*, July 20, 2015; Eric Morath, "Jobs at a Crossroads: Hiring Up, Pay Flat," *Wall Street Journal*, July 2, 2015; and Rachel Louise Ensign and Lisa Beilfuss, "U.S. Bancorp Says Pressure from Low Rates Looks to Ease," *Wall Street Journal*, July 15, 2015.

Economics in Your Life

Should You Change Your Career Plans if You Graduate during a Recession?

Suppose that you are a sophomore majoring in either economics or finance. You plan to find a job in the banking industry after graduation. The economy is now in a deep recession, and the unemployment rate is the highest in your lifetime, at more than 10 percent. Sizable layoffs have occurred in the banking industry. Should you change your major? Should you still consider a job in the banking industry? As you read this module, try to answer these questions.

nemployment and inflation are the macroeconomic problems that are most often discussed in the media and during political campaigns. For many people, the state of the economy can be summarized in just two measures: the unemployment rate and the inflation rate. In the 1960s, Arthur Okun, who was chairman of the Council of Economic Advisers during President Lyndon Johnson's administration, coined the term *misery index*, which adds together the inflation rate and the unemployment rate to give a rough measure of the state of the economy. As we will see in later modules, although unemployment and inflation are important problems in the short run, the long-run success of an economy is best judged by its ability to generate high levels of real GDP per person. We devote this module to discussing how the government measures the unemployment and inflation rates. In particular, we will look closely at the statistics on unemployment and inflation that the federal government issues each month.

1.1 Measuring the Unemployment Rate, the Labor Force Participation Rate, and the Employment–Population Ratio

LEARNING OBJECTIVE: Define the unemployment rate, the labor force participation rate, and the employment-population ratio and understand how they are computed.

At 8:30 A.M. on a Friday early in each month, the U.S. Department of Labor reports its estimate of the previous month's unemployment rate. If the unemployment rate is higher or lower than expected, investors are likely to change their views on the health of the economy. The result is seen an hour later, when trading begins on the New York Stock Exchange. Good news about unemployment usually causes stock prices to rise, and bad news causes stock prices to fall. The unemployment rate can also have important political implications. In most presidential elections, the incumbent president is reelected if the unemployment rate is falling early in the election year but is defeated if the unemployment rate is rising. This relationship held true in 2012, when the unemployment rate was lower during the first six months of 2012 than it had been during the last six months of 2011, and incumbent Barack Obama was reelected.

The unemployment rate is a key macroeconomic statistic. But how does the Department of Labor prepare its estimates of the unemployment rate, and how accurate are these estimates? We will explore the answers to these questions in this section.

The Household Survey

Each month, the U.S. Bureau of the Census conducts the *Current Population Survey* (often called the *household survey*) to collect data needed to compute the unemployment rate. The bureau interviews adults in a sample of 60,000 households, chosen to represent the U.S. population, about the employment status of everyone in the household 16 years of age and older. The Department of Labor's Bureau of Labor Statistics (BLS) uses these data to calculate the monthly unemployment rate. People are considered:

Employed In government statistics, someone who currently has a job or who is temporarily away from his or her job.

- **Employed** if they worked during the week before the survey or if they were temporarily away from their jobs because they were ill, on vacation, on strike, or for other reasons.

Unemployed In government statistics, someone who is not currently at work but who is available for work and who has actively looked for work during the previous month.

- **Unemployed** if they did not work in the previous week but were available for work and had actively looked for work at some time during the previous four weeks.

The **labor force** is the sum of the *employed* and the *unemployed*. The **unemployment rate** is the percentage of the labor force that is unemployed.

Labor force The sum of employed and unemployed workers in the economy.

The BLS classifies the following groups of people who do not have a job and who are not actively looking for a job as *not in the labor force*:

Unemployment rate The percentage of the labor force that is unemployed.

- Retirees, homemakers, full-time students, and those on active military service, in prison, or in hospitals.

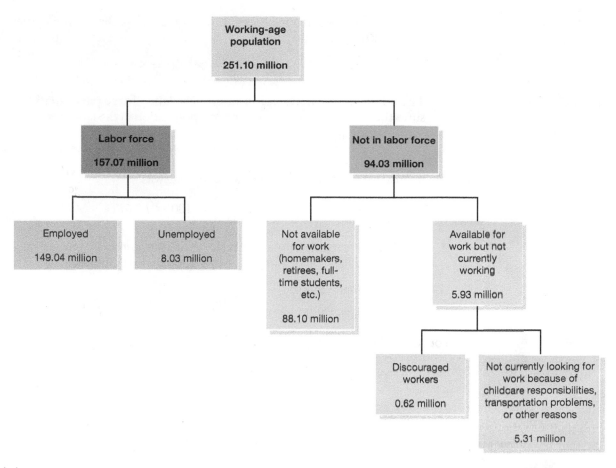

MyEconLab Animation

Figure 1.1 **The Employment Status of the Civilian Working-Age Population, August 2015**

In August 2015, the working-age population of the United States was 251.10 million. The working-age population is divided into those in the labor force (157.07 million) and those not in the labor force (94.03 million). The labor force is divided into the employed (149.04 million) and the unemployed (8.03 million). Those not in the labor force are divided into those not available for work (88.10 million) and those available for work but not

currently working (5.93 million). Finally, those available for work but not in the labor force are divided into discouraged workers (0.62 million) and those not currently looking for work for other reasons (5.31 million).

Source: U.S. Department of Labor, Bureau of Labor Statistics, *The Employment Situation—August 2015*, September 4, 2015.

- People who are available for work and who have actively looked for a job at some point during the previous 12 months but have not looked during the previous 4 weeks. Some people are not actively looking for work for reasons such as transportation difficulties or childcare responsibilities.

- People who are available for work but have *not* actively looked for a job during the previous four weeks because they believe no jobs are available for them. These people are labeled **discouraged workers**.

Figure 1.1 shows the employment status of the civilian working-age population in August 2015.

We can use the information in the figure to calculate three important macroeconomic indicators:

- **The unemployment rate.** The unemployment rate measures the percentage of the labor force that is unemployed:

$$\frac{\text{Number of unemployed}}{\text{Labor force}} \times 100 = \text{Unemployment rate.}$$

Discouraged workers People who are available for work but have not looked for a job during the previous four weeks because they believe no jobs are available for them.

Using the numbers from Figure 1.1, we can calculate the unemployment rate for August 2015:

$$\frac{8.03 \text{ million}}{157.07 \text{ million}} \times 100 = 5.1\%.$$

Labor force participation rate The percentage of the working-age population in the labor force.

- **The labor force participation rate.** The **labor force participation rate** measures the percentage of the working-age population in the labor force:

$$\frac{\text{Labor force}}{\text{Working-age population}} \times 100 = \text{Labor force participation rate.}$$

For August 2015, the labor force participation rate was:

$$\frac{157.07 \text{ million}}{251.10 \text{ million}} \times 100 = 62.6\%.$$

- **The employment–population ratio.** The *employment–population ratio* measures the percentage of the working-age population that is employed:

$$\frac{\text{Employment}}{\text{Working-age population}} \times 100 = \text{Employment} - \text{population ratio.}$$

For August 2015, the employment–population ratio was:

$$\frac{149.04 \text{ million}}{251.10 \text{ million}} \times 100 = 59.3\%. \quad \text{MyEconLab Concept Check}$$

Solved Problem 1.1

MyEconLab Interactive Animation

What Happens if the BLS Includes the Military?

In the BLS household survey, people on active military service are not included in the totals for employment, the labor force, or the working-age population. Suppose the BLS included the military in these categories. How would the unemployment rate, the labor force participation rate, and the employment–population ratio change?

Solving the Problem

Step 1: **Review the module material.** This problem is about calculating the unemployment rate, the labor force participation rate, and the employment–population ratio, so you may want to review the section "Measuring the Unemployment Rate, the Labor Force Participation Rate, and the Employment–Population Ratio," which begins on page 4.

Step 2: **Show that including people in the military decreases the measured unemployment rate.** The unemployment rate is calculated as:

$$\frac{\text{Number of unemployed}}{\text{Labor force}} \times 100.$$

Including people in the military would increase the number of people counted as being in the labor force but would leave unchanged the number of people counted as unemployed. Therefore, the unemployment rate would decrease.

Step 3: **Show how including people in the military would affect the measured labor force participation rate and the measured employment–population ratio.** The labor force participation rate is calculated as:

$$\frac{\text{Labor force}}{\text{Working-age population}} \times 100,$$

and the employment–population ratio is calculated as:

$$\frac{\text{Employment}}{\text{Working-age population}} \times 100.$$

Including people in the military would increase the number of people in the labor force, the number of people employed, and the number of people in the working-age population, all by the same amount. The labor force participation rate and the employment–population ratio would both increase because adding the same number to both the numerator and the denominator of a fraction that is less than one increases the value of the fraction.

To help see this point, consider the following simple example. Suppose that 100,000,000 people are in the working-age population and 50,000,000 are in the labor force, not counting people in the military. Suppose that 1,000,000 people are in the military. Then, the labor force participation rate excluding the military is:

$$\frac{50,000,000}{100,000,000} \times 100 = 50\%,$$

and the labor force participation rate including the military is:

$$\frac{51,000,000}{101,000,000} \times 100 = 50.5\%.$$

A similar calculation shows that including the military would also increase the employment–population ratio.

Your Turn: For more practice, do related problem 1.8 on page 19 at the end of this module.   MyEconLab Study Plan

Problems with Measuring the Unemployment Rate

Although the BLS reports the unemployment rate measured to the tenth of a percentage point, it is not a perfect measure of the actual state of joblessness in the economy. One problem that the BLS confronts is distinguishing between the unemployed and people who are not in the labor force. During an economic recession, for example, an increase in discouraged workers usually occurs, as people who have had trouble finding a job stop actively looking. Because these workers are not counted as unemployed, the unemployment rate as measured by the BLS may understate the true degree of joblessness in the economy. The BLS also counts people as being employed if they hold part-time jobs even though they would prefer to hold full-time jobs. In a recession, counting as "employed" a part-time worker who wants to work full time understates the degree of joblessness in the economy and makes the employment situation appear better than it is.

Not counting discouraged workers as unemployed and counting people as employed who are working part time, although they would prefer to be working full time, has a substantial effect on the measured unemployment rate. In Figure 1.2, the red line shows the official measure of the unemployment rate. The blue line shows what the unemployment rate would be if the BLS had counted as unemployed (1) all people who were available for work but not actively looking for jobs, and (2) all people who were in part-time jobs but wanted full-time jobs. The difference between the two measures of the unemployment rate is substantial and was particularly large during the slow recovery following the 2007–2009 recession. For example, in August 2015, using the broader definition of unemployment would have increased the measured unemployment rate from 5.1 percent to 10.3 percent.

There are other measurement problems, however, that cause the measured unemployment rate to *overstate* the true extent of joblessness. These problems arise because the BLS does not verify the responses of people included in the survey. Some people who claim to be unemployed and actively looking for work may not really be actively looking. A person might claim to be actively looking for a job in order to remain eligible for government payments to the unemployed. In this case, a person who is actually not in the labor force is counted as unemployed. Other people might be employed but

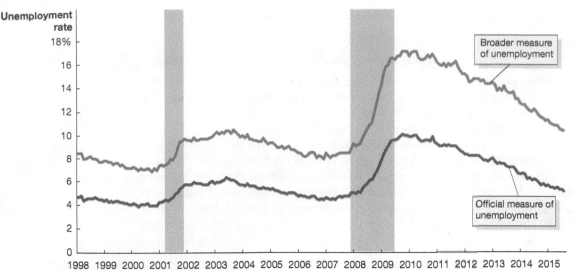

Figure 1.2   **The Official Unemployment Rate and a Broad Measure of the Unemployment Rate, 1998–2015**

The red line shows the official measure of the unemployment rate. The blue line shows what the unemployment rate would be if the BLS had counted as unemployed (1) all people who were available for work but not actively looking for jobs, and (2) all people who were in part-time jobs but wanted full-time jobs. The difference between the measures was particularly large

during the 2007–2009 recession and the weak recovery that followed. Shaded areas indicate months of recession.

Note: The official measure (red line) is BLS series U-3, and the broader measure (blue line) is BLS series U-6.
Source: U.S. Bureau of Labor Statistics.

engaged in illegal activity—such as drug dealing—or might want to conceal a legitimate job to avoid paying taxes. In these cases, individuals who are actually employed are counted as unemployed. These inaccurate responses to the survey bias the unemployment rate as measured by the BLS toward overstating the true extent of joblessness. We can conclude that, although the unemployment rate provides some useful information about the employment situation in the country, it is far from an exact measure of joblessness in the economy.   MyEconLab Concept Check

Trends in Labor Force Participation

The labor force participation rate is important because it determines the amount of labor that will be available to the economy from a given population. The higher the labor force participation rate, the more labor that will be available and the higher a country's levels of GDP and GDP per person. Figure 1.3 highlights two important trends in the

Figure 1.3

Trends in the Labor Force: Participation Rates of Adult Men and Women since 1948

The labor force participation rate of adult men has declined gradually since 1948, but the labor force participation rate of adult women has increased significantly, making the overall labor force participation rate higher today than it was in 1948.
Source: U.S. Bureau of Labor Statistics.

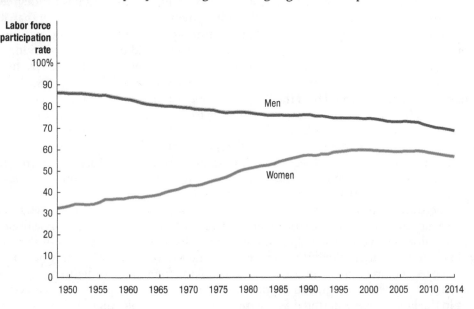

labor force participation rates of adults aged 16 years and over in the United States since 1948: the falling labor force participation rate of adult men and the rising labor force participation rate of adult women. (Note, though, that by 2014, the labor force participation rate of women had not yet fully recovered from the effects of the recession.)

The labor force participation rate of adult males fell from 87 percent in 1948 to 69 percent in 2014. Most of this decline is due to older men retiring earlier and younger men remaining in school longer. There has also been a decline in labor force participation among males who are not in school but who are too young to retire. Over the longer term, this decline in labor force participation among prime-age males appears to be partly due to Congress having made it easier for people to receive cash payments under the Social Security Disability Insurance program. In the shorter term, the decline is due to the severity of the 2007–2009 recession and the weak recovery that followed the recession.

The decline in the labor force participation rate of adult men has been more than offset by a sharp increase in the labor force participation rate of adult women, which rose from 33 percent in 1948 to 57 percent in 2014. As a result, the overall labor force participation rate rose from 59 percent in 1948 to 63 percent in 2014. The increase in the labor force participation rate of women has several causes, including changing social attitudes due in part to the women's movement, federal legislation outlawing discrimination, increasing wages for women, the typical family having fewer children, and an increase in female-headed households.   MyEconLab Concept Check

Unemployment Rates for Different Groups

Different groups in the population can have very different unemployment rates. Figure 1.4 shows unemployment rates in August 2015 for different ethnic groups and for groups with different levels of education. While the overall unemployment rate was 5.1 percent, Asians had an unemployment rate of 3.5 percent, and African Americans had an unemployment rate of 9.5 percent. The unemployment rate for people over age 25 without a high school degree was 7.7 percent, while the unemployment rate for college graduates was only 2.5 percent.   MyEconLab Concept Check

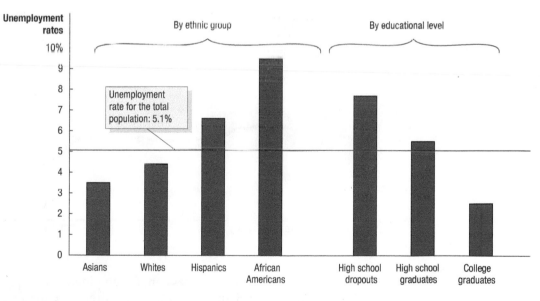

MyEconLab Real-time data

Figure 1.4   Unemployment Rates in the United States, August 2015

The unemployment rate of African Americans is the highest of the four ethnic groups shown, while the unemployment rate of Asians is the lowest. High school dropouts have an unemployment rate that is triple the unemployment rate for college graduates.

Notes: The unemployment rates for ethnic groups apply to people 16 years and older; the unemployment rates by educational attainment apply to people 25 years and older. People identified as Hispanic may be of any race.
Source: U.S. Department of Labor, Bureau of Labor Statistics, *The Employment Situation—August 2015*, September 4, 2015.

How Long Are People Typically Unemployed?

The longer a person is unemployed, the greater the hardship. During the Great Depression of the 1930s, some people were unemployed for years at a time. In the modern U.S. economy, a typical unemployed person stays unemployed for a relatively brief period of time, although that time lengthens significantly during a severe recession. For example, when the economy was expanding in early 2007, fewer than 20 percent of the unemployed had been jobless for more than six months. By the end of the 2007–2009 recession, though, half of the unemployed had been jobless for more than six months. The average period of unemployment had more than doubled from about 4 months to about 10 months. The severity of unemployment during and after the 2007–2009 recession was a sharp break with the normal U.S. experience in which the typical person who loses a job will find another one or be recalled to a previous job within a few months.   MyEconLab Concept Check

Making the Connection

Eight Million Workers Are Missing!

Although the unemployment rate is the most widely followed measure of the state of the labor market, during the recovery from the 2007–2009 recession, many economists and policymakers became concerned about the employment–population ratio. As we saw earlier, the employment–population ratio measures the percentage of the working-age population that is employed. Figure 1.2 on page 8 shows that by mid-2015, the unemployment rate had fallen from its high of 10 percent in 2009 to 5.1 percent, or to roughly normal levels. But the red line in the figure below shows that the employment–population ratio did not recover completely from its decline during the 2007–2009 recession.

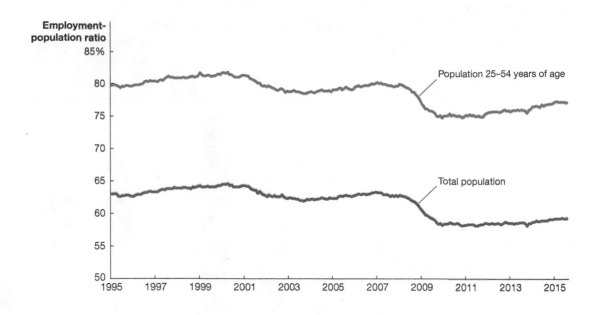

In 2006, before the start of the recession, the employment–population ratio was 63.4 percent. In August 2015, more than six years after the end of the recession, the ratio was still only 59.4 percent. If the employment–population had regained its pre-recession level, an additional 8 million people would have been working in 2015 than actually were. With 8 million additional workers, GDP would have been significantly larger than it was.

Why hasn't the employment–population ratio returned to its pre-recession levels? Part of the explanation is that as the baby boom generation—people born between the years 1946 and 1964—has gotten older, the average age of the population has increased. People in their late 50s and early 60s are less likely to have jobs than are younger people. This fact is illustrated by the blue line, which shows the employment–population ratio just for people aged 25 to 54—the age range in which people are most likely to be working. The employment–population ratio for this age range declined by about 3 percentage points between 2006 and 2015, or about one-fourth less than the decline in employment–population ratio for the whole working-age population. Economists have not reached a consensus in explaining the remainder of the decline in the employment–population ratio. Some economists note that not only did many people lose their jobs during the recession, but the slow recovery from the recession meant that some people were out of work for years. Often people who have not held a job for a long period have difficulty finding a new one because their skills deteriorate and employers therefore become more reluctant to hire them. This "labor-market scarring" may help explain some of the decline in the employment–population ratio. Other economists point to the increased number of people who receive Social Security Disability Insurance. Under this program, people with disabilities receive cash payments from the federal government and receive medical benefits under the Medicaid program. Some people who might otherwise be working are being supported by disability payments instead.

Economists at the Congressional Budget Office (CBO) estimate that the Affordable Care Act, which provides subsidies to buy medical insurance and expands Medicare coverage, has resulted in a decline in employment. According to a CBO report, as a result of the act, "some people will decide not to work or to work fewer hours than would otherwise be the case—including some people who will choose to retire earlier than they would have otherwise, and some people who will work less themselves and rely more on a spouse's earnings."

Economists Jeffrey Clemens and Michael Wither of the University of California, San Diego, have analyzed the effects of the increase in the federal minimum wage from $5.15 an hour in 2007 to $7.25 an hour in 2009. They find that by making it more difficult for low-skilled workers to find jobs, the increase in the minimum wage reduced the employment–population ratio. They estimate that this effect accounts for about 14 percent of the total decline in the ratio.

Finally, new businesses are being started at lower rates than in past years and barriers to entering certain occupations have increased as some states have imposed additional licensing requirements. Difficulties in starting new businesses mean that some people who would otherwise be self-employed as small business owners may have left the labor force instead.

As we will see in later modules, economic growth in the United States has slowed in recent years. Many economists believe that one key to increasing growth and living standards is for the government to develop policies that will help to reverse the decline in the employment–population ratio.

Sources: Josh Zumbrun, "Labor-Market Dropouts Stay on the Sidelines," *Wall Street Journal*, December 28, 2014; Doug Elmendorf, "Frequently Asked Questions about CBO's Estimates of the Labor Market Effects of the Affordable Care Act," cbo.gov, February 10, 2014; Jeffrey Clemens and Michael Wither, "The Minimum Wage and the Great Recession: Evidence of Effects on the Employment and Income Trajectories of Low-Skilled Workers," Working Paper, University of California, San Diego, November 24, 2014; Janet L. Yellen, "Labor Market Dynamics and Monetary Policy," Speech at the Federal Reserve Bank of Kansas City Economic Symposium, Jackson Hole, Wyoming, August 22, 2014; Samuel Kapon and Joseph Tracy, "A Mis-Leading Labor Market Indicator," libertystreeteconomics.nyfed.org, February 3, 2014; and U.S. Bureau of Labor Statistics.

Your Turn: Test your understanding by doing related problem 1.10 on page 20 at the end of this module.

MyEconLab Study Plan

The Establishment Survey: Another Measure of Employment

In addition to the household survey, the BLS uses the *establishment survey*, sometimes called the *payroll survey*, to measure total employment in the economy. This monthly survey samples about 300,000 business establishments (such as factories, stores, and offices). A small company typically operates only one establishment, but a large company may operate many establishments. The establishment survey provides

TABLE 1.1   Household and Establishment Survey Data for July and August 2015   MyEconLab Real-time data

	Household Survey			Establishment Survey		
	July	August	Change	July	August	Change
Employed	148,840,000	149,036,000	196,000	142,115,000	142,288,000	173,000
Unemployed	8,266,000	8,029,000	−237,000			
Labor force	157,106,000	157,065,000	−41,000			
Unemployment rate	5.3%	5.1%	−0.2%			

Source: U.S. Department of Labor, Bureau of Labor Statistics, *The Employment Situation—August 2015*, September 4, 2015.

information on the total number of persons who are employed and *on a company payroll.* The establishment survey has four drawbacks:

1. The survey does not provide information on the number of self-employed persons because they are not on a company payroll.

2. The survey may fail to count some persons employed at newly opened firms that are not included in the survey.

3. The survey provides no information on unemployment.

4. The values for employment that the BLS initially announces can be significantly revised as data from additional establishments become available.

Despite these drawbacks, the establishment survey has the advantage of being determined by actual payrolls rather than by unverified answers, as is the case with the household survey. As a result, many economists rely more on establishment survey data than on household survey data in analyzing current labor market conditions. Some financial analysts who forecast the future state of the economy to help forecast stock prices also rely more on establishment survey data than on household survey data.

Table 1.1 shows household survey and establishment survey data for the months of July and August 2015. Notice that the household survey, because it includes the self-employed, gives a larger total for employment than does the establishment survey. The household survey provides information on the number of persons unemployed and on the number of persons in the labor force. This information is not available in the establishment survey. Between July and August 2015, employment rose by 196,000 in the household survey, but rose by only 173,000 in the establishment survey. This discrepancy is due partly to the slightly different groups covered by the two surveys and partly to inaccuracies in the surveys.   MyEconLab Concept Check

Revisions in the Establishment Survey Employment Data: How Bad Was the 2007–2009 Recession?

Economists and policymakers rely on government economic data, such as the employment data from the establishment survey, to understand the current state of the economy. Given the size of the U.S. economy, though, government agencies, such as the Bureau of Economic Analysis, the Bureau of Labor Statistics, and the Census Bureau, need considerable time to gather complete and accurate data on GDP, employment, and other macroeconomic variables. To avoid long waits in supplying data to policymakers and the general public, government agencies typically issue preliminary estimates that they revise as additional information becomes available. As we noted earlier, the data on employment from the establishment survey can be subject to particularly large revisions over time.

Figure 1.5 shows for each month from December 2007 to December 2010 the difference between the value for the change in employment as initially reported in the establishment survey and the revised value available in September 2015. The green bars show months for which the BLS revised its preliminary estimates to show that fewer jobs were lost (or more jobs were created) than originally reported, and the red bars show months for which the BLS revised its preliminary estimates to show that more jobs were lost (or fewer jobs were created). For example, the BLS initially reported that

MyEconLab Animation

Figure 1.5

Revisions to Employment Changes, as Reported in the Establishment Survey, 2007–2010

Over time, the BLS revises its preliminary estimates of changes in employment. During the 2007–2009 recession, many more jobs were lost than the preliminary estimates showed. The green bars show months for which the BLS revised its preliminary estimates to show fewer jobs were lost (or more jobs were created), and the red bars show months for which the BLS revised its preliminary estimates to show more jobs were lost (or fewer jobs were created).

Source: U.S. Bureau of Labor Statistics.

employment declined by 159,000 jobs during September 2008. In fact, after additional data became available, the BLS revised its estimate to show that employment had declined by 452,000 jobs during the month—a difference of nearly 300,000 more jobs lost. As the recession deepened between April 2008 and April 2009, the BLS's initial reports underestimated the number of jobs lost by 2.3 million. In other words, the recession of 2007–2009 turned out to be much more severe than economists and policymakers realized at the time.   MyEconLab Concept Check

Job Creation and Job Destruction over Time

One important fact about employment is not very well known: The U.S. economy creates and destroys millions of jobs every year. In 2014, for example, about 29.1 million jobs were created, and about 26.1 million jobs were destroyed. This degree of job creation and destruction is not surprising in a vibrant market system where new firms are constantly being started, some existing firms are expanding, some existing firms are contracting, and some firms are going out of business. The creation and destruction of jobs results from changes in consumer tastes, technological progress, and the successes and failures of entrepreneurs in responding to the opportunities and challenges of shifting consumer tastes and technological change. The large volume of job creation and job destruction helps explain why during most years, the typical person who loses a job is unemployed for a relatively brief period of time.

When the BLS announces each month the increases or decreases in the number of persons employed and unemployed, these are net *figures.* That is, the change in the number of persons employed is equal to the total number of jobs created minus the number of jobs eliminated. Take, for example, the months from September to December 2014. During that period, 7,635,000 jobs were created, and 6,526,000 jobs were eliminated, for a net increase of 1,109,000 jobs. Because the net change is so much smaller than the total job increases and decreases, the net change doesn't fully represent how dynamic the U.S. job market really is.   MyEconLab Concept Check

MyEconLab Study Plan

1.2 Types of Unemployment

LEARNING OBJECTIVE: Identify the three types of unemployment.

Figure 1.6 illustrates that the unemployment rate follows the business cycle, rising during recessions and falling during expansions. Notice, though, that the unemployment rate never falls to zero. To understand why, we need to discuss the three types of unemployment:

1. Frictional unemployment
2. Structural unemployment
3. Cyclical unemployment

MyEconLab Real-time data

Figure 1.6

The Annual Unemployment Rate in the United States, 1950–2014

The unemployment rate rises during recessions and falls during expansions. Shaded areas indicate recessions. **Source:** U.S. Bureau of Labor Statistics.

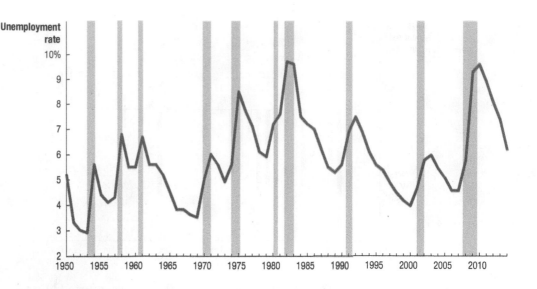

Frictional unemployment Short-term unemployment that arises from the process of matching workers with jobs.

Frictional Unemployment and Job Search

Workers have different skills, interests, and abilities, and jobs have different skill requirements, working conditions, and pay levels. As a result, a new worker entering the labor force or a worker who has lost a job probably will not find an acceptable job right away. Most workers spend at least some time in *job search*, just as most firms spend time searching for a new person to fill a job opening. **Frictional unemployment** is short-term unemployment that arises from the process of matching workers with jobs. Some frictional unemployment is unavoidable. As we have seen, the U.S. economy creates and destroys millions of jobs each year. The process of job search takes time, so there will always be some workers who are frictionally unemployed because they are between jobs and in the process of searching for new ones.

Some frictional unemployment is due to seasonal factors, such as weather or fluctuations in demand for some products or services during different times of the year. For example, stores located in beach resort areas reduce their hiring during the winter, and ski resorts reduce their hiring during the summer. Department stores increase their hiring in November and December and reduce their hiring after New Year's Day. In agricultural areas, employment increases during harvest season and declines thereafter. Construction workers in many parts of the United States experience greater unemployment during the winter than during the summer. *Seasonal unemployment* refers to unemployment due to factors such as weather, variations in tourism, and other calendar-related events. Because seasonal unemployment can make the unemployment rate seem artificially high during some months and artificially low during other months, the BLS reports two unemployment rates each month—one that is *seasonally adjusted* and one that is not seasonally adjusted. The seasonally adjusted data eliminate the effects of seasonal unemployment. Economists and policymakers rely on the seasonally adjusted data as a more accurate measure of the current state of the labor market.

Would eliminating all frictional unemployment be good for the economy? No, because some frictional unemployment actually increases economic efficiency. Frictional unemployment occurs because workers and firms take the time necessary to ensure a good match between the attributes of workers and the characteristics of jobs. By devoting time to job search, workers end up with jobs they find satisfying and in which they can be productive. Of course, having workers who are satisfied and productive is also in the best interest of firms.   MyEconLab Concept Check

Structural Unemployment

Computer-generated three-dimensional animation, which has been used in movies such as *Inside Out* and *Minions*, has become much more popular than traditional hand-drawn two-dimensional animation. As a result, many people who are highly skilled in hand-drawn animation lost their jobs at movie studios such as Walt Disney Pictures and DreamWorks. To become employed again, many of these people either became skilled in computer-generated animation or found new occupations. In the meantime, they were unemployed. Economists consider these animators *structurally unemployed*. **Structural unemployment** arises from a persistent mismatch between the job skills or attributes of workers and the requirements of jobs. While frictional unemployment is short term, structural unemployment can last for longer periods because workers need time to learn new skills. For example, employment by U.S. steel firms fell by more than half between the early 1980s and the early 2000s as a result of competition from foreign producers and technological change that substituted machines for workers. Many steelworkers found new jobs in other industries only after lengthy periods of retraining.

> **Structural unemployment**
> Unemployment that arises from a persistent mismatch between the skills or attributes of workers and the requirements of jobs.

Some workers lack even basic skills, such as literacy, or have addictions to alcohol or other drugs that make it difficult for them to perform adequately the duties of almost any job. These workers may remain structurally unemployed for long periods.   MyEconLab Concept Check

Cyclical Unemployment

When the economy moves into recession, many firms find their sales falling and cut back on production. As production falls, firms start laying off workers. Workers who lose their jobs because of a recession are experiencing **cyclical unemployment**. For example, Ford Motor Company laid off workers during the recession of 2007–2009. As the economy slowly recovered from the recession, Ford began rehiring those workers. The Ford workers who had been laid off from their jobs during the recession and then rehired during the following expansion had experienced cyclical unemployment.   MyEconLab Concept Check

> **Cyclical unemployment**
> Unemployment caused by a business cycle recession.

Full Employment

As the economy moves through the expansion phase of the business cycle, cyclical unemployment eventually drops to zero. The unemployment rate will not be zero, however, because of frictional and structural unemployment. As Figure 1.6 shows, the unemployment rate in the United States is rarely less than 4 percent. The fluctuations that we see in Figure 1.6 are mainly due to the changes in the level of cyclical unemployment. When the only remaining unemployment is structural and frictional unemployment, the economy is said to be at *full employment*.

Economists consider the sum of frictional and structural unemployment to be the normal underlying level of unemployment in the economy, or the **natural rate of unemployment**. Economists disagree on the exact value of the natural rate of unemployment, and there is good reason to believe that it doesn't remain constant over long periods of a decade or more. Currently, most economists estimate the natural rate to be between 5.0 percent and 5.5 percent. The natural rate of unemployment is also sometimes called the *full-employment rate of unemployment*.   MyEconLab Concept Check

> **Natural rate of unemployment**
> The normal rate of unemployment, consisting of frictional unemployment and structural unemployment.

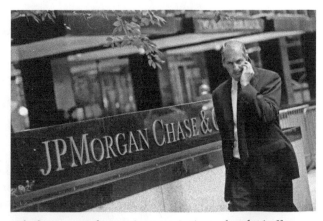

Making the Connection
MyEconLab Video

How Should We Categorize Unemployment at JPMorgan Chase?

We saw at the beginning of the module that JPMorgan Chase announced in 2015 that it was laying off 5,000 employees, with each bank branch losing on average two tellers. In addition, the bank was exiting certain lines of business, including making student loans. Did the layoffs at JPMorgan result in an increase in frictional unemployment, structural unemployment, or cyclical unemployment? In answering this question, we should acknowledge that dividing unemployment into these three categories is useful in understanding the sources of unemployment, but it can be difficult to apply these categories in a particular case.

Which category of unemployment do the workers laid off at JPMorgan Chase fit into?

The BLS, for instance, provides estimates of total unemployment but does not classify it as frictional, structural, or cyclical.

Despite these difficulties, we can roughly categorize the unemployment resulting from the layoffs at JPMorgan. At the time of the layoffs, the U.S. economy was expanding, and the demand for loans and other services the bank offered was increasing, so the unemployment at JPMorgan was not cyclical, and the firm was unlikely to rehire the workers it was laying off, even if the economic recovery became even stronger.

The decision to lay off bank tellers was the result of technological change. As more people deposit checks and make their loan payments online using smartphone apps, fewer people visit bank branches, so JPMorgan doesn't need as many bank tellers. Because other banks are affected by the same changes in technology, the laid-off bank tellers were likely to need to retrain for other jobs to find employment again. So, these workers were structurally unemployed.

As the largest U.S. bank, JPMorgan is subject to federal regulations that do not affect smaller banks. The bank was dropping some types of services, including making student loans, because new federal regulations had increased the costs facing the largest U.S. banks. So, if JPMorgan's employees who were providing these services were able to find employment with smaller banks not subject to the new regulations, during the time the employees were out of work they would have been frictionally unemployed.

It therefore seems likely that some of the unemployment at JPMorgan Chase in 2015 was structural and some was frictional. Given the state of the economy, none of it was likely cyclical.

Sources: Emily Glazer, "J.P. Morgan Aims to Cut 5,000 Jobs," *Wall Street Journal*, May 28, 2015; and Ryan Tracy, Victoria McGrane, and Justin Baer, "Fed Lifts Capital Requirements for Banks," *Wall Street Journal*, July 20, 2015.

MyEconLab Study Plan

Your Turn: Test your understanding by doing related problems 2.6, 2.7, and 2.8 on pages 20-21 at the end of this module.

Explaining Unemployment

1.3

LEARNING OBJECTIVE: Explain what factors determine the unemployment rate.

We have seen that some unemployment is a result of the business cycle. In later modules, we will explore the causes of the business cycle, which will help us understand cyclical unemployment. In this section, we look at the factors that determine the levels of frictional and structural unemployment.

Government Policies and the Unemployment Rate

Workers search for jobs by sending out résumés, registering with Internet job sites such as Monster.com, and getting job referrals from friends and relatives. Firms fill job openings by advertising in newspapers, listing openings online, participating in job fairs, and recruiting on college campuses. Here's how government policies can aid these private employment efforts:

- Governments can help reduce the level of frictional unemployment by pursuing policies that help speed up the process of matching unemployed workers with unfilled jobs.

- Governments can help reduce structural unemployment by implementing policies that aid worker retraining. For example, the federal government's Trade Adjustment Assistance program offers training to workers who lose their jobs as a result of competition from foreign firms.

Some government policies, however, can add to the level of frictional and structural unemployment. These government policies increase the unemployment rate either by increasing the time workers devote to searching for jobs, by providing disincentives for firms to hire workers, or by keeping wages above their market level.

Unemployment Insurance and Other Payments to the Unemployed

Suppose you have been in the labor force for a few years but have just lost your job. You could probably find a low-wage job immediately if you needed to—perhaps at Walmart or McDonald's. But you might decide to search for a better, higher-paying job by sending out résumés and responding to want ads and Internet job postings. Remember that the *opportunity cost* of any activity is the highest-valued alternative that you must give up to engage in that activity. In this case, the opportunity cost of continuing to search for a job is the salary you are giving up at the job you could have taken. The longer you search, the greater your chances of finding a better, higher-paying job, but the longer you search, the more salary you have given up by not working, so the greater the opportunity cost.

In the United States and most other high-income countries, the unemployed are eligible for *unemployment insurance payments* from the government. In the United States, these payments vary by state but are generally equal to about half the average wage. The unemployed spend more time searching for jobs because they receive these payments. This additional time spent searching raises the unemployment rate. Can we conclude that the unemployment insurance program is a bad idea? Most economists would say "no." Before Congress established the unemployment insurance program at the end of the 1930s, unemployed workers suffered very large declines in their incomes, which led them to greatly reduce their spending. This reduced spending contributed to the severity of recessions. Unemployment insurance helps the unemployed maintain their income and spending, which lessens the personal hardship of being unemployed and also helps reduce the severity of recessions.

In the United States, unemployed workers are generally eligible to receive unemployment insurance payments for only six months, although this period is typically extended during recessions, as happened during and after the recession of 2007–2009. After that, the opportunity cost of continuing to search for a job rises. In many other high-income countries, such as Canada and most of the countries of Western Europe, workers are eligible to receive unemployment payments for a year or more, and the payments may equal as much as 70 percent of their previous wage. In addition, many of these countries have generous *social insurance programs* that allow unemployed adults to receive some government payments even after their eligibility for unemployment insurance has ended. In the United States, very few government programs make payments to healthy adults, with the exception of the Temporary Assistance for Needy Families program, which allows single parents to receive payments for up to five years. Although there are many reasons unemployment rates may differ across countries, most economists believe that because the opportunity cost of job search is lower in Canada and the countries of Western Europe, unemployed workers in those countries search longer for jobs and, therefore, the unemployment rates in those countries tend to be higher than in the United States. During the 2007–2009 recession, however, unemployment rates were lower in Canada and Germany than in the United States.

Minimum Wage Laws In 1938, the federal government enacted a national minimum wage law. At first, the lowest legal wage firms could pay workers was $0.25 per hour. Over the years, Congress has gradually raised the minimum wage; in 2015, it was $7.25 per hour. Some states and cities also have minimum wage laws. For example, in 2015, the minimum wage in California was $9.00 per hour, and the minimum wage in San Francisco was $12.25 per hour. If the minimum wage is set above the market wage determined by the demand and supply of labor, the quantity of labor supplied will be greater than the quantity of labor demanded. Some workers will become unemployed who would have been employed if there was no minimum wage. As a result, the unemployment rate will be higher than it would be without a minimum wage. Economists agree that the current minimum wage is above the market wage for some workers, but they disagree on the amount of unemployment that has resulted. Because teenagers generally have relatively few job-related skills, they are the group most likely to receive the minimum wage. Studies estimate that a 10 percent increase in the minimum wage reduces teenage employment by about 2 percent. Because teenagers and others receiving the minimum wage are a relatively small part of the labor force, most economists believe that, at the minimum wage's current level, it has a fairly small effect on the unemployment rate in the United States.   MyEconLab Concept Check

Labor Unions

Labor unions are organizations of workers that bargain with employers for higher wages and better working conditions for their members. In unionized industries, the wage is usually above what otherwise would be the market wage. This above-market wage results in employers in unionized industries hiring fewer workers, but does it also significantly increase the overall unemployment rate in the economy? Most economists would say the answer is "no" because in the United States only about 9 percent of workers outside the government sector are unionized. Although unions remain strong in a few industries, such as airlines, automobiles, steel, and telecommunications, most industries are not unionized. The result is that most workers who can't find jobs in unionized industries because the wage is above its market level can find jobs in other industries.   MyEconLab Concept Check

Efficiency Wages

Some firms pay above-market wages not because the government requires them to or because they are unionized but because they believe doing so will increase their profits. Because wages are the largest cost for many employers, so paying higher wages seems like a good way for firms to *lower* profits rather than to increase them. The key to understanding this wage policy is that the level of wages can affect the level of workers' productivity. Many studies have shown that workers are motivated by higher wages to work harder. An **efficiency wage** is an above-market wage that a firm pays to motivate workers to be more productive. Can't firms ensure that workers work hard by supervising them? In some cases, they can. For example, a telemarketing firm can monitor workers electronically to ensure that they make the required number of phone calls per hour. In many business situations, however, it is much more difficult to monitor workers. Many firms must rely on workers being motivated enough to work hard. By paying an above-market wage, a firm raises the cost to workers of losing their jobs because many alternative jobs will pay only the market wage. The increase in productivity that results from paying the high wage can more than offset the extra cost of the wage, thereby lowering the firm's costs of production.

Efficiency wage An above-market wage that a firm pays to increase workers' productivity.

Because the efficiency wage is above the market wage, it results in the quantity of labor supplied being greater than the quantity of labor demanded, just as do minimum wage laws and labor unions. So, efficiency wages also contribute to economies experiencing some unemployment even when cyclical unemployment is zero.   MyEconLab Concept Check

MyEconLab Study Plan

Key Terms

Cyclical unemployment, p. 15	Frictional unemployment, p. 14	Natural rate of unemployment, p. 15	Unemployment rate, p. 4
Discouraged workers, p. 5	Labor force, p. 4		
Efficiency wage, p. 18	Labor force participation rate, p. 6	Structural unemployment, p. 15	
Employed, p. 4		Unemployed, p. 4	

1.1 **Measuring the Unemployment Rate, the Labor Force Participation Rate, and the Employment–Population Ratio, pages 13–16**

LEARNING OBJECTIVE: Define the unemployment rate, the labor force participation rate, and the employment–population ratio and understand how they are computed.

Summary

The U.S. Bureau of Labor Statistics uses the results of the monthly household survey to calculate the *unemployment rate*, the *labor force participation rate*, and the *employment–population ratio*. The **labor force** is the total number of people who have jobs (the **employed**) plus the number of people who do not have jobs but are actively looking for them (the **unemployed**). The **unemployment rate** is the percentage of the labor force that is unemployed. **Discouraged workers** are people who are available for work but who are not actively looking for a job because they believe no jobs are available for them. Discouraged workers are not counted as unemployed. The **labor force participation rate** is the percentage of the working-age population in the labor force. Since 1950, the labor force participation rate of women has been rising, while the labor force participation rate of men has been falling. The employment–population ratio measures the percentage of the working-age population that is employed. Asians, whites, and college graduates have below-average unemployment rates. African Americans, Hispanics, and high school dropouts have above-average unemployment rates. Except during severe recessions, a typical unemployed person finds a new job or returns to his or her previous job within a few months. Each year, millions of jobs are created in the United States, and millions of jobs are destroyed.

MyEconLab   Visit **www.myeconlab.com** to complete these exercises online and get instant feedback.

Review Questions

1.1 How is the unemployment rate measured? What are the three conditions someone needs to meet to be counted as unemployed?

1.2 What are the problems in measuring the unemployment rate? In what ways does the official BLS measure of the unemployment rate *understate* the true degree of unemployment? In what ways does the official BLS measure *overstate* the true degree of unemployment?

1.3 Which groups tend to have above-average unemployment rates, and which groups tend to have below-average unemployment rates?

1.4 What does the labor force participation rate measure? Since 1950, how have the labor force participation rates of men and women changed?

1.5 What does the employment–population ratio measure? How does an unemployed person dropping out of the labor force affect the unemployment rate? How does it affect the employment–population ratio?

1.6 What is the difference between the household survey and the establishment survey? Which survey do many economists prefer for measuring changes in employment? Why?

Problems and Applications

1.7 Fill in the blank cells in the following table of data collected in the household survey for June 2015:

Working-age population	
Employment	148,739,000
Unemployment	
Unemployment rate	5.3%
Labor force	
Labor force participation rate	62.6%
Employment–population ratio	

1.8 **(Related to** Solved Problem 1.1 **on page 6)** Homemakers are not included in the employment or labor force totals compiled in the BLS household survey. They are included in the working-age population totals. Suppose that homemakers were counted as employed and included in labor force statistics. How would that change affect the unemployment rate, the labor force participation rate, and the employment–population ratio?

1.9 In June 2015, the unemployment rate declined to 5.3 percent from 5.5 percent in May. The labor force participation rate also declined from May to June, from 62.9 percent to 62.6 percent. If the labor force participation rate had remained unchanged from May to June, would the unemployment rate for June have been lower than, higher than, or equal to 5.3 percent? Briefly explain.

1.10 (Related to the Making the Connection **on page 10)** In discussing the labor market during the recovery from the 2007–2009 recession, Federal Reserve Chair Janet Yellen noted that "the employment-to-population ratio has increased far less over the past several years than the unemployment rate alone would indicate, based on past experience."

   a. During an economic expansion, why would we normally expect the employment–population ratio to increase as the unemployment rate falls?

   b. Why didn't the employment–population ratio increase as much as might have been expected during the recovery from the 2007–2009 recession?

Source: Janet L. Yellen, "Labor Market Dynamics and Monetary Policy," Speech at the Federal Reserve Bank of Kansas City Economic Symposium, Jackson Hole, Wyoming, August 22, 2014.

1.11 In early 2015, the employment–population ratio was increasing while the labor force participation rate remained largely unchanged. Shouldn't both of these data series move in the same direction? Briefly explain how it is possible that they didn't.

1.12 An article in the *Wall Street Journal* contained the following observation: "Every month, millions of workers leave the job market because of retirement, to care for children or aging parents, to pursue more education, or out of discouragement. Millions of others jump in after graduating."

   a. Are the millions of workers leaving the job market for the reasons given counted as unemployed in the BLS data? Briefly explain.

   b. Will the BLS count people entering the job market after graduating from high school or college as part of the labor force even if they don't find a job right away? Briefly explain.

Source: Josh Zumbrun, "Labor-Market Dropouts Stay on the Sidelines," *Wall Street Journal*, December 28, 2014.

1.13 An article in the *Wall Street Journal* noted that over a four-month period in late 2014, employment in the state of Georgia "rose 1% even as the state's jobless rate climbed 1.2 percentage points." Briefly explain how the state's unemployment rate could have increased at the same time that employment in the state was increasing.

Source: Cameron McWhirter and Ben Leubsdorf, "Rising Jobless Rates Are a Southern Mystery," *Wall Street Journal*, October 5, 2014.

1.14 In his 2015 State of the Union address, President Barack Obama observed that "over the past five years, our businesses have created more than 11 million new jobs." Is it likely that the U.S. economy created only 11 million jobs during this time period? If not, what was President Obama referring to?

Source: Barack Obama, "Remarks by the President in State of the Union Address," whitehouse.gov, January 20, 2015.

 1.2 **Types of Unemployment, pages 13–16**

LEARNING OBJECTIVE: Identify the three types of unemployment.

Summary

There are three types of unemployment: frictional, structural, and cyclical. **Frictional unemployment** is short-term unemployment that arises from the process of matching workers with jobs. One type of frictional unemployment is *seasonal unemployment*, which refers to unemployment due to factors such as weather, variations in tourism, and other calendar-related events. **Structural unemployment** arises from a persistent mismatch between the job skills or attributes of workers and the requirements of jobs. **Cyclical unemployment** is caused by a business cycle recession. The **natural rate of unemployment** is the normal rate of unemployment, consisting of structural unemployment and frictional unemployment. The natural rate of unemployment is also sometimes called the *full-employment rate of unemployment*.

MyEconLab   Visit **www.myeconlab.com** to complete these exercises online and get instant feedback.

Review Questions

2.1 What are the three types of unemployment? Which type of unemployment do you consider most likely to result in hardship for people who are unemployed? Briefly explain.

2.2 What is the relationship between frictional unemployment and job search?

2.3 What is the natural rate of unemployment? What is the relationship between the natural rate of unemployment and full employment?

Problems and Applications

2.4 (Related to the Module Opener **on page 3)** Ford Motor Company employed fewer people in 2015 than it did in 1980. Is this decline in employment frictional, structural, cyclical, or some combination of these factors? What information would you need to arrive at a definite answer?

2.5 A politician makes the following argument: "The economy would operate more efficiently if frictional unemployment were eliminated. Therefore, a goal of government policy should be to reduce the frictional rate of unemployment to the lowest possible level." Briefly explain whether you agree with this argument.

2.6 (Related to the Making the Connection **on page 15)** What advice for finding a job would you give someone who is frictionally unemployed? What advice would you give someone who is structurally unemployed? What advice would you give someone who is cyclically unemployed?

2.7 (Related to the Making the Connection on page 15) The BLS estimated that there were 2.7 million job "quits" in May 2015. The BLS defines a job quit as a "voluntary separation initiated by an employee."

a. Economists distinguish three types of unemployment: frictional, structural, and cyclical. How would you classify unemployment caused by an increase in job quits?

b. Would an increase in the number of job quits suggest that it was becoming easier or more difficult for people to find jobs? Briefly explain.

Source: Bureau of Labor Statistics, "Job Openings and Labor Turnover Survey," July 7, 2015.

2.8 (Related to the Making the Connection on page 15) The headline on an article in the *New York Times* was "Unemployed in Europe Stymied by Lack of Technology Skills." Are these workers likely to be cyclically, frictionally, or structurally unemployed? Briefly explain.

Source: Liz Alderman, "Unemployed in Europe Stymied by Lack of Technology Skills," *New York Times*, January 3, 2014.

1.3 **Explaining Unemployment, pages 16–18**
LEARNING OBJECTIVE: Explain what factors determine the unemployment rate.

Summary

Government policies can reduce the level of frictional and structural unemployment by aiding the search for jobs and the retraining of workers. Some government policies, however, can add to the level of frictional and structural unemployment. Unemployment insurance payments can raise the unemployment rate by extending the time that unemployed workers search for jobs. Government policies have caused the unemployment rates in most other high-income countries typically to be higher than in the United States. Wages above market levels can also increase unemployment. Wages may be above market levels because of the minimum wage, labor unions, and *efficiency wages*. An **efficiency wage** is a higher-than-market wage that a firm pays to increase workers' productivity.

MyEconLab   Visit **www.myeconlab.com** to complete these exercises online and get instant feedback.

Review Questions

3.1 What effect does the payment of government unemployment insurance have on the unemployment rate? On the severity of recessions?

3.2 Discuss the effect of each of the following on the unemployment rate.
a. The federal minimum wage law
b. Labor unions
c. Efficiency wages

3.3 Why has the unemployment rate in the United States typically been lower than the unemployment rates in Canada and the countries in Western Europe?

Problems and Applications

3.4 When Ségolène Royal was running unsuccessfully for president of France, she proposed that workers who lost their jobs would receive unemployment payments equal to 90 percent of their previous wages during their first year of unemployment. If this proposal had been enacted, what would the effect likely have been on the unemployment rate in France? Briefly explain.

Source: Alessandra Galloni and David Gauthier-Villars, "France's Royal Introduces Platform Ahead of Election," *Wall Street Journal*, February 12, 2007.

3.5 Jared Bernstein, an economist at the Center on Budget and Policy Priorities, has stated: "I want to see receipt of unemployment insurance … go up in recessions." If government unemployment insurance payments didn't go up, he explains, it "would be a sign that something's very wrong." What would be very wrong about government unemployment insurance payments failing to rise during a recession? What would be the consequences for the unemployed and for the economy?

Source: Jared Bernstein, "Lessons of the Great Recession: How the Safety Net Performed," *New York Times*, June 24, 2013.

3.6 Discuss the likely effect of each of the following on the unemployment rate.
a. The length of time workers are eligible to receive unemployment insurance payments doubles.
b. The minimum wage is abolished.
c. Most U.S. workers join labor unions.
d. More companies make information about job openings easily available on Internet job sites.

3.7 In 1914, Henry Ford increased the wage he paid workers in his car factory in Dearborn, Michigan, to $5 per day. This wage was more than twice as much as other car manufacturers were paying. Ford was quoted as saying, "The payment of five dollars a day for an eight-hour day was one of the finest cost-cutting moves we ever made." How can paying an above-market wage result in a firm cutting its costs?

3.8 In 2015, an article on bloomberg.com noted that Walmart, Starbucks, TJ Maxx, IKEA, Gap, and several other big retailers had announced increases in the wages they were paying newly hired workers. The same article also noted that "[labor] turnover in the retail sector has been steadily rising and now stands at 5 percent a month."
a. What do the authors mean by labor turnover?
b. Is it likely that the increase in labor turnover is connected to the increases in entry-level wages being paid by large retailers? Briefly explain.

Source: Kyle Stock and Kim Bhasin, "Why Retailers Are Suddenly Desperate to Keep Their Least-Valuable Workers," bloomberg.com, March 6, 2015.

Inflation

2.1 ## Measuring Inflation
LEARNING OBJECTIVE: Define the price level and the inflation rate and understand how they are computed.

One of the facts of economic life is that the prices of most goods and services rise over time. As a result, the cost of living continually rises. In 1914, Henry Ford began paying his workers a wage of $5 per day, which was more than twice as much as other automobile manufacturers were paying. Ford's $5-a-day wage provided his workers with a middle-class income because prices were so low. In 1914, Ford's Model T, the best-selling car in the country, sold for less than $600, the price of a man's suit was $15, the price of a ticket to a movie theater was $0.15, and the price of a box of Kellogg's Corn Flakes was $0.08. In 2015, with the cost of living being much higher than it was in 1914, the federal minimum wage law required firms to pay a wage of at least $7.25 per *hour*, more than Ford's highly paid workers earned in a day.

Knowing how the government compiles the employment and unemployment statistics is important in interpreting them. The same is true of the government's statistics on the cost of living. The **price level** measures the average prices of goods and services in the economy (see Module 3). The **inflation rate** is the percentage increase in the price level from one year to the next. We have introduced the *GDP deflator* as a measure of the price level. The GDP deflator is the broadest measure we have of the price level because it includes the price of every final good and service. But for some purposes, it is too broad. For example, if we want to know how inflation affects a typical household, the GDP price deflator may be misleading because it includes the prices of products such as large electric generators and machine tools that are part of the investment component of GDP but are not purchased by a typical household. In this module, we will focus on measuring the inflation rate by changes in the *consumer price index* because changes in this index come closest to measuring changes in the cost of living as experienced by a typical household. We will also briefly discuss a third measure of inflation: the *producer price index*.

Price level A measure of the average prices of goods and services in the economy.

Inflation rate The percentage increase in the price level from one year to the next.

The Consumer Price Index

To obtain prices of a representative group of goods and services, the BLS surveys 14,000 households nationwide on their spending habits. It uses the results of this survey to construct a *market basket* of 211 types of goods and services purchased by a typical urban family of four. Figure 2.1 shows the goods and services in the market basket, grouped into eight broad categories. Almost three-quarters of the market basket falls into just three categories: housing, transportation, and food. Each month, hundreds of BLS employees visit 23,000 stores in 87 cities and record prices of the goods and services in the market basket. Each price in the consumer price index is given a weight equal to the fraction of a typical family's budget spent on that good or service.

The **consumer price index (CPI)** is a measure of the average change over time in the prices a typical urban family of four pays for the goods and services they purchase. One year is chosen as the base year, and the value of the CPI is set equal to 100 for that year. In any year other than the base year, the CPI is equal to the ratio of the dollar amount necessary to buy the market basket of goods in that year divided by the dollar amount necessary to buy the market basket of goods in the base year, multiplied by 100. Because the CPI measures the cost to a typical family of buying a representative basket of goods and services, it is sometimes called the *cost-of-living index*.

A simple example can clarify how the CPI is constructed. For purposes of this example, we assume that the market basket has only three products: eye examinations, pizzas, and books:

Consumer price index (CPI) A measure of the average change over time in the prices a typical urban family of four pays for the goods and services they purchase.

Figure 2.1

The CPI Market Basket, December 2014

The Bureau of Labor Statistics surveys 14,000 households on their spending habits. The results are used to construct a *market basket* of goods and services purchased by a typical urban family of four. The chart shows these goods and services, grouped into eight broad categories. The percentages represent the expenditure shares of the categories within the market basket. The categories housing, transportation, and food make up about three-quarters of the market basket.
Source: U.S. Bureau of Labor Statistics.

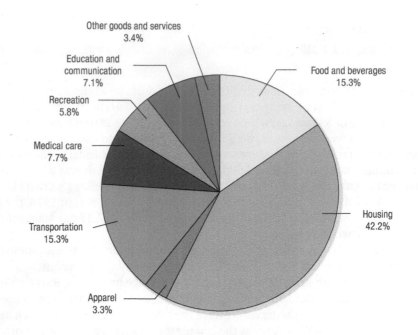

Other goods and services 3.4%
Education and communication 7.1%
Recreation 5.8%
Medical care 7.7%
Transportation 15.3%
Apparel 3.3%
Food and beverages 15.3%
Housing 42.2%

Product	Base Year (1999)			2016		2017	
	Quantity	Price	Expenditures	Price	Expenditures (on base-year quantities)	Price	Expenditures (on base-year quantities)
Eye examinations	1	$50.00	$50.00	$100.00	$100.00	$85.00	$85.00
Pizzas	20	10.00	200.00	15.00	300.00	14.00	280.00
Books	20	25.00	500.00	25.00	500.00	27.50	550.00
TOTAL			$750.00		$900.00		$915.00

Suppose that during the base year, 1999, a survey determines that each month, a typical family purchases 1 eye examination, 20 pizzas, and 20 books. At 1999 prices, a family must spend $750.00 to purchase this market basket of goods and services. The CPI for every year after the base year is determined by dividing the amount necessary to purchase the market basket in that year by the amount required in the base year, then multiplying by 100. Notice that the quantities of the products purchased in 2016 and 2017 are irrelevant in calculating the CPI because *we are assuming that households buy the same market basket of products each month.* Using the numbers in the table, we can calculate the CPI for 2016 and 2017:

Formula	Applied to 2016	Applied to 2017
$\text{CPI} = \dfrac{\text{Expenditures in the current year}}{\text{Expenditures in the base year}} \times 100$	$\left(\dfrac{\$900}{\$750}\right) \times 100 = 120$	$\left(\dfrac{\$915}{\$750}\right) \times 100 = 122$

How do we interpret values such as 120 and 122? First, recognize that they are *index numbers*, which means they are not measured in dollars or any other units. *The CPI is intended to measure changes in the price level over time.* We can't use the CPI to tell us in an absolute sense how high the price level is—only how much it has changed over time. We measure the inflation rate as the percentage increase in the CPI from one year to the next. For our simple example, the inflation rate in 2017 would be the percentage change in the CPI from 2016 to 2017:

$$\left(\frac{122 - 120}{120}\right) \times 100 = 1.7\%.$$

Because the CPI is designed to measure the cost of living, we can also say that the cost of living increased by 1.7 percent during 2017.   MyEconLab Concept Check

Is the CPI Accurate?

The CPI is the most widely used measure of inflation. Policymakers use the CPI to track the state of the economy. Businesses use it to help set the prices of their products and the wages and salaries of their employees. Each year, the federal government increases the Social Security payments made to retired workers by an amount equal to the percentage increase in the CPI during the previous year. In setting alimony and child support payments in divorce cases, judges often order that the payments increase each year by the inflation rate, as measured by the CPI.

Don't Let This Happen to You

Don't Miscalculate the Inflation Rate

Suppose you are given the data in the following table and are asked to calculate the inflation rate for 2014:

Year	CPI
2013	233
2014	237

It is tempting to avoid any calculations and simply report that the inflation rate in 2014 was 137 percent because 237 is a 137 percent increase from 100. But 137 percent would be the wrong answer. A value for the CPI of 237 in 2014

tells us that the price level in 2014 was 137 percent higher than in the *base year*, but the inflation rate is the percentage increase in the price level from the *previous year*, not the percentage increase from the base year. The correct calculation of the inflation rate for 2014 is:

$$\left(\frac{237 - 233}{233}\right) \times 100 = 1.7\%.$$

MyEconLab Study Plan

Your Turn: Test your understanding by doing related problem 1.5 and 1.6 on page 34 at the end of this module.

It is important that the CPI be as accurate as possible, but four biases cause changes in the CPI to overstate the true inflation rate:

1. **Substitution bias.** In constructing the CPI, the BLS assumes that each month, consumers purchase the same amount of each product in the market basket. In fact, consumers are likely to buy fewer of those products that increase most in price and more of those products that increase least in price (or fall the most in price). For instance, if apple prices rise rapidly during a particular month while orange prices fall, consumers will reduce their apple purchases and increase their orange purchases. Therefore, the prices of the market basket consumers actually buy will rise less than the prices of the market basket the BLS uses to compute the CPI.
2. **Increase in quality bias.** Over time, most products included in the CPI improve in quality: Automobiles become more durable and side air bags become standard equipment, smartphones have better processors and more memory, dishwashers use less water while getting dishes cleaner, and so on. Increases in the prices of these products partly reflect their improved quality and partly are pure inflation. The BLS attempts to make adjustments so that only the pure inflation part of price increases is included in the CPI. These adjustments are difficult to make, however, so the recorded price increases overstate the pure inflation in some products.
3. **New product bias.** For many years, the BLS updated the market basket of goods used in computing the CPI only every 10 years. So, new products introduced between updates were not included in the market basket. For example, the 1987 update took place before cellphones were introduced. Although millions of U.S.

households used cellphones by the mid-1990s, they were not included in the CPI until the 1997 update. The prices of many products, such as cellphones, Blu-ray players, and 4K televisions, decrease in the years immediately after they are introduced. If the market basket is not updated frequently, these price decreases are not included in the CPI.

4. **Outlet bias.**   During the mid-1990s, many consumers began to increase their purchases from discount stores such as Sam's Club and Costco. By the late 1990s, the Internet began to account for a significant fraction of sales of some products. Because the BLS continued to collect price statistics from traditional full-price retail stores, the CPI did not reflect the prices some consumers actually paid.

Most economists believe these biases cause changes in the CPI to overstate the true inflation rate by 0.5 percentage point to 1 percentage point. That is, if the CPI indicates that the inflation rate is 3 percent, it is probably between 2 percent and 2.5 percent. The BLS continues to take steps to reduce the size of the bias. For example, the BLS has reduced the size of the substitution and new product biases by updating the market basket every 2 years rather than every 10 years. The BLS has reduced the size of the outlet bias by conducting a point-of-purchase survey to track where consumers actually make their purchases. Finally, the BLS has used statistical methods to reduce the size of the quality bias. Prior to these changes, the size of the total bias in the CPI was probably greater than 1 percentage point.   MyEconLab Concept Check

The Producer Price Index

Producer price index (PPI)
An average of the prices received by producers of goods and services at all stages of the production process.

In addition to the GDP deflator and the CPI, the government also computes the **producer price index (PPI)**. Like the CPI, the PPI tracks the prices of a market basket of goods. But while the CPI tracks the prices of goods and services purchased by a typical household, the PPI tracks the prices firms receive for goods and services at all stages of production. The PPI includes the prices of intermediate goods, such as flour, yarn, steel, and lumber; and raw materials, such as raw cotton, coal, and crude petroleum. If the prices of these goods rise, the cost to firms of producing final goods and services will rise, which may lead firms to increase the prices of goods and services purchased by consumers. Changes in the PPI therefore can give an early warning of future movements in the CPI.

MyEconLab Study Plan

MyEconLab Concept Check

2.2   **Using Price Indexes to Adjust for the Effects of Inflation**

LEARNING OBJECTIVE: Use price indexes to adjust for the effects of inflation.

You are likely to receive a much higher salary after graduation than your parents did 25 or more years ago, but prices 25 years ago were, on average, much lower than prices today. In other words, the purchasing power of a dollar was much higher 25 years ago because the prices of most goods and services were much lower. Price indexes such as the CPI give us a way of adjusting for the effects of inflation so that we can compare dollar values from different years.

For example, suppose your mother received a salary of $25,000 in 1989. By using the CPI, we can calculate what $25,000 in 1989 was equivalent to in 2014. The CPI is 124 for 1989 and 237 for 2014. Because 237/124 = 1.9, we know that, on average, prices were almost twice as high in 2014 as in 1989. We can use this result to inflate a salary of $25,000 received in 1989 to its value in terms of 2014 purchasing power:

$$\text{Value in 2014 dollars} = \text{Value in 1989 dollars} \times \left(\frac{\text{CPI in 2014}}{\text{CPI in 1989}} \right)$$

$$= \$25,000 \times \left(\frac{237}{124} \right) = \$47,782.$$

Our calculation shows that if you were paid a salary of $47,782 in 2014, you would be able to purchase roughly the same amount of goods and services that your mother could have purchased with a salary of $25,000 in 1989. Economic variables that are calculated in current-year prices are referred to as *nominal variables*. The calculation we have just made uses a price index to adjust a nominal variable—your mother's salary—for the effects of inflation.

For some purposes, we are interested in tracking changes in an economic variable over time rather than in seeing what its value would be in today's dollars. In that case, to correct for the effects of inflation, we can divide the nominal variable by a price index and multiply by 100 to obtain a *real variable*. The real variable will be measured in dollars of the base year for the price index. Currently, the base year for the CPI is the average of prices in the years 1982 to 1984.　　　　MyEconLab Concept Check

---

Solved Problem 2.2

MyEconLab Interactive Animation

What Has Been Happening with Real Wages in the United States?

In addition to data on employment, the BLS establishment survey gathers data on average hourly earnings of production workers. Production workers are all workers, except for managers and professionals. Average hourly earnings are the wages or salaries earned by these workers per hour. Economists and policymakers closely follow changes in average hourly earnings because they are a broad measure of a typical worker's income. Note, though, that in order to measure changes in the purchasing power of these wages, we have to convert the nominal values reported by the BLS to real values. Use the information in the following table to compute real average hourly earnings

for each year. Compare the percentage change in nominal average hourly earnings between 2013 and 2014 with the percentage change in real average hourly earnings. Be sure to explain what the values you calculate for real average hourly earnings represent.

Year	Nominal Average Hourly Earnings	CPI (1982–1984 = 100)
2012	$19.73	230
2013	$20.14	233
2014	$20.60	237

Solving the Problem

Step 1:   **Review the module material.** This problem is about using price indexes to correct for the effects of inflation, so you may want to review the section "Using Price Indexes to Adjust for the Effects of Inflation," which begins on page 26.

Step 2:   **Begin by defining real average hourly earnings, calculating the value of real average hourly earnings for each year, and explaining what the values you calculated represent.** Nominal average hourly earnings are the number of dollars a worker receives. To calculate real average hourly earnings, we have to divide the nominal average earnings by the CPI for that year and multiply by 100. For example, real average hourly earnings for 2012 equal:

$$\left(\frac{\$19.73}{230}\right) \times 100 = \$8.59$$

The results for all three years are:

Year	Nominal Average Hourly Earnings	CPI (1982–1984 = 100)	Real Average Hourly Earnings (1982–1984 dollars)
2012	$19.73	230	$8.59
2013	$20.14	233	$8.65
2014	$20.60	237	$8.70

The base year for the CPI is the average of prices during the period 1982–1984. So, the values for the real average hourly earnings we calculated are in 1982–1984 dollars. In other words, these values for the real wage tell us that in 2013, $20.14 would buy what $8.65 would have bought in 1982–1984 and that in 2014, $20.60 would buy what $8.70 would have bought in 1982–1984.

Step 3: **Complete your answer by calculating the percentage change in nominal average hourly earnings and in real average hourly earnings between 2013 and 2014.** The percentage change in nominal average hourly earnings equals:

$$\left(\frac{\$20.60 - \$20.14}{\$20.14} \right) \times 100 = 2.3\%.$$

And the percentage change real average hourly earnings equals:

$$\left(\frac{\$8.70 - \$8.65}{\$8.65} \right) \times 100 = 0.6\%.$$

We can conclude that although nominal average hourly earnings increased by more than 2 percent, real average hourly earnings increased by less than 1 percent.

Extra Credit: The values we computed for the real average hourly earnings are measured in 1982–1984 dollars. Because this period is more than 30 years ago, the values are somewhat difficult to interpret. We can convert the earnings to 2014 dollars by using the method we used on page 26 to calculate your mother's salary. But for purposes of calculating the *change* in the value of real average hourly earnings over time, converting the earnings to 2014 dollars doesn't matter. The change from 2013 to 2014 would still be 0.6 percent. You can check this point by using the "mother's salary" method to calculate the real average hourly earnings for 2013 and 2014 in 2014 dollars. Then calculate the percentage change. Unless you make an arithmetic error, you should find that the answer is still 0.6 percent. Finally, keep in mind that average hourly earnings do not include employee benefits, such as employer contributions to retirement programs or the value of employer provided medical insurance. Because benefits have increased over the years relative to wages and salaries, changes in average hourly earnings can be a misleading measure of changes in the typical worker's standard of living.

 MyEconLab Study Plan

Your Turn: For more practice, do related problems 2.4, 2.5, 2.6, and 2.7 on pages 35–36 at the end of this module.

2.3 Nominal Interest Rates versus Real Interest Rates

LEARNING OBJECTIVE: Distinguish between the nominal interest rate and the real interest rate.

The difference between nominal and real values is important when money is being borrowed and lent. The *interest rate* is the cost of borrowing funds, expressed as a percentage of the amount borrowed (see Module 6). If you lend someone $1,000 for one year and charge an interest rate of 6 percent, the borrower will pay back $1,060, or 6 percent more than the amount you lent. But is $1,060 received one year from now really 6 percent more than $1,000 today? If prices rise during the year, you will not be able to buy as much with $1,060 one year from now as you could with that amount today. Your true return from lending the $1,000 is equal to the percentage change in your purchasing power after taking into account the effects of inflation.

The stated interest rate on a loan is the **nominal interest rate**. The **real interest rate** corrects the nominal interest rate for the effect of inflation on purchasing power. As a simple example, suppose that the only good you purchase is DVDs, and at the beginning of

Nominal interest rate The stated interest rate on a loan.

Real interest rate The nominal interest rate minus the inflation rate.

the year the price of DVDs is $10.00. With $1,000, you can purchase 100 DVDs. If you lend the $1,000 out for one year at an interest rate of 6 percent, you will receive $1,060 at the end of the year. Suppose the inflation rate during the year is 2 percent, so that the price of DVDs has risen to $10.20 by the end of the year. How has your purchasing power increased as a result of making the loan? At the beginning of the year, your $1,000 could purchase 100 DVDs. At the end of the year, your $1,060 can purchase $1,060/$10.20 = 103.92 DVDs. In other words, you can purchase almost 4 percent more DVDs. So, in this case, the real interest rate you received from lending was a little less than 4 percent (actually, 3.92 percent). For low rates of inflation, a convenient approximation for the real interest rate is:

Real interest rate = Nominal interest rate − Inflation rate.

We can calculate the real interest rate in our example using this formula as 6 percent − 2 percent = 4 percent, which is close to the actual value of 3.92 percent. If the inflation rate during the year was 5 percent, the real interest rate would be only 1 percent. Holding the nominal interest rate constant, the higher the inflation rate, the lower the real interest rate. Notice that if the inflation rate turns out to be higher than expected, borrowers pay and lenders receive a lower real interest rate than either of them expected. For example, if both you and the person to whom you lent the $1,000 to expected the inflation rate to be 2 percent, you both expected the real interest rate on the loan to be 4 percent. If the inflation rate turns out actually to be 4 percent, the real interest rate on the loan will be 2 percent: That's bad news for you but good news for your borrower.

For the economy as a whole, we can measure the nominal interest rate as the interest rate on three-month U.S. Treasury bills. U.S. Treasury bills are short-term loans investors make to the federal government. We can use the inflation rate as measured by changes in the CPI to calculate the real interest rate on Treasury bills. Figure 2.2 shows the nominal and real interest rates for the period from 1970 through the beginning of

MyEconLab Real-time data

Figure 2.2   Nominal and Real Interest Rates, 1970–2015

The real interest rate is equal to the nominal interest rate minus the inflation rate. The real interest rate provides a better measure of the true cost of borrowing and the true return to lending than does the nominal interest rate. The nominal interest rate in the figure is the interest rate on three-month U.S. Treasury bills. The inflation rate is measured by the percentage change in the CPI from the same quarter during the previous year.

Source: Federal Reserve Bank of St. Louis.

2015. Notice that when the inflation rate is low, as it has been during most years since the early 1990s, the gap between the nominal and real interest rates is small. When the inflation rate is high, as it was during the mid- to late 1970s, the gap between the nominal and real interest rates becomes large. In fact, a particular nominal interest rate can be associated in different periods with very different real interest rates. For example, during late 1975, the nominal interest rate was about 5.5 percent, but because the inflation rate was 7 percent, the real interest rate was −1.5 percent. In early 1987, the nominal interest rate was also 5.5 percent, but because the inflation rate was only 2 percent, the real interest rate was 3.5 percent.

This example shows that it is impossible to know whether a particular nominal interest rate is "high" or "low." It all depends on the inflation rate. *The real interest rate provides a better measure of the true cost of borrowing and the true return from lending than does the nominal interest rate.* When firms are deciding whether to borrow the funds to buy an investment good, such as a new factory, they will look at the real interest rate because it measures the true cost to the firm of borrowing.

Is it possible for the nominal interest rate to be less than the real interest rate? Yes, but only when the inflation rate is negative. A negative inflation rate is referred to as **deflation** and occurs on the rare occasions when the price level falls. During the years shown in Figure 2.2, the inflation rate as measured by changes in the CPI was negative only during the first nine months of 2009 and three months in early 2015.   MyEconLab Concept Check

Deflation A decline in the price level.

MyEconLab Study Plan

2.4 Does Inflation Impose Costs on the Economy?
LEARNING OBJECTIVE: Discuss the problems that inflation causes.

Imagine waking up tomorrow morning and finding that every price in the economy has doubled. The prices of food, gasoline, clothing, laptops, houses, and haircuts have all doubled. But suppose that all wages and salaries have also doubled. Will this doubling of prices and wages matter? Think about walking into McDonald's, expecting to find a Big Mac selling for $4.50. Instead, you find it selling for $9.00. Will you turn around and walk out? Probably not, because your salary has also increased overnight from $45,000 per year to $90,000 per year. So, the purchasing power of your salary has remained the same, and you are just as likely to buy the Big Mac today as you were yesterday.

This hypothetical situation makes an important point: Nominal incomes generally increase with inflation. Remember that we can think of the $4.50 price of a Big Mac as representing either the value of the product or the value of all the income generated in producing the product (see Module 3). The two amounts are the same, whether the Big Mac sells for $4.50 or $9.00. When the price of the Big Mac rises from $4.50 to $9.00, that extra $4.50 ends up as income that goes to the workers at McDonald's, the firms selling supplies to McDonald's, or the stockholders of McDonald's, just as the first $4.50 did.

It's tempting to think that the problem with inflation is that, as prices rise, consumers can no longer afford to buy as many goods and services, but our example shows that this conclusion is a fallacy. An expected inflation rate of 10 percent will raise the average price of goods and services by 10 percent, but it will also raise average incomes by 10 percent. Goods and services will be as affordable to an average consumer as they would be if there were no inflation.

Inflation Affects the Distribution of Income

If inflation will not reduce the affordability of goods and services to an average consumer, why do people dislike inflation? One reason is that the argument in the previous section applies to the *average* person but not to every person. Some people will find their incomes rising faster than the rate of inflation, and so their purchasing power will rise. Other people will find their incomes rising more slowly than the rate of inflation—or not at all—and their purchasing power will fall. People on fixed incomes are particularly likely to be hurt by inflation. If a retired worker receives a pension fixed at $3,000 per month, over time, inflation will reduce the purchasing power of that payment. In that way, inflation can change the distribution of income in a manner that seems unfair to many people.

The extent to which inflation redistributes income depends in part on whether the inflation is *anticipated*—in which case consumers, workers, and firms can see it coming and can prepare for it—or *unanticipated*—in which case they do not see it coming and do not prepare for it. MyEconLab Concept Check

The Problem with Anticipated Inflation

Like many of life's problems, inflation is easier to manage if you see it coming. Suppose that everyone knows that the inflation rate for the next 10 years will be 10 percent per year. Workers know that unless their wages go up by at least 10 percent per year, the real purchasing power of their wages will fall. Businesses will be willing to increase workers' wages enough to compensate for inflation because they know that the prices of the products they sell will increase. Lenders will realize that the loans they make will be paid back with dollars that are losing 10 percent of their value each year, so they will charge higher interest rates to compensate. Borrowers will be willing to pay the higher interest rates because they also know they are paying back these loans with dollars that are losing value. So far, there don't seem to be costs to anticipated inflation.

Even when inflation is perfectly anticipated, however, some individuals and firms will experience a cost:

1. Inevitably, there will be a redistribution of income, as some people's incomes fall behind even an anticipated level of inflation.

2. Firms and consumers have to hold some paper money to facilitate their buying and selling. Anyone holding paper money will find its purchasing power decreasing each year by the rate of inflation. To avoid this cost, workers and firms will try to hold as little paper money as possible, but they will have to hold some.

3. Firms that have catalogs listing the prices of their products will have to update them more frequently. Supermarkets and other stores that mark prices on packages or on store shelves will have to devote more time and labor to changing the marked prices. The costs to firms of changing prices are called **menu costs**. At moderate rates of anticipated inflation, menu costs are relatively small, but at high rates of inflation, such as those experienced in some developing countries, menu costs can become substantial.

4. Taxes paid by investors will increase because investors are taxed on the nominal payments they receive from owning stocks and bonds or from making loans, rather than on the real payments—the nominal payments corrected for inflation. Because investors are interested in the real, after-tax return they receive when investing in firms, the higher taxes that investors pay as a result of inflation mean that firms must pay more for the funds they need to expand. MyEconLab Concept Check

Menu costs The costs to firms of changing prices.

The Problem with Unanticipated Inflation

In any high-income economy—such as the United States—households, workers, and firms routinely enter into contracts that commit them to make or receive certain payments for years in the future. For example, when firms sign wage contracts, they commit to paying a specified wage for the duration of the contract. When people buy homes, they usually borrow most of the amount they need from banks. These loans, called *mortgage loans*, commit a borrower to make a fixed monthly payment for the length of the loan. Most mortgage loans are for long periods, often as long as 30 years.

To make these long-term commitments, households, workers, and firms must forecast the rate of inflation. If a firm believes the inflation rate over the next three years will be 6 percent per year, signing a three-year contract with a union that calls for wage increases of 8 percent per year may seem reasonable because the firm may be able to raise its prices by at least the rate of inflation each year. If the firm believes that the inflation rate will be only 2 percent over the next three years, paying wage increases of 8 percent may significantly reduce its profit or even force it out of business.

When people borrow money or a bank like JPMorgan Chase lends money, they must forecast the inflation rate so they can calculate the real rate of interest on a loan. In 1980, banks were charging interest rates of 18 percent or more on mortgage loans. This rate seems very high compared to the less than 5 percent charged on such loans in 2015, but the inflation rate in 1980 was more than 13 percent and was expected to remain high. In fact, the inflation rate *declined* unexpectedly, and by 1983 it was only about 3 percent. People who borrowed money for 30 years at the high interest rates of 1980 soon found that the real interest rate on their loans was much higher than they had expected.

When the actual inflation rate turns out to be very different from the expected inflation rate, some people gain, and other people lose. This outcome seems unfair to most people because they are either winning or losing only because something unanticipated has happened. This apparently unfair redistribution is a key reason people dislike unanticipated inflation.   MyEconLab Concept Check

Making the Connection
MyEconLab Video

What's So Bad about Falling Prices?

We have just discussed how inflation being higher than expected can cause problems for consumers, workers, and firms. But what if an economy begins to experience falling prices—*deflation*, rather than inflation? A falling price level might seem like good news for the economy. After all, falling prices should encourage consumers to increase their spending as goods and services become less expensive. In fact, though, deflation tends to have the opposite effect on consumers. Episodes of deflation are relatively rare, but we can draw some lessons from two important deflationary episodes: the United States during the 1930s and Japan during the 1990s. In both cases, many consumers reduced their spending in the face of falling prices, apparently because they were waiting for prices to go even lower. Waiting for prices to fall even lower was also a problem for the U.S. housing market in the late 2000s. A large run-up in housing prices took place from 2002 to 2006. When prices began to decline, many potential buyers postponed purchases in the expectation that prices would continue to fall.

The following figure shows changes in the CPI in the United States during the years between 1925 and 1940. The beginning of the Great Depression in 1929 caused the country to experience severe deflation.

The deflation of the 1930s hurt the U.S. economy not just because it may have led some consumers to postpone purchases but also because it increased the burden on borrowers. Suppose that in 1929 you had borrowed money for five years at a nominal interest rate of 5 percent. What real interest rate would you have paid during those years? We have seen that to calculate the real interest rate, we need to subtract the inflation rate from the nominal interest rate. With deflation, the change in the price level is negative, so to calculate the real interest rate, we are in effect *adding* the change in the price level to the nominal interest rate. The following table uses the actual deflation rate in each year to calculate the resulting real interest rates on your loan:

	1929	1930	1931	1932	1933
Nominal interest rate	5%	5%	5%	5%	5%
Change in the consumer price index	0	−2.3	−9.0	−9.9	−5.1
Real interest rate	5.0	7.3	14.0	14.9	10.1

The bottom row of the table shows that although the nominal interest rate on your loan is only 5 percent, in three of the five years the real interest rate you pay is greater than 10 percent. In fact, high real interest rates inflicted serious losses on both household and business borrowers during the early 1930s and contributed to the severity of the Great Depression.

During the 2001 and 2007–2009 recessions, some policymakers and economists feared that the U.S. economy would experience deflation. Fortunately, significant deflation did not occur. If it had, those recessions would likely have been more severe than they were.

MyEconLab Concept Check

Your Turn: Test your understanding by doing related problems 4.9 and 4.10 on page 37 at the end of this module.

MyEconLab Study Plan

Continued from page 3

Economics in Your Life

Should You Change Your Career Plans if You Graduate during a Recession?

At the beginning of this module, we asked whether layoffs in the banking industry should cause you to change your major and give up your plans to pursue a career in banking. We have seen in this module that unemployment rates are higher and layoffs are more common in a recession than in an economic expansion. Because you are a sophomore, you will graduate a few years later, when the recession will likely have ended and the unemployment rate will have declined. You might also want to investigate whether the layoffs in the banking industry represent a permanent contraction in the size of the industry or a temporary decline caused by the recession. If the reduction of banking jobs is more likely to be permanent, then you might consider a career in another industry. If the layoffs appear to be related to the current recession, then you probably do not need to change your career plans.

Conclusion

Inflation and unemployment are key macroeconomic problems. Presidential elections are often won and lost on the basis of which candidate is able to convince the public that he or she can best deal with these problems. Many economists, however, would argue that, in the long run, maintaining high rates of growth of real GDP per person is the most important macroeconomic concern. Only when real GDP per person is increasing will a country's standard of living increase. In the next module, we look more closely at the important topic of economic growth.

Visit MyEconLab for a news article and analysis related to the concepts in this module.

Key Terms

Consumer price index (CPI), p. 23

Deflation, p. 30

Inflation rate, p. 23

Menu costs, p. 31

Nominal interest rate, p. 28

Price level, p. 23

Producer price index (PPI), p. 26

Real interest rate, p. 28

2.1 Measuring Inflation, pages 23–26

LEARNING OBJECTIVE: Define the price level and the inflation rate and understand how they are computed.

Summary

The **price level** measures the average prices of goods and services. The **inflation rate** is equal to the percentage change in the price level from one year to the next. The federal government compiles statistics on three different measures of the price level: the consumer price index, the GDP price deflator, and the producer price index. The **consumer price index (CPI)** is a measure of the average change over time in the prices a typical urban family of four pays for the goods and services they purchase. Changes in the CPI are the best measure of changes in the cost of living as experienced by a typical household. Biases in the construction of the CPI cause changes in it to overstate the true inflation rate by 0.5 percentage point to 1 percentage point. The **producer price index (PPI)** is an average of prices received by producers of goods and services at all stages of production.

MyEconLab Visit **www.myeconlab.com** to complete these exercises online and get instant feedback.

Review Questions

1.1 Briefly describe the three major measures of the price level.
1.2 Which price index does the government use to measure changes in the cost of living?
1.3 What potential biases exist in calculating the CPI? What steps has the Bureau of Labor Statistics taken to reduce the size of the biases?
1.4 What is the difference between the CPI and the PPI?

Problems and Applications

1.5 **(Related to the** Don't Let This Happen to You **on page 25)** Briefly explain whether you agree with the following statement: "I don't believe the government price statistics. The CPI for 2014 was 237, but I know that the inflation rate couldn't have been as high as 137 percent in 2014."

1.6 **(Related to the** Don't Let This Happen to You **on page 25)** An article in the *Wall Street Journal* asks the question "How can inflation be low when everything is so expensive?" The article also notes that "the CPI shows that prices are the highest they've ever been." Is there a contradiction between a low inflation rate as measured by the CPI and the observations that prices are "the highest they've ever been" and everything is "so expensive"? Briefly explain.

Source: Josh Zumbrun, "5 Things You Always Wanted to Know about Inflation Statistics," *Wall Street Journal*, May 15, 2014.

1.7 Consider a simple economy that produces only three products: haircuts, hamburgers, and Blu-rays. Use the information in the following table to calculate the inflation rate for 2016, as measured by the CPI.

Product	Base Year (1999) Quantity	Base Year (1999) Price	2015 Price	2016 Price
Haircuts	2	$10.00	$11.00	$16.20
Hamburgers	10	2.00	2.45	2.40
Blu-rays	6	15.00	15.00	14.00

1.8 The Standard & Poor's/Case-Shiller Home Price Index is one of the leading indicators of housing price trends in the United States. The base year for the index is January 2000. The following table lists index numbers for April 2014 and April 2015 for five cities.

City	April 2014	April 2015
New York	174.5	179.3
Miami	183.2	198.5
Phoenix	145.4	150.4
Dallas	136.8	148.8
San Francisco	192.5	211.5

a. In which of these five cities did housing prices increase the fastest from April 2014 to April 2015? In which did they increase the slowest? Briefly explain the basis for your answers.

b. Can you determine from these numbers which city had the highest house prices in April 2015? Briefly explain.

Source: "House Price Indices," Federal Reserve Bank of St. Louis (FRED), research.stlouisfed.org/fred2/.

1.9 Suppose the CPI of a country follows the path shown in the following figure.

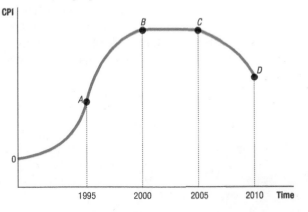

a. During which period did the country experience zero inflation?

b. During which period did the country experience an increasing rate of inflation?

c. During which period did the country experience a slow-down in inflation, although the inflation rate remained positive? (This situation is called "disinflation.")

d. During which period did the country experience deflation?

1.10 An article in the *Wall Street Journal* notes that the BLS has changed the methods it uses to calculate the CPI with the result that the measured inflation rate is lower than it would have been if the BLS had still used the old methods. The article notes, "But this is not a massive conspiracy to hide runaway inflation." What was the BLS's motivation in changing its methods of calculating the CPI?

Source: Josh Zumbrun, "5 Things You Always Wanted to Know about Inflation Statistics," *Wall Street Journal*, May 15, 2014.

1.11 In the fall of 2015, Apple introduced a new model of its iPhone. The new model had a faster processor and a better camera than the previous model but sold for the same price. How was the CPI affected by the introduction of the new model of the iPhone?

2.2 Using Price Indexes to Adjust for the Effects of Inflation, pages 26–28

LEARNING OBJECTIVE: Use price indexes to adjust for the effects of inflation.

Summary

Price indexes are designed to measure changes in the price level over time, not the absolute level of prices. To correct for the effects of inflation, we can divide a *nominal variable* by a price index and multiply by 100 to obtain a *real variable*. The real variable will be measured in dollars of the base year for the price index.

MyEconLab   Visit www.myeconlab.com to complete these exercises online and get instant feedback.

Review Questions

2.1 What is the difference between a nominal variable and a real variable?

2.2 During a period of deflation, which is likely to increase faster: nominal average hourly earnings or real average hourly earnings? Briefly explain.

Problems and Applications

2.3 The Great Depression was the worst economic disaster in U.S. history in terms of declines in real GDP and increases in the unemployment rate. Use the data in the following table to calculate the percentage decline in real GDP between 1929 and 1933:

Year	Nominal GDP (billions of dollars)	GDP Price Deflator (2009 = 100)
1929	$104.6	9.9
1933	57.2	7.3

Source: U.S. Bureau of Economic Analysis.

2.4 (**Related to** Solved Problem 2.2 **on page 27-28**) In 1924, the famous novelist F. Scott Fitzgerald wrote an article for the *Saturday Evening Post* titled "How to Live on $36,000 a Year," in which he wondered how he and his wife had managed to spend all of that very high income without saving any of it. The CPI in 1924 was 17, and the CPI in 2014 was 237. What income would you have needed in 2014 to have had the same purchasing power that Fitzgerald's $36,000 had in 1924? Be sure to show your calculation.

Source: F. Scott Fitzgerald, "How to Live on $36,000 a Year," *Saturday Evening Post*, April 5, 1924.

2.5 (**Related to** Solved Problem 2.2 **on page 27-28**) Use the information in the following table to determine the percentage changes in the U.S. and French *real* minimum wages between 1957 and 2014. Does it matter for your answer that you have not been told the base year for the U.S. CPI or the French CPI? Was the percentage increase in the price level greater in the United States or in France during these years?

	United States		France	
Year	Minimum Wage (dollars per hour)	CPI	Minimum Wage (euros per hour)	CPI
1957	$1.00	27	€0.19	8
2014	7.25	237	9.61	106

Sources: John M. Abowd, Francis Kramarz, Thomas Lemieux, and David N. Margolis, "Minimum Wages and Youth Employment in France and the United States," in D. Blanchflower and R. Freeman, eds., *Youth Employment and Joblessness in Advanced Countries*, Chicago: University of Chicago Press, 1999, pp. 427–472 (the value for the minimum wage is given in francs; it was converted to euros at a conversion rate of 1 euro = 6.55957 francs); Insee online data bank, www.insee.fr; U.S. Department of Labor; and U.S. Bureau of Labor Statistics.

2.6 (**Related to** Solved Problem 2.2 **on page 27-28**) In an article in the *Wall Street Journal*, a professor of financial planning noted the effect of rising prices on purchasing power: "Today, $2,000 a month seems reasonable [as an income for a retired person in addition to the person's Social Security payments], but 40 years from now that's going to be three cups of coffee and a donut." Suppose that currently three cups of coffee and a donut can be purchased for $10. The CPI in 2014 was 237. What would the CPI have to be in 2054 for $2,000 to be able to purchase only three cups of coffee and a donut? Assume that the prices of coffee and donuts increase at the same rate as the CPI during these 40 years.

Source: Matthias Rieker, "Rising Use of Immediate Annuities Raises Some Concerns," *Wall Street Journal*, December 4, 2014.

2.7 (**Related to** Solved Problem 2.2 **on page 27-28**) The table on the next page shows the top 10 films of all time through July 2015, measured by box office receipts in the United States, as well as several other notable films farther down the list.

The CPI in 2015 was 238. Use this information and the data in the table to calculate the box office receipts for each film in 2015 dollars. Assume that each film generated all of its box office receipts during the year it was released. Use your results to prepare a new list of the top 10 films, based on their earnings in 2015 dollars. (Some of the films, such as the first *Star Wars* film, *Gone with the Wind*, and *Snow White and the Seven Dwarfs*, were re-released to theaters several times, so their receipts were actually earned during several different years, but we will ignore that complication.)

Source: boxofficemojo.com and the U.S. Bureau of Labor Statistics.

Rank	Film	Total Box Office Receipts	Year Released	CPI
1	*Avatar*	$760,507,625	2009	215
2	*Titanic*	658,672,302	1997	161
3	*Jurassic World*	628,700,000	2015	238
4	*Marvel's The Avengers*	623,357,910	2012	230
5	*The Dark Knight*	534,858,444	2008	215
6	*Star Wars: Episode I—The Phantom Menace*	474,544,677	1999	167
7	*Star Wars*	460,998,007	1977	61
8	*Avengers: Age of Ultron*	456,774,004	2015	238
9	*The Dark Knight Rises*	448,139,099	2012	230
10	*Shrek 2*	441,226,247	2004	189
11	*ET: The Extra-Terrestrial*	435,110,554	1982	97
79	*Jaws*	260,000,000	1975	54
161	*Gone with the Wind*	198,676,459	1939	14
183	*Snow White and the Seven Dwarfs*	184,925,486	1937	14
257	*The Sound of Music*	158,671,368	1965	32
303	*101 Dalmatians*	144,880,014	1961	30

2.3 Nominal Interest Rates versus Real Interest Rates, pages 28–30

LEARNING OBJECTIVE: Distinguish between the nominal interest rate and the real interest rate.

Summary

The stated interest rate on a loan is the **nominal interest rate**. The **real interest rate** is the nominal interest rate minus the inflation rate. Because it is corrected for the effects of inflation, the real interest rate provides a better measure of the true cost of borrowing and the true return from lending than does the nominal interest rate. The nominal interest rate is always greater than the real interest rate unless the economy experiences **deflation**, which is a decline in the price level.

MyEconLab   Visit **www.myeconlab.com** to complete these exercises online and get instant feedback.

Review Questions

3.1 What is the difference between the nominal interest rate and the real interest rate?

3.2 If inflation is expected to increase, what will happen to the nominal interest rate? Briefly explain.

3.3 The module states that it is impossible to know whether a particular nominal interest rate is "high" or "low." Briefly explain why.

3.4 If the economy is experiencing deflation, will the nominal interest rate be higher or lower than the real interest rate?

Problems and Applications

3.5 The following appeared in a news article: "Inflation in the Lehigh Valley during the first quarter of … [the year] was less than half the national rate. … So, unlike much of the nation, the fear here is deflation—when prices sink so low the CPI drops below zero." Do you agree with the reporter's definition of deflation? Briefly explain.

Source: Dan Shope, "Valley's Inflation Rate Slides," (Allentown, PA) *Morning Call*, July 9, 1996.

3.6 Suppose you were borrowing money to buy a car.
   a. Which of these situations would you prefer: The interest rate on your car loan is 20 percent and the inflation rate is 19 percent, or the interest rate on your car loan is 5 percent and the inflation rate is 2 percent? Briefly explain.
   b. Now suppose you are JPMorgan Chase, and you are making car loans. Which situation in part (a) would you now prefer? Briefly explain.

3.7 In June 2014, the nominal interest rate on a one-year Treasury bill was 0.10 percent. From June 2014 to June 2015, the consumer price index rose from 237.3 to 237.8. If you bought the one-year Treasury bill in May 2014, calculate the real interest rate you earned over the following 12-month period. Given the results of your calculation, why were investors willing to buy Treasury bills in May 2014?

3.8 Describing the situation in England in 1920, the historian Robert Skidelsky wrote the following: "Who would not borrow at 4 percent a year, with prices going up 4 percent a *month*?" What was the real interest rate paid by borrowers in this situation? (*Hint:* What is the annual inflation rate, if the monthly inflation rate is 4 percent?)

Source: Robert Skidelsky, *John Maynard Keynes: Volume 2, The Economist as Saviour 1920–1937*, New York: The Penguin Press, 1992, p. 39.

3.9 Suppose that the only good you purchase is hamburgers, and that at the beginning of the year, the price of a hamburger is $2.00. Suppose you lend $1,000 for one year at an interest rate of 5 percent. At the end of the year, a hamburger costs $2.08. What is the real rate of interest you earned on your loan?

2.4 **Does Inflation Impose Costs on the Economy? pages 30–33**
LEARNING OBJECTIVE: Discuss the problems that inflation causes.

Summary

Inflation does not reduce the affordability of goods and services to an average consumer, but it does impose costs on the economy. When inflation is anticipated, its main costs are that paper money loses some of its value and firms incur *menu costs*. **Menu costs** include the costs of changing prices on products and updating catalogs. When inflation is unanticipated, the actual inflation rate can turn out to be different from the expected inflation rate. As a result, income is redistributed as some people gain and some people lose.

MyEconLab   Visit **www.myeconlab.com** to complete these exercises online and get instant feedback.

Review Questions

4.1 Why do nominal incomes generally increase with inflation? If nominal incomes increase with inflation, does inflation reduce the purchasing power of an average consumer? Briefly explain.

4.2 How can inflation affect the distribution of income?

4.3 Which is a greater problem: anticipated inflation or unanticipated inflation? Briefly explain.

4.4 What are menu costs? What effect has the Internet had on the size of menu costs?

4.5 What problems does deflation cause?

Problems and Applications

4.6 Suppose that the inflation rate turns out to be much higher than most people expected. In that case, would you rather have been a borrower or a lender? Briefly explain.

4.7 Suppose James and Frank both retire this year. For income during retirement, James will rely on a pension from his company that pays him a fixed $2,500 per month for as long as he lives. James hasn't saved anything for retirement. Frank has no pension but has saved a considerable amount, which he has invested in certificates of deposit (CDs) at his bank. Currently, Frank's CDs pay him interest of $2,300 per month.
  a. Ten years from now, is James or Frank likely to have a higher real income? In your answer, be sure to define *real income*.
  b. Now suppose that instead of being a constant amount, James's pension increases each year by the same percentage as the CPI. For example, if the CPI increases by 5 percent in the first year after James retires, then his pension in the second year equals $2,500 + ($2,500 × 0.05) = $2,625. In this case, 10 years from now, is James or Frank likely to have a higher real income?

4.8 Suppose that Apple and the investors buying the firm's bonds both expect a 2 percent inflation rate for the year. Given this expectation, suppose the nominal interest rate on the bonds is 6 percent and the real interest rate is 4 percent. Suppose that a year after the investors purchase the bonds, the inflation rate turns out to be 6 percent, rather than the 2 percent that had been expected. Who gains and who loses from the unexpectedly high inflation rate?

4.9 **(Related to the** Making the Connection **on page 32)** During the spring of 2015, the United Kingdom experienced a brief period of deflation. According to an article in the *Wall Street Journal*, "The U.K.'s history of sticky and hard-to-control inflation suggests that a short period of falling prices will be taken as a reprieve for consumers, not as a signal to defer purchases." Why might consumers see deflation as a "signal to defer purchases"? Shouldn't lower prices cause consumers to buy more, not less? Briefly explain.

Source: Richard Barley, "U.K. Deflation More Curiosity Than Concern," *Wall Street Journal*, May 19, 2015.

4.10 **(Related to the** Making the Connection **on page 32)** During the late nineteenth century in the United States, many farmers borrowed heavily to buy land. During most of the period between 1870 and the mid-1890s, the United States experienced mild deflation: The price level declined each year. Many farmers engaged in political protests during these years, and deflation was often a subject of their protests. Explain why farmers would have felt burdened by deflation.

Real-Time Data Exercises

D2.1 **(Using the CPI to measure inflation)** Go to the Web site of the Federal Reserve Bank of St. Louis (FRED) (research. stlouisfed.org/fred2/).
  a. Find values for the most recent month and for the same month one year earlier for the Consumer Price Index (CPIAUCSL).
  b. Use the values you found in part (a) to calculate the inflation rate for the past year.

D2.2 **(Using CPI data and Excel to calculate the inflation rate)** Go to the Web site of the Federal Reserve Bank of St. Louis (FRED) (research.stlouisfed.org/fred2/).
  a. Locate the data for the Consumer Price Index (CPIAUCSL). Click on the "Download Data" link on the left of the page. Change the beginning date to six years prior to the most recent observation. You can leave the ending date as it is. Then click on the "Download Data" button to download the data and save it to your computer. Finally, open the Excel file that you just

downloaded. (*Note:* You can also use another compatible spreadsheet program, such as OpenOffice's Calc.)

   b. Using Excel, calculate the percentage change in CPI from a year earlier for each observation, beginning with the observation one year later than the first observation. To make this calculation, click on the blank cell next to the observation corresponding to that date and then enter the following formula (note that in Excel, the symbol for multiplication is *):

$$\text{Percentage change} = \left(\frac{CPI_t - CPI_{t-1}}{CPI_{t-1}} \right) \times 100,$$

where $t-1$ is the first observation and t is the observation one year later. Repeat this process for the remaining observations. (You can use the copy and paste functions to avoid having to retype the formula.)

   c. Using your calculations from part (b), create a graph of the percentage changes from a year earlier.

   d. Use your calculations from part (b) to explain which period experienced the highest inflation rate. What was the inflation rate during that period?

D2.3 (Using CPI data and Excel to calculate an alternative measure of the inflation rate) In addition to the usual CPI, the BLS also calculates a CPI that does not include the prices of food and energy. Because the prices of food and energy tend to fluctuate more than other prices, some economists believe that omitting them provides a better measure of the long-run inflation rate. Go to the Web site of the Federal Reserve Bank of St. Louis (FRED) (research. stlouisfed.org/fred2/).

   a. Locate the data for the Consumer Price Index (CPI-AUCSL) and the Consumer Price Index less Food and Energy (CPILFESL). Click on the "Download Data" link on the left of the page. Change the beginning date to 2006-07-01. You can leave the ending date as it is. Then click on the "Download Data" button to download the data and save it to your computer. Finally, open the Excel file that you just downloaded. (*Note:* You can also use another compatible spreadsheet program, such as OpenOffice's Calc.)

   b. Using Excel, calculate the percentage change in each CPI from a year ago for each of the observations, beginning with the observation 2007-07-01. To make this calculation, click on the blank cell next to the observation corresponding to 2007-07-01, and then enter the following formula (note that in Excel, the symbol for multiplication is *):

$$\text{Percentage change} = \left(\frac{CPI_t - CPI_{t-1}}{CPI_{t-1}} \right) \times 100$$

where $t-1 = 2007\text{-}07\text{-}01$ and $t = 2006\text{-}07\text{-}01$. Repeat this process for the remaining observations. (You can use the copy and paste functions to avoid having to retype the formula.)

   c. Using your calculations from part (b), create a graph of the percentage changes from a year ago for both indexes. Make sure both data lines are on the same graph.

   d. Discuss differences between the two measures of the inflation rate. For instance, from your calculations, what was the inflation rate in June 2009 using the two CPI measures?

D2.4 (Analyzing inflation in CPI categories) Calculating inflation rates for categories of goods and services in the CPI market basket (see page 23) can provide insight into inflation in different sectors of the economy. Go to the Web site of the Federal Reserve Bank of St. Louis (FRED) (research.stlouisfed.org/fred2/).

   a. Find the most recent values and values from the same month in 2010 for the following four categories of the Consumer Price Index: (1) Food and Beverages (CPIFABSL), (2) Apparel (CPIAPPSL), (3) Transportation (CPITRNSL), and (4) Medical Care (CPIMEDSL).

   b. Using the data from part (a), calculate the inflation rate over the period from 2010 to the present period for each of the four CPI categories.

   c. According to your calculations, which category experienced the least amount of inflation and which category experienced the most inflation?

D2.5 (Analyzing the labor force and unemployment) Go to the Web site of the Federal Reserve Bank of St. Louis (FRED) (research.stlouisfed.org/fred2/).

   a. Find the most recent values for these three variables: (1) Unemployed (UNEMPLOY), (2) Civilian Labor Force (CLF16OV), and (3) Employment Level – Part-Time for Economic Reasons, Slack Work or Business Conditions (LNS12032195). Are these data reported annually, quarterly, or monthly? What units are these values reported in?

   b. Using the values you found in part (a), calculate the civilian unemployment rate and the civilian unemployment rate including persons who are underemployed (part-time for economic reasons).

D2.6 (Calculating the unemployment rate for different groups) Go to the Web site of the Federal Reserve Bank of St. Louis (FRED) (research.stlouisfed.org/fred2/).

   a. Find the most recent values for these four variables: (1) Unemployment Level – Men (LNS13000001), (2) Unemployment Level – Women (LNS13000002), (3) Civilian Labor Force Level – Men (LNS11000001), and (4) Civilian Labor Force Level – Women (LNS11000002). Are these data reported annually, quarterly, or monthly? What units are these values reported in?

   b. Using the values you found in part (a), calculate the unemployment rate for men and the unemployment rate for women.

   c. Explain why some people are considered discouraged workers. What will happen to the unemployment rate if there is an increase in discouraged workers?

D2.7 (Calculating the employment-population ratio) Go to the Web site of the Federal Reserve Bank of St. Louis (FRED) (research.stlouisfed.org/fred2/).

   a. Find the most recent values for these three variables: (1) Unemployed (UNEMPLOY), (2) Civilian Employment (CE16OV), and (3) Not in Labor Force (LNS15000000).

   b. Using the values you found in part (a), calculate the working-age population (in thousands) and the employment–population ratio.

   c. Holding all other factors constant, what would you expect to happen to the employment–population ratio if the economy entered a recession? Briefly explain.

D2.8 (Calculating the cyclical unemployment rate) Go to the Web site of the Federal Reserve Bank of St. Louis (FRED) (research.stlouisfed.org/fred2/).
  a. Find the value for the most recent month and for the same month two years earlier for the Civilian Unemployment Rate (UNRATE) and the Natural Rate of Unemployment (NROU).
  b. Using the values you found in part (a), calculate the cyclical rate of unemployment.
  c. Given the change in cyclical unemployment over this two-year period, what can you conclude about the state of the economy?

D2.9 (The unemployment rate and the business cycle) Go to the Web site of the Federal Reserve Bank of St. Louis (FRED) (research.stlouisfed.org/fred2/).
  a. Find the most recent values for these three variables: (1) Unemployed (UNEMPLOY), Civilian Employment (CE16OV), (2) Employment Level – Part-Time for Economic Reasons, All Industries (LNS12032194), and (3) Not in Labor Force, Searched for Work and Available (LNU05026642).
  b. Using the values you found in part (a), calculate the official unemployment rate.
  c. Some economists argue that the official unemployment rate understates the degree of joblessness in the economy because it uses too narrow a definition of unemployment. The BLS also calculates a broader measure of the unemployment rate, which includes people who work part time for economic reasons and people who are available for work but not actively searching. Using the data you found in part (a), calculate this broader measure of the unemployment rate.
  d. How would you expect the gap between the official rate of unemployment and the broader rate to change over the course of the business cycle?

D2.10 (Calculating the real interest rate) Go to the Web site of the Federal Reserve Bank of St. Louis (FRED) (research.stlouisfed.org/fred2/).
  a. Find the most recent values for the 3-Month Treasury Bill: Secondary Market Rate (TB3MS) and the University of Michigan Inflation Expectation (MICH).
  b. Using the data you found in part (a), calculate the expected real interest rate.
  c. If the actual inflation rate is greater than the expected inflation rate, how are borrowers and lenders affected?

D2.11 (Calculating the effect of inflation on real wages) Go to the Web site of the Federal Reserve Bank of St. Louis (FRED) (research.stlouisfed.org/fred2/).
  a. Find the values for the most recent month and for the month one year earlier for the Consumer Price Index for All Urban Consumers: All Items (CPIAUCNS) and Average Hourly Earnings of Production and Nonsupervisory Employees: Total Private (AHETPI).
  b. Using the data you found in part (a), calculate the average hourly real wage for each year.
  c. Calculate the percentage change in the average hourly nominal wage and the average hourly real wage during this year.
  d. Given your calculation in part (c), explain whether an average worker was better or worse off than a year earlier.

GDP: Measuring Total Production and Income

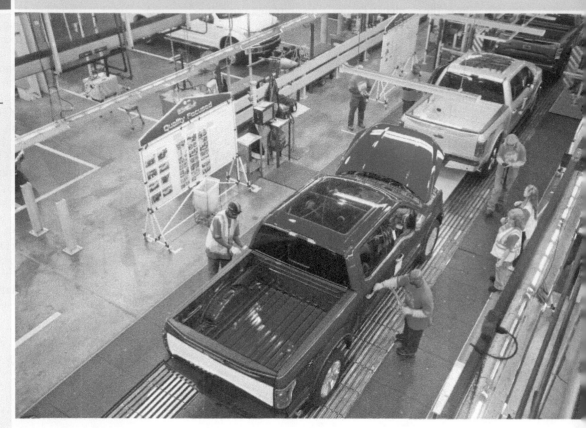

Ford Motor Company Rides the Business Cycle

In the more than 100 years that the Ford Motor Company has been in business, its experiences have often mirrored those of the U.S. economy. So, it was no surprise that in 2008, with the U.S. economy suffering from its worst downturn since the 1930s, sales of Ford cars and trucks plummeted. Overall, the automobile industry, which sold 16.1 million new vehicles in 2007, saw sales tumble to 10.4 million in 2009. Although Ford was hit hard, General Motors and Chrysler, Ford's two great American rivals, were even worse off, and both declared bankruptcy. Those firms survived largely because the federal government invested more than $62 billion in them. Ford suffered heavy losses but did not require direct government aid.

In 2015, the economy was several years into its recovery from the downturn, and Ford's sales had risen by more than one-third since their low point in 2009. With these fluctuations in sales, Ford and the automobile industry as a whole were experiencing the effects of the *business cycle*, which refers to alternating periods of economic expansion and recession. Production and employment increase during expansions and decrease during recessions.

Whether the general level of economic activity is increasing is important not just to firms such as Ford but also to workers wondering whether they will be able to keep their jobs and to college students wondering whether they will be able to find jobs when they graduate. One study found that during the slow recovery from the 2007–2009 recession, only 56 percent of those students who graduated from college in the spring of 2010 had found a job a year later. The average salary of graduates who did find a job was $27,000, down from an average of $30,000 for the classes of 2006 to 2008. What's more, students who graduate during recessions will continue to earn less for as long as 15 years after they graduate. The overall state of the economy is clearly important!

Sources: Vehicle sales data are from the U.S. Bureau of Economic Analysis and the Ford Motor Company; Catherine Rampell, "Many with New College Degrees Find the Job Market Humbling," *New York Times*, May 18, 2011; and Lisa B. Kahn, "The Long-Term Labor Market Consequences of Graduating from College in a Bad Economy," *Labour Economics*, Vol. 17, No. 2, April 2010, pp. 233–246.

Economics in Your Life

What's the Best Country for You to Work In?

Suppose that Ford offers you a job after graduation in 2016. The firm has vacancies in Canada and China, and because you are fluent in Mandarin, you get to choose the country where you will work and live. Gross domestic product (GDP) is a measure of an economy's total production of goods and services, so one factor in your decision is likely to be the growth rate of GDP in each country. Based on the International Monetary Fund's forecasts for 2016, GDP would increase by 2.4 percent in Canada but by 6.8 percent in China. What effect do these two very different growth rates have on your decision to work and live in one country or the other? If China's much higher growth rate does not necessarily lead you to decide to work and live in China, why not? As you read this module, try to answer these questions. You can check your answers against those we provide on **page 59** at the end of this module.

Microeconomics The study of how households and firms make choices, how they interact in markets, and how the government attempts to influence their choices.

Macroeconomics The study of the economy as a whole, including topics such as inflation, unemployment, and economic growth.

Business cycle Alternating periods of economic expansion and economic recession.

Expansion The period of a business cycle during which total production and total employment are increasing.

Recession The period of a business cycle during which total production and total employment are decreasing.

Economic growth The ability of an economy to produce increasing quantities of goods and services.

Inflation rate The percentage increase in the price level from one year to the next.

We can divide economics into the subfields of microeconomics and macroeconomics. **Microeconomics** is the study of how households and firms make choices, how they interact in markets, and how the government attempts to influence their choices.

Macroeconomics is the study of the economy as a whole, including topics such as inflation, unemployment, and economic growth. In microeconomic analysis, economists generally study individual markets, such as the market for smartphones. In macroeconomic analysis, economists study factors that affect many markets at the same time.

In the following modules, we will deal with many key macroeconomic issues, including:

- The **business cycle**, which refers to the alternating periods of expansion and recession that the U.S. economy has experienced since at least the early nineteenth century. A business cycle **expansion** is a period during which total production and total employment are increasing. A business cycle **recession** is a period during which total production and total employment are decreasing. We will discuss the factors that influence the business cycle and policies the government may use to reduce its effects.

- **Economic growth**, which refers to the ability of an economy to produce increasing quantities of goods and services. Economic growth is important because an economy that grows too slowly fails to raise living standards. In some countries in Africa, little economic growth has occurred in the past 50 years, and many people remain in severe poverty. Macroeconomics analyzes both what determines a country's rate of economic growth and the reasons growth rates differ so greatly across countries.

- Fluctuations in the total level of employment in an economy. In the short run, the level of employment is significantly affected by the business cycle, but in the long run, the effects of the business cycle disappear, and other factors determine the level of employment. A related question is why some economies are more successful than others at maintaining high levels of employment over time.

- Fluctuations in the **inflation rate**, which is the percentage increase in the average level of prices from one year to the next. Like employment, inflation is affected both by the business cycle and by long-run factors.

- Linkages among economies in the form of international trade and international finance.

Macroeconomic analysis provides information that consumers and firms need in order to understand current economic conditions and to help predict future conditions. A family may be reluctant to buy a house if employment in the economy is declining because some family members may be at risk of losing their jobs. Similarly, firms may be willing to invest in building new factories or to undertake major new expenditures on information technology only if they expect future sales to be strong. For example, in 2015, Ford opened two new factories in China and announced that it would spend more than $1 billion to expand an existing factory. Ford was relying on macroeconomic forecasts indicating that the Chinese economy would continue to grow rapidly and that sales of cars in the country would increase from 24 million in 2014 to 32 million in 2020. Macroeconomic analysis can also assist the federal government design policies that help the U.S. economy perform more efficiently.

In this and the following modules, we begin our study of macroeconomics by considering how best to measure key macroeconomic variables. We start by considering measures of total production and total income in an economy.

Gross Domestic Product Measures Total Production

LEARNING OBJECTIVE: Explain how total production is measured.

"U.S. GDP Swings to Contraction in First Quarter"

"Canada GDP Posts Surprise Drop in April"

"Brazil GDP Shrinks in First Quarter"

"5 Things You Need to Know about India's GDP Growth"

"China Maintains 7% GDP Growth in Second Quarter"

These headlines are from articles that appeared in the *Wall Street Journal* during 2015. Why is GDP so often the focus of news stories? In this section, we explore what GDP is and how it is measured. We also explore why understanding GDP is important to consumers, firms, and government policymakers.

Measuring Total Production: Gross Domestic Product

Economists use **gross domestic product (GDP)** to measure total production. GDP is the market *value* of all *final* goods and services produced in a country during a period of time, typically one year. In the United States, the Bureau of Economic Analysis (BEA) in the Department of Commerce compiles the data needed to calculate GDP. The BEA issues reports on the GDP every three months. GDP is a central concept in macroeconomics, so we need to consider its definition carefully.

Gross domestic product (GDP) The market value of all final goods and services produced in a country during a period of time, typically one year.

GDP Is Measured Using Market Values, Not Quantities The word
value is important in the definition of GDP. In microeconomics, we measure production in quantity terms: the number of cars Ford produces, the tons of wheat U.S. farmers grow, or the number of burritos Chipotle sells. When we measure total production in the economy, we can't just add together the quantities of every good and service because the result would be a meaningless jumble. Tons of wheat would be added to gallons of milk, numbers of burritos, and so on. Instead, we measure production by taking the *value*, in dollar terms, of all the goods and services produced.

GDP Includes Only the Market Value of Final Goods In measuring
GDP, we include only the value of *final goods and services*. A **final good or service** is one that is purchased by its final user and is not included in the production of any other good or service. Examples of final goods are a hamburger purchased by a consumer and a computer purchased by a business. In contrast, **intermediate goods and services** become part of other goods and services. For example, Ford does not produce tires for its cars and trucks; it buys them from tire companies, such as Goodyear and Michelin. The tires are an *intermediate good*, while a Ford truck is a *final good*. In calculating GDP, we include the value of the Ford truck but not the value of the tire. If we included the value of the tire, we would be *double counting*: The value of the tire would be counted once when the tire company sold it to Ford and a second time when Ford sold the truck, with the tire installed, to a consumer.

Final good or service A good or service purchased by a final user.

Intermediate good or service A good or service that is an input into another good or service, such as a tire on a truck.

GDP Includes Only Current Production GDP includes only production
that takes place during the indicated time period. For example, GDP in 2016 includes only the goods and services produced during that year. In particular, GDP does *not* include the value of used goods. If you buy a Blu-ray of *Star Wars: The Force Awakens* from Amazon.com, the purchase is included in GDP. If six months later you resell the Blu-ray on eBay, that transaction is not included in GDP. MyEconLab Concept Check

Solved Problem 3.1

Calculating GDP

Suppose that a very simple economy produces only four goods and services: eye examinations, pizzas, shoes, and cheese. Assume that all the cheese in this economy is used in the production of pizzas. Use the information in the following table to compute GDP for the year 2017.

Production and Price Statistics for 2017		
Product	**(1)** **Quantity**	**(2)** **Price per Unit**
Eye examinations	100	$50.00
Pizzas	80	10.00
Shoes	20	100.00
Cheese	80	2.00

Solving the Problem

Step 1: **Review the module material.** This problem is about GDP, so you may want to review the section "Measuring Total Production: Gross Domestic Product," which begins on page 43.

Step 2: **Determine which goods and services listed in the table should be included in the calculation of GDP.** GDP is the value of all final goods and services. Therefore, we need to calculate the value of the final goods and services listed in the table. Eye examinations, pizzas, and shoes are final goods. Cheese would also be a final good if, for instance, a consumer bought it to use in a meal. However, here we are assuming that restaurants buy all the cheese to use in making pizzas, so the cheese is an intermediate good, and its value is not included in GDP.

Step 3: **Calculate the value of the three final goods and services listed in the table.** Value is equal to the quantity produced multiplied by the price per unit, so we multiply the numbers in column (1) by the numbers in column (2) to calculate the numbers in column (3).

Product	**(1)** **Quantity**	**(2)** **Price per Unit**	**(3)** **Value**
Eye examinations	100	$50	$5,000
Pizzas	80	10	800
Shoes	20	100	2,000

Step 4: **Add the value for each of the three final goods and services to find GDP.** GDP = Value of eye examinations produced + Value of pizzas produced + Value of shoes produced = $5,000 + $800 + $2,000 = $7,800.

Your Turn: For more practice, do related problem 1.11 on page 70 at the end of this module.

Production, Income, and the Circular-Flow Diagram

When we measure the value of total production in the economy by calculating GDP, we are at the same time measuring the value of total income. To see why the value of total production is equal to the value of total income, consider what happens to the money you spend on a single product. Suppose you buy a pair of New Balance running shoes for $149 at a Foot Locker store. *All* of that $149 must end up as someone's income. New Balance and Foot Locker will receive some of the $149 as profits, workers at New Balance will receive some as wages, the salesperson who sold you the shoes will receive some as salary, the firms that sell components to New Balance will receive some as profits, the workers for those firms will receive some as wages, and so on. Every penny must end up as someone's income. (Note, though, that any sales tax on the shoes will be collected by the store and sent to the government, without ending up as anyone's income.) There-fore, if we add up the values of every good and service sold in the economy, we must get a total that is exactly equal to the value of all the income in the economy.

The circular-flow diagram illustrates the flow of spending and money in the economy. Firms sell goods and services to three groups: domestic households, foreign firms and households, and the government. Expenditures by foreign firms and households (shown as "Rest of the World" in the diagram) on domestically produced goods and services are called *exports*. For example, American Airlines sells many tickets to passengers in Europe and Asia. As noted at the bottom of Figure 3.1, we can measure GDP by adding up the total expenditures of these groups on goods and services.

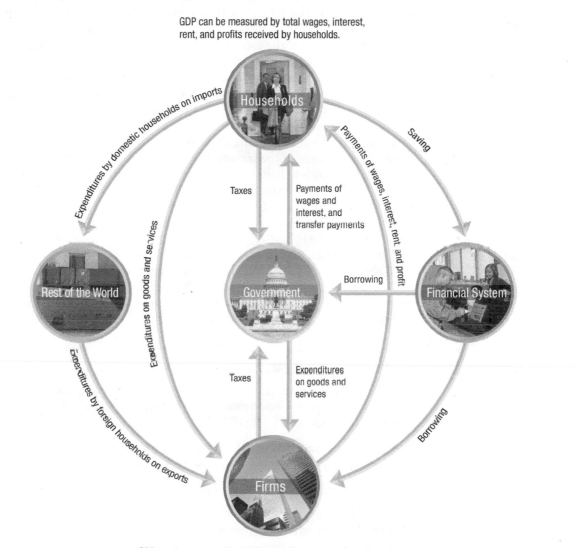

GDP can be measured by total wages, interest, rent, and profits received by households.

GDP can be measured by total expenditures on goods and services by households, firms, government, and the rest of the world.

MyEconLab Animation

Figure 3.1   The Circular Flow and the Measurement of GDP

The circular-flow diagram illustrates the flow of spending and money in the economy. Firms sell goods and services to three groups: domestic households, foreign firms and households, and the government. To produce goods and services, firms use factors of production: labor, capital, natural resources, and entrepreneurship. Households supply the factors of production to firms in exchange for income in the form of wages, interest, profit, and rent. Firms make payments of wages and interest to households in exchange for hiring workers and other factors of production. The sum of wages, interest, rent, and profit is total income in the economy. We can measure GDP as the total income received by households. The diagram also shows that households use their income to purchase goods and services, pay taxes, and save for the future. Firms and the government borrow the funds that flow from households into the financial system. We can measure GDP either by calculating the total value of expenditures on final goods and services or by calculating the value of total income.

Firms use the *factors of production*—labor, capital, natural resources, and entrepreneurial ability—to produce goods and services. Households supply the factors of production to firms in exchange for income. We divide income into four categories: wages, interest, rent, and profit. Firms pay wages to households in exchange for labor services, interest for the use of capital, and rent for natural resources such as land. Profit is the income that remains after a firm has paid wages, interest, and rent. Profit is the return to entrepreneurs and other business owners for bearing the risk of producing and selling goods and services. As Figure 3.1 shows, federal, state, and local governments make payments of wages and interest to households in exchange for hiring workers and other factors of production. Governments also make *transfer payments* to households. **Transfer payments** include Social Security payments to retired and disabled people and unemployment insurance payments to unemployed workers. These payments are not included in GDP because they are not received in exchange for production of a new good or service. The sum of wages, interest, rent, and profit is total income in the economy. As noted at the top of Figure 3.1, we can measure GDP as the total income received by households.

> **Transfer payments** Payments by the government to households for which the government does not receive a new good or service in return.

The diagram also allows us to trace the ways that households use their income. Households spend some of their income on goods and services. Some of this spending is on domestically produced goods and services, and some is on *imports*, which are foreign-produced goods and services. Households use some of their income to pay taxes to the government. (Note that firms also pay taxes to the government.) Households also use some of the income they earn to save by making deposits in checking or savings accounts in banks or by buying stocks or bonds. Banks and stock and bond markets make up the *financial system*. The flow of funds from households into the financial system makes it possible for the government and firms to borrow. As we will see, the health of the financial system is vital to an economy. Without the ability to borrow funds through the financial system, firms will have difficulty expanding and adopting new technologies. In fact, no country without a well-developed financial system has been able to sustain high levels of economic growth.

The circular-flow diagram shows that we can measure GDP either by calculating the total value of expenditures on final goods and services or by calculating the value of total income. We get the same dollar amount of GDP with either approach.

MyEconLab Concept Check

Components of GDP

The BEA divides its statistics on GDP into four major categories of expenditures: consumption, investment, government purchases, and net exports. Economists use these categories to understand why GDP fluctuates and to forecast future GDP.

Personal Consumption Expenditures, or "Consumption" Consumption expenditures are made by households and are divided into three categories:

> **Consumption** Spending by households on goods and services, not including spending on new houses.

1. Expenditures on *services*, such as medical care, education, and haircuts
2. Expenditures on *nondurable goods*, such as food and clothing
3. Expenditures on *durable goods*, such as automobiles and furniture

The spending by households on new houses is not included in consumption. Instead, spending on new houses is included in the investment category, which we discuss next.

Gross Private Domestic Investment, or "Investment" Spending on *gross private domestic investment*, or simply **investment**, is also divided into three categories.

> **Investment** Spending by firms on new factories, office buildings, machinery, and additions to inventories, plus spending by households and firms on new houses.

1. *Business fixed investment* is spending by firms on new factories, office buildings, and machinery used to produce other goods. Since 2013, this category of investment has included business spending on research and development. The BEA had previously considered such spending to be an intermediate good.

Don't Let This Happen to You

Remember What Economists Mean by *Investment*

Notice that the definition of *investment* in this module is narrower than in everyday use. For example, people often say they are investing in the stock market or in rare coins. As we have seen, economists reserve the word *investment* for purchases of machinery, factories, and houses. Economists don't include purchases of shares of stock or rare coins or deposits in savings accounts in the definition of investment because these activities don't result in the production of new goods. For example, a share of Twitter's stock represents part ownership of that company. When you buy a share of Twitter's stock, nothing new is produced; there is just a transfer from the seller to you of that small piece of ownership of Twitter. Similarly, buying a rare coin or putting $1,000 into a savings account does not result in an increase in production. GDP is not affected by any of these activities, so they are not included in the economic definition of investment.

MyEconLab Study Plan

Your Turn: Test your understanding by doing related problem 1.12 on page 71 at the end of this module.

2. *Residential investment* is spending by households and firms on new single-family and multi-unit houses.

3. *Changes in business inventories* are changes in the stocks of goods that have been produced but not yet sold. If Ford has $200 million worth of unsold cars at the beginning of the year and $350 million worth of unsold cars at the end of the year, then the firm has spent $150 million on inventory investment during the year.

Government Consumption and Gross Investment, or "Government Purchases" Government purchases are spending by federal, state, and local governments on goods and services, such as teachers' salaries, highways, and aircraft carriers. Again, government spending on transfer payments is not included in government purchases because it does not result in the production of new goods and services.

Government purchases Spending by federal, state, and local governments on goods and services.

Net Exports of Goods and Services, or "Net Exports" Net exports are equal to *exports* minus *imports*. Exports are goods and services produced in the United States and purchased by foreign firms, households, and governments. We add exports to our other categories of expenditures because otherwise we would not be including all spending on new goods and services produced in the United States. For example, if a farmer in South Dakota sells wheat to China, the value of the wheat is included in GDP because it represents production in the United States. Imports are goods and services produced in foreign countries and purchased by U.S. firms, households, and governments. We subtract imports from total expenditures because otherwise we would be including spending that does not result in production of new goods and services in the United States. For example, if U.S. consumers buy $1 billion worth of furniture manufactured in China, that spending is included in consumption expenditures. But the value of those imports is subtracted from GDP because the imports do not represent production in the United States.

Net exports Exports minus imports.

MyEconLab Concept Check

An Equation for GDP and Some Actual Values

A simple equation sums up the components of GDP:

$$Y = C + I + G + NX.$$

The equation tells us that GDP (denoted as *Y*) equals consumption (*C*) plus investment (*I*) plus government purchases (*G*) plus net exports (*NX*). Figure 3.2 shows the values of the components of GDP for the year 2014. The graph in the figure highlights the fact

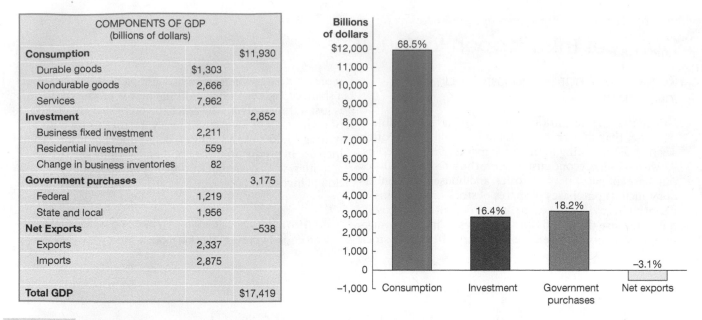

COMPONENTS OF GDP (billions of dollars)		
Consumption		$11,930
Durable goods	$1,303	
Nondurable goods	2,666	
Services	7,962	
Investment		2,852
Business fixed investment	2,211	
Residential investment	559	
Change in business inventories	82	
Government purchases		3,175
Federal	1,219	
State and local	1,956	
Net Exports		–538
Exports	2,337	
Imports	2,875	
Total GDP		$17,419

Figure 3.2   Components of GDP in 2014

Consumption accounts for a much larger percentage of GDP than any of the other components. In recent years, net exports have typically been negative, which reduces GDP. Note that the subtotals may not sum to the totals for each category because of rounding.
Source: U.S. Bureau of Economic Analysis.

that consumption is by far the largest component of GDP. The table provides a more detailed breakdown and shows several interesting points:

- Consumer spending on services is greater than the sum of spending on durable and nondurable goods. There has been a continuing trend in the United States and other high-income countries away from the production of goods and toward the production of services. As the populations of these countries have become, on average, both older and wealthier, their demand for services such as medical care and financial advice has increased faster than their demand for goods.

- Business fixed investment is the largest component of investment. As we will see in later modules, spending by firms on new factories, computers, and machinery can fluctuate. For example, a decline in business fixed investment played an important role in the 2007–2009 recession.

- Purchases made by state and local governments are greater than purchases made by the federal government. Because basic government activities, such as education and law enforcement, occur largely at the state and local levels, state and local government spending is greater than federal government spending.

- Imports are greater than exports, so net exports are negative. We will discuss in Module 9 why imports have typically been larger than exports for the U.S. economy.   MyEconLab Concept Check

Making the Connection
MyEconLab Video

Adding More of Lady Gaga to GDP

The Bureau of Economic Analysis (BEA) is always researching to improve its measurement of GDP. A few years ago, the BEA changed how it accounts for spending on research and development (R&D). Prior to 2013, the BEA considered R&D by firms or the government to be an intermediate good, just as tires or batteries are considered intermediate goods in automobile manufacturing. But spending on R&D is similar to investment spending. For example, when Ford buys new machine tools—which are included in investment spending—it does so to help manufacture automobiles now and in the future. Similarly, when Ford spends on R&D to improve the battery in its Ford Focus electric car, it does so to help improve the car now and in the future. The BEA now counts spending on R&D as investment. In other words, the BEA shifted from not counting spending on R&D as part of GDP to counting it.

The term *research and development* brings to mind scientists working in laboratories, trying to develop new pharmaceutical drugs or improved computer chips. But just as firms and the government devote resources to R&D, movie and television studios, book authors, and musicians devote time and resources to producing new movies, television programs, books, and recordings. In past years, the BEA counted spending by firms and individuals on developing entertainment products as part of the cost of producing those products, in the same way that it counted the cost of labor and materials. So the cost of developing entertainment products was *not* included in GDP. But in 2013, the BEA changed its procedures to include those costs as part of investment and began including it in GDP. For example, prior to 2013, sales of Lady Gaga's songs on iTunes and on CDs as well as ticket sales for her concerts were included in GDP, but the cost to Lady Gaga and her record company of writing and recording her songs was not included. Now both types of spending are included in GDP.

The cost to Lady Gaga and her record company of writing and recording her songs is now part of GDP.

By broadening the definition of investment spending, the BEA increased measured GDP in 2013 by about 3 percent. The BEA adjusted its historical data on GDP back to 1929, so while the levels of GDP increased, the changes in GDP from one year to the next were not greatly affected. The BEA makes changes to its calculations of GDP after consulting with government statistical agencies in other countries. The objective is to allow economists, firms, and policymakers to more accurately compare GDP in different countries. The broadening of the definition of investment was meant to increase the importance of *intellectual property* (IP), such as software, movies, and books, in GDP. A study by the U.S. Patent and Trademark Office estimated that in the United States, IP-intensive industries, including pharmaceuticals, computers and software, telecommunications, book publishing, and radio and television broadcasting, account for about 40 million jobs and more than one-third of GDP.

As the economy changes over time, the BEA evaluates whether to adjust the way it measures GDP.

Sources: David Kestenbaum, "Lady Gaga Writing a New Song Is Like a Factory Investing in a New Machine," www.npr.org, April 25, 2013; Osagie Imasogie and Thaddeus J. Kobylarz, "Yes, Lady Gaga's Songs Contribute to GDP," *Wall Street Journal*, May 27, 2013; U.S. Bureau of Economic Analysis, "Preview of the 2013 Comprehensive Revision of the National Income and Product Accounts," *Survey of Current Business*, Vol. 93, No. 3, March 2013; and U.S. Department of Commerce, *Intellectual Property and the U.S. Economy: Industries in Focus*, March 2012.

Your Turn: Test your understanding by doing related problem 1.13 on page 71 at the end of this module.

MyEconLab Study Plan

Measuring GDP Using the Value-Added Method

We have seen that GDP can be calculated by adding together all expenditures on final goods and services. An alternative way of calculating GDP is the *value-added method*. **Value added** refers to the additional market value a firm gives to a product and is equal to the difference between the price for which the firm sells a good and the price it paid other firms for intermediate goods. Table 3.1 gives a hypothetical example of the value added by each firm involved in the production of a shirt offered for sale on L.L.Bean's Web site.

Suppose a cotton farmer sells $1 of raw cotton to a textile mill. If, for simplicity, we ignore any inputs the farmer may have purchased from other firms—such as cottonseed

Value added The market value a firm adds to a product.

Table 3.1

Calculating Value Added

Firm	Value of Product	Value Added		
Cotton farmer	Value of raw cotton = $1	Value added by cotton farmer	=	$1
Textile mill	Value of raw cotton woven into cotton fabric = $3	Value added by textile mill = ($3 − $1)	=	$2
Shirt company	Value of cotton fabric made into a shirt = $15	Value added by shirt company = ($15 − $3)	=	$12
L.L.Bean	Value of shirt for sale on L.L.Bean's Web site = $35	Value added by L.L.Bean = ($35 − $15)	=	$20
	Total Value Added		**=**	**$35**

or fertilizer—then the farmer's value added is $1. The textile mill then weaves the raw cotton into cotton fabric, which it sells to a shirt company for $3. The textile mill's value added ($2) is the difference between the price it paid for the raw cotton ($1) and the price for which it can sell the cotton fabric ($3). Similarly, the shirt company's value added is the difference between the price it paid for the cotton fabric ($3) and the price it receives for the shirt from L.L.Bean ($15). L.L.Bean's value added is the difference between the price it pays for the shirt ($15) and the price for which it can sell the shirt on its Web site ($35). Notice that *the price of the shirt on L.L.Bean's Web site is exactly equal to the sum of the value added by each firm involved in the production of the shirt.* We can calculate GDP by adding up the market value of every final good and service produced during a particular period. Or, we can arrive at the same value for GDP by adding up the value added by every firm involved in producing those final goods and services.

 MyEconLab Study Plan

MyEconLab Concept Check

 3.2 ## Does GDP Measure What We Want It to Measure?

LEARNING OBJECTIVE: Discuss whether GDP is a good measure of well-being.

Economists use GDP to measure total production in the economy. For that purpose, we would like GDP to be as comprehensive as possible, not overlooking any significant production that takes place in the economy. Most economists believe that GDP does a good— but not flawless—job of measuring production. GDP is also sometimes used as a measure of well-being. Although it is generally true that the more goods and services people have, the better off they are, we will see that GDP provides only a rough measure of well-being.

Shortcomings in GDP as a Measure of Total Production

When the BEA calculates GDP, it does not include two types of production: production in the home and production in the underground economy.

Household Production With few exceptions, the BEA does not attempt to estimate the value of goods and services that are not bought and sold in markets. If a carpenter makes and sells bookcases, the value of those bookcases will be counted in GDP. If the carpenter makes a bookcase for personal use, it will not be counted in GDP. *Household production* refers to goods and services people produce for themselves. The most important type of household production is the services a homemaker provides to the homemaker's family. If a person has been caring for children, cleaning the house, and preparing the family meals, the value of such services is not included in GDP. If the person then decides to work outside the home, enrolls the children in day care, hires a cleaning service, and begins buying the family's meals in restaurants, the value of GDP will rise by the amount paid for day care, cleaning services, and restaurant meals, even though production of these services has not actually increased.

The Underground Economy Individuals and firms sometimes conceal the buying and selling of goods and services, in which case their production isn't counted in GDP. Individuals and firms conceal what they buy and sell for three main reasons: They are dealing in illegal goods and services, such as drugs or prostitution; they want to avoid paying taxes on the income they earn; or they want to avoid government regulations. This concealed buying and selling is called the **underground economy**. Estimates of the size of the underground economy in the United States vary widely, but

Underground economy Buying and selling of goods and services that is concealed from the government to avoid taxes or regulations or because the goods and services are illegal.

it is probably at most 10 percent of measured GDP, or about $1.8 trillion. The underground economy in some low-income countries, such as Zimbabwe or Peru, may be more than 50 percent of measured GDP. Recently, countries in Western Europe have decided to include estimates of spending on illegal drugs and prostitution in their measures of GDP. To this point, the BEA has decided not to follow this approach. If it did, estimates are that measured U.S. GDP would increase by about 3 percent.

Is not counting household production or production in the underground economy a serious shortcoming of GDP? Most economists would answer "no" because the most important use of GDP is to measure changes in how the economy is performing over short periods of time, such as from one year to the next. For this purpose, omitting household production and production in the underground economy doesn't matter because there is not likely to be much change in household production or the size of the underground economy from one year to the next.

We also use GDP to measure how production of goods and services grows over fairly long periods of a decade or more. For this purpose, omitting household production and production in the underground economy may be more important. For example, beginning in the 1970s, the number of women working outside the home increased dramatically. Some of the goods and services—such as childcare and restaurant meals—produced in the following years were not true additions to total production; rather, they were replacing what had been household production.   MyEconLab Concept Check

Making the Connection
MyEconLab Video

Why Do Many Developing Countries Have Such Large Underground Economies?

Recent estimates put the size of the underground economy at 8 percent of measured GDP in the United States and 13 percent in Western Europe. The underground economy is much larger in many developing countries—perhaps 50 percent or more of measured GDP. In developing countries, the underground economy is often referred to as the *informal sector*, as opposed to the *formal sector*, in which output of goods and services is measured. Although it might not seem to matter whether production of goods and services is measured and included in GDP or unmeasured, a large informal sector can be a sign of government policies that are retarding economic growth.

Because firms in the informal sector are operating illegally, they tend to be smaller and have less capital than firms operating legally. The entrepreneurs who start firms in the informal sector may be afraid the government could someday close or confiscate their firms. Therefore, the entrepreneurs limit their investments in these firms. As a consequence, workers in these firms have less machinery and equipment to work with and so can produce fewer goods and services. Entrepreneurs in the informal sector also have to pay the costs of avoiding government authorities. For example, construction firms operating in the informal sector in Brazil have to employ lookouts who can warn workers to hide when government inspectors come around. In many countries, firms in the informal sector have to pay substantial bribes to government officials to remain in business. The informal sector is large in some developing economies because taxes are high and government regulations are extensive. For example, firms in Brazil pay 85 percent of all taxes collected, as compared with 40 percent in the United States. Not surprisingly, about half of all Brazilian workers are employed in the informal sector. According to one estimate, firms in the informal sector in Brazil can earn three times the profit of similar-sized firms in the formal sector. In Zimbabwe and Peru, the fraction of workers in the informal sector may be as high as 60 or 70 percent. One estimate puts the size of the informal sector in India at nearly 50 percent.

Many economists believe taxes in developing countries are so high because these countries are attempting to pay for government sectors that are as large relative to their economies as the government sectors of industrial economies. Including transfer payments, government spending in Brazil, for example, is 41 percent of measured GDP, compared to 36 percent in the United States. In the early twentieth century,

In some developing countries, more than half the workers may be in the underground economy.

when the United States was much poorer than it is today, government spending was only about 8 percent of GDP, so the tax burden on U.S. firms was much lower. In countries such as Brazil, bringing firms into the formal sector from the informal sector may require reductions in government spending and taxes. In most developing countries, however, voters are reluctant to see government services reduced.

Sources: "The Price Is Wrong," *Economist*, September 28, 2013; "Dynamic but Dirty," *Economist*, December 2, 2010; "Notes from the Underground," *Economist*, April 2, 2009; Mary Anastasia O'Grady, "Why Brazil's Underground Economy Grows and Grows," *Wall Street Journal*, September 10, 2004; and the International Monetary Fund.

MyEconLab Study Plan

Your Turn: Test your understanding by doing related problems 2.8 and 2.9 on page 72 at the end of this module.

Shortcomings of GDP as a Measure of Well-Being

The main purpose of GDP is to measure a country's total production. GDP is also frequently used, though, as a measure of well-being. For example, news stories often include tables that show for different countries the levels of GDP per person, which is usually called *GDP per capita*. GDP per capita is calculated by dividing the value of GDP for a country by the country's population. These articles imply that people in the countries with higher levels of GDP per capita are better off. Although increases in GDP often do lead to increases in the well-being of the population, it is important to be aware that GDP is not a perfect measure of well-being for several reasons.

The Value of Leisure Is Not Included in GDP If an economic consultant decides to retire, GDP will decline even though the consultant may value increased leisure more than the income he or she was earning from running a consulting firm. The consultant's well-being has increased, but GDP has decreased. In 1890, the typical American worked 60 hours per week. Today, the typical American works fewer than 40 hours per week. If Americans still worked 60-hour weeks, GDP would be much higher than it is now, but the well-being of a typical person would be lower because less time would be available for leisure activities.

GDP Is Not Adjusted for Pollution or Other Negative Effects of Production When a dry cleaner cleans and presses clothes, the value of this service is included in GDP. If the chemicals the dry cleaner uses pollute the air or water, GDP is not adjusted to compensate for the cost of the pollution. Similarly, the value of cigarettes produced is included in GDP, with no adjustment made for the cost of the lung cancer that some smokers develop.

We should note, though, that increasing GDP often leads countries to devote more resources to pollution reduction. For example, in the United States between 1970 and 2013, as GDP was steadily increasing, emissions of the six main air pollutants declined by more than 50 percent. Developing countries often have higher levels of pollution than high-income countries because the lower GDPs of the developing countries make them more reluctant to spend resources on pollution reduction. Levels of pollution in China are much higher than those in the United States, Japan, or the countries of Western Europe. According to the World Health Organization, 7 of the 10 most polluted cities in the world are in China, but as Chinese GDP continues to rise, the country is likely to devote more resources to reducing pollution.

GDP Is Not Adjusted for Changes in Crime and Other Social Problems An increase in crime reduces well-being but may actually increase GDP if it leads to greater spending on police, security guards, and alarm systems. GDP is also not adjusted for changes in divorce rates, drug addiction, or other factors that may affect people's well-being.

GDP Measures the Size of the Pie but Not How the Pie Is Divided When a country's GDP increases, the country has more goods and services, but those goods and services may be very unequally distributed. Therefore, GDP may not provide good information about the goods and services consumed by a typical person.

To summarize, we can say that a person's well-being depends on many factors that are not considered in calculating GDP. Because GDP is designed to measure total production, it should not be surprising that it does an imperfect job of measuring well-being.

MyEconLab Concept Check

3.3 Real GDP versus Nominal GDP

LEARNING OBJECTIVE: Discuss the difference between real GDP and nominal GDP.

Because GDP is measured in value terms, we have to be careful about interpreting changes over time. To see why, consider interpreting an increase in the total value of pickup truck production from $40 billion in 2016 to $44 billion in 2017. Because $44 billion is 10 percent greater than $40 billion, were 10 percent more trucks produced in 2017 than in 2016? We can draw this conclusion only if the average price of trucks did not change between 2016 and 2017. In fact, when GDP increases from one year to the next, the increase is due partly to increases in production of goods and services and partly to increases in prices. Because we are mainly interested in GDP as a measure of production, we need a way of separating the price changes from the quantity changes.

Calculating Real GDP

The BEA separates price changes from quantity changes by calculating a measure of production called *real GDP*. **Nominal GDP** is calculated by summing the current values of final goods and services. **Real GDP** is calculated by designating a particular year as the *base year* and then using the prices of goods and services in the base year to calculate the value of goods and services in all other years. For instance, if the base year is 2009, real GDP for 2017 would be calculated by using prices of goods and services from 2009. By keeping prices constant, we know that changes in real GDP represent changes in the quantity of goods and services produced in the economy.

Nominal GDP The value of final goods and services evaluated at current-year prices.

Real GDP The value of final goods and services evaluated at base-year prices.

Solved Problem 3.3

MyEconLab Interactive Animation

Calculating Real GDP

Suppose that a very simple economy produces only the following three final goods and services: eye examinations, pizzas, and shoes. Use the information in the table on the right to compute real GDP for the year 2017. Assume that the base year is 2009.

Product	2009		2017	
	Quantity	Price	Quantity	Price
Eye examinations	80	$40	100	$50
Pizzas	90	11	80	10
Shoes	15	90	20	100

Solving the Problem

Step 1: **Review the module material.** This problem is about calculating real GDP, so you may want to review the section, "Calculating Real GDP," which begins on this page.

Step 2: **Calculate the value of the three goods and services listed in the table, using the quantities for 2017 and the prices for 2009.** Real GDP is the value of all final goods and services, evaluated at base-year prices. In this case, the base year is 2009, and we have the price of each product in that year:

Product	2017 Quantity	2009 Price	Value
Eye examinations	100	$40	$4,000
Pizzas	80	11	880
Shoes	20	90	1,800

Step 3: **Add up the values of the three products to find real GDP.** Real GDP for 2017 equals the sum of:

Quantity of eye examinations in 2017 $\times$ Price of eye examinations in 2009 = \$4,000
Quantity of pizzas produced in 2017 $\times$ Price of pizzas in 2009 = \$880
Quantity of shoes produced in 2017 $\times$ Price of shoes in 2009 = \$1,800
or, \$6,680

Extra Credit: Notice that the quantities of each good produced in 2009 were irrelevant for calculating real GDP in 2017. Notice also that the value of \$6,680 for real GDP in 2017 is lower than the value of \$7,800 for nominal GDP in 2017 that we calculated in Solved Problem 3.1 on page 44.

MyEconLab Study Plan

Your Turn: For more practice, do related problem 3.4 on page 73 at the end of this module.

One drawback to calculating real GDP using base-year prices is that, over time, prices may change relative to each other. For example, the price of smartphones may fall relative to the price of milk. Because this change is not reflected in the fixed prices from the base year, the estimate of real GDP is somewhat distorted. The further away the current year is from the base year, the worse the problem becomes. To make the calculation of real GDP more accurate, in 1996, the BEA switched to using *chain-weighted prices*, and it now publishes statistics on real GDP in "chained (2009) dollars."

The details of calculating real GDP using chain-weighted prices are more complicated than we need to discuss here, but the basic idea is straightforward: Starting with the base year, the BEA takes an average of prices in that year and prices in the following year. It then uses this average to calculate real GDP in the year following the base year (currently the year 2009). For the next year—in other words, the year that is two years after the base year—the BEA calculates real GDP by taking an average of prices in that year and the previous year. In this way, prices in each year are "chained" to prices from the previous year, and the distortion from changes in relative prices is minimized.

Holding prices constant means that the *purchasing power* of a dollar remains the same from one year to the next. Ordinarily, the purchasing power of the dollar falls every year as price increases reduce the amount of goods and services that a dollar can buy.   MyEconLab Concept Check

Comparing Real GDP and Nominal GDP

Real GDP holds prices constant, which makes it a better measure than nominal GDP of changes in the production of goods and services from one year to the next. In fact, growth in the economy is almost always measured as growth in real GDP. If a headline in the *Wall Street Journal* states "U.S. Economy Grew 2.3% Last Year," the article will report that real GDP increased by 2.3 percent during the previous year.

We describe real GDP as being measured in "base-year dollars." For example, nominal GDP in 2014 was \$17,419 billion, and, with a base year of 2009, real GDP in 2014 was \$16,086 billion in 2009 dollars. Because, on average, prices rise from one year to the next, real GDP is greater than nominal GDP in years before the base year and less than nominal GDP for years after the base year. In the base year, real GDP and nominal GDP are the same because both are calculated for the base year using the same prices and quantities. Figure 3.3 shows movements in nominal GDP and real GDP between 1990 and 2014. In the years before 2009, prices were, on average, lower than in 2009, so nominal GDP was lower than real GDP. In 2009, nominal and real GDP were equal. Since 2009, prices have been, on average, higher than in 2009, so nominal GDP is higher than real GDP.   MyEconLab Concept Check

The GDP Deflator

Price level A measure of the average prices of goods and services in the economy.

Economists and policymakers are interested not just in the level of total production, as measured by real GDP, but also in the *price level*. The **price level** measures the average prices of goods and services in the economy. One of the goals of economic policy is to maintain a

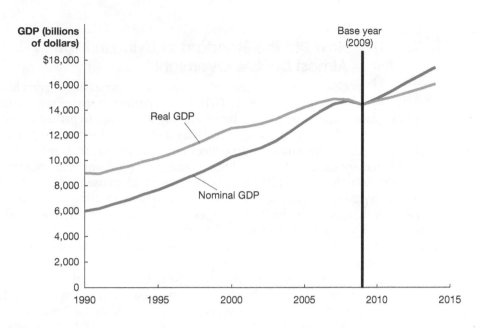

MyEconLab Real-time data

Figure 3.3

Nominal GDP and Real GDP, 1990–2014

Currently, the base year for calculating GDP is 2009. In the years before 2009, prices were, on average, lower than in 2009, so nominal GDP was lower than real GDP. In 2009, nominal and real GDP were equal. Since 2009, prices have been, on average, higher than in 2009, so nominal GDP is higher than real GDP.

Source: U.S. Bureau of Economic Analysis.

stable price level. We can use values for nominal GDP and real GDP to compute a measure of the price level called the *GDP deflator*. We calculate the **GDP deflator** using this formula:

$$\text{GDP deflator} = \frac{\text{Nominal GDP}}{\text{Real GDP}} \times 100.$$

GDP deflator A measure of the price level, calculated by dividing nominal GDP by real GDP and multiplying by 100.

To see why the GDP deflator is a measure of the price level, think about what would happen if prices of goods and services rose while production remained the same. In that case, nominal GDP would increase, but real GDP would remain constant, so the GDP deflator would increase. In reality, both prices and production usually increase each year, but the more prices increase relative to the increase in production, the more nominal GDP increases relative to real GDP, and the higher the value for the GDP deflator. Increases in the GDP deflator allow economists and policymakers to track increases in the price level over time.

Remember that in the base year (currently 2009), nominal GDP is equal to real GDP, so the value of the GDP price deflator will always be 100 in the base year. The following table gives the values for nominal and real GDP for 2013 and 2014:

	2013	2014
Nominal GDP	$16,768 billion	$17,419 billion
Real GDP	$15,710 billion	$16,086 billion

We can use the information from this table to calculate values for the GDP price deflator for 2013 and 2014:

Formula	Applied to 2013	Applied to 2014
GDP deflator $= \left(\dfrac{\text{Nominal GDP}}{\text{Real GDP}}\right) \times 100$	$\left(\dfrac{\$16,768 \text{ billion}}{\$15,710 \text{ billion}}\right) \times 100 = 106.7$	$\left(\dfrac{\$17,419 \text{ billion}}{\$16,086 \text{ billion}}\right) \times 100 = 108.3$

From these values for the deflator, we can calculate that the price level increased by 1.5 percent between 2013 and 2014:

$$\left(\frac{108.3 - 106.7}{106.7}\right) \times 100 = 1.5\%.$$

In the next module, we will see that economists and policymakers also rely on another measure of the price level, known as the consumer price index. In addition, we will discuss the strengths and weaknesses of different measures of the price level.

MyEconLab Concept Check

How Did the Standard of Living in Nigeria Almost Double Overnight?

Government agencies in developing countries like Nigeria have difficulty measuring GDP for two primary reasons: First, the size of the underground economy may be large, making it difficult to gather data on many businesses. Second, government agencies may lack the budgets or the trained staff to accurately process the data they do collect or to use the same approaches to calculating GDP that are used in the United States and other high-income countries. For example, we've seen that in calculating real GDP, governments use base-year prices that, over time, may change relative to each other, potentially distorting the measurement. To deal with this problem, the BEA changes the base year fairly frequently and uses chain-weighted prices. This approach, though, can be difficult for developing countries to implement because it can be expensive to have government employees collect large amounts of price data.

By 2010, the government of Nigeria knew that the data it was publishing on real GDP were inaccurate because it was still using 1990 as its base year, even though the economy had changed dramatically over the years. The Nigerian National Bureau of Statistics was given a larger budget and the task of both changing the real GDP base year to 2010 and gathering data on previously unrecorded output in the underground economy. As an article in the *Wall Street Journal* put it, "Nigerian number crunchers traversed the West African nation by motorcycle and speedboat, visiting Internet cafe owners, movie producers and other businesspeople to record previously uncaptured commercial activity." The number of businesses being surveyed for data increased from 85,000 to 850,000.

When the new data on GDP were released in 2014, the results were dramatic. The estimate for real GDP for 2013 was changed from $270 billion to $510 billion, an 89 percent increase. The increase was large enough for Nigeria to pass South Africa as the largest economy in Africa. As the figure below shows, the new data also gave a more accurate picture of the structure of the Nigerian economy. For instance, where previously the service sector was believed to make up less than one-third of the economy, it was shown to actually be more than half the economy. In addition, although not shown in the figure, the telecommunications sector actually makes up 9 percent of the economy, rather than the 1 percent in previous estimates, and the oil industry is only 14 percent of the economy rather than 33 percent.

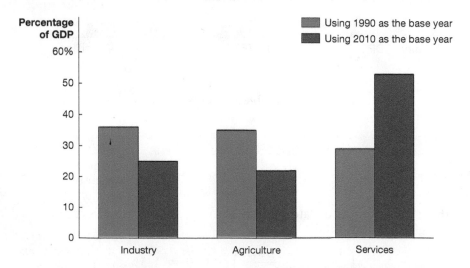

But had the standard of living of the typical Nigerian actually increased? The new estimates made it appear so, with real GDP per person increasing from $1,500 to $2,688. Of course, all that had really changed was how accurately the government was measuring real GDP. The country was producing no more goods and services on April 6, 2014, when the new GDP data were announced, than it had been the day before.

Nigeria's experience with measuring its GDP demonstrates the problems governments have in accurately constructing these statistics and how misleading it can be to rely on them as measures of a country's standard of living.

Sources: Drew Hinshaw and Patrick McGroarty, "Nigeria's Economy Surpasses South Africa's in Size," *Wall Street Journal*, April 6, 2014; Javier Blas and William Wallis, "Nigeria Almost Doubles GDP in Recalculation," *Financial Times*, April 7, 2014; and "How Nigeria's Economy Grew by 89% Overnight," *Economist*, April 7, 2014.

Your Turn: Test your understanding by doing related problem 3.10 on page 73 at the end of this module.

MyEconLab Study Plan

3.4 Other Measures of Total Production and Total Income

MyEconLab Study Plan

LEARNING OBJECTIVE: Describe other measures of total production and total income.

National income accounting refers to the methods the BEA uses to track total production and total income in the economy. The statistical tables containing this information are called the *National Income and Product Accounts (NIPA)* tables. Every quarter, the BEA releases NIPA tables containing data on several measures of total production and total income. We have already discussed GDP, which is the most important measure of total production and total income. In addition to computing GDP, the BEA computes the following four measures of production and income: gross national product, national income, personal income, and disposable personal income.

Gross National Product

We have seen that GDP is the value of final goods and services produced within the United States. *Gross national product (GNP)* is the value of final goods and services produced by residents of the United States, even if the production takes place *outside* the United States. U.S. firms have facilities in foreign countries, and foreign firms have facilities in the United States. Ford, for example, has assembly plants in the United Kingdom, and Toyota has assembly plants in the United States. GNP includes foreign production by U.S. firms but excludes U.S. production by foreign firms. For the United States, GNP is almost the same as GDP. For example, in 2014, GDP was $17,419 billion, and GNP was $17,631 billion, or only about 1.2 percent more than GDP.

For many years, GNP was the main measure of total production compiled by the federal government and used by economists and policymakers in the United States. However, in many countries other than the United States, a significant percentage of domestic production takes place in foreign-owned facilities. For those countries, GDP is much larger than GNP and is a more accurate measure of the level of production within the country's borders. As a result, many countries and international agencies had long preferred using GDP to using GNP. In 1991, the United States joined those countries in using GDP as its main measure of total production.   MyEconLab Concept Check

National Income

In the production of goods and services, some machinery, equipment, and buildings wear out and have to be replaced. The value of this worn-out machinery, equipment, and buildings is called *depreciation*. In the NIPA tables, depreciation is called the *consumption of fixed capital*. If we subtract this value from GDP, we are left with *national income*.

Earlier in this module, we stressed that the value of total production is equal to the value of total income. This point is not strictly true if by "value of total production" we mean GDP and by "value of total income" we mean national income because national income will always be smaller than GDP by an amount equal to depreciation. In practice, though, the difference between the value of GDP and value of national income does not matter for most macroeconomic issues.   MyEconLab Concept Check

Personal Income

Personal income is income received by households. To calculate personal income, we subtract the earnings that corporations retain rather than pay to shareholders in the form of dividends. We also add in the payments received by households from the government in the form of *transfer payments* or interest on government bonds.   MyEconLab Concept Check

Disposable Personal Income

Disposable personal income is equal to personal income minus personal tax payments, such as the federal personal income tax. It is the best measure of the income households actually have available to spend.

Figure 3.4 shows the values of these measures of total production and total income for 2014 in a table and a graph.   MyEconLab Concept Check

The Division of Income

Figure 3.1 on page 45 illustrates the important fact that we can measure GDP in terms of total expenditure or as the total income received by households. GDP calculated as the sum of income payments to households is sometimes called *gross domestic income*. Figure 3.5 shows the division of total income among wages, interest, rent, profit, and certain non-income items. The non-income items are included in gross domestic income because sales taxes, depreciation, and a few other items are included in the value of goods and services produced but are not directly received by households as income. *Wages* include all compensation received by employees, including fringe benefits such as health insurance. *Interest* is net interest received by households, or the difference between the interest received on savings accounts, government bonds, and other investments and the interest paid on car loans, home mortgages, and other debts. *Rent* is rent received by households. *Profits* include the profits of sole proprietorships, which are usually small businesses, and the profits of corporations. Figure 3.5 shows that the largest component of gross domestic income is wages, which are about three times as large as profits.   MyEconLab Concept Check

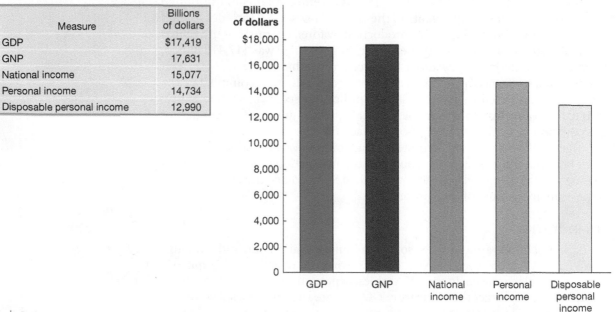

Measure	Billions of dollars
GDP	$17,419
GNP	17,631
National income	15,077
Personal income	14,734
Disposable personal income	12,990

MyEconLab Real-time data

Figure 3.4   Measures of Total Production and Total Income, 2014

The most important measure of total production and total income is gross domestic product (GDP). As we will see in later modules, for some purposes, the other measures of total production and total income shown in the figure turn out to be more useful than GDP.
Source: U.S. Bureau of Economic Analysis.

	Billions of dollars
Wages	$9,237
Interest	660
Rent	640
Profit	3,076
Profits of sole proprietors	1,380
Profits of corporations	1,696
Taxes, depreciation, and statistical discrepancy	3,989

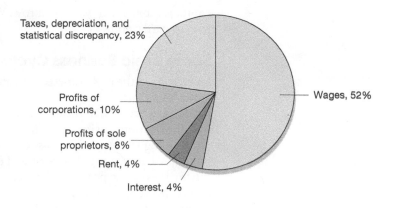

MyEconLab Animation

Figure 3.5   The Division of Income, 2014

We can measure GDP in terms of total expenditure or as the total income received by households. The largest component of income received by households is wages, which are more than three times as large as the profits received by sole proprietors and the profits received by corporations combined.

Note: The components in the figure do not sum to 100 percent because of rounding.
Source: U.S. Bureau of Economic Analysis.

Continued from page 41

Economics in Your Life

What's the Best Country for You to Work In?

At the beginning of the module, we posed two questions: What effect should Canada's and China's two very different growth rates have on your decision to work and live in one country or the other? And if China's much higher growth rate does not necessarily lead you to decide to work and live there, why not? This module has shown that although it is *generally* true that the more goods and services people have, the better off they are, GDP provides only a rough measure of well-being. GDP does not include the value of leisure; nor is it adjusted for pollution and other negative effects of production or crime and other social problems. So, in deciding where to live and work, you would need to balance China's much higher growth rate of GDP against these other considerations. You would also need to take into account that although China's *growth rate* is higher than Canada's, Canada's current *level* of real GDP is higher than China's.

Conclusion

In this module, we have begun the study of macroeconomics by examining an important concept: how a country's total production and income can be measured. Understanding GDP is important for understanding the business cycle and the process of long-run economic growth. In the further modules, we discuss the issues involved in measuring two other key economic variables: the unemployment rate and the inflation rate.

Visit MyEconLab for a news article and analysis related to the concepts in this module.

3.5 The Business Cycle

LEARNING OBJECTIVE: Explain what happens during the business cycle.

There was a tremendous increase during the past century in the standard of living of the average American. But close inspection real GDP per capita did not increase every year during this time. For example, during the first half of the 1930s, real GDP per capita *fell* for several years in a row. What accounts for these fluctuations in the long-run upward trend?

Some Basic Business Cycle Definitions

Since at least the early nineteenth century, the U.S. economy has experienced business cycles that consist of alternating periods of expanding and contracting economic activity. Because real GDP is our best measure of economic activity, the business cycle is usually illustrated using movements in real GDP.

During the *expansion phase* of the business cycle, production, employment, and income are increasing. The period of expansion ends with a *business cycle peak*. Following the business cycle peak, production, employment, and income decline as the economy enters the *recession phase* of the cycle. The recession comes to an end with a *business cycle trough*, after which another period of expansion begins. Figure 3.6 illustrates the phases of the business cycle. Panel (a) shows an idealized business cycle, with real GDP increasing smoothly in an expansion to a business cycle peak and then decreasing smoothly in a recession to a business cycle trough, which is followed by another expansion. Panel (b) shows the somewhat messier reality of an actual business cycle by plotting fluctuations in real GDP during the period from 2006 to 2015. The figure shows that the expansion that began in 2001 continued until a business cycle peak was reached in December 2007. The following recession was the longest and the most severe since the Great Depression of the 1930s. The severity of the recession led some economists to refer to it as the "Great Recession." The economy reached a business cycle trough in June 2009, when the next expansion began. Although real GDP grew following the business cycle trough, the growth was slower than is typical at the beginning of a business cycle expansion.

MyEconLab Concept Check

How Do We Know When the Economy Is in a Recession?

The federal government produces many statistics that make it possible to monitor the economy. But the federal government does not officially decide when a recession begins or when it ends. Instead, most economists and policymakers accept the decisions of the Business Cycle Dating Committee of the National Bureau of Economic Research (NBER), a private research group located in Cambridge, Massachusetts.

(a) An idealized business cycle

(b) Movements in real GDP, 2006–2015

MyEconLab Real-time data

Figure 3.6 **The Business Cycle**

Panel (a) shows an idealized business cycle, with real GDP increasing smoothly in an expansion to a business cycle peak and then decreasing smoothly in a recession to a business cycle trough, which is followed by another expansion. The periods of expansion are shown in green, and the period of recession is shown in red. Panel (b) shows the actual movements in real GDP from 2006 to 2015. The recession that began following the business cycle peak in December 2007 was the longest and the most severe since the Great Depression of the 1930s.

Although writers for newspapers and magazines often define a recession as two consecutive quarters of declining real GDP, the NBER has a broader definition: "A recession is a significant decline in activity spread across the economy, lasting more than a few months, visible in industrial production, employment, real income, and wholesale–retail trade."

The NBER is fairly slow in announcing business cycle dates because gathering and analyzing economic statistics takes time. Typically, the NBER will announce that the economy is in a recession only well after the recession has begun. For instance, it did not announce that a recession had begun in December 2007 until 11 months later, at the end of November 2008. Table 3.2 lists the business cycle peaks and troughs identified by the NBER for the years since 1950. The length of each recession is the number of months from each peak to the following trough.   MyEconLab Concept Check

Making the Connection

MyEconLab Video

Can a Recession Be a Good Time for a Business to Expand?

During a recession, business managers have to quickly make many decisions, such as whether to reduce production, cut prices, close stores or other facilities, or lay off workers. In addition to making decisions aimed at dealing with the immediate effects of the recession, managers have to consider how to prepare for the expansion that will follow the recession. Managers know that every recession, even one as severe as the recession of 2007–2009, will be followed by an expansion during which demand for their products is likely to increase. But it can be difficult to commit resources to future expansion when current conditions are bleak and when the end of the recession is difficult to predict.

The payoff to preparing for future growth can be very large, however. For example, at the end of World War II in 1945, many economists and business managers expected that the U.S. economy would enter a severe recession. Sears and Montgomery Ward were the two largest department store chains in the country. Robert Wood, CEO of Sears, expected continuing prosperity and moved to open new stores across the country. Sewell Avery, CEO of Montgomery Ward, expected falling incomes and rising unemployment and refused to authorize any new stores and closed a number of existing ones. As a result, when strong economic growth occurred during the late 1940s, Sears rapidly gained market share at Montgomery Ward's expense.

Following the September 11, 2001, terrorist attacks in the United States, the managers of many hotels expected a prolonged period of reduced travel. They responded by laying off workers and postponing or canceling new construction. Isadore Sharp, the chairman and CEO of Four Seasons Hotels, decided that although the recession would severely hurt the hotel industry, the effects would be short-lived. He decided to finish construction of 18 hotels and begin construction of 10 more. By his own account: "We

Businesses such as VF viewed the recession of 2007–2009 as an opportunity to expand operations.

Peak	Trough	Length of Recession
July 1953	May 1954	10 months
August 1957	April 1958	8 months
April 1960	February 1961	10 months
December 1969	November 1970	11 months
November 1973	March 1975	16 months
January 1980	July 1980	6 months
July 1981	November 1982	16 months
July 1990	March 1991	8 months
March 2001	November 2001	8 months
December 2007	June 2009	18 months

Source: National Bureau of Economic Research.

Table 3.2

The U.S. Business Cycle Since 1950

maintained or enhanced our market share in most regions, contrary to the predictions of various industry experts." In a letter to his shareholders in March 2002, he wrote: "We are well positioned for the economic recovery expected later this year."

During the severe recession of 2007–2009, managers had similar decisions to make. Based in Greensboro, North Carolina, VF Corporation is the largest apparel maker in the world. Among its brands are North Face, Timberland, and Wrangler. While many firms, such as J.Crew, Anne Klein, and Liz Claiborne, were closing stores or postponing opening new ones, Eric Wiseman, CEO of VF, pushed ahead, opening 89 stores in 2008 and 70 in 2009. One retail analyst was quoted as saying, "Unfortunately, many companies pull in the reins in a downturn, but these are often the best opportunities to grow." Similarly, Intel, the computer chip manufacturer, decided in early 2009 to proceed with a $7 billion expansion of its factories in the United States, while many rival firms were reducing their spending on new factories as computer sales declined. Paul Otellini, CEO of Intel, was quoted as saying, "I thought it was important for a company like Intel to stand up and say we have confidence." Heavy equipment manufacturer Caterpillar, Inc., announced that it would build several new facilities and expand some existing ones "to meet the expected increase in customer demand."

By 2015, the recovery from the 2007–2009 recession was well underway, although it was slower than a typical recovery. VF's decision to expand appeared to have been a good one as sales and profits continued to increase and its stock price was near an all-time high. The company continued to open new stores and was operating nearly 1,500 stores worldwide. The verdict for Caterpillar and Intel was more mixed, although both firms remained profitable. Intel's announcement in mid-2015 that technical problems would delay its latest generation of computer chips until late 2017 might represent a temporary setback, or it could indicate that it was beginning to fall behind rival chipmakers. Caterpillar was being hurt by declining prices for coal, iron ore, oil, and other commodities, which was reducing demand for equipment used for mining and oil exploration. Still, Caterpillar's CEO expected that sales would increase in the future as growth in the world economy caused a turnaround in commodity prices.

Over the long run, betting on the future of the U.S. economy has paid off for most firms.

Sources: Lisa Beilfuss, "VF Corp. Tops Expectations on Strength in Outdoor Sales," *Wall Street Journal*, July 24, 2015; Tiernan Ray, "Is Intel in Trouble?" *Barrons*, July 18, 2015; James R. Hagerty, "Caterpillar Resists Calls to Slash Spending," *Wall Street Journal*, July 23, 2015; Robert Sobel, *When Giants Stumble*, Paramus, NJ: Prentice Hall, 1999; Isadore Sharp, *Four Seasons: The Story of a Business Philosophy*, New York: Portfolio, 2009; Bob Tita, "Caterpillar to Expand Kansas Plant," *Wall Street Journal*, August 18, 2011; Rachel Dodes, "VF Dresses Up Its Operations, Bucking Recession," *Wall Street Journal*, March 31, 2009; and Don Clark, "Intel to Spend Heavily on U.S. Plants," *Wall Street Journal*, February 10, 2009.

MyEconLab Study Plan   **Your Turn:** Test your understanding by doing related problem 5.6 on page 75 at the end of this module.

What Happens during the Business Cycle?

Each business cycle is different. The lengths of the expansion and recession phases and the sectors of the economy that are most affected are rarely the same in any two cycles. But most business cycles share these characteristics:

1. As the economy nears the end of an expansion, interest rates are usually rising, and the wages of workers are usually increasing faster than prices. As a result of rising interest rates and wages, the profits of firms will be falling. Typically, toward the end of an expansion, both households and firms will have substantially increased their debts. These debts are the result of the borrowing that firms and households undertake to help finance their spending during the expansion. Rising debts can eventually lead households and firms to reduce their spending.
2. A recession will often begin with a decline in spending by firms on capital goods, such as machinery, equipment, new factories, and new office buildings, or by households on new houses and consumer durables, such as furniture and automobiles. As spending declines, firms that build houses and firms that sell capital goods

and consumer durables will find their sales declining. As sales decline, firms cut back on production and begin to lay off workers. Rising unemployment and falling profits reduce income, which leads to further declines in spending.

3. As the recession continues, economic conditions eventually begin to improve. The declines in spending finally come to an end; households and firms begin to reduce their debts, thereby increasing their ability to spend; and interest rates decline, making it more likely that households and firms will borrow to finance new spending. Firms begin to increase their spending on capital goods as they anticipate the need for additional production during the next expansion. Increased spending by households on new houses and consumer durables and by businesses on capital goods will finally bring the recession to an end and begin the next expansion.

Corning, Technology, and the Business Cycle We have seen that long-run economic growth depends on the development of new technologies, such as those introduced over the years by firms like Corning. Often, though, these firms are exposed to the effects of the business cycle because new technologies are embodied in *durables*, which are goods that are expected to last for three or more years. Consumer durables include automobiles, laptops, and appliances. Producer durables include machine tools, electric generators, and commercial airplanes. *Nondurables* are goods that are expected to last for fewer than three years. Consumer nondurables include goods such as food and clothing. Durables are affected more by the business cycle than are nondurables. During a recession, workers reduce spending if they lose their jobs, fear losing their jobs, or suffer wage cuts. Because people can often continue using their existing automobiles, appliances, and smartphones, they are more likely to postpone spending on durables than spending on nondurables. Similarly, when firms experience declining sales and profits during a recession, they often cut back on purchases of producer durables.

We mentioned in our discussion of Corning at the beginning of this module that the firm has substantial sales to firms that produce automobiles, televisions, and

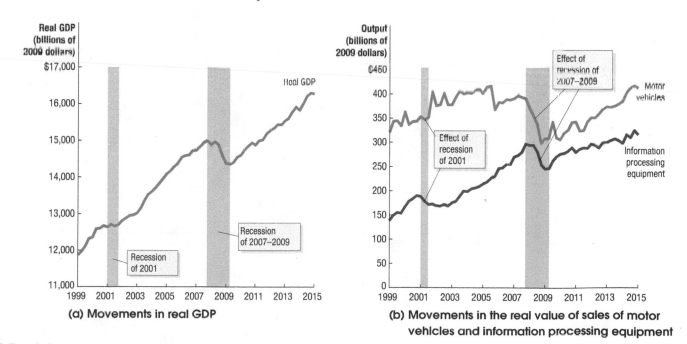

(a) Movements in real GDP

(b) Movements in the real value of sales of motor vehicles and information processing equipment

MyEconLab Real-time data

Figure 3.7   The Effect of the Business Cycle on Corning

Panel (a) shows movements in real GDP for each quarter from the beginning of 1999 through the beginning of 2015. Panel (b) shows movements in the real value of automobile production and the real value of production of information processing equipment for the same years. In panel (b), the effects of the recessions on the sales of firms that Corning sells its products to are more dramatic than the effects on the economy as a whole.

Sources: U.S. Bureau of Economic Analysis.

computers. As a result, Corning's sales are significantly affected by the business cycle. Panel (a) of Figure 3.7 shows movements in real GDP for each quarter from the beginning of 1999 through the beginning of 2015. We can see both the upward trend in real GDP over time and the effects of the recessions of 2001 and 2007–2009. Data for Corning's sales of individual products are not available, but panel (b) shows movements in the real value of automobile production and the real value of production of information processing equipment, such as computers. Panel (b) shows that recessions affect these industries more than they affect the economy as a whole. For example, during the 2007–2009 recession, real GDP declined by about 4 percent, while motor vehicle production declined by nearly 25 percent, and production of information processing equipment declined by 17 percent. As production declined in these industries, Corning's sales of ceramics for automobile emissions systems and display panels for computers dropped as well. As these industries recovered from the recession, so did Corning's sales.

The Effect of the Business Cycle on the Inflation Rate The *price level* measures the average prices of goods and services in the economy, and the *inflation rate* is the percentage increase in the price level from one year to the next (see Modules 1 and 2). An important fact about the business cycle is that the inflation rate usually increases during economic expansions—particularly near the end of an expansion—and the inflation rate usually decreases during recessions. Figure 3.8 illustrates this pattern for the three recessions since 1990.

In every recession since 1950, the inflation rate has been lower during the 12 months after the recession ends than it was during the 12 months before the recession began. The average decline in the inflation rate has been about 2.5 percentage points. This result is not surprising. During a business cycle expansion, spending by businesses and

MyEconLab Real-time data

Figure 3.8 **The Effect of Recessions on the Inflation Rate**

Toward the end of a typical expansion, the inflation rate begins to rise. During recessions, marked by the shaded vertical bars, the inflation rate declines. By the end of a recession, the inflation rate is significantly below what it had been at the beginning of the recession.

Note: The points on the figure represent the annual inflation rate measured by the percentage change in the consumer price index from the same month during the previous year.

Source: U.S. Bureau of Labor Statistics.

households is strong, and producers of goods and services find it easier to raise prices. As spending declines during a recession, firms have a more difficult time selling their goods and services and are likely to increase prices less than they otherwise might have.

Don't Let This Happen to You

Don't Confuse the Price Level and the Inflation Rate

Do you agree with the following statement: "The consumer price index is a widely used measure of the inflation rate"? This statement may sound plausible, but it is incorrect. The consumer price index (CPI) tells us what a typical urban family of four pays for the goods and services they purchase relative to a base year, but values for the CPI do not directly measure the inflation rate (see Modules 1 and 2). We can measure the inflation rate as the *percentage*

change in the CPI from one year to the next. In macroeconomics, it is important not to confuse the level of a variable with the change in the variable. To give another example, real GDP does not measure economic growth. Economic growth is measured by the percentage change in real GDP from one year to the next.

MyEconLab Study Plan

Your Turn: Test your understanding by doing related problem 5.8 on page 76 at the end of this module.

The Effect of the Business Cycle on the Unemployment Rate Recessions cause the inflation rate to fall, but they cause the unemployment rate to increase. As firms see their sales decline, they begin to reduce production and lay off workers. Figure 3.9 illustrates this pattern for the three recessions since 1990. Notice in the figure

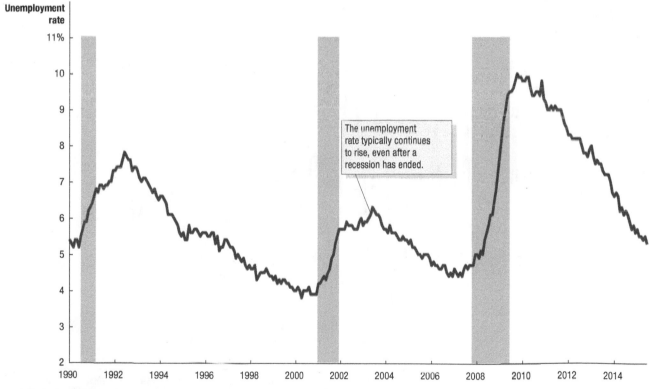

MyEconLab Real-time data

Figure 3.9   How Recessions Affect the Unemployment Rate

Unemployment rises during recessions and falls during expansions. The reluctance of firms to hire new employees during the early stages of a recovery usually causes the unemployment rate to continue to rise even after a recession has ended.

Source: U.S. Bureau of Labor Statistics.

that the unemployment rate continued to rise even after the recessions of 1990–1991, 2001, and 2007–2009 had ended. This lag before the unemployment rate begins to decline is typical and is due to two factors. First, even though employment begins to increase as a recession ends, it may be increasing more slowly than the increase in the labor force resulting from population growth. If employment increases slowly enough relative to the growth in the labor force, it is possible for the unemployment rate to rise. Second, some firms continue to operate well below their capacity even after a recession has ended and sales have begun to increase. As a result, at first, firms may not hire back all the workers they have laid off and may even continue for a while to lay off more workers.

During the recessions since 1950, the unemployment rate has risen on average by about 1.2 percentage points during the 12 months after a recession has begun. So, on average, more than 1 million more workers have been unemployed during the 12 months after a recession has begun than during the previous 12 months.

Is the "Great Moderation" Over? Figure 3.10, which shows the year-to-year percentage changes in real GDP since 1900, illustrates a striking change in fluctuations in real GDP beginning around 1950. Before 1950, real GDP went through much greater year-to-year fluctuations than it has since that time. Fluctuations since the mid-1980s have been particularly mild. By the early twenty-first century, some economists had begun referring to the absence of severe recessions in the United States as the *Great Moderation*. However, economists began questioning this view with the recession that began in December 2007. That recession was the longest and the most severe since the Great Depression of the 1930s and has been called the *Great Recession*.

Figure 3.10 **Fluctuations in Real GDP, 1900–2014**

Fluctuations in real GDP were greater before 1950 than they have been since 1950.

Sources: Samuel H. Williamson, "What Was the U.S. GDP Then?" MeasuringWorth, July 2015; and U.S. Bureau of Economic Analysis.

Period	Average Length of Expansions	Average Length of Recessions
1870–1900	26 months	26 months
1900–1950	25 months	19 months
1950–2009	61 months	11 months

Table 3.3

Until 2007, the Business Cycle Had Become Milder

The percentage decline in real GDP during 2009 was the largest since 1932. Economists and policymakers remain unsure whether the Great Moderation will return even as the economy continued to expand more than six years after the end of the Great Recession.

The unusual severity of the 2007–2009 recession can be seen by comparing its length to those of other recessions. Table 3.3 shows that in the late nineteenth century, the average length of recessions was the same as the average length of expansions. During the first half of the twentieth century, the average length of expansions decreased slightly, and the average length of recessions decreased significantly. As a result, expansions were about six months longer than recessions during these years. The most striking change came after 1950, when the length of expansions greatly increased and the length of recessions decreased. After 1950, expansions were more than five times as long as recessions. In other words, in the late nineteenth century, the U.S. economy spent as much time in recession as it did in expansion. After 1950, the U.S. economy experienced long expansions interrupted by relatively short recessions.

The recession of 2007–2009 is an exception to this experience of relatively short, mild recessions. The recession lasted 18 months, the longest of the post-1950 period. Does the length and depth of the 2007–2009 recession indicate that the United States is returning to an era of severe fluctuations in real GDP? A full answer to this question will not be possible for at least several years. But in the next section, we provide some perspective on the question by considering why the period from 1950 to 2007 was one of relative macroeconomic stability.   MyEconLab Concept Check

Will the U.S. Economy Return to Stability?

Shorter recessions, longer expansions, and less severe fluctuations in real GDP have resulted in a significant improvement in the economic well-being of Americans. Economists have offered several explanations for why the U.S. economy experienced a period of relative stability from 1950 to 2007:

- **The increasing importance of services and the declining importance of goods.** As services such as medical care and investment advice have become a much larger fraction of GDP, there has been a corresponding relative decline in the production of goods. For example, at one time, manufacturing production accounted for about 40 percent of GDP, but in 2015, it accounted for about 12 percent. Manufacturing production, particularly of durable goods such as automobiles, fluctuates more than the production of services because during a recession, households will cut back more on purchases of durables than they will on purchases of services.

- **The establishment of unemployment insurance and other government transfer programs that provide funds to the unemployed.** Before the 1930s, programs such as unemployment insurance, which provides government payments to workers who lose their jobs, and Social Security, which provides government payments to retired and disabled workers, did not exist. These and other government programs make it possible for workers who lose their jobs during recessions to have higher incomes and, therefore, to spend more than they would otherwise. This additional spending may have helped to shorten recessions.

- **Active federal government policies to stabilize the economy.** Before the Great Depression of the 1930s, the federal government did not attempt to end recessions or prolong expansions. Because the Great Depression was so severe, with the unemployment rate rising to more than 20 percent of the labor force and real GDP declining by almost 30 percent, public opinion began favoring government attempts to stabilize the economy. In the years since World War II, the federal government has actively used macroeconomic policy measures to try to end recessions and prolong expansions. Many economists believe that these government policies have played a key role in stabilizing the economy. Other economists, however, argue that active government policy has had little effect. The debate over the role of macroeconomic policy became particularly intense during and after the 2007–2009 recession (see Modules 7A and 8A).

- **The increased stability of the financial system.** The severity of the Great Depression of the 1930s was caused in part by instability in the financial system. More than 5,000 banks failed between 1929 and 1933, reducing the savings of many households and making it difficult for households and firms to obtain the credit needed to maintain their spending. In addition, a decline of more than 80 percent in stock prices greatly reduced the wealth of many households and made it difficult for firms to raise funds by selling stock. Most economists believe that the return of financial instability during the 2007–2009 recession is a key reason the recession was so severe. If the United States is to return to macroeconomic stability, stability will first have to return to the financial system.

MyEconLab Study Plan

MyEconLab Concept Check

Economics in Your Life

Do You Help the Economy More if You Spend or if You Save?

Which of your two roommates is right—the one who argues that you would help the economy more by saving your tax refund, or the one who argues that you should spend it? In this module, we have seen that consumption spending promotes the production of more consumption goods and services—such as jeans and haircuts—and fewer investment goods and services—such as physical capital and research and development. Saving (or not consuming) is necessary to fund investment expenditure. So, saving your refund will help the economy over the long run. But if the economy is in a recession, spending your refund will spur more production of consumption goods. In a sense, then, both of your roommates are correct: Spending your refund will help stimulate the economy during a recession, while saving it will help the economy grow over the long run.

Conclusion

The U.S. economy remains a remarkable engine for improving the well-being of Americans. The standard of living of Americans today is much higher than it was 100 years ago. But households and firms are still subject to the ups and downs of the business cycle. In the following modules, we will continue our analysis of this basic fact of macroeconomics: Ever-increasing long-run prosperity is achieved in the context of short-run instability.

Visit MyEconLab for a news article and analysis related to the concepts in this module.

Key Terms

3.1 Gross Domestic Product Measures Total Production, pages 43–50

LEARNING OBJECTIVE: Explain how total production is measured.

Summary

Economics is divided into the subfields of **microeconomics**—which studies how households and firms make choices—and **macroeconomics**—which studies the economy as a whole. An important macroeconomic topic is the **business cycle**, which refers to alternating periods of economic expansion and economic recession. An **expansion** is a period during which production and employment are increasing. A **recession** is a period during which production and employment are decreasing. Another important macroeconomic topic is **economic growth**, which refers to the ability of the economy to produce increasing quantities of goods and services. Macroeconomics also studies the **inflation rate**, or the percentage increase in the price level from one year to the next. Economists measure total production by **gross domestic product (GDP)**, which is the value of all *final goods and services* produced in an economy during a period of time. A **final good or service** is purchased by a final user. An **intermediate good or service** is an input into another good or service and is not included in GDP. When we measure the value of total production in the economy by calculating GDP, we are simultaneously measuring the value of total income. GDP is divided into four major categories of expenditures: consumption, investment, government purchases, and net exports. **Consumption** is spending by households on goods and services, not including spending on new houses. **Investment** is spending by firms on new factories, office buildings, machinery, research and development, and additions to inventories, plus spending by households and firms on new houses. **Government purchases** is spending by federal, state, and local governments on goods and services. **Net exports** are equal to exports minus imports. Government **transfer payments** are not included in GDP because they are payments to individuals for which the government does not receive a good or service in return. We can also calculate GDP by adding up the **value added** by every firm involved in producing final goods and services.

MyEconLab   Visit www.myeconlab.com to complete these exercises online and get instant feedback.

Review Questions

1.1 Why in microeconomics do we measure production in terms of quantity, but in macroeconomics we measure production in terms of market value?

1.2 If the U.S. Bureau of Economic Analysis added up the values of every good and service sold during the year, would the total be larger, smaller, or equal to GDP? Briefly explain.

1.3 In the circular flow of income, why must the value of total production in an economy equal the value of total income?

1.4 Describe the four major components of expenditures in GDP and write the equation that represents the relationship between GDP and the four expenditure components.

1.5 What is meant by a firm's "value added"?

Problems and Applications

1.6 A student remarks, "It doesn't make sense that intermediate goods are not counted in GDP. A computer chip is an intermediate good, and without it, a laptop won't work. So, why don't we count the computer chip in GDP?" Provide an answer to the student's question.

1.7 Briefly explain whether each of the following transactions represents the purchase of a final good.
   a. The purchase of flour by a bakery
   b. The purchase of an aircraft carrier by the federal government
   c. The purchase of French wine by a U.S. consumer
   d. The purchase of a new airliner by American Airlines

1.8 An article in the *Wall Street Journal* states that a "change in … inventories subtracted 0.57 percentage point from" what would have been the increase in GDP. For this result to occur, must there have been an increase or a decrease in inventories? Briefly explain.

   Source: Eric Morath and Ben Leubsdorf, "GDP Slows to Crawl in First Quarter, up 0.1%," *Wall Street Journal*, April 30, 2014.

1.9 **(Related to the** Module Opener **on page 41)** Which component of GDP will be affected by each of the following transactions involving Ford Motor Company? If you believe that none of the components of GDP will be affected by a transaction, briefly explain why.
   a. You purchase a new Ford Escape hybrid from a Ford dealer.
   b. You purchase a 2011 Ford Escape hybrid from a friend.
   c. Ford purchases door handles for the Escape from an auto parts manufacturer in Indiana.
   d. Ford produces 1,000 Escapes in a factory in Missouri and ships them to a car dealer in Shanghai, China.

e. Ford purchases new machine tools to use in its Missouri Escape factory.

f. The state of Missouri builds a new highway to help improve access to the Ford Escape plant.

1.10 Is the value of a house built in 2006 and resold in 2017 included in the GDP of 2017? Briefly explain. Would the services of the real estate agent who helped sell (or buy) the house in 2017 be counted in GDP for 2017? Briefly explain.

1.11 (Related to Solved Problem 3.1 **on page 44)** Suppose that a simple economy produces only four goods: shoes, hamburgers, shirts, and cotton. Assume that all the cotton is used in the production of shirts. Use the information in the following table to calculate nominal GDP for 2017.

Production and Price Statistics for 2017		
Product	Quantity	Price
Shoes	100	$60.00
Hamburgers	100	2.00
Shirts	50	25.00
Cotton	80	0.60

1.12 (Related to the Don't Let This Happen to You **on page 47)** Briefly explain whether you agree with the following statement: "In years when people buy many shares of stock, investment will be high and, therefore, so will GDP."

1.13 (Related to the Making the Connection **on page 48)** According to Dan Sichel, an economist at Wellesley College, the amount of time a singer spends working on a record album in a recording studio is "quite analogous to a factory investing in a new machine." Do you agree? Briefly explain.

Source: David Kestenbaum, "Lady Gaga Writing a New Song Is Like a Factory Investing in a New Machine," www.npr.org, April 25, 2013.

1.14 An artist buys scrap metal from a local steel mill as a raw material for her metal sculptures. Last year, she bought $5,000 worth of the scrap metal. During the year, she produced 10 metal sculptures that she sold for $800 each to a local art store. The local art store sold all of the sculptures to local art collectors, at an average price of $1,000 each. For the 10 metal sculptures, what was the total value added by the artist, and what was the total value added by the local art store?

3.2
Does GDP Measure What We Want It to Measure? pages 50–53
LEARNING OBJECTIVE: Discuss whether GDP is a good measure of well-being.

Summary

GDP does not include household production, which refers to goods and services people produce for themselves, nor does it include production in the **underground economy**, which consists of concealed buying and selling. The underground economy in some developing countries may be more than half of measured GDP. GDP is not a perfect measure of well-being because it does not include the value of leisure, it is not adjusted for pollution or other negative effects of production, and it is not adjusted for changes in crime and other social problems.

MyEconLab   Visit www.myeconlab.com to complete these exercises online and get instant feedback.

Review Questions

2.1 Why does the size of a country's GDP matter? How does it affect the quality of life of the country's people?

2.2 What is the underground economy? Why do some countries have larger underground economies than other countries?

2.3 Why is GDP an imperfect measure of economic well-being? What types of production does GDP not measure? If GDP included these types of production, would it still be an imperfect measure of economic well-being?

Problems and Applications

2.4 Which of the following are likely to increase measured GDP, and which are likely to reduce it?

a. The fraction of women working outside the home increases.

b. There is a sharp increase in the crime rate.

c. Higher tax rates cause some people to hide more of the income they earn.

2.5 Michael Burda of Humboldt University in Germany and Daniel Hamermesh of the University of Texas examined how workers in the United States who lost their jobs spent their time. They discovered that during the period when the workers were unemployed, the decline in the number of hours of paid work these workers did was almost the same as the increase in the number of hours these workers devoted to household production. Do Burda and Hamermesh's findings allow us to draw any conclusions about whether total production in the economy—whether that production is included in GDP or not—decreased when these workers became unemployed? Does your answer depend on whether the household production they carried out while unemployed were activities, such as childcare, that the workers had been paying other people to perform before they lost their jobs? Briefly explain.

Source: Michael Burda and Daniel S. Hamermesh, "Unemployment, Market Work, and Household Production," *Economic Letters*, Vol. 107, May 2010, pp. 131–133.

2.6 A typical U.S. worker today works fewer than 40 hours per week, while in 1890, he or she worked 60 hours per week. Does this difference in the length of work weeks matter in comparing the economic well-being of U.S. workers today with that of 1890? Or can we use the difference between real GDP per capita today and in 1890 to measure differences in economic well-being while ignoring differences in the number of hours worked per week? Briefly explain.

2.7 Economic historians Roger Ransom and Richard Sutch have estimated that African-American farmers in the U.S. South worked about 30 percent fewer hours per year after the Civil War than they had as slaves before the Civil War. If after the Civil War, African-American farmers had continued to work these additional hours, their production and income would have been higher, and U.S. GDP would have been higher. Would the farmers' well-being also have been higher as a result of working these additional hours? Does your answer affect how we should interpret changes in U.S. GDP from before the Civil War to after it? Briefly explain.

Source: Roger L. Ransom and Richard Sutch, *One Kind of Freedom: The Economic Consequences of Emancipation*, 2nd edition, New York: Cambridge University Press, 2001.

2.8 (Related to the Making the Connection **on page 51)** An article in the *New York Times* describes the much greater use of cash, as opposed to checks and credit cards, in buying and selling in China. The article describes someone bringing several bags of cash containing the equivalent of $130,000 into a car dealership to buy a new BMW. Another article notes, "Many economists believe that the rise in [use of] cash is strongly related to growth in the so-called underground economy."
a. What is the underground economy?
b. Why might buyers and sellers in the underground economy prefer to use cash?

Sources: David Barboza, "Chinese Way of Doing Business: In Cash We Trust," *New York Times*, April 30, 2013; and Bruce Bartlett, "America's Most Profitable Export Is Cash," *New York Times*, April 9, 2013.

2.9 (Related to the Making the Connection **on page 51)** An article in the *Wall Street Journal* notes that many economists believe that GDP data for India are unreliable because "the average firm employs just a handful of people and the overwhelming majority of the adult population works off the books and far from major cities."
a. What does the article mean by working "off the books"?
b. Why would the problems listed make it difficult for the Indian government to accurately measure GDP?

c. What problems can be caused for a government or for businesses in a country if the government cannot accurately measure GDP?

Source: Raymond Zhong, "Just How Bad Are India's Official GDP Numbers?" *Wall Street Journal*, August 27, 2014.

2.10 The following table shows data from the Organization for Economic Co-operation and Development (OECD) on the average number of hours employed people worked per week and on real GDP per capita for seven countries.

	Average Hours Worked	Real per Capita GDP
Germany	26.2	$41,007
Canada	32.8	$41,475
Japan	33.3	$34,929
OECD average (34 nations)	34.0	$36,074
United States	34.4	$50,429
Greece	39.6	$23,919
Korea	41.6	$32,711
Mexico	43.0	$16,022

The average German worker worked 8 fewer hours but earned $9,000 less per year than did the average worker in the United States. Can we conclude anything about the well-being of the average German worker versus the well-being of the average worker in the United States from these data? What measures besides average number of hours worked and real per capita GDP would you like to see in evaluating the well-being of workers in OECD countries?

Sources: Eric Morath, "Are Americans Working Less Than the Rest of the World?" *Wall Street Journal*, July 10, 2015; and OECD Data, https://data.oecd.org/emp/hours-worked.htm#indicator-chart.

3.3 ## Real GDP versus Nominal GDP, pages 53–57

LEARNING OBJECTIVE: Discuss the difference between real GDP and nominal GDP.

Summary

Nominal GDP is the value of final goods and services evaluated at current-year prices. **Real GDP** is the value of final goods and services evaluated at *base-year* prices. By keeping prices constant, we know that changes in real GDP represent changes in the quantity of goods and services produced in the economy. When the **price level**, the average prices of goods and services in the economy, is increasing, real GDP is greater than nominal GDP in years before the base year and less than nominal GDP for years after the base year. The **GDP deflator** is a measure of the price level and is calculated by dividing nominal GDP by real GDP and multiplying by 100.

Review Questions

3.1 Why does inflation make nominal GDP a poor measure of the increase in total production from one year to the next? How does the U.S. Bureau of Economic Analysis deal with this drawback?
3.2 What is the GDP deflator, and how is it calculated?
3.3 Assuming that inflation has occurred over time, what is the relationship between nominal GDP and real GDP in each of the following situations?
a. In the years after the base year
b. In the base year
c. In the years before the base year

Problems and Applications

3.4 **(Related to** Solved Problem 3.3 **on page 53)** Suppose the information in the following table is for a simple economy that produces only four goods and services: shoes, hamburgers, shirts, and cotton. Assume that all the cotton is used in the production of shirts.

	2009		2016		2017	
Product	Quantity	Price	Quantity	Price	Quantity	Price
Shoes	90	$50.00	100	$60.00	100	$65.00
Hamburgers	75	2.00	100	2.00	120	2.25
Shirts	50	30.00	50	25.00	65	25.00
Cotton	100	0.80	800	0.60	120	0.70

    a. Use the information in the table to calculate real GDP for 2016 and 2017, assuming that the base year is 2009.

    b. What is the growth rate of real GDP during 2017?

3.5 Briefly explain whether you agree with the following statements.

    a. "If nominal GDP is less than real GDP, then the price level must have fallen during the year."

    b. "Whenever real GDP declines, nominal GDP must also decline."

    c. "If a recession is so severe that the price level declines, then we know that both real GDP and nominal GDP must decline."

    d. "Nominal GDP declined between 2008 and 2009; therefore, the GDP deflator must also have declined."

3.6 An article in the *Wall Street Journal* discussed the views of Canadian Minister of Finance Joe Oliver on the effect of falling oil prices on the Canadian economy. According to the article, Oliver argued that "lower oil prices would have a broadly neutral impact on real ... gross domestic product, but have a negative effect on nominal GDP." Given this view, can we tell what Oliver must be expecting the effect of lower oil prices to be on the inflation rate? Briefly explain.

Source: Scott Hagget, "Canada Pushes Back Budget to April Due to Market Instability," *New York Times*, January 15, 2015.

3.7 The following table lists hypothetical values.

(1) Year	(2) Nominal GDP	(3) GDP Deflator (base year = 2014)	(4) Real GDP (base year = 2014)	(5) Percentage Change in Real GDP	(6) GDP Deflator (base year = 2016)	(7) Real GDP (base year = 2016)	(8) Percentage Change in Real GDP
2012	$980.00	90			81.8		
2013	1,020.00	92			83.6		
2014	1,050.00	100			90.9		
2015	1,200.00	105			95.5		
2016	1,400.00	110			100.0		

    a. Fill in column (4) by calculating real GDP using the GDP deflator with a base year of 2014 from column (3). Fill in column (7) by calculating real GDP using the GDP deflator with a base year of 2016 from column (6).

    b. Fill in column (5) by calculating the annual percentage change in real GDP for each year, using the values from column (4), and fill in column (8) by calculating the annual percentage change in real GDP by using the values from column (7).

    c. What effect does the change in the base year used to compute real GDP have on your calculations of the percentage changes in real GDP?

3.8 According to an article in the *Economist*, "China's GDP grew by 7% in the second quarter, which was higher than had been expected." Is it likely that the article is referring to the change in nominal GDP or the change in real GDP? Briefly explain.

Source: "World This Week," *Economist*, July 15, 2015.

3.9 Use the data in the following table to calculate the GDP deflator for each year (values are in billions of dollars):

Year	Nominal GDP	Real GDP
2010	$14,964	$14,784
2011	15,518	15,021
2012	16,163	15,369
2013	16,768	15,710
2014	16,245	16,086

Which year from 2011 to 2014 saw the largest percentage increase in the price level, as measured by changes in the GDP deflator? Briefly explain.

3.10 **(Related to the** Making the Connection **on page 56)** An article in the *Economist* on the revisions to Nigeria's GDP commented, "The GDP revision is not mere trickery. It provides a truer picture of Nigeria's size by giving due weight to the bits of the economy, such as telecoms, banking and the Nollywood film industry, that have been growing fast in recent years."

    a. What does the article mean by "giving due weight" to the sectors of the economy that have been growing quickly?

    b. How did the Nigerian National Bureau of Statistics accomplish the task of giving these sectors their due weight?

    c. Why does making this change in calculating GDP provide a truer picture of the size of Nigeria's economy?

Source: "Africa's New Number One," *Economist*, April 12, 2014.

3.4   **Other Measures of Total Production and Total Income, pages 57–59**
LEARNING OBJECTIVE: Describe other measures of total production and total income.

Summary

The most important measure of total production and total income is gross domestic product (GDP). As we will see in later modules, for some purposes, other measures of total production and total income are actually more useful than GDP. These measures are gross national product (GNP), national income, personal income, and disposable personal income.

MyEconLab   Visit **www.myeconlab.com** to complete these exercises online and get instant feedback.

Review Questions

4.1 What is the difference between GDP and GNP? Briefly explain whether the difference is important for the United States.

4.2 What are the differences between national income, personal income, and disposable personal income?

4.3 What is gross domestic income? Which component of gross domestic income is the largest?

Problems and Applications

4.4 Suppose Turkey has many of its citizens temporarily working in other countries, and many of its firms have facilities in other countries. Furthermore, relatively few citizens of foreign countries are working in Turkey, and relatively few foreign firms have facilities in Turkey. In these circumstances, which would you expect to be larger for Turkey, GDP or GNP? Briefly explain.

4.5 An article in the *Economist* on the Irish economy argues, "Irish progress, both economic and fiscal, is typically measured using GDP.... But for an economy where foreign firms are so dominant, GNP ... is more relevant." Briefly explain the writer's reasoning.
Source: "Fitter, yet Fragile," *Economist*, January 5, 2013.

4.6 Suppose the amount the federal government collects in personal income taxes increases, while the level of GDP remains the same. What will happen to the values of national income, personal income, and disposable personal income?

4.7 If you were attempting to forecast the level of consumption spending by households, which measure of total production or total income might be most helpful to you in making your forecast? Briefly explain.

4.8 Briefly discuss the accuracy of the following statement: "Corporate profits are much too high: Most corporations make profits equal to 50 percent of the price of the products they sell."

Real-Time Data Exercises

D3.1 **(Analyzing the components of personal consumption expenditures)** Go to the Web site of the Federal Reserve Bank of St. Louis (FRED) (research.stlouisfed.org/fred2/).

a. Find the values for the most recent quarter for these four variables: (1) Personal Consumption Expenditures (PCEC); (2) Personal Consumption Expenditures: Durable Goods (PCDG): (3) Personal Consumption Expenditures: Nondurable Goods (PCND); and (4) Personal Consumption Expenditures: Services (PCESV).

b. What percentage of total household expenditures is devoted to the consumption of goods (both durable and nondurable goods)?

D3.2 **(Analyzing the components of investment)** Go to the Web site of the Federal Reserve Bank of St. Louis (FRED) (research.stlouisfed.org/fred2/).

a. Find the values for the most recent quarter for these three variables: (1) Gross Private Domestic Investment (GPDI); (2) Private Nonresidential Fixed Investment (PNFI); and (3) Private Residential Fixed Investment (PRFI).

b. Use these values to calculate the difference between private domestic investment and residential and nonresidential fixed private investment. What component of GDP does the value calculated represent?

D3.3 **(Calculating net exports)** Go to the Web site of the Federal Reserve Bank of St. Louis (FRED) (research.stlouisfed.org/fred2/).

a. Find the values for the most recent two years for Real Exports of Goods and Services (EXPGSCA) and Real Imports of Goods and Services (IMPGSCA).

b. Compute the value of net exports for each of the two most recent years.

D3.4 **(Comparing GDP and GNP)** Go to the Web site of the Federal Reserve Bank of St. Louis (FRED) (research.stlouisfed.org/fred2/).

a. Find the values for the most recent quarter for Gross Domestic Product (GDP) and Gross National Product (GNP).

b. Given these values, explain whether foreign production by U.S. firms exceeded U.S. production by foreign firms.

D3.5 **(Analyzing the components of personal income)** Go to the Web site of the Federal Reserve Bank of St. Louis (FRED) (research.stlouisfed.org/fred2/).

a. Find the values for the most recent quarter for these three variables: (1) Personal Income (PINCOME); (2) Disposable Personal Income (DPI); and (3) Personal Consumption Expenditures (PCEC).

b. Use these values to calculate the difference between personal income and disposable personal income. What does this value represent?

D3.6 **(Calculating the GDP deflator and the inflation rate)** Go to the Web site of the Federal Reserve Bank of St. Louis (FRED) (research.stlouisfed.org/fred2/).

a. Find the values for the most recent quarter and the values for the same quarter one year ago for nominal Gross Domestic Product (GDP) and Real Gross Domestic Product (GDPC1).

b. Use these values to calculate the GDP price deflator for the most recent quarter and the GDP price deflator for the quarter one year ago.

c. Using the two GDP price deflators, calculate the inflation rate during this year.
d. Look again at Figure 3.3 on page 55. Briefly explain why the nominal and real GDP lines intersect at the base year. What is the value of the GDP deflator in the year when the nominal and real GDP lines intersect?

D3.7 (Calculating real GDP and the real growth rate) Go to the Web site of the Federal Reserve Bank of St. Louis (FRED) (research.stlouisfed.org/fred2/).

a. Find the values for the most recent quarter and the same quarter one year ago for nominal Gross Domestic Product (GDP) and the GDP Implicit Price Deflator (GDPDEF)
b. Use these values to calculate real GDP for the most recent quarter and for the quarter one year ago.
c. Use the two real GDP values to calculate the real growth rate of the economy during this year.

3.5 The Business Cycle, pages 59–69
LEARNING OBJECTIVE: Explain what happens during the business cycle.

Summary

During the expansion phase of the business cycle, production, employment, and income are increasing. The period of expansion ends with a business cycle peak. Following the business cycle peak, production, employment, and income decline during the recession phase of the cycle. The recession comes to an end with a business cycle trough, after which another period of expansion begins. The inflation rate usually rises near the end of a business cycle expansion and then falls during a recession. The unemployment rate declines during the latter part of an expansion and increases during a recession. The unemployment rate often continues to increase even after an expansion has begun. Until the severe recession of 2007–2009, recessions had been milder and the economy had been more stable in the period since 1950. Economists debate whether the economy will return to the stability it experienced during the period of the Great Moderation.

MyEconLab   Visit www.myeconlab.com to complete these exercises online and get instant feedback.

Review Questions

5.1 What are the names of the following events that occur during a business cycle?
a. The high point of economic activity
b. The low point of economic activity
c. The period between the high point of economic activity and the following low point
d. The period between the low point of economic activity and the following high point

5.2 Briefly describe the effect of the business cycle on the inflation rate and the unemployment rate. Why might the unemployment rate continue to rise during the early stages of an expansion?

5.3 Briefly compare the severity of recessions before and after 1950. What explanations have economists offered for the period of relative macroeconomic stability from 1950 to 2007?

Problems and Applications

5.4 (Related to the Module Opener **on page 79)** Briefly explain whether production of each of the following goods is likely to fluctuate more or less than real GDP does during the business cycle.

a. Ford F-150 trucks
b. McDonald's Big Macs
c. Corning's screens for 4K televisions
d. Huggies diapers
e. Boeing passenger aircraft

5.5 The National Bureau of Economic Research, a private group, is responsible for declaring when recessions begin and end in the United States. Can you think of reasons the Bureau of Economic Analysis, part of the federal government, might not want to take on this responsibility?

5.6 (Related to the Making the Connection **on page 61)** As we have seen, some firms prosper by expanding during recessions. What risks do firms take when they pursue this strategy? Are there circumstances in particular industries that might cause firms to be more cautious during a recession? Briefly explain.

5.7 An article in the *Wall Street Journal* noted that at the end of 2014, "U.S. families' debt burdens have settled at their lowest level in over a decade." Does this information indicate that the U.S. economy was close to the end of an economic expansion in late 2014? Briefly explain.
Source: Neil Shah, "Americans' Debt-Cutting Levels Off," *Wall Street Journal*, December 11, 2014.

5.8 (Related to the Don't Let This Happen to You **on page 65)** Briefly explain whether you agree with this statement: "Real GDP in 2014 was $16.1 trillion. This value is a large number. Therefore, economic growth must have been high during 2014."

5.9 (Related to the Module Opener **on page 79)** In its annual report for 2009, Corning noted declines in sales for most of its products. But it also said that these declines were "offset somewhat by an increase in sales of Gorilla glass, a protective cover glass that is optimized for portable display devices. Sales of Gorilla glass have continued to increase as the Company moves to capitalize on market opportunities for this product." Why might sales of Gorilla glass be less affected by the business cycle than sales of some of the firm's other products, such as screen for LCD televisions or ceramics used in automobile emission systems?
Source: Corning, Inc., "Form 10-K (Annual Report), 2010, p. 34.

5.10 Robert Samuelson, a columnist for the *Washington Post*, argues that the Great Moderation actually caused the Great Recession. During the Great Moderation, "consumers could assume more debt—and lenders could lend more freely." Why might consumers have been willing to assume more debt and banks and other lenders have been willing to make loans more freely during the Great Moderation? Why might these actions have made the severe recession of 2007–2009 more likely?

Source: Robert J. Samuelson, "Is the Economy Experiencing Another Great Moderation?" *Washington Post*, June 4, 2014.

Real-Time Data Exercises

D 3.1 (Analyzing real GDP over the business cycle) Go to the Web site of the Federal Reserve Bank of St. Louis (FRED) (research.stlouisfed.org/fred2/).
  a. Find the values for the most recent quarter for the following three variables: (1) Nominal Gross Domestic Product (GDP), (2) Real Gross Domestic Product (GDPC1), and (3) Real Potential Gross Domestic Product (GDPPOT).
  b. Using the data from part (a), calculate the GDP Price Deflator for the most recent quarter.
  c. Calculate for this quarter the percentage difference between real GDP and potential GDP.
  d. Using Figure 3A.2 on page 88, describe the relationship between real GDP and potential GDP over the past 10 years.

D 3.2 (Analyzing saving and investment) Go to the Web site of the Federal Reserve Bank of St. Louis (FRED) (research.stlouisfed.org/fred2/).
  a. Find the most recent values and the values from the same quarter three years earlier for Gross Private Saving (GPSAVE) and Gross Government Saving (GGSAVE).
  b. Using the values found in part (a), calculate the value of total saving in the economy for these two periods.
  c. Draw a graph to show the loanable funds market in equilibrium. Explain which curve represents total saving.
  d. On the graph you drew in part (c), show the effect on the loanable funds market from the change you calculated in part (b) for total saving between the two periods.

D 3.3 (Analyzing saving and investment) Go to the Web site of the Federal Reserve Bank of St. Louis (FRED) (research.stlouisfed.org/fred2/).
  a. Find the most recent value and the value from the same quarter four years earlier for Gross Government Saving (GGSAVE).
  b. Total saving in the economy is composed of private saving and government saving. What does government saving represent?
  c. Using the values found in part (a), explain whether the government budget in each of the two periods is balanced, in a surplus, or in a deficit. From the first period to the most recent period, has government saving increased, decreased, or remained constant?
  d. Draw a graph showing the loanable funds market in equilibrium. Use the graph to show the effect of the change in government saving that you calculated in part (c) on the loanable funds market. (Assume that the level of private saving is unchanged.) Explain what will happen to the level of investment in the economy.

Long-Run Economic Growth: Sources and Policies

Economic Growth and the Business Cycle at Corning, Inc.

Amory Houghton founded the company that became Corning, Inc., in 1851. At first, the company manufactured basic glass products such as jars. Over time, though, the company developed a number of new products using innovative technologies. For instance, in 1921, a Corning employee invented a machine that made millions of light bulbs for Thomas Edison. In the 1970s, Corning developed fiber-optic cable that eventually became the means for carrying the electronic signals needed for modern telecommunications and the Internet. In 2007, researchers at the company developed a damage-resistant glass called Gorilla glass that is used on the screens of iPhones and many other portable electronic devices. By 2015, Corning, headquartered in Corning, New York, had more than 34,000 employees and sales of nearly $10 billion.

Corning is one of many firms responsible for the technological progress that has been the basis for the growth of the U.S. economy and the rise in U.S. living standards. Corning's experiences have mirrored two key macroeconomic facts: In the long run, the U.S. economy has experienced economic growth, and in the short run, the economy has experienced a series of business cycles. During the 2001 recession, Corning suffered a $5 billion loss as the market for fiber-optic cable collapsed as a result of the bursting of the "dot-com" stock market bubble. Similarly, the recession of 2007–2009 caused a sharp decline in the demand for durable goods, including automobiles, televisions, and computers. Because Corning supplies ceramics for automobile emissions systems, as well as display panels for televisions and computers, its sales declined and its profits fell by more than 60 percent between 2008 and 2009.

Unlike many firms, Corning did continue to earn a profit during the recession. The company managed to remain profitable due to products like Gorilla glass that continue to sell well even during recessions. The next success for Corning could be a thinner version of Gorilla glass, called Willow glass, that can be wound and shipped in rolls, which might make it possible for Apple and other firms to produce foldable smartphones and other electronic devices.

In this module, we provide an overview of long-run growth and the business cycle and discuss their importance for firms, consumers, and the economy as a whole.

Sources: Robin Goldwyn Blumenthal, "Corning's Latest Magic: Turning Glass into Cash," *Barron's*, June 6, 2015; Connie Guglielmo, "Working with Innovators from Thomas Edison to Steve Jobs, Corning Finds a Glass Fix," *Forbes*, September 23, 2013; and Corning, Inc., Annual Reports on corning.com.

Economics in Your Life

Do You Help the Economy More if You Spend or if You Save?

Suppose the U.S. government sends you an income tax refund. You're not sure what to do with the money, so you ask your two roommates for advice. One roommate tells you that if you want to help the economy, you should save all the money because a country's economic growth depends on the amount of saving by households. The other roommate disagrees and advises you to spend all the money because consumer spending is a major component of gross domestic product (GDP), and your spending would help increase production and create more jobs. Which of your two roommates is right? As you read this module, try to answer this question. You can check your answer against the one we provide on **page 120** at the end of this module.

A successful economy is capable of increasing production of goods and services faster than the growth in population. Attaining this level of growth is the only way that the standard of living of the average person in a country can increase. Unfortunately, some economies around the world are not growing at all or are growing very slowly. Most people in those countries live on about the same levels of income as their ancestors did decades, or even centuries, ago. In the United States and other developed countries, however, incomes and living standards are much higher today than they were 50 years ago. An important macroeconomic topic is why some countries grow much faster than others.

As we will see, one determinant of economic growth is the ability of firms to expand their operations, buy additional equipment, train workers, and adopt new technologies. To carry out these activities, firms must acquire funds from households, either directly through financial markets—such as the stock and bond markets—or indirectly through financial intermediaries—such as banks. Financial markets and financial intermediaries together comprise the *financial system*. In this module, we present an overview of the financial system and see how funds flow from households to firms through the *market for loanable funds*.

Since at least the early nineteenth century, the U.S. economy has experienced periods of expanding production and employment followed by periods of recession during which production and employment decline. These alternating periods of expansion and recession are called the **business cycle**. Business cycles are not uniform: Periods of expansion are not the same length, nor are periods of recession. But every period of expansion in U.S. history has been followed by a period of recession, and every period of recession has been followed by a period of expansion.

Business cycle Alternating periods of economic expansion and economic recession.

In this module, we begin to explore two key aspects of macroeconomics: the long-run growth that has steadily raised living standards in the United States and the short-run fluctuations of the business cycle.

3A.1 Long-Run Economic Growth

LEARNING OBJECTIVE: Discuss the importance of long-run economic growth.

Most people in high-income countries such as the United States, Canada, Japan, and the countries in Western Europe expect that over time, their standard of living will improve. They expect that year after year, firms will introduce new and improved products, new prescription drugs and better surgical techniques will overcome more diseases, and their ability to afford these goods and services will increase. For most people, these are reasonable expectations.

In 1900, the United States was already enjoying the highest standard of living in the world. Yet in that year, only 3 percent of U.S. homes had electricity, only 15 percent had indoor flush toilets, and only 25 percent had running water. The lack of running water meant that before people could cook or bathe, they had to pump water from wells and haul it to their homes in buckets—on average about 10,000 gallons per year per family. Not surprisingly, water consumption averaged only about 5 gallons per person per day, compared with about 150 gallons today. The result was that people washed themselves and their clothing only infrequently. A majority of families living in cities had to use outdoor toilets, which they shared with other families. Diseases such as smallpox, typhus, dysentery, and cholera were still common. In 1900, 5,000 of the 45,000 children born in Chicago died before their first birthday. Life expectancy at birth was about 47 years, compared with 80 years in 2015. Few families had electric lights, relying instead on burning candles or burning kerosene or coal oil in lamps. Many homes were heated in the winter by burning coal, which contributed to the severe pollution that fouled the air of most large cities. In 1900, there were no modern appliances, so housework was time-consuming and physically demanding. The typical American homemaker baked a half-ton of bread per year.

The process of **long-run economic growth** brought the typical American from the standard of living of 1900 to the standard of living of today. The best measure of the standard of living is real GDP per person, which is usually called *real GDP per capita*. So, we measure long-run economic growth by increases in real GDP per capita over long periods of time, generally decades or more. We use real GDP rather than nominal GDP to adjust for changes in the price level over time. Figure 3A.1 shows the growth in real GDP per capita in the United States from 1900 to 2014. The figure shows that the trend in real GDP per capita is strongly upward, although it fluctuates in the short run because of the business cycle. It is the upward trend in real GDP per capita that we focus on when discussing long-run economic growth.

The values in Figure 3A.1 are measured in prices of 2009, so they represent constant amounts of purchasing power. In 1900, real GDP per capita was about $6,000. More than a century later, in 2014, it had risen to about $50,010, which means that an average American in 2014 could purchase more than eight times as many goods and services as an average American in 1900. Large as it is, this increase in real GDP per capita actually understates the true increase in the standard of living of Americans in 2014 compared with 1900. Many of today's goods and services were not available in 1900. For example, if you lived in 1900 and became ill with a serious infection, you could not purchase antibiotics to treat your illness—no matter how high your income. You might have died from an illness for which even a very poor person in today's society could receive effective medical treatment. Of course, the quantity of goods and services that a person can buy is not a perfect measure of how happy or contented that person may be. A person's happiness also depends on education, health, spiritual well-being, and many other factors ignored in calculating GDP. Nevertheless, economists rely heavily on comparisons of real GDP per capita because it is the best means of comparing the performance of one economy over time or the performance of different economies at any particular time.   MyEconLab Concept Check

Long-run economic growth The process by which rising productivity increases the average standard of living.

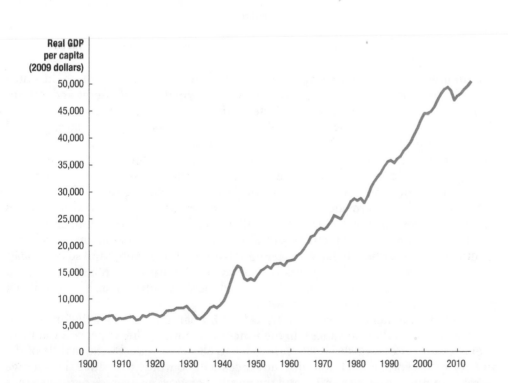

Figure 3A.1

The Growth in Real GDP per Capita, 1900–2014

Measured in 2009 dollars, real GDP per capita in the United States grew from about $6,000 in 1900 to about $50,010 in 2014. An average American in 2014 could buy more than eight times as many goods and services as an average American in 1900.

Sources: Samuel H. Williamson, "What Was the U.S. GDP Then?" Measuring-Worth, July 2015; and U.S. Bureau of Economic Analysis.

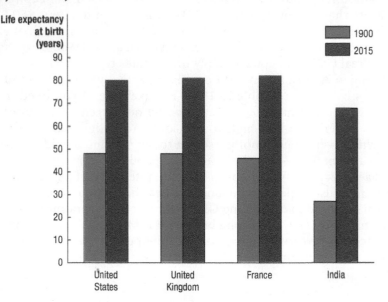

Making
the
Connection
MyEconLab Video

The Connection between Economic Prosperity and Health

We can see the direct effect of economic growth on living standards by looking at improvements in health in high-income countries over the past 100 years. The research of the late Robert Fogel, winner of the Nobel Prize in Economics, highlights the close connection between economic growth, improvements in technology, and improvements in human physiology. One important measure of health is life expectancy at birth. As the following graph shows, in 1900, life expectancy was less than 50 years in the United States, the United Kingdom, and France. Today, life expectancy is about 80 years. Although life expectancies in the lowest-income countries remain very short, some countries that have begun to experience economic growth have seen dramatic increases in life expectancies. For example, life expectancy in India has more than doubled from 27 years in 1900 to 68 years today.

Many economists believe there is a link between health and economic growth. In the United States and Western Europe during the nineteenth century, improvements in agricultural technology and rising incomes led to dramatic improvements in the nutrition of the average person. The development of the germ theory of disease and technological progress in the purification of water in the late nineteenth century led to sharp declines in sickness due to waterborne diseases. As people became taller, stronger, and less susceptible to disease, they also became more productive. There is also evidence that over time, people have become more intelligent, with scores on intelligence tests having increased about 30 percent over the past 100 years. These increases may be the result of rising incomes that both increase the health of children, allowing them to learn more in schools, and provide the means by which parents can afford to keep children in school longer. The greater learning will allow these children to be more productive as adults. Their higher productivity will allow them to earn higher incomes and have healthier children who will have greater opportunities for learning, and so on. Today, economists studying economic development have put increasing emphasis on the need for low-income countries to reduce disease and increase nutrition as important first steps toward increasing economic growth.

Many researchers believe that the state of human physiology will continue to improve as technology advances. In high-income countries, life expectancy at birth is expected to rise from about 80 years today to about 90 years by the middle of the twenty-first century. Technological advances will continue to reduce the average number of hours worked per day and the number of years an average person spends in the paid workforce. Individuals spend about 10 hours per day sleeping, eating, and bathing. Their remaining "discretionary hours" are divided between paid work and leisure. The following graph is based on estimates by Robert Fogel that contrast how individuals in the United States will divide their time in 2040 compared with 1880 and 1995. Not only will technology and economic growth allow people in the near future to live longer lives, but a much smaller fraction of those lives will need to be spent at paid work.

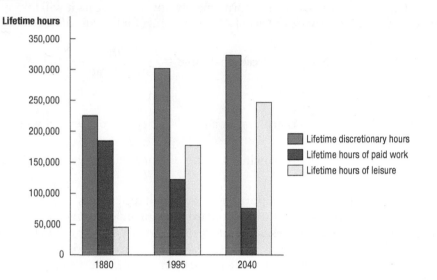

Sources: Robert William Fogel, *The Escape from Hunger and Premature Death, 1700–2100*, New York: Cambridge University Press, 2004; Alison Gopnik, "Smarter Every Year? Mystery of the Rising IQs," *Wall Street Journal*, May 27, 2015; and U.S. Central Intelligence Agency, *The 2015 World Factbook*, online version.

Your Turn: Test your understanding by doing related problem 1.7 on page 120 at the end of this module.

MyEconLab Study Plan

Calculating Growth Rates and the Rule of 70

The growth rate of real GDP or real GDP per capita during a particular year is equal to the percentage change from the previous year. For example, measured in 2009 prices, real GDP equaled $15,710 billion in 2013 and rose to $16,086 billion in 2014. We calculate the growth of real GDP in 2014 as:

$$\left(\frac{\$16,086 \text{ billion} - \$15,710 \text{ billion}}{\$15,710 \text{ billion}} \right) \times 100 = 2.4\%.$$

For longer periods of time, we can use the *average annual growth rate*. For example, real GDP in the United States was $2,184 billion in 1950 and $16,086 billion in 2014. To find the average annual growth rate during this 64-year period, we compute the annual growth rate that would result in $2,184 billion increasing to $16,086 billion over 64 years. In this case, the growth rate is 3.2 percent. That is, if $2,184 billion grows at an average rate of 3.2 percent per year, after 64 years, it will have grown to $16,086 billion.

For shorter periods of time, we get approximately the same answer by averaging the growth rate for each year. For example, real GDP in the United States grew by 2.3 percent in 2012, 2.2 percent in 2013, and 2.4 percent in 2014. So, the average annual growth rate of real GDP for the period 2012–2014 was 2.3 percent, which is the average of the three annual growth rates:

$$\frac{2.3\% + 2.2\% + 2.4\%}{3} = 2.3\%.$$

Finally, when discussing long-run economic growth, we usually shorten "average annual growth rate" to "growth rate."

We can judge how rapidly an economic variable is growing by calculating the number of years it would take to double. For example, if real GDP per capita in a country doubles, say, every 20 years, most people in the country will experience significant increases in their standard of living over the course of their lives. If real GDP per capita doubles only every 100 years, increases in the standard of living will occur too slowly to notice. One easy way to calculate approximately how many years it will take real GDP per capita to double is to use the *rule of 70*. The formula for the rule of 70 is:

$$\text{Number of years to double} = \frac{70}{\text{Growth rate}}.$$

For example:

- If real GDP per capita is growing at a rate of 5 percent per year, it will double in $70/5 = 14$ years.
- If real GDP per capita is growing at a rate of 2 percent per year, it will double in $70/2 = 35$ years.

These examples illustrate an important point: Small differences in growth rates can have large effects on how rapidly the standard of living in a country increases. Finally, notice that the rule of 70 applies not just to growth in real GDP per capita but to growth in any variable. For example, if you invest $1,000 in the stock market, and your investment grows at an average annual rate of 7 percent, your investment will double to $2,000 in 10 years. MyEconLab Concept Check

What Determines the Rate of Long-Run Growth?

Labor productivity The quantity of goods and services that can be produced by one worker or by one hour of work.

A key point in explaining long-run growth is that *increases in real GDP per capita depend on increases in labor productivity*. **Labor productivity** is the quantity of goods and services that can be produced by one worker or by one hour of work. In analyzing long-run growth, economists usually measure labor productivity as output per hour of work to avoid the effects of fluctuations in the length of the workday and in the fraction of the population employed. If the quantity of goods and services consumed by the average person is to increase, the quantity of goods and services produced per hour of work must also increase. Why in 2014 was the average American able to consume more than eight times as many goods and services as the average American in 1900? Because the average American worker in 2014 was eight times as productive as the average American worker in 1900.

If increases in labor productivity are the key to long-run economic growth, what causes labor productivity to increase? Economists believe two key factors determine labor productivity:

1. The quantity of capital per hour worked
2. The level of technology

Therefore, economic growth occurs if the quantity of capital per hour worked increases and if there is technological change.

Capital Manufactured goods that are used to produce other goods and services.

Increases in Capital per Hour Worked Workers today in high-income countries such as the United States have more physical capital available than workers in low-income countries or workers in the high-income countries of 100 years ago. Recall that **capital** refers to manufactured goods that are used to produce other goods and services. Examples of capital are computers, factory buildings, machine tools, warehouses, and trucks. The total amount of physical capital available in a country is known as the country's *capital stock*.

As the amount of capital per hour worked increases, worker productivity increases. An accountant who records a firm's revenues and costs using Excel is more productive than an accountant who uses only pen and paper. A worker who uses a backhoe can excavate more earth than a worker who uses only a shovel.

In explaining economic growth, economists take into account not just *physical capital*, like computers and factories, but also *human capital*, which is the accumulated knowledge and skills workers acquire from education and training or from their life experiences. For example, workers with a college education generally have more skills and are more productive than workers who have only a high school degree. Increases in human capital are particularly important in stimulating economic growth.

Technological Change Economic growth depends more on *technological change* than on increases in capital per hour worked. *Technology* refers to the processes a firm uses to turn inputs into outputs of goods and services. Technological change is an increase in the quantity of output firms can produce, using a given quantity of inputs. Technological change can come from many sources. For example, a firm's managers may rearrange a factory floor or the layout of a retail store to increase production and sales. Most technological change, however, is embodied in new machinery, equipment, or software.

A very important point is that just accumulating more inputs—such as labor, capital, and natural resources—will not ensure that an economy experiences economic growth unless technological change also occurs. For example, the Soviet Union failed to maintain a high rate of economic growth, even though it continued to increase the quantity of capital available per hour worked, because it experienced relatively little technological change.

Entrepreneurs are critical for implementing technological change. Recall that an entrepreneur is someone who operates a business, bringing together the factors of production—labor, capital, and natural resources—to produce goods and services. In a market economy, entrepreneurs make the crucial decisions about whether to introduce new technology to produce better or lower-cost products. Entrepreneurs also decide whether to allocate a firm's resources to research and development that can result in new technologies. One of the difficulties centrally planned economies have in sustaining economic growth is that managers employed by the government are usually much slower to develop and adopt new technologies than are entrepreneurs in a market system.

Solved Problem 3A.1

MyEconLab Interactive Animation

Where Does Productivity Come From?

A column in the *Wall Street Journal* argued that "productivity growth is a key ingredient to prosperity." What did the columnist mean by "prosperity"? What is the connection between productivity growth and prosperity?

Solving the Problem

Step 1: Review the module material. This problem is about what determines the rate of long-run growth, so you may want to review the section "What Determines the Rate of Long-Run Growth?" which begins on page 84.

Step 2: **Answer the first question by explaining what the columnist meant by the word "prosperity" in this context.** By *prosperity*, most people mean a high standard of living. In the context of economic growth, the key measure of the standard of living is real GDP per capita.

Step 3: **Answer the second question by explaining the connection between productivity growth and prosperity.** *Productivity* refers to the amount of goods and services produced per worker. As we have seen, per capita real GDP increases only if productivity increases. Therefore, increases in a country's standard of living—its prosperity—are tied to increases in productivity.

Source: Jon Hilsenrath, "More Disturbing Findings Emerge on U.S. Productivity Path," *Wall Street Journal*, February 12, 2015.

Your Turn: For more practice, do related problems 1.10 and 1.11 on page 120 at the end of this module.

MyEconLab Study Plan

Property Rights Finally, an additional requirement for economic growth is that the government must provide secure rights to private property. A market system cannot function unless rights to private property are secure. In addition, the government can aid economic growth by establishing an independent court system that enforces contracts between private individuals. Many economists would also say that the government has a role in facilitating the development of an efficient financial system, as well as systems of education, transportation, and communication. Economist Richard Sylla of New York University has argued that every country that has experienced economic growth first experienced a "financial revolution." For example, before the United States was able to experience significant economic growth in the early nineteenth century, the country's banking and monetary systems were reformed under the guidance of Alexander Hamilton, who was appointed the country's first secretary of the Treasury in 1789. Without supportive government policies, long-run economic growth is unlikely to occur.   MyEconLab Concept Check

Making the Connection

MyEconLab Video

Can India Sustain Its Rapid Growth?

When you have a computer problem and need technical support, the person who takes your call may well be in India. In addition to information technology, in recent years Indian firms have made gains in the global markets for steel, oil, and automobiles, among other goods.

To many people in the United States, the rapid economic rise of India has been unexpected. As the following figure shows, Indian real GDP per capita increased very slowly up to the time India became independent from England in 1947. As a result, in 1950, India was desperately poor. India's real GDP per capita in 1950 was less than $1,000 measured in 2015 dollars, or less than 7 percent of 1950 U.S. real GDP per capita. During the first 40 years of independence, India's growth rate increased but was still too slow to significantly reduce the country's poverty. Recent years tell a much different story, however. In 1991, the Indian government decided to scale back central planning, reduce regulations, and introduce market-based reforms. The result was that the growth rate doubled over the following decade. In the most recent period, growth has been even more rapid.

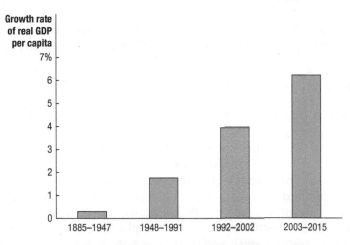

Still, India remains a very poor country. Nearly half of its population of 1.3 billion is employed in agriculture, and many can barely produce enough to feed themselves. Infant mortality rates are still at 10 times the levels in high-income countries, and about 40 percent of adult women and 20 percent of adult men are unable to read and write. The rapid economic growth that began in 1991 will have to continue in the coming decades if the average person in India is eventually to enjoy a standard of living equal to that in the United States and other high-income countries. But can India continue its rapid growth?

Some economists and policymakers worry that India's growth rates may begin to decline, leaving hundreds of millions of its people stuck in deep poverty. These economists point to several problems facing the Indian economy. The public education system has struggled to provide basic instruction, particularly in rural and poorer urban areas. India's expenditures on education rank 134th out of 173 countries, and are far below the levels in most successful developing countries. As a result, many adults lack the basic skills needed for a productive workforce. Even many high school and college graduates lack the skills to work in firms that compete in global markets. High rates of infectious disease also reduce the productivity of the workforce. Only 60 percent of urban residents have access to modern sewage systems, and fewer than one-quarter of rural residents do. In general, India has struggled to meet its infrastructure needs, as highways, bridges, and its train system—which dates from the British colonial period—have deteriorated.

India also suffers from political problems with ethnic, religious, cultural, and geographic divisions—there are 15 official languages—often making it difficult for the government to successfully implement policy reforms. Many observers believe that government corruption has increased, making it more difficult for businesses to obtain the permits necessary to operate. One estimate puts the size of the underground economy at more than 50 percent of GDP. Laws restricting the sale of agricultural land for industrial use have slowed the growth of manufacturing. Although Narendra Modi was elected prime minister in 2014 partly by promising new policies to spur economic growth, some economists and policymakers worry that the pace of market-oriented reforms has slowed over the years. They also urge the government to allow greater foreign investment in the financial and retail sectors. Greater foreign investment would allow these sectors to gain access to new technology and to increase productivity.

The economic progress India has made in the past 25 years has already lifted hundreds of millions of people out of poverty. For that progress to continue, however, many economists believe that the Indian government will need to upgrade infrastructure, improve the provision of educational and health services, and renew its commitment to the rule of law and to market-based reforms.

Sources: "Ready, Steady, Go," *Economist*, April 18, 2015; Ellen Barry, "After a Year of Outsize Expectations, Narendra Modi Adjusts His Plan for India," *New York Times*, May 25, 2015; Amartya Sen, "Why India Trails China," *New York Times*, June 19, 2013; Geeta Anand, "India Graduates Millions, but Too Few Are Fit to Hire," *Wall Street Journal*, April 5, 2011, data in graph are authors' calculations from the Maddison Project database, www.ggdc.net/maddison/maddison-project/home.htm, and International Monetary Fund, *World Economic Outlook Database*.

Your Turn: Test your understanding by doing related problems 1.13 and 1.14 on page 121 at the end of this module.

MyEconLab Study Plan

Potential GDP

Because economists take a long-run perspective in discussing economic growth, the concept of *potential GDP* is useful. **Potential GDP** is the level of real GDP attained when all firms are producing at *capacity*. The capacity of a firm is *not* the maximum output the firm is capable of producing. A Corning factory could operate 24 hours per day for 52 weeks per year and would be at its maximum production level. The factory's capacity, however, is measured by its production when operating on normal hours, using a normal workforce. If all firms in the economy were operating at capacity, the level of total production of final goods and services would equal potential GDP. Potential GDP increases over time as the labor force grows, new factories and office buildings are built, new machinery and equipment are installed, and technological change takes place.

Potential GDP The level of real GDP attained when all firms are producing at capacity.

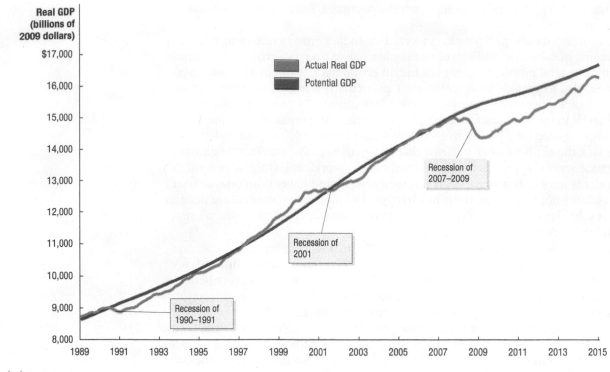

Figure 3A.2   Actual and Potential GDP

Potential GDP increases every year as the labor force and the capital stock grow and technological change occurs. The red line represents potential GDP, and the blue line represents actual real GDP. During the

three recessions since 1989, actual real GDP has been less than potential GDP.

Source: Federal Reserve Bank of St. Louis.

From 1949 to 2015, potential GDP in the United States grew at an average annual rate of 3.2 percent. In other words, each year, on average, the capacity of the economy to produce final goods and services expanded by 3.2 percent. In any particular year, the *actual* level of real GDP increased by more or less than 3.2 percent as the economy moved through the business cycle. Figure 3A.2 shows movements in actual and potential GDP for the years since 1989. The red line represents potential GDP, and the blue line represents actual real GDP. Notice that in each of the three recessions since 1989, actual real GDP has fallen below potential GDP. During the 2007–2009 recession, the gap between actual real GDP and potential GDP was particularly large, which shows the severity of the recession.

Will Economic Reforms in Mexico Boost Growth?

Founded in 1947, Flambeau, Inc., is a family firm based in Middlefield, Ohio, that makes plastic products including Duncan yo-yos, hunting decoys, and storage containers used in homes and businesses. In recent years, the company has faced strong competition from imports and has sought ways to reduce costs. The firm considered building a factory in China but chose instead to build in Saltillo, Mexico, because it was closer, and managers from the company could more easily oversee production. Flambeau President Jason Sauey explained, "It's not just about cost; it's about speed of response and quality."

Flambeau is not alone in choosing to locate plants in Mexico rather than China. More than 18,000 U.S. companies, including many Fortune 500 firms, have operations in Mexico. As Christopher Wilson, an economist at the Woodrow Wilson International Center for Scholars in Washington, observed: "Mexico has become the most competitive place to manufacture goods for the North American market." Proximity to the United States is an advantage of doing business in Mexico, rather than China or India, but investing in Mexico can be risky. Organized crime and corruption are major concerns. Coca-Cola, for example, suspended its operations in Chilpancingo because of attacks on its employees. Some local Mexican firms have been reluctant to expand because they fear attracting the attention of criminal gangs who might demand payments or government inspectors who might demand bribes.

These problems indicate that the Mexican government has failed to fully establish the rule of law, which is critical for the long-term prospects of the Mexican economy. Without the rule of law, entrepreneurs cannot fulfill their role in the market system of bringing together the factors of production—labor, capital, and natural resources—to produce goods and services. Mexican entrepreneurs also suffer from problems in the banking system that make it difficult to obtain the funding needed to finance expansion.

Although Mexico has experienced some increases in real GDP per capita during the past 30 years, its record of economic growth has been disappointing, particularly in comparison with China and other rapidly growing countries in the developing world. Being able to attain faster rates of growth would benefit people in Mexico—particularly those with low incomes—and the wider world economy.

Sources: Damien Cave, "As Ties with China Unravel, U.S. Companies Head to Mexico," *New York Times*, May 31, 2014; Matthias Rieker, "Making Yo-Yos and More," *Wall Street Journal*, July 16, 2012; Dolia Estevez, "U.S. Warns against Rising Costs of Doing Business in Mexico Due to Criminal Activity," *Forbes*, June 5, 2014; and flambeau.com.

Economics in Your Life

Would You Be Better Off without China?

For decades, China was a very poor country whose economy was growing very slowly. The government introduced economic reforms in 1978, which spurred rapid economic growth. Suppose that you could choose to live and work in a world with the Chinese economy growing very rapidly or in a world with the Chinese economy growing as slowly as it did before 1978. In which world would you choose to live? How does the current high-growth, high-export Chinese economy affect you as a consumer? How does it affect you as someone about to start a career? As you read the module, try to answer these questions. You can check your answers against those we provide on **page 118** at the end of this module.

E conomic growth is not inevitable. For most of human history, no sustained increases in output per capita occurred, and, in the words of the philosopher Thomas Hobbes, the lives of most people were "poor, nasty, brutish, and short." Sustained economic growth first began with the Industrial Revolution in England in the late eighteenth century. From there, economic growth spread to the United States, Canada, and the countries of Western Europe. Following the end of World War II in 1945, rapid economic growth also began in Japan and, eventually, in several other Asian countries, but the economies of many other countries stagnated, leaving their people trapped in poverty.

Real GDP per capita is the best measure of a country's standard of living because it represents the ability of the average person to buy goods and services. Economic growth occurs when real GDP per capita increases. In this module, we will develop a *model of economic growth* that will help us answer important questions like these:

- Why have countries such as the United States and the United Kingdom, which had high standards of living at the beginning of the twentieth century, continued to grow rapidly?

- Why have countries such as Argentina, which at one time had relatively high standards of living, failed to keep pace?

- Why was the Soviet Union unable to sustain the rapid growth rates of its early years?

- Why are some countries that were very poor at the beginning of the twentieth century still very poor?

- Why have some countries, such as South Korea and Japan, that once were very poor now become much richer?

- What explains China's very rapid recent growth rates?

3A.2 Economic Growth over Time and around the World

LEARNING OBJECTIVE: Define economic growth, calculate economic growth rates, and describe global trends in economic growth.

You live in a world that is very different from the world when your grandparents were young. You can listen to music on an iPhone that fits in your pocket; your grandparents played vinyl records on large stereo systems. You can send a text message to someone in another city, state, or country; your grandparents mailed letters that took days or weeks to arrive. More importantly, you have access to health care and medicines that have prolonged life and improved its quality. In many poorer countries, however, people endure grinding poverty and have only the bare necessities of life, just as their parents, grandparents, and great-grandparents did.

The difference between you and people in poor countries is that you live in a country that has experienced substantial economic growth. A growing economy produces both increasing quantities of goods and services and better goods and services. It is only through economic growth that living standards can increase, but through most of human history, no economic growth took place. Even today, billions of people are living in countries where economic growth is extremely slow.

Economic Growth from 1,000,000 B.C. to the Present

In 1,000,000 B.C., our ancestors survived by hunting animals and gathering edible plants. Farming was many years in the future, and production was limited to food, clothing, shelter, and simple tools. Bradford DeLong, an economist at the University of California, Berkeley, estimates that in those primitive circumstances, GDP per capita was about $145 per year in 2015 dollars, which was the minimum amount necessary to sustain life. DeLong estimates that real GDP per capita worldwide was still $145 in the year A.D. 1300. In other words, no sustained economic growth occurred between 1,000,000 B.C. and A.D. 1300. A peasant toiling on a farm in France in the year 1300 was no better off than his ancestors thousands of years before. In fact, for most of human existence, the typical person had only the bare minimum of food, clothing, and shelter necessary to sustain life. Few people survived beyond age 40, and most people suffered from debilitating illnesses.

Sustained economic growth did not begin until the **Industrial Revolution**, which started in England around the year 1750. The production of cotton cloth in factories using machinery powered by steam engines marked the beginning of the Industrial Revolution. Before that time, production of goods had relied almost exclusively on human or animal power. The use of mechanical power spread to the production of many other goods, greatly increasing the quantity of goods each worker could produce. First England and then other countries, such as the United States, France, and Germany, experienced *long-run economic growth*, with sustained increases in real GDP per capita that eventually raised living standards in those countries to the high levels of today.

Industrial Revolution The application of mechanical power to the production of goods, beginning in England around 1750.

Making the Connection
MyEconLab Video

Why Did the Industrial Revolution Begin in England?

The Industrial Revolution was a key turning point in human history. Before it, economic growth was slow and halting. After it, economic growth became rapid and sustained in a number of countries. Although historians and economists agree on the importance of the Industrial Revolution, they have not reached a consensus on why it happened in the time and place that it did. Why the eighteenth century and not the sixteenth century or the twenty-first century? Why England and not China or India or Africa or Japan?

There is always a temptation to read history backward. We know when and where the Industrial Revolution occurred; therefore, it had to happen where it did and when it did. But what was so special about England in the eighteenth century? Nobel Laureate Douglass North of Washington University in St. Louis has argued that institutions in England differed significantly from those in other countries in ways that greatly aided economic growth. North believes that the Glorious Revolution of 1688 was a key turning point. After that date, the British Parliament, rather than the king, controlled the government. The British court system also became independent of the king. As a result, the British government was credible when it committed to upholding private property rights, protecting wealth, and eliminating arbitrary increases in taxes. These institutional changes gave entrepreneurs the confidence and the incentive to make the investments necessary to use the important technological developments of the second half of the eighteenth century—particularly the spinning jenny and the water frame, which were used in the production of cotton textiles, and the steam engine, which was used in mining and in the manufacture of textiles and other products. Without the institutional changes, entrepreneurs would have been reluctant to risk their property or their wealth by starting new businesses.

Although not all economists agree with North's specific argument about the origins of the Industrial Revolution, we will see that most economists accept the idea that economic growth is not likely to occur unless a country's government provides the type of institutional framework North describes.

The British government's guarantee of property rights set the stage for the Industrial Revolution.

Sources: Douglass C. North, *Understanding the Process of Economic Change*, Princeton, NJ: Princeton University Press, 2005; and Douglass C. North and Barry R. Weingast, "Constitutions and Commitment: The Evolution of Institutions Governing Public Choice in Seventeenth-Century England," *Journal of Economic History*, Vol. 49, No. 4, December 1989, pp. 803–832.

Your Turn: Test your understanding by doing related problem 2.3 on page 121 at the end of this module.

MyEconLab Study Plan

MyEconLab Animation

Figure 3A.3

Average Annual Growth Rates for the World Economy

World economic growth was essentially zero in the years before 1300, and it was very slow—an average of only 0.2 percent per year—between 1300 and 1800. The Industrial Revolution made possible the sustained increases in real GDP per capita that have allowed some countries to attain high standards of living.
Source: J. Bradford DeLong, "Estimates World GDP, One Million B.C.–Present," Working paper, University of California, Berkeley.

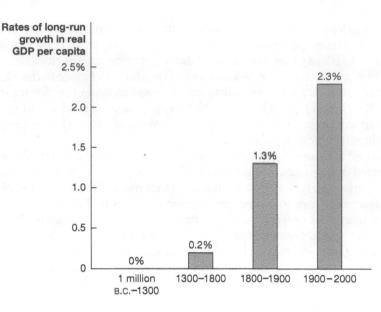

Figure 3A.3 shows how growth rates of real GDP per capita for the entire world have changed over long periods. Prior to A.D. 1300, there were no sustained increases in real GDP per capita. Over the next 500 years, to 1800, there was very slow growth. Significant growth began in the nineteenth century, as a result of the Industrial Revolution. A further acceleration in growth occurred during the twentieth century, as the average growth rate increased from 1.3 percent per year to 2.3 percent per year.   MyEconLab Concept Check

Small Differences in Growth Rates Are Important

The difference between 1.3 percent and 2.3 percent may seem trivial, but over long periods, small differences in growth rates can have a large effect. Suppose you have $100 in a savings account earning an interest rate of 1.3 percent, which means you will receive an interest payment of $1.30 this year. If the interest rate on the account is 2.3 percent, you will earn $2.30. The difference of an extra $1.00 interest payment seems insignificant. But if you leave the interest as well as the original $100 in your account for another year, the difference becomes greater because now the higher interest rate is applied to a larger amount—$102.30—and the lower interest rate is applied to a smaller amount—$101.30. This process, known as *compounding*, magnifies even small differences in interest rates over long periods of time. Over a period of 50 years, your $100 would grow to $312 at an interest rate of 2.3 percent but to only $191 at an interest rate of 1.3 percent.

The principle of compounding applies to economic growth rates as well as to interest rates. For example, in 1950, real GDP per capita in Argentina was $5,474 (measured in 2005 dollars), which was larger than Italy's real GDP per capita of $5,361. Over the next 64 years, the economic growth rate in Italy averaged 2.5 percent per year, while in Argentina, the growth rate was only 1.5 percent per year. Although this difference in growth rates of only 1 percentage point may seem small, in 2014, real GDP per capita in Italy had risen to $26,550, while real GDP per capita in Argentina was only $13,980. In other words, because of a relatively small difference in the growth rates of the two economies, the standard of living of a typical person in Italy went from being a little below that of a typical person in Argentina to being much higher. Here is the key point to keep in mind: *In the long run, small differences in economic growth rates result in big differences in living standards.*   MyEconLab Concept Check

Why Do Growth Rates Matter?

Why should anyone care about growth rates? Growth rates matter because an economy that grows too slowly fails to raise living standards. In some countries in Africa and

Asia, very little economic growth has occurred in the past 50 years, so many people remain in severe poverty. In high-income countries, only 4 out of every 1,000 babies die before they are one year old. In the poorest countries, more than 100 out of every 1,000 babies die before they are one year old, and millions of children die annually from diseases that could be avoided by having access to clean water or that could be cured by using medicines that cost only a few dollars.

Although their problems are less dramatic, countries that experience slow growth have also missed opportunities to improve the lives of their citizens. For example, the failure of Argentina to grow as rapidly as other countries that had similar levels of GDP per capita in 1950 has left many of its people in poverty. Life expectancy in Argentina is lower than in the United States and other high-income countries, and about 50 percent more babies in Argentina die before the age of one.   MyEconLab Concept Check

Don't Let This Happen to You

Don't Confuse the Average Annual Percentage Change with the Total Percentage Change

When economists talk about growth rates over a period of more than one year, the numbers are always *average annual percentage changes* and *not* total percentage changes. For example, in the United States, real GDP per capita was $14,398 in 1950 and $50,398 in 2014. The percentage change in real GDP per capita between these two years is:

$$\left(\frac{\$50,398 - \$14,398}{\$14,398}\right) \times 100 = 250\%.$$

However, this is *not* the growth rate between the two years. The growth rate between these two years is the rate at which $14,398 in 1950 would have to grow on average *each year* to end up as $50,398 in 2014, which is 2.0 percent.

MyEconLab Study Plan
Your Turn: Test your understanding by doing related problem 2.6 on page 122 at the end of this module.

"The Rich Get Richer and … "

We can divide the world's economies into two groups:

1. The *high-income countries,* sometimes also referred to as the *industrial countries* or the *developed countries,* including Australia, Canada, Japan, New Zealand, the United States, and the countries of Western Europe

2. The lower-income countries, or *developing countries,* including most of the countries of Africa, Asia, and Latin America

In the 1980s and 1990s, a small group of countries, mostly East Asian countries such as Singapore, South Korea, and Taiwan, began to experience high rates of growth and are sometimes referred to as the *newly industrializing countries.*

Figure 3A.4 shows the levels of GDP per capita around the world in 2014. GDP is measured in U.S. dollars, corrected for differences across countries in the cost of living. In 2014, GDP per capita ranged from a high of $144,400 in the Persian Gulf country of Qatar to a low of $600 in the Central African Republic. To understand why the gap between rich and poor countries exists, we need to look at what causes economies to grow.   MyEconLab Concept Check

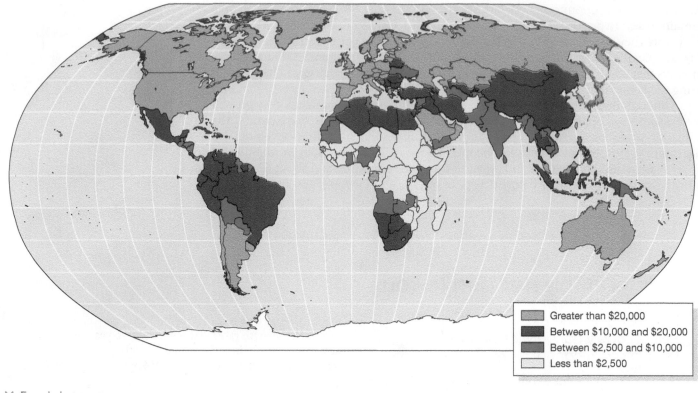

Greater than $20,000
Between $10,000 and $20,000
Between $2,500 and $10,000
Less than $2,500

MyEconLab Animation

Figure 3A.4   GDP per Capita, 2014

GDP per capita is measured in U.S. dollars, corrected for differences across countries in the cost of living.

Making the Connection

MyEconLab Video

Is Income All That Matters?

The more income you have, the more goods and services you can buy. When people are surviving on very low incomes of $2 per day or less, their ability to buy even minimal amounts of food, clothing, and housing is limited. So, most economists argue that unless the incomes of the very poor increase significantly, they will be unable to attain a higher standard of living. In some countries—primarily those colored yellow in Figure 3A.4—the growth in average income has been very slow, or even negative, over a period of decades. Most economists and policymakers have concluded that the standard of living in these countries has been largely unchanged for many years.

Some economists argue, though, that if we look beyond income to other measures of the standard of living, we can see that even the poorest countries have made significant progress in recent decades. For example, Charles Kenny, an economist with the Center for Global Development, argues that "those countries with the lowest quality of life are making the fastest progress in improving it—across a range of measures including health, education, and civil and political liberties." For example, since

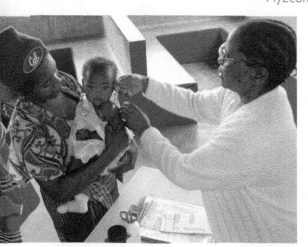

In sub-Saharan Africa and other parts of the world, increases in technology and knowledge are leading to improvements in health care and the standard of living.

1960 deaths among children have declined, often by more than 50 percent, in nearly all countries, including most of those with the lowest incomes. Even in sub-Saharan Africa, where growth in incomes has been very slow, the percentage of children dying before age five has decreased by more than 30 percent over the past 50 years. Similarly, the percentage of people able to read and write has more than doubled in sub-Saharan Africa since 1970. Many more people now live in democracies where basic civil rights are respected than at any other time in world history. Although some countries, such as Somalia, the Democratic Republic of the Congo, Syria, and Afghanistan, have suffered from civil wars, improved political stability in many countries has reduced the likelihood of dying from violence.

What explains these improvements in health, education, democracy, and political stability? William Easterly, an economist at New York University, has found that although, at any given time, countries that have a higher income also have a higher standard of living, over time, increases in income *within a particular country* are typically not the main cause of improvements in its standard of living in terms of health, education, individual rights, political stability, and similar factors. Kenny's argument and Easterly's finding are connected: Some increases in living standards do not require significant increases in income. The key factors in raising living standards in low-income countries have been increases in technology and knowledge—such as the development of inexpensive vaccines that reduce epidemics or the use of mosquito-resistant netting that reduces the prevalence of malaria—that are inexpensive enough to be widely available. Changes in attitudes, such as placing a greater value on education, particularly for girls, or increasing support for political freedoms, have also played a role in improving conditions in low-income countries.

There are limits, of course, to how much living standards can increase if incomes stagnate. Ultimately, much higher rates of economic growth will be necessary for low-income countries to significantly close the gap in living standards with high-income countries.

Sources: Charles Kenny, *Getting Better*, New York: Basic Books, 2011; Ursula Casabonne and Charles Kenny, "The Best Things in Life Are (Nearly) Free: Technology, Knowledge, and Global Health," *World Development*, Vol. 40, No. 1, January 2012, pp. 21–35; and William Easterly, "Life during Growth," *Journal of Economic Growth*, Vol. 4, No. 3, September 1999, pp. 239–276.

Your Turn: Test your understanding by doing related problems 2.7 and 2.8 on page 122 at the end of this module.

MyEconLab Study Plan

3A.3 | What Determines How Fast Economies Grow?

LEARNING OBJECTIVE: Use the economic growth model to explain why growth rates differ across countries.

To explain changes in economic growth rates over time within countries and differences in growth rates among countries, we need to develop an *economic growth model*. An **economic growth model** explains growth rates in real GDP per capita over the long run. As we have seen, the average person can buy more goods and services only if the average worker produces more goods and services. Recall that **labor productivity** is the quantity of goods and services that can be produced by one worker or by one hour of work. Because of the importance of labor productivity in explaining economic growth, the economic growth model focuses on the causes of long-run increases in labor productivity.

How can a country's workers become more productive? Economists believe two key factors determine labor productivity:

1. The quantity of capital available to workers
2. The level of technology

Therefore, to explain changes in real GDP per capita, the economic growth model focuses on technological change and changes over time in the quantity of capital available to workers. Recall that **technological change** is a change in the quantity of output firms can produce using a given quantity of inputs.

There are three main sources of technological change:

1. **Better machinery and equipment.** Beginning with the steam engine during the Industrial Revolution, the invention of new machinery has been an important source of rising labor productivity. Today, continuing improvements in computers, factory machine tools, electric generators, and many other machines contribute to increases in labor productivity.

Economic growth model A model that explains growth rates in real GDP per capita over the long run.

Labor productivity The quantity of goods and services that can be produced by one worker or by one hour of work.

Technological change A change in the quantity of output a firm can produce using a given quantity of inputs.

Human capital The accumulated knowledge and skills that workers acquire from education and training or from their life experiences.

2. **Increases in human capital.** Capital refers to *physical capital*, including computers, factory buildings, machine tools, warehouses, and trucks. The more physical capital workers have available, the more output they can produce. **Human capital** is the accumulated knowledge and skills that workers acquire from education and training or from their life experiences. As workers increase their human capital through education or on-the-job training, their productivity also increases. The more educated workers are, the greater is their human capital.

3. **Better means of organizing and managing production.** Labor productivity increases if managers can do a better job of organizing production. For example, the *just-in-time system*, first developed by Toyota Motor Corporation, involves assembling goods from parts that arrive at the factory at exactly the time they are needed. With this system, firms need fewer workers to store and keep track of parts in the factory, so the quantity of goods produced per hour worked increases.

Note that technological change is *not* the same thing as more physical capital. New capital can *embody* technological change, as when a faster computer chip is embodied in a new computer. But simply adding more capital that is the same as existing capital is not technological change. To summarize: A country's standard of living will be higher the more capital workers have available on their jobs, the better the capital, the more human capital workers have, and the better the job managers do in organizing production.

The Per-Worker Production Function

Per-worker production function The relationship between real GDP per hour worked and capital per hour worked, holding the level of technology constant.

Often when analyzing economic growth, we look at increases in real GDP *per hour worked* and increases in capital *per hour worked*. We use measures of GDP per hour and capital per hour rather than per person, so we can analyze changes in the underlying ability of an economy to produce more goods with a given amount of labor without having to worry about changes in the fraction of the population working or in the length of the workday. We can illustrate the economic growth model using the **per-worker production function**, which is the relationship between real GDP per hour worked and capital per hour worked, *holding the level of technology constant*. For simplicity, from now on we will shorten "per-worker production function" to just "production function." Figure 3A.5 shows the production function as a graph. We measure capital per hour worked along the horizontal axis and real GDP per hour worked along the vertical axis. Letting K stand for capital, L stand for labor, and Y stand for real GDP, real GDP per hour worked is Y/L, and capital per hour worked is K/L. The curve represents the production function. Notice that we do not explicitly show technological change in the

Figure 3A.5

The Per-Worker Production Function

The per-worker production function shows the relationship between capital per hour worked and real GDP per hour worked, holding technology constant. Increases in capital per hour worked increase output per hour worked but at a diminishing rate. For example, an increase in capital per hour worked from $75 to $100 increases real GDP per hour worked from $48 to $53. An increase in capital per hour worked from $100 to $125 increases real GDP per hour worked by a smaller amount, from $53 to $57. Each additional $25 increase in capital per hour worked results in a progressively smaller increase in output per hour worked.

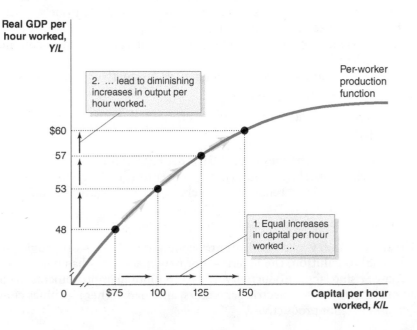

figure. We assume that as we move along the production function, the level of technology remains constant. As we will see, we can illustrate technological change using this graph by *shifting up* the curve representing the production function.

The figure shows that increases in the quantity of capital per hour worked result in movements up along the production function, increasing the quantity of output each worker produces. When *we hold technology constant*, however, equal increases in the amount of capital per hour worked lead to *diminishing* increases in output per hour worked. For example, increasing capital per hour worked from $75 to $100 increases real GDP per hour worked from $48 to $53, an increase of $5. Another $25 increase in capital per hour worked, from $100 to $125, increases real GDP per hour worked from $53 to $57, an increase of only $4. Each additional $25 increase in capital per hour worked results in progressively smaller increases in real GDP per hour worked. In fact, at very high levels of capital per hour worked, further increases in capital per hour worked will not result in any increase in real GDP per hour worked. This effect results from the *law of diminishing returns*, which states that as we add more of one input—in this case, capital—to a fixed quantity of another input—in this case, labor—output increases by smaller additional amounts.

Why are there diminishing returns to capital? Consider a simple example in which you own a copy store. At first you have 10 employees but only 1 copy machine, so each of your workers is able to produce relatively few copies per day. When you buy a second copy machine, your employees will be able to produce more copies. Adding additional copy machines will continue to increase your output—but by increasingly smaller amounts. For example, adding a twentieth copy machine to the 19 you already have will not increase the copies each worker is able to make by nearly as much as adding a second copy machine did. Eventually, adding additional copying machines will not increase your output at all.   MyEconLab Concept Check

Which Is More Important for Economic Growth: More Capital or Technological Change?

Technological change helps economies avoid diminishing returns to capital. Let's consider two simple examples of the effects of technological change. First, suppose you have 10 copy machines in your copy store. Each copy machine can produce 10 copies per minute. You don't believe that adding an eleventh machine identical to the 10 you already have will significantly increase the number of copies your employees can produce in a day. Then you find out that a new copy machine has become available that produces 20 copies per minute. If you replace your existing machines with the new machines, the productivity of your workers will increase. The replacement of existing capital with more productive capital is an example of technological change.

Or suppose you realize that the layout of your store could be improved. Maybe the paper for the machines is on shelves at the back of the store, which requires your workers to spend time walking back and forth whenever the machines run out of paper. By placing the paper closer to the copy machines, you can improve the productivity of your workers. Reorganizing how production takes place so as to increase output is also an example of technological change.   MyEconLab Concept Check

Technological Change: The Key to Sustaining Economic Growth

Figure 3A.6 shows the effect of technological change on the production function. Technological change shifts up the production function and allows an economy to produce more real GDP per hour worked with the same quantity of capital per hour worked. For example, if the current level of technology puts the economy on Production function$_1$, then when capital per hour worked is $150, real GDP per hour worked is $60. Technological change that shifts the economy to Production function$_2$ makes it possible to produce $65 in goods and services per hour worked with the same level of capital per hour worked. Further increases in technology that shift the economy to higher production functions result in further increases in real GDP per hour worked. Because of diminishing returns to capital, continuing increases in real GDP per hour worked can be sustained only if there is technological change. Remember that a country will

Figure 3A.6

Technological Change Increases Output per Hour Worked

Technological change shifts up the production function and allows more output per hour worked with the same amount of capital per hour worked. For example, along Production function₁ with $150 in capital per hour worked, the economy can produce $60 in real GDP per hour worked. However, an increase in technology that shifts the economy to Production function₂ makes it possible to produce $65 in real GDP per hour worked with the same level of capital per hour worked.

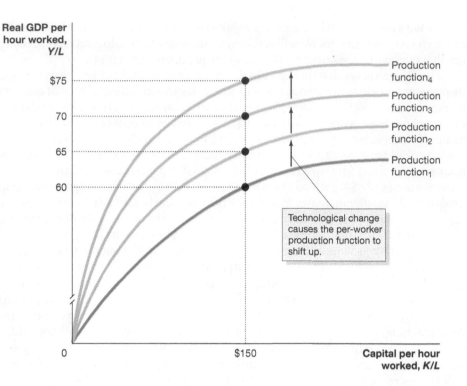

experience increases in its standard of living only if it experiences increases in real GDP per hour worked. Therefore, we can draw the following important conclusion: *In the long run, a country will experience an increasing standard of living only if it experiences continuing technological change.*   MyEconLab Concept Check

Making the Connection
MyEconLab Video

What Explains the Economic Failure of the Soviet Union?

The economic growth model can help explain one of the most striking events of the twentieth century: the economic collapse of the Soviet Union. The Soviet Union was formed from the old Russian Empire following the Russian Revolution of 1917. Under Communism, the Soviet Union was a centrally planned economy in which the government owned nearly every business and made all production and pricing decisions. In 1960, Nikita Khrushchev, the leader of the Soviet Union, addressed the United Nations in New York City. He declared to the United States and the other democracies: "We will bury you. Your grandchildren will live under Communism."

Many people at the time took Khrushchev's boast seriously. Capital per hour worked grew rapidly in the Soviet Union from 1950 through the 1980s. At first, these increases in capital per hour worked also produced rapid increases in real GDP per hour worked. Rapid increases in real GDP per hour worked during the 1950s caused some economists in the United States to predict incorrectly that the Soviet Union would someday surpass the United States economically. In fact, diminishing returns to capital meant that the additional factories the Soviet Union was building resulted in smaller and smaller increases in real GDP per hour worked.

In the former Soviet Union there were frequent shortages, and unhappy consumers often had to wait in long lines to shop for groceries and other goods.

The Soviet Union did experience some technological change—but at a rate much slower than in the United States and other high-income countries. Why did the Soviet Union fail the crucial requirement for growth: implementing new technologies? The key reason is that in a centrally planned economy, the people managing most businesses are government employees and not entrepreneurs or independent businesspeople, as is the case in market economies. Soviet managers had little incentive to adopt new ways of producing goods and services. Their pay depended on producing the quantity of output specified in the government's economic plan, not on discovering new, better, and lower-cost ways to produce goods. In addition, these managers did not have to worry about competition from either domestic or foreign firms.

Entrepreneurs and managers of firms in the United States, by contrast, are under intense competitive pressure from other firms. They must constantly search for better ways of producing the goods and services they sell. Developing and using new technologies is an important way to gain a competitive edge and earn a higher profit. The drive for profit provides an incentive for technological change that centrally planned economies are unable to duplicate. In market economies, entrepreneurs and managers who have their own money on the line make decisions about which investments to make and which technologies to adopt. Nothing concentrates the mind like having your own funds at risk.

In hindsight, it is clear that a centrally planned economy, such as the Soviet Union's, could not, over the long run, grow faster than a market economy. The Soviet Union collapsed in 1991, and contemporary Russia now has a more market-oriented system, although the government continues to play a much larger role in the economy than does the government in the United States.

Your Turn: Test your understanding by doing related problem 3.7 on page 123 at the end of this module.

MyEconLab Study Plan

Solved Problem 3A.3

MyEconLab Interactive Animation

Using the Economic Growth Model to Analyze the Failure of the Soviet Economy

Use the economic growth model and the information in the *Making the Connection* on page 98 to analyze the economic problems the Soviet Union encountered.

Solving the Problem

Step 1: **Review the module material.** This problem is about using the economic growth model to explain the failure of the Soviet economy, so you may want to review the *Making the Connection* on page 98.

Step 2: **Draw a graph like Figure 3A.5 on page 96 to illustrate the economic problems of the Soviet Union.** For simplicity, assume that the Soviet Union experienced no technological change.

The Soviet Union experienced rapid increases in capital per hour worked from 1950 through the 1980s, but its failure to implement new technology meant that output per hour worked grew at a slower and slower rate.

Extra Credit: The Soviet Union hoped to raise the standard of living of its citizens above that enjoyed in the United States and other high-income countries. Its strategy was to make continuous increases in the quantity of capital available to its workers. The economic growth model helps us understand the flaws in this policy for achieving economic growth.

MyEconLab Study Plan

Your Turn: For more practice, do related problems 3.8, 3.9, and 3.10 on page 123–124 at the end of this module.

New Growth Theory

The economic growth model we have been using was first developed in the 1950s by Nobel Laureate Robert Solow of MIT. According to this model, productivity growth is the key factor in explaining long-run growth in real GDP per capita. In recent years, some economists have become dissatisfied with this model because it does not explain the factors that determine productivity growth. Paul Romer, of New York University, developed the **new growth theory** to provide a better explanation of the sources of technological change that underlie productivity growth. Romer argues that the rate of technological change is influenced by how individuals and firms respond to economic incentives. Earlier accounts of economic growth did not explain technological change or attributed it to factors such as chance scientific discoveries.

Romer argues that the accumulation of *knowledge capital* is a key determinant of economic growth. Firms add to an economy's stock of knowledge capital when they engage in research and development or otherwise contribute to technological change. We have seen that accumulation of physical capital is subject to diminishing returns: Increases in capital per hour worked lead to increases in real GDP per hour worked but at a decreasing rate. Romer argues that the same is true of knowledge capital *at the firm level.* As firms add to their stock of knowledge capital, they increase their output but at a decreasing rate. At the level of the entire economy, however, Romer argues that knowledge capital is subject to *increasing returns.* Increasing returns can exist because knowledge, once discovered, becomes available to everyone. The use of physical capital, such as a computer or machine tool, is *rival* because if one firm uses it, other firms cannot, and it is *excludable* because the firm that owns the capital can keep other firms from using it. The use of knowledge capital, such as the chemical formula for a drug that cures cancer, is nonrival, however, because one firm's using that knowledge does not prevent another firm from using it. Knowledge capital is also nonexcludable because once something like a chemical formula becomes known, it becomes widely available for other firms to use (unless, as we discuss shortly, the government gives the firm that invents a new product the legal right to its exclusive use).

Because knowledge capital is nonrival and nonexcludable, firms can *free ride* on the research and development of other firms. Firms free ride when they benefit from the results of research and development they did not pay for. For example, transistor technology was first developed at Western Electric's Bell Laboratories in the 1950s and served as the basic technology of the information revolution. Bell Laboratories, however, received only a tiny fraction of the immense profits that were eventually made by all the firms that used this technology. Romer points out that firms are unlikely to invest in research and development up to the point where the marginal cost of the research equals the marginal return from the knowledge gained because *other* firms gain much of the marginal return. Therefore, there is likely to be an inefficiently small amount of research and development, slowing the accumulation of knowledge capital and economic growth.

Government policy can help increase the accumulation of knowledge capital in three ways:

1. **Protecting intellectual property with patents and copyrights.** Governments can increase the incentive to engage in research and development by giving firms the exclusive rights to their discoveries for a period of years. The U.S. government

New growth theory A model of long-run economic growth that emphasizes that technological change is influenced by economic incentives and so is determined by the working of the market system.

grants patents to companies that develop new products or new ways of making existing products. A **patent** gives a firm the exclusive legal right to a new product for a period of 20 years from the date the patent is filed with the government. For example, a pharmaceutical firm that develops a drug that cures cancer can secure a patent on the drug, keeping other firms from manufacturing the drug without permission. The profit earned during the period the patent is in force provides firms with an incentive for undertaking research and development. The patent system has drawbacks, however. In filing for a patent, a firm must disclose information about the product or process. This information enters the public record and may help competing firms develop products or processes that are similar but that do not infringe on the patent. To avoid this problem, a firm may try to keep the results of its research a *trade secret*, without patenting it. (A famous example of a trade secret is the formula for Coca-Cola.) Tension also arises between the government's objectives of providing patent protection that gives firms the incentive to engage in research and development and making sure that the knowledge gained through the research is widely available, which increases the positive effect of the knowledge on the economy. Economists debate the features of an ideal patent system.

Patent The exclusive right to produce a product for a period of 20 years from the date the patent is applied for.

2. **Supporting research and development.** The government can help increase the quantity of research and development that takes place. In the United States, the federal government conducts some research directly. For example, the National Institutes of Health conducts medical research. The forerunner of the Internet—the Advanced Research Project Agency Network (ARPANET)—was developed by the U.S. Department of Defense to improve communication among defense researchers around the country. The government also subsidizes research by providing grants and other payments to researchers in universities through the National Science Foundation and other agencies. Finally, the government provides tax benefits to firms that invest in research and development.

3. **Subsidizing education.** People with technical training carry out research and development. If firms are unable to capture all the profit from research and development, they will pay lower wages and salaries to technical workers. These lower wages and salaries reduce the incentive to workers to receive this training. If the government subsidizes education, it can increase the number of workers who have technical training. In the United States, the government subsidizes education by directly providing free education from grades kindergarten through 12 and by providing support for public colleges and universities. The government also provides student loans at reduced interest rates.

These government policies can bring the accumulation of knowledge capital closer to the optimal level.

MyEconLab Concept Check

Joseph Schumpeter and Creative Destruction

The new growth theory has revived interest in the ideas of Joseph Schumpeter. Born in Austria in 1883, Schumpeter served briefly as that country's finance minister. In 1932, he became an economics professor at Harvard University. Schumpeter developed a model of growth that emphasized his view that new products unleash a "gale of creative destruction" that drives older products—and, often, the firms that produced them—out of the market. According to Schumpeter, the key to rising living standards is not small changes to existing products but, rather, new products that meet consumer wants in qualitatively better ways. For example, in the early twentieth century, the automobile displaced the horse-drawn carriage by meeting consumer demand for personal transportation in a way that was qualitatively better. In the early twenty-first century, the DVD and the DVD player displaced the VHS tape and the VCR by better meeting consumer demand for watching films at home. Downloading or streaming movies from the Internet are now in the process of displacing the DVD just as the DVD displaced the VHS tape.

To Schumpeter, the entrepreneur is central to economic growth: "The function of entrepreneurs is to reform or revolutionize the pattern of production by exploiting an invention or, more generally, an untried technological possibility for producing new commodities or producing an old one in a new way."

The profit an entrepreneur hopes to earn provides the incentive for bringing together the factors of production—labor, capital, and natural resources—to start new firms and introduce new goods and services. Successful entrepreneurs can use their profits to finance the development of new products and are better able to attract funds from investors.   MyEconLab Concept Check

  Economic Growth in the United States

3A.4 LEARNING OBJECTIVE: Discuss fluctuations in productivity growth in the United States.

The economic growth model can help us understand the record of growth in the United States. Figure 3A.7 shows average annual growth rates in real GDP per hour worked since 1800. As the United States experienced the Industrial Revolution during the nineteenth century, U.S. firms increased the quantities of capital per hour worked. New technologies such as the steam engine, the railroad, and the telegraph also became available. Together, these factors resulted in an average annual growth rate of real GDP per worker of 1.3 percent from 1800 to 1900. Real GDP *per capita* grew at a slower rate of 1.1 percent during this period. At this growth rate, real GDP per capita would double about every 63 years, which means that living standards were growing steadily but relatively slowly.

By the twentieth century, technological change had been institutionalized. Many large corporations began to set up research and development facilities to improve the quality of their products and the efficiency with which they produced them. Universities also began to conduct research that had business applications. After World War II, many corporations began to provide significant funds to universities to help pay for research. In 1950, the federal government created the National Science Foundation, whose main goal is to support university researchers. The accelerating rate of technological change led to more rapid growth rates.

MyEconLab Animation

Figure 3A.7

Average Annual Growth Rates in Real GDP per Hour Worked in the United States, 1800–2014

The growth rate in the United States increased from 1800 through the mid-1970s. Then, for more than 20 years, growth slowed before increasing for a 10-year period beginning in the mid-1990s. During the past 10 years, growth has slowed again.
Note: The values for 1800–1900 are real GDP per worker. The values for 1900–2014 are real GDP per hour worked; for the period 1900–2014 they are the authors' calculations, based on the methods used in Neville Francis and Valerie A. Ramey, "The Source of Historical Economic Fluctuations: An Analysis Using Long-Run Restrictions," in Jeffrey Frankel, Richard Clarida, and Francesco Giavazzi, eds., *International Seminar in Macroeconomics*, Chicago: University of Chicago Press, 2005; the authors thank Neville Francis for kindly providing some of the data used.

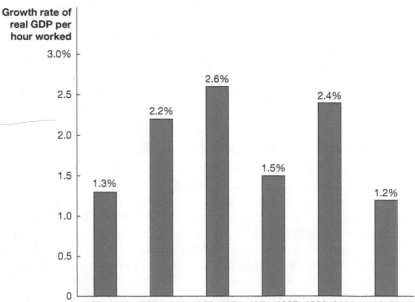

Economic Growth in the United States since 1950

Continuing technological change allowed the U.S. economy to avoid the diminishing returns to capital that stifled growth in the Soviet economy. In fact, until the 1970s, the growth rate of the U.S. economy accelerated over time. As Figure 3A.7 shows, growth in the first half of the twentieth century was faster than growth during the nineteenth century, and growth in the immediate post–World War II period from 1950 to 1973 was faster yet. Then the unexpected happened: For more than 20 years, from 1974 to 1995, the growth rate of real GDP per hour worked slowed. The growth rate during these years was more than 1 percentage point per year lower than during the 1950–1973 period. Beginning in the mid-1990s, the growth rate picked up again, and many economists argued that the effects of the revolution in *information technology* (IT), including increased use of computers, software, cellphones, and related innovations, were causing a return to higher rates of long-run growth. But, then, beginning in 2006, growth again slowed.   MyEconLab Concept Check

Is the United States Headed for a Long Period of Slow Growth?

Economists have not reached a consensus in explaining the swings in U.S. productivity growth since the mid-1970s. Broadly speaking, economists' views fall into two camps:

- **The optimistic view.** Some economists argue that although productivity has become more difficult to measure, the United States is likely to experience high rates of productivity growth in the long run, which will significantly increase the standard of living of the average person in the decades ahead.

- **The pessimistic view.** Other economists believe that productivity growth entered a long-run decline in the mid-1970s that was overcome for only a brief period of time by the initial effects of the revolution in information technology. These economists argue that future productivity growth rates are likely to remain low and, therefore, the standard of living of the average person in the United States will increase only slowly.

We can briefly discuss some of the key issues involved in this debate.

Measurement Issues Some economists argue that recent productivity growth rates may appear worse than they are because of problems in measuring output. If growth in real GDP understates the true growth rate of output, then measured productivity growth will also understate the true growth rate of productivity. After 1970, services—such as haircuts and financial advice—became a larger fraction of GDP, and goods—such as automobiles and hamburgers—became a smaller fraction. It is more difficult to measure increases in the output of services than to measure increases in the output of goods. For example, before banks began using automated teller machines (ATMs) in the 1980s, you could withdraw money only by going to a bank before closing time—which was usually 3:00 P.M. Once ATMs became available, you could withdraw money at any time of the day or night at a variety of locations. This increased convenience from ATMs does not show up in GDP. If this and similar improvements in the quality and convenience of services were included in GDP, measured output per hour worked would have grown more rapidly.

There may also be a measurement problem in accounting for improvements in the environment and in health and safety. Beginning in 1970, new laws required firms to spend billions of dollars reducing pollution, improving workplace safety, and redesigning products to improve their safety. This spending did not result in additional output that would be included in GDP—although it may have increased overall well-being. If these increases in well-being had been included in GDP, measured output per hour worked would have grown more rapidly.

All the high-income countries have experienced roughly similar movements in productivity growth rates. Because they all began producing more services and fewer goods and enacted stricter environmental regulations at about the same time, explanations of the productivity slowdown that emphasize measurement problems become more plausible.

The Role of Information Technology Some economists argue that the development of information technology (IT) caused the higher productivity growth that began in the mid-1990s. As computers became less expensive and faster, they made it possible for people and organizations to communicate and process data more efficiently. Today, a single laptop computer has more computing power than all the mainframe computers NASA used to control the *Apollo* spacecrafts that landed on the moon in the late 1960s and early 1970s.

Faster data processing has had a major effect on nearly every firm. Business record keeping, once done laboriously by hand, is now done more quickly and accurately by computers. During the 1990s, firms used the Internet to market and sell products. Smartphones, tablets, laptop computers, and wireless Internet access allow people to work at home and while traveling. These developments in IT have significantly increased labor productivity.

Despite the wonders of IT, productivity growth since 2006 has fallen to an even lower rate than during the period of slow growth from the mid-1970s to the mid-1990s. Is IT no longer a productivity booster, or are the data not capturing some of IT's benefits? What insight do the answers to these questions give us about how rapid growth will be in the coming decades?

Some economists believe that developments in IT have improved the delivery of services to both consumers and firms in ways that the GDP statistics fail to capture. For instance, receiving detailed driving directions using TomTom or a similar app is much easier than before smartphones were developed. In recent years the widespread use of apps to arrange for car rides, make short-term room rentals, locate friends, and so on have provided benefits to consumers that are not measured or are only partially measured by GDP. Similarly, a store manager can quickly check on available warehouse inventory using a dedicated smartphone or tablet app.

Economists who believe that IT is having large, but difficult to measure, effects on the economy are usually also optimistic about future growth rates. They believe that continuing advances in semiconductor technology—which underlie progress in IT—will result in substantial gains in labor productivity. The gains will come from higher productivity in the IT sector itself and in other sectors of the economy as the result of progress made possible by advances in IT. For example, ever more rapid and inexpensive computing lowers the cost and speeds the adoption of existing products, such as 3D printers, and helps innovators develop new products, which, in turn, raise productivity growth above its current levels.

Other economists doubt that the unmeasured benefits of the IT revolution are any greater than the unmeasured benefits of earlier innovations. Robert J. Gordon of Northwestern University has argued that productivity increases from the IT revolution were in fact much smaller than increases resulting from earlier innovations, such as the railroad, electrification of homes and businesses, petroleum refining, and the automobile. Moreover, Gordon and some other economists argue that most of the gains from the IT revolution occurred in the 1990s, as a result of the development of the World Wide Web, Windows 95, and computerized inventory control systems. These innovations raised labor productivity because they changed how businesses operated. By the early 2000s, the IT revolution was having a greater effect on consumer products, such as smartphones and tablets, than on labor productivity. Gordon identifies other factors, such as an aging population, declining educational achievement, and the consequences of increased regulations and higher taxes, that will lead to lower productivity growth rates. Gordon forecasts an extended period of productivity growth rates of 0.5 percent or less.

"Secular Stagnation ... " In the late 1930s, toward the end of the Great Depression, Alvin Hansen of Harvard University predicted that the U.S. economy would experience an extended period of slow growth, or *secular stagnation*. The rapid growth rates the U.S. economy experienced beginning in 1950 indicate that Hansen's analysis was incorrect. Recently, however, Lawrence Summers of Harvard, along with some other economists, has revived the term in arguing that growth rates are likely to remain low in future years. These economists do not focus on potentially slow rates of technological progress. Instead, they believe that real GDP may grow slowly because of insufficient demand for investment spending.

We have seen that in the loanable funds model, the equilibrium level of saving and investment is determined at the level of the real interest rate where the quantity of loanable funds demanded equals the quantity of loanable funds supplied. Economists who forecast a future of secular stagnation believe that the demand for loanable funds may be low in coming years for three main reasons:

1. Slowing population growth in the United States will reduce the demand for housing.
2. Modern information technology firms, such as Twitter, Google, and Facebook, require much less capital than older industrial firms, such as General Motors or Whirlpool.
3. The price of capital, particularly information technology goods such as computers, has been falling relative to the prices of other goods. Accordingly, firms can meet their needs for capital with lower levels of expenditure.

As a result of these factors, the real interest rate that brings equality to the loanable funds market may be very low—possibly even negative. So, investment spending will be very low. With this component of GDP growing slowly, GDP will itself only grow slowly.

… or a Return to Faster Growth? Critics of the secular stagnation view believe that low rates of investment in recent years have resulted from the severity of the recession of 2007–2009 and the relatively slow recovery from that recession. They argue that as the economic recovery continues, the demand for investment goods will increase. In addition, they argue that economic growth in other countries may increase the demand for U.S. goods, allowing exports to increase, thereby offsetting the effects on GDP of lower production of investment goods.

The debate over future growth rates is an important one. If the optimistic forecasts are correct, then in future decades, the U.S. standard of living will be much higher than if the pessimistic forecasts are correct. A large difference in the standard of living will have an enormous effect on nearly every aspect of life in the United States, including the extent of poverty, the ability of individuals and the government to finance increasing medical costs, and the ability of the country to deal with the effects of an aging population.   MyEconLab Concept Check   MyEconLab Study Plan

Why Isn't the Whole World Rich?

3A.5

LEARNING OBJECTIVE: Explain economic catch-up and discuss why many poor countries have not experienced rapid economic growth.

The economic growth model tells us that economies grow when the quantity of capital per hour worked increases and when technological change occurs. This model seems to provide a good blueprint for developing countries to become rich:

1. Increase the quantity of capital per hour worked.
2. Use the best available technology.

There are economic incentives for both of these things to happen in poor countries. The profitability of using additional capital or better technology is generally greater in a developing country than in a high-income country. For example, replacing an existing computer with a new, faster computer will generally have a relatively small payoff for a firm in the United States. In contrast, installing a new computer in a Zambian firm where records have been kept by hand is likely to have an enormous payoff.

This observation leads to an important conclusion: *The economic growth model predicts that poor countries will grow faster than rich countries.* If this prediction is correct, we should observe poor countries catching up to rich countries in levels of GDP per capita (or income per capita). Has this **catch-up**—or *convergence*—actually occurred? Here we come to a paradox: If we look only at the countries that currently have high incomes, we see that the lower-income countries have been catching up to the higher-income

Catch-up The prediction that the level of GDP per capita (or income per capita) in poor countries will grow faster than in rich countries.

countries, but the developing countries as a group have not been catching up to the high-income countries as a group.

Catch-up: Sometimes but Not Always

We can construct a graph that makes it easier to see whether catch-up is happening. In Figure 3A.8, the horizontal axis shows the initial level of real GDP per capita, and the vertical axis shows the rate at which real GDP per capita is growing. We can then plot points on the graph for rich and poor countries. Each point represents the combination of a country's initial level of real GDP per capita and its growth rate over the following years. The catch-up line in the figure shows the situation where the catch-up prediction holds exactly: Low-income countries should be on the upper-left section of the line because they would have low initial levels of real GDP per capita but fast growth rates. High-income countries should be in the lower-right section of the line because they would have high initial levels of real GDP per capita but slow growth rates. When we plot the actual observations for each country, the closer the points for each country are to the line, the more accurate the catch-up prediction is.

Catch-up among the High-Income Countries If we look at only the countries that currently have high incomes, we can see the catch-up predicted by the economic growth model. Figure 3A.9 shows that the high-income countries that had the lowest incomes in 1960, such as Taiwan, Korea, and Hong Kong, grew the fastest between 1960 and 2011 (which is the most recent year for which comprehensive data are available). Countries that had the highest incomes in 1960, such as Switzerland, Australia, and the United States, grew the slowest.

Are the Developing Countries Catching Up to the High-Income Countries? If we expand our analysis to include every country for which statistics are available, it becomes more difficult to find the catch-up predicted by the economic growth model. Figure 3A.10 does not show a consistent relationship between the level of real GDP per capita in 1960 and growth from 1960 to 2011. Some countries that had low levels of real GDP per capita in 1960, such as Niger and the Democratic Republic of the Congo, actually experienced *negative* economic growth: They had *lower* levels of real GDP per capita in 2011 than in 1960. Other countries that started with low levels of real GDP per capita, such as Malaysia and China, grew rapidly. Some middle-income countries in 1960, such as Venezuela, grew slowly between 1960 and 2011, while others, such as Ireland, grew much more rapidly.   MyEconLab Concept Check

MyEconLab Animation

Figure 3A.8

The Catch-up Predicted by the Economic Growth Model

According to the economic growth model, countries that start with lower levels of real GDP per capita should grow faster (points near the upper-left section of the line) than countries that start with higher levels of real GDP per capita (points near the lower-right section of the line).

Growth in real GDP per capita

Poorer countries should grow faster and be on this section of the line.

Catch-up line

Richer countries should grow more slowly and be on this section of the line.

Initial level of real GDP per capita

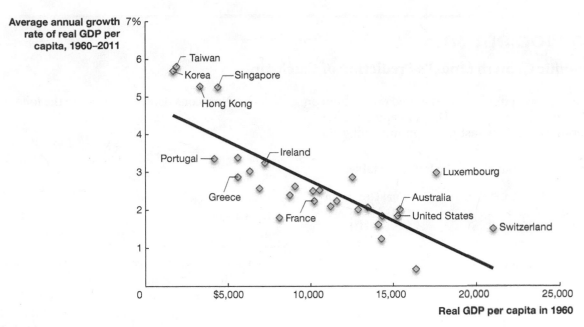

Figure 3A.9 **There Has Been Catch-up among High-Income Countries**

If we look only at countries that currently have high incomes, we see that countries such as Taiwan, Korea, and Singapore that had the lowest incomes in 1960 grew the fastest between 1960 and 2011. Countries such as Switzerland and the United States that had the highest incomes in 1960 grew the slowest.

Note: Data are real GDP per capita in 2005 dollars. Each point in the figure represents one high-income country.
Source: Authors' calculations from data in *Penn World Table Version 8.1;* Robert C. Feenstra, Robert Inklaar, and Marcel P. Timmer, "The Next Generation of the Penn World Table" www.ggdc.net/pwt, April 2015.

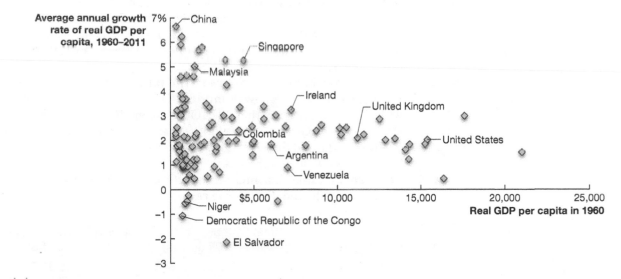

Figure 3A.10 **Most of the World Hasn't Been Catching Up**

If we look at all countries for which statistics are available, we do not see the catch-up predicted by the economic growth model. Some countries that had low levels of real GDP per capita in 1960, such as Niger and the Democratic Republic of the Congo, actually experienced *negative* economic growth. Other countries that started with low levels of real GDP per capita, such as Malaysia and China, grew rapidly. Some middle-income countries in 1960, such as Venezuela, hardly grew between 1960 and 2011, while others, such as Ireland, experienced significant growth.

Note: Data are real GDP per capita in 2005 dollars. Each point in the figure represents one country.
Source: Authors' calculations from data in *Penn World Table Version 8.1;* Robert C. Feenstra, Robert Inklaar, and Marcel P. Timmer, "The Next Generation of the Penn World Table" www.ggdc.net/pwt, April 2015.

Solved Problem 3A.5

MyEconLab Interactive Animation

The Economic Growth Model's Prediction of Catch-Up

The economic growth model makes a prediction about an economy's initial level of real GDP per capita relative to other economies and how fast the economy will grow in the future.

a. Consider the statistics in the following table:

Country	Real GDP per Capita, 1960 (2005 dollars)	Annual Growth in Real GDP per Capita, 1960–2011
Taiwan	$1,861	5.81%
Panama	2,120	3.50
Brazil	2,483	2.73
Costa Rica	4,920	1.42
Venezuela	7,015	0.91

Are these statistics consistent with the economic growth model? Briefly explain.

b. Now consider the statistics in the following table:

Country	Real GDP per Capita, 1960 (2005 dollars)	Annual Growth in Real GDP per Capita, 1960–2011
Japan	$5,586	3.39%
Belgium	10,132	2.50
United Kingdom	11,204	2.10
Australia	15,255	1.85

Are these statistics consistent with the economic growth model? Briefly explain.

c. Construct a new table that lists all nine countries, from the lowest real GDP per capita in 1960 to the highest, along with their growth rates. Are the statistics in your new table consistent with the economic growth model?

Solving the Problem

Step 1: Review the module material. This problem is about catch-up in the economic growth model, so you may want to review the section "Why Isn't the Whole World Rich?" which begins on page 105.

Step 2: Explain whether the statistics in the table in part (a) are consistent with the economic growth model. These statistics are consistent with the economic growth model. The countries with the lowest levels of real GDP per capita in 1960 had the fastest growth rates between 1960 and 2011, and the countries with the highest levels of real GDP per capita had the slowest growth rates.

Step 3: Explain whether the statistics in the table in part (b) are consistent with the economic growth model. These statistics are also consistent with the economic growth model. Once again, the countries with the lowest levels of real GDP per capita in 1960 had the fastest growth rates between 1960 and 2011, and the countries with the highest levels of real GDP per capita had the slowest growth rates.

Step 4: Construct a table that includes all nine countries from the tables in parts (a) and (b) and discuss the results.

Country	Real GDP per Capita, 1960 (2005 dollars)	Annual Growth in Real GDP per Capita, 1960–2011
Taiwan	$1,861	5.81%
Panama	2,120	3.50
Brazil	2,483	2.73
Costa Rica	4,920	1.42
Japan	5,586	3.39
Venezuela	7,015	0.91
Belgium	10,132	2.50
United Kingdom	11,204	2.10
Australia	15,255	1.85

The statistics in the new table are *not* consistent with the predictions of the economic growth model. For example, Australia and the United Kingdom had higher levels of real GDP per capita in 1960 than did Costa Rica and Venezuela. The economic growth model predicts that Australia and the United Kingdom should, therefore, have grown more slowly than Costa Rica and Venezuela. The data in the table show, however, that Australia and the United Kingdom grew faster. Similarly, Belgium grew faster than Costa Rica, even though its real GDP per capita was already much higher than Costa Rica's in 1960.

Extra Credit: The statistics in these tables confirm what we saw in Figures 3A.9 and 3A.10 on page 107: There has been catch-up among the high-income countries, but there has not been catch-up if we include in the analysis all the countries of the world.

Your Turn: For more practice, do related problems 5.4 and 5.5 on page 125 at the end of this module.

MyEconLab Study Plan

Why Haven't Most Western European Countries, Canada, and Japan Caught Up to the United States?

Figure 3A.9 on page 107 indicates that there has been catch-up among the high-income countries over the past 50 years. If we look at the catch-up of other high-income countries to the United States during the most recent period, we discover a surprising fact: Over the past 25 years, other high-income countries have actually fallen further behind the United States rather than catching up to it. Figure 3A.11 shows real GDP per capita in Canada, Japan, and the five largest economies in Western Europe relative to real GDP per capita in the United States. The blue bars show real GDP per capita in 1990 relative to the United States, and the red bars show real GDP per capita in 2014 relative to the United States. In each case, relative levels of real GDP per capita were lower in 2014 than they were in 1990. Each of these countries experienced significant catch-up to the United States between 1960 and 1990, but they have experienced no catch-up since 1990.

Why have other high-income countries had trouble completely closing the gap in real GDP per capita with the United States? Many economists believe there are two

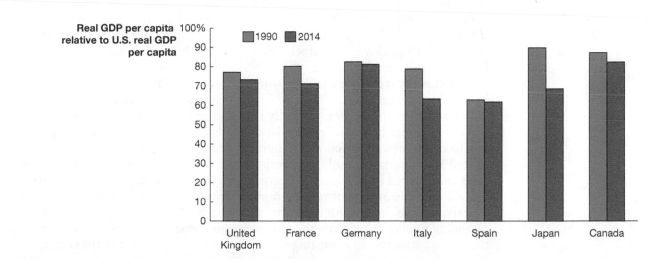

MyEconLab Real-time data

Figure 3A.11   **Other High-Income Countries Have Stopped Catching Up to the United States**

The blue bars show real GDP per capita in 1990 relative to the United States, and the red bars show real GDP per capita in 2014 relative to the United States. In each case, relative levels of real GDP per capita are lower in 2014 than they were in 1990, which means that these countries have ceased catching up to the United States.

Source: Authors' calculations from data in Organization for Economic Co-operation and Development, stat.oecd.org.

main explanations: the greater flexibility of U.S. labor markets and the greater efficiency of the U.S. financial system. U.S. labor markets are more flexible than labor markets in other countries for several reasons. In many European countries, government regulations make it difficult for firms to fire workers and thereby make firms reluctant to hire workers in the first place. As a result, many younger workers have difficulty finding jobs, and once a job is found, a worker tends to remain in it even if his or her skills and preferences are not a good match for the characteristics of the job. In the United States, by contrast, government regulations are less restrictive, workers have an easier time finding jobs, and workers change jobs fairly frequently. This high rate of job mobility ensures a better match between workers' skills and preferences and the characteristics of jobs, which increases labor productivity. Many European countries also have restrictive work rules that limit the ability of firms to implement new technologies. These rules restrict the tasks firms can ask workers to perform and the number of hours they work. The rules reduce the ability of firms to use new technologies that may require workers to learn new skills, perform new tasks, or work during the night or early mornings.

Workers in the United States tend to enter the labor force earlier, retire later, and experience fewer long spells of unemployment than do workers in Europe. Unemployed workers in the United States typically receive smaller government payments for a shorter period of time than do unemployed workers in Canada and most of the countries of Western Europe. Because the opportunity cost of being unemployed is lower in those countries, the unemployment rate tends to be higher, and the fraction of the labor force that is unemployed for more than one year also tends to be higher. Studies have shown that workers who are employed for longer periods tend to have greater skills, greater productivity, and higher wages. Many economists believe that the design of the U.S. unemployment insurance program has contributed to the greater flexibility of U.S. labor markets and to higher rates of growth in labor productivity and real GDP per capita.

As we have seen, technological change is essential for rapid productivity growth. To obtain the funds needed to implement new technologies, firms turn to the financial system. It is important that funds for investment be not only available but also allocated efficiently. Large corporations can raise funds by selling stocks and bonds in financial markets. U.S. corporations benefit from the efficiency of U.S. financial markets. The level of legal protection of investors is relatively high in U.S. financial markets, which encourages both U.S. and foreign investors to buy stocks and bonds issued by U.S. firms. The volume of trading in U.S. financial markets also ensures that investors will be able to quickly sell the stocks and bonds they buy. This *liquidity* serves to attract investors to U.S. markets.

Smaller firms that are unable to issue stocks and bonds often obtain funding from banks. Entrepreneurs founding new firms—"startups"—particularly firms that are based on new technologies, generally find that investors are unwilling to buy their stocks and bonds because the firms lack records of profitability. Banks are also reluctant to lend to new firms founded to introduce new and unfamiliar technologies. In the United States, some technology startups obtain funds from *venture capital firms*, which raise funds from institutional investors, such as pension funds, and from wealthy individuals. The owners of venture capital firms closely examine the business plans of startup firms, looking for those that appear most likely to succeed. In exchange for providing funding, a venture capital firm often becomes part owner of the startup and may even play a role in managing the firm. A successful venture capital firm is able to attract investors who would not otherwise be willing to provide funds to startups because the investors lack enough information about the startup. A number of well-known U.S. high-technology firms, such as Google, relied on venture capital firms to fund their early expansion. The ability of venture capital firms to finance technology-driven startup firms may be giving the United States an advantage in bringing new products and new processes to market.

The U.S. financial system suffered severe problems between 2007 and 2009. But, over the long run, it has succeeded in efficiently allocating investment funds.

Why Don't More Low-Income Countries Experience Rapid Growth?

The economic growth model predicts that the countries that were very poor in 1960 should have grown rapidly over the next 50 years. As we have just seen, some did, but many did not. Why are many low-income countries growing so slowly? There is no single answer, but most economists point to four key factors:

1. Failure to enforce the rule of law
2. Wars and revolutions
3. Poor public education and health
4. Low rates of saving and investment

Failure to Enforce the Rule of Law In the years since 1960, increasing numbers of developing countries, including China, have abandoned centrally planned economies in favor of more market-oriented economies. For entrepreneurs in a market economy to succeed, however, the government must guarantee private **property rights** and enforce contracts. Unless entrepreneurs feel secure in their property, they will not risk starting a business. Business owners also have difficulty being successful unless they can use an independent court system to enforce contracts. The **rule of law** refers to the ability of a government to enforce the laws of the country, particularly with respect to protecting private property and enforcing contracts. The failure of many developing countries to guarantee property rights and to enforce contracts has hindered their economic growth.

Consider, for example, the production of shoes. Suppose the owner of a shoe factory signs a contract with a leather tannery to deliver a specific quantity of leather on a particular date for a particular price. On the basis of this contract, the owner of the shoe factory signs a contract to deliver a specific quantity of shoes to a shoe wholesaler. This contract states the quantity of shoes to be delivered, the quality of the shoes, the delivery date, and the price. The owner of the leather tannery uses the contract with the shoe factory to enter into a contract with cattle ranchers for the delivery of hides. The shoe wholesaler enters into contracts to deliver shoes to retail stores, where they are sold to consumers. For the flow of goods from cattle ranchers to shoe customers to operate efficiently, each business must carry out the terms of the contract it has signed. In developed countries, such as the United States, businesses know that if they fail to carry out a contract, they may be sued in court and forced to compensate the other party for any economic damages.

Many developing countries do not have functioning, independent court systems. Even if a court system does exist, a case may not be heard for many years. In some countries, bribery of judges and political favoritism in court rulings are common. If firms cannot enforce contracts through the court system, they may insist on carrying out only face-to-face cash transactions. For example, the shoe manufacturer will wait until the leather producer brings the hides to the factory and will then buy the hides for cash. The wholesaler will wait until the shoes have been produced before making plans for sales to retail stores. Production still takes place, but it is carried out more slowly and inefficiently. With slow and inefficient production, firms have difficulty finding investors willing to provide them with the funds they need to expand.

Property rights The rights individuals or firms have to the exclusive use of their property, including the right to buy or sell it.

Rule of law The ability of a government to enforce the laws of the country, particularly with respect to protecting private property and enforcing contracts.

Making the Connection MyEconLab Video

Why Hasn't Mexico Grown as Fast as China?

Many people consider China *the* great economic growth success story. The decision by Chinese government leaders in the 1970s to turn away from a centrally planned economy and toward a market system unleashed economic growth that has lifted more than a billion people in China out of poverty. As we will discuss in Section 3A.6, the Chinese economy still faces significant obstacles to maintaining high growth rates, and the Chinese Communist Party has maintained its dictatorship over the country. Despite these problems, many economists and policymakers see China as an example of the rapid growth that low-income countries can attain.

As we saw in the module opener, some U.S. firms have chosen in recent years to locate factories and other facilities in Mexico rather than in China because Mexico is closer to the United States and because labor costs have been increasing more rapidly in China. This trend has been good news for the Mexican economy because it has increased factory employment and given the country easier access to U.S. technology. Overall, though, the growth rates of the Mexican economy have been disappointing. The graph below compares the growth rates of real GDP per capita for the Mexican and Chinese economies over the past 35 years.

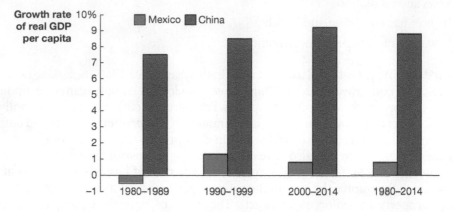

Taking the whole period between 1980 and 2014, the average annual growth rate for the Chinese economy has been 8.8 percent, while the growth rate for the Mexican economy has been a very slow 0.8 percent. We have seen that if we divide a growth rate into 70, the result is approximately the number of years it will take real GDP per capita to double. When we apply that rule here, we find that it will take real GDP per capita more than 85 years to double in Mexico but only 8 years in China.

What explains the slow growth of the Mexican economy? For most of the period from the Mexican Revolution of 1910 until 2000, the Institutional Revolutionary Party (PRI) dominated the Mexican government. For decades, the party followed a policy of limiting imports and foreign investment, concentrating on building up domestic industry behind high tariff walls. The Mexican government took over, or nationalized, some businesses, including the oil industry. By the 1980s, dissatisfaction with the country's poor economic performance led the PRI, under President Miguel de la Madrid, to institute a series of reforms. The reforms, which were broadened in the 1990s, included allowing banks again to be private businesses; signing the North American Free Trade Agreement (NAFTA) with the United States and Canada, which greatly reduced tariffs on imports; and allowing foreign investment in most sectors of the economy apart from the oil industry. As the graph above shows, though, these reforms have not resulted in high rates of economic growth.

Some economic historians believe that the Spanish colonial background of the nineteenth century and earlier hobbled the Mexican economy. Unlike in the United States, in Mexico and other Spanish and Portuguese colonies, land was often concentrated in very large estates, which led to highly unequal distributions of income and may have made it difficult for a broad-based middle class capable of supporting a large manufacturing base to develop. Other countries in Latin America, though, including Chile and Uruguay, with similar colonial backgrounds have experienced much more rapid growth.

Some economists believe that the financial sector has been an important obstacle to growth. The Mexican legal system makes it difficult for banks to seize a business's assets when the business defaults on a loan. As a result, Mexican banks are reluctant to make loans to businesses. As we noted in the module opener, Mexico also suffers from government corruption that either makes businesses reluctant to expand or forces them to operate in the underground economy. In either case, the businesses are unable to take advantage of economies of scale and may be unwilling to make large investments in machinery or buildings. In certain areas of Mexico, criminal gangs have also disrupted business. The educational system in Mexico has failed to provide many students with the skills needed to find work at firms competing in the global marketplace. Finally, infrastructure, including poor roads and inconsistent and expensive provision of electricity—with occasional blackouts—have also hindered business expansion.

Timothy J. Kehoe of the University of Minnesota and Kim J. Ruhl of New York University note that China also suffers from institutional problems, but it has grown much faster than Mexico. China, though, began its rapid growth from very low levels of income, so that in 2014, real GDP per capita in Mexico was still more than twice the level in China. Kehoe and Ruhl argue that, as a middle-income country, Mexico has already taken advantage of many of the relatively easy ways of increasing real GDP— including moving resources out of the low-productivity agricultural sector, accumulating capital in manufacturing, and adopting modern technology. We saw in the discussion of Figure 3A.11 that, probably for institutional reasons, many high-income countries have made no progress in closing the gap in real GDP per capita between themselves and the United States during the past 25 years. Mexico may now be in a similar situation of having difficulty growing fast enough to close the gap with higher-income countries. Because Mexico's institutional barriers to growth are more severe than those in European countries, the gap in real GDP per capita between the United States and Mexico may persist at a high level.

Economists and policymakers in Mexico continue to look for ways to increase growth rates. Without an increase in growth, it may be decades before millions of low-income people in Mexico are able to escape poverty.

Sources: "The 100-Year View," *Economist*, May 2, 2015; Gordon H. Hanson, "Why Isn't Mexico Rich?" *Journal of Economic Literature*, Vol. 48, No. 4, December 2010, pp. 987–1004; Timothy J. Kehoe and Kim J. Ruhl, "Why Have Economic Reforms in Mexico Not Generated Growth?" *Journal of Economic Literature*, Vol. 48, No. 4, December 2010, pp. 1004–1027; Nora Lustig, "Life Is Not Easy: Mexico's Quest for Stability and Growth," *Journal of Economic Perspectives*, Vol. 15, No. 1, Winter 2001, pp. 85–106; and Federal Reserve Bank of St. Louis.

Your Turn: Test your understanding by doing related problems 5.8 and 5.9 on page 126 at the end of this module.

MyEconLab Study Plan

Wars and Revolutions Many of the countries that were very poor in 1960 have experienced extended periods of war or violent changes of government during the years since. These wars have made it impossible for countries such as Afghanistan, Angola, Ethiopia, the Central African Republic, and the Democratic Republic of the Congo to accumulate capital or adopt new technologies. In fact, conducting any kind of business has been very difficult. Ending war has a positive effect on growth, as shown by the case of Mozambique, which suffered through almost two decades of civil war and declining real GDP per capita. With the end of civil war, Mozambique experienced a strong annual growth rate of 8 percent in real GDP per capita from 1990 to 2014.

Poor Public Education and Health We have seen that human capital is one of the determinants of labor productivity. Many low-income countries have weak public school systems, so many workers are unable to read and write. Few workers acquire the skills necessary to use the latest technology.

People in many low-income countries suffer from diseases that are either nonexistent or easily treated in high-income countries. For example, few people in developed countries suffer from malaria, but about 500,000 Africans die from it each year. Treatments for AIDS have greatly reduced deaths from this disease in the United States and Europe. But millions of people in low-income countries continue to die from AIDS. These countries often lack the resources, and their governments are often too ineffective, to provide even routine medical care, such as childhood vaccinations.

People who are sick work less and are less productive when they do work. Poor nutrition or exposure to certain diseases in childhood can leave people permanently weakened and can affect their intelligence as adults. Poor health has a significant negative effect on the human capital of workers in developing countries.

Low Rates of Saving and Investment To invest in factories, machinery, and computers, firms need funds. Some of the funds can come from the owners of the firm and from their friends and families, but firms in high-income countries raise most of their funds from bank loans and the sale of stocks and bonds in financial markets. In most developing countries, stock and bond markets do not exist, and often the banking system is very weak. In high-income countries, the funds that banks lend to businesses come from the savings of households. In high-income countries, many households are able to save a significant fraction of their income. In developing countries, many households barely survive on their incomes and, therefore, have little or no savings.

The low saving rates in developing countries can contribute to a *vicious cycle of poverty*. Because households have low incomes, they save very little. Because households save very little, few funds are available for firms to borrow. Lacking funds, firms do not invest in the new factories, machinery, and equipment needed for economic growth. Because the economy does not grow, household incomes remain low, as do their savings, and so on.   MyEconLab Concept Check

The Benefits of Globalization

One way for a developing country to break out of the vicious cycle of low saving and investment and low growth is through foreign investment. **Foreign direct investment (FDI)** occurs when corporations build or purchase facilities in foreign countries. **Foreign portfolio investment** occurs when an individual or a firm buys stocks or bonds issued in another country. Foreign direct investment and foreign portfolio investment can give a low-income country access to technology and funds that otherwise would not be available. Until fairly recently, many developing countries were reluctant to take advantage of this opportunity.

From the 1940s through the 1970s, many developing countries closed themselves off from the global economy. During the 1930s and early 1940s, the global trading and financial system collapsed as a result of the Great Depression and World War II. Developing countries that relied on exporting to the high-income countries were hurt economically. Also, many countries in Africa and Asia achieved independence from the colonial powers of Europe during the 1950s and 1960s and were afraid of being dominated by them economically. As a result, many developing countries imposed high tariffs on foreign imports and strongly discouraged or even prohibited foreign investment. These policies made it difficult to break out of the vicious cycle of poverty.

The policies of erecting high tariff barriers and avoiding foreign investment failed to produce much growth, so by the 1980s, many developing countries began to change policies. The result was **globalization**, which refers to the process of countries becoming more open to foreign trade and investment. Developing countries that are more globalized have grown faster than developing countries that are less globalized. Globalization has benefited developing countries by making it easier for them to obtain technology and investment funds.   MyEconLab Concept Check

Foreign direct investment (FDI) The purchase or building by a corporation of a facility in a foreign country.

Foreign portfolio investment The purchase by an individual or a firm of stocks or bonds issued in another country.

Globalization The process of countries becoming more open to foreign trade and investment.

MyEconLab Study Plan

3A.6 Growth Policies

LEARNING OBJECTIVE: Discuss government policies that foster economic growth.

What can governments do to promote long-run economic growth? We have seen that even small differences in growth rates compounded over the years can lead to major differences in standards of living. Therefore, there is potentially a very high payoff to government policies that increase growth rates. We have already discussed some of these policies in this module. In this section, we explore additional policies.

Enhancing Property Rights and the Rule of Law

A market system cannot work well unless property rights are enforced. Entrepreneurs are unlikely to risk their own funds, and investors are unlikely to lend their funds to entrepreneurs, if property is not protected from being arbitrarily seized. We have seen that in many developing countries, the rule of law and property rights are undermined by government *corruption*. In some developing countries, it is impossible for an entrepreneur to obtain a permit to start a business without paying bribes, often to several different government officials. Is it possible for a country to reform a corrupt government bureaucracy?

Although today the United States ranks among the least corrupt countries, recent research by economists Edward Glaeser and Claudia Goldin of Harvard University has shown that in the late nineteenth and early twentieth centuries, corruption was a significant problem in the United States. The fact that political reform movements and crusading newspapers helped to reduce corruption in the United States to relatively low levels by the 1920s provides some hope for reform movements that aim to reduce corruption in developing countries today.

Property rights are unlikely to be secure in countries that are afflicted by wars and civil strife. For a number of countries, increased political stability is a necessary prerequisite to economic growth.   MyEconLab Concept Check

<table>
<tr><td>**Making**
the
Connection
MyEconLab Video</td><td>**Will China's Standard of Living Ever Exceed**
That of the United States?</td></tr>
</table>

In 2014, GDP per capita in the United States was more than four times higher than GDP per capita in China. However, the growth rate of real GDP per capita in the United States has averaged only 1.7 percent per year since 1980, compared to China's average growth rate of 8.8 percent per year over the same time period. If these growth rates were to continue, China's standard of living, as measured by real GDP per capita, would exceed the U.S. standard of living in the year 2036.

Some economists argue that China may have overinvested in physical capital, such as bullet trains.

For China to maintain its high rates of growth in real GDP per capita, however, it would have to maintain high rates of productivity growth, which is unlikely for several reasons. First, the United States invests more in activities, such as research and development, that result in new technologies and increases in productivity. Although China has been successful in adopting existing technologies developed in the United States and other countries, it has been much less successful in developing new technologies. Second, a good part of China's growth is due to the transition from a centrally planned economy to a market economy, so China's growth rate is likely to decrease as the transition is completed. Third, China's economic growth has depended on moving workers from agriculture, where their productivity was low, to manufacturing jobs in cities, where their productivity is much higher. The large supply of low-wage agricultural workers helped to keep manufacturing wages low and provided China with a cost advantage in manufacturing goods compared with the United States and other high-income countries. China has exhausted much of its supply of low-wage agricultural workers, so manufacturing wages have begun to rise, eroding China's cost advantage. As we saw in the module opener, some U.S. firms have reacted to rising labor costs in China by moving factories to Mexico—or back to the United States.

Another looming problem is demographic. Because of China's low birth rate, the country will soon experience a decline in its labor force. Over the next two decades, the population of men and women between the ages of 15 and 29 will fall by roughly 100 million, or about 30 percent. China will also experience a large increase in older workers, a group that will on average be less productive and less healthy than younger workers. Given current trends, the U.S. Census Bureau projects fewer people under age 50 in China in 2030 than today, including fewer people in their 20s and early 30s, and many more people in their 60s and older. China still has potential sources for enhancing productivity, including the wider application of technology and the movement of workers into high-productivity industries, such as the manufacture of automobiles and household appliances, provided that domestic demand increases rapidly. These factors can fuel future growth, but at some point, China's demographic problems could slow growth.

Perhaps most troubling for China is the fact that the country remains autocratic, with the Communist Party refusing to allow meaningful elections and continuing to limit freedom of expression. The government has yet to establish secure property rights and the rule of law. Some observers believe that the lack of political freedom in China may ultimately lead to civil unrest, which could slow growth rates. Whether or not civil unrest eventually develops, the lack of democracy in China may already be resulting in problems that could slow growth in the near future. Large, state-owned firms, controlled by Communist Party members, continue to receive government subsidies. The result is that these firms, which typically have low productivity and are not globally competitive, receive funds that otherwise would have allowed high-productivity firms to expand.

Nouriel Roubini, an economist at New York University, argues that China's Communist Party may be repeating some of the mistakes the Soviet Communist Party committed decades ago. He argues that by employing policies that have resulted in investment spending being 50 percent of GDP, the government may have boosted short-term growth at the expense of the health of the economy in the long term. He notes:

> China is rife with overinvestment in physical capital, infrastructure, and property. To a visitor, this is evident in sleek but empty airports and bullet trains ... highways to nowhere, thousands of colossal new central and provincial government buildings, ghost towns, and brand-new aluminum smelters kept closed to prevent global prices from plunging.

Growth in China is already showing signs of slowing. Between 2010 and 2014, real GDP per capita grew at an annual rate of 6.0 percent. While still rapid, this growth rate is well below what the Chinese economy had achieved in previous decades. In early 2015, Chinese Premier Li Keqiang noted, "The downward pressure on economic growth continues to increase."

China has been engaged in an economic experiment: Can a country maintain high rates of economic growth in the long run while denying its citizens basic political rights?

Sources: Mark Magnier, "China's First-Quarter Growth Slowest in Six Years at 7%," *Wall Street Journal*, April 15, 2015; Pranab Bardhan, "The Slowing of Two Economic Giants," *New York Times*, July 14, 2013; Alex Frangos and Eric Bellman, "China Slump Ripples Globally," *Wall Street Journal*, July 15, 2013; Nicholas Eberstadt, "The Demographic Future," *Foreign Affairs*, Vol. 89, No. 6, November/December 2010, pp. 54–64; and Nouriel Roubini, "Beijing's Empty Bullet Trains," *Slate*, April 14, 2011.

MyEconLab Study Plan   **Your Turn:** Test your understanding by doing related problems 6.4 and 6.5 on page 127 at the end of this module.

Improving Health and Education

Recently, many economists have become convinced that poor health is a major impediment to growth in some countries. The research of the late Nobel Laureate Robert Fogel emphasizes the important interaction between health and economic growth (see module 10). As people's health improves and they become stronger and less susceptible to diseases, they also become more productive. Recent initiatives in developing countries to increase vaccinations against infectious diseases, to improve access to treated water, and to improve sanitation have begun to reduce rates of illness and death.

We discussed earlier in this module Paul Romer's argument that there are increasing returns to knowledge capital. Nobel Laureate Robert Lucas of the University of Chicago similarly argues that there are increasing returns to *human* capital. Lucas argues that productivity increases as the total stock of human capital increases but that these productivity increases are not completely captured by individuals as they decide how much education to purchase. Therefore, the market may produce an inefficiently low level of education and training unless the government subsidizes education. Some researchers have been unable to find evidence of increasing returns to human capital, but many economists believe that government subsidies for education have played an important role in promoting economic growth.

The rising incomes that result from economic growth can help developing countries deal with the *brain drain*, which refers to highly educated and successful individuals leaving developing countries for high-income countries. This migration occurs when successful individuals believe that economic opportunities are very limited in the domestic economy. Rapid economic growth in India and China in recent years has resulted in more entrepreneurs, engineers, and scientists deciding to remain in those countries rather than leave for the United States or other high-income countries.   MyEconLab Concept Check

Policies That Promote Technological Change

One of the lessons of the economic growth model is that technological change is more important than increases in capital in explaining long-run growth. Government policies that facilitate access to technology are crucial for low-income countries. The easiest way for developing countries to gain access to technology is through foreign direct investment, where foreign firms are allowed to build new facilities or to buy domestic firms. Recent economic growth in India has been greatly aided by the Indian government's relaxation of regulations on foreign investment. Relaxing these regulations made it possible for India to gain access to the technology of Dell, Microsoft, and other multinational corporations.

In high-income countries, government policies can aid the growth of technology by subsidizing research and development. As we noted previously, in the United States, the federal government conducts some research and development on its own and also provides grants to researchers in universities. Tax breaks to firms undertaking research and development also facilitate technological change.   MyEconLab Concept Check

Policies That Promote Saving and Investment

Firms turn to the loanable funds market to finance expansion and research and development (see module 10). Policies that increase the incentives to save and invest will increase the equilibrium level of loanable funds and may increase the level of real GDP per capita. For instance, governments can use tax incentives to increase saving. In the United States, many workers are able to save for retirement by placing funds in 401(k) or 403(b) plans or in Individual Retirement Accounts (IRAs). Income placed in these accounts is not taxed until it is withdrawn during retirement. Because the funds are allowed to accumulate tax-free, the return is increased, which raises the incentive to save.

Governments also increase incentives for firms to engage in investment in physical capital by using *investment tax credits*. Investment tax credits allow firms to deduct from their taxes some fraction of the funds they have spent on investment. Reductions in the taxes firms pay on their profits also increase the after-tax return on investments.   MyEconLab Concept Check

Is Economic Growth Good or Bad?

Although we didn't state so explicitly, in this module we have assumed that economic growth is desirable and that governments should undertake policies that will increase growth rates. It seems undeniable that increasing the growth rates of very low-income countries would help relieve the daily suffering that many people in those countries endure. But some people are unconvinced that, at least in the high-income countries, further economic growth is desirable.

The arguments against further economic growth reflect concern about the effects of growth on the environment or concern about the effects of the globalization process that has accompanied economic growth. In 1972, the Club of Rome published a controversial book titled *The Limits to Growth*, which predicted that economic growth would likely grind to a halt in the United States and other high-income countries because of increasing pollution and the depletion of natural resources, such as oil. Although these dire predictions have not yet come to pass, many people remain concerned that economic growth may be contributing to global warming, the destruction of rain forests, and other environmental problems.

In an earlier module, we discussed the opposition to globalization. We noted that some people believe that globalization has undermined the distinctive cultures of many countries, as imports of food, clothing, movies, and other goods have displaced domestically produced goods. We have seen that allowing foreign direct investment is an important way in which low-income countries can gain access to the latest technology. Some people, however, believe multinational firms behave unethically in low-income countries because they claim the firms pay very low wages and fail to follow the same safety and environmental regulations the firms are required to follow in high-income countries.

As with many other normative questions, economic analysis can contribute to the ongoing political debate over the consequences of economic growth, but it cannot settle the issue.

MyEconLab Study Plan   MyEconLab Concept Check

Continued from page 89

Economics in Your Life

Would You Be Better Off without China?

At the end of section 3A.1, we asked you to imagine that you could choose to live and work in a world with the Chinese economy growing very rapidly or in a world with the Chinese economy as it was before 1978—very poor and growing slowly. In which world would you choose to live? How does the current high-growth, high-export Chinese economy affect you as a consumer? How does it affect you as someone about to start a career?

It's impossible to walk into most stores in the United States without seeing products imported from China. Many of these products were at one time made in the United States. Imports from China replace domestically produced goods when the imports are either priced lower or have higher quality than the domestic goods they replace. Therefore, the rapid economic growth that has enabled Chinese firms to be competitive with firms in the United States has benefited you as a consumer: You have lower-priced goods and better goods available for purchase than you would if China had remained very poor. As you begin your career, there are some U.S. industries that, because of competition from Chinese firms, will have fewer jobs to offer. As we saw when discussing international trade, expanding trade changes the types of products each country makes, and, therefore, the types of jobs available, but it does not affect the total number of jobs. So, the economic rise of China will affect the mix of jobs available to you in the United States but will not make finding a job any more difficult.

Conclusion

For much of human history, most people have had to struggle to survive. Even today, a large fraction of the world's population lives in extreme poverty. The differences in living standards among countries today are a result of many decades of sharply different rates of economic growth. According to the economic growth model, increases in the quantity of capital per hour worked and increases in technology determine the growth in real GDP per hour worked and a country's standard of living. The keys to higher living standards seem straightforward:

1. Establish the rule of law.
2. Provide basic education and health care for the population.
3. Increase the amount of capital per hour worked.
4. Adopt the best technology.
5. Participate in the global economy.

However, for many countries, these policies have proved very difficult to implement.

Having discussed what determines the growth rate of economies, we will turn in the following modules to the question of why economies experience short-run fluctuations in output, employment, and inflation.

Visit MyEconLab for a news article and analysis related to the concepts in this module.

MODULE SUMMARY AND PROBLEMS

Key Terms

Business cycle, p. 80

Capital, p. 84

Catch-up, p. 105

Economic growth model, p. 95

Foreign direct investment (FDI), p. 114

Foreign portfolio investment, p. 114

Globalization, p. 114

Human capital, p. 96

Industrial Revolution, p. 91

Labor productivity, p. 95

Long-run economic growth, p. 81

New growth theory, p. 100

Patent, p. 101

Per-worker production function, p. 96

Potential GDP, p. 87

Property rights, p. 111

Rule of law, p. 111

Technological change, p. 95

3A.1 **Long-Run Economic Growth, pages 80–88**

LEARNING OBJECTIVE: Discuss the importance of long-run economic growth.

Summary

The U.S. economy has experienced both *long-run economic growth* and the *business cycle*. The **business cycle** refers to alternating periods of economic expansion and economic recession. **Long-run economic growth** is the process by which rising productivity increases the standard of living of the typical person. Because of economic growth, the typical American today can buy almost eight times as much as the typical American of 1900. Long-run growth is measured by increases in real GDP per capita. Increases in real GDP per capita depend on increases in labor productivity. **Labor productivity** is the quantity of goods and services that can be produced by one worker or by one hour of work. Economists believe two key factors determine labor productivity: the quantity of capital per hour worked and the level of technology. **Capital** refers to manufactured goods that are used to produce other goods and services. *Human capital* is the accumulated knowledge and skills workers acquire from education, training, or their life experiences. Economic growth occurs if the quantity of capital per hour worked increases and if technological change occurs. Economists often discuss economic growth in terms of growth in **potential GDP**, which is the level of GDP attained when all firms are producing at capacity.

MyEconLab   Visit **www.myeconlab.com** to complete these exercises online and get instant feedback.

Review Questions

1.1 By how much did real GDP per capita increase in the United States between 1900 and 2014? Discuss whether the increase in real GDP per capita is likely to be greater or smaller than the true increase in living standards.

1.2 What is the rule of 70? If real GDP per capita grows at a rate of 5 percent per year, how many years will it take to double?

1.3 What two key factors cause labor productivity to increase over time?

1.4 What is potential GDP? Does potential GDP remain constant over time?

Problems and Applications

1.5 Briefly discuss whether you would rather live in the United States of 1900 with an income of $1,000,000 per year or the United States of 2016 with an income of $50,000 per year. Assume that the incomes for both years are measured in 2016 dollars.

1.6 Based on what you read about economic growth in this module, discuss the importance of growth in GDP, particularly real GDP per capita, to the quality of life of a country's citizens.

1.7 **(Related to the** Making the Connection **on page 82)** Think about the relationship between economic prosperity and life expectancy. What implications does this relationship have for the size of an economy's health care sector? In particular, is this sector of the U.S. economy likely to expand or contract in coming years?

1.8 Use the following table to answer the questions.

Year	Real GDP (billions of 2009 dollars)
1990	$8,955
1991	8,948
1992	9,267
1993	9,521
1994	9,905

a. Calculate the growth rate of real GDP for each year from 1991 to 1994.

b. Calculate the average annual growth rate of real GDP for the period from 1991 to 1994.

1.9 As discussed in this module, real GDP per capita in the United States grew from about $6,000 in 1900 to about $50,010 in 2014, which represents an average annual growth rate of 1.9 percent. If the U.S. economy continues to grow at this rate, how many years will it take for real GDP per capita to double? If government economic policies meant to stimulate economic growth result in the annual growth rate increasing to 2.2 percent, how many years will it take for real GDP per capita to double?

1.10 **(Related to** Solved Problem 3A.1 **on page 85)** The business consulting firm McKinsey & Company released a report on world economic growth that contained the observation "productivity needs to drive growth." Is it likely that McKinsey was referring to growth in real GDP or growth in real GDP per capita? Do you agree with this observation? Briefly explain.

Source: McKinsey Global Institute, "Global Growth: Can Productivity Save the Day in an Aging World?" January 2015.

1.11 (Related to Solved Problem 3A.1 **on page 85)** An article in the *Wall Street Journal* notes that "raising productivity in the long run is the most effective way to elevate standards of living." Do you agree? Briefly explain.

Source: Greg Ip, "Politicians Should Pay Heed to Productivity Problem," *Wall Street Journal*, July 22, 2015.

1.12 An article in the *Economist* notes, "For 60 years, from 1770 to 1830, growth in British wages, adjusted for inflation, was imperceptible because productivity growth was restricted to a few industries." Not until the late nineteenth, when productivity "gains had spread across the whole economy," did a sustained increase in real wages begin. Why would you expect there to be a close relationship between productivity gains and increases in real wages?

Source: "The Onrushing Wave," *Economist*, January 18, 2014.

1.13 (Related to the Making the Connection **on page 86)** Amartya Sen, a professor of economics at Harvard University and a Nobel Laureate, has argued, "For India to match China in its range of manufacturing capacity … it needs a better-educated and healthier labor force at all levels of society." What role do education and health care play in economic growth? How has India been able to experience rapid economic growth since 1991 despite poor education and health care systems?

Source: Amartya Sen, "Why India Trails China," *New York Times*, June 19, 2013.

1.14 (Related to the Making the Connection **on page 86)** India's labor force has been gradually shifting out of the low-productivity agricultural sector into the higher-productivity service and industrial sectors.
a. Briefly explain how this shift is affecting India's real GDP per capita.
b. Is this shift likely to result in continuing increases in India's growth rate in coming decades? Briefly explain.

3A.2 | **Economic Growth over Time and around the World, pages 90–95**

LEARNING OBJECTIVE: Define economic growth, calculate economic growth rates, and describe global trends in economic growth.

Summary

For most of history, the average person survived with barely enough food. Living standards began to rise significantly only after the start of the **Industrial Revolution** in England in the 1700s, with the application of mechanical power to the production of goods. The best measure of a country's standard of living is its level of real GDP per capita. Economic growth occurs when real GDP per capita increases, thereby increasing the country's standard of living.

Review Questions

2.1 Why does a country's economic growth rate matter?
2.2 Explain the difference between the total percentage increase in real GDP between 2005 and 2015 and the average annual growth rate in real GDP between the same years.

Problems and Applications

2.3 **(Related to the** Making the Connection **on page 91)** Economists Carol Shiue and Wolfgang Keller of the University of Colorado published a study of "market efficiency" in the eighteenth century in England, other European countries, and China. If the markets in a country are efficient, a product should have the same price wherever in the country it is sold, allowing for the effect of transportation costs. If prices are not the same in two areas within a country, it is possible to make a profit by buying the product where its price is low and reselling it

where its price is high. This trading will drive prices to equality. Trade is most likely to occur, however, if entrepreneurs feel confident that the government will not seize their gains and the courts will enforce contracts. Therefore, in the eighteenth century, the more efficient a country's markets, the more its institutions favored long-run growth. Shiue and Keller found that in 1770, the efficiency of markets in England was significantly greater than the efficiency of markets elsewhere in Europe and in China. How does this finding relate to Douglass North's argument concerning why the Industrial Revolution occurred in England?

Source: Carol H. Shiue and Wolfgang Keller, "Markets in China and Europe on the Eve of the Industrial Revolution," *American Economic Review*, Vol. 97, No. 4, September 2007, pp. 1189–1216.

2.4 Use the data on real GDP in the following table to answer the following questions. The values are measured in each country's domestic currency. The base year for Brazil is 1995; the base year for Mexico is 2008; and the base year for Thailand is 1988.

Country	2011	2012	2013	2014
Brazil	1,192	1,213	1,247	1,248
Mexico	12,774	13,286	13,471	13,757
Thailand	4,600	4,898	5,040	5,076

a. Which country experienced the highest rate of economic growth during 2012 (that is, for which country did real GDP increase the most from 2011 to 2012)?
b. Which country experienced the highest average annual growth rate between 2012 and 2014?

c. Does it matter for your answers to parts (a) and (b) that each country's real GDP is measured in a different currency and uses a different base year? Briefly explain.

Source: International Monetary Fund, *World Economic Outlook Database*, April 2015.

2.5 Andover Bank and Lowell Bank each sell one-year certificates of deposit (CDs). The interest rates on these CDs are given in the following table for a three-year period.

Bank	2016	2017	2018
Andover Bank	5%	5%	5%
Lowell Bank	2%	6%	7%

Suppose you deposit $1,000 in a CD in each bank at the beginning of 2016. At the end of 2016, you take your $1,000 and any interest earned and invest it in a CD for the following year. You do this again at the end of 2017. At the end of 2018, will you have earned more on your Andover Bank CDs or on your Lowell Bank CDs? Briefly explain.

2.6 **(Related to the** Don't Let This Happen to You **on page 93)** Use the data for the United States in this table to answer the following questions.

Year	Real GDP per Capita (2009 prices)
2010	$47,719
2011	48,116
2012	48,822
2013	49,184
2014	50,010

a. What was the percentage change in real GDP per capita between 2010 and 2014?
b. What was the average annual growth rate in real GDP per capita between 2010 and 2014? (*Hint:* Remember that the average annual growth rate for relatively short periods can be approximated by averaging the growth rates for each year during the period.)

2.7 **(Related to the** Making the Connection **on page 94)** In his book *The White Man's Burden*, William Easterly reports:

A vaccination campaign in southern Africa virtually eliminated measles as a killer of children. Routine childhood immunization combined with measles vaccination in seven southern African nations starting in 1996 virtually eliminated measles in those countries by 2000. A national campaign in Egypt to make parents aware of the use of oral rehydration therapy from 1982 to 1989 cut childhood deaths from diarrhea by 82 percent over that period.

a. Is it likely that real GDP per capita increased significantly in southern Africa and Egypt as a result of the near elimination of measles and the large decrease in childhood deaths from diarrhea? If these events did not increase real GDP per capita, is it still possible that they increased the standard of living in southern Africa and Egypt? Briefly explain.
b. Which seems more achievable for a developing country: the elimination of measles and childhood deaths from diarrhea or sustained increases in real GDP per capita? Briefly explain.

Source: William Easterly, *The White Man's Burden: Why the West's Efforts to Aid the Rest Have Done So Much Ill and So Little Good*, New York: The Penguin Press, 2006, p. 241.

2.8 **(Related to the** Making the Connection **on page 94)** Economist Charles Kenny of the Center for Global Development has argued:

The process technologies—institutions like laws and inventory management systems—that appear central to raising incomes per capita flow less like water and more like bricks. But ideas and inventions—the importance of [education] and vaccines for DPT—really might flow more easily across borders and over distances.

If Kenny is correct, what are the implications of these facts for the ability of low-income countries to rapidly increase their rates of growth of real GDP per capita in the decades ahead? What are the implications for the ability of these countries to increase their standards of living? Briefly explain.

Source: Charles Kenny, *Getting Better*, New York: Basic Books, 2011, p. 117.

3A.3 **What Determines How Fast Economies Grow? pages 95–102**

LEARNING OBJECTIVE: Use the economic growth model to explain why growth rates differ across countries.

Summary

An **economic growth model** explains changes in real GDP per capita in the long run. **Labor productivity** is the quantity of goods and services that can be produced by one worker or by one hour of work. Economic growth depends on increases in labor productivity. Labor productivity will increase if there is an increase in the amount of *capital* available to each worker or if there is an improvement in *technology*. **Technological change** is a change in the ability of a firm to produce a given level of output with a given quantity of inputs. There are three main sources of technological change: better machinery and equipment, increases in human capital, and better means of organizing and managing production. **Human capital** is the accumulated knowledge and skills that workers acquire from education and training or from their life experiences. We can say that an economy will have a higher standard of living the more capital it has per hour worked, the more human capital its workers have, the better its capital, and the better the job its business managers do in organizing production.

The **per-worker production function** shows the relationship between capital per hour worked and output per hour worked, holding technology constant. *Diminishing returns to capital* means that increases in the quantity of capital per hour worked will result in diminishing increases in output per hour worked. Technological change shifts up the per-worker production function, resulting in more output per hour worked at every level of capital per hour worked. The economic growth model stresses the importance of changes in capital per hour worked and technological change in explaining growth in output per hour worked. **New growth theory** is a model of long-run economic growth that emphasizes that technological change is influenced by how individuals and firms respond to economic incentives.

One way governments can promote technological change is by granting **patents**, which are exclusive rights to a product for a period of 20 years from the date the patent is filed with the government. To Joseph Schumpeter, the entrepreneur is central to the "creative destruction" by which the standard of living increases as qualitatively better products replace existing products.

MyEconLab   Visit www.myeconlab.com to complete these exercises online and get instant feedback.

Review Questions

3.1 Using the per-worker production function graph from Figures 3A.5 and 3A.6 on pages 96 and 98, show the effect on real GDP per hour worked of an increase in capital per hour worked, holding technology constant. Now, again using the per-worker production function graph, show the effect on real GDP per hour worked of an increase in technology, holding constant the quantity of capital per hour worked.

3.2 What are the consequences for growth of diminishing returns to capital? How are some economies able to maintain high growth rates despite diminishing returns to capital?

3.3 What is the *new growth theory*? How does the new growth theory differ from the growth theory developed by Robert Solow?

3.4 Why are firms likely to underinvest in research and development? Briefly discuss three ways in which government policy can increase the accumulation of knowledge capital.

3.5 Why does knowledge capital experience increasing returns at the economy level while physical capital experiences decreasing returns?

Problems and Applications

3.6 Which of the following will result in a movement along China's per-worker production function, and which will result in a shift of China's per-worker production function? Briefly explain.
   a. Capital per hour worked increases from 200 yuan per hour worked to 250 yuan per hour worked.
   b. The Chinese government doubles its spending on support for university research.
   c. A reform of the Chinese school system results in more highly trained Chinese workers.

3.7 **(Related to the** Making the Connection **on page 98)** The *Making the Connection* emphasizes that a key difference between market economies and centrally planned economies, like that of the former Soviet Union, is as follows:

> In market economies, entrepreneurs and managers who have their own money on the line make decisions about which investments to make and which technologies to adopt. Nothing concentrates the mind like having your own funds at risk.

But in large corporations, investment decisions are often made by salaried managers who do not have their own money on the line. These managers are spending the money of the firm's shareholders rather than their own money. Why, then, do the investment decisions of salaried managers in the United States tend to be better for the long-term growth of the economy than were the decisions of salaried bureaucrats in the Soviet Union?

3.8 **(Related to** Solved Problem 3A.3 **on page 99)** Use the following graph to answer the questions. In each case, briefly explain your answer.

   a. True or false: The movement from point A to point B shows the effects of technological change.
   b. True or false: The economy can move from point B to point C only if there are no diminishing returns to capital.
   c. True or false: To move from point A to point C, the economy must increase the amount of capital per hour worked *and* experience technological change.

3.9 **(Related to** Solved Problem 3A.3 **on page 99)** If the per-worker production function were shaped as shown in the following graph, what would be the implications for economic growth of a country that was accumulating increasing quantities of capital per hour worked? Briefly explain.

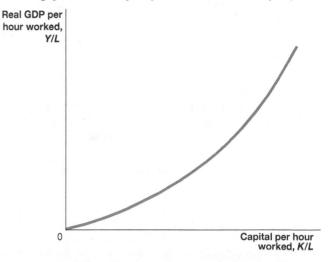

3.10 **(Related to** Solved Problem 3A.3 **on page 99)** Shortly before the fall of the Soviet Union, the economist Gur Ofer of Hebrew University of Jerusalem wrote, "The most outstanding characteristic of Soviet growth strategy is its consistent policy of very high rates of investment, leading to a rapid growth rate of [the] capital stock." Explain why this economic growth strategy turned out to be a very poor one.

Source: Gur Ofer, "Soviet Economic Growth, 1928–1985," *Journal of Economic Literature*, Vol. 25, No. 4, December 1987, p. 1,784.

3.11 People who live in rural areas often have less access to capital and, as a result, their productivity is lower on average than the productivity of people who live in cities. An article in the *New York Times* quotes a financial analyst as arguing that "the core driver" of economic growth in China "is the simple process of urbanization."
   a. What does the analyst mean by the "process of urbanization"?
   b. If the analyst is correct that urbanization is the core driver of economic growth in China, would we expect that China will be able to continue to experience high rates of economic growth in the long run? Briefly explain.

Source: Neil Irwin, "China Will Keep Growing. Just Ask the Soviets," *New York Times*, October 24, 2014.

3.12 Why is the role of entrepreneurs much more important in the new growth theory than in the traditional economic growth model?

3A.4 Economic Growth in the United States, pages 102–105

LEARNING OBJECTIVE: Discuss fluctuations in productivity growth in the United States.

Summary

Productivity in the United States grew rapidly from the end of World War II until the mid-1970s. Growth then slowed down for 20 years before increasing again for a decade after 1995. Growth has slowed again during the most recent period. Economists debate whether this growth slowdown will be long-lived or whether the U.S. economy will return to the faster growth rates of earlier years.

MyEconLab   Visit **www.myeconlab.com** to complete these exercises online and get instant feedback.

Review Questions

4.1 Describe the record of productivity growth in the United States from 1800 to the present.

4.2 Briefly describe the debate among economists over how high U.S. productivity growth rates are likely to be in the future.

Problems and Applications

4.3 Figure 3A.7 on page 102 shows growth rates in real GDP per hour worked in the United States for various periods from 1800 onward. How might the growth rates in the figure be different if they were calculated for real GDP *per capita* instead of per hour worked? (*Hint:* How do you think the number of hours worked per person has changed in the United States since 1800?)

4.4 A column in the *Wall Street Journal* considers two observations about the U.S. economy: "We live in an era of accelerating technological progress. …" and "In the years since the recession … the economy has been growing very slowly." The writer concludes that "Both statements can't be completely correct." Do you agree with this conclusion? Briefly explain.

Source: Josh Zumbrun, "Goldman Sachs and J.P. Morgan Can't Agree Why the Economy's Productivity Has Slumped," *Wall Street Journal*, June 16, 2015.

4.5 Economist Robert Gordon of Northwestern University has argued:

My interpretation of the [information] revolution is that it is increasingly burdened by diminishing returns. The push to ever smaller devices runs up against the fixed size of the human finger that must enter information on the device. Most of the innovations since 2000 have been directed to consumer enjoyment rather than business productivity, including video games, DVD players, and iPods. iPhones are nice, but the ability to reschedule business meetings and look up corporate documents while on the road already existed by 2003.

If Gordon's observations about the information revolution are correct, what are the implications for future labor productivity growth rates in the United States?

Source: Robert J. Gordon, "Revisiting U.S. Productivity Growth over the Past Century with a View of the Future," National Bureau of Economic Research, Working Paper 15834, March 2010.

4.6 Some economists argue that the apparent slowdown in productivity growth in the United States in recent years is a measurement problem resulting from the failure of GDP to capture the effects of many recent innovations, such as cloud computing. James Manyika, head of technology at McKinsey & Company, argues that for many of these innovations, "we have all these benefits but we're not paying for them."
   a. Before the arrival of the Internet, people looking for facts, such as the population of France or the salary of the president of the United States, had to go to the library to look them up. Now people can find that information in a few seconds with a Google search. Are the benefits to you of being able to do a Google search included in GDP? Briefly explain.
   b. Does your answer to part (a) indicate that the slowdown in U.S. productivity growth in recent years is just a measurement problem? What other information would you need to arrive at a definite answer?

Source: Timothy Aeppel, "Silicon Valley Doesn't Believe U.S. Productivity Is Down," *Wall Street Journal*, July 16, 2015.

3A.5 Why Isn't the Whole World Rich? pages 105–114

LEARNING OBJECTIVE: Explain economic catch-up and discuss why many poor countries have not experienced rapid economic growth.

Summary

The economic growth model predicts that poor countries will grow faster than rich countries, resulting in **catch-up**. In recent decades, some poor countries have grown faster than rich countries, but many have not. Some poor countries have not experienced rapid growth for four main reasons: wars and revolutions, poor public education and health, failure to enforce the rule of law, and low rates of saving and investment. The **rule of law** refers to the ability of a government to enforce the laws of the country, particularly with respect to protecting **property rights** and enforcing contracts. **Globalization** has aided countries that have opened their economies to foreign trade and investment. **Foreign direct investment (FDI)** is the purchase or building by a corporation of a facility in a foreign country. **Foreign portfolio investment** is the purchase by an individual or firm of stocks or bonds issued in another country.

MyEconLab   Visit www.myeconlab.com to complete these exercises online and get instant feedback.

Review Questions

5.1 Why does the economic growth model predict that poor countries should catch up to rich countries in real GDP per capita? Have poor countries been catching up to rich countries?

5.2 What are the main reasons many poor countries have experienced slow growth?

5.3 What does *globalization* mean? How have developing countries benefited from globalization?

Problems and Applications

5.4 **(Related to** Solved Problem 3A.5 **on page 108)** Briefly explain whether the statistics in the following table are consistent with the economic growth model's predictions of catch-up.

Country	Real GDP per Capita, 1960 (2005 dollars)	Growth in Real GDP per Capita, 1960–2011
China	$331	6.66%
Uganda	657	1.37
Madagascar	1,051	−0.23
Ireland	7,223	3.25
United States	15,398	2.02

Source: Authors' calculations from data in *Penn World Table Version 8.1*; Robert C. Feenstra, Robert Inklaar, and Marcel P. Timmer, "The Next Generation of the Penn World Table" www.ggdc.net/pwt, April 2015.

5.5 **(Related to** Solved Problem 3A.5 **on page 108)** In the following graph, each dot represents a particular country's initial level of real GDP per capita and its growth rate of real GDP per capita.

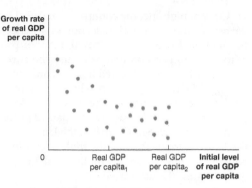

a. For the range of initial GDP per capita from 0 to Real GDP per capita$_2$, does the figure support the economic growth model's prediction of catch-up? Briefly explain.

b. For the range of initial GDP per capita from 0 to Real GDP per capita$_1$, does the figure support the catch-up prediction? Briefly explain.

c. For the range from initial Real GDP per capita$_1$ to Real GDP per capita$_2$, does the figure support the catch-up prediction? Briefly explain.

5.6 Refer to Figures 3A.9–3A.11 on pages 107 and 109. The lines in the following three graphs show the average relationship between the initial level of real GDP per capita and the growth rate of real GDP per capita for three groups of countries over a given time period. Match each group of countries with the graph that best depicts the relationship between the initial level of real GDP per capita and the growth rate of real GDP per capita for that group.

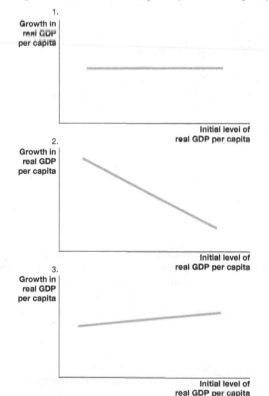

a. All countries for which statistics are available, 1960–2011

b. United States, Western Europe, Canada, and Japan, 1990–2014

c. Current high-income countries, 1960–2011

5.7 An article in the *New York Times* notes that since 2001 Italy has had the lowest rate of growth in labor productivity among European countries that use the euro common currency. The article quoted Italy's economy minister as saying, "The real tragedy for Italy is falling productivity." At the time the minister made these remarks, the unemployment rate in Italy was greater than 12 percent—more than twice the rate in Germany, the United Kingdom, or the United States. Despite the high unemployment rate, why might Italy's economy minister call low productivity growth rates "the real tragedy"?

Source: Reuters, "Italy Economy Minister Warns Deflation Would Be 'Disaster,'" *New York Times*, May 31, 2014.

5.8 **(Related to the** Making the Connection **on page 111)** A study by the McKinsey Global Institute reported that labor productivity increased at an average annual rate of 5.8 percent between 1999 and 2013 in Mexico's large companies, but it fell at an average annual rate of 6.5 percent over the same period for its smaller firms, such as family-owned stores and bakeries. Briefly explain why productivity growth would be much higher for Mexico's largest companies than for its smaller companies.

Source: Anthony Harrup, "Two Economies Explain Mexico's Productivity Quandary," *Wall Street Journal*, March 27, 2014.

5.9 **(Related to the** Making the Connection **on page 111)** In 2014, real GDP per capita in Mexico increased by 0.9 percent. A Mexican economist was quoted in an article in the *Wall Street Journal* as saying, "It's clearly insufficient if we want to significantly reduce poverty and move Mexico toward a middle-class country."

a. Given that growth rate, how long would it take the standard of living of the average person in Mexico to double?

b. Why isn't the Mexican economy growing more rapidly?

Source: Juan Montes, "Mexican Economy Expanded Modestly in 2014," *Wall Street Journal*, February 20, 2015.

5.10 In 2015, President Barack Obama was quoted in an article in the *Wall Street Journal* as warning against "rising anti-globalization sentiment," which the president called "a big mistake."

a. What did President Obama mean by "anti-globalization sentiment"?

b. Why might he have considered such sentiment to be a big mistake for the U.S. economy?

c. Is there an argument to be made that globalization hurts rather than helps the U.S. economy? Briefly explain.

Source: Gerald F. Seib, "Obama Presses Case for Asia Trade Deal, Warns Failure Would Benefit China," *Wall Street Journal*, April 27, 2015.

5.11 A columnist in the *New York Times* observes that "many analysts agree that economic reform, of which integration into the global economy was a key element, has lifted millions of people out of poverty in India." What does "integration into the global economy" mean? How might integration into the global economy reduce poverty in India?

Source: Vivek Dehejia, "Has Globalization Helped India's Poor?" *New York Times*, October 7, 2011.

5.12 The Roman Empire lasted from 27 B.C. to A.D. 476. The empire was wealthy enough to build such monuments as the Roman Coliseum. Roman engineering skill was at a level high enough that aqueducts built during the empire to carry water long distances remained in use for hundreds of years. Yet, although the empire experienced some periods of growth in real GDP per capita, these periods did not last, and there is little evidence that growth would have been sustained even if the empire had survived. Why didn't the Roman Empire experience sustained economic growth? What would the world be like today if it had? (*Note:* There are no definite answers to these questions; they are intended to get you to think about the preconditions for economic growth. Looking beyond this problem, if you are interested in the macroeconomics of the Roman economy, see Peter Temin, *The Roman Market Economy*, Princeton: Princeton University Press, 2013, modules 1–3A.)

3A.6	**Growth Policies, pages 114–119**

LEARNING OBJECTIVE: Discuss government policies that foster economic growth.

Summary

Governments can attempt to increase economic growth through policies that enhance property rights and the rule of law, improve health and education, subsidize research and development, and provide incentives for saving and investment. Whether continued economic growth is desirable is a normative question that cannot be settled by economic analysis.

Review Questions

6.1 Briefly describe three government policies that can increase economic growth.

6.2 Can economic analysis arrive at the conclusion that economic growth will always improve economic well-being? Briefly explain.

Problems and Applications

6.3 **(Related to the** module Opener **on page 89)** An article on the Mexican economy in the *Economist* notes, "A huge, unproductive informal sector and general lawlessness also drag the economy down." If these factors were the main barriers to more rapid economic growth in Mexico, would that be good news or bad news for the Mexican government's attempts to increase its economy's growth rate? Briefly explain.

Source: "The 100-Year View," *Economist*, May 2, 2015.

6.4 (Related to the Making the Connection **on page 115)** In China, why may a lower birth rate lead to slower growth in real GDP per capita? Why might high levels of spending on investment in China lead to high rates of growth in the short run but not in the long run?

6.5 (Related to the Making the Connection **on page 115)** Pranab Bardhan, an economist at the University of California, Berkeley, argues: "China may be close to exhausting the possibilities of technological catch-up with the West, particularly in manufacturing."
   a. What does Bardhan mean by "technological catch-up"?
   b. If Bardhan is correct, what problems might the Chinese economy encounter in the future?
   c. Briefly discuss the similarities and differences between the Chinese economy today and the Soviet economy in the 1980s.

Source: Pranab Bardhan, "The Slowing of Two Economic Giants," *New York Times*, July 14, 2013.

6.6 Briefly explain which of the following policies are likely to increase the rate of economic growth in the United States.
   a. Congress passes an investment tax credit, which reduces a firm's taxes if it installs new machinery and equipment.
   b. Congress passes a law that allows taxpayers to reduce their income taxes by the amount of state sales taxes they pay.
   c. Congress provides more funds for low-interest loans to college students.

6.7 In an interview on PBS about economic development in Africa, economist George Ayittey stated that of the 54 African countries, only 8 had a free press. For Africa's economic development, Ayittey argued strongly for the establishment of a free press. Why would a free press be vital for the enhancement of property rights and the rule of law? How could a free press help reduce corruption?

Source: George Ayittey, *Border Jumpers*, Anchor Interview Transcript, WideAngle, PBS.org, July 24, 2005.

6.8 More people in high-income countries than in low-income countries tend to believe that rapid rates of economic growth are not desirable. Recall the concept of a "normal good". Does this concept provide insight into why some people in high-income countries might be more concerned with certain consequences of rapid economic growth than are people in low-income countries?

Real-Time Data Exercises

D3A.1 (Analyzing labor productivity) Using data from the St. Louis Federal Reserve (FRED) (research.stlouisfed.org/fred2/), analyze the relationship between labor productivity in the manufacturing sector and in the non-farm business sector as a whole.
   a. Download data since 1987 on output per hour of all persons in the manufacturing sector (OPHMFG) and in the non-farm business sector (OPHNFB).
   b. Which has increased more since 1987, labor productivity in manufacturing or in the non-farm business sector?
   c. The manufacturing sector has been shrinking relative to the size of the economy in the United States and other advanced economies. What do your results imply about future labor productivity growth in advanced economies?

D3A.2 (Comparing labor productivity across countries) Using data from the St. Louis Federal Reserve (FRED) (research.stlouisfed.org/fred2/), analyze differences in labor productivity among China, India, and the United States.
   a. From 1952 to the present, chart the following series on the same graph: real GDP per worker for China (RGDPL2CNA627NUPN), real GDP per worker for India (RGDPLWINA627NUPN), and real GDP per worker for the United States (RGDPLWUSA627NUPN). To chart the series on the same graph follow these steps: (1) On the page for real GDP per worker for China, click on the "Edit graph" link under the graph; (2) on the bottom of the next page, click on the "Add Data Series" link; (3) search for the other two series and click on them to add them to your graph.
   b. Calculate the relative productivity of workers in China and the United States by dividing U.S. labor productivity by China's labor productivity. Describe the change in this measure of relative productivity since 1952.
   c. Repeat part (b) for the United States and India.

D3A.3 (The U.S. economy in a world context) The U.S. Central Intelligence Agency's World Factbook (https://www.cia.gov/library/publications/the-world-factbook/) offers many comparative tables of world data. Go to this site and find the following:
   a. The countries with the highest and lowest real GDPs
   b. The countries with the highest and lowest per capita real GDPs, adjusted for purchasing power
   c. The countries with the most equal and least equal income distributions
   d. The countries with the highest and lowest real GDP growth rates
   e. The rank of the United States in these categories

MODULE

4

Aggregate Demand and Aggregate Supply Analysis

Module Outline and Learning Objectives

4.1 Aggregate Demand, page 130
Identify the determinants of aggregate demand and distinguish between a movement along the aggregate demand curve and a shift of the curve.

4.2 Aggregate Supply, page 138
Identify the determinants of aggregate supply and distinguish between a movement along the short-run aggregate supply curve and a shift of the curve.

The Fortunes of Delta Airlines Follow the Business Cycle

An infestation of insects that threatened cotton fields in Southern states led B. R. Coad and Collett E. Woolman to form a crop-dusting business, the Huff Daland Dusters, in 1924. By 1930 the company was renamed the Delta Air Corporation and offered airmail and passenger service. Delta Air Lines has grown into the world's largest airline, flying over 170 million passengers to more than 300 destinations worldwide in 2015 and earning revenue of more than $40 billion.

Despite Delta's long-run success, its fortunes and the fortunes of the other U.S. airlines are dependent on the ups and downs of the business cycle. As a *Wall Street Journal* article put it: "Year after year, domestic revenue came in at 0.73% of GDP." That relationship is good news during economic expansions, when GDP is increasing, but it's bad news during recessions, when GDP is falling. During the severe 2007–2009 recession, Delta both sold fewer passenger tickets and had to cut the prices of the tickets it did sell. The result was a $1.2 billion loss in 2009.

By 2015, with GDP steadily growing during the economic expansion, Delta was earning a record profit as both the number of passengers flown and ticket prices were increasing. Delta was also benefiting from falling jet fuel prices as increased output from U.S. shale oil fields led to a worldwide decline in oil prices. Many business analysts consider Delta to be the best managed of the four large U.S. airlines—the other three being Southwest, American Airlines, and United. Still, Delta management was taking steps to reduce the problems the airline would experience when—inevitably—the next recession occurred. Domestically, Delta was attempting to reduce costs by "upgauging," or adding seats to existing planes and replacing small planes with larger planes. Internationally, Delta continued a strategy of buying partial ownership of foreign airlines. In 2015, it purchased part of China Eastern Airlines. Under terms of the deal, the two airlines would list each other's flights on their reservation systems and share some facilities at Chinese airports. By expanding overseas, Delta was not only participating in rapidly growing markets but also insulating itself to some extent from the fluctuations of the U.S. business cycle.

To better understand how the business cycle affects Delta Air Lines and other firms, we need to explore the effects that recessions and expansions have on production, employment, and prices.

Sources: Susan Carey, "Delta Air Lines to Buy China Eastern Stake for $450 Million," *Wall Street Journal*, July 27, 2015; Bob McAdoo and Scott Buck, "American Airlines Shares Have Over 70% Upside," barrons.com, July 27, 2015; Susan Carey, "Airline Industry Sees Pain Extending Beyond the Recession," *Wall Street Journal*, August 17, 2009; and Delta Air Lines, "Earnings Releases," various dates.

Economics in Your Life

Is an Employer Likely to Cut Your Pay during a Recession?

Suppose that you have worked as a barista for a local coffeehouse for two years. From on-the-job training and experience, you have honed your coffee-making skills and mastered the perfect latte. Then the economy moves into a recession, and sales at the coffeehouse decline. Is the owner of the coffeehouse likely to cut the prices of lattes and other drinks? Suppose the owner asks to meet with you to discuss your wages for next year. Is the owner likely to cut your pay? As you read this module, try to answer these questions.

W e have seen that the U.S. economy has experienced a long-run upward trend in real GDP. These increases in real GDP have raised the standard of living in the United States to a level much higher today than it was 100 years ago. In the short run, however, real GDP fluctuates around this long-run upward trend because of the business cycle. Fluctuations in GDP lead to fluctuations in employment. These fluctuations in real GDP and employment are the most visible and dramatic part of the business cycle. During recessions, we are more likely to see factories close, small businesses declare bankruptcy, and workers lose their jobs. During expansions, we are more likely to see new businesses open and new jobs created. In addition to these changes in output and employment, the business cycle causes changes in wages and prices. Some firms react to a decline in sales by cutting back on production, but they may also cut the prices they charge and the wages they pay. Other firms respond to a recession by raising prices and workers' wages by less than they otherwise would have.

In this module, we expand our discussion of the business cycle by developing the aggregate demand and aggregate supply model. This model will help us analyze the effects of recessions and expansions on production, employment, and prices.

4.1 Aggregate Demand

LEARNING OBJECTIVE: Identify the determinants of aggregate demand and distinguish between a movement along the aggregate demand curve and a shift of the curve.

Aggregate demand and aggregate supply model A model that explains short-run fluctuations in real GDP and the price level.

Aggregate demand (AD) curve A curve that shows the relationship between the price level and the quantity of real GDP demanded by households, firms, and the government.

Short-run aggregate supply (SRAS) curve A curve that shows the relationship in the short run between the price level and the quantity of real GDP supplied by firms.

To understand what happens during the business cycle, we need an explanation of why real GDP, the unemployment rate, and the inflation rate fluctuate. We have already seen that fluctuations in the unemployment rate are caused mainly by fluctuations in real GDP. In this module, we use the **aggregate demand and aggregate supply model** to explain short-run fluctuations in real GDP and the price level. As Figure 4.1 shows, real GDP and the price level in this model are determined in the short run by the intersection of the *aggregate demand curve* and the *aggregate supply curve*. Fluctuations in real GDP and the price level are caused by shifts in the aggregate demand curve or in the aggregate supply curve.

The **aggregate demand (AD) curve** shows the relationship between the price level and the quantity of real GDP demanded by households, firms, and the government. The **short-run aggregate supply (SRAS) curve** shows the relationship in the short run between the price level and the quantity of real GDP supplied by firms. The aggregate demand and short-run aggregate supply curves in Figure 4.1 look similar to the individual market demand and supply curves. However, because these curves apply to the whole economy, rather than to just a single market, the aggregate demand and aggregate supply model is very different from the model of demand and supply in individual markets. Because we are dealing with the economy as a whole, we need *macroeconomic* explanations of why the aggregate demand curve is downward sloping, why the short-run aggregate supply curve is upward sloping, and why the curves shift. We begin by explaining why the aggregate demand curve is downward sloping.

Why Is the Aggregate Demand Curve Downward Sloping?

We have seen that GDP has four components:

- Consumption (C)
- Investment (I)
- Government purchases (G)
- Net exports (NX)

Figure 4.1   Aggregate Demand and Aggregate Supply

In the short run, real GDP and the price level are determined by the intersection of the aggregate demand curve and the short-run aggregate supply curve. In the figure, real GDP is measured on the horizontal axis, and the price level is measured on the vertical axis by the GDP deflator. In this example, the equilibrium real GDP is $17.0 trillion, and the equilibrium price level is 110.

If we let Y stand for GDP, we have the following relationship:

$$Y = C + I + G + NX.$$

The aggregate demand curve is downward sloping because a fall in the price level increases the quantity of real GDP demanded. To understand why, we need to look at how changes in the price level affect each component of aggregate demand. We begin with the assumption that government purchases are determined by the policy decisions of lawmakers and are not affected by changes in the price level. We can then consider the effect of changes in the price level on the three other components: consumption, investment, and net exports.

The Wealth Effect: How a Change in the Price Level Affects Consumption
Current income is the most important variable determining consumption by households. As income rises, consumption will rise, and as income falls, consumption will fall. But consumption also depends on household wealth, which is the difference between the value of a household's assets and the value of its debts. Consider two households, both with incomes of $80,000 per year. The first household has wealth of $5 million, and the second household has wealth of $50,000. The first household is likely to spend more of its income than the second household. So, as total household wealth rises, consumption will rise. Some household wealth is held in cash or other *nominal assets* that lose value as the price level rises and gain value as the price level falls. For instance, if you have $10,000 in cash, a 10 percent increase in the price level will reduce the purchasing power of that cash by 10 percent. When the price level rises, the *real value* of household wealth declines, and so will consumption, thereby reducing the demand for goods and services. When the price level falls, the real value of household wealth rises, and so will consumption and the demand for goods and services. The effect of the price level on consumption is called the *wealth effect*, and it is one reason the aggregate demand curve is downward sloping.

The Interest-Rate Effect: How a Change in the Price Level Affects Investment When prices rise, households and firms need more money to finance buying and selling. Therefore, when the price level rises, households and firms will try to increase the amount of money they hold by withdrawing funds from banks, borrowing from banks, or selling financial assets, such as bonds. These actions tend to drive up the interest rate banks charge on loans and the interest rate on bonds. (In Module 8A, we analyze in more detail the relationship between money and interest rates.) A higher interest rate raises the cost of borrowing for households and firms. As a result, firms will borrow less to build new factories or install new machinery and equipment, and households will borrow less to buy new houses. To summarize:

- A higher price level will increase the interest rate and reduce investment spending, thereby reducing the quantity of goods and services demanded.
- A lower price level will decrease the interest rate and increase investment spending, thereby increasing the quantity of goods and services demanded.

To a smaller extent, consumption will also fall when the interest rate rises as households borrow less to finance spending on automobiles, furniture, and other durable goods.

The effect of the price level on investment and consumption is known as the *interest-rate effect*, and it is a second reason the aggregate demand curve is downward sloping.

The International-Trade Effect: How a Change in the Price Level Affects Net Exports *Net exports* equals spending by foreign households and firms on goods and services produced in the United States minus spending by U.S. households and firms on goods and services produced in other countries. If the price level in the United States rises relative to the price levels in other countries, U.S. exports will become relatively more expensive, and foreign imports will become relatively less expensive. Some consumers in foreign countries will shift from buying U.S. products to buying domestic products, and some U.S. consumers will also shift from buying U.S. products to buying imported products. U.S. exports will fall and U.S. imports will rise, causing net exports to fall, thereby reducing the quantity of goods and services demanded. A lower price level in the United States relative to other countries has the reverse effect, causing net exports to rise, thereby increasing the quantity of goods and services demanded. The effect of the price level on net exports is known as the *international-trade effect*, and it is a third reason the aggregate demand curve is downward sloping. MyEconLab Concept Check

Shifts of the Aggregate Demand Curve versus Movements along It

An important point to remember is that the aggregate demand curve tells us the relationship between the price level and the quantity of real GDP demanded, *holding everything else constant*. If the price level changes but other variables that affect the willingness of households, firms, and the government to spend are unchanged, the result is a movement up or down a stationary aggregate demand curve. If any variable other than the price level changes, the aggregate demand curve will shift. For example, if government purchases increase and the price level remains unchanged, the aggregate demand curve will shift to the right at every price level. Or, if firms become pessimistic about the future profitability of investment and cut back spending on factories and machinery, the aggregate demand curve will shift to the left. MyEconLab Concept Check

The Variables That Shift the Aggregate Demand Curve

The variables that cause the aggregate demand curve to shift fall into three categories:

1. Changes in government policies
2. Changes in the expectations of households and firms
3. Changes in foreign variables

Changes in Government Policies As we will discuss further in Module 7A and 8A, the federal government uses monetary policy and fiscal policy to shift the aggregate demand curve. **Monetary policy** is the actions the Federal Reserve—the nation's central bank—takes to manage the money supply and interest rates and to ensure the flow of funds from lenders to borrowers. The Federal Reserve takes these actions to achieve macroeconomic policy objectives, such as high employment, price stability, high rates of economic growth, and stability of the financial system. For example, the Federal Reserve can lower the cost to firms and households of borrowing by taking actions that reduce interest rates. Lower borrowing costs increase consumption and investment spending, which shifts the aggregate demand curve to the right. Higher interest rates shift the aggregate demand curve to the left.

Monetary policy The actions the Federal Reserve takes to manage the money supply and interest rates to achieve macroeconomic policy objectives.

Fiscal policy is the changes in federal taxes and purchases that are intended to achieve macroeconomic policy objectives. Because government purchases are one component of aggregate demand:

Fiscal policy Changes in federal taxes and purchases that are intended to achieve macroeconomic policy objectives.

- An increase in *government purchases* shifts the aggregate demand curve to the right, and a decrease in government purchases shifts the aggregate demand curve to the left.

- An increase in *personal income taxes* reduces the amount of spendable income available to households, which reduces consumption spending and shifts the aggregate demand curve to the left. A decrease in personal income taxes shifts the aggregate demand curve to the right.

- An increase in *business taxes* reduces the profitability of investment spending and shifts the aggregate demand curve to the left. A decrease in business taxes shifts the aggregate demand curve to the right.

Changes in the Expectations of Households and Firms If households become more optimistic about their future incomes, they are likely to increase their current consumption. This increased consumption will shift the aggregate demand curve to the right. If households become more pessimistic about their future incomes, the aggregate demand curve will shift to the left. Similarly, if firms become more optimistic about the future profitability of investment spending, the aggregate demand curve will shift to the right. If firms become more pessimistic, the aggregate demand curve will shift to the left.

Don't Let This Happen to You

Understand Why the Aggregate Demand Curve Is Downward Sloping

The aggregate demand curve and the demand curve for a single product are both downward sloping—but for different reasons. When we draw a demand curve for a single product, such as apples, we know that it will slope downward because as the price of apples rises, apples become more expensive relative to other products—such as oranges—and consumers will buy fewer apples and more of the other products. In other words, consumers substitute other products for apples. When the overall price level rises, the prices of all domestically produced goods and services are rising, so consumers have no other

domestic products to which they can switch. The aggregate demand curve slopes downward because a higher price level:

- Reduces the real value of household wealth, which decreases consumption

- Raises interest rates, which decreases investment and consumption

- Makes U.S. exports more expensive and foreign imports less expensive, which decreases net exports

MyEconLab Study Plan

Your Turn: Test your understanding by doing related problem 1.8 on pages 140–141 at the end of this module.

Changes in Foreign Variables If households and firms in other countries buy fewer U.S. goods or if households and firms in the United States buy more foreign goods, net exports will fall, and the aggregate demand curve will shift to the left. When real GDP increases, so does the income available for consumers to spend. If real GDP in the United States increases faster than real GDP in other countries, U.S. imports will increase faster than U.S. exports, and net exports will fall. Net exports will also fall if the *exchange rate* between the dollar and foreign currencies rises because the price in foreign currency of U.S. products sold in other countries will rise, and the dollar price of foreign products sold in the United States will fall. For example, if the current exchange rate between the dollar and the euro is $1 = €1 then:

- A $20 Blu-ray disc exported from the United States to France will cost €20 in France.
- A €50 bottle of wine exported from France will cost $50 in the United States.

But if the exchange rate rises to $1 = €1.50 then:

- The disc's price will rise from €20 to €30 in France, causing its sales to decline.
- The price of the French wine will fall from $50 to $33.33 per bottle in the United States, causing its sales to increase.

As a result, U.S. exports will fall, U.S. imports will rise, and the aggregate demand curve will shift to the left.

An increase in net exports at every price level will shift the aggregate demand curve to the right. Net exports will increase if real GDP grows more slowly in the United States than in other countries or if the value of the dollar falls against other currencies. A change in net exports that results from a change in the price level in the United States will result in a movement along the aggregate demand curve, *not* a shift of the aggregate demand curve.

MyEconLab Concept Check

Solved Problem 4.1

MyEconLab Interactive Animation

Movements along the Aggregate Demand Curve versus Shifts of the Aggregate Demand Curve

Germany, along with 18 other countries in Europe, uses the euro as its currency. According to an article in the *Wall Street Journal*, in 2014 German net exports rose to "€217 billion ($246 billion), shattering the previous record of €195.3 billion set in 2007." The story quoted an economist working for a German bank as saying, "I think that due to the weaker euro we should get stronger exports."

a. At the time this article was written, what was the exchange rate between the U.S. dollar and the euro?

b. What does the economist mean by a "weaker euro"?
c. Why would a weaker euro cause an increase in German net exports?
d. Briefly explain whether a weaker euro will cause a shift in the aggregate demand curve of the German economy or a movement along the aggregate demand curve. Illustrate your answer with a graph.

Solving the Problem

Step 1: **Review the module material.** This problem is about understanding the difference between movements along an aggregate demand curve and shifts of an aggregate demand curve, so you may want to review the section "Shifts of the Aggregate Demand Curve versus Movements along It," and the section "The Variables that Shift the Aggregate Demand Curve," which both begin on page 132.

Step 2: **Answer part (a) by calculating the exchange rate between the euro and the U.S. dollar at the time the article was written.** If €217 billion was the equivalent of $246 billion at the time the article was written, then the exchange rate must have been $246 billion/€217 billion = $1.13 dollars per euro, or $1 = €0.88.

Step 3: **Answer part (b) by explaining what the economist meant by a "weaker euro."** A weaker euro means an exchange rate such that a dollar (or a unit of another foreign currency) would buy more euros, or, equivalently, a euro would buy fewer dollars (or units of another foreign currency).

Step 4: **Answer part (c) by explaining why a weaker euro would cause an increase in German net exports.** If it takes fewer dollars to buy German goods priced in euros, then U.S. consumers will buy more of them, increasing German exports. If it takes more euros to buy U.S. goods priced in dollars, then German consumers will buy fewer of them, decreasing German imports. We can apply similar reasoning to the products of other countries outside the eurozone. So we would expect that a weaker euro will result in an increase in German net exports.

Step 5: **Answer part (d) by explaining whether a weaker euro would cause a shift in the aggregate demand curve for the German economy or a movement along it and by drawing a graph to illustrate your answer.** Only changes in the price level in Germany will cause a movement along the aggregate demand curve for the German economy. Although a decline in the value of the euro affects the prices of exports from Germany and imports to Germany, it doesn't directly affect the price level in Germany. By increasing German net exports, the weaker euro will cause the aggregate demand curve for the German economy to shift to the right at every price level, as shown in the following graph:

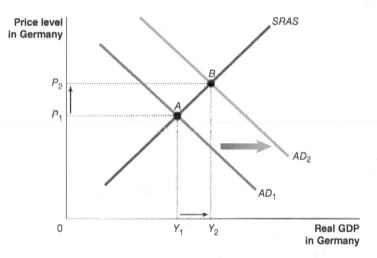

Source: Todd Buell and Bertrand Benoit, "Germany Enjoys Record Year for Trade," *Wall Street Journal*, February 9, 2015.

Your Turn: For more practice, do related problems 1.9 and 1.10 on page 141 at the end of this module.

MyEconLab Study Plan

Table 4.1 summarizes the most important variables that cause the aggregate demand curve to shift. The table shows the shift in the aggregate demand curve that results from an increase in each of the variables. A *decrease* in these variables will cause the aggregate demand curve to shift in the opposite direction.

Table 4.1

Variables That Shift the Aggregate Demand Curve

An increase in . . .	shifts the aggregate demand curve . . .	because . . .
interest rates		higher interest rates raise the cost to households and firms of borrowing, reducing consumption and investment spending.
government purchases		government purchases are a component of aggregate demand.
personal income taxes or business taxes		consumption spending falls when personal taxes rise, and investment falls when business taxes rise.
households' expectations of their future incomes		consumption spending increases.
firms' expectations of the future profitability of investment spending		investment spending increases.
the growth rate of domestic GDP relative to the growth rate of foreign GDP		imports will increase faster than exports, reducing net exports.
the exchange rate (the value of the dollar) relative to foreign currencies		imports will rise and exports will fall, reducing net exports.

Which Components of Aggregate Demand Changed the Most during the 2007–2009 Recession?

The recession of 2007–2009 was the longest and most severe since the Great Depression of the 1930s. We can better understand what happened during the 2007–2009 recession by looking at changes over time in the components of aggregate demand. In the following graphs, we show changes in the three components of aggregate demand that had the largest movements between the first quarter of 2005 and the second quarter of 2015: consumption, residential investment spending on new homes and apartments, and net exports. The shaded area represents the 2007–2009 recession. We know that potential GDP, or the level of GDP when all firms are producing at capacity, grows over time. So, economists are often interested in measuring changes in the components of aggregate demand *relative to potential GDP*, which is what we have done in these graphs.

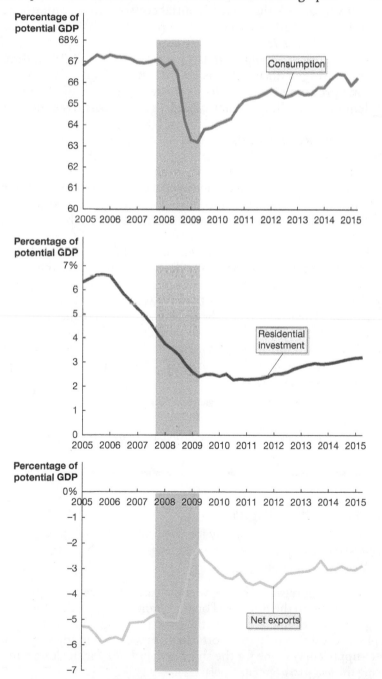

The graphs illustrate a number of facts about the 2007–2009 recession:

- In the two years before the beginning of the recession, spending on residential investment had already declined significantly relative to potential GDP.
- For the first two years following the end of the recession, spending on residential investment did not increase relative to potential GDP. Beginning in late 2011, spending on residential investment began to increase slowly, but in mid-2015, it was still far below its 2005–2006 level.
- Consumption, which usually remains relatively stable during a recession, declined significantly relative to potential GDP during the recession and had still not quite regained its 2007 level six years after the recession had ended.
- Net exports increased during the recession. (Because net exports was negative throughout this period, it increased by becoming a smaller negative number.)

Although not shown in the graphs, business fixed investment and changes in business inventories—the nonresidential construction components of investment spending—actually rose relative to potential GDP during the recession. Government purchases remained fairly stable relative to potential GDP during the recession, before declining from late 2010 through mid-2015. Federal government purchases surged during the recession but declined in later years as temporary spending programs intended to fight the recession ended and Congress and the president cut spending further to address concerns over the federal budget deficit.

We can briefly account for the four facts listed above. The housing sector underwent a boom from 2002 to 2005, with rapid increases in both housing prices and spending on new housing. But the housing boom turned into a housing bust beginning in 2006, which explains the sharp decline in residential investment. The continued low levels of residential investment help explain why the recession was the longest since the Great Depression and why the economic expansion that began in June 2009 was relatively weak.

High levels of unemployment reduced household incomes and led to declines in consumption spending. In addition, many households increased their saving and paid off debts, further reducing consumption spending. The low levels of consumption spending also contributed to the severity of the recession and the weakness of the following expansion. Finally, efforts by the Federal Reserve to reduce interest rates helped to lower the value of the U.S. dollar, thereby reducing the prices of U.S. exports and increasing the prices of foreign imports. The result was an increase in net exports during the recession. (We will further discuss the effect of Federal Reserve policy on net exports in Modules 8A and 9.)

Sources: U.S. Bureau of Economic Analysis and Congressional Budget Office.

 MyEconLab Study Plan

Your Turn: Test your understanding by doing related problem 1.11 on page 141 at the end of this module.

4.2 Aggregate Supply

LEARNING OBJECTIVE: Identify the determinants of aggregate supply and distinguish between a movement along the short-run aggregate supply curve and a shift of the curve.

Having discussed aggregate demand, we now turn to aggregate supply, which shows the effect of changes in the price level on the quantity of goods and services that firms are willing and able to supply. Because the effect of changes in the price level on aggregate supply is very different in the short run from what it is in the long run, we use two aggregate supply curves: one for the short run and one for the long run. We start by considering the *long-run aggregate supply curve*.

MyEconLab Animation

Figure 4.2

The Long-Run Aggregate Supply Curve

Changes in the price level do not affect the level of aggregate supply in the long run. Therefore, the long-run aggregate supply (*LRAS*) curve is a vertical line at the potential level of real GDP. For instance, the price level was 109 in 2015, and potential GDP was $16.8 trillion. If the price level had been 119, or if it had been 99, long-run aggregate supply would still have been a constant $16.8 trillion. Each year, the long-run aggregate supply curve shifts to the right, as the number of workers in the economy increases, more machinery and equipment are accumulated, and technological change occurs.

The Long-Run Aggregate Supply Curve

In the long run, the level of real GDP is determined by the number of workers, the *capital stock*—including factories, office buildings, and machinery and equipment—and the available technology (see Module 3A). Because changes in the price level do not affect the number of workers, the capital stock, or technology, *in the long run, changes in the price level do not affect the level of real GDP*. Remember that the level of real GDP in the long run is called *potential GDP,* or *full-employment GDP*. At potential GDP, firms will operate at their normal level of capacity, and everyone who wants a job will have one, except the structurally and frictionally unemployed. There is no reason for this normal level of capacity to change just because the price level has changed. The **long-run aggregate supply (LRAS) curve** shows the relationship in the long run between the price level and the quantity of real GDP supplied. As Figure 4.2 shows, in 2015, the price level was 109, and potential GDP was $16.8 trillion. If the price level had been 119, or if it had been 99, long-run aggregate supply would still have been a constant $16.8 trillion. Therefore, the *LRAS* curve is a vertical line.

Figure 4.2 also shows that the long-run aggregate supply curve shifts to the right each year. This shift occurs because potential GDP increases each year, as (1) the number of workers in the economy increases, (2) the economy accumulates more machinery and equipment, and (3) technological change occurs. Figure 4.2 shows potential GDP increasing from $16.8 trillion in 2015 to $17.1 trillion in 2016 and to $17.5 trillion in 2017.

Long-run aggregate supply (LRAS) curve A curve that shows the relationship in the long run between the price level and the quantity of real GDP supplied.

MyEconLab Concept Check

MODULE SUMMARY AND PROBLEMS

Key Terms

4.1 Aggregate Demand, pages 130–138

LEARNING OBJECTIVE: Identify the determinants of aggregate demand and distinguish between a movement along the aggregate demand curve and a shift of the curve.

Summary

The **aggregate demand and aggregate supply model** enables us to explain short-run fluctuations in real GDP and the price level. The **aggregate demand (AD) curve** shows the relationship between the price level and the level of planned aggregate expenditures by households, firms, and the government. The **short-run aggregate supply (SRAS) curve** shows the relationship in the short run between the price level and the quantity of real GDP supplied by firms. The long-run aggregate supply curve shows the relationship in the long run between the price level and the quantity of real GDP supplied. The four components of aggregate demand are consumption (C), investment (I), government purchases (G), and net exports (NX). The aggregate demand curve is downward sloping because a decline in the price level causes consumption, investment, and net exports to increase. If the price level changes but all else remains constant, the result is a movement up or down a stationary aggregate demand curve. If any variable other than the price level changes, the aggregate demand curve will shift. The variables that cause the aggregate demand curve to shift are divided into three categories: changes in government policies, changes in the expectations of households and firms, and changes in foreign variables. For example, **monetary policy** involves the actions the Federal Reserve takes to manage the money supply and interest rates to pursue macroeconomic policy objectives. When the Federal Reserve takes actions to change interest rates, consumption and investment spending will change, shifting the aggregate demand curve. **Fiscal policy** involves changes in the federal government's taxes and purchases that are intended to achieve macroeconomic policy objectives. Changes in federal taxes and purchases shift the aggregate demand curve.

MyEconLab   Visit **www.myeconlab.com** to complete these exercises online and get instant feedback.

Review Questions

1.1 What relationship does the aggregate demand curve show? What relationship does the aggregate supply curve show?

1.2 Explain the three reasons the aggregate demand curve slopes downward.

1.3 What are the differences between the AD curve and the demand curve for an individual product, such as apples?

1.4 What variables cause the AD curve to shift? For each variable, identify whether an increase in that variable will cause the AD curve to shift to the right or to the left and also indicate which component(s) of GDP—consumption, investment, government purchases, or net exports—will change.

Problems and Applications

1.5 Explain how each of the following events would affect the aggregate demand curve.
a. An increase in the price level
b. An increase in government purchases
c. Higher state income taxes
d. Higher interest rates
e. Faster income growth in other countries
f. A higher exchange rate between the dollar and foreign currencies

1.6 From August 2009 to August 2015, the Standard & Poor's Index of 500 stock prices more than doubled, while the consumer price index increased by just over 10 percent. Briefly explain what effect, if any, these changes had on the aggregate demand curve.

1.7 Consider the two aggregate demand curves in the following graph. What would cause a movement from point A to point B on AD_1? What would cause a movement from point A to point C?

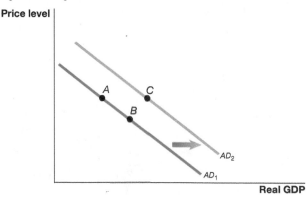

1.8 **(Related to the** Don't Let This Happen to You **on page 133)** An economics student makes the following statement: "It's easy to understand why the aggregate demand curve is downward sloping: When the price level increases, consumers substitute into less expensive products, which decreases total spending in the economy." Briefly explain whether you agree.

1.9 **(Related to** Solved Problem 4.1 **on page 134)** Explain whether each of the following will cause a shift of the *AD* curve or a movement along the *AD* curve.

   a. Firms become more optimistic and increase their spending on machinery and equipment.

   b. The federal government increases taxes in an attempt to reduce a budget deficit.

   c. The U.S. economy experiences 4 percent inflation.

1.10 **(Related to** Solved Problem 4.1 **on page 134)** A reporter for the *Wall Street Journal* wrote, "A strong dollar and weak growth overseas portend downward pressure on U.S. exports."

   a. What does the reporter mean by a "strong dollar"?

   b. What does the reporter mean by "weak growth overseas"?

   c. Briefly explain why the combination of a strong dollar and weak growth overseas might result in lower U.S. exports.

   d. Will the result of a strong dollar be a movement along the U.S. aggregate demand curve or a shift of the aggregate demand curve? Briefly explain.

Source: Jon Hilsenrath, "Rising Dollar and Falling Oil Could Be Recipe for a U.S. Asset Boom," *Wall Street Journal*, December 11, 2014.

1.11 **(Related to the** Making the Connection **on page 137)** If real GDP in the United States declined by more during the 2007–2009 recession than did real GDP in Canada, China, and other trading partners of the United States, would the effect be to increase or decrease U.S. net exports? Briefly explain.

Aggregate Supply and Aggregate Demand Analysis

Module Outline and Learning Objectives

4A.1 Aggregate Supply

LEARNING OBJECTIVE: Identify the determinants of aggregate supply and distinguish between a movement along the short-run aggregate supply curve and a shift of the curve.

The Short-Run Aggregate Supply Curve

While the *LRAS* curve is vertical, the *SRAS* curve is upward sloping because, over the short run, as the price level increases, the quantity of goods and services firms are willing to supply will increase. Firms supply more goods and services as the price level increases for two key reasons:

1. As prices of final goods and services rise, prices of inputs—such as the wages of workers or the price of natural resources—rise more slowly. Profits rise when the prices of goods and services firms sell rise more rapidly than the prices they pay for inputs. Therefore, a higher price level leads to higher profits and increases the willingness of firms to supply more goods and services.

2. As the price level rises, some firms are slow to adjust their prices. A firm that is slow to raise its prices when the price level is increasing may find its sales increasing and, therefore, will increase production.

Why do some firms adjust prices more slowly than others, and why might the wages of workers and the prices of other inputs change more slowly than the prices of final goods and services? Most economists believe the explanation is that *some firms and workers fail to accurately predict changes in the price level.* If firms and workers could predict the future price level exactly, the short-run aggregate supply curve would be the same as the long-run aggregate supply curve.

But how does the failure of workers and firms to predict the price level accurately result in an upward-sloping *SRAS* curve? Economists are not in complete agreement on this point, but we can briefly discuss the three most common explanations:

1. Contracts make some wages and prices "sticky."
2. Firms are often slow to adjust wages.
3. Menu costs make some prices sticky

Contracts Make Some Wages and Prices "Sticky" Prices or wages are said to be "sticky" when they do not respond quickly to changes in demand or supply. Contracts can make wages or prices sticky. For example, suppose Delta Air Lines negotiates a three-year contract with the Air Line Pilots Association, the union for the pilots who fly the company's planes, during a time when the economy is in recession and the number of passenger tickets being sold is falling. Suppose that after the union signs the contract, the economy begins to expand rapidly, and the number of tickets sold increases, so that Delta can raise ticket prices. Delta will find that flying more passengers will be profitable because the prices it charges are rising, while the wages it pays its pilots are fixed by contract. Or a steel mill might sign a multiyear contract to buy coal, which is used in making steel, at a time when the demand for steel is falling. If demand for steel and steel prices begin to rise rapidly, producing additional steel will be profitable because coal prices will remain fixed by contract. In both of these cases, rising prices lead to higher output. If these examples are representative of enough firms in the economy, a rising price level should lead to a greater quantity of goods and services supplied. In other words, the short-run aggregate supply curve will be upward sloping.

Notice, though, that if the pilots working for Delta or the managers of the coal companies had accurately predicted what would happen to prices, this prediction would have been reflected in the contracts, and Delta and the steel mill would not have earned greater profits when prices rose. In that case, rising prices would not have led to higher output.

Firms Are Often Slow to Adjust Wages We just noted that the wages of many union workers remain fixed by contract for several years. Many nonunion workers have their wages or salaries adjusted only once a year. Suppose you accept a job at a management consulting firm in June, at a salary of $45,000 per year. The firm probably will not adjust your salary until the following June, even if the prices it can charge for its services later in the year are higher or lower than the firm had expected them to be when it hired you. If firms are slow to adjust wages, a rise in the price level will increase the profitability of hiring more workers and producing more output. A fall in the price level will decrease the profitability of hiring more workers and producing more output. Once again, we have an explanation for why the short-run aggregate supply curve slopes upward.

Firms are often slower to *cut* wages than to increase them. Cutting wages can have a negative effect on the morale and productivity of workers and can also cause some of a firm's best workers to quit and look for jobs elsewhere.

Making the Connection
MyEconLab Video

How Sticky Are Wages?

When we have discussed the model of demand and supply, we have assumed that if the demand curve or supply curve for a product shifted, the price would adjust quickly from the old equilibrium to the new equilibrium. As we have just discussed, though, many economists argue that at least some wages and prices are sticky and do *not* adjust quickly to changes in demand or supply. Other economists argue that stickiness in wages and prices is not widespread enough to be important in macroeconomic analysis. In other words, these economists believe that the aggregate supply curve may be vertical in the short run, as well as in the long run.

Recently, a number of economists have examined the evidence for wage stickiness. Each month, the Bureau of Labor Statistics (BLS) collects data on average hourly earnings for all workers and for various subcategories of workers, such as workers in manufacturing. Using these data is not the best way to measure wage stickiness, though, because each of the BLS categories contains many workers. As a result, the average hourly earnings data the BLS reports represent the average change in wages but do not show how many workers received wage increases, wage decreases, or unchanged wages or how large those changes may have been. To better understand how frequently employers change wages, economists have looked instead at data on individual workers.

Separate studies of data on individual workers have arrived at similar results. One important result from these studies is that during a recession, firms are much more likely to reduce wages offered to newly hired workers than to reduce wages paid to current workers in the same job. For example, Mary C. Daly, Bart Hobijn, and Timothy Ni of the Federal Reserve Bank of San Francisco have shown that rather than cut wages during a recession, many firms reduce the *raises* they give workers, with more workers having their wages frozen, sometimes for long periods. Recall that the nominal wage is the number of dollars a firm pays a worker, while the real wage is the nominal wage divided by a price index. If a firm freezes a worker's nominal wage, the worker's real wage will gradually decline over time because of inflation. Most workers appear to be less upset if their real wage falls because of inflation than if it falls because of a cut in their nominal wage.

Daly, Hobijn, and Ni have used census data on individual workers to calculate the percentage of workers who each month were paid the same wage as they received in the same month during the previous year. The following figure shows these data for the years from 1997 through 2014. (The shaded areas are periods of recession.) Note that the percentage of workers with unchanged wages increases dramatically during recessions and the following months as the unemployment rate rises. The persistence of high rates of workers with frozen wages several years after the end of the 2007–2009 recession is an indication of how slowly the labor market recovered and how low the inflation rate has been since the recession. Other researchers using data for other countries have also found that firms are reluctant to cut nominal wages during recessions but instead freeze workers' nominal wages and allow inflation to gradually reduce real wages.

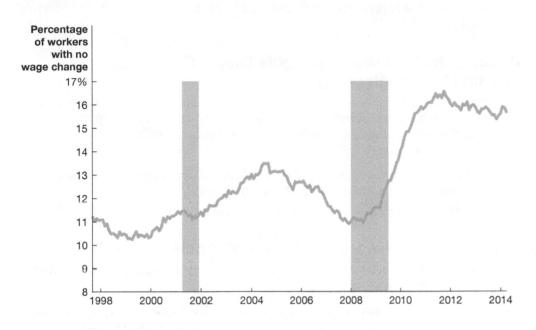

During recessions, why do firms often freeze nominal wages—frequently for extended periods—while they also lay off workers? Many economists believe that the main reason is that wage cuts upset workers. As a consequence, the productivity of workers who receive wage cuts may fall, and some workers may quit to find new jobs, either immediately or once the economy improves and the unemployment rate falls. As Truman Bewley, an economist at Yale, puts it, "The advantage of layoffs over pay reductions was that they 'get misery out of the door.'"

Sources: Mary C. Daly, Bart Hobijn, and Timothy Ni, "The Path of Wage Growth and Unemployment," *Federal Reserve Bank of San Francisco Economic Letter*, July 15, 2013; Anabela Carneiro, Paulo Guimarães, and Pedro Portugal, "Real Wages and the Business Cycle: Accounting for Worker, Firm, and Job Title Heterogeneity," *American Economic Review: Macroeconomics*, Vol. 4, No. 2, April 2012, pp. 133–152; Hervé Le Bihan, Jérémi Montornès, and Thomas Heckel, "Sticky Wages: Evidence from Quarterly Microeconomic Data," *American Economic Review: Macroeconomics*, Vol. 4, No. 3, July 2012, pp. 1–32; Alessando Barattieri, Susanto Basu, and Peter Gottschalk, "Some Evidence on the Importance of Sticky Wages," National Bureau of Economic Research, Working Paper 16130, June 2010; William T. Dickens et al., "How Wages Change: Micro Evidence from the International Wage Flexibility Project," *Journal of Economic Perspectives*, Vol. 21, No. 2, Spring 2007, pp. 195–214; and data from Federal Reserve Bank of San Francisco, "Nominal Wage Rigidity Data Releases."

Your Turn: Test your understanding by doing related problems 1.12 and 1.13 on pages 163–164 at the end of this module.

MyEconLab Study Plan

Menu Costs Make Some Prices Sticky Firms base their prices today partly on what they expect future prices to be. For instance, if you own a restaurant, you will determine the prices printed on your menu based on what you expect the demand to be for the meals you sell and what you expect to pay for labor, rent, ingredients, and other inputs. Similarly, many firms list the prices of their products on their Web sites.

Menu costs The costs to firms of changing prices.

If demand for their products or their production costs are higher or lower than the firms had expected, they may want to charge prices that are different from the ones in their menus or on their Web sites. Changing prices would be costly, however, because it would require printing new menus or entering new prices on their Web sites. The costs to firms of changing prices are called **menu costs**. To see why menu costs can lead to an upward-sloping short-run aggregate supply curve, consider the effect of an unexpected increase in the price level. In this case, firms will want to increase the prices they charge. Some firms, however, may not be willing to increase prices because of menu costs. Because their prices are now lower relative to competitors, these firms will find their sales increasing, which will cause them to increase output. Once again, a higher price level leads to a larger quantity of goods and services supplied.

Shifts of the Short-Run Aggregate Supply Curve versus Movements along It

Keep in mind the difference between a shift in a curve and a movement along a curve. The short-run aggregate supply curve tells us the short-run relationship between the price level and the quantity of goods and services firms are willing to supply, *holding constant all other variables that affect the willingness of firms to supply goods and services:*

- If the price level changes but other variables are unchanged, the economy will move up or down a stationary aggregate supply curve.

- If any variable other than the price level changes, the aggregate supply curve will shift.

Variables That Shift the Short-Run Aggregate Supply Curve

We now briefly discuss the five most important variables that cause the short-run aggregate supply curve to shift.

Increases in the Labor Force and in the Capital Stock A firm will supply more output at every price if it has more workers and more physical capital. The same is true of the economy as a whole. So, as the labor force and the capital stock grow, firms will supply more output at every price level, and the short-run aggregate supply curve will shift to the right. In Japan, the population is aging, and the labor force is decreasing. Holding other variables constant, this decrease in the labor force causes the short-run aggregate supply curve in Japan to shift to the left.

Technological Change As positive technological change takes place, the productivity of workers and machinery increases, which means firms can produce more goods and services with the same amount of labor and machinery. This increase in productivity reduces the firms' costs of production and allows them to produce more output at every price level. As a result, the short-run aggregate supply curve shifts to the right.

Expected Changes in the Future Price Level If workers and firms believe that the price level is going to increase by 3 percent during the next year, they will try to adjust their wages and prices accordingly. For instance, if a labor union believes there will be 3 percent inflation next year, it knows that wages must rise 3 percent to preserve the purchasing power of those wages. Similar adjustments by other workers and firms will result in costs increasing throughout the economy by 3 percent. The result, shown in Figure 4A.1, is that the short-run aggregate supply curve will shift to the left, so that any level of real GDP is now associated with a price level that is 3 percent higher. In general, *if workers and firms expect the price level to increase by a certain percentage, the SRAS curve will shift by an equivalent amount,* holding constant all other variables that affect the *SRAS* curve.

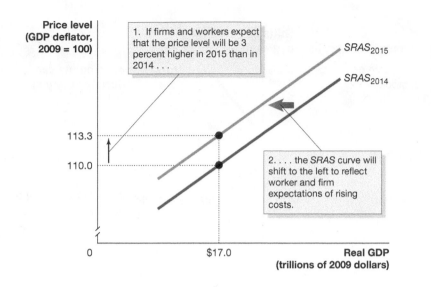

MyEconLab Animation

Figure 4A.1

How Expectations of the Future Price Level Affect the Short-Run Aggregate Supply Curve

The *SRAS* curve shifts to reflect worker and firm expectations of future prices.

1. If workers and firms expect that the price level will rise by 3 percent, from 110.0 to 113.3, they will adjust their wages and prices by that amount.
2. Holding constant all other variables that affect aggregate supply, the short-run aggregate supply curve will shift to the left.

If workers and firms expect that the price level will be lower in the future, the short-run aggregate supply curve will shift to the right.

Adjustments of Workers and Firms to Errors in Past Expectations about the Price Level Workers and firms sometimes make incorrect predictions about the price level. As time passes, they will attempt to compensate for these errors. Suppose that the Air Line Pilots Association signs a contract with Delta that provides for only small wage increases because the company and the union both expect only small increases in the price level. If increases in the price level turn out to be unexpectedly large, the union will take this into account when negotiating the next contract. The higher wages Delta pilots receive under the new contract will increase the company's costs and result in its needing to receive higher prices to produce the same level of output. If workers and firms across the economy are adjusting to the price level being higher than expected, the *SRAS* curve will shift to the left. If they are adjusting to the price level being lower than expected, the *SRAS* curve will shift to the right.

Unexpected Changes in the Price of an Important Natural Resource An unexpected event that causes the short-run aggregate supply curve to shift is called a **supply shock**. Supply shocks are often caused by unexpected increases or decreases in the prices of important natural resources that cause firms' costs to be different from what they had expected. Oil prices can be particularly volatile. Some firms use oil in the production process. Other firms use products, such as plastics, that are made from oil. If oil prices rise unexpectedly, the costs of production will rise for these firms. Some utilities also burn oil to generate electricity, so electricity prices will rise. Rising oil prices lead to rising gasoline prices, which raise transportation costs for many firms. Because firms face rising costs, they will supply the same level of output only if they receive higher prices, and the short-run aggregate supply curve will shift to the left.

The U.S. economy has experienced at least some inflation every year since the 1930s, so workers and firms always expect next year's price level to be higher than this year's price level. Holding everything else constant, expectations of a higher price level will cause the *SRAS* curve to shift to the left. But everything else is not constant because every year, the U.S. labor force and the U.S. capital stock expand and changes in technology occur, and these factors cause the *SRAS* curve to shift to the right. Whether in any particular year the *SRAS* curve shifts to the left or to the right depends on how large an effect these variables have during that year.

Table 4A.1 summarizes the most important variables that cause the *SRAS* curve to shift. The table shows the shift in the *SRAS* curve that results from an *increase* in each of the variables. A *decrease* in these variables would cause the *SRAS* curve to shift in the opposite direction.

Supply shock An unexpected event that causes the short-run aggregate supply curve to shift.

MyEconLab Concept Check   MyEconLab Study Plan

Table 4A.1

Variables That Shift the Short-Run Aggregate Supply Curve

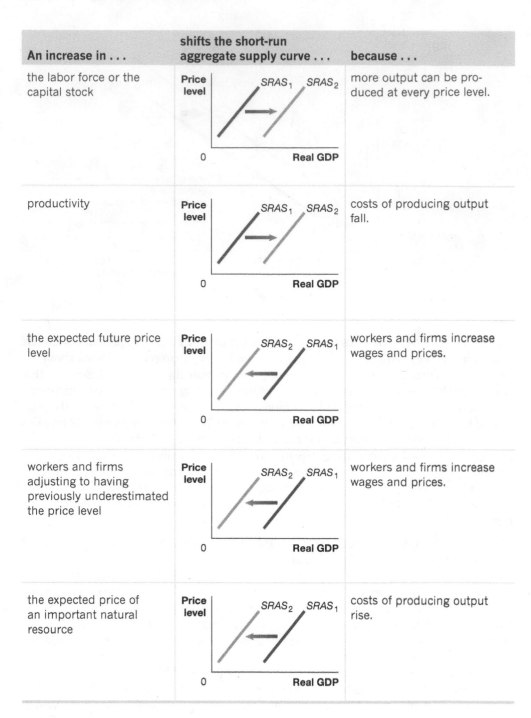

An increase in ...	shifts the short-run aggregate supply curve ...	because ...
the labor force or the capital stock		more output can be produced at every price level.
productivity		costs of producing output fall.
the expected future price level		workers and firms increase wages and prices.
workers and firms adjusting to having previously underestimated the price level		workers and firms increase wages and prices.
the expected price of an important natural resource		costs of producing output rise.

4A.2 Macroeconomic Equilibrium in the Long Run and the Short Run

LEARNING OBJECTIVE: Use the aggregate demand and aggregate supply model to illustrate the difference between short-run and long-run macroeconomic equilibrium.

Now that we have discussed the components of the aggregate demand and aggregate supply model, we can use it to analyze changes in real GDP and the price level. In Figure 4A.2, we bring the aggregate demand curve, the short-run aggregate supply curve, and the long-run aggregate supply curve together in one graph, to show the *long-run macroeconomic equilibrium* for the economy. In the figure, equilibrium occurs at real GDP of $17.0 trillion and a price level of 110. Notice that in long-run equilibrium, the short-run aggregate

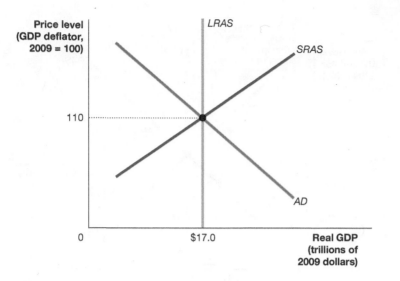

Figure 4A.2

Long-Run Macroeconomic Equilibrium

In long-run macroeconomic equilibrium, the *AD* and *SRAS* curves intersect at a point on the *LRAS* curve. In this case, equilibrium occurs at real GDP of $17.0 trillion and a price level of 110.

supply curve and the aggregate demand curve intersect at a point on the long-run aggregate supply curve. Because equilibrium occurs at a point along the long-run aggregate supply curve, we know the economy is at potential GDP: Firms will be operating at their normal level of capacity, and everyone who wants a job will have one, except the structurally and frictionally unemployed. We know, however, that the economy is often not in long-run macroeconomic equilibrium. In the following section, we discuss the economic forces that can push the economy away from long-run equilibrium.

Recessions, Expansions, and Supply Shocks

Because the full analysis of the aggregate demand and aggregate supply model can be complicated, we begin with a simplified case, using two assumptions:

1. The economy has not been experiencing any inflation. The price level is currently 110, and workers and firms expect it to remain at 110 in the future.

2. The economy is not experiencing any long-run growth. Potential GDP is $17.0 trillion and will remain at that level in the future.

These assumptions are simplifications because in reality, the U.S. economy has experienced at least some inflation every year since the 1930s, and potential GDP also increases every year. However, the assumptions allow us to understand more easily the key ideas of the aggregate demand and aggregate supply model. In this section, we examine the short-run and long-run effects of recessions, expansions, and supply shocks.

Recession

The Short-Run Effect of a Decline in Aggregate Demand Suppose that rising interest rates cause firms to reduce spending on factories and equipment and cause households to reduce spending on new homes. The decline in investment that results will shift the aggregate demand curve to the left, from AD_1 to AD_2, as shown in Figure 4A.3. The economy moves from point A to a new *short-run macroeconomic equilibrium*, where the AD_2 curve intersects the $SRAS_1$ curve at point B. In the new short-run equilibrium, real GDP has declined from $17.0 trillion to $16.8 trillion and is below its potential level. This lower level of GDP will result in declining profits for many firms and layoffs for some workers: The economy will be in recession.

Adjustment Back to Potential GDP in the Long Run We know that a recession will eventually end because there are forces at work that push the economy back to potential GDP in the long run. Figure 4A.3 shows how the economy moves from recession back to potential GDP. The shift from AD_1 to AD_2 initially leads to a short-run equilibrium, with the price level having fallen from 110 to 108 (point B). Workers and firms will begin to adjust to the price level being lower than they had expected it to be. Workers will be

Figure 4A.3

The Short-Run and Long-Run Effects of a Decrease in Aggregate Demand

In the short run, a decrease in aggregate demand causes a recession. In the long run, it causes only a decline in the price level.

1. A decline in investment shifts *AD* to the left, causing a recession.

2. As firms and workers adjust to the price level being lower than they had expected, costs will fall and cause *SRAS* to shift to the right.

3. Equilibrium moves from point *B* back to potential GDP at point *C*, with a lower price level.

willing to accept lower wages—because each dollar of wages is able to buy more goods and services—and firms will be willing to accept lower prices. In addition, the unemployment resulting from the recession will make workers more willing to accept lower wages, and the decline in demand will make firms more willing to accept lower prices. As a result, the $SRAS$ curve will shift to the right, from $SRAS_1$ to $SRAS_2$. At this point, the economy will be back in long-run equilibrium (point *C*). The shift from $SRAS_1$ to $SRAS_2$ will not happen instantly. It may take the economy several years to return to potential GDP. The important conclusion is that a decline in aggregate demand causes a recession in the short run, but in the long run it causes only a decline in the price level.

Economists refer to the process of adjustment back to potential GDP just described as an *automatic mechanism* because it occurs without any actions by the government. An alternative to waiting for the automatic mechanism to end a recession is for the government to use monetary policy or fiscal policy to shift the *AD* curve to the right and restore potential GDP more quickly. We will discuss monetary policy and fiscal policy in Modules 7A and 8A. Economists debate whether it is better to wait for the automatic mechanism to end recessions or to use monetary policy and fiscal policy.

Making the Connection

Does It Matter What Causes a Decline in Aggregate Demand?

We have seen that GDP has four components and that a decrease in any of them can cause the aggregate demand curve to shift to the left, leading to a recession. In practice, most recessions in the United States since World War II have begun with a decline in residential construction. Edward Leamer of the University of California, Los Angeles, has gone so far as to argue that "housing *is* the business cycle," meaning that declines in residential construction are the most important reason for the declines in aggregate demand that lead to recessions. The shaded periods in the graph on the next page represent recessions. The graph shows that spending on residential construction has declined prior to every recession since 1955.

The graph also highlights a fact that we noted earlier in this module: The decline in residential construction during the 2007–2009 recession was particularly severe. Spending on residential construction declined by almost 60 percent from the fourth quarter of 2005 to the third quarter of 2010. Largely because of these problems in the housing sector, the decline in real GDP during the recession of 2007–2009 was larger than during any other recession since the Great Depression of the 1930s.

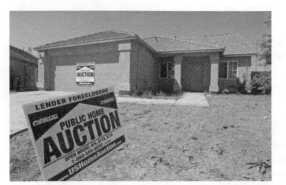

The collapse in spending on housing added to the severity of the 2007–2009 recession.

What typically causes declines in spending on residential construction? Late in a business cycle expansion, the inflation rate and interest rates start to increase (see Module 3 & 3A). Higher interest rates often result from monetary policy actions as the Federal Reserve tries to slow down the economy and reduce the rate of inflation (see Module 8A). Higher interest rates reduce consumer demand for new houses by increasing the cost of loans.

But the collapse in residential construction prior to and during the recession of 2007–2009 was due more to the deflating of the "housing bubble" of 2002–2005 and to the financial crisis that began in 2007 than to higher interest rates. We will discuss both the housing bubble and the financial crisis later in this module. At this point, we can note that research by Carmen M. Reinhart and Kenneth S. Rogoff of Harvard University shows that declines in aggregate demand that result from financial crises tend to be larger and longer-lasting than declines due to other factors. So, the experience of 2007–2009 indicates that, in fact, the source of the decline in aggregate demand can be important in determining the severity of a recession.

Sources: Edward E. Leamer, "Housing *Is* the Business Cycle," in *Housing, Housing Finance, and Monetary Policy*, Federal Reserve Bank of Kansas City, August 2007; Carmen M. Reinhart and Kenneth S. Rogoff, "The Aftermath of Financial Crises," *American Economic Review*, Vol. 99, No. 2, May 2009, pp. 466–472; and U.S. Bureau of Economic Analysis.

Your Turn: Test your understanding by doing related problem 2.6 on page 165 at the end of this module.

MyEconLab Study Plan

Expansion

The Short-Run Effect of an Increase in Aggregate Demand Suppose that instead of becoming pessimistic, many firms become optimistic about the future profitability of new investment, as happened during the information technology and telecommunications booms of the late 1990s. The resulting increase in investment will shift the *AD* curve to the right, as shown in Figure 4A.4. Equilibrium moves from point *A* to point *B*. Real GDP rises from $17.0 trillion to $17.3 trillion, and the price level rises from 110 to 113. Real GDP will be above potential GDP: Firms are operating beyond their normal level of capacity, and some workers who would ordinarily be structurally or frictionally unemployed or who would not be in the labor force are employed.

Figure 4A.4

The Short-Run and Long-Run Effects of an Increase in Aggregate Demand

In the short run, an increase in aggregate demand causes an increase in real GDP. In the long run, it causes only an increase in the price level.

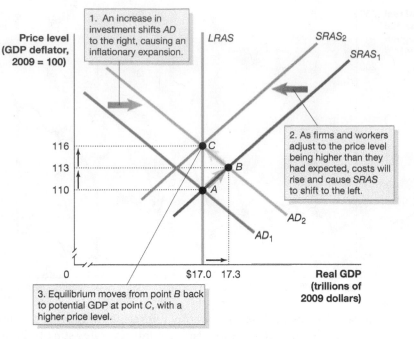

Adjustment Back to Potential GDP in the Long Run Just as an automatic mechanism brings the economy back to potential GDP from a recession, an automatic mechanism brings the economy back from a short-run equilibrium beyond potential GDP. Figure 4A.4 illustrates this mechanism. The shift from AD_1 to AD_2 initially leads to a short-run equilibrium, with the price level rising from 110 to 113 (point B). Workers and firms will begin to adjust to the price level being higher than they had expected. Workers will push for higher wages—because each dollar of wages is able to buy fewer goods and services—and firms will charge higher prices. In addition, the low levels of unemployment resulting from the expansion will make it easier for workers to negotiate for higher wages, and the increase in demand will make it easier for firms to receive higher prices. As a result, the $SRAS$ curve will shift to the left, from $SRAS_1$ to $SRAS_2$. At this point, the economy will be back in long-run equilibrium. Once again, the shift from $SRAS_1$ to $SRAS_2$ will not happen instantly. The process of returning to potential GDP may stretch out for more than a year.

Supply Shock

The Short-Run Effect of a Supply Shock Suppose oil prices increase substantially. This supply shock will increase many firms' costs and cause the $SRAS$ curve to shift to the left, as shown in panel (a) of Figure 4A.5. Notice that the price level is higher in the new short-run equilibrium (112 rather than 110), but real GDP is lower ($16.7 trillion rather than $17.0 trillion). This unpleasant combination of inflation and recession is called **stagflation**.

Stagflation A combination of inflation and recession, usually resulting from a supply shock.

Adjustment Back to Potential GDP in the Long Run A recession caused by a supply shock increases unemployment and reduces output. Workers will eventually be willing to accept lower wages, and firms will be willing to accept lower prices. In panel (b) of Figure 4A.5, the short-run aggregate supply curve shifts from $SRAS_2$ to $SRAS_1$, moving equilibrium from point B back to point A. Real GDP is back to potential GDP at the original price level. It may take several years for this process to be completed. An alternative would be to use monetary and fiscal policy to shift the aggregate demand curve to the right. Using policy in this way would bring real GDP back to potential GDP more quickly but would result in a permanently higher price level.

(a) A recession with a rising price level—the short-run effect of a supply shock

(b) Adjustment back to potential GDP—the long-run effect of a supply shock

MyEconLab Animation

Figure 4A.5   The Short-Run and Long-Run Effects of a Supply Shock

Panel (a) shows that a supply shock, such as a large increase in oil prices, will cause a recession and a higher price level in the short run. The recession caused by the supply shock increases unemployment and reduces output. Panel (b) shows that rising unemployment and falling output result in workers being willing to accept lower wages and firms being willing to accept lower prices. The short-run aggregate supply curve shifts from $SRAS_2$ to $SRAS_1$. Equilibrium moves from point B back to potential GDP and the original price level at point A.

Making the Connection

MyEconLab Video

How Long Is the Long Run in Macroeconomics?

Once a recession starts, how long does it take for real GDP and employment to return to the levels they had achieved at the business cycle peak? On average, in the recessions since 1950, it has taken six quarters, or about a year and a half, for real GDP to return to its cyclical peak. During the same period, it has taken employment on average about 9.5 quarters, or nearly two and a half years, to return to its cycle peak. But these averages disguise great variation across recessions.

The figure at the top of the next page shows the recessions of 1981–1982, 1990–1991, 2001, and 2007–2009. The value of real GDP at the business cycle peak is set equal to 100. Therefore, values less than 100 represent levels of real GDP below the level at the business cycle peak. The horizontal axis shows the number of quarters since the business cycle peak. The severity of the 2007–2009 recession can be seen clearly in the figure. Real GDP reached a cyclical peak in the fourth quarter of 2007. Real GDP didn't return to this level until the second quarter of 2011, which was 14 quarters, or *three and a half years*, after the recession began. That was far longer than in any other recession since 1950. Some economists describe the 1981–1982 recession as a V-shaped recession because although the decline in real GDP was large, real GDP returned to its cyclical peak relatively quickly. The 2007–2009 recession, in contrast, was a U-shaped recession because it took an extended period for real GDP to return to its cyclical peak.

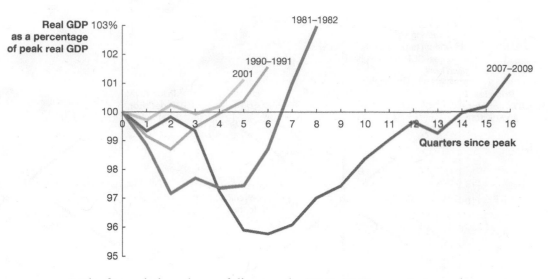

As the figure below shows, following the 2007–2009 recession, employment was very slow to return to its cyclical peak: It took 25 quarters, or more than six years. This period was far longer than in any other recession since 1950, and more than twice as long as following a typical recession. The second-slowest return to peak employment was following the 2001 recession, which has led some economists to consider whether changes in the U.S. labor market have made it more difficult for employment to return to normal levels following a recession.

The severity of the 2007–2009 recession took most economists and policymakers by surprise because they did not predict that the decline in housing prices that began in 2006 would eventually lead to a major financial crisis in 2008. Even as the recession was ending in 2009, members of President Obama's economic staff, economists at the Federal Reserve, and economists at the Congressional Budget Office all expected that the economy would return to normal levels of real GDP and employment far sooner than it did.

In Modules 7A and 8A, we will discuss the disagreements among economists and policymakers over why the U.S. economy took so long to return to potential GDP and full employment following the 2007–2009 recession.

Sources: Board of Governors of the Federal Reserve System, "Economic Projections of Federal Reserve Board Members and Federal Reserve Bank Presidents," various dates; Congressional Budget Office, "Data Underlying Selected Economic Figures, Real Gross Domestic Product," various dates; Christina Romer and Jared Bernstein, "The Job Impact of the American Recovery and Reinvestment Plan," January 9, 2009; U.S. Bureau of Economic Analysis; U.S. Bureau of Labor Statistics; and National Bureau of Economic Research.

4A.3 A Dynamic Aggregate Demand and Aggregate Supply Model*

LEARNING OBJECTIVE: Use the dynamic aggregate demand and aggregate supply model to analyze macroeconomic conditions.

The basic aggregate demand and aggregate supply model used so far in this module provides important insights into how short-run macroeconomic equilibrium is determined. Unfortunately, the model also provides some misleading results. For instance, it incorrectly predicts that a recession caused by the aggregate demand curve shifting to the left will result in a lower price level, which has not happened over an entire year since the 1930s. The difficulty with the basic model arises because we assumed that (1) the economy does not experience continuing inflation and (2) the economy does not experience long-run growth. We can develop a more useful aggregate demand and aggregate supply model by dropping these assumptions. The result will be a model that takes into account that the economy is not *static*, with an unchanging level of potential GDP and no continuing inflation, but *dynamic*, with potential GDP that grows over time and inflation that continues every year. We can create a *dynamic aggregate demand and aggregate supply model* by making changes to the basic model that incorporate the following important macroeconomic facts:

- Potential GDP increases continually, shifting the long-run aggregate supply curve to the right.
- During most years, the aggregate demand curve shifts to the right.
- Except during periods when workers and firms expect high rates of inflation, the short-run aggregate supply curve shifts to the right.

Figure 4A.6 illustrates how incorporating these macroeconomic facts changes the basic aggregate demand and aggregate supply model. We start with $SRAS_1$ and AD_1 intersecting at point A, at a price level of 110 and real GDP of $17.0 trillion. Because this intersection occurs at a point on $LRAS_1$, we know the economy is in long-run equilibrium. We show the long-run aggregate supply curve shifting to the right, from $LRAS_1$ to $LRAS_2$, because during the year, potential GDP increases as the U.S. labor force and the U.S. capital stock increase and technological progress occurs. The short-run aggregate supply curve shifts from $SRAS_1$ to $SRAS_2$ because the same variables that cause the long-run aggregate supply curve to shift to the right will also increase the quantity of goods and services that firms are willing to supply in the short run. Finally, the aggregate demand curve shifts to the right, from AD_1 to AD_2. The aggregate demand curve shifts for several reasons: As the population grows and incomes rise, consumption will increase over time. As the economy grows, firms will expand capacity, and new firms will be formed, increasing investment. An expanding population and an expanding economy require increased government services, such as more police officers and teachers, so government purchases will increase.

The new equilibrium in Figure 4A.6 occurs at point B, where AD_2 intersects $SRAS_2$ on $LRAS_2$. In the new equilibrium, the price level remains at 110, while real GDP increases to $17.4 trillion. Notice that there has been no inflation because the price level is unchanged, at 110. There has been no inflation because aggregate demand and aggregate supply shifted to the right by exactly as much as long-run aggregate supply. In fact, though, we wouldn't expect that all three curves will typically shift by the same amount. For instance, the $SRAS$ curve is also affected by workers' and firms' expectations of future changes in the price level and by supply shocks. These variables can partially or completely offset the normal tendency of the $SRAS$ curve to shift to the right over the course of a year. We also know that changes in the expenditures of consumers, firms, and the government may result in the AD curve shifting to the right by more or less than the $SRAS$ and $LRAS$ curves. In fact, as we will see shortly, *changes in the price level and in real GDP in the short run are determined by how much the SRAS and AD curves shift.*

* This section may be omitted without loss of continuity.

1. The economy begins in equilibrium at point *A*, with $SRAS_1$ and AD_1 intersecting at a point on $LRAS_1$.

MyEconLab Animation

Figure 4A.6 A Dynamic Aggregate Demand and Aggregate Supply Model

We start with the basic aggregate demand and aggregate supply model.

What Is the Usual Cause of Inflation?

The dynamic aggregate demand and aggregate supply model provides a more accurate explanation of the source of most inflation. If total spending in the economy grows faster than total production, prices rise. Figure 4A.7 illustrates this point by showing that if the *AD* curve shifts to the right by more than the *LRAS* curve, inflation results because equilibrium occurs at a higher price level, point *B*. In the new equilibrium, the *SRAS* curve has shifted to the right by less than the *LRAS* curve because the anticipated increase in prices offsets some of the effect of the technological change and increases in the labor force and capital stock that occur during the year. Although inflation generally results from total spending growing faster than total production, a shift to the left of the short-run aggregate supply curve can also cause an increase in the price level, as we noted in Section 13.3 when discussing supply shocks.

As we saw in Figure 4A.6, if aggregate demand increases by the same amount as short-run and long-run aggregate supply, the price level will not change. In this case, the economy experiences economic growth without inflation.

The Recession of 2007–2009

We can use the dynamic aggregate demand and aggregate supply model to analyze the recession of 2007–2009. The recession began in December 2007, with the end of the

MyEconLab Animation

Figure 4A.7   Using Dynamic Aggregate Demand and Aggregate Supply to Understand Inflation

The most common cause of inflation is total spending increasing faster than total production.
1. The economy begins at point A, with real GDP of $17.0 trillion and a price level of 110. An increase in full-employment real GDP from $17.0 trillion to $17.4 trillion causes long-run aggregate supply to

shift to the right from $LRAS_1$ to $LRAS_2$. Aggregate demand shifts to the right from AD_1 to AD_2.
2. Because AD shifts to the right by more than the LRAS curve, the price level in the new equilibrium rises from 110 to 114.

economic expansion that started in November 2001. Several factors combined to cause the recession:

- **The end of the housing bubble.**   The figure in the *Making the Connection* on page 151 shows that spending on residential construction increased rapidly from 2002 to 2005, before declining more than 60 percent between the end of 2005 and the beginning of 2010. The increase in spending on housing through 2005 was partly the result of actions the Federal Reserve had taken to lower interest rates during and after the recession of 2001. As interest rates on mortgage loans declined, more consumers began to buy new homes. But by 2005, it was clear that a speculative bubble was partly responsible for the rapidly rising prices of both newly built and existing homes. A bubble occurs when people become less concerned with the underlying value of an asset—either a physical asset, such as a house, or a financial asset, such as a stock—and focus instead on expectations of the price of the asset increasing. In some areas of the country, such as California, Arizona, and Florida, many homes were purchased by investors who intended to resell them for higher prices than they paid for them and did not intend to live in them. Some popular television programs explored ways that people could "flip" houses by buying and quickly reselling them. Speculative bubbles eventually end, and the housing bubble started to deflate in 2006. Both new home sales and housing prices began to decline. The growth of aggregate demand slowed as spending on residential construction—a component of investment spending—fell.

- **The financial crisis.**   Problems in the housing market were bad news for workers and firms involved with residential construction. In addition, falling housing prices led to an increased number of borrowers defaulting on their mortgage loans. These defaults caused banks and some other financial institutions to suffer heavy losses. Beginning in the spring of 2008, the U.S. Department of the Treasury and the Federal Reserve intervened to save several large financial institutions from bankruptcy. We will look at the details of the financial crisis in Modules 8 and 8A. For now we can note that the financial crisis led to a *credit crunch* that made it difficult for many households and firms to obtain the loans they needed to finance their spending. This drying up of credit contributed to declines in consumption spending and investment spending.

- **The rapid increase in oil prices during 2008.** Oil prices, which had been as low as $34 per barrel in 2004, had risen to $140 per barrel by mid-2008. The increase in the price of oil appeared to be caused by increased demand in rapidly growing economies, particularly India and China, and by the difficulty in developing new supplies of oil in the short run. With the deepening of the recession, worldwide demand for oil declined, and oil prices fell to about $40 per barrel in early 2009. As we have seen in this module, rising oil prices can result in a *supply shock* that causes the short-run aggregate supply curve to shift to the left, increasing the severity of a recession.

Figure 4A.8 illustrates the beginning of the recession by showing the economy's short-run macroeconomic equilibrium in 2007 and 2008. In the figure, short-run equilibrium for 2007 occurs where AD_{2007} intersects $SRAS_{2007}$ at real GDP of $14.87 trillion and a price level of 97.3. Real GDP in 2007 was below potential GDP of $14.95 trillion, shown by $LRAS_{2007}$. During 2008, aggregate demand shifted to the

MyEconLab Animation

Figure 4A.8   The Beginning of the Recession of 2007–2009

Between 2007 and 2008, the *AD* curve shifted to the right but not by nearly enough to offset the shift to the right of the *LRAS* curve, which represented the increase in potential GDP from $14.95 trillion to $15.26 trillion. Because of a sharp increase in oil prices, short-run aggregate supply shifted to the left, from $SRAS_{2007}$ to $SRAS_{2008}$.

Real GDP decreased from $14.87 trillion in 2007 to $14.83 trillion in 2008, which was far below the potential GDP, shown by $LRAS_{2008}$. Because the increase in aggregate demand was small, the price level increased only from 97.3 in 2007 to 99.2 in 2008, so the inflation rate for 2008 was only 2.0 percent.

right, from AD_{2007} to AD_{2008}. Aggregate demand increased by less than potential GDP because of the negative effects of the bursting of the housing bubble and the financial crisis on consumption spending and investment spending. The supply shock from higher oil prices caused short-run aggregate supply to shift to the left, from $SRAS_{2007}$ to $SRAS_{2008}$.

Short-run equilibrium for 2008 occurred at real GDP of $14.83 trillion and a price level of 99.2. A large gap opened between short-run equilibrium real GDP and potential GDP. Not surprisingly, unemployment rose from 4.6 percent in 2007 to 5.8 percent in 2008. The price level increased only from 97.3 to 99.2, so the inflation rate was a low 2.0 percent.

The recession persisted into 2009, as potential GDP increased to $15.50 trillion, while real GDP fell to $14.42 trillion. (The situation in 2009 is not shown in Figure 4A.8.) The increased gap between real GDP and potential GDP caused the unemployment rate to soar to 9.3 percent—the highest unemployment rate since the recession of 1981–1982 and the second highest since the Great Depression of the 1930s. Although the recession ended in June 2009, real GDP grew only slowly during 2010 and 2011, leaving the unemployment rate above 8.5 percent.

The severity of the recession of 2007–2009 resulted in some of the most dramatic changes in government economic policy since the Great Depression. We will explore these new policies in Modules 8 and 7,7A.   MyEconLab Concept Check

Solved Problem 4A.3

MyEconLab Interactive Animation

Showing the Oil Shock of 1974–1975 on a Dynamic Aggregate Demand and Aggregate Supply Graph

The 1974–1975 recession clearly illustrates how a supply shock affects the economy. Following the Arab–Israeli War of 1973, the Organization of the Petroleum Exporting Countries (OPEC) took actions that increased the price of a barrel of oil from less than $3 to more than $10. Use this information and the statistics in the following table to draw a dynamic aggregate demand and aggregate supply graph showing macroeconomic equilibrium for 1974 and 1975. Assume that the aggregate demand curve did not shift

between 1974 and 1975. Provide a brief explanation of your graph.

	Actual Real GDP	Potential GDP	Price Level
1974	$5.40 trillion	$5.43 trillion	28.7
1975	$5.39 trillion	$5.63 trillion	31.4

Sources: U.S. Bureau of Economic Analysis; and Federal Reserve Bank of St. Louis.

Solving the Problem

Step 1: Review the module material. This problem is about applying the dynamic aggregate demand and aggregate supply model, so you may want to review the section "A Dynamic Aggregate Demand and Aggregate Supply Model," which begins on page 155.

Step 2: Use the information in the table to draw the graph. You need to draw five curves: SRAS and LRAS for both 1974 and 1975 and AD, which is the same for both years. You know that the two LRAS curves will be vertical lines at the values given for potential GDP in the table. Because of the large supply shock, you know that the SRAS curve shifted to the left. The problem asks you to assume that the AD curve did not shift. Your graph should look like the following:

Step 3: **Explain your graph.** $LRAS_{1974}$ and $LRAS_{1975}$ are at the levels of potential
GDP for each year. Macroeconomic equilibrium for 1974 occurs where the
AD curve intersects the $SRAS_{1974}$ curve, with real GDP of $5.40 trillion and
a price level of 28.7. Macroeconomic equilibrium for 1975 occurs where the
AD curve intersects the $SRAS_{1975}$ curve, with real GDP of $5.39 trillion and a
price level of 31.4.

Extra Credit: As a result of the supply shock, equilibrium real GDP moved from just
below potential GDP in 1974 (the recession actually began right at the end of 1973) to
well below potential GDP in 1975. With real GDP in 1975 about 4.3 percent below its
potential level, the unemployment rate soared from 5.6 percent in 1974 to 8.5 percent
in 1975.

MyEconLab Study Plan   **Your Turn:** For more practice, do related problems 3.5 and 3.6 on page 166 at the end of this
module.

Economics in Your Life

Is an Employer Likely to Cut Your Pay during a Recession?

Consider whether during a recession your employer is likely to reduce your pay and cut the prices of the products he or she sells. We have seen that even during a recession, the price level rarely falls. In fact, in the United States, the GDP deflator has not fallen for an entire year since the 1930s. Although some firms reduced prices during the recession of 2007–2009, most firms did not. So, the owner of the coffeehouse where you work will probably not cut the price of lattes unless sales have declined drastically. We also saw that most firms are more reluctant to cut wages than to increase them because wage cuts can lower worker morale and productivity. Because the recession of 2007–2009 was particularly severe, some firms did cut wages. But given that you are a highly skilled barista, your employer is unlikely to cut your wages for fear that you might quit and work for a competitor.

Conclusion

This module showed that we need a model other than the microeconomic model of demand and supply to explain the behavior of the whole economy. We saw that the macroeconomic model of aggregate demand and aggregate supply explains fluctuations in real GDP and the price level.

Fluctuations in real GDP, employment, and the price level have led the federal government to implement macroeconomic policies. We will explore these policies in later modules after first considering the role money plays in the economy.

Visit MyEconLab for a news article and analysis related to the concepts in this module.

Key Terms

Menu costs, p. 146   Stagflation, p. 152   Supply shock, p. 148

4A.1 ## Aggregate Supply, pages 143–148

LEARNING OBJECTIVE: Identify the determinants of aggregate supply and distinguish between a movement along the short-run aggregate supply curve and a shift of the curve.

Summary

The **long-run aggregate supply (LRAS) curve** is a vertical line because in the long run, real GDP is always at its potential level and is unaffected by the price level. The short-run aggregate supply curve slopes upward because workers and firms fail to predict accurately the future price level. The three main explanations of why this failure results in an upward-sloping aggregate supply curve are that (1) contracts make wages and prices "sticky," (2) businesses often adjust wages slowly, and (3) menu costs make some prices sticky. **Menu costs** are the costs to firms of changing prices. If the price level changes but all else remains constant, the result is a movement up or down a stationary aggregate supply curve. If any other variable that affects the willingness of firms to supply goods and services changes, the aggregate supply curve will shift. The aggregate supply curve shifts as a result of increases in the labor force and capital stock, technological change, expected increases or decreases in the future price level, adjustments of workers and firms to errors in past expectations about the price level, and unexpected increases or decreases in the price of an important raw material. A **supply shock** is an unexpected event that causes the short-run aggregate supply curve to shift.

MyEconLab   Visit **www.myeconlab.com** to complete these exercises online and get instant feedback.

Review Questions

1.1 Explain why the long-run aggregate supply curve is vertical.

1.2 What variables cause the long-run aggregate supply curve to shift? For each variable, identify whether an increase in that variable will cause the long-run aggregate supply curve to shift to the right or to the left.

1.3 Why does the short-run aggregate supply curve slope upward?

1.4 What variables cause the short-run aggregate supply curve to shift? For each variable, identify whether an increase in that variable will cause the short-run aggregate supply curve to shift to the right or to the left.

Problems and Applications

1.5 Explain how each of the following events would affect the long-run aggregate supply curve.
  a. A higher price level
  b. An increase in the labor force
  c. An increase in the quantity of capital goods
  d. Technological change

1.6 A student was asked to draw an aggregate demand and aggregate supply graph to illustrate the effect of an increase in aggregate supply. The student drew the following graph:

The student explains the graph as follows:

An increase in aggregate supply causes a shift from $SRAS_1$ to $SRAS_2$. Because this shift in the aggregate supply curve results in a lower price level, consumption, investment, and net exports will increase. This change causes the aggregate demand curve to shift to the right, from AD_1 to AD_2. We know that real GDP will increase, but we can't be sure whether the price level will rise or fall because that depends on whether the aggregate supply curve or the aggregate demand curve has shifted farther to the right. I assume that aggregate supply shifts out farther than aggregate demand, so I show the final price level, P_3, as being lower than the initial price level, P_1.

Explain whether you agree with the student's analysis. Be careful to explain exactly what—if anything—you find wrong with this analysis.

1.7 Consider the short-run aggregate supply curves in the following graph. What would cause a movement from point A to point B on $SRAS_1$? What would cause a movement from point A to point C?

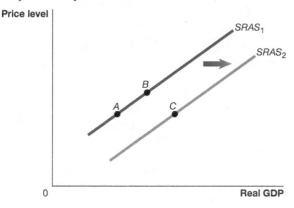

1.8 An article in the *Economist* noted that "the economy's potential to supply goods and services [is] determined by such things as the labour force and capital stock, as well as inflation expectations." Do you agree with this list of the determinants of potential GDP? Briefly explain.

Source: "Money's Muddled Message," *Economist*, March 19, 2009.

1.9 Explain how each of the following events would affect the short-run aggregate supply curve.
a. An increase in the price level
b. An increase in what the price level is expected to be in the future
c. A price level that is currently higher than expected
d. An unexpected increase in the price of an important raw material
e. An increase in the labor force participation rate

1.10 Consider the variables that shift long-run aggregate supply and the variables that shift short-run aggregate supply. Match each of the following scenarios with one of the three graphs of long-run aggregate supply and short-run aggregate supply.

a. The expected future price level decreases.
b. Workers and firms adjust to having previously underestimated the price level
c. A positive technological change occurs.

1.11 The American Trucking Association anticipates a shortage of truck drivers in coming years as the number of retirees exceeds the number of new drivers who enter the profession. The number of train boxcars is also expected to fall by over 40 percent in coming years because federal regulations limit boxcars to 50 years of service and many currently in use will reach that limit by 2020. Lumber and paper producers that depend on boxcars for their shipments fear that they will have to depend more on trucks for transportation, which will cost as much as 20 percent more than shipping by rail. Is the reduction in the number of trucks and boxcars likely to affect the short-run aggregate supply curve? Is it likely to affect the long-run aggregate supply curve? Briefly explain.

Sources: Lindsay Ellis and Laura Stevens, "International Paper Focuses on Improving Shipment Planning," *Wall Street Journal*, July 30, 2015; and Bob Tita, "Why Railroads Can't Keep Enough Boxcars in Service," *Wall Street Journal*, June 21, 2015.

1.12 (Related to the Making the Connection **on page 144)** Economists Mary Daly, Bart Hobijn, and Timothy Ni of the Federal Reserve Bank of San Francisco argue that "employers hesitate to reduce wages and workers are reluctant to accept wage cuts, even during recessions." If a firm faces declining sales during a recession, why might the firm's managers decide to lay off some workers and freeze the wages of other workers rather than cut workers' nominal wages?

Source: Mary C. Daly, Bart Hobijn, and Timothy Ni, "The Path of Wage Growth and Unemployment," *Federal Reserve Bank of San Francisco Economic Letter*, July 15, 2013.

1.13 (Related to the Making the Connection on page 144) An article in the *Economist* discussing the 2007–2009 recession states that "employers found it difficult to reduce the cash value of the wages paid to their staff. (Foisting a pay cut on your entire workforce hardly boosts morale.)"
   a. During a recession, couldn't firms reduce their labor costs by the same, or possibly more, if they laid off fewer workers while cutting wages? Why did few firms use this approach?
   b. What does the article mean by firms reducing the "cash value" of workers' wages? Is it possible for firms to reduce workers' wages over time without reducing their cash value? Briefly explain.

Source: "Careful Now," *Economist*, April 11, 2015.

1.14 What are menu costs? If menu costs were eliminated, would the short-run aggregate supply curve be a vertical line? Briefly explain.

4A.2   ## Macroeconomic Equilibrium in the Long Run and the Short Run, pages 148–154

LEARNING OBJECTIVE: Use the aggregate demand and aggregate supply model to illustrate the difference between short-run and long-run macroeconomic equilibrium.

Summary

In long-run macroeconomic equilibrium, the aggregate demand and short-run aggregate supply curves intersect at a point *on* the long-run aggregate supply curve. In short-run macroeconomic equilibrium, the aggregate demand and short-run aggregate supply curves often intersect at a point *off* the long-run aggregate supply curve. An automatic mechanism drives the economy to long-run equilibrium. If short-run equilibrium occurs at a point below potential GDP, wages and prices will fall, and the short-run aggregate supply curve will shift to the right until potential GDP is restored. If short-run equilibrium occurs at a point beyond potential GDP, wages and prices will rise, and the short-run aggregate supply curve will shift to the left until potential GDP is restored. Real GDP can be temporarily above or below its potential level, either because of shifts in the aggregate demand curve or because supply shocks lead to shifts in the short-run aggregate supply curve. **Stagflation** is a combination of inflation and recession, usually resulting from a supply shock.

MyEconLab   Visit **www.myeconlab.com** to complete these exercises online and get instant feedback.

Review Questions

2.1 Describe the relationship of the *AD*, *SRAS*, and *LRAS* curves when the economy is in long-run macroeconomic equilibrium.
2.2 Why might a supply shock lead to stagflation?
2.3 Suppose the economy enters a recession. If government policymakers—Congress, the president, and members of the Federal Reserve—do not take any policy actions in response to the recession, which of the alternatives listed below is the likely result? Be sure to carefully explain why you chose the answer you did.
   1. The unemployment rate will rise and remain higher even in the long run, and real GDP will drop below potential GDP and remain lower than potential GDP in the long run.
   2. The unemployment rate will rise in the short run but return to the natural rate of unemployment in the long run, and real GDP will drop below potential GDP in the short run but return to potential GDP in the long run.

3. The unemployment rate will rise and remain higher even in the long run, and real GDP will drop below potential GDP in the short run but return to potential GDP in the long run.
4. The unemployment rate will rise in the short run but return to the natural rate of unemployment in the long run, and real GDP will drop below potential GDP in the short run and remain lower than potential GDP in the long run.

Problems and Applications

2.4 An article in the *Economist* noted that in the first half of 2015, the value of Canadian oil exports declined and that "energy firms, which account for around a third of capital spending, are expected to slash investment by nearly 40% this year." As a result, real GDP in Canada declined during the first six months of 2015.
   a. Use a basic aggregate demand and aggregate supply graph (with *LRAS* constant) to illustrate this situation.
   b. On your graph show the adjustment back to long-run equilibrium.

Source: "A Rough Ride," *Economist*, July 11, 2015.

2.5 Draw a basic aggregate demand and aggregate supply graph (with *LRAS* constant) that shows the economy in long-run equilibrium.
   a. Assume that there is a large increase in demand for U.S. exports. Show the resulting short-run equilibrium on your graph. In this short-run equilibrium, is the unemployment rate likely to be higher or lower than it was before the increase in exports? Briefly explain. Explain how the economy adjusts back to long-run equilibrium. When the economy has adjusted back to long-run equilibrium, how have the values of each of the following changed relative to what they were before the increase in exports:
      i.   Real GDP
      ii. The price level
      iii. The unemployment rate
   b. Assume that there is an unexpected increase in the price of oil. Show the resulting short-run equilibrium on your

graph. Explain how the economy adjusts back to long-run equilibrium. In this short-run equilibrium, is the unemployment rate likely to be higher or lower than it was before the unexpected increase in the price of oil? Briefly explain. When the economy has adjusted back to long-run equilibrium, how have the values of each of the following changed relative to what they were before the unexpected increase in the price of oil:

   i. Real GDP
   ii. The price level
   iii. The unemployment rate

2.6 (Related to the Making the Connection **on page 150)** Edward Leamer of the University of California, Los Angeles, has argued that "housing is the business cycle." Why would spending on housing be likely to fluctuate more than spending by households on consumer durables, such as automobiles or furniture, or spending by firms on plant and equipment?

Source: Edward E. Leamer, "Housing *Is* the Business Cycle," in *Housing, Housing Finance, and Monetary Policy*, Federal Reserve Bank of Kansas City, August 2007.

2.7 Consider the data in the following table for 1969 and 1970 (where the values for real GDP and potential GDP are in 2009 dollars):

Year	Actual Real GDP	Potential GDP	Unemployment Rate
1969	$4.71 trillion	$4.57 trillion	3.5%
1970	$4.72 trillion	$4.74 trillion	4.9%

Sources: U.S. Bureau of Labor Statistics; and Federal Reserve Bank of St. Louis.

   a. In 1969, actual real GDP was greater than potential GDP. Briefly explain how this is possible.
   b. Even though real GDP in 1970 was slightly greater than real GDP in 1969, the unemployment rate increased substantially from 1969 to 1970. Why did this increase in unemployment occur?
   c. Was the inflation rate in 1970 likely to have been higher or lower than the inflation rate in 1969? Does your answer depend on whether the recession that began in December 1969 was caused by a change in a component of aggregate demand or by a supply shock?

2.8 Use the graph below to answer the following questions.

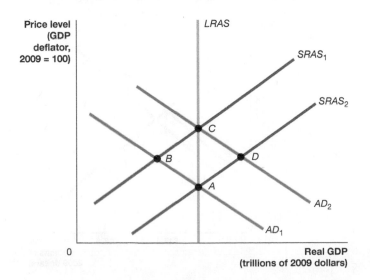

   a. Which of the points *A*, *B*, *C*, or *D* can represent a long-run equilibrium?
   b. Suppose that initially the economy is at point *A*. If aggregate demand increases from AD_1 to AD_2, which point represents short-run equilibrium? Which point represents the eventual long-run equilibrium? Briefly explain how the economy adjusts from the short-run equilibrium to the long-run equilibrium.

2.9 (Related to the Making the Connection **on page 153)** In early 2009, Christina Romer, who was then the chair of the Council of Economic Advisers, and Jared Bernstein, who was then an economic adviser to Vice President Joseph Biden, forecast how long they expected it would take for real GDP to return to potential GDP, assuming that Congress passed fiscal policy legislation proposed by President Obama:

   It should be understood that all of the estimates presented in this memo are subject to significant margins of error. There is the obvious uncertainty that comes from modeling a hypothetical package rather than the final legislation passed by the Congress. But there is the more fundamental uncertainty that comes with any estimate of the effects of a program. Our estimates of economic relationships … are derived from historical experience and so will not apply exactly in any given episode. Furthermore, the uncertainty is surely higher than normal now because the current recession is unusual both in its fundamental causes and its severity.

Why would the causes of a recession and its severity affect the accuracy of forecasts of when the economy would return to potential GDP?

Source: Christina Romer and Jared Bernstein, *The Job Impact of the American Recovery and Reinvestment Plan*, January 9, 2009, p. 2.

2.10 The following graphs show either aggregate demand or short-run aggregate supply shifting to the right or to the left.

a. Match the following scenarios to the appropriate graph.
  i.   An increase in the expected price level
  ii. An increase in households' expectations of their future income
  iii. A decrease in the price of an important natural resource
  iv. A decrease in firms' expectations of the future profitability of investment spending

b. Match one or more of the four graphs to each of the following scenarios:
  i.   The economy experiences a recession
  ii. The economy experiences short-term inflation
  iii. The economy experiences stagflation

4A.3 **A Dynamic Aggregate Demand and Aggregate Supply Model, pages 155–161**
LEARNING OBJECTIVE: Use the dynamic aggregate demand and aggregate supply model to analyze macroeconomic conditions.

Summary

To make the aggregate demand and aggregate supply model more realistic, we need to make it *dynamic* by incorporating three facts that were left out of the basic model: (1) Potential GDP increases continually, shifting the long-run aggregate supply curve to the right; (2) during most years, aggregate demand shifts to the right; and (3) except during periods when workers and firms expect high rates of inflation, the aggregate supply curve shifts to the right. The dynamic aggregate demand and aggregate supply model allows us to analyze macroeconomic conditions, including the beginning of the 2007–2009 recession.

MyEconLab   Visit **www.myeconlab.com** to complete these exercises online and get instant feedback.

Review Questions

3.1 What are the key differences between the basic aggregate demand and aggregate supply model and the dynamic aggregate demand and aggregate supply model?
3.2 In the dynamic aggregate demand and aggregate supply model, what is the result of aggregate demand increasing more than potential GDP increases? What is the result of aggregate demand increasing less than potential GDP increases?
3.3 Briefly discuss the factors that caused the recession of 2007–2009.

Problems and Applications

3.4 Draw a dynamic aggregate demand and aggregate supply graph showing the economy moving from potential GDP in 2017 to potential GDP in 2018, with no inflation. Your graph should contain the *AD*, *SRAS*, and *LRAS* curves for both 2017 and 2018 and should indicate the short-run macroeconomic equilibrium for each year and the directions in which the curves have shifted. Identify what must happen to have growth during 2018 without inflation.
3.5 **(Related to** Solved Problem 4A.3 **on page 159)** Consider the information in the following table for the first two years of the Great Depression (where the values for real GDP and potential GDP are in 2009 dollars):

Year	Actual Real GDP	Potential GDP	Price Level
1929	$1,056.6 billion	$1,006.3 billion	10.6
1930	$966.7 billion	$1,094.1 billion	10.2

Sources: U.S. Bureau of Labor Statistics; and Federal Reserve Bank of St. Louis.

a. The table shows that something happened during 1929–1930 that has not happened during the recessions of the past 50 years. What is it?
b. Draw a dynamic aggregate demand and aggregate supply graph to illustrate what happened during these years. Your graph should contain the *AD*, *SRAS*, and *LRAS* curves for both 1929 and 1930 and should indicate the short-run macroeconomic equilibrium for each year and the directions in which the curves shifted.
3.6 **(Related to** Solved Problem 4A.3 **on page 159)** An article in the *New York Times* in early 2015 stated that economists at the Federal Reserve were forecasting that "real GDP would expand at a faster pace than potential output in 2015" and that the inflation rate during 2015 would be about 1 percent.
a. Fill in the blank cells in the table with estimates that are consistent with these forecasts.

	2015	2016
Real GDP	$16.5 trillion	
Potential GDP	$16.8 trillion	$17.1 trillion
GDP deflator	119.2	

b. Draw a dynamic aggregate demand and aggregate supply graph to illustrate your answer to part a.
Source: Reuters, "Factbox: Fed Staff Forecasts from FOMC Minutes," *New York Times*, April 8, 2015.

3.7 In the following graph, suppose that the economy moves from point *A* in year 1 to point *B* in year 2. Using the graph, briefly explain your answer to each of the questions.

a. What is the growth rate in potential GDP from year 1 to year 2?

b. Is the unemployment rate in year 2 higher or lower than in year 1?

c. What is the inflation rate in year 2?

d. What is the growth rate of real GDP in year 2?

3.8 Explain whether you agree with the following statement:

> The dynamic aggregate demand and aggregate supply model predicts that a recession caused by a decline in *AD* will cause the inflation rate to fall. I know that the 2007–2009 recession was caused by a fall in *AD*, but the inflation rate was not lower as a result of the recession. The prices of most products were definitely higher in 2008 than they were in 2007, so the inflation rate could not have fallen.

3.9 In a speech in late 2011, President Barack Obama argued, "Probably the single greatest cause of the financial crisis and this brutal recession has been the housing bubble that burst four years ago." What did the president mean by the "housing bubble"? How can a housing bubble bring on a recession?

Source: Laura Meckler, "Obama Says Plan Will Cut Mortgage Payments for Millions," *Wall Street Journal*, October 24, 2011.

3.10 **(Related to the** Module Opener **on page 143)** Jet fuel is the largest operating cost for Delta Air Lines. In 2015, Delta's CEO Richard Anderson announced that the firm was likely to save more than $2 billion during the year because of lower fuel prices. Are firms like airlines that have costs that are dependent on raw material prices likely to be more or less affected by the business cycle than firms like automobile companies whose costs are not as dependent on raw material prices? Briefly explain.

Source: Paul R. La Monica, "Delta Air Lines Is Saving $2 Billion on Fuel," money.cnn.com, January 20, 2015.

Real-Time Data Exercises

D4A.1(Showing movements in equilibrium real GDP and the price level) Go to the Web site of the Federal Reserve Bank of St. Louis (FRED) (research.stlouisfed.org/fred2/) and find data on real GDP (GDPCA) and the GDP price deflator (USAGDPDEFAISMEI) for 1960, 1973, 1975, and 2007.

a. In an *AD–AS* graph, using the actual values for real GDP and the GDP price deflator, show equilibrium for 1960 and for 2007. Assume that the economy was at equilibrium at potential GDP in both years. From 1960 to 2007, what happened to long-run aggregate supply? Given the change in the GDP implicit price deflator, did aggregate demand grow more or less than long-run aggregate supply?

b. In an *AD–AS* graph, using the actual values for real GDP and the GDP price deflator, show equilibrium for 1973 and for 1975. Assume that the economy was in equilibrium at potential GDP in 1973 but in only a short-run equilibrium in 1975. Given the changes in real GDP and the GDP implicit price deflator, briefly explain what happened to short-run aggregate supply from 1973 to 1975.

D4A.2(The effects of a positive supply shock) Using data from the St. Louis Federal Reserve (research.stlouisfed.org/fred2/) FRED database, examine the experience of the U.S. economy during the 1990s. The U.S. economy experienced a positive supply shock with the spread of information communication technology and the Internet after 1995.

a. Download monthly data on the Personal Consumption Expenditure Price Index (PCEPI) from 1981 to the present. Calculate the inflation rate from 1982 to 2007 as the percentage change in the PCEPI from the same month in the previous year.

b. Calculate the average inflation rate from 1982 through 1994 and the average inflation rate from 1995 through 2007.

c. Are your calculations consistent with a positive supply shock after 1994? Briefly explain.

D4A.3(Comparing business cycles across countries) During the 2007–2009 period, the economies of the United Kingdom and the United States experienced similar problems. High oil prices and a housing bubble affected both economies. The financial crisis in the United States also affected investment in the United Kingdom, both by limiting credit and by increasing risk premiums. Using data from the St. Louis Federal Reserve (research.stlouisfed.org/fred2/) FRED database, examine the behavior of the U.K. economy since 2007.

a. Download quarterly data for real GDP (GBRRGDPQDSNAQ) and the GDP deflator (GBRGDPDEFQISMEI) for the United Kingdom from 2006 to the present. Calculate the growth rate of real GDP as the percentage change from the same quarter in the previous year and calculate the inflation rate as the percentage change in the GDP deflator from the same quarter in the previous year. Download data on the unemployment rate (GBRURHARMMDSMEI) for the same time period. For the frequency of the unemployment rate data, select quarterly, to match the frequency of the real GDP and GDP deflator data.

b. Download the three data series from 2007 to the present in the same graph. What do the data indicate about how similar the experience of the United Kingdom was to that of the United States during those years?

Appendix

Macroeconomic Schools of Thought

LEARNING OBJECTIVE: Compare macroeconomic schools of thought.

Macroeconomics became a separate field of economics in 1936, with the publication of John Maynard Keynes's book *The General Theory of Employment, Interest, and Money*. Keynes, an economist at the University of Cambridge in England, was attempting to explain the devastating Great Depression of the 1930s. Real GDP in the United States declined more than 25 percent between 1929 and 1933 and did not return to its potential level until the United States entered World War II in 1941 (see Module 5). The unemployment rate soared above 20 percent by 1933 and did not return to its 1929 level until 1942. Keynes developed a version of the aggregate demand and aggregate supply model to explain these facts. The widespread acceptance of Keynes's model during the 1930s and 1940s became known as the **Keynesian revolution**.

Keynesian revolution The name given to the widespread acceptance during the 1930s and 1940s of John Maynard Keynes's macroeconomic model.

In fact, using the aggregate demand and aggregate supply model remains the most widely accepted approach to analyzing macroeconomic issues. Because the model has been modified significantly from Keynes's day, many economists who use the model today refer to themselves as *new Keynesians*. The new Keynesians emphasize the importance of the stickiness of wages and prices in explaining fluctuations in real GDP. A significant number of economists, however, dispute whether using the aggregate demand and aggregate supply model, as we have discussed it in this module, is the best way to analyze macroeconomic issues. These alternative *schools of thought* use models that differ significantly from the standard aggregate demand and aggregate supply model. We can briefly consider four major alternative models:

1. The monetarist model
2. The new classical model
3. The real business cycle model
4. The Austrian model

The Monetarist Model

The monetarist model—also known as the neo-quantity theory of money model—was developed beginning in the 1940s by Milton Friedman, an economist at the University of Chicago who was awarded the Nobel Prize in Economics in 1976. Friedman argued that the Keynesian approach overstates the amount of macroeconomic instability in the economy. In particular, he argued that the economy will ordinarily be at potential GDP. In the book *A Monetary History of the United States: 1867–1960*, written with Anna Jacobson Schwartz, Friedman argued that most fluctuations in real output are caused by fluctuations in the money supply rather than by fluctuations in consumption spending or investment spending. Friedman and Schwartz argued that the severity of the Great Depression was caused by the Federal Reserve allowing the quantity of money in the economy to fall by more than 25 percent between 1929 and 1933.

Monetary growth rule A plan for increasing the quantity of money at a fixed rate that does not respond to changes in economic conditions.

In the United States, the Federal Reserve is responsible for managing the quantity of money. As we will discuss further in Module 8A, the Federal Reserve has typically focused more on controlling interest rates than on controlling the money supply. Friedman argued that the Federal Reserve should change its practices and adopt a **monetary growth rule**, which is a plan for increasing the quantity of money at a fixed rate. He believed that adopting a monetary growth rule would reduce fluctuations in real GDP, employment, and inflation.

Monetarism The macroeconomic theories of Milton Friedman and his followers, particularly the idea that the quantity of money should be increased at a constant rate.

Friedman's ideas, which are referred to as **monetarism**, attracted significant support during the 1970s and early 1980s, when the U.S. economy experienced high rates of unemployment and inflation. The support for monetarism declined during the late 1980s and 1990s, when the unemployment and inflation rates were relatively low. In Module 8, we will discuss the *quantity theory of money*, which underlies the monetarist model.

The New Classical Model

The new classical model was developed in the mid-1970s by a group of economists including Nobel Laureate Robert Lucas of the University of Chicago, Nobel Laureate Thomas Sargent of New York University, and Robert Barro of Harvard University. Some of the views held by the new classical macroeconomists are similar to those held by economists before the Great Depression. Keynes referred to the economists before the Great Depression as *classical economists*. Like the classical economists, the new classical macroeconomists believe that the economy normally will be at potential GDP. They also believe that wages and prices adjust quickly to changes in demand and supply. Put another way, they believe the stickiness in wages and prices emphasized by the new Keynesians is unimportant.

Lucas argues that workers and firms have *rational expectations*, meaning that they form their expectations of the future values of economic variables, such as the inflation rate, by making use of all available information, including information on changes in the quantity of money and other factors that might affect aggregate demand. Fluctuations in output and employment occur if households and firms form incorrect expectations of the inflation rate. If the actual inflation rate is lower than the expected inflation rate, the actual real wage will be higher than the expected real wage. Higher real wages will lead to a recession because firms will hire fewer workers and cut back on production. As workers and firms adjust their expectations to the lower inflation rate, the real wage will decline, and employment and production will expand, bringing the economy out of recession. The ideas of Lucas and his followers are referred to as the **new classical macroeconomics**. Supporters of the new classical model agree with supporters of the monetarist model that the Federal Reserve should adopt a monetary growth rule. They argue that a monetary growth rule will make it easier for workers and firms to accurately forecast the price level, thereby reducing fluctuations in real GDP. MyEconLab Concept Check

New classical macroeconomics
The macroeconomic theories of Robert Lucas and others, particularly the idea that workers and firms have rational expectations.

The Real Business Cycle Model

In the 1980s, some economists, including Nobel Laureates Finn Kydland of the University of California, Santa Barbara, and Edward Prescott of Arizona State University, argued that Lucas was correct in assuming that workers and firms formed their expectations rationally and that wages and prices adjust quickly to supply and demand but was wrong about the source of fluctuations in real GDP. They argued that fluctuations in real GDP are caused by temporary shocks to productivity and not by inaccurate forecasts of the price level. These shocks can be negative, such as a decline in the availability of oil or other raw materials, or positive, such as technological change that makes it possible to produce more output with the same quantity of inputs.

According to this school of thought, shifts in the aggregate demand curve have no effect on real GDP because the short-run aggregate supply curve is vertical. (Other schools of thought believe that the short-run aggregate supply curve is upward sloping and that only the *long-run* aggregate supply curve is vertical.) Fluctuations in real GDP occur when a negative productivity shock causes the short-run aggregate supply curve to shift to the left—reducing real GDP—or a positive productivity shock causes the short-run aggregate supply curve to shift to the right—increasing real GDP. Because this model focuses on "real" factors—productivity shocks—rather than changes in the quantity of money to explain fluctuations in real GDP, it is known as the **real business cycle model**. MyEconLab Concept Check

Real business cycle model
A macroeconomic model that focuses on real, rather than monetary, causes of the business cycle.

The Austrian Model

The *Austrian school* of economics began in the late nineteenth century with the writings of Carl Menger, an economist at the University of Vienna. Important later contributors to this school of thought were Ludwig von Mises, who spent the later years of his career at New York University, and Friedrich von Hayek, who spent most of his career at the London School of Economics. The Austrian school is best known for arguing the superiority of the market system over government economic planning. Hayek, in particular, emphasized that only the price system operating through markets could make use of the dispersed information available to households and firms to bring about an efficient allocation of resources.

During the 1930s, Hayek developed a theory of the business cycle that emphasized the problems arising from central banks forcing interest rates to very low levels. Low interest rates cause businesses to spend more on factories, machinery, office buildings, and other types of capital. Initially, the surge in investment spending will produce an economic expansion, but the additional capital goods eventually produce more output than firms can sell for a profit. Businesses suffer losses, reduce output, and lay off workers, resulting in a recession. The lower the central bank drives interest rates, the greater the increase in investment spending, the larger the economic expansion, and the deeper the eventual recession.

For a time in the early 1930s, Hayek's theory of the business cycle attracted significant interest from economists, particularly in the United Kingdom. After the publication of Keynes's *General Theory* in 1936, interest in Hayek's theory declined, and today only a relatively few economists belong to the Austrian school. In the past few years, however, Austrian economists have argued that the events of the 2007–2009 recession fit their model well: The Federal Reserve lowered interest rates to fight the 2001 recession, and the low interest rates sparked a surge in capital spending—in this case, spending on houses rather than on factories or office buildings. Eventually, the excessive investment in housing ended with a housing bust and a severe recession. MyEconLab Concept Check

Making the Connection

Karl Marx: Capitalism's Severest Critic

The schools of macroeconomic thought we have discussed in this appendix are considered part of mainstream economic theory because of their acceptance of the market system as the best means of raising living standards in the long run. One quite influential critic of mainstream economic theory was Karl Marx. Marx was born in Trier, Germany, in 1818. After graduating from the University of Berlin in 1841, he began a career as a political journalist and agitator. His political activities caused him to be expelled first from Germany and then from France and Belgium. In 1849, he moved to London, where he spent the remainder of his life.

In 1867, Marx published the first volume of his greatest work, *Das Kapital*. Marx read closely the most prominent mainstream economists, including Adam Smith, David Ricardo, and John Stuart Mill. But Marx believed that he understood how market systems would evolve in the long run much better than those earlier authors. He argued that the market system would eventually be replaced by a Communist economy, in which the workers would control production. He believed in the *labor theory of value*, which attributed all the value of a good or service to the labor embodied in it. According to Marx, the owners of businesses—capitalists—did not earn profits by contributing anything of value to the production of goods or services. Instead, they earned profits because their "monopoly of the means of production"—their ownership of factories and machinery—allowed them to exploit workers by paying them wages that were much lower than the value of workers' contributions to production.

Marx argued that the wages of workers would be driven to levels that allowed only bare survival. He also argued that small firms would eventually be driven out of business by larger firms, forcing owners of small firms into the working class. Control of production would ultimately be concentrated in the hands of a few firms, which would have difficulty selling the goods they produced to the impoverished masses. A final economic crisis would lead the working classes to rise up, seize control of the economy, and establish Communism. Marx died in 1883, without having provided a detailed explanation of how the Communist economy would operate.

Marx had relatively little influence on mainstream thinking in the United States, but several political parties in Europe were guided by his ideas. In 1917, the Bolshevik

Karl Marx predicted that a final economic crisis would lead to the collapse of the market system.

Party seized control of Russia and established the Soviet Union, the first Communist state. Although the Soviet Union was a vicious dictatorship under Vladimir Lenin and his successor, Joseph Stalin, its prestige rose when it avoided the macroeconomic difficulties that plagued the market economies during the 1930s. By the late 1940s, Communist parties had also come to power in China and the countries of Eastern Europe. Poor economic performance contributed to the eventual collapse of the Soviet Union and its replacement by a market system, although one with significant government intervention in the economy. The Communist Party remains in power in China, but the economy is evolving toward a market system. Today, only North Korea and Cuba have economies that claim to be based on the ideas of Karl Marx.

Key Terms

Keynesian revolution, p. 168

Monetarism, p. 168

Monetary growth rule, p. 168

New classical macroeconomics, p. 169

Real business cycle model, p. 169

Aggregate Expenditure and Output in the Short Run

Module Outline and Learning Objectives

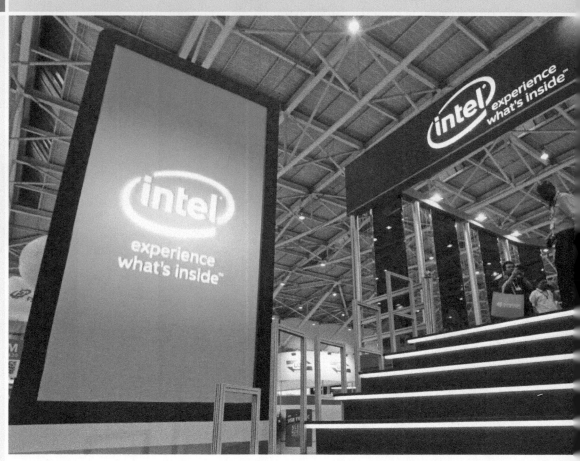

Fluctuating Demand Helps—and Hurts—Intel and Other Firms

Robert Noyce and Gordon Moore founded Intel in 1968. Today, the company is the world's largest semiconductor manufacturer and a major supplier of the microprocessors and memory chips that power desktop and laptop computers sold by Dell, Apple, Lenovo, Hewlett-Packard, and other computer manufacturers.

To this point, Intel's success has depended on the health of the computer market. As a result, the firm faces two problems: First, in the past few years, sales of computers have declined because many consumers and some businesses have switched to using tablets and smartphones to access the Internet. Second, Intel is vulnerable to the swings of the business cycle because sales of computers rise during economic expansions and fall during recessions. Intel was particularly hurt by the 2007–2009 recession. During the last quarter of 2008, Intel's revenues fell 90 percent, and the firm laid off 6,000 workers. Conditions improved for the firm beginning in 2010, as the U.S. economy recovered from the recession, although the firm was still struggling to reduce its dependence on selling chips to computer manufacturers. In 2015, Intel decided to lay off several hundred employees because businesses were only slowly increasing spending on computers and other information processing equipment.

The recovery from the 2007–2009 recession was by some measures the weakest since the end of World War II in 1945. By 2015, though, some industries were prospering. For example, sales of automobiles reached pre-recession levels. However, other industries still struggled. A weak recovery in spending by businesses on factories, office buildings, and other structures was bad news for some firms, including steelmakers. Worthington Industries, an Ohio-based steelmaker, announced that it would lay off 555 employees in 2015. Other U.S. steel companies also suffered from sluggish domestic and foreign demand. "Clearly, this is a rough patch," said Christopher Plummer, president and CEO of Metal Strategies.

These firms were dealing with changes in total spending, or *aggregate expenditure*. In this module, we will explore how changes in aggregate expenditure affect the level of total production in the economy.

Sources: Don Clark and Angela Chen, "Intel President Renée James to Leave as Others Also Depart," *Wall Street Journal*, July 2, 2015; Dan Gearino, "Worthington Industries to lay off 555 nationwide, including 80 in Fairfield County," *Columbus Dispatch*, March 25, 2015; John Carney, "Raising the Roof on Home Sales," *Wall Street Journal*, June 29, 2015; and Don Clark, "The Lawmaker: How Gordon Moore Predicted the Digital Revolution," *Wall Street Journal*, April 17, 2015.

Economics in Your Life

When Consumer Confidence Falls, Is Your Job at Risk?

Suppose that while attending college, you work part time at a company that manufactures door handles that it sells to automobile companies. One morning, you read in a news story online that consumer confidence in the economy has fallen, and, as a result, many households expect their future income to be well below their current income. Should you be concerned about losing your job? What factors should you consider in deciding how likely your company is to lay you off? As you read this module, try to answer these questions. You can check your answers against those we provide on **page 207** at the end of this module.

Aggregate expenditure (AE) Total spending in the economy: the sum of consumption, planned investment, government purchases, and net exports.

I n Module 3A, we discussed the determinants of long-run growth in the economy. We now turn to exploring the causes of the business cycle. We begin by examining the effect of changes in total spending on real gross domestic product (GDP).

During some years, total spending in the economy, or **aggregate expenditure (AE)**, and total production of goods and services increase by the same amount. In this case, most firms will sell about as much as they expected to sell, and they probably will not increase or decrease production or the number of workers they hire. During other years, total spending in the economy increases more than the production of goods and services. In those years, firms will increase production and hire more workers. But there are times, such as 2008 and early 2009, when total spending does not increase as much as total production. As a result, firms cut back on production and lay off workers, and the economy moves into a recession. In this module, we will explore why changes in total spending play such an important role in the economy.

5.1 The Aggregate Expenditure Model

LEARNING OBJECTIVE: Understand how macroeconomic equilibrium is determined in the aggregate expenditure model.

Aggregate expenditure model A macroeconomic model that focuses on the short-run relationship between total spending and real GDP, assuming that the price level is constant.

The business cycle involves the interaction of many economic variables. A simple model called the *aggregate expenditure model* can help us understand the relationships among some of these variables. Recall that GDP is the value of all the final goods and services produced in an economy during a particular year. Real GDP corrects nominal GDP for the effects of inflation. The **aggregate expenditure model** focuses on the short-run relationship between total spending and real GDP. An important assumption of the model is that the price level is constant. In Modules 4 and 4A, we developed a more complete model of the business cycle that relaxes the assumption of constant prices.

The key idea of the aggregate expenditure model is that *in any particular year, the level of GDP is determined mainly by the level of aggregate expenditure*. To understand the relationship between aggregate expenditure and real GDP, we need to look more closely at the components of aggregate expenditure.

Aggregate Expenditure

Economists first began to study the relationship between changes in aggregate expenditure and changes in GDP during the Great Depression of the 1930s. The United States, the United Kingdom, and other industrial countries suffered declines in real GDP of 20 percent or more during the early 1930s. In 1936, the English economist John Maynard Keynes published a book, *The General Theory of Employment, Interest, and Money*, that systematically analyzed the relationship between changes in aggregate expenditure and changes in GDP. Keynes identified four components of aggregate expenditure that together equal GDP (these are the same four components we discussed in Module 8):

- *Consumption (C).* Spending by households on goods and services, such as automobiles and haircuts.
- *Planned investment (I).* Planned spending by firms on capital goods, such as factories, office buildings, and machine tools, and on research and development, and spending by households and firms on new houses.
- *Government purchases (G).* Spending by local, state, and federal governments on goods and services, such as aircraft carriers, bridges, and the salaries of FBI agents.
- *Net exports (NX).* Spending by foreign firms and households on goods and services produced in the United States minus spending by U.S. firms and households on goods and services produced in other countries.

So, we can write:

$$\text{Aggregate expenditure} = \text{Consumption} + \text{Planned investment}$$
$$+ \text{Government purchases} + \text{Net exports,}$$

or:

$$AE = C + I + G + NX.$$

Governments around the world gather statistics on aggregate expenditure on the basis of these four components. And economists and business analysts usually explain changes in GDP in terms of changes in these four components of spending.   MyEconLab Concept Check

The Difference between Planned Investment and Actual Investment

Before considering further the relationship between aggregate expenditure and GDP, we need to consider an important distinction: Notice that *planned* investment spending, rather than actual investment spending, is a component of aggregate expenditure. You might wonder how the amount that businesses plan to spend on investment can be different from the amount they actually spend. We can begin resolving this puzzle by remembering that goods that have been produced but have not yet been sold are referred to as **inventories**. Changes in inventories are included as part of investment spending, along with spending on machinery, equipment, office buildings, and factories. We assume that the amount businesses plan to spend on machinery and office buildings is equal to the amount they actually spend, but the amount businesses plan to spend on inventories may be different from the amount they actually spend.

Inventories Goods that have been produced but not yet sold.

For example, Doubleday Publishing may print 1.5 million copies of the latest John Grisham novel, expecting to sell them all. If Doubleday does sell all 1.5 million, its inventories will be unchanged, but if it sells only 1.2 million, it will have an unplanned increase in inventories. In other words, changes in inventories depend on sales of goods, which firms cannot always forecast with perfect accuracy.

For the economy as a whole, we can say that actual investment spending will be greater than planned investment spending when there is an unplanned increase in inventories. Actual investment spending will be less than planned investment spending when there is an unplanned decrease in inventories. *Therefore, actual investment will equal planned investment only when there is no unplanned change in inventories.* In this module, we will use *I* to represent planned investment. We will also assume that the government data on investment spending compiled by the U.S. Bureau of Economic Analysis represents planned investment spending. This assumption is a simplification, however, because the government collects data on actual investment spending, which equals planned investment spending only when unplanned changes in inventories are zero.   MyEconLab Concept Check

Macroeconomic Equilibrium

Macroeconomic equilibrium is similar to microeconomic equilibrium. In microeconomics, equilibrium in the apple market occurs when the quantity of apples demanded equals the quantity of apples supplied. When the apple market is in equilibrium, the quantity of apples produced and sold will not change unless the demand for apples or the supply of apples changes. For the economy as a whole, macroeconomic equilibrium occurs when total spending, or aggregate expenditure, equals total production, or GDP:

$$\text{Aggregate expenditure} = \text{GDP.}$$

As we have seen, over the *long run*, real GDP in the United States increases, and the standard of living rises (see Module 3A). In this module, we are interested in understanding why GDP fluctuates in the *short run*. To simplify the analysis of macroeconomic equilibrium, we assume that the economy is not growing. In Module 4 & 4A, we will discuss the more realistic case of macroeconomic equilibrium in a growing economy. If we assume that the economy is not growing, then equilibrium GDP will not change unless aggregate expenditure changes.   MyEconLab Concept Check

Adjustments to Macroeconomic Equilibrium

The apple market isn't always in equilibrium because sometimes the quantity of apples demanded is greater than the quantity supplied, and sometimes the quantity supplied is greater than the quantity demanded. The same outcome holds for the economy as a whole. Sometimes the economy is in macroeconomic equilibrium, and sometimes it isn't. When aggregate expenditure is greater than GDP, the total amount of spending in the economy is greater than the total amount of production. With spending being greater than production, many businesses will sell more goods and services than they had expected to sell. For example, the manager of a Home Depot store might like to keep 50 refrigerators in stock to give customers the opportunity to see a variety of different sizes and models. If sales are unexpectedly high, the store may have only 20 refrigerators in stock. In that case, the store will have an unplanned decrease in inventories: Its inventory of refrigerators will decline by 30.

How will the store manager react when more refrigerators are sold than expected? The manager is likely to order more refrigerators. If other stores selling refrigerators are experiencing similar sales increases and are also increasing their orders, then Whirlpool, KitchenAid, and other refrigerator manufacturers will significantly increase their production. These manufacturers may also increase the number of workers they hire. If the increase in sales is affecting not just refrigerators but also other appliances, automobiles, furniture, and other goods and services, then GDP and total employment will begin to increase. In summary, *when aggregate expenditure is greater than GDP, inventories will decline, and GDP and total employment will increase.*

Now suppose that aggregate expenditure is less than GDP. With spending being less than production, many businesses will sell fewer goods and services than they had expected to sell, so their inventories will increase. For example, the manager of the Home Depot store who wants 50 refrigerators in stock may find that because of slow sales, the store has 75 refrigerators, so the store manager will cut back on orders for new refrigerators. If other stores also cut back on their orders, General Electric and Whirlpool will reduce production and lay off workers.

If the decrease in sales is affecting not just refrigerators but also many other goods and services, GDP and total employment will begin to decrease. Falling sales followed by reductions in production and employment occurred at many firms during 2008. In summary, *when aggregate expenditure is less than GDP, inventories will increase, and GDP and total employment will decrease.*

Only when aggregate expenditure equals GDP will firms sell what they expected to sell. In that case, their inventories will be unchanged, and they will not have an incentive to increase or decrease production. The economy will be in macroeconomic equilibrium. Table 5.1 summarizes the relationship between aggregate expenditure and GDP.

Increases and decreases in aggregate expenditure cause the year-to-year changes we see in GDP. Economists devote considerable time and energy to forecasting what will happen to each component of aggregate expenditure. If economists forecast that

Table 5.1

The Relationship between Aggregate Expenditure and GDP

If . . .	then . . .	and . . .
aggregate expenditure is *equal* to GDP	inventories are *unchanged*	the economy is in *macroeconomic equilibrium.*
aggregate expenditure is *less* than GDP	inventories *rise*	GDP and employment *decrease.*
aggregate expenditure is *greater* than GDP	inventories *fall*	GDP and employment *increase.*

aggregate expenditure will decline in the future, that is equivalent to forecasting that GDP will decline and that the economy will enter a recession. Firms, policymakers, and individuals closely watch these forecasts because changes in GDP can have dramatic consequences. When GDP is increasing, so are wages, profits, and job opportunities. Declining GDP can be bad news for workers, firms, and job seekers.

When economists forecast that aggregate expenditure is likely to decline and that the economy is headed for a recession, the federal government may implement *macroeconomic policies* in an attempt to head off the decrease in expenditure and keep the economy from falling into recession. We will discuss these macroeconomic policies in Modules 7A and 8A.   MyEconLab Concept Check   MyEconLab Study Plan

5.2 Determining the Level of Aggregate Expenditure in the Economy

LEARNING OBJECTIVE: Discuss the determinants of the four components of aggregate expenditure and define marginal propensity to consume and marginal propensity to save.

To better understand how macroeconomic equilibrium is determined in the aggregate expenditure model, we look more closely at the components of aggregate expenditure. Table 5.2 lists the four components of aggregate expenditure for 2014. The components are measured in *real* terms, which means that their values are corrected for inflation by being measured in billions of 2009 dollars. Consumption is clearly the largest component of aggregate expenditure. Investment and government purchases are of roughly similar size. Net exports was negative because in 2014, as in most years since the early 1970s, the United States imported more goods and services than it exported. Next, we consider the variables that determine each of the four components of aggregate expenditure.

Consumption

Figure 5.1 shows movements in real consumption from 1979 through the second quarter of 2015. Notice that consumption follows a smooth, upward trend. Only during periods of recession does the growth in consumption decline.

Here are the five most important variables that determine the level of consumption:

1. Current disposable income
2. Household wealth
3. Expected future income
4. The price level
5. The interest rate

Next we discuss how changes in each of these variables affect consumption.

Current Disposable Income The most important determinant of consumption is the current disposable income of households. Recall that disposable income is the income remaining to households after they have paid the personal income tax and received government *transfer payments*, such as Social Security payments (see Module 3). For most households, the higher their disposable income, the more they spend, and the lower their income, the less they spend. Macroeconomic consumption

MyEconLab Real-time data

Expenditure Category	Real Expenditure (billions of 2009 dollars)
Consumption	$10,876
Planned investment	2,718
Government purchases	2,838
Net exports	−443

Source: U.S. Bureau of Economic Analysis.

Table 5.2

Components of Real Aggregate Expenditure, 2014

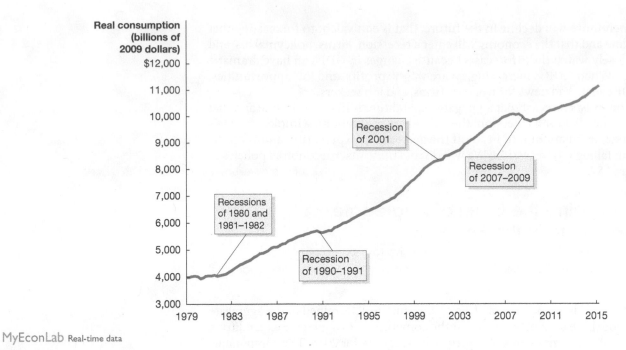

Figure 5.1   Real Consumption, 1979–2015

Consumption follows a smooth, upward trend, interrupted only infrequently by brief recessions.

Note: The values are quarterly data seasonally adjusted at an annual rate.

Source: U.S. Bureau of Economic Analysis.

is the total of all the consumption of U.S. households. We would expect consumption to increase when the current disposable income of households increases and to decrease when the current disposable income of households decreases. As we have seen, total income in the United States expands during most years. Only during recessions, which happen infrequently, does total income decline. The main reason for the general upward trend in consumption shown in Figure 5.1 is that disposable income has followed a similar upward trend.

Household Wealth Consumption depends in part on the wealth of households. A household's *wealth* is the value of its *assets* minus the value of its *liabilities*. Recall that an asset is anything of value owned by a person or a firm, and a liability is anything owed by a person or a firm (see Module 6). A household's assets include its home, stock and bond holdings, and bank accounts. A household's liabilities include any loans that it owes. A household with $10 million in wealth is likely to spend more than a household with $10,000 in wealth, even if both households have the same disposable income. Therefore, when the wealth of households increases, consumption should increase, and when the wealth of households decreases, consumption should decrease. Shares of stock are an important category of household wealth. When stock prices increase, household wealth will increase, and so should consumption. For example, a family whose stock holdings increase in value from $30,000 to $100,000 may be willing to spend a larger fraction of its income because it is less concerned with adding to its savings. A decline in stock prices should lead to a decline in consumption. Economists who have studied the determinants of consumption have concluded that permanent increases in wealth have a larger impact than temporary increases. One estimate of the effect of changes in wealth on consumption spending indicates that, for every permanent $1 increase in household wealth, consumption spending will increase by between 4 and 5 cents per year.

Expected Future Income Consumption depends in part on expected future income. Most people prefer to keep their consumption fairly stable from year to year, even if their income fluctuates significantly. Some salespeople, for example, earn most of their income from commissions, which are fixed percentages of the prices of the products they sell. A salesperson might have a high income in some years and a much lower income in other years. Most people in this situation keep their consumption steady and do not increase it during good years and then drastically cut it back during slower years. If we looked only at the current income of someone in this situation, we might have difficulty estimating the person's current consumption. Instead, we need to take into account the person's expected future income. We can conclude that current income explains current consumption well *but only when current income is not unusually high or unusually low compared with expected future income.*

The Price Level Recall that the *price level* measures the average prices of goods and services in the economy (see Modules 1 and 2). Changes in the price level affect consumption. It is tempting to think that an increase in prices will reduce consumption by making goods and services less affordable. In fact, the effect of an increase in the price of *one* product on the quantity demanded of that product is different from the effect of an increase in the price level on *total* spending by households on goods and services. Changes in the price level affect consumption mainly through their effect on household wealth. An increase in the price level will result in a decrease in the *real* value of household wealth. For example, if you have $2,000 in a checking account, the higher the price level, the fewer goods and services you can buy with your money. Therefore, as the price level rises, the real value of your wealth declines, and so will your consumption, at least a little. Conversely, if the price level falls—which happens rarely in the United States—the real value of your $2,000 increases, and your consumption will also increase.

The Interest Rate Finally, consumption depends on the interest rate. When the interest rate is high, the reward for saving is increased, and households are likely to save more and spend less. Recall the distinction between the *nominal interest rate* and the *real interest rate* (see Modules 1 and 2):

- The nominal interest rate is the stated interest rate on a loan or a financial investment such as a bond.
- The real interest rate corrects the nominal interest rate for the effect of inflation and is equal to the nominal interest rate minus the inflation rate.

Because households are concerned with the payments they will make or receive after the effects of inflation are taken into account, consumption spending depends on the real interest rate.

We have seen that consumption spending is divided into three categories:

1. Spending on *services*, such as medical care, education, and haircuts
2. Spending on *nondurable goods*, such as food and clothing
3. Spending on *durable goods*, such as automobiles and furniture

Spending on durable goods is most likely to be affected by changes in the interest rate because a high real interest rate increases the cost of spending financed by borrowing. The monthly payment on a four-year car loan will be higher if the real interest rate on the loan is 6 percent than if it is 4 percent.

The Consumption Function Panel (a) in Figure 5.2 illustrates the relationship between consumption and disposable income during the years 1960 to 2014. In panel (b), we draw a straight line through the points representing consumption and disposable income. The fact that most of the points lie almost on the line shows the close relationship between consumption and disposable income. Because changes in consumption depend on changes in disposable income, we can say that *consumption is a function of disposable income.* The relationship between consumption spending and disposable income illustrated in panel (b) of Figure 5.2 is called the **consumption function**.

Consumption function The relationship between consumption spending and disposable income.

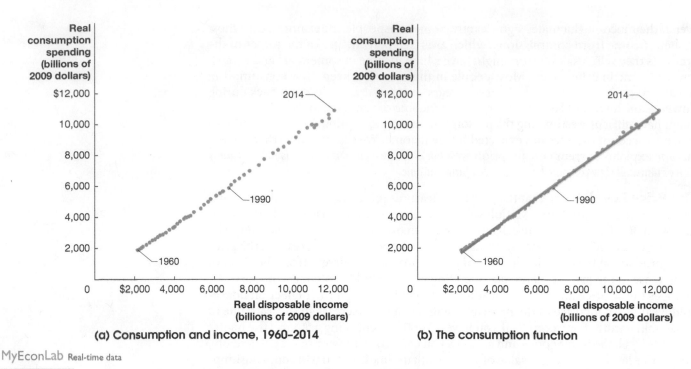

(a) Consumption and income, 1960–2014

(b) The consumption function

MyEconLab Real-time data

Figure 5.2   The Relationship between Consumption and Income, 1960–2014

Panel (a) shows the relationship between consumption and income. The points represent combinations of real consumption spending and real disposable income for the years 1960 to 2014. In panel (b), we draw a straight line through the points from panel (a). The line, which represents the relationship between consumption and disposable income, is called the *consumption function*. The slope of the consumption function is the marginal propensity to consume.

Source: U.S. Bureau of Economic Analysis.

Marginal propensity to consume (MPC) The slope of the consumption function: The amount by which consumption spending changes when disposable income changes.

The slope of the consumption function, which is equal to the change in consumption divided by the change in disposable income, is called the **marginal propensity to consume (MPC)**. Using the Greek letter delta, Δ, to represent "change in," C to represent consumption spending, and YD to represent disposable income, we can write the expression for the MPC as follows:

$$MPC = \frac{\text{Change in consumption}}{\text{Change in disposable income}} = \frac{\Delta C}{\Delta YD}.$$

For example, between 2013 and 2014, consumption spending increased by $285 billion, while disposable income increased by $313 billion. The marginal propensity to consume was, therefore:

$$\frac{\Delta C}{\Delta YD} = \frac{\$285\,\text{billion}}{\$313\,\text{billion}} = 0.91.$$

The value for the MPC tells us that households in 2014 spent 91 percent of the increase in their disposable income.

We can also use the MPC to determine how much consumption will change as income changes. To see this relationship, we rewrite the expression for the MPC:

$$\text{Change in consumption} = \text{Change in disposable income} \times MPC.$$

For example, with an MPC of 0.91, a $10 billion increase in disposable income will increase consumption by $10 billion $\times$ 0.91, or $9.1 billion.   MyEconLab Concept Check

The Relationship between Consumption and National Income

We have seen that consumption spending by households depends on disposable income. We now shift our focus slightly to the similar relationship that exists between consumption spending and GDP. We make this shift because we are interested in using the aggregate expenditure model to explain changes in real GDP rather than changes in disposable income. The first step in examining the relationship between consumption and GDP is to recall that the differences between GDP and national income are small and can be ignored without affecting our analysis (see Module 8). In fact, in this and the following modules, we will use the terms *GDP* and *national income* interchangeably. Also recall that disposable income is equal to national income plus government transfer payments minus taxes. Taxes minus government transfer payments are called *net taxes*. So, we can write the following:

$$\text{Disposable income} = \text{National income} - \text{Net taxes}.$$

We can rearrange the equation like this:

$$\text{National income} = \text{GDP} = \text{Disposable income} + \text{Net taxes}.$$

The table in Figure 5.3 shows hypothetical values for national income (or GDP), net taxes, disposable income, and consumption spending. Notice that national income and disposable income differ by a constant amount, which is equal to net taxes of $1,000 billion. In reality, net taxes are not a constant amount because they are affected by changes in income. As income rises, net taxes rise because some taxes, such as the personal income tax, increase and some government transfer payments, such as government payments to unemployed workers, fall. Nothing important is affected in our analysis, however, by our simplifying assumption that net taxes are constant.

National Income or GDP (billions of dollars)	Net Taxes (billions of dollars)	Disposable Income (billions of dollars)	Consumption (billions of dollars)	Change in National Income (billions of dollars)	Change in Disposable Income (billions of dollars)
$1,000	$1,000	$0	$750	—	—
3,000	1,000	2,000	2,250	$2,000	$2,000
5,000	1,000	4,000	3,750	2,000	2,000
7,000	1,000	6,000	5,250	2,000	2,000
9,000	1,000	8,000	6,750	2,000	2,000
11,000	1,000	10,000	8,250	2,000	2,000
13,000	1,000	12,000	9,750	2,000	2,000

MyEconLab Animation

Figure 5.3

The Relationship between Consumption and National Income

Because national income differs from disposable income only by net taxes—which, for simplicity, we assume are constant—we can graph the consumption function using national income rather than disposable income. We can also calculate the *MPC*, which is the slope of the consumption function, using either the change in national income or the change in disposable income and always get the same value. The slope of the consumption function between points *A* and *B* is equal to the change in consumption—$1,500 billion—divided by the change in national income—$2,000 billion—or 0.75.

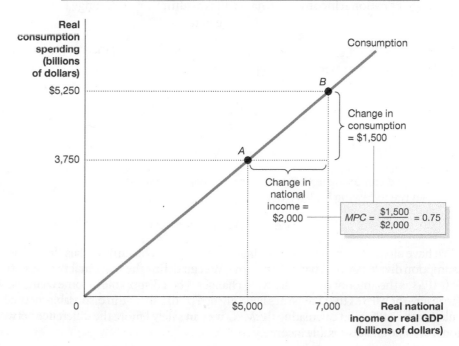

The graph in Figure 5.3 shows a line representing the relationship between consumption and national income. The line is very similar to the consumption function shown in panel (b) of Figure 5.2. We defined the marginal propensity to consume (MPC) as the change in consumption divided by the change in disposable income, which is the slope of the consumption function. In fact, notice that if we calculate the slope of the line in Figure 5.3 between points A and B, we get a result that will not change whether we use the values for national income or the values for disposable income. Using the values for national income:

$$\frac{\Delta C}{\Delta Y} = \frac{\$5{,}250 \text{ billion} - \$3{,}750 \text{ billion}}{\$7{,}000 \text{ billion} - \$5{,}000 \text{ billion}} = 0.75.$$

Using the corresponding values for disposable income from the table:

$$\frac{\Delta C}{\Delta YD} = \frac{\$5{,}250 \text{ billion} - \$3{,}750 \text{ billion}}{\$6{,}000 \text{ billion} - \$4{,}000 \text{ billion}} = 0.75.$$

It should not be surprising that we get the same result in either case. National income and disposable income differ by a constant amount, so changes in the two numbers always give us the same value, as shown in the last two columns of the table in Figure 5.3. Therefore, we can graph the consumption function using national income rather than using disposable income. We can also calculate the MPC using either the change in national income or the change in disposable income and always get the same value.   MyEconLab Concept Check

Income, Consumption, and Saving

To complete our discussion of consumption, we can look briefly at the relationships among income, consumption, and saving. Households spend their income, save it, or use it to pay taxes. For the economy as a whole, we can write the following:

National income = Consumption + Saving + Taxes.

When national income increases, there must be some combination of an increase in consumption, an increase in saving, and an increase in taxes:

Change in national income = Change in consumption + Change in saving + Change in taxes.

Using symbols, where Y represents national income (and GDP), C represents consumption, S represents saving, and T represents taxes, we can write the following:

$$Y = C + S + T$$

and:

$$\Delta Y = \Delta C + \Delta S + \Delta T.$$

To simplify, we can assume that taxes are always a constant amount, in which case $\Delta T = 0$, so the following is also true:

$$\Delta Y = \Delta C + \Delta S.$$

Marginal propensity to save (MPS) The amount by which saving changes when disposable income changes.

We have already seen that the marginal propensity to consume equals the change in consumption divided by the change in income. We can define the **marginal propensity to save (MPS)** as the amount by which saving changes when disposable income changes. We can measure the MPS as the change in saving divided by the change in disposable income. In calculating the MPS, as in calculating the MPC, we can safely ignore the difference between national income and disposable income.

If we divide the previous equation by the change in income, ΔY, we get an equation that shows the relationship between the marginal propensity to consume and the marginal propensity to save:

$$\frac{\Delta Y}{\Delta Y} = \frac{\Delta C}{\Delta Y} + \frac{\Delta S}{\Delta Y},$$

or:

$$1 = MPC + MPS.$$

This equation tells us that when taxes are constant, the marginal propensity to consume plus the marginal propensity to save must always equal 1. They must add up to 1 because part of any increase in income is consumed, and whatever remains must be saved.

MyEconLab Concept Check

Solved Problem 5.2

Calculating the Marginal Propensity to Consume and the Marginal Propensity to Save

Fill in the blank cells in the following table. For simplicity, assume that taxes are zero. Show that the MPC plus the MPS equals 1.

National Income and Real GDP (Y)	Consumption (C)	Saving (S)	Marginal Propensity to Consume (MPC)	Marginal Propensity to Save (MPS)
$9,000	$8,000			
10,000	8,600			
11,000	9,200			
12,000	9,800			
13,000	10,400			

Solving the Problem

Step 1: **Review the module material.** This problem is about the relationship among income, consumption, and saving, so you may want to review the section "Income, Consumption, and Saving," which begins on page 182.

Step 2: **Fill in the table.** We know that $Y = C + S + T$. With taxes equal to zero, this equation becomes $Y = C + S$. We can use this equation to fill in the "Saving" column. We can use the equations for the MPC and the MPS to fill in the other two columns:

$$MPC = \frac{\Delta C}{\Delta Y}$$

$$MPS = \frac{\Delta S}{\Delta Y}$$

For example, to calculate the value of the MPC in the second row, we have:

$$MPC = \frac{\Delta C}{\Delta Y} = \frac{\$8,600 - \$8,000}{\$10,000 - \$9,000} = \frac{\$600}{\$1,000} = 0.6.$$

To calculate the value of the MPS in the second row, we have:

$$MPS = \frac{\Delta S}{\Delta Y} = \frac{\$1,400 - \$1,000}{\$10,000 - \$9,000} = \frac{\$400}{\$1,000} = 0.4.$$

National Income and Real GDP (Y)	Consumption (C)	Saving (S)	Marginal Propensity to Consume (MPC)	Marginal Propensity to Save (MPS)
$9,000	$8,000	$1,000	—	—
10,000	8,600	1,400	0.6	0.4
11,000	9,200	1,800	0.6	0.4
12,000	9,800	2,200	0.6	0.4
13,000	10,400	2,600	0.6	0.4

Step 3: **Show that the MPC plus the MPS equals 1.** At every level of national income, the MPC is 0.6 and the MPS is 0.4. Therefore, the MPC plus the MPS is always equal to 1.

Your Turn: For more practice, do related problem 2.10 on page 209 at the end of this module.

Planned Investment

Figure 5.4 shows movements in real investment spending from 1979 through the second quarter of 2015. Notice that, unlike consumption, investment does not follow a smooth, upward trend. Investment declined significantly during the recessions of 1980, 1981–1982, 1990–1991, 2001, and 2007–2009.

These are the four most important variables that determine the level of investment:

1. Expectations of future profitability
2. The interest rate
3. Taxes
4. Cash flow

Expectations of Future Profitability Investment goods, such as factories, office buildings, and machinery and equipment, are long-lived. A firm is unlikely to build a new factory unless it is optimistic that the demand for its product will remain strong for at least several years. When the economy moves into a recession, many firms postpone buying investment goods even if the demand for their own product is strong

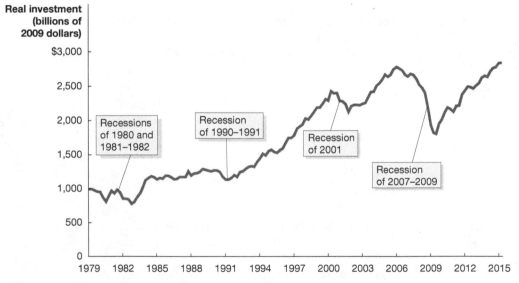

Figure 5.4   **Real Investment, 1979–2015**

Investment is subject to larger changes than is consumption. Investment declined significantly during the recessions of 1980, 1981–1982, 1990–1991, 2001, and 2007–2009.

Note: The values are quarterly data, seasonally adjusted at an annual rate.

Source: U.S. Bureau of Economic Analysis.

because they are afraid that the recession may become worse. During an expansion, some firms may become optimistic and begin to increase spending on investment goods even before the demand for their own product has increased. The key point is that *the optimism or pessimism of firms is an important determinant of investment spending.*

Residential construction is included in investment spending. Since 1990, residential construction has averaged about 30 percent of total investment spending. But the swings in residential construction have been quite substantial, ranging from a high of 36 percent of investment spending at the height of the housing boom in 2005 down to 18 percent in 2011. The sharp decline in spending on residential construction beginning in 2006 helped to cause the 2007–2009 recession and contributed to its severity.

The Interest Rate Some business investment is financed by borrowing, as firms issue corporate bonds or receive loans from banks. Households also borrow to finance most of their spending on new homes. The higher the interest rate, the more expensive it is for firms and households to borrow. Because households and firms are interested in the cost of borrowing after taking into account the effects of inflation, investment spending depends on the real interest rate. Therefore, holding constant the other factors that affect investment spending, there is an inverse relationship between the real interest rate and investment spending: *A higher real interest rate results in less investment spending, and a lower real interest rate results in more investment spending.* The ability of households to borrow money at very low real interest rates helps explain the rapid increase in spending on residential construction from 2002 to 2006.

Taxes Taxes affect the level of investment spending. Firms focus on the profits that remain after they have paid taxes. The federal government imposes a *corporate income tax* on the profits corporations earn, including profits from the new buildings, equipment, and other investment goods they purchase. A reduction in the corporate income tax increases the after-tax profitability of investment spending. An increase in the corporate income tax decreases the after-tax profitability of investment spending. *Investment tax incentives* increase investment spending. An investment tax incentive provides firms with a tax reduction when they buy new investment goods.

Cash Flow Most firms do not borrow to finance spending on new factories, machinery, and equipment. Instead, they use their own funds. **Cash flow** is the difference between the cash revenues received by a firm and the cash spending by the firm. Neither noncash receipts nor noncash spending is included in cash flow. For example, tax laws allow firms to count the depreciation of worn-out or obsolete machinery and equipment as a cost, even if new machinery and equipment have not actually been purchased. Because this is noncash spending, firms do not include it when calculating cash flow. The largest contributor to cash flow is profit. The more profitable a firm is, the greater its cash flow and the greater its ability to finance investment. During periods of recession, many firms experience reduced profits, which in turn reduces their ability to finance spending on new factories or machinery and equipment.

Cash flow The difference between the cash revenues received by a firm and the cash spending by the firm.

Making the Connection
MyEconLab Video

Is Student Loan Debt Causing Fewer Young People to Buy Houses?

Although our discussion in this section has concentrated on the components of investment that represent spending by businesses, household purchases of new homes are an important part of investment spending. As the graph on the next page shows, spending on residential construction rose rapidly in the period just before the recession of 2007–2009, declined dramatically during the recession, and recovered only slowly thereafter. The slow recovery in spending on residential construction is one reason the recovery from the recession was weaker than most recoveries.

Some economists believe that one factor holding back recovery in the housing market was low home-buying rates among younger households. In 2014, homeownership rates among people younger than 35 were the lowest they have been in the United States in at least 25 years. Do high levels of student debt explain why young people are buying fewer homes? If you have a college degree, you are likely to earn more than

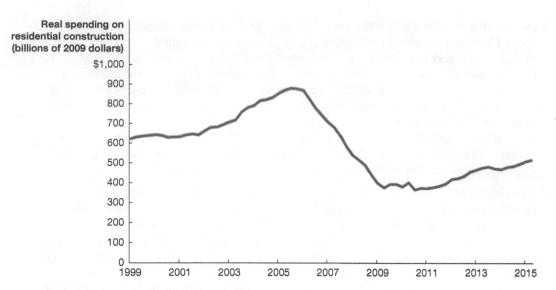

people without a college degree. So, many people consider student debt taken on to earn a degree to be a good investment. For the class of 2014, the average student debt per borrower was a record $33,000. Total student debt in 2014 was $1.1 trillion, more than the amount that all Americans owe on credit cards or automobile loans, and twice the level of student debt in 2007. Does increasing student debt explain the decline in home purchases among younger households? Economists differ in their answers to this question because other factors may be affecting homeownership rates.

Harvard economist and former Obama administration economic adviser Larry Summers argues that many college graduates have trouble accumulating the funds for a down payment on a house because they are making student loan payments. He also argues that these payments have led young college graduates to delay forming families, thereby reducing their need to move from an apartment to a house. One survey indicates that 45 percent of college graduates under age 24 are living at home or with another family member. Some economists point to rising delinquency rates on student loans as a factor that makes it difficult for some young college graduates to qualify for a mortgage loan necessary to buy a house.

Other economists are skeptical of a link between student debt and a reduced demand for housing by young college graduates. Economists who have carried out statistical studies of the link have arrived at mixed results. In testifying before Congress, Federal Reserve Chair Janet Yellen remarked of the connection between students' debt and the demand for housing that "I don't know of clear evidence of it."

Some economists believe that new government lending guidelines may be playing a role. When deciding whether to grant a mortgage loan, banks and other lenders have interpreted the guidelines to mean that they must give greater consideration to how much debt graduates have. As a result, fewer young college graduates qualify for mortgage loans. Finally, some economists argue that the weak recovery of the U.S. labor market from the recession of 2007–2009 is the key reason that young college graduates have been buying fewer houses. With unemployment rates remaining high and wages growing slowly, many young people have difficulty affording homes, even if they have limited or no student debt. As the recovery became stronger in 2015, these economists expected that younger people would be increasing their demand for housing.

Sources: Mitchell E. Daniels, "How Student Debt Harms the Economy," *Wall Street Journal*, January 27, 2015; Zeppo Mitchell, "Larry Summers: Student Debt Is Slowing the U.S. Housing Recovery," *Wall Street Journal*, May 21, 2014; Josh Mitchell, "Student Debt Takes a Toll on Some Home Buyers," *Wall Street Journal*, June 20, 2014; Susan Dynarski, "Remember the Problems with Mortgage Defaults? They're Coming Back with Student Loans," *New York Times*, June 12, 2014; Meta Brown, et al., "Measuring Student Debt and Its Performance," Federal Reserve Bank of New York, Staff Report No. 668, April 2014; and U.S. Bureau of Economic Analysis.

Your Turn: Test your understanding by doing related problem 2.11 on page 209 at the end of this module.

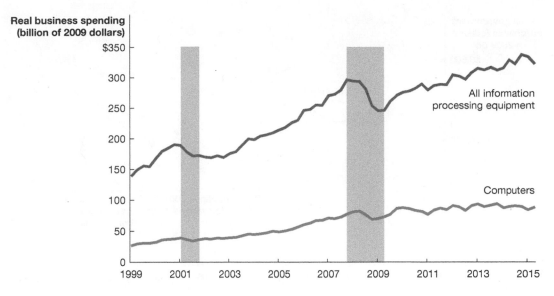

Figure 5.5   Spending on Information Processing Equipment, 1999–2015

Business spending on information processing equipment, particularly computers, has grown only slowly since the end of the recession of 2007–2009.

Source: U.S. Bureau of Economic Analysis.

The Surprisingly Slow Growth of Business Spending on Information Processing Equipment

In recent years, most businesses have increased their use of information technology in a variety of ways, including expanding their presence on the Internet, especially by using social networking apps such as Twitter, Instagram, and Facebook; designing company apps; and providing employees with tablets and smartphones. As Figure 5.5 shows, though, the focus of many businesses on information technology is not reflected in spending on information processing equipment. The blue line shows spending on computers, printers, and related equipment, while the red line shows spending on all information processing equipment, which in addition to computers, includes photocopiers, fax machines, and other office equipment. In 2015, total spending on information processing equipment had grown by less than 10 percent from its levels at the beginning of the recession in 2007. Spending on computers was also growing slowly and in 2015 was barely above 2010 levels.

A key reason for this slow growth in spending on information technology equipment is that over time, the frontier of developments in information technology has shifted away from equipment—particularly computers and servers—and toward software, such as apps used on smartphones and tablets. This shift has been bad news for firms like Intel, whose sales of processors are heavily dependent on sales of computers. Intel has had only mixed success in reducing its dependence on sales to computer manufacturers by shifting toward making components for tablets, smartwatches, and smartphones, including a modem chip for Apple's iPhone.

Government Purchases

Total government purchases include all spending by federal, local, and state governments for goods and services. Recall that government purchases do not include transfer payments, such as Social Security payments by the federal government or pension payments by local governments to retired police officers and firefighters, because the government does not receive a good or service in return (see Module 3).

Figure 5.6 shows levels of real government purchases from 1979 through the second quarter of 2015. Government purchases grew steadily for most of this period,

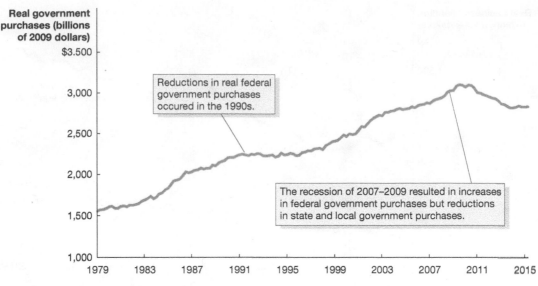

Figure 5.6 **Real Government Purchases, 1979–2015**

Government purchases grew steadily for most of the 1979–2015 period, with the exception of the early 1990s, when concern about the federal budget deficit caused real government purchases to fall for three years, beginning in 1992, and the period following the recession of 2007–2009 when many state and local governments reduced spending.

Note: The values are quarterly data, seasonally adjusted at an annual rate.

Source: U.S. Bureau of Economic Analysis.

with the exception of the early 1990s and the period following the end of the recession of 2007–2009. During the early 1990s, Congress and Presidents George H. W. Bush and Bill Clinton enacted a series of spending reductions after they became concerned that spending by the federal government was growing much faster than tax receipts. As a result, real government purchases declined for three years beginning in 1992. Contributing to the slow growth of government purchases during the 1990s was the end of the Cold War between the United States and the Soviet Union in 1989. Real federal government spending on national defense declined by 24 percent from 1990 to 1998, before rising by 60 percent between 1998 and 2010 in response to the war on terrorism and the wars in Iraq and Afghanistan. As those wars wound down, defense spending declined by 18 percent between 2010 and 2015. Total federal government purchases increased in 2009 and 2010, as President Barack Obama and Congress attempted to offset declining consumption and investment spending during the recession. Federal government purchases then declined beginning in 2011 and continuing through 2015. The recession and the slow recovery resulted in declining tax revenues to state and local governments. As a result, real state and local government purchases declined between 2009 and 2013, before increasing, along with tax revenues, beginning in 2014. MyEconLab Concept Check

Net Exports

Net exports equal exports minus imports. We can calculate net exports by taking the value of spending by foreign firms and households on goods and services produced in the United States and *subtracting* the value of spending by U.S. firms and households on goods and services produced in other countries. Figure 5.7 illustrates movements in real net exports from 1979 through the second quarter of 2015. During nearly all these years, the United States imported more goods and services than it exported, so net exports were negative. Net exports usually increase when the U.S. economy is in a recession—although they fell during the 2001 recession—and fall when the U.S. economy is in an expansion.

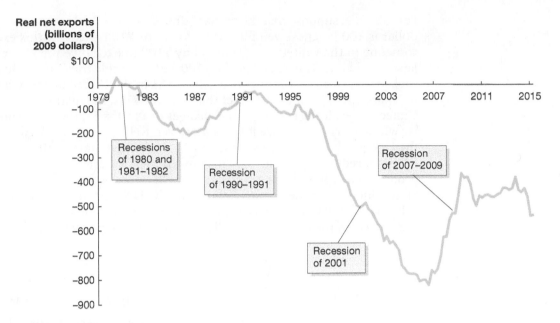

Figure 5.7   **Real Net Exports, 1979–2015**

Net exports were negative in most years between 1979 and 2015. Net exports have usually increased when the U.S. economy is in a recession and decreased when the U.S. economy is in an expansion, although they fell during the 2001 recession.

Note: The values are quarterly data, seasonally adjusted at an annual rate.

Source: U.S. Bureau of Economic Analysis.

The following are the three most important variables that determine the level of net exports:

1. The price level in the United States relative to the price levels in other countries
2. The growth rate of GDP in the United States relative to the growth rates of GDP in other countries
3. The exchange rate between the dollar and other currencies

The Price Level in the United States Relative to the Price Levels in Other Countries
If inflation in the United States is lower than inflation in other countries, prices of U.S. products increase more slowly than the prices of products in other countries. This slower increase in the U.S. price level increases the demand for U.S. products relative to the demand for foreign products. So, U.S. exports increase and U.S. imports decrease, which increases net exports. The reverse happens during periods when the inflation rate in the United States is higher than the inflation rates in other countries: U.S. exports decrease and U.S. imports increase, which decreases net exports.

The Growth Rate of GDP in the United States Relative to the Growth Rates of GDP in Other Countries
As GDP increases in the United States, the incomes of households rise, leading them to increase their purchases of goods and services. Some of the additional goods and services purchased with rising incomes are produced in the United States, but some are imported. When incomes rise faster in the United States than in other countries, U.S. consumers' purchases of foreign goods and services increase faster than foreign consumers' purchases of U.S. goods and services. As a result, net exports fall. When incomes in the United States rise more slowly than incomes in other countries, net exports rise.

The Exchange Rate between the Dollar and Other Currencies
As the value of the U.S. dollar rises, the foreign currency price of U.S. products sold in other countries rises, and the dollar price of foreign products sold in the United States falls.

For example, suppose that the exchange rate between the Japanese yen and the U.S. dollar is 100 Japanese yen for 1 U.S. dollar, or ¥100 = $1. At this exchange rate, someone in the United States could buy ¥100 in exchange for $1, or someone in Japan could buy $1 in exchange for ¥100. Leaving aside transportation costs, at this exchange rate, a U.S. product that sells for $1 in the United States will sell for ¥100 in Japan, and a Japanese product that sells for ¥100 in Japan will sell for $1 in the United States. If the exchange rate changes to ¥150 = $1, then the value of the dollar will have risen because it takes more yen to buy $1. At the new exchange rate, the U.S. product that still sells for $1 in the United States will now sell for ¥150 in Japan, reducing the quantity demanded by Japanese consumers. The Japanese product that still sells for ¥100 in Japan will now sell for only $0.67 in the United States, increasing the quantity demanded by U.S. consumers. An increase in the value of the dollar will reduce exports and increase imports, so net exports will fall. A decrease in the value of the dollar will increase exports and reduce imports, so net exports will rise.   MyEconLab Concept Check

Making the Connection

MyEconLab Video

The box says iPhones are made in China, but are they?

The iPhone Is Made in China ... or Is It?

Designers and software engineers at Apple in Cupertino, California, designed the iPhone. However, the iPhone is sold in a box labeled "Made in China." The price of the iPhone when it is shipped from a factory in China is about $275. (The retail price is higher because Apple adds a markup, as do Best Buy and other stores that sell the iPhone.) So if you buy an iPhone, the purchase enters the GDP statistics as a $275 import to the United States from China. Recently, economists have begun to question whether the standard way of keeping track of imports and exports accurately reflects how modern businesses operate.

The iPhone contains components that are produced by a number of firms, based in several different countries, including the United States. Apple uses this *global supply chain* to take advantage of both lower production costs in other countries and the ability of different firms to use their engineering and manufacturing skills to produce the iPhone's many components. Apple arranges for these firms to ship the components to factories in China for final assembly. These Chinese factories are owned by Foxconn, a firm based in Taiwan. So, only final assembly of the iPhone takes place in China; no Chinese firm makes any of the iPhone's components.

How much of the price of the iPhone is accounted for by the value of final assembly? According to a study by economists Yuqing Xing and Neal Detert of the Asian Development Bank, less than 4 percent. In fact, they note that the value of the iPhone components China imports from U.S. firms is greater than the value of assembling the iPhones in Chinese factories. As measured in the GDP statistics, in 2015 the United States imported more than $20 billion worth of iPhones from China. In fact, most of that $20 billion represents the value of the iPhone's components, none of which are made in China.

The current system of accounting for imports and exports in the GDP statistics dates to a time when most products were produced entirely within one country. So a good the United States imported from France or Japan would have been produced completely in that country. As large firms have increasingly relied on global supply chains, the statistics on imports and exports have failed to keep up. As Pascal Lamy of the World Trade Organization put it: "The concept of country of origin for manufactured goods has gradually become obsolete." In other words, "trade statistics can mislead as much as inform," as economists Kenneth Kraemer of the University of

California, Irvine, Greg Linden of the University of California, Berkeley, and Jason Dedrick of Syracuse University put it. The U.S. Bureau of Economic Analysis and the government statistical agencies in other countries are all aware of the flaws that have developed in accounting for imports and exports. But the complexity of global supply chains makes it difficult to develop more accurate measures of imports and exports.

Sources: Izabella Kaminska, "iPhone6, the GDP Effect," ftalphaville.ft.com, September 2, 2014; Phil Izzo, "Who Gets Credit for iPhone Trade," *Wall Street Journal*, March 17, 2012; Kenneth L. Kraemer, Greg Linden, and Jason Dedrick, "Capturing Value in Global Networks: Apple's iPad and iPhone," University of California, Irvine, Working paper, July 2011; Yuqing Xing and Neal Detert, "How the iPhone Widens the United States Trade Deficit with the People's Republic of China," ADBI Working Paper Series, No. 257, May 2011; and Andrew Batson, "Not Really, 'Made in China,'" *Wall Street Journal*, December 15, 2010.

Your Turn: Test your understanding by doing related problems 2.13 and 2.14 on page 210 at the end of this module.

MyEconLab Study Plan

Graphing Macroeconomic Equilibrium

5.3 LEARNING OBJECTIVE: Use a 45°-line diagram to illustrate macroeconomic equilibrium.

Having examined the components of aggregate expenditure, we can now look more closely at macroeconomic equilibrium. We saw earlier in the module that macroeconomic equilibrium occurs when GDP is equal to aggregate expenditure. We can use a graph called the *45°-line diagram* to illustrate macroeconomic equilibrium. (The 45°-line diagram is also sometimes called the *Keynesian cross* because it is based on the analysis of John Maynard Keynes.) To become familiar with this diagram, consider Figure 5.8, which is a 45°-line diagram that shows the relationship between the quantity of Pepsi sold (on the vertical axis) and the quantity of Pepsi produced (on the horizontal axis).

The line on the diagram forms an angle of 45° with the horizontal axis. The line represents all the points that are equal distances from both axes. So, points such as

MyEconLab Animation

Figure 5.8

An Example of a 45°-Line Diagram

The 45° line shows all the points that are equal distances from both axes. Points such as *A* and *B*, at which the quantity produced equals the quantity sold, are on the 45° line. Points such as *C*, at which the quantity sold is greater than the quantity produced, lie above the line. Points such as *D*, at which the quantity sold is less than the quantity produced, lie below the line.

Figure 5.9

The Relationship between Planned Aggregate Expenditure and GDP on a 45°-Line Diagram

Every point of macroeconomic equilibrium is on the 45° line, where planned aggregate expenditure equals GDP. At points above the line, planned aggregate expenditure is greater than GDP. At points below the line, planned aggregate expenditure is less than GDP.

A and B, where the number of bottles of Pepsi produced equals the number of bottles sold, are on the 45° line. Points such as C, where the quantity sold is greater than the quantity produced, lie above the line. Points such as D, where the quantity sold is less than the quantity produced, lie below the line.

Figure 5.9 is similar to Figure 5.8 except that it measures real national income, or real GDP (Y), on the horizontal axis and planned real aggregate expenditure (AE) on the vertical axis. Because macroeconomic equilibrium occurs where planned aggregate expenditure equals GDP, *we know that all points of macroeconomic equilibrium must lie along the 45° line.* For all points above the 45° line, planned aggregate expenditure will be greater than GDP. For all points below the 45° line, planned aggregate expenditure will be less than GDP.

The 45° line shows many potential points of macroeconomic equilibrium. During any particular year, only one of these points will represent the actual level of equilibrium real GDP, given the actual level of planned real expenditure. To determine this point, we need to draw a line on the graph to represent the *aggregate expenditure function,* which shows the amount of planned aggregate expenditure that will occur at every level of national income, or GDP.

Changes in GDP have a much greater effect on consumption than on planned investment, government purchases, or net exports. For simplicity, we assume that changes in GDP have no effect on planned investment, government purchases, or net exports. We also assume that the other variables that determine planned investment, government purchases, and net exports all remain constant, as do the variables other than GDP that affect consumption. For example, we assume that a firm's level of planned investment at the beginning of the year will not change during the year, even if the level of GDP changes.

Figure 5.10 shows the aggregate expenditure function on the 45°-line diagram. The lowest upward-sloping line, C, represents the consumption function, as shown in Figure 5.2, panel (b), on page 180. The quantities of planned investment, government purchases, and net exports are constant because we assumed that the variables they depend on are constant. So, the level of planned aggregate expenditure at any

MyEconLab Animation

Figure 5.10

Macroeconomic Equilibrium on the 45°-Line Diagram

Macroeconomic equilibrium occurs where the aggregate expenditure (AE) line crosses the 45° line. The lowest upward-sloping line, C, represents the consumption function. The quantities of planned investment, government purchases, and net exports are constant because we assumed that the variables they depend on are constant. So, the total of planned aggregate expenditure at any level of GDP is the amount of consumption at that level of GDP plus the sum of the constant amounts of planned investment, government purchases, and net exports. We successively add each component of spending to the consumption function line to arrive at the gray line representing aggregate expenditure.

level of GDP is the amount of consumption spending at that level of GDP plus the sum of the constant amounts of planned investment, government purchases, and net exports. In Figure 5.10, we add each component of spending successively to the consumption function line to arrive at the line representing planned aggregate expenditure (AE). The C + I line is higher than the C line by the constant amount of planned investment; the C + I + G line is higher than the C + I line by the constant amount of government purchases; and the C + I + G + NX line is higher than the C + I + G line by the constant amount of NX. (In many years, however, NX is negative, which would cause the C + I + G + NX line to be *below* the C + I + G line.) The C + I + G + NX line shows all four components of expenditure and is the aggregate expenditure (AE) function. At the point where the AE line crosses the 45° line, planned aggregate expenditure is equal to GDP, and the economy is in macroeconomic equilibrium.

Figure 5.11 makes the relationship between planned aggregate expenditure and GDP clearer by showing only the 45° line and the AE line. The figure shows that the AE line intersects the 45° line at a level of real GDP of $10 trillion. Therefore, $10 trillion represents the equilibrium level of real GDP. To see why, consider the situation if real GDP were only $8 trillion. By moving vertically from $8 trillion on the horizontal axis up to the AE line, we see that planned aggregate expenditure will be greater than $8 trillion at this level of real GDP. Whenever total spending is greater than total production, firms' inventories will fall. The fall in inventories is equal to the vertical distance between the AE line, which shows the level of total spending, and the 45° line, which shows the $8 trillion of total production. Unplanned declines in inventories lead firms to increase their production. As real GDP increases from $8 trillion, so will total income and, therefore, consumption. The economy will move up the AE line as consumption increases. The gap between total spending and total production will fall, but as long as the AE line is above the 45° line, inventories will continue to decline, and firms will

Figure 5.11

Macroeconomic Equilibrium

Macroeconomic equilibrium occurs where the *AE* line crosses the 45° line, which occurs at GDP of $10 trillion. If GDP is less than $10 trillion, the corresponding point on the *AE* line is above the 45° line, planned aggregate expenditure is greater than total production, firms will experience an unplanned decrease in inventories, and GDP will increase. If GDP is greater than $10 trillion, the corresponding point on the *AE* line is below the 45° line, planned aggregate expenditure is less than total production, firms will experience an unplanned increase in inventories, and GDP will decrease.

continue to expand production. When real GDP rises to $10 trillion, inventories stop falling, and the economy will be in macroeconomic equilibrium.

As Figure 5.11 shows, if GDP is initially $12 trillion, planned aggregate expenditure will be less than GDP, and firms will experience an unplanned increase in inventories. Rising inventories lead firms to decrease production. As GDP falls from $12 trillion, consumption will also fall, which causes the economy to move down the *AE* line. The gap between planned aggregate expenditure and GDP will fall, but as long as the *AE* line is below the 45° line, inventories will continue to rise, and firms will continue to cut production. When GDP falls to $10 trillion, inventories will stop rising, and the economy will be in macroeconomic equilibrium.

Showing a Recession on the 45°-Line Diagram

Notice that *macroeconomic equilibrium can occur at any point on the 45° line*. Ideally, equilibrium will occur at *potential GDP*. At potential GDP, firms will be operating at their normal level of capacity, and the economy will be at the *natural rate of unemployment*. As we have seen, at the natural rate of unemployment, the economy will be at *full employment*: Everyone in the labor force who wants a job will have one, except the structurally and frictionally unemployed (see Modules 1 and 2). However, for equilibrium to occur at potential GDP, planned aggregate expenditure must be high enough. As Figure 5.12 shows, if there is insufficient total spending, equilibrium will occur at a lower level of real GDP. In this situation, many firms will be operating below their normal capacity, and the unemployment rate will be above the natural rate of unemployment.

Suppose that the level of potential GDP is $10 trillion. As Figure 5.12 shows, when GDP is $10 trillion, planned aggregate expenditure is below $10 trillion, perhaps because firms have become pessimistic about their future profitability and have reduced their investment spending. The shortfall in planned aggregate expenditure

Figure 5.12

Showing a Recession on the 45°-Line Diagram

When the aggregate expenditure line intersects the 45° line at a level of GDP below potential GDP, the economy is in recession. The figure shows that potential GDP is $10 trillion, but because planned aggregate expenditure is too low, the equilibrium level of GDP is only $9.8 trillion, where the *AE* line intersects the 45° line. As a result, some firms will be operating below their normal capacity, and unemployment will be above the natural rate of unemployment. We can measure the shortfall in planned aggregate expenditure as the vertical distance between the *AE* line and the 45° line at the level of potential GDP.

that leads to the recession can be measured as the vertical distance between the *AE* line and the 45° line at the level of potential GDP. The shortfall in planned aggregate expenditure is exactly equal to the unplanned increase in inventories that would occur if the economy were initially at a level of GDP of $10 trillion. The unplanned increase in inventories measures the amount by which current planned aggregate expenditure is too low for the current level of production to be the equilibrium level. Put another way, if any of the four components of aggregate expenditure increased by this amount, the *AE* line would shift upward and intersect the 45° line at GDP of $10 trillion, and the economy would be in macroeconomic equilibrium at full employment.

Figure 5.12 shows that macroeconomic equilibrium will occur when real GDP is $9.8 trillion. Because real GDP is 2 percent below potential GDP of $10 trillion, many firms will be operating below their normal capacity, and the unemployment rate will be well above the natural rate of unemployment. The economy will remain at this level of real GDP until there is an increase in one or more of the components of aggregate expenditure.   MyEconLab Concept Check

The Important Role of Inventories

Whenever planned aggregate expenditure is less than real GDP, some firms will experience unplanned increases in inventories. If firms do not cut back their production promptly when spending declines, they will accumulate inventories. If firms accumulate excess inventories, then even if spending quickly returns to its normal level, firms will have to sell their excess inventories before they can return to producing at normal levels. For example, more than half of the sharp 5.4 percent annual rate of decline in real GDP during the first quarter of 2009 resulted from firms cutting production as they sold off unintended accumulations of inventories.   MyEconLab Concept Check

Table 5.3   **Macroeconomic Equilibrium**

Real GDP (Y)	Consumption (C)	Planned Investment (I)	Government Purchases (G)	Net Exports (NX)	Planned Aggregate Expenditure (AE)	Unplanned Change in Inventories	Real GDP Will . . .
$8,000	$6,200	$1,500	$1,500	−$500	$8,700	−$700	increase
9,000	6,850	1,500	1,500	−500	9,350	−350	increase
10,000	7,500	1,500	1,500	−500	10,000	0	be in equilibrium
11,000	8,150	1,500	1,500	−500	10,650	+350	decrease
12,000	8,800	1,500	1,500	−500	11,300	+700	decrease

Note: The values are in billions of 2009 dollars.

A Numerical Example of Macroeconomic Equilibrium

In forecasting real GDP, economists rely on quantitative models of the economy. We can increase our understanding of the causes of changes in real GDP by considering a simple numerical example of macroeconomic equilibrium. Although simplified, this example captures some of the key features contained in the quantitative models that economic forecasters use. Table 5.3 shows several hypothetical combinations of real GDP and planned aggregate expenditure. The first column lists real GDP. The next four columns list levels of the four components of planned aggregate expenditure that occur at the corresponding level of real GDP. We assume that planned investment, government purchases, and net exports do not change as GDP changes. Because consumption depends on GDP, it increases as GDP increases.

Don't Let This Happen to You

Don't Confuse Aggregate Expenditure with Consumption Spending

Macroeconomic equilibrium occurs where planned aggregate expenditure equals GDP. But remember that planned aggregate expenditure equals the sum of consumption spending, planned investment spending, government purchases, and net exports, *not* consumption spending alone. If GDP were equal to consumption, the economy would not be in equilibrium. Planned investment plus government purchases plus net exports will always be a positive number. Therefore, if consumption were equal to GDP, aggregate expenditure would have to be greater than GDP. In that case, inventories would be decreasing, and GDP would be *increasing*; GDP would not be in equilibrium.

Test your understanding of macroeconomic equilibrium with this problem:

Question: Do you agree with the following argument?

This module says macroeconomic equilibrium occurs where planned aggregate expenditure equals GDP. GDP is equal to national income. So, at equilibrium, planned aggregate expenditure must equal national income. But we know

that consumers do not spend all of their income: They save at least some and use some to pay taxes. Therefore, aggregate expenditure will never equal national income, and the basic macroeconomic story is incorrect.

Answer: Remember that national income equals GDP (disregarding depreciation, as we have done throughout this module). So, it is correct to say that in macroeconomic equilibrium, planned aggregate expenditure must equal national income. But the last sentence of the argument is incorrect because it assumes that aggregate expenditure is the same as consumption spending. Because of saving and taxes, consumption spending is always much less than national income, but in equilibrium, the sum of consumption spending, planned investment spending, government purchases, and net exports does, in fact, equal GDP and national income. So, the argument is incorrect because it confuses consumption spending with aggregate expenditure.

MyEconLab Study Plan

Your Turn: Test your understanding by doing related problem 3.11 on page 211 at the end of this module.

In the first row of the table, GDP of $8,000 billion (or $8 trillion) results in consumption of $6,200 billion. Adding consumption, planned investment, government purchases, and net exports across the row gives planned aggregate expenditure of $8,700 billion, which is shown in the sixth column. Because planned aggregate expenditure is greater than GDP, inventories will fall by $700 billion. This unplanned decline in inventories will lead firms to increase production, and GDP will increase. GDP will continue to increase until it reaches $10,000 billion. At that level of GDP, planned aggregate expenditure is also $10,000 billion, unplanned changes in inventories are zero, and the economy is in macroeconomic equilibrium.

In the last row, GDP of $12,000 billion results in consumption of $8,800 billion and planned aggregate expenditure of $11,300 billion. Because planned aggregate expenditure is less than GDP, inventories will increase by $700 billion. This unplanned increase in inventories will lead firms to decrease production, and GDP will decrease. GDP will continue to decrease until it reaches $10,000 billion, unplanned changes in inventories are zero, and the economy is in macroeconomic equilibrium.

Only when real GDP equals $10,000 billion will the economy be in macroeconomic equilibrium. At other levels of real GDP, planned aggregate expenditure will be higher or lower than GDP, and the economy will be expanding or contracting. MyEconLab Concept Check

---

Solved Problem 5.3

MyEconLab Interactive Animation

Determining Macroeconomic Equilibrium

Fill in the blank cells in the following table and determine the equilibrium level of real GDP.

Real GDP (Y)	Consumption (C)	Planned Investment (I)	Government Purchases (G)	Net Exports (NX)	Planned Aggregate Expenditure (AE)	Unplanned Change in Inventories
$8,000	$6,200	$1,675	$1,675	−$500		
9,000	6,850	1,675	1,675	−500		
10,000	7,500	1,675	1,675	−500		
11,000	8,150	1,675	1,675	−500		
12,000	8,800	1,675	1,675	−500		

Solving the Problem

Step 1: **Review the module material.** This problem is about determining macroeconomic equilibrium, so you may want to review the section "A Numerical Example of Macroeconomic Equilibrium," which begins on page 196.

Step 2: **Fill in the missing values in the table.** We can calculate the missing values in the last two columns by using two equations:

Planned aggregate expenditure (AE) = Consumption (C)
  + Planned investment (I) + Government purchases (G)
  + Net exports (NX)

and:

Unplanned change in inventories = Real GDP (Y)
  − Planned aggregate expenditure (AE).

For example, to fill in the first row, we have AE = $6,200 billion + $1,675 billion + $1,675 billion + (−$500 billion) = $9,050 billion, and unplanned change in inventories = $8,000 billion − $9,050 billion = −$1,050 billion.

Real GDP (Y)	Consumption (C)	Planned Investment (I)	Government Purchases (G)	Net Exports (NX)	Planned Aggregate Expenditure (AE)	Unplanned Change in Inventories
$8,000	$6,200	$1,675	$1,675	−$500	$9,050	−1,050
9,000	6,850	1,675	1,675	−500	9,700	−700
10,000	7,500	1,675	1,675	−500	10,350	−350
11,000	8,150	1,675	1,675	−500	11,000	0
12,000	8,800	1,675	1,675	−500	11,650	350

Step 3: **Determine the equilibrium level of real GDP.** Once you fill in the table, you should see that equilibrium real GDP must be $11,000 billion because only at that level is real GDP equal to planned aggregate expenditure.

MyEconLab Study Plan

Your Turn: For more practice, do related problem 3.12 on page 211 at the end of this module.

 5.4

The Multiplier Effect

LEARNING OBJECTIVE: Describe the multiplier effect and use the multiplier formula to calculate changes in equilibrium GDP.

So far, we have seen that aggregate expenditure determines real GDP in the short run, and we have seen how the economy adjusts if it is not in equilibrium. We have also seen that whenever aggregate expenditure changes, there will be a new level of equilibrium real GDP. In this section, we will look more closely at the effects of a change in aggregate expenditure on equilibrium real GDP. We begin the discussion with Figure 5.13, which illustrates the effect of an increase in planned investment spending. We assume that the economy starts in equilibrium at point A, at which real GDP is $9.6 trillion. Firms then become more optimistic about the future profitability of investment and increase spending on factories, machinery, and equipment by $100 billion. This increase in investment spending shifts the AE line up by

MyEconLab Animation

Figure 5.13

The Multiplier Effect

The economy begins at point A, at which equilibrium real GDP is $9.6 trillion. A $100 billion increase in planned investment shifts up aggregate expenditure from AE_1 to AE_2. The new equilibrium is at point B, where real GDP is $10.0 trillion, which is potential real GDP. Because of the multiplier effect, a $100 billion increase in investment results in a $400 billion increase in equilibrium real GDP.

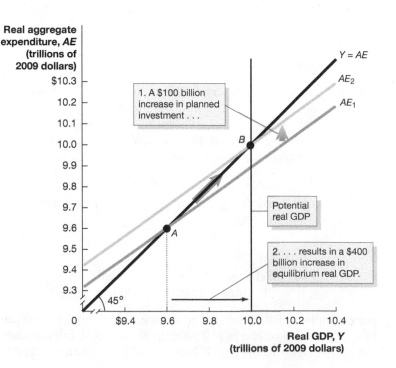

$100 billion, from AE_1 to AE_2. The new equilibrium occurs at point *B*, at which real GDP is $10.0 trillion, which equals potential real GDP.

Notice that the initial $100 billion increase in planned investment spending results in a $400 billion increase in equilibrium real GDP. The increase in planned investment spending has had a *multiplied effect* on equilibrium real GDP. It is not only investment spending that will have this multiplied effect; any increase in *autonomous expenditure* will shift up the aggregate expenditure function and lead to a multiplied increase in equilibrium GDP. **Autonomous expenditure** does not depend on the level of GDP. In the aggregate expenditure model we have been using, planned investment spending, government spending, and net exports are all autonomous expenditures. Consumption has both an autonomous component, which does not depend on the level of GDP, and a nonautonomous—or *induced*—component, which does depend on the level of GDP. For example, if households decide to spend more of their incomes—and save less—at every level of income, there will be an autonomous increase in consumption spending, and the aggregate expenditure function will shift up. If, however, real GDP increases and households increase their consumption spending, as indicated by the consumption function, there will be a movement up along the aggregate expenditure function, and the increase in consumption spending will be nonautonomous.

The ratio of the increase in equilibrium real GDP to the increase in autonomous expenditure is called the **multiplier**. The series of induced increases in consumption spending that results from an initial increase in autonomous expenditure is called the **multiplier effect**. The multiplier effect occurs because an initial increase in autonomous expenditure sets off a series of increases in real GDP.

We can look more closely at the multiplier effect. Suppose the whole $100 billion increase in investment spending shown in Figure 5.13 consists of firms building additional factories and office buildings. Initially, this additional spending will cause the construction of factories and office buildings to increase by $100 billion, so GDP will also increase by $100 billion. Remember that increases in production result in equal increases in national income. So, this increase in real GDP of $100 billion is also an increase in national income of $100 billion. In this example, the income is received as wages and salaries by the employees of the construction firms, as profit by the owners of the firms, and so on. After receiving this additional income, these workers, managers, and owners will increase their consumption of cars, appliances, furniture, and many other products. If the marginal propensity to consume (*MPC*) is 0.75, we know the increase in consumption spending will be $75 billion. This additional $75 billion in spending will cause the firms making the cars, appliances, and other products to increase production by $75 billion, so GDP will rise by $75 billion. This increase in GDP means national income has also increased by another $75 billion. This increased income will be received by the owners and employees of the firms producing the cars, appliances, and other products. These workers, managers, and owners in turn will increase their consumption spending, and the process of increasing production, income, and consumption will continue.

Eventually, the total increase in consumption will be $300 billion. (We will soon show how we determined this value.) The $300 billion increase in consumption combined with the initial $100 billion increase in investment spending will result in a total change in equilibrium GDP of $400 billion. Table 5.4 summarizes how changes in GDP and spending caused by the initial $100 billion increase in investment will result in equilibrium GDP rising by $400 billion. We can think of the multiplier effect occurring in rounds of spending. In round 1, there is an increase of $100 billion in autonomous expenditure—the $100 billion in planned investment spending in our example—which causes GDP to rise by $100 billion. In round 2, induced expenditure rises by $75 billion (which equals the $100 billion increase in real GDP in round 1 multiplied by the *MPC*). The $75 billion in induced expenditure in round 2 causes a $75 billion increase in real GDP, which leads to a $56 billion increase in induced expenditure in round 3, and so on. The final column adds up the total increases in expenditure, which equal the total increase in GDP. In each round, the additional induced

Autonomous expenditure An expenditure that does not depend on the level of GDP.

Multiplier The increase in equilibrium real GDP divided by the increase in autonomous expenditure.

Multiplier effect The process by which an increase in autonomous expenditure leads to a larger increase in real GDP.

Table 5.4

The Multiplier Effect in Action

	Additional Autonomous Expenditure (investment)	Additional Induced Expenditure (consumption)	Total Additional Expenditure = Total Additional GDP
Round 1	$100 billion	$0	$100 billion
Round 2	0	75 billion	175 billion
Round 3	0	56 billion	231 billion
Round 4	0	42 billion	273 billion
Round 5	0	32 billion	305 billion
.	.	.	.
.	.	.	.
Round 10	0	8 billion	377 billion
.	.	.	.
Round 15	0	2 billion	395 billion
.	.	.	.
.	.	.	.
Round 19	0	1 billion	398 billion
.	.	.	.
.	.	.	.
Round n	0	0	400 billion

expenditure becomes smaller because the *MPC* is less than 1. By round 10, additional induced expenditure is only $8 billion, and the total increase in GDP from the beginning of the process is $377 billion. By round 19, the process is almost complete: Additional induced expenditure is only about $1 billion, and the total increase in GDP is $398 billion. Eventually, the process will be finished, although we cannot say precisely how many spending rounds it will take, so we simply label the last round *n* rather than give it a specific number.

We can calculate the value of the multiplier in our example by dividing the increase in equilibrium real GDP by the increase in autonomous expenditure:

$$\frac{\Delta Y}{\Delta I} = \frac{\text{Change in real GDP}}{\text{Change in investment spending}} = \frac{\$400 \text{ billion}}{\$100 \text{ billion}} = 4.$$

With a multiplier of 4, each increase in autonomous expenditure of $1 will result in an increase in equilibrium GDP of $4.

Making the Connection

MyEconLab Video

The Multiplier in Reverse: The Great Depression of the 1930s

An increase in autonomous expenditure causes an increase in equilibrium real GDP, but the reverse is also true: A decrease in autonomous expenditure causes a decrease in real GDP. Many Americans became aware of this fact in the 1930s, when reductions in autonomous expenditure were magnified by the multiplier into the largest decline in real GDP in U.S. history.

In August 1929, the economy reached a business cycle peak, and a downturn in production began. In October, the stock market crashed, destroying billions of dollars of wealth and increasing pessimism among households and firms. Both consumption spending and planned investment spending declined. The passage by the U.S. Congress of the Smoot-Hawley Tariff Act in June 1930 helped set off a trade war that reduced exports. A series of banking crises that began in the fall of 1930 limited the ability of households and firms to finance consumption and investment. As aggregate expenditure declined, many firms experienced declining sales and began to lay off workers. Falling levels of production and income induced further declines in consumption spending, which led to further cutbacks in production and employment, leading to further declines in income, and so on, in a downward spiral. The following table shows the severity of the economic downturn by contrasting the business cycle peak of 1929 with the business cycle trough of 1933:

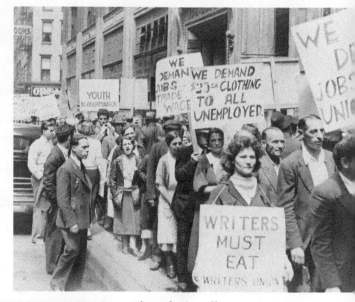

Year	Consumption	Investment	Exports	Real GDP	Unemployment Rate
1929	$781 billion	$124 billion	$41 billion	$1,057 billion	2.9%
1933	$638 billion	$27 billion	$22 billion	$778 billion	20.9%

Note: The values are in 2009 dollars.

Sources: U.S. Bureau of Economic Analysis; and David R. Weir, "A Century of U.S. Unemployment, 1890–1990," in Roger L. Ransom, Richard Sutch, and Susan B. Carter, eds., *Research in Economic History*, Vol. 14, San Diego, CA: JAI Press, 1992, Table D3, pp. 341–343.

We can use a 45°-line diagram to illustrate the multiplier effect working in reverse during these years. The economy was at potential real GDP in 1929, before the declines in aggregate expenditure began. Declining consumption, planned investment, and net exports shifted the aggregate expenditure function down from AE_{1929} to AE_{1933}, reducing equilibrium real GDP from $1,057 billion in 1929 to $778 billion in 1933. The depth and length of this economic downturn led to its being labeled the Great Depression.

The multiplier effect contributed to the very high levels of unemployment during the Great Depression.

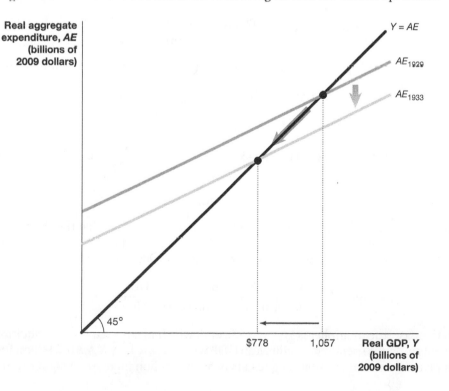

The severity of the Great Depression forced thousands of firms to declare bankruptcy. Even firms that survived experienced sharp declines in sales. By 1933, production at U.S. Steel had declined 90 percent, and production at General Motors had declined more than 75 percent. High rates of unemployment forced many families into poverty and a daily struggle for survival. Recovery from the business cycle trough in 1933 was slow. Real GDP did not regain its 1929 level until 1936, and a growing labor force meant that the unemployment rate did not return to its 1929 level until 1942, after the United States entered World War II.

MyEconLab Study Plan

Your Turn: Test your understanding by doing related problem 4.6 on page 212 at the end of this module.

A Formula for the Multiplier

Table 5.4 on page 200 shows that during the multiplier process, each round of increases in consumption is smaller than in the previous round, so eventually, the increases will come to an end, and we will have a new macroeconomic equilibrium. But how do we know that when we add all the increases in GDP, the total will be $400 billion? We can verify this result by first writing out the total change in equilibrium GDP:

> The total change in equilibrium real GDP equals the initial increase in planned investment spending $= 100$ billion
>
> *Plus* the first induced increase in consumption $= MPC \times \$100$ billion
>
> *Plus* the second induced increase in consumption $= MPC \times (MPC \times \$100$ billion$)$
> $= MPC^2 \times \$100$ billion
>
> *Plus* the third induced increase in consumption $= MPC \times (MPC^2 \times \$100$ billion$)$
> $= MPC^3 \times \$100$ billion
>
> *Plus* the fourth induced increase in consumption $= MPC \times (MPC^3 \times \$100$ billion$)$
> $= MPC^4 \times \$100$ billion

and so on ...

Or:

> Total change in GDP $= \$100$ billion $+ (MPC \times \$100$ billion$) + (MPC^2 \times \$100$ billion$) + (MPC^3 \times \$100$ billion$) + (MPC^4 \times \$100$ billion$) + \ldots$

where the ellipsis (...) indicates that the expression contains an infinite number of similar terms.

If we factor out the $100 billion from each expression, we have:

> Total change in GDP $= \$100$ billion $\times (1 + MPC + MPC^2 + MPC^3 + MPC^4 + \ldots)$

Mathematicians have shown that an expression like the one in the parentheses sums to:

$$\frac{1}{1 - MPC}.$$

In this case, the MPC is equal to 0.75. So, we can now calculate that the change in equilibrium GDP $= \$100$ billion $\times [1/(1 - 0.75)] = \$100$ billion $\times 4 = \$400$ billion, as shown in Table 5.4. We have also derived a general formula for the multiplier:

$$\text{Multiplier} = \frac{\text{Change in equilibrium real GDP}}{\text{Change in autonomous expenditure}} = \frac{1}{1 - MPC}.$$

In this case, the multiplier is $1/(1 - 0.75)$, or 4, which means that for each additional $1 of autonomous spending, equilibrium GDP will increase by $4. A $100 billion increase in planned investment spending results in a $400 billion increase in equilibrium GDP.

Notice that the value of the multiplier depends on the value of the MPC. In particular, the larger the value of the MPC, the larger the value of the multiplier. For example, if the MPC were 0.9 instead of 0.75, the value of the multiplier would increase from 4 to $1/(1 - 0.9) = 10$. MyEconLab Concept Check

Summarizing the Multiplier Effect

You should note four key points about the multiplier effect:

1. The multiplier effect occurs both when autonomous expenditure increases and when it decreases. For example, with an MPC of 0.75, a *decrease* in planned investment of $100 billion will lead to a *decrease* in equilibrium income of $400 billion.

2. The multiplier effect makes the economy more sensitive to changes in autonomous expenditure than it would otherwise be. Between the fourth quarter of 2005 and the second quarter of 2009, spending on residential construction declined by 57 percent. This decline in investment set off a series of declines in production, income, and spending so that firms such as automobile dealerships and clothing stores, which are far removed from the housing industry, also experienced declines in sales. Because of the multiplier effect, a decline in spending and production in one sector of the economy can lead to declines in spending and production in many other sectors of the economy.

3. The larger the MPC, the larger the value of the multiplier. With an MPC of 0.75, the multiplier is 4, but with an MPC of 0.50, the multiplier is only 2. This direct relationship between the value of the MPC and the value of the multiplier holds true because the larger the MPC, the larger the change in consumption that takes place after each change in income during the multiplier process.

4. The formula for the multiplier, $1/(1 - MPC)$, is oversimplified because it ignores some real-world complications, such as the effect that increases in GDP have on imports, inflation, interest rates, and individual income taxes. These effects combine to cause the simple formula to overstate the true value of the multiplier. In Modules 4 and 4A, we started to take into account these real-world complications. MyEconLab Concept Check

Solved Problem 5.4

MyEconLab Interactive Animation

Using the Multiplier Formula

Use the information in the table to answer the following questions:

Real GDP (Y)	Consumption (C)	Planned Investment (I)	Government Purchases (G)	Net Exports (NX)
$8,000	$6,900	$1,000	$1,000	-$500
9,000	7,700	1,000	1,000	-500
10,000	8,500	1,000	1,000	-500
11,000	9,300	1,000	1,000	-500
12,000	10,100	1,000	1,000	-500

Note: The values are in billions of 2009 dollars.

a. What is the equilibrium level of real GDP?

b. What is the MPC?

c. Suppose government purchases increase by $200 billion. What will be the new equilibrium level of real GDP? Use the multiplier formula to determine your answer.

Solving the Problem

Step 1: **Review the module material.** This problem is about the multiplier process, so you may want to review the section "The Multiplier Effect," which begins on page 198.

Step 2: **Answer part (a) by determining equilibrium real GDP.** Just as in Solved Problem 5.2 on page 183, we can find macroeconomic equilibrium by calculating the level of planned aggregate expenditure for each level of real GDP:

Real GDP (Y)	Consumption (C)	Planned Investment (I)	Government Purchases (G)	Net Exports (NX)	Planned Aggregate Expenditure (AE)
$8,000	$6,900	$1,000	$1,000	−$500	$8,400
9,000	7,700	1,000	1,000	−500	9,200
10,000	8,500	1,000	1,000	−500	10,000
11,000	9,300	1,000	1,000	−500	10,800
12,000	10,100	1,000	1,000	−500	11,600

We can see that macroeconomic equilibrium will occur when real GDP equals $10,000 billion.

Step 3: **Answer part (b) by calculating the MPC.**

$$MPC = \frac{\Delta C}{\Delta Y}.$$

In this case:

$$MPC = \frac{\$800 \text{ billion}}{\$1,000 \text{ billion}} = 0.8.$$

Step 4: **Answer part (c) by using the multiplier formula to calculate the new equilibrium level of real GDP.** We could find the new level of equilibrium real GDP by constructing a new table with government purchases increased from $1,000 to $1,200. But the multiplier allows us to calculate the answer directly. In this case:

$$\text{Multiplier} = \frac{1}{1 - MPC} = \frac{1}{1 - 0.8} = 5.$$

So:

Change in equilibrium real GDP = Change in autonomous expenditure × 5.

Or:

Change in equilibrium real GDP = $200 billion × 5 = $1,000 billion.

Therefore:

New level of equilibrium GDP = $10,000 billion + $1,000 billion = $11,000 billion.

MyEconLab Study Plan **Your Turn:** For more practice, do related problem 4.7 on page 212 at the end of this module.

The Paradox of Thrift

We have seen that an increase in saving can increase the rate of economic growth in the long run by providing funds for investment (see Modules 1 & 2 and 3 & 3A). But in the short run, if households save more of their income and spend less of it, aggregate expenditure and real GDP will decline. In discussing the aggregate expenditure model, John Maynard Keynes argued that if many households decide at the same time to increase their saving and reduce their spending, they may make themselves worse off by causing aggregate expenditure to fall, thereby pushing the economy into a recession. The lower incomes in the recession might mean that total saving does not increase, despite the attempts by many individuals to increase their own saving. Keynes called this outcome the *paradox of thrift* because what appears to be something favorable to the long-run performance of the economy might be counterproductive in the short run.

Households saved very little of their income in the mid-2000s but increased their saving markedly in late 2008 and 2009. The personal saving rate is saving by households as a percentage of disposable personal income. By mid-2009, the personal saving rate had increased to 6 percent. Some economists argued that this increase in saving contributed to the recession and weak recovery by reducing consumption spending. Other economists are skeptical of the reasoning behind the paradox of thrift. An increase in saving, by increasing the supply of loanable funds, should lower the real interest rate and increase the level of investment spending. This increase in investment spending might offset some or all of the decline in consumption spending attributable to increased saving. Economists continue to debate the short-run effects of an increase in saving.   MyEconLab Concept Check   MyEconLab Study Plan

5.5 | The Aggregate Demand Curve

LEARNING OBJECTIVE: Understand the relationship between the aggregate demand curve and aggregate expenditure.

When demand for a product increases, firms usually respond by increasing production, but they are also likely to increase prices. Similarly, when demand falls, production falls, but prices may also fall. We would expect, then, that an increase or a decrease in aggregate expenditure would affect not just real GDP but also the *price level*. Will a change in the price level, in turn, affect the components of aggregate expenditure? In fact, as we will see, increases in the price level cause aggregate expenditure to fall, and decreases in the price level cause aggregate expenditure to rise. There are three main reasons for this inverse relationship between changes in the price level and changes in aggregate expenditure. We discussed the first two reasons in Section 5.2 when considering the factors that determine consumption and net exports:

1. A rising price level decreases consumption by decreasing the real value of household wealth; a falling price level has the reverse effect.

2. If the price level in the United States rises relative to the price levels in other countries, U.S. exports will become relatively more expensive, and foreign imports will become relatively less expensive, causing net exports to fall. A falling price level in the United States has the reverse effect.

3. When prices rise, firms and households need more money to finance buying and selling. If the central bank (the Federal Reserve in the United States) does not increase the money supply, the result will be an increase in the interest rate. In Module 8, we will analyze in more detail why the interest rate increases. As we discussed in Section 5.2, at a higher interest rate, investment spending falls as firms borrow less money to build new factories or to install new machinery and equipment and households borrow less money to buy new houses. A falling price level has the reverse effect: Other things being equal, interest rates will fall, and investment spending will rise.

We can now incorporate the effect of a change in the price level into the basic aggregate expenditure model, in which equilibrium real GDP is determined by the intersection of the aggregate expenditure (*AE*) line and the 45° line. Remember that we measure the price level as an index number with a value of 100 in the base year. If the price level rises from, say, 100 to 103, consumption, planned investment, and net exports will all fall, causing the *AE* line to shift down in the 45°-line diagram. The *AE* line shifts down because with higher prices, less spending will occur in the economy at every level of GDP. Panel (a) of Figure 5.14 shows that the downward shift of the *AE* line results in a lower level of equilibrium real GDP.

If the price level falls from, say, 100 to 97, then investment, consumption, and net exports will all rise. As panel (b) of Figure 5.14 shows, the *AE* line will shift up, which will cause equilibrium real GDP to increase.

(a) The effect of a higher price level on real GDP

(b) The effect of a lower price level on real GDP

Figure 5.14 **The Effect of a Change in the Price Level on Real GDP**

In panel (a), an increase in the price level results in declining consumption, planned investment, and net exports and causes the aggregate expenditure line to shift down from AE_1 to AE_2. As a result, equilibrium real GDP declines from $10.0 trillion to $9.8 trillion.

In panel (b), a decrease in the price level results in rising consumption, planned investment, and net exports and causes the aggregate expenditure line to shift up from AE_1 to AE_2. As a result, equilibrium real GDP increases from $10.0 trillion to $10.2 trillion.

Aggregate demand (AD) curve
A curve that shows the relationship between the price level and the level of planned aggregate expenditure in the economy, holding constant all other factors that affect aggregate expenditure.

Figure 5.15 summarizes the effect of changes in the price level on real GDP. The table shows the combinations of price level and real GDP from Figure 5.14. The graph plots the numbers from the table. In the graph, the price level is measured on the vertical axis, and real GDP is measured on the horizontal axis. The relationship shown in Figure 5.15 between the price level and the level of planned aggregate expenditure is known as the **aggregate demand (AD) curve**.

Figure 5.15

The Aggregate Demand Curve

The aggregate demand (AD) curve shows the relationship between the price level and the level of planned aggregate expenditure in the economy. When the price level is 97, real GDP is $10.2 trillion. An increase in the price level to 100 causes consumption, investment, and net exports to fall, which reduces real GDP to $10.0 trillion.

Price level	Equilibrium real GDP
97	$10.2 trillion
100	10.0 trillion
103	9.8 trillion

Continued from page 173

Economics in Your Life

When Consumer Confidence Falls, Is Your Job at Risk?

At the beginning of this module, we asked you to suppose that you work part time for a company that manufacturers door handles for automobiles. You have learned that consumer confidence in the economy has fallen and that many households expect their future income to be well below their current income. Should you be concerned about losing your job? We have seen in this module that if consumers expect their future income to decline, they will cut their consumption spending, and consumption spending is more than two-thirds of aggregate expenditure. So, if the decline in consumer confidence is correctly forecasting a decline in consumption spending, then aggregate expenditure and GDP will also likely decline. In deciding how likely your company is to lay you off, you should consider the following factors: If the economy moves into a recession, spending on automobiles by households and firms is likely to fall, which could reduce your firm's sales and possibly cost you a job. Before you panic, though, keep in mind that surveys of consumer confidence do not have a good track record in predicting recessions, so you may not have to move back in with your parents after all.

Conclusion

In this module, we examined a key macroeconomic idea: In the short run, the level of GDP is determined mainly by the level of aggregate expenditure. When economists forecast changes in GDP, they do so by forecasting changes in the four components of aggregate expenditure. We constructed an aggregate demand curve by taking into account how changes in the price level affect aggregate expenditure.

But our story is incomplete. In Module 4 & 4A, we will analyze the *aggregate supply curve*. Then we will use the aggregate demand curve and the aggregate supply curve to show how equilibrium real GDP and the equilibrium price level are simultaneously determined.

We also need to discuss the roles that the financial system and government policy play in determining real GDP and the price level in the short run. We will cover these important topics in the following modules.

Visit MyEconLab for a news article and analysis related to the concepts in this module.

Key Terms

Aggregate demand (*AD*) curve, p. 206

Aggregate expenditure (*AE*), p. 174

Aggregate expenditure model, p. 174

Autonomous expenditure, p. 199

Cash flow, p. 185

Consumption function, p. 179

Inventories, p. 175

Marginal propensity to consume (*MPC*), p. 180

Marginal propensity to save (*MPS*), p. 182

Multiplier, p. 199

Multiplier effect, p. 199

5.1 | ## The Aggregate Expenditure Model, pages 174–177
LEARNING OBJECTIVE: Understand how macroeconomic equilibrium is determined in the aggregate expenditure model.

Summary

Aggregate expenditure (AE) is the total amount of spending in the economy. The **aggregate expenditure model** focuses on the relationship between total spending and real GDP in the short run, assuming that the price level is constant. In any particular year, the level of GDP is determined by the level of total spending, or aggregate expenditure, in the economy. The four components of aggregate expenditure are consumption (*C*), planned investment (*I*), government purchases (*G*), and net exports (*NX*). When aggregate expenditure is greater than GDP, there is an unplanned decrease in **inventories**, which are goods that have been produced but not yet sold, and GDP and total employment will increase. When aggregate expenditure is less than GDP, there is an unplanned increase in inventories, and GDP and total employment will decline. When aggregate expenditure is equal to GDP, firms will sell what they expected to sell, production and employment will be unchanged, and the economy will be in macroeconomic equilibrium.

MyEconLab   Visit **www.myeconlab.com** to complete these exercises online and get instant feedback.

Review Questions

1.1 What is the key idea in the aggregate expenditure macroeconomic model?

1.2 What are inventories? What usually happens to inventories at the beginning of a recession? At the beginning of an expansion?

1.3 Which of the following does the aggregate expenditure model seek to explain: long-run economic growth, the business cycle, inflation, or cyclical unemployment?

Problems and Applications

1.4 Into which category of aggregate expenditure would each of the following transactions fall?
a. The Jones family buys a new car.
b. The San Diego Unified School District buys 12 new school buses.
c. The Jones family buys a newly constructed house from the Garcia Construction Co.

d. Joe Jones orders a Burberry coat from an online site in the United Kingdom.
e. Prudential insurance company purchases 250 new iPads from Apple.

1.5 Assume that Intel sells $1 billion of computer chips to Dell, Inc., for use in Dell's personal computers. How does this transaction affect aggregate expenditure?

1.6 In reporting on real GDP growth in the second quarter of 2015, an article in the *Wall Street Journal* noted that the 2.3 percent annual growth rate "would have been stronger if it hadn't been for companies drawing down inventories."
a. If companies are "drawing down inventories," is aggregate expenditure likely to have been larger or smaller than GDP?
b. Assume that the reduction in inventories was unplanned. What would you expect to happen to production in the future following an unplanned reduction in inventories?
Source: Justin Lahart, "Consumers Priming U.S. Pump," *Wall Street Journal*, July 30, 2015.

1.7 In the third quarter of 2015, business inventories in the United States increased by $62 billion. Can we tell from this information whether aggregate expenditure was higher or lower than GDP during the third quarter of 2015? If not, what other information do we need?
Source: Bureau of Economic Analysis.

1.8 An article in the *Wall Street Journal* stated that in China, "carmakers continue to grapple with ... rising inventories." Why might carmakers in China find that their inventories are unexpectedly rising? How are these carmakers likely to react to the increase in inventories?
Source: Colum Murphy, "China's Automobile Sales to Slow Further in 2015," *Wall Street Journal*, January 12, 2015.

1.9 According to an article in the *Wall Street Journal*, in late 2014, the Japanese economy experienced a large increase in business inventories. The article noted, "The large buildup of inventories is a reflection that the ... drop in demand was bigger than expected." Does it matter that Japanese firms didn't expect the drop in demand? Won't a decline in demand always lead to an increase in firms' holdings of inventories? Briefly explain.
Source: Eleanor Warnock, "Rising Inventories Hamper Japan Recovery," *Wall Street Journal*, September 30, 2014.

5.2 Determining the Level of Aggregate Expenditure in the Economy, pages 177–191

LEARNING OBJECTIVE: Discuss the determinants of the four components of aggregate expenditure and define marginal propensity to consume and marginal propensity to save.

Summary

The five determinants of consumption are current disposable income, household wealth, expected future income, the price level, and the interest rate. The **consumption function** is the relationship between consumption and disposable income. The **marginal propensity to consume (MPC)** is the change in consumption divided by the change in disposable income. The **marginal propensity to save (MPS)** is the change in saving divided by the change in disposable income. The determinants of planned investment are expectations of future profitability, the real interest rate, taxes, and **cash flow**, which is the difference between the cash revenues received by a firm and the cash spending by the firm. Government purchases include spending by the federal government and by local and state governments for goods and services. Government purchases do not include *transfer payments*, such as Social Security payments by the federal government or pension payments by local governments to retired police officers and firefighters. The three determinants of net exports are changes in the price level in the United States relative to changes in the price levels in other countries, the growth rate of GDP in the United States relative to the growth rates of GDP in other countries, and the exchange rate between the dollar and other currencies.

MyEconLab   Visit www.myeconlab.com to complete these exercises online and get instant feedback.

Review Questions

2.1 In the aggregate expenditure model, why is it important to know the factors that determine consumption spending, investment spending, government purchases, and net exports?

2.2 What are the five main determinants of consumption spending? Which of these is the most important? How would a rise in stock prices or housing prices affect consumption spending?

2.3 Compare what happened to real investment between 1979 and the second quarter of 2015 with what happened to real consumption during that period.

2.4 What are the four main determinants of investment? How would a change in interest rates affect investment?

2.5 What are the three main determinants of net exports? How would an increase in the growth rate of GDP in the BRIC nations (Brazil, Russia, India, and China) affect U.S. net exports?

Problems and Applications

2.6 **(Related to the** Module Opener **on page 183)** Suppose a major U.S. appliance manufacturer is forecasting demand for its products during the next year. How will the forecast be affected by each of the following?
a. A survey shows a sharp rise in consumer confidence that income growth will be increasing.

b. Real interest rates are expected to increase.
c. The value of the U.S. dollar is expected to increase versus foreign currencies.
d. Planned investment spending in the economy is expected to decrease.

2.7 Draw the consumption function and label each axis. Show the effect of an increase in income on consumption spending. Does the change in income cause a movement along the consumption function or a shift of the consumption function? How would an increase in expected future income or an increase in household wealth affect the consumption function? Would these increases cause a movement along the consumption function or a shift of the consumption function? Briefly explain.

2.8 An economics student raises the following objection: "The textbook said that a higher interest rate lowers investment, but this doesn't make sense. I know that if I can get a higher interest rate, I am certainly going to invest more in my savings account." Briefly explain whether you agree with this reasoning.

2.9 Unemployed workers receive unemployment insurance payments from the government. Does the existence of unemployment insurance make it likely that consumption will fluctuate more or less over the business cycle than it would in the absence of unemployment insurance? Briefly explain.

2.10 **(Related to** Solved Problem 5.2 **on page 183)** Fill in the blank cells in the following table. Assume for simplicity that taxes are zero. Also assume that the values represent billions of 2009 dollars.

National Income and Real GDP (Y)	Consumption (C)	Saving (S)	Marginal Propensity to Consume (MPC)	Marginal Propensity to Save (MPS)
$9,000	$8,000			
10,000	8,750			
11,000	9,500			
12,000	10,250			
13,000	11,000			

2.11 **(Related to the** Making the Connection **on page 185)** In an opinion column in the *Wall Street Journal*, Purdue University President Mitchell Daniels wrote that "today's 20- and 30-year-olds are delaying marriage and delaying childbearing, both unhelpful trends from an economic and social standpoint." Why might young people be delaying marriage and childbearing? Why would this trend be unhelpful from an economic point of view? Is the trend possibly connected with the slow recovery from the 2007–2009 recession? Briefly explain.

Source: Mitchell E, Daniels, "How Student Debt Harms the Economy," *Wall Street Journal*, January 27, 2015.

2.12 An article in the *Wall Street Journal* on changes in Intel's sales noted, "Intel sells its chips to customers in U.S. dollars, but many PC makers that buy those chips sell their products in local currencies." In these circumstances, would an increase in the value of the dollar relative to foreign currencies be likely to help or hurt Intel's sales? Briefly explain.

Source: Tess Stynes, "Intel Earnings: What to Watch," *Wall Street Journal*, July 15, 2015.

2.13 (Related to the Making the Connection **on page 190)** Briefly explain which of the following statement is correct.
  a. The iPhone is made in China, using Chinese-made parts.
  b. The iPhone is made in the United States, using U.S.-made parts.
  c. The iPhone is made in the United States, using Chinese-made parts.
  d. The iPhone is made China, using parts that are all made outside China.

What relevance does your answer have to how the Bureau of Economic Analysis calculates data on U.S. imports?

2.14 (Related to the Making the Connection **on page 190)** In a speech to a conference of government trade officials, Angel Gurría, secretary general of the Organization for Economic Co-operation and Development, made the following observation: "As goods and services cross borders several times at different stages of processing, conventional trade statistics may not tell the whole story."
  a. What does Gurría mean by "conventional trade statistics"?
  b. Why might conventional trade statistics no longer be as reliable as they once were?
  c. What difficulties might the problems with trade statistics cause for policymakers?

Source: Angel Gurría, "Understanding Global Value Chains," Speech delivered at the G20 trade ministers conference in Puerto Vallarta, Mexico, April 19, 2012, www.oecd.org/about/secretary-general/g20understandingglobalvaluechains.htm.

5.3 Graphing Macroeconomic Equilibrium, pages 191–198

LEARNING OBJECTIVE: Use a 45°-line diagram to illustrate macroeconomic equilibrium.

Summary

The 45°-line diagram shows all the points where aggregate expenditure equals real GDP. On the 45°-line diagram, macroeconomic equilibrium occurs where the line representing the aggregate expenditure function crosses the 45° line. The economy is in recession when the aggregate expenditure line intersects the 45° line at a level of GDP that is below potential GDP. Numerically, macroeconomic equilibrium occurs when:

$$\text{Consumption} + \text{Planned investment} +$$
$$\text{Government purchases} + \text{Net exports} = \text{GDP.}$$

MyEconLab   Visit **www.myeconlab.com** to complete these exercises online and get instant feedback.

Review Questions

3.1 What is the meaning of the 45° line in the 45°-line diagram?

3.2 Use a 45°-line diagram to illustrate macroeconomic equilibrium. Make sure your diagram shows the aggregate expenditure function and the level of equilibrium real GDP and that your axes are properly labeled.

3.3 What does the slope of the aggregate expenditure line equal? How is the slope of the aggregate expenditure line related to the slope of the consumption function?

3.4 What is likely to happen if firms accumulate large amounts of unplanned inventory at the beginning of a recession?

3.5 What is the difference between aggregate expenditure and consumption spending?

Problems and Applications

3.6 At point A in the following graph, is planned aggregate expenditure greater than, equal to, or less than GDP? What about at point B? At point C? For points A and C, indicate the vertical distance that measures the unintended change in inventories.

3.7 Suppose we drop the assumption that net exports do not depend on real GDP. Draw a graph with the value of net exports on the vertical axis and the value of real GDP on the horizontal axis. Now, add a line representing the relationship between net exports and real GDP. Does your net exports line have a positive or negative slope? Briefly explain.

3.8 A Federal Reserve publication notes that "the shedding of unwanted inventories often accounts for a large portion of the decline in gross domestic product (GDP) during economic recessions." What does the author mean be "shedding of unwanted inventories"? What makes the inventories unwanted? Why would shedding inventories lead to a decline in GDP?

Source: Jeremy M. Piger, "Is the Business Cycle Still an Inventory Cycle?" *Economic Synopses*, Federal Reserve Bank of St. Louis, No. 2, 2005.

3.9 An article on bloomberg.com about the Japanese economy noted, "Whether the 2.4 percent annualized gain in gross domestic product reported Wednesday can be maintained depends on consumers stepping in to buy the products that companies are piling up in warehouses."
a. Did business inventories in Japan increase or decrease during this period? Briefly explain.
b. What would happen if consumers do not buy the products that companies are piling up? Illustrate your answer with a 45°-line diagram.

Source: Keiko Ujikane and Toru Fujioka, "Japan's Economy Grows as Investment Gains, Inventories Rise," bloomberg.com, May 20, 2015.

3.10 Consider the table in the next column, which shows the change in inventories for each quarter from the first quarter of 2007 (2007:I) through the fourth quarter of 2010 (2010:IV) measured in billions of 2009 dollars. Provide a macroeconomic explanation for this pattern. (*Hint:* When did the recession during this period begin and end?)

Accompanies problem 3.10.

Year	Quarter	Change in Inventories
2007	I	$19.6
	II	49.4
	III	50.2
	IV	23.0
2008	I	−20.2
	II	−26.4
	III	−20.7
	IV	−67.4
2009	I	−144.5
	II	−190.1
	III	−206.1
	IV	−49.6
2010	I	9.8
	II	48.8
	III	116.2
	IV	58.1

3.11 (**Related to the** Don't Let This Happen to You **on page 196)** Briefly explain whether you agree with the following argument: "The equilibrium level of GDP is determined by the level of aggregate expenditure. Therefore, GDP will decline only if households decide to spend less on goods and services."

3.12 (**Related to** Solved Problem 5.3 **on page 197)** Fill in the blank cells in the table below. Assume that the value of the MPC does not change as real GDP changes. Also assume that the values represent billions of 2009 dollars.
a. What is the value of the MPC?
b. What is the value of equilibrium real GDP?

Accompanies problem 5.12.

Real GDP (Y)	Consumption (C)	Planned Investment (I)	Government Purchases (G)	Net Exports (NX)	Planned Aggregate Expenditure (AE)	Unplanned Change in Inventories
$9,000	$7,600	$1,200	$1,200	−$400		
10,000	8,400	1,200	1,200	−400		
11,000		1,200	1,200	−400		
12,000		1,200	1,200	−400		
13,000		1,200	1,200	−400		

5.4	**The Multiplier Effect, pages 198–205**

LEARNING OBJECTIVE: Describe the multiplier effect and use the multiplier formula to calculate changes in equilibrium GDP.

Summary

Autonomous expenditure is expenditure that does not depend on the level of GDP. An autonomous change is a change in expenditure not caused by a change in income. An *induced change* is a change in aggregate expenditure caused by a change in income. An autonomous change in expenditure will cause rounds of induced changes in expenditure. Therefore, an autonomous change in expenditure will have a *multiplier effect* on equilibrium GDP. The **multiplier effect** is the process by which an increase in autonomous expenditure leads to a larger increase in real GDP. The **multiplier** is the ratio of the change in equilibrium GDP to the change in autonomous expenditure. The formula for the multiplier is:

$$\frac{1}{1 - MPC}.$$

Because of the paradox of thrift, an attempt by many individuals to increase their saving may lead to a reduction in aggregate expenditure and a recession.

MyEconLab   Visit **www.myeconlab.com** to complete these exercises online and get instant feedback.

Review Questions

4.1 The following graph contains two aggregate expenditure functions. Consider a movement from point A to point B and a movement from point B to point C. Which movement shows a change in *autonomous* expenditure? Which movement shows a change in *induced* expenditure? Briefly explain your answers.

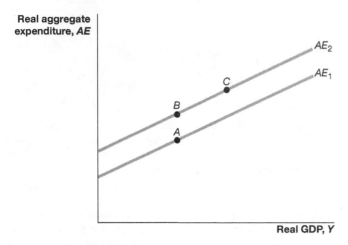

4.2 What is the multiplier effect? Use a 45°-line diagram to illustrate the multiplier effect of a decrease in government purchases.

4.3 What is the formula for the multiplier? Explain why this formula is considered to be too simple.

Problems and Applications

4.4 In Figure 5.13 on page 198, the economy is initially in equilibrium at point A. Aggregate expenditure and real GDP both equal $9.6 trillion. The increase in investment of $100 billion increases aggregate expenditure to $9.7 trillion. If real GDP increases to $9.7 trillion, will the economy be in equilibrium? Briefly explain. What happens to aggregate expenditure when real GDP increases to $9.7 trillion?

4.5 An opinion column in the *New York Times* quotes an economist's analysis of the effect of government infrastructure spending on new bridges and highways in the United States: "The investment multiplier would give a further kick to the U.S. economy."
a. What does the economist mean by the "investment multiplier"?
b. Briefly explain what the economist means by saying that the investment multiplier would "give a further kick to the U.S. economy."
Source: Thomas L. Friedman, "Why 2014 Is a Big Deal," *New York Times*, December 13, 2014.

4.6 **(Related to the** Making the Connection **on page 200)** If the multiplier had a value of 4 in 1929, how large must the change in autonomous expenditure have been to have caused the decline in real GDP between 1929 and 1933 shown in the table on page 201? If the multiplier had a value of 2, how large must the change in autonomous expenditure have been?

4.7 **(Related to** Solved Problem 5.4 **on page 203)** Use the information in the following table to answer the questions. Assume that the values represent billions of 2009 dollars.

Real GDP (Y)	Consumption (C)	Planned Investment (I)	Government Purchases (G)	Net Exports (NX)
$8,000	$7,300	$1,000	$1,000	-$500
9,000	7,900	1,000	1,000	-500
10,000	8,500	1,000	1,000	-500
11,000	9,100	1,000	1,000	-500
12,000	9,700	1,000	1,000	-500

a. What is the equilibrium level of real GDP?
b. What is the MPC?
c. Suppose net exports increase by $400 billion. What will be the new equilibrium level of real GDP? Use the multiplier formula to determine your answer.

4.8 An article published in an economics journal found the following: "For the poorest households, the marginal propensity to consume was close to 70%. For the richest households, the MPC was only 35%." Assume that the macroeconomy can be divided into three sections. Section A consists of the poorest households, Section B consists of the richest households, and Section C consists of all other households.
a. Compute the value of the multiplier for Section A.
b. Compute the value of the multiplier for Section B.
c. Assume that there was an increase in planned investment of $4 billion. Compute the change in equilibrium real GDP if the MPC for the economy was 70 percent (or 0.70). Compute the change in equilibrium real GDP if the MPC for the economy was 35 percent (or 0.35).
Source: Atif Mian and Amir Sufi, "Who Spends Extra Cash?" *House of Debt*, April 13, 2014.

4.9 Explain whether each of the following would cause the value of the multiplier to be larger or smaller.
a. An increase in real GDP increases imports.
b. An increase in real GDP increases interest rates.
c. An increase in real GDP increases the marginal propensity to consume.
d. An increase in real GDP causes the average tax rate paid by households to decrease.
e. An increase in real GDP increases the price level.

4.10 Suppose the rate of growth of the economies in the BRIC nations (Brazil, Russia, India, and China) slows down, causing U.S. net exports to fall by $75 billion. If the MPC is 0.8, what will be the change in equilibrium U.S. GDP?

4.11 Would a larger multiplier lead to longer and more severe recessions or shorter and less severe recessions? Briefly explain.

4.12 A study by the management consulting company McKinsey & Company recommended that the U.S. increase spending on infrastructure, such as bridges and highways, by between $150 and $180 billion per year. The study estimated that the result would be an increase in GDP of between $270 billion and $320 billion per year. What is the implied value of the multiplier if the McKinsey study's estimate of the effect of infrastructure spending on GDP is correct?

Source: David Harrison, "Nation's Crumbling Roads Put a Dent in Drivers' Wallets," *Wall Street Journal*, July 31, 2015.

4.13 Use the following graph to answer the questions.
  a. What is the value of equilibrium real GDP?
  b. What is the value of the *MPC*?
  c. What is the value of the multiplier?
  d. What is the value of unplanned changes in inventories when real GDP has each of the following values?
    i. $10 trillion
    ii. $12 trillion
    iii. $14 trillion

5.5 **The Aggregate Demand Curve, pages 205–206**

LEARNING OBJECTIVE: Understand the relationship between the aggregate demand curve and aggregate expenditure.

Summary

Increases in the price level cause a reduction in consumption, investment, and net exports. This causes the aggregate expenditure function to shift down on the 45°-line diagram, leading to a lower equilibrium real GDP. A decrease in the price level leads to a higher equilibrium real GDP. The **aggregate demand (AD) curve** shows the relationship between the price level and the level of aggregate expenditure, holding constant all factors other than the price level that affect aggregate expenditure.

MyEconLab   Visit **www.myeconlab.com** to complete these exercises online and get instant feedback.

Review Questions

5.1 Explain the difference between aggregate expenditure and aggregate demand.

5.2 Explain which components of aggregate expenditure are affected by a change in the price level.

5.3 Does a change in the price level cause a movement along the aggregate expenditure line or a shift of the aggregate expenditure line? Does a change in the price level cause a movement along the aggregate demand curve or a shift of the aggregate demand curve?

Problems and Applications

5.4 Explain why the aggregate expenditure line is upward sloping, while the aggregate demand curve is downward sloping.

5.5 Explain whether you agree with the following statement: "The reason the aggregate demand curve slopes downward is that when the price level is higher, people cannot afford to buy as many goods and services."

5.6 Suppose that exports become more sensitive to changes in the price level in the United States. That is, when the price level in the United States rises, exports decline by more than they previously did. Will this change make the aggregate demand curve steeper or less steep? Briefly explain.

Real-Time Data Exercises

D5.1 **(Calculating the multiplier effect)** Using data from the Federal Reserve Bank of St. Louis (FRED) (research.stlouisfed.org/fred2/), analyze the effect of a decline in exports on GDP.
  a. Download data since 1990 on Real Exports of Goods and Services (EXPGSC1).
  b. What was the dollar value of the decline in real exports between the second quarter of 2008 and the first quarter of 2009? If the multiplier is 2, holding everything else constant, what was the effect of this decline in exports on real GDP?

Appendix

The Algebra of Macroeconomic Equilibrium

LEARNING OBJECTIVE: Apply the algebra of macroeconomic equilibrium.

In this module, we relied primarily on graphs and tables to illustrate the aggregate expenditure model of short-run real GDP. Graphs help us understand economic change *qualitatively*. When we write an economic model using equations, we make it easier to make *quantitative estimates*. When economists forecast future movements in GDP, they often rely on *econometric models*. An econometric model is an economic model written in the form of equations, where each equation has been statistically estimated using methods similar to the methods used in estimating demand curves that we briefly described in Module 3. We can use equations to represent the aggregate expenditure model described in this module.

The following equations are based on the example shown in Table 5.3 on page 196. Y stands for real GDP, and the numbers (with the exception of the *MPC*) represent billions of dollars.

1. $C = 1,000 + 0.65Y$ Consumption function
2. $I = 1,500$ Planned investment function
3. $G = 1,500$ Government purchases function
4. $NX = -500$ Net export function
5. $Y = C + I + G + NX$ Equilibrium condition

The first equation is the consumption function. The *MPC* is 0.65, and 1,000 is autonomous consumption, which is the level of consumption that does not depend on income. If we think of the consumption function as a line on the 45°-line diagram, 1,000 would be the intercept, and 0.65 would be the slope. The "functions" for the other three components of planned aggregate expenditure are very simple because we have assumed that these components are not affected by GDP and, therefore, are constant. Economists who use this type of model to forecast GDP would, of course, use more realistic investment, government, and net export functions. The *parameters* of the functions—such as the value of autonomous consumption and the value of the *MPC* in the consumption function—would be estimated statistically, using data on the values of each variable over a period of years.

In this model, GDP is in equilibrium when it equals planned aggregate expenditure. Equation 5—the equilibrium condition—shows us how to calculate equilibrium in the model: We need to substitute equations 1 through 4 into equation 5. Doing so gives us the following:

$$Y = 1,000 + 0.65Y + 1,500 + 1,500 - 500.$$

We need to solve this expression for Y to find equilibrium GDP. The first step is to subtract 0.65Y from both sides of the equation:

$$Y - 0.65Y = 1,000 + 1,500 + 1,500 - 500.$$

Then, we solve for Y:

$$0.35Y = 3,500.$$

Or:

$$Y = \frac{3,500}{0.35} = 10,000.$$

To make this result more general, we can replace particular values with general values represented by letters:

1. $C = \bar{C} + MPC(Y)$ Consumption function
2. $I = \bar{I}$ Planned investment function
3. $G = \bar{G}$ Government purchases function
4. $NX = \overline{NX}$ Net export function
5. $Y = C + I + G + NX$ Equilibrium condition

The letters with bars over them represent fixed, or autonomous, values. So, for example, $\bar{C}$ represents autonomous consumption, which had a value of 1,000 in our original example. Now, solving for equilibrium, we get:

$$Y = \bar{C} + MPC(Y) + \bar{I} + \bar{G} + \overline{NX},$$

or:

$$Y - MPC(Y) = \bar{C} + \bar{I} + \bar{G} + \overline{NX},$$

or:

$$Y(1 - MPC) = \bar{C} + \bar{I} + \bar{G} + \overline{NX},$$

or:

$$Y = \frac{\bar{C} + \bar{I} + \bar{G} + \overline{NX}}{1 - MPC}.$$

Remember that $1/(1 - MPC)$ is the multiplier, and all four variables in the numerator of the equation represent autonomous expenditure. Therefore, an alternative expression for equilibrium GDP is:

Equilibrium GDP = Autonomous expenditure × Multiplier.

MyEconLab Concept Check

5A   The Algebra of Macroeconomic Equilibrium, pages 214–215

LEARNING OBJECTIVE: Apply the algebra of macroeconomic equilibrium.

MyEconLab   Visit www.myeconlab.com to complete these exercises online and get instant feedback.

Review Questions

5A.1 Write a general expression for the aggregate expenditure function. If you think of the aggregate expenditure function as a line on the 45°-line diagram, what would be the intercept and what would be the slope, using the general values represented by letters?

5A.2 Find equilibrium GDP using the following macroeconomic model (where the numbers, with the exception of the *MPC*, represent billions of dollars).

1. $C = 1,500 + 0.75Y$ Consumption function
2. $I = 1,250$ Planned investment function
3. $G = 1,250$ Government purchases function
4. $NX = -250$ Net export function
5. $Y = C + I + G + NX$ Equilibrium condition

5A.3 For the macroeconomic model in problem 5A.2, write the aggregate expenditure function. For GDP of $16,000, what is the value of aggregate expenditure, and what is the value of the unintended change in inventories? For GDP of $12,000, what is the value of aggregate expenditure, and what is the value of the unintended change in inventories?

5A.4 Suppose that autonomous consumption is 500, government purchases are 1,000, planned investment spending is 1,250, net exports are −250, and the *MPC* is 0.8. What is equilibrium GDP?

Firms, the Stock Market, and Corporate Governance

Module Outline and Learning Objectives

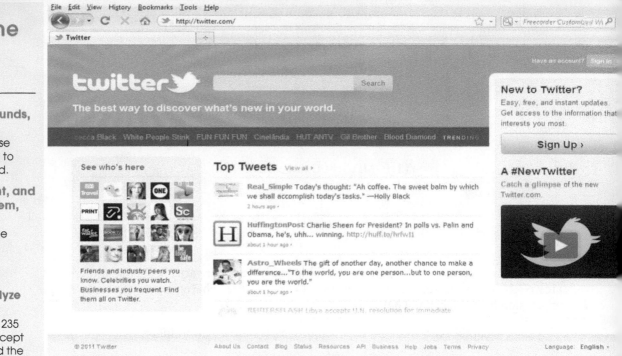

Is Twitter the Next Facebook?

Most people today have trouble imagining a world without Facebook, Twitter, Snapchat, and Instagram. All four of these social networking applications ("apps") are businesses that started small but have since grown rapidly. To finance that growth, they needed to raise funds. Some businesses raise funds by borrowing from banks. Once firms grow large enough, they can become *public firms* and sell stocks and bonds to investors in financial markets, such as the New York Stock Exchange. Firms that do not sell stock are called *private firms*. Both Facebook and Twitter have made the transition to being public firms. The founders of Snapchat, the mobile photo-sharing app, took a different approach: In 2012, they sold their company to Facebook for $1 billion. In the summer of 2015, Instagram, which allows people to share photos and 15-second videos, was still a private company. It was relying on investments from venture capital firms, which provide funds to private companies in exchange for part ownership.

A major decision for a successful social media startup is whether to remain a private firm, to become a public firm, or to sell itself to a larger firm as Snapchat did. Becoming a public firm provides access to greater financing but can also have drawbacks. From the time Mark Zuckerberg started Facebook in 2004 as a sophomore in college until the company went public in 2012, he was the unquestioned leader of the company. But buyers of Facebook's stock have partial ownership of the firm and a claim on its profits and can question Zuckerberg's decisions. Twitter became a public firm in 2013.

Stockholders want to invest in companies that can earn a profit. During its first year as a public company, Facebook struggled to meet the expectations of its investors. Eventually, Facebook was able to find a better way to target advertising on its app, and its stock more than doubled from its initial price in 2012 of $38 per share.

Twitter, however, found life as a public company to be more challenging. By 2015, it had more than 300 million active users and had become an important part of many people's lives. But advertisers who provided most of the company's revenue weren't convinced that advertising on the site was actually effective.

As we will see in this module, the ability of firms such as Twitter and Facebook to raise funds in financial markets is crucial to the health of the economy. Financial markets are also an important source of investment opportunities to households as they accumulate savings to buy houses, pay for college, and prepare for retirement.

Sources: Jack Marshall and Yoree Koh, "The Problem with Twitter Ads," *Wall Street Journal*, April 30, 2015; Douglas MacMillan, "Snapchat Raises Another $500 Million From Investors," *Wall Street Journal*, May 29, 2015; and Vindu Goel, "An Early Twitter Investor Calls for Change," *New York Times*, June 3, 2015.

Economics in Your Life

Would You Pay to Use Facebook or Twitter?

You can use Facebook or Twitter for free—or can you? Social media apps don't charge you directly; instead they earn their revenue primarily by displaying ads as you use the app. Most sites collect data about your Web searches and browsing habits and then display ads for products they think you might buy. But many people see targeted ads as an invasion of their privacy. Some of these people would be willing to pay to use these apps if they could do so without having to see advertisements. Would you be willing to pay to use social media apps? Do you think other users would be willing to pay enough that firms could rely on that source of revenue? As you read this module, try to answer these questions. You can check your answers against those we provide on **page 244** at the end of this module.

I n this module, we look at firms: how they are organized, how they raise funds, and the information they provide to investors. As we have discussed in earlier modules, firms in a market system are responsible for organizing the factors of production to produce goods and services. Entrepreneurs start firms to earn a profit by offering a good or service. To succeed, entrepreneurs must meet consumers' wants by producing new or better goods and services or by finding ways to produce existing goods and services at a lower cost so that they can be sold at a lower price. Entrepreneurs also need access to sufficient funds, and they must be able to efficiently organize production. As the typical firm in many industries has become larger over the past 100 years, the task of efficiently organizing production has become more difficult. In the final section of this module, we look at problems of *corporate governance* that have occurred in recent years. We also look at the steps firms and the government have taken to avoid similar problems in the future.

 ## 6.1   How Firms Raise Funds

LEARNING OBJECTIVE: Explain how firms raise the funds they need to operate and expand.

Owners and managers of firms try to earn a profit. To succeed, a firm must raise funds to pay for its operations, including paying its employees and buying or renting computers and other machinery and equipment. In fact, a central challenge for anyone running a firm, whether that person is a sole proprietor or a top manager of a large corporation, is raising the funds needed to operate and expand the business. Suppose you develop a new social networking app, and you decide to start a business using $100,000 you have saved in a bank. You use the $100,000 to rent an office for your firm, buy computers, and pay other startup expenses. Your firm is a great success, and you decide to expand it by moving to a larger office and buying more computers. As the owner of a small business, you can raise the funds for this expansion in three ways:

1. If you are making a profit, you could reinvest the profits back into your firm. Profits that are reinvested in a firm rather than taken out of the firm and paid to the firm's owners are called *retained earnings*.
2. You could raise funds by recruiting additional owners to invest in the firm. This arrangement would increase the firm's *financial capital*.
3. Finally, you could borrow the funds from relatives, friends, or a bank.

The managers of a large public firm have some additional ways to raise funds, as we will see in the next section.

Sources of External Funds

Unless firms rely on retained earnings, they have to raise the *external funds* they need from those who have funds available to invest. It is the role of an economy's *financial system* to transfer funds from savers to borrowers.

Most firms raise external funds in two ways. The first way, called **indirect finance**, relies on financial intermediaries such as banks. If you put $1,000 in a checking account or in a certificate of deposit (CD), the bank will loan most of those funds to borrowers. The bank will combine your funds with those of other depositors and, for example, make a $100,000 loan to a local business. Small businesses rely heavily on bank loans as their primary source of external funds.

A second way for firms to acquire external funds is through *financial markets*. Raising funds in these markets, such as the New York Stock Exchange on Wall Street in New York City, is called **direct finance**. Direct finance usually takes the form of the borrower selling the lender a *financial security*. A financial security is a document—sometimes in electronic form—that states the terms under which the funds are passed from the buyer of the security (who is lending funds) to the borrower. *Bonds* and *stocks* are the two main types of financial securities. Typically, only large corporations are able to sell bonds and stocks on financial markets. Investors are generally unwilling to buy securities issued by small and medium-sized firms because the investors lack sufficient information on the financial health of smaller firms.

Indirect finance A flow of funds from savers to borrowers through financial intermediaries such as banks. Intermediaries raise funds from savers to lend to firms (and other borrowers).

Direct finance A flow of funds from savers to firms through financial markets, such as the New York Stock Exchange.

Bonds **Bonds** are financial securities that represent promises to repay a fixed amount of funds. When Apple sells a bond to raise funds, it promises to pay the purchaser of the bond an interest payment each year for the term of the bond, as well as a payment of the loan amount, or the *principal*, at the end of the term. Apple may need to raise many millions of dollars to build new offices, but each individual bond has a principal, or *face value*, of $1,000, which is the amount each bond purchaser is lending Apple. So, Apple must sell many bonds to raise all the funds it needs. Suppose Apple promises it will pay interest of $40 per year to anyone who buys one of its bonds. The interest payments on a bond are called **coupon payments**. The **interest rate** is the cost of borrowing funds, usually expressed as a percentage of the amount borrowed. We can calculate the interest rate on the bond, called the *coupon rate*, by dividing the coupon by the face value of the bond. In this case, the coupon rate is:

$$\frac{\$40}{\$1,000} = 0.04, \text{ or } 4\%.$$

Many bonds that corporations issue have terms, or *maturities*, of 30 years. In this example, if you bought a bond from Apple, Apple would pay you $40 per year for 30 years, and at the end of the thirtieth year, Apple would repay the $1,000 principal to you.

The interest rate that a corporation selling a bond has to pay depends on how likely bond buyers—investors—think that the corporation is to default, or not make the promised coupon or principal payments. The higher the *default risk* on a bond, the higher the interest rate will be. For example, investors see the federal government as being very unlikely to default on its bonds, so federal government bonds pay a lower interest rate than do bonds of a firm such as Apple. In turn, Apple pays a lower interest rate on its bonds than does a corporation that investors believe is not as likely to make its bond payments.

Bond A financial security that represents a promise to repay a fixed amount of funds.

Coupon payment An interest payment on a bond.

Interest rate The cost of borrowing funds, usually expressed as a percentage of the amount borrowed.

Making the Connection
MyEconLab Video

The Rating Game: Is the U.S. Treasury Likely to Default on Its Bonds?

Federal regulations require that before they can sell bonds to investors, firms and governments must first have bonds rated by one of the credit-rating agencies. The three largest rating agencies are Moody's Investors Service, Standard & Poor's Corporation, and Fitch Ratings. These private firms rate bonds by giving them letter grades—AAA or Aaa being the highest—that reflect the likelihood that the firm or government will be able to make the payments on the bond. The following table shows the ratings:

	Moody's Investors Service	Standard & Poor's (S&P)	Fitch Ratings	Meaning of the Ratings
Investment-grade bonds	Aaa	AAA	AAA	Highest credit quality
	Aa	AA	AA	Very high credit quality
	A	A	A	High credit quality
	Baa	BBB	BBB	Good credit quality
Non-investment-grade bonds	Ba	BB	BB	Speculative
	B	B	B	Highly speculative
	Caa	CCC	CCC	Substantial default risk
	Ca	CC	CC	Very high levels of default risk
	C	C	C	Exceptionally high levels of default risk
	—	D	D	Default

Note: The entries in the "Meaning of the Ratings" column are slightly modified from those that Fitch uses. The other two rating agencies have similar descriptions. For each rating from Aa to Caa, Moody's adds a numerical modifier of 1, 2, or 3. The rating Aa1 is higher than the rating Aa2, and the rating Aa2 is higher than the rating Aa3. Similarly, Standard & Poor's and Fitch Ratings add a plus (+) or minus (−) sign. The rating AA+ is higher than the rating AA, and the rating AA is higher than the rating AA-.

Source: *Money, Banking, and the Financial System,* 2nd edition, by R. Glenn Hubbard and Anthony P. O'Brien. Copyright © 2014 by Pearson Education, Inc. Reprinted and electronically reproduced by permission of Pearson Education, Inc., Upper Saddle River, New Jersey.

Investors can use the ratings in deciding how much risk they are willing to accept when buying a bond. Generally, the lower the rating, the higher the interest rate an investor will receive but also the higher the risk that the issuer of the bond will default.

The rating agencies charge firms and governments—rather than investors—for their services. This arrangement raises the question of whether rating agencies face a conflict of interest. Because firms issuing bonds can choose which of the agencies to hire to rate their bonds, the agencies may have an incentive to give higher ratings than might be justified in order to keep the firms' business. During the housing boom of the mid-2000s, some financial firms issued *mortgage-backed bonds*. These bonds were similar to regular corporate bonds except that the interest payments came from mortgage loans people had taken out to buy houses. The money from those mortgage payments was passed along to investors who had bought the mortgage-backed bonds. The rating agencies gave many of these bonds AAA ratings, even though when housing prices began to decline in 2006, many homeowners stopped making their mortgage payments and the value of the bonds declined sharply. Some economists and policymakers believe the rating agencies provided the high ratings primarily to ensure that the firms that issued the bonds would continue to hire them.

Some investors worry that the U.S. government might someday default on the bonds that it has sold. Over the past 15 years, the federal government has been spending more than it has been collecting in taxes. The result is a federal budget deficit, which forces the Treasury to sell bonds equal to the amount of the deficit. The budget deficit was particularly large during and immediately after the 2007–2009 recession, which resulted in sharp declines in tax receipts and increases in government spending. Forecasts from the U.S. Congressional Budget Office indicate that large budget deficits will continue indefinitely because spending on Social Security, Medicare, Medicaid, and other government programs is expected to increase faster than tax revenues.

In 2011, Standard & Poor's (S&P) decided that because of these continuing deficits, it would downgrade U.S. Treasury bonds from AAA to AA+. Never before had a rating agency given Treasury bonds less than an AAA rating.

Is it likely that the U.S. Treasury will default on its bonds? S&P argued that while a default is still unlikely, the continuing large deficits increased the chance that someday the Treasury might not make the interest payments on its bonds. Most investors, though, appear confident that the Treasury will not default and are willing to buy Treasury bonds despite the historically low interest rates on the bonds. Like the Ghost of Christmas Yet to Come in Charles Dickens's *A Christmas Carol*, S&P was giving a warning of something that might happen rather than something that necessarily must happen.

Sources: Mary Williams Walsh, "Credit Ratings Services Give Mixed Reviews to Tax Deal," *New York Times*, January 3, 2013; and Cyrus Sanati, "S.E.C. Urges Changes to Ratings-Agency Rules," *New York Times*, August 28, 2009.

MyEconLab Study Plan

Your Turn: Test your understanding by doing related problems 1.8 and 1.9 on page 244 at the end of this module.

Stock A financial security that represents partial ownership of a firm.

Stocks When you buy a newly issued bond from a firm, you are lending funds to that firm. When you buy **stock** issued by a firm, you are actually buying part ownership of the firm. When a corporation sells stock, it is doing the same thing the owner of a small business does when he or she takes on a partner: The firm is increasing its financial capital by bringing additional owners into the firm. Any one shareholder usually owns only a small fraction of the total shares of stock issued by a corporation.

Many small investors buy shares of *mutual funds* rather than directly buying stocks issued by individual companies. Mutual funds, such as Fidelity Investment's Magellan Fund, sell shares to investors and use the funds to invest in a portfolio of financial assets, such as stocks and bonds. By buying shares in a mutual fund, small investors reduce the costs they would pay to buy many individual stocks and bonds. Small savers who have only enough money to buy a few individual stocks and bonds can use mutual funds to *diversify*, which lowers their investment risk because most mutual funds hold a large number of stocks and bonds. If a firm issuing a stock or bond declares bankruptcy, causing the stock or bond to lose all of its value, the effect on a mutual fund's portfolio is likely to be small. The effect might be devastating, though, to a small investor who invested most of his or her savings in the stock or bond. Because mutual funds are willing to buy back their shares at any time, they also provide savers with easy access to their money.

Exchange-traded funds (ETFs) are similar to mutual funds in that when you buy shares in an ETF, you are buying a claim to a portfolio of stocks or bonds. But mutual funds can only be bought from or sold back to the firm that issues them. ETFs can be bought and sold to other investors in financial markets, just as individual stocks or bonds can.

A shareholder is entitled to a portion of the corporation's profits, if there are any. Corporations generally keep some of their profits as retained earnings to finance future expansion. The remaining profits are paid to shareholders as **dividends**. If a firm uses its retained earnings to grow and earn economic profits, its share price rises, which provides a *capital gain* for investors. If a corporation is unable to make a profit, it usually does not pay a dividend. Under the law, corporations must make payments on any debt they have before making payments to their owners. That is, a corporation must make promised payments to bondholders before it can make any dividend payments to shareholders. Unlike bonds, stocks do not have a maturity date, so the firm is not obliged to return the investor's funds at any particular date.   MyEconLab Concept Check

Dividends Payments by a corporation to its shareholders.

Stock and Bond Markets Provide Capital—and Information

The original purchasers of stocks and bonds may resell them to other investors. In fact, most of the buying and selling of stocks and bonds that takes place each day involves investors reselling existing stocks and bonds to each other rather than corporations selling new stocks and bonds to investors. The buyers and sellers of stocks and bonds together make up the *stock and bond markets*. There is no single place where stocks and bonds are bought and sold. Some trading of stocks and bonds takes place in buildings known as *exchanges*, such as the New York Stock Exchange or the Tokyo Stock Exchange. In the United States, the stocks and bonds of the largest corporations are traded on the New York Stock Exchange. The development of computer technology has spread the trading of stocks and bonds outside exchanges to *securities dealers* linked by computers. These dealers comprise the *over-the-counter market*. The stocks of many high-technology firms—including Apple, Twitter, and Facebook—are traded in the most important of the over-the-counter markets, the *National Association of Securities Dealers Automated Quotations* system, which is referred to by its acronym, NASDAQ.

Shares of stock represent claims on the profits of the firms that issue them. Therefore, as the fortunes of the firms change and they earn more or less profit, the prices of the stock the firms have issued should also change. Similarly, bonds represent claims to receive coupon payments and one final payment of the principal. Therefore, a particular bond that was issued in the past may have its price go up or down, depending on whether the coupon payments being offered on newly issued bonds are higher or lower than those on existing bonds. If you hold a bond with a coupon of $30 per year, and similar newly issued bonds have coupons of $40 per year, the price of your bond will fall because it is less attractive to investors. The price of a bond will also be affected by changes in *default risk*, which reflects investors' expectations of the issuing firm's ability to make the coupon payments. For example, if investors begin to believe that a firm may soon go out of business and stop making coupon payments to its bondholders, the price of the firm's bonds will fall to very low levels.

Changes in the value of a firm's stocks and bonds provide important information for a firm's managers, as well as for investors. An increase in the stock price means that investors are more optimistic about the firm's profit prospects, and the firm's managers might want to expand the firm's operations as a result. By contrast, a decrease in the firm's stock price indicates that investors are less optimistic about the firm's profit prospects, so management may want to shrink the firm's operations. Similarly, changes in the value of the firm's bonds imply changes in the cost of external funds to finance the firm's investment in research and development or in new factories. A higher bond price indicates a lower cost of new external funds, while a lower bond price indicates a higher cost of new external funds.   MyEconLab Concept Check

Don't Let This Happen to You

When Twitter Shares Are Sold, Twitter Doesn't Get the Money

Twitter is a popular investment, with investors buying and selling shares often as their views about the value of the firm shift. That's great for Twitter, right? Think of Twitter collecting all that money as shares change hands and the stock price goes up. *Wrong.* Twitter raises funds in a primary market, but its shares trade in a secondary market. Those trades don't put money into Twitter's hands, but they do give important information to the firm's managers. Let's see why.

Primary markets are markets in which firms sell newly issued stocks and bonds to initial buyers. Businesses can raise funds in a primary financial market in two ways—by borrowing (selling bonds) or selling shares of stock—which result in different types of claims on the borrowing firm's future income. Although you may hear about the stock market fluctuations every day in news updates, bonds actually account for more of the funds raised by borrowers. The total value of bonds in the United States is typically about twice the value of stocks.

In *secondary markets*, stocks and bonds that have already been issued are sold by one investor to another.

If Twitter sells shares to the public, it is turning to a primary market for new funds. Once Twitter shares are issued, investors trade the shares in the secondary market. Twitter does not receive any new funds when its shares are traded. The initial seller of a stock or bond raises funds from an investor only in the primary market. Secondary markets convey information to firms' managers and investors by determining the price of stocks and bonds. For example, a major increase in Twitter's stock price conveys the market's optimism about the firm, and Twitter may decide to raise funds to expand. So, secondary markets are valuable sources of information for corporations that are considering raising funds.

Primary and secondary markets are both important, but they play different roles. As an investor, you principally trade stocks and bonds in a secondary market. As a corporate manager, you may help decide how to raise new funds to expand the firm where you work.

MyEconLab Study Plan

Your Turn: Test your understanding by doing related problem 1.11 on page 245 at the end of this module.

The Fluctuating Stock Market

The performance of the U.S. stock market is often measured using *stock market indexes*. Stock market indexes are averages of stock prices, with the value of the index set equal to 100 in a particular year, called the *base year*. Because the stock indexes are intended to show movements in prices from one year to the next, rather than the actual dollar values of the underlying stocks, the year chosen for the base year is unimportant. Figure 6.1 shows movements from January 1998 to June 2015 in the three most widely followed stock indexes (the shaded areas represent months in which the U.S. economy was in a business cycle recession when the production and profits of many firms are falling):

- The Dow Jones Industrial Average, which is an index of the stock prices of 30 large U.S. corporations.
- The S&P 500, which is an index prepared by Standard & Poor's Corporation and includes the stock prices of 500 large U.S. firms.
- The NASDAQ Composite Index, which includes the stock prices of more than 4,000 firms whose shares are traded in the NASDAQ stock market. NASDAQ is an over-the-counter market, meaning that buying and selling on NASDAQ is carried out between dealers who are linked together by computer. The listings on NASDAQ are dominated by high-tech firms such as Apple, Facebook, and Twitter.

As we have seen, ownership of a firm's stock represents a claim on the firm's profits. So, the larger the firm's profits are, the higher its stock price will be. When the overall economy is expanding, incomes, employment, and spending will all increase, as will corporate profits. When the economy is in a recession, incomes, employment, and spending will fall, as will corporate profits. Therefore, we would expect that stock prices will rise when the economy is expanding and fall when the economy is in recession. We see this pattern reflected in the three stock market indexes shown in Figure 6.1. All three

(a) Dow Jones Industrial Average   (b) S&P 500   (c) NASDAQ

MyEconLab Real-time data

Figure 6.1 Movements in Stock Market Indexes, January 1998 to June 2015

The performance of the U.S. stock market is often measured by market indexes, which are averages of stock prices. The three most important indexes are the Dow Jones Industrial Average, the S&P 500, and the NAS-DAQ. During the period from 1998 to 2015, the three indexes followed similar patterns, rising when the U.S. economy was expanding and falling when the economy was in recession. Note that in all three panels, the vertical axis does not start at zero.

indexes follow a roughly similar pattern: increases in stock prices during the economic expansion of the late 1990s, declines after the "dot-com crash" of 2000 and the recession of 2001, increases from late 2001 to late 2007, declines as the U.S. economy entered a recession at the end of 2007, and then increases beginning in early 2009.

The stock prices of many early Internet companies soared in the late 1990s, as some analysts made what turned out to be overly optimistic predictions about how rapidly online retailing would grow. In 2000, when investors realized that many dot-coms would never be profitable, their stock prices crashed. Because the NASDAQ is dominated by high-tech stocks, it experienced greater swings during the dot-com boom and bust of the late 1990s and early 2000s than did the other two indexes. The sharp declines in all three indexes beginning in late 2007 reflected the severity of the recession that began in December of that year. The severity of the recession was due in part to problems with financial firms. By 2015, as recovery from the recession continued, all three indexes had reached their highest values ever.   MyEconLab Concept Check

Making the Connection
MyEconLab Video

Why Are Many People Poor Stock Market Investors?

You've probably heard this standard advice about investing: "Buy low and sell high." That is, you should buy shares of stocks and other financial assets when their prices are low and sell them when their prices are high. Unfortunately, many people do the opposite. For instance, many people bought shares of Apple stock when it was selling for more than $700 per share in September 2012 and sold when it was below $400 per share in April 2013.

Stock prices are difficult to predict, but many people convince themselves that a stock whose price has been rising will continue to rise and that a stock whose price has been falling will continual to fall. As a result, people end up buying high and selling low rather than the reverse. Studies have shown that individual investors consistently earn lower returns on their investments when they frequently buy and sell stock hoping to predict changes in stock prices.

New information about Twitter's future profitability would cause the price of its stock to change.

But why are stock prices so difficult to predict? The key reason is that stock prices are based less on the *current* profitability of firms than on their *expected* future profitability. After all, few investors would be willing to pay a high price for a stock that was profitable today but was expected to suffer large losses tomorrow. Similarly, investors in late 2015 were willing to pay $30 per share for Twitter even though the firm was suffering losses because they expected it would earn profits in the future. If you look carefully at Figure 6.1, you can see that stock prices start to rise when investors begin to expect an economic recovery will soon begin rather than after the recovery has already begun.

Many Wall Street investment professionals spend a lot of time and money gathering all possible information about the future profitability of firms, hoping to buy stock in the most profitable firms. As a result, all of the information publicly available about a firm is reflected in the firm's stock price. For example, if at the end of a particular day, Twitter is selling for $30 per share, that price reflects all of the information available about Twitter's future profitability. What might cause Twitter's stock price to change? *Only new information about its future profitability.* For example, if Twitter releases new data showing that its advertising sales have been lower than investors had expected, its stock price will fall.

Even highly paid professional investors cannot consistently predict stock prices. The managers of mutual funds who try to earn high returns by frequently buying and selling stocks are rarely able to beat the stock market averages, such as the S&P 500. One study found that, in a typical year, only one-third of mutual fund managers were able to earn their investors a higher return than a small investor could earn by investing in an index mutual that buys only the stocks in the S&P 500. Only 10 percent of mutual fund managers earned a higher return than an index fund for two consecutive years.

Whichever way you—or Wall Street professionals—predict stock prices will move in the future, you are as likely to be wrong as you are to be right.

Sources: Morgan Housel, "Three Mistakes Investors Keep Making Again and Again," *Wall Street Journal*, September 12, 2014; Joe Light, "How to Find a Fund Manager Who Can Beat the Market," *Wall Street Journal*, January 11, 2013; and Howard Gold, "Almost No One Can Beat the Market," marketwatch.com, October 25, 2013.

MyEconLab Study Plan   **Your Turn:** Test your understanding by doing related problem 1.12 on page 245 at the end of this module.

Solved Problem 6.1

MyEconLab Interactive Animation

Why Does Warren Buffett Like Mutual Funds?

Warren Buffett is considered one of the greatest investors who has ever lived. His ability to predict which firms' stocks are likely to rise in price helped make him one of the richest people in the world. Yet Buffett advises that individual investors not try to pick individual stocks but instead use 90 percent of their savings to buy shares in mutual funds that charge low fees, such as those offered by the Vanguard Group. Is it likely that anyone investing mostly in mutual funds will become as wealthy as Buffett? Why would Buffett give this advice?

Solving the Problem

Step 1: **Review the module material.** This problem is about investing in the stock market, so you may want to review the section "The Fluctuating Stock Market" on page 222 and the *Making the Connection*, "Why Are Many People Poor Stock Market Investors?" which begins on page 223.

Step 2: **Answer the first question by discussing whether investing in low-cost mutual funds is a way to become as wealthy as Warren Buffett.** Most investors who have become wealthy have done so by making large investments in just a few firms. Mutual funds typically hold large numbers of stocks and bonds, so even if one or two of the stocks do extremely well, the total investment return from the fund will be held back by the smaller increases (or losses) in the other stocks in the fund. By investing in mutual funds, you can accumulate significant amounts to pay for a house, a college education, or retirement. Many people who have earned only middle-class incomes have accumulated a million dollars or more by retirement age by investing in low-cost mutual funds. But no one is known to have become fabulously wealthy with this approach to saving.

Step 3: **Answer the second question by explaining why Warren Buffett would advise most people to put their savings in mutual funds, even though they are unlikely to become wealthy by doing so.** Mutual funds give individual investors a low-cost way to diversify. Although it's possible to earn a high return investing in the stocks of individual firms, it's also easy for a small investor to lose all of his or her money if those firms run into financial problems.

Extra Credit: Warren Buffett may have become a billionaire by being better than other investors at predicting the future profits of the firms he invests in. Or he may have become a billionaire because he was lucky that the firms he invested in did particularly well—in which case he may not be better at forecasting the future profitability of firms than are other investors. Given that nearly all other equally intelligent and hardworking professional investors have been unable to consistently "beat the market" by earning higher returns than those earned by the typical low-cost, well-diversified mutual fund, it is impossible to know with certainty the true reasons for Buffett's success.

Source: Warren Buffett, *Letter to Berkshire Shareholders*, March 1, 2014, p. 20.

Your Turn: For more practice, do related problem 1.13 on page 245 at the end of this module.

MyEconLab Study Plan

6.2 Saving, Investment, and the Financial System

LEARNING OBJECTIVE: Discuss the role of the financial system in facilitating long-run economic growth.

The process of economic growth depends on the ability of firms to expand their operations, buy additional equipment, train workers, and adopt new technologies. Firms can finance some of these activities from *retained earnings*, which are profits that are reinvested in the firm rather than paid to the firm's owners. For many firms, retained earnings are not sufficient to finance the rapid expansion required in economies experiencing high rates of economic growth. Firms can acquire funds from households, either directly through financial markets—such as the stock and bond markets—or indirectly through financial intermediaries—such as banks. Financial markets and financial intermediaries together comprise the **financial system**. Without a well-functioning financial system, economic growth is impossible because firms will be unable to expand and adopt new technologies. As we noted earlier, no country without a well-developed financial system has been able to sustain high levels of economic growth.

> **Financial system** The system of financial markets and financial intermediaries through which firms acquire funds from households.

An Overview of the Financial System

The financial system channels funds from savers to borrowers and channels returns on the borrowed funds back to savers. In this section, we discuss the key components of the financial system and the services they provide to households and firms.

Financial markets Markets where financial securities, such as stocks and bonds, are bought and sold.

Financial Markets In **financial markets**, such as the stock market or the bond market, firms raise funds by selling financial securities directly to savers (see Module 6). A *financial security* is a document—sometimes in electronic form—that states the terms under which funds pass from the buyer of the security—who is providing funds—to the seller. *Stocks* are financial securities that represent partial ownership of a firm. If you buy one share of stock in Corning, you become one of millions of owners of that firm. *Bonds* are financial securities that represent promises to repay a fixed amount of funds. When Corning sells a bond, the firm promises to pay the purchaser of the bond an interest payment each year for the term of the bond, as well as a final payment of the amount of the loan.

Financial intermediaries Firms, such as banks, mutual funds, pension funds, and insurance companies, that borrow funds from savers and lend them to borrowers.

Financial Intermediaries **Financial intermediaries**, such as banks, mutual funds, pension funds, and insurance companies, act as go-betweens for borrowers and lenders. In effect, financial intermediaries borrow funds from savers and lend them to borrowers. When you deposit funds in your checking account, you are lending your funds to the bank. The bank may lend your funds (together with the funds of other savers) to an entrepreneur who wants to start a business. Suppose Lena wants to open a laundry. Rather than your lending money directly to Lena's Laundry, the bank acts as a go-between for you and Lena. Intermediaries pool the funds of many small savers to lend to many individual borrowers. The intermediaries pay interest to savers in exchange for the use of savers' funds and earn a profit by lending money to borrowers and charging them a higher rate of interest on the loans. For example, a bank might pay you as a depositor a 2 percent rate of interest, while it lends the money to Lena's Laundry at a 6 percent rate of interest.

Banks, mutual funds, pension funds, and insurance companies also make investments in stocks and bonds on behalf of savers. For example, *mutual funds* sell shares to savers and then use the funds to buy a portfolio of stocks, bonds, mortgages, and other financial securities. Large mutual fund companies, such as Fidelity, Vanguard, and Dreyfus, offer many stock and bond funds. Some funds hold a wide range of stocks or bonds; others specialize in securities issued by a particular industry or sector, such as health care; and others invest as index funds in fixed market baskets of securities, such as shares of the Standard & Poor's 500 firms. Over the past 30 years, the role of mutual funds in the financial system has increased dramatically. Today, competition among hundreds of mutual fund firms gives investors thousands of funds from which to choose.

The Services the Financial System Provides: Risk Sharing, Liquidity, and Information In addition to matching households that have excess funds with firms that want to borrow funds, the financial system provides three key services for savers and borrowers: risk sharing, liquidity, and information. *Risk* is the chance that the value of a financial security will change relative to what you expect. For example, you may buy a share of stock in Corning at a price of $25, only to have the price fall to $5. Most individual savers are not gamblers and seek a steady return on their savings rather than erratic swings between high and low earnings. The financial system provides *risk sharing* by allowing savers to spread their money among many financial investments. For example, you can divide your money among a bank certificate of deposit, individual bonds, and a stock mutual fund.

Liquidity is the ease with which a financial security can be exchanged for money. The financial system provides the service of liquidity by offering savers markets where they can sell their holdings of financial securities. For example, savers can easily sell their holdings of the stocks and bonds issued by large corporations on the major stock and bond markets.

A third service that the financial system provides savers is the collection and communication of *information*, or facts about borrowers and expectations about returns on financial securities. For example, Lena's Laundry may want to borrow $10,000 from you. Finding out what Lena intends to do with the funds and how likely she is to pay you back may be costly and time-consuming. By depositing $10,000 in the bank, you are, in effect, allowing the bank to gather this information for you. Because banks specialize in gathering information about borrowers, they are able to do it faster and at a lower cost than can individual savers. The financial system plays an important role in communicating information. If you read a news story announcing that an automobile firm has invented a car with an engine that runs on water, how would you determine the effect of that discovery on the firm's profits? Financial markets do the job for you by incorporating information into the prices of stocks, bonds, and other financial securities. In this example, the expectation of higher future profits would boost the prices of the automobile firm's stock and bonds.   MyEconLab Concept Check

The Macroeconomics of Saving and Investment

As we have seen, the funds available to firms through the financial system come from saving. When firms use funds to purchase machinery, factories, and office buildings, they are engaging in investment. In this section, we explore the macroeconomics of saving and investment. A key point we will develop is that *the total value of saving in the economy must equal the total value of investment. National income accounting* refers to the methods the Bureau of Economic Analysis uses to keep track of total production and total income in the economy (see Module 3). We can use some relationships from national income accounting to understand why total saving must equal total investment.

We begin with the relationship between gross domestic product, GDP (Y), and its components, consumption (C), investment (I), government purchases (G), and net exports (NX):

$$Y = C + I + G + NX.$$

Remember that GDP is a measure of both total production in the economy and total income.

In an *open economy*, there is interaction with other economies in terms of both trading of goods and services and borrowing and lending. All economies today are open economies, although they vary significantly in the extent of their openness. In a *closed economy*, there is no trading or borrowing and lending with other economies. For simplicity, we will develop the relationship between saving and investment for a closed economy, which allows us to focus on the most important points in a simpler framework. (See Module 9 for the case of an open economy.)

In a closed economy, net exports are zero, so we can rewrite the relationship between GDP and its components as:

$$Y = C + I + G.$$

The Savings Equals Investment Condition   If we rearrange the equation showing the relationship between GDP and its components, we have an expression for investment in terms of the other variables:

$$I = Y - C - G.$$

This expression tells us that in a closed economy, investment spending is equal to total income minus consumption spending and minus government purchases.

We can also derive an expression for total saving. *Private saving* is equal to what households retain of their income after purchasing goods and services (C) and paying taxes (T). Households receive income for supplying the factors of production to firms. This portion of household income is equal to Y. Households also receive income from government in the form of *transfer payments* (TR), which include Social Security payments and unemployment insurance payments. We can write this expression for private saving ($S_{Private}$):

$$S_{Private} = Y + TR - C - T.$$

The government also engages in saving. *Public saving* (S_{Public}) equals the amount of tax revenue the government retains after paying for government purchases and making transfer payments to households:

$$S_{Public} = T - G - TR.$$

So, total saving in the economy (S) is equal to the sum of private saving and public saving:

$$S = S_{Private} + S_{Public},$$

or:

$$S = (Y + TR - C - T) + (T - G - TR),$$

or:

$$S = Y - C - G.$$

The right side of this expression is identical to the expression we derived earlier for investment spending. So, we can conclude that total saving must equal total investment:

$$S = I.$$

Budget Deficits and Budget Surpluses When the government spends the same amount that it collects in taxes, there is a *balanced budget*. When the government spends more than it collects in taxes, there is a *budget deficit*. In the case of a deficit, T is less than $G + TR$, which means that public saving is negative. Negative saving is also known as *dissaving*. How can public saving be negative? When the federal government runs a budget deficit, the U.S. Department of the Treasury sells Treasury bonds to borrow the money necessary to fund the gap between taxes and spending. In this case, rather than adding to the total amount of saving available to be borrowed for investment spending, the government is subtracting from it. (Notice that if households borrow more than they save, the total amount of saving will also fall.) With less saving, investment must also be lower. We can conclude that, holding constant all other factors, there is a lower level of investment spending in the economy when there is a budget deficit than when there is a balanced budget.

When the government spends less than it collects in taxes, there is a *budget surplus*. A budget surplus increases public saving and the total level of saving in the economy. A higher level of saving results in a higher level of investment spending. Therefore, holding constant all other factors, there is a higher level of investment spending in the economy when there is a budget surplus than when there is a balanced budget.

The U.S. federal government has experienced dramatic swings in the state of its budget over the past 20 years. In 1992, the federal budget deficit was $297.4 billion. The federal budget had a surplus of $189.5 billion in 2000, but a sharp decline in taxes and increase in government spending resulting from the recession of 2007–2009 led to a record budget deficit of $1.4 trillion in 2009. By 2015, the budget deficit had declined to less than $500 billion.   MyEconLab Concept Check

The Market for Loanable Funds

We have seen that the value of total saving must equal the value of total investment, but we have not yet discussed how this equality is actually brought about in the financial system. We can think of the financial system as being composed of many markets through which funds flow from lenders to borrowers: the market for certificates of deposit at banks, the market for stocks, the market for bonds, the market for mutual

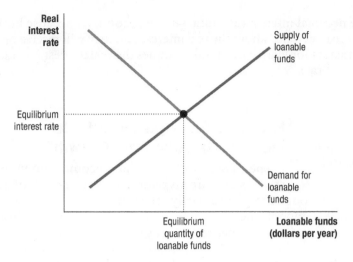

MyEconLab Animation

Figure 6.2   The Market for Loanable Funds

The demand for loanable funds is determined by the willingness of firms to borrow money to engage in new investment projects. The supply of loanable funds is determined by the willingness of households to save and by the extent of government saving or dissaving. Equilibrium in the market for loanable funds determines the real interest rate and the quantity of loanable funds exchanged.

fund shares, and so on. For simplicity, we can combine these markets into a single market for *loanable funds*. In the model of the **market for loanable funds**, the interaction of borrowers and lenders determines the market interest rate and the quantity of loanable funds exchanged. As we will discuss in a later module, firms can also borrow from savers in other countries (see Module 9). For the remainder of this section, we will assume that there are no interactions between households and firms in the United States and those in other countries.

Market for loanable funds The interaction of borrowers and lenders that determines the market interest rate and the quantity of loanable funds exchanged.

Demand and Supply in the Loanable Funds Market   The demand for
loanable funds is determined by the willingness of firms to borrow money to engage in new investment projects, such as building new factories or carrying out research and development of new products. In determining whether to borrow funds, firms compare the return they expect to make on an investment with the interest rate they must pay to borrow the necessary funds. For example, if Home Depot is considering opening several new stores and expects to earn a return of 12 percent on its investment, the investment will be profitable if Home Depot can borrow the funds at an interest rate of 8 percent but will not be profitable if the interest rate is 15 percent. In Figure 6.2, the demand for loanable funds is downward sloping because the lower the interest rate, the more investment projects firms can profitably undertake, and the greater the quantity of loanable funds they will demand.

The supply of loanable funds is determined by the willingness of households to save and by the extent of government saving or dissaving. When households save, they reduce the amount of goods and services they can consume and enjoy today. The willingness of households to save rather than consume their incomes today will be determined in part by the interest rate they receive when they lend their savings. The higher the interest rate, the greater the reward for saving and the larger the amount of funds households will save. Therefore, the supply curve for loanable funds in Figure 6.2 is upward sloping because the higher the interest rate, the greater the quantity of saving supplied.

Recall the distinction between the *nominal interest rate* and the *real interest rate* (see Modules 1 and 2). The nominal interest rate is the stated interest rate on a loan. The real interest rate corrects the nominal interest rate for the effect of inflation and is equal to the nominal interest rate minus the inflation rate. Because both borrowers and lenders are concerned about the real interest rate they will receive or pay, equilibrium in the market for loanable funds determines the real interest rate rather than the nominal interest rate.

Who was better for economic growth: Scrooge the saver or Scrooge the spender?

Making the Connection
MyEconLab Video

Ebenezer Scrooge: Accidental Promoter of Economic Growth?

Ebenezer Scrooge's name has become synonymous with miserliness. Before his reform at the end of Charles Dickens's *A Christmas Carol*, Scrooge is extraordinarily reluctant to spend money. Although he earns a substantial income, he lives in a cold, dark house that he refuses to heat or light adequately, and he eats a meager diet of gruel because he refuses to buy more expensive food. Throughout most of the book, Dickens portrays Scrooge's behavior in a negative way. Only at the end of the book, when the reformed Scrooge begins to spend lavishly on himself and others, does Dickens praise his behavior.

As economist Steven Landsburg of the University of Rochester points out, however, economically speaking, it may be the pre-reform Scrooge who is more worthy of praise:

> In this whole world, there is nobody more generous than the miser—the man who could deplete the world's resources but chooses not to. The only difference between miserliness and philanthropy is that the philanthropist serves a favored few while the miser spreads his largess far and wide.

We can extend Landsburg's discussion to consider whether the actions of the pre-reform Scrooge or the actions of the post-reform Scrooge are more helpful to economic growth. Pre-reform Scrooge spends very little, investing most of his income in the financial markets. These funds became available for firms to borrow to build new factories and to carry out research and development. Post-reform Scrooge spends much more—and saves much less. Funds that he had previously saved are now spent on food for Bob Cratchit's family and on "making merry" at Christmas. In other words, the actions of post-reform Scrooge contribute to more consumption goods being produced and fewer investment goods. We can conclude that Scrooge's reform caused economic growth to slow down—if only by a little. The larger point is, of course, that savers provide the funds that are indispensable for the investment spending that economic growth requires, and the only way to save is to not consume.

Source: Steven Landsburg, "What I Like about Scrooge," *Slate*, December 9, 2004.

MyEconLab Study Plan **Your Turn:** Test your understanding by doing related problems 2.14 and 2.15 on page 247 at the end of this module.

Explaining Movements in Saving, Investment, and Interest Rates Equilibrium in the market for loanable funds determines the quantity of loanable funds that will flow from lenders to borrowers each period. Equilibrium also determines the real interest rate that lenders will receive and that borrowers must pay. We draw the demand curve for loanable funds by holding constant all factors, other than the interest rate, that affect the willingness of borrowers to demand funds. We draw the supply curve by holding constant all factors, other than the interest rate, that affect the willingness of lenders to supply funds. A shift in either the demand curve or the supply curve will change the equilibrium interest rate and the equilibrium quantity of loanable funds.

If, for example, the profitability of new investment increases due to technological change or because the government reduces corporate taxes, firms will increase their

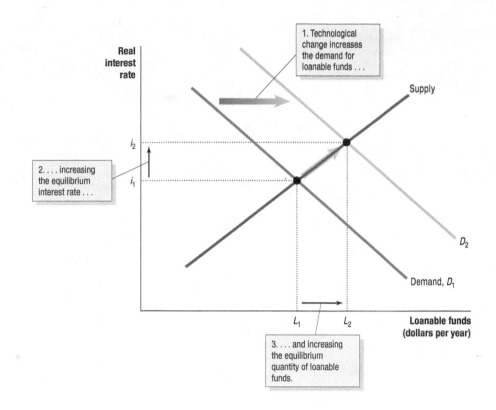

MyEconLab Animation

Figure 6.3

An Increase in the Demand for Loanable Funds

An increase in the demand for loanable funds increases the equilibrium interest rate from i_1 to i_2 and increases the equilibrium quantity of loanable funds from L_1 to L_2. As a result, saving and investment both increase.

demand for loanable funds. Figure 6.3 shows the effect of an increase in demand in the market for loanable funds. As in the markets for goods and services, an increase in demand in the market for loanable funds shifts the demand curve to the right. In the new equilibrium, the interest rate increases from i_1 to i_2, and the equilibrium quantity of loanable funds increases from L_1 to L_2. Notice that an increase in the quantity of loanable funds means that both the quantity of saving by households and the quantity of investment by firms have increased. Increasing investment increases the capital stock and the quantity of capital per hour worked, helping to increase economic growth.

We can also use the market for loanable funds to examine the effect of a government budget deficit. Putting aside the effects of foreign saving, recall that if the government begins running a budget deficit, it reduces the total amount of saving in the economy. Suppose the government increases spending, which results in a budget deficit. We illustrate the effects of the budget deficit in Figure 6.4 by shifting the supply curve for loanable funds to the left. In the new equilibrium, the interest rate is higher, and the equilibrium quantity of loanable funds is lower. Running a deficit has reduced the level of total saving in the economy and, by increasing the interest rate, has also reduced the level of investment spending by firms. By borrowing to finance its budget deficit, the government will have *crowded out* some firms that would otherwise have been able to borrow to finance investment. **Crowding out** refers to a decline in private expenditures (in this case, investment spending) as a result of an increase in government purchases. In Figure 6.4, the decline in investment spending due to crowding out is shown by the movement from L_1 to L_2 on the demand for loanable funds curve. Lower investment spending means that the capital stock and the quantity of capital per hour worked will not increase as much.

A government budget surplus has the opposite effect of a deficit: A budget surplus increases the total amount of saving in the economy, shifting the supply curve for loanable funds to the right. In the new equilibrium, the interest rate will be lower, and the quantity of loanable funds will be higher. We can conclude that a budget surplus increases the level of saving and investment.

Crowding out A decline in private expenditures as a result of an increase in government purchases.

MyEconLab Animation

Figure 6.4

The Effect of a Budget Deficit on the Market for Loanable Funds

When the government begins running a budget deficit, the supply curve for loanable funds shifts to the left. The equilibrium interest rate increases from i_1 to i_2, and the equilibrium quantity of loanable funds falls from L_1 to L_2. As a result, saving and investment both decline.

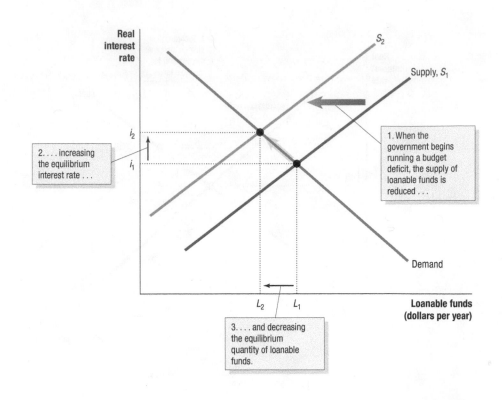

2. . . . increasing the equilibrium interest rate . . .

1. When the government begins running a budget deficit, the supply of loanable funds is reduced . . .

Supply, S_1

Demand

3. . . . and decreasing the equilibrium quantity of loanable funds.

Loanable funds (dollars per year)

In practice, however, the effect of government budget deficits and surpluses on the equilibrium interest rate is relatively small. (This finding reflects in part the importance of global saving in determining the interest rate.) For example, one study found that increasing government borrowing by an amount equal to 1 percent of GDP would increase the equilibrium real interest rate by only about 0.003 percentage point. However, this small effect on interest rates does not imply that we can ignore the effect of deficits on economic growth. Paying off government debt in the future may require higher taxes, which can depress economic growth. In 2015, many economists and policymakers were concerned that the large deficits projected for future years might be an obstacle to growth.

In addition to budget deficits, other government policies can affect the supply of loanable funds. The federal government gives special tax incentives for saving. For example, individuals can delay paying taxes on income they put into 401(k) retirement accounts until they actually retire. The delay in paying taxes increases the after-tax return to saving, so this policy encourages individuals to save.

Solved Problem 6.2

Are Future Budget Deficits a Threat to the Economy?

Congress gives the Congressional Budget Office (CBO) the responsibility of estimating the effects of federal spending and taxing policies on the economy. An *Associated Press* news story on a CBO report noted that federal budget deficits in the United States were likely to increase in future years. According to the CBO, these higher deficits might "pose a threat to the economy by crowding out business investment and threatening a spike in interest rates."

a. What did the CBO mean by a "spike in interest rates"? Why might increased federal budget deficits lead to a spike in interest rates? Illustrate your answer with a graph.

b. Is the spike in interest rates connected to crowding out? Why might crowding out be considered a threat to the economy?

Solving the Problem

Step 1: **Review the module material.** This problem is about applying the market for loanable funds model, so you may want to review the section "Explaining Movements in Saving, Investment, and Interest Rates," which begins on page 230.

Step 2: **Answer part (a) by explaining what the CBO meant by a "spike in interest rates," explaining why increased federal budget deficits could lead to such a spike, and drawing a graph to illustrate your answer.** By a "spike in interest rates" the CBO meant that interest rates might be significantly higher in the future. The figure below is the same as Figure 6.4 and shows that a higher budget deficit will shift the supply curve for loanable funds to the left, resulting in an increase in the equilibrium real interest rate.

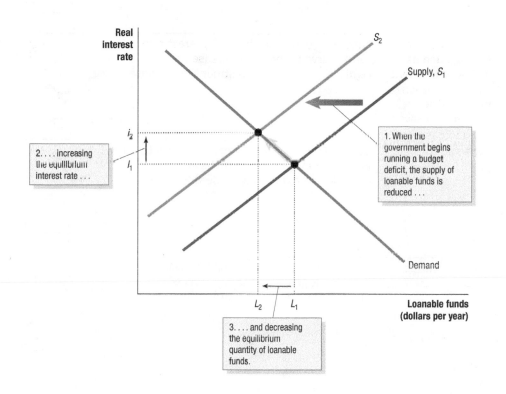

Step 3: **Answer part (b) by explaining how a spike in interest rates is connected to crowding out and why crowding out might be considered a threat to the economy.** A spike in interest rates is the way that higher budget deficits can cause crowding out. The higher interest rates will result in a decline in investment spending by firms. Lower investment spending can reduce economic growth. It is this possibility of higher deficits leading to slower economic growth that the CBO was referring to as a threat to the economy.

Source: Andrew Taylor, "CBO: Deficits to Drift Lower on Lower Health Costs," *Associated Press*, April 14, 2014.

Your Turn: For more practice, do related problem 2.16 on page 247 at the end of this module.

Table 6.1

Summary of Loanable Funds Model

An increase in ...	will shift the ...	causing ...	Graph of the effect on equilibrium in the loanable funds market
the government's budget deficit	supply of loanable funds curve to the left	the real interest rate to increase and investment to decrease.	
the desire of households to consume today	supply of loanable funds curve to the left	the real interest rate to increase and investment to decrease.	
tax benefits for saving, such as 401(k) retirement accounts, which increase the incentive to save	supply of loanable funds curve to the right	the real interest rate to decrease and investment to increase.	
expected future profits	demand for loanable funds curve to the right	the real interest rate and the level of investment to increase.	
corporate taxes	demand for loanable funds curve to the left	the real interest rate and the level of investment to decrease.	

Table 6.1 summarizes the key factors that cause shifts in the demand and supply curves for loanable funds.

Appendix

Tools to Analyze Firms' Financial Information

LEARNING OBJECTIVE: Understand the concept of present value and the information contained on a firm's income statement and balance sheet.

As we saw in the module, modern firms are not just "black boxes" transforming inputs into output. The majority of business revenues and profits are earned by large corporations. Unlike founder-dominated firms, the typical large corporation is run by managers who generally do not own a controlling interest in the firm. Large firms raise funds from outside investors, and outside investors seek information on firms and the assurance that the managers of firms will act in the interests of the investors.

This module shows how corporations raise funds by issuing stocks and bonds. This appendix provides more detail to support that discussion. We begin by analyzing *present value* as a key concept in determining the prices of financial securities. We then provide greater information on *financial statements* issued by corporations, using Twitter as an example.

Using Present Value to Make Investment Decisions

Firms raise funds by selling equity (stock) and debt (bonds and loans) to investors and lenders. If you own shares of stock or a bond, you will receive payments in the form of dividends or coupons over a number of years. Most people value funds they already have more highly than funds they will receive some time in the future. For example, you would probably not trade $1,000 you already have for $1,000 you will not receive for one year. The longer you have to wait to receive a payment, the less value it will have for you. One thousand dollars you will not receive for two years is worth less to you than $1,000 you will receive after one year. The value you give today to money you will receive in the future is called the future payment's **present value**. The present value of $1,000 you will receive in one year will be less than $1,000.

Why is the $1,000 you will not receive for one year less valuable to you than the $1,000 you already have? The most important reason is that if you have $1,000 today, you can use that $1,000 today. You can buy goods and services with the money and receive enjoyment from them. The $1,000 you receive in one year does not have direct use to you now.

Also, prices will likely rise during the year you are waiting to receive your $1,000. So, when you finally do receive the $1,000 in one year, you will not be able to buy as much with it as you could with $1,000 today. Finally, there is some risk that you will not receive the $1,000 in one year. The risk may be very great if an unreliable friend borrows $1,000 from you and vaguely promises to pay you back in one year. The risk may be very small if you lend money to the federal government by buying a U.S. Treasury bond. In either case, though, there is at least some risk that you will not receive the funds promised.

When someone lends money, the lender expects to be paid back both the amount of the loan and some additional interest. Say you are willing to lend $1,000 today if you are paid back $1,100 one year from now. In this case, you are charging $100/$1,000 = 0.10, or 10 percent interest on the funds you have loaned. Economists would say that you value $1,000 today as equivalent to the $1,100 to be received one year in the future.

Notice that $1,100 can be written as $1,000(1 + 0.10). That is, the value of money received in the future is equal to the value of money in the present multiplied by 1 plus the interest rate, with the interest rate expressed as a decimal. Or:

$$\$1,100 = \$1,000(1 + 0.10).$$

Present value The value in today's dollars of funds to be paid or received in the future.

Notice, also, that if we divide both sides by $(1 + 0.10)$, we can rewrite this formula as:

$$\$1,000 = \frac{\$1,100}{(1 + 0.10)}.$$

The rewritten formula states that the present value is equal to the future value to be received in one year divided by 1 plus the interest rate. This formula is important because you can use it to convert any amount to be received in one year into its present value. Writing the formula generally, we have:

$$\text{Present value} = \frac{\text{Future value}_1}{(1 + i)}.$$

The present value of funds to be received in one year—Future value$_1$—can be calculated by dividing the amount of those funds to be received by 1 plus the interest rate. With an interest rate of 10 percent, the present value of $1,000,000 to be received one year from now is:

$$\frac{\$1,000,000}{(1 + 0.10)} = \$909,090.91.$$

This formula allows us to calculate the value today of funds that will be received in one year. But financial securities such as stocks and bonds involve promises to pay funds over many years. Therefore, it would be useful if we could expand this formula to calculate the present value of funds to be received more than one year in the future.

Go back to the original example, where we assumed you were willing to loan out your $1,000 for one year, provided that you received 10 percent interest. Suppose you are asked to lend the funds for two years and that you are promised 10 percent interest per year for each year of the loan. That is, you are lending $1,000, which at 10 percent interest will grow to $1,100 after one year, and you are agreeing to loan that $1,100 for a second year at 10 percent interest. So, after two years, you will be paid back $1,100(1 + 0.10)$, or $1,210. Or:

$$\$1,210 = \$1,000(1 + 0.10)(1 + 0.10),$$

or:

$$\$1,210 = \$1,000(1 + 0.10)^2.$$

This formula can also be rewritten as:

$$\$1,000 = \frac{\$1.210}{(1 + 0.10)^2}.$$

To put this formula in words, the $1,210 you receive two years from now has a present value equal to $1,210 divided by the quantity 1 plus the interest rate squared. If you agree to lend out your $1,000 for three years at 10 percent interest, you will receive:

$$\$1,331 = \$1,000(1 + 0.10)^3.$$

Notice, again, that:

$$\$1,000 = \frac{\$1,331}{(1 + 0.10)^3}.$$

You can probably see a pattern here. We can generalize the concept to say that the present value of funds to be received n years in the future—whether n is 1, 20, or 85 does not matter—equals the amount of the funds to be received divided by the quantity 1 plus the interest rate raised to the nth power. For instance, with an interest rate of 10 percent, the value of $1,000,000 to be received 25 years in the future is:

$$\text{Present value} = \frac{\$1,000,000}{(1 + 0.10)^{25}} = \$92,296.$$

Or, more generally:

$$\text{Present value} = \frac{\text{Future value}_n}{(1 + i)^n},$$

where Future value$_n$ represents funds that will be received in n years.

Solved Problem 6A.1

MyEconLab Interactive Animation

How to Receive Your Contest Winnings

Suppose you win a contest and are given the choice of the following prizes:

> **Prize 1:** $50,000 to be received right away, with four additional payments of $50,000 to be received each year for the next four years

Prize 2: $175,000 to be received right away

Explain which prize you would choose and the basis for your decision.

Solving the Problem

Step 1: **Review the material.** This problem involves applying the concept of present value, so you may want to review the section "Using Present Value to Make Investment Decisions," which begins on page 235.

Step 2: **Explain the basis for choosing the prize.** Unless you need cash immediately, you should choose the prize with the highest present value.

Step 3: **Calculate the present value of each prize.** Prize 2 consists of one payment of $175,000 received right away, so its present value is $175,000. Prize 1 consists of five payments spread out over time. To find the present value of the prize, we must find the present value of each of these payments and add them together. To calculate present value, we must use an interest rate. Let's assume an interest rate of 10 percent. In that case, the present value of Prize 1 is:

$$\$50,000 + \frac{\$50,000}{(1 + 0.10)} + \frac{\$50,000}{(1 + 0.10)^2} + \frac{\$50,000}{(1 + 0.10)^3} + \frac{\$50,000}{(1 + 0.10)^4}$$

$$= \$50,000 + \$45,454.55 + \$41,322.31 + \$37,565.74 + \$34,150.67$$

$$= \$208,493.27$$

Step 4: **State your conclusion.** Prize 1 has the greater present value, so you should choose it rather than Prize 2.

Your Turn: For more practice, do related problems 6A.6, 6A.7, 6A.8, and 6A.9 on page 242 at the end of this appendix.

MyEconLab Study Plan

Using Present Value to Calculate Bond Prices

Anyone who buys stocks or bonds is really buying a promise to receive certain payments—dividends in the case of stocks or coupons in the case of bonds. The price investors are willing to pay for a financial asset should be equal to the value of the payments they will receive as a result of owning the asset. Because most of the coupon or dividend payments will be received in the future, it is their present value that matters. We therefore have the following important idea: *The price of a financial asset should be equal to the present value of the payments to be received from owning that asset.*

Let's look at an example. Suppose that in 1988, General Electric issued a bond with an $80 coupon that will mature in 2018. It is now 2016, and that bond has been bought and sold by investors many times. You are considering buying it. If you buy the bond, you will receive two years of coupon payments plus a final payment of the bond's principal, or face value, of $1,000. Suppose, once again, that you need an interest rate of 10 percent to invest your funds. If the bond has a coupon of $80, the present value of the payments you receive from owning the bond—and, therefore, the present value of the bond—will be:

$$\text{Present value} = \frac{\$80}{(1+0.10)} + \frac{\$80}{(1+0.10)^2} + \frac{\$1,000}{(1+0.10)^2} = \$965.29.$$

That is, the present value of the bond will equal the present value of the three payments you will receive during the two years you own the bond. You should, therefore, be willing to pay $965.29 to own this bond and have the right to receive these payments from GE. This process of calculating present values of future payments is used to determine bond prices, with one qualification: The relevant interest rate used by investors in the bond market to calculate the present value and, therefore, the price of an existing bond is usually the coupon rate on comparable newly issued bonds. Therefore, the general formula for the price of a bond is:

$$\text{Bond price} = \frac{\text{Coupon}_1}{(1+i)} + \frac{\text{Coupon}_2}{(1+i)^2} + \cdots + \frac{\text{Coupon}_n}{(1+i)^n} + \frac{\text{Face value}}{(1+i)^n},$$

where:

- Coupon_1 is the coupon payment to be received after one year.
- Coupon_2 is the coupon payment to be received after two years.
- Coupon_n is the coupon payment received in the year the bond matures.
- The ellipsis takes the place of the coupon payments—if any—received between the second year and the year when the bond matures.
- Face value is the amount that will be received when the bond matures.
- i is the interest rate on comparable newly issued bonds.   MyEconLab Concept Check

Using Present Value to Calculate Stock Prices

When you own a firm's stock, you are legally entitled to your share of the firm's profits. Remember that the profits a firm pays out to its shareholders are called *dividends*. The price of a share of stock should equal the present value of the dividends investors expect to receive as a result of owning that stock. Therefore, the general formula for the price of a stock is:

$$\text{Stock price} = \frac{\text{Dividend}_1}{(1+i)} + \frac{\text{Dividend}_2}{(1+i)^2} + \cdots$$

Notice that this formula looks very similar to the one we used to calculate the price of a bond, with a couple of important differences:

- First, unlike a bond, a share of stock has no maturity date, so we have to calculate the present value of an infinite number of dividend payments. It may seem that the stock's price must be infinite as well, but remember that dollars you don't receive for many years are worth very little today. For instance, a dividend payment of $10 that will be received 40 years in the future is worth only a little more than $0.20 today at a 10 percent interest rate.
- Second, you know with certainty the coupon payments you will receive from owning the bond because they are set when the bond is issued and cannot be changed. However, you don't know for sure what the dividend payments from owning a stock will be. How large a dividend payment you will receive depends on how profitable the company will be in the future.

Although it is possible to forecast the future profitability of a company, this cannot be done with perfect accuracy. To emphasize this point, some economists rewrite the basic stock price formula by adding a superscript *e* to each dividend term to emphasize that these are *expected* dividend payments. Because the future profitability of companies is often very difficult to forecast, it is not surprising that differences of opinion exist over what the price of a particular stock should be. Some investors will be optimistic about the future profitability of a company and will, therefore, believe that the company's stock should have a high price. Other investors might be pessimistic and believe that the company's stock should have a low price.   MyEconLab Concept Check

A Simple Formula for Calculating Stock Prices

It is possible to simplify the formula for determining the price of a stock. If we assume that dividends will grow at a constant rate, we get the following equation:

$$\text{Stock price} = \frac{\text{Dividend}}{(i - \text{Growth rate})}.$$

In this equation, Dividend is the dividend expected to be received one year from now, and Growth rate is the rate at which those dividends are expected to grow. If a company pays a dividend of $1 per share to be received one year from now and Growth rate is 10 percent, the company is expected to pay a dividend of $1.10 the following year, $1.21 the year after that, and so on.

Now suppose that IBM will pay a dividend of $5 per share at the end of year, the consensus of investors is that these dividends will increase at a rate of 5 percent per year for the indefinite future, and the interest rate is 10 percent. Then the price of IBM's stock should be:

$$\text{Stock price} = \frac{\$5.00}{(0.10 - 0.05)} = \$100.00.$$

In recent years, investors have debated whether the high prices of the stocks of many high-tech firms, including Twitter, were justified, given that many of these companies had not made any profit yet and so had not paid any dividends. Is there any way that a rational investor would pay a high price for the stock of a company currently not earning profits? The formula for determining stock prices shows that it is possible, provided that the investor's assumptions are optimistic enough! For example, during 2015, one stock analyst predicted that Twitter would soon be earning $1 per share of stock. That is, Twitter's total earnings divided by the number of shares of its stock outstanding would be $1. Suppose Twitter pays out that $1 in dividends and that the $1 will grow rapidly over the years, by, say, 7 percent per year. Then the formula indicates that the price of Twitter's stock should be:

$$\text{Stock price} = \frac{\$1.00}{(0.10 - 0.07)} = \$33.33.$$

If you are sufficiently optimistic about the future prospects of a company, a high stock price can be justified even if the company is not currently earning a profit. But investors in stocks must be careful. Suppose investors decide that growth prospects for Twitter are only 4 percent per year instead of 7 percent because the firm turns out not to be as profitable as initially believed. Then our formula indicates that the price of Twitter's stock should be:

$$\text{Stock price} = \frac{\$1.00}{(0.10 - 0.04)} = \$16.67.$$

This price is only half the price determined assuming a more optimistic growth rate. We can conclude that investors use information about a firm's profitability and growth prospects to determine what the firm is worth.   MyEconLab Concept Check

Going Deeper into Financial Statements

Corporations disclose substantial information about their business operations and financial position to actual and potential investors. Some of this information meets the demands of participants in financial markets and of information-collection agencies, such as Moody's Investors Service, which develops credit ratings that help investors judge how risky corporate bonds are. Other information meets the reporting requirements of the U.S. Securities and Exchange Commission.

Key sources of information about a corporation's profitability and financial position are its principal financial statements—the *income statement* and the *balance sheet*. These important information sources were first introduced in the module. In the following section we go into more detail, using recent data for Twitter as an example.

Analyzing Income Statements

As discussed in the module, a firm's income statement summarizes its revenues, costs, and profit over a period of time. Figure 6A.1 shows Twitter's income statement for 2014.

Twitter's income statement presents the results of the company's operations during the year. Listed first are the revenues it earned, largely from selling advertising on its app, from January 1, 2014, to December 31, 2014: $1,403 million. Listed next are Twitter's operating expenses, the most important of which is its *cost of revenue*—which is commonly known as *cost of sales* or *cost of goods sold*: $446 million. Cost of revenue is the direct cost of producing the products sold, including in this case the salaries of the computer programmers Twitter hires to write the software for its app. Twitter also has substantial costs for researching and developing its products ($692 million) and for advertising and marketing them ($614 million). General and administrative expenses ($190 million) include costs such as the salaries of top managers.

The difference between a firm's revenue and its costs is its *profit*. Profit shows up in several forms on an income statement. A firm's *operating income* is the difference between its revenue and its operating expenses. Most corporations, including Twitter, also have interest expenses and income from investments, such as government and corporate bonds. In this case, Twitter paid $39 million more in interest expenses than it earned on its investments. Because its costs were greater than its revenue, Twitter's *income before taxes* was a loss (a loss in financial statements is indicated by the use of parenthesis) of $578 million. The federal government taxes the profits of corporations, but because Twitter experienced a

Note: All numbers are in millions of dollars.

Figure 6A.1 **Twitter's Income Statement for 2014**

Twitter's income statement shows the company's revenue, costs, and profit for 2014. The difference between its revenue ($1,403 million) and its operating expenses ($1,942 million) is its operating income (a loss of $539 million). Most corporations also have interest expenses and income from investments, such as government and corporate bonds. In this case, Twitter paid $39 million more in interest expenses than it earned on its investments, so its *income before taxes* was a loss of $578 million. Twitter had a net loss, or accounting loss, of $578 million for the year.

Note: Negative values in the figure are shown in parentheses.
Source: Twitter, *Annual Report, 2014.*

loss in 2014, it paid no taxes. Therefore, Twitter's *net income* after taxes was also a loss of $578 million. The fact that Twitter could experience a loss while still having a high stock price is an indication that investors were expecting Twitter to earn significant profits in the future. The net income that firms report on their income statements is referred to as their after-tax *accounting profit*.

MyEconLab Concept Check

Analyzing Balance Sheets

As discussed in the module, while a firm's income statement reports the firm's activities for a period of time, a firm's balance sheet summarizes its financial position on a particular day, usually the end of a quarter or year. To understand how a balance sheet is organized, first recall that an asset is anything of value that the firm owns, and a liability is a debt or an obligation that the firm owes. Subtracting the value of a firm's liabilities from the value of its assets leaves its *net worth*. Because a corporation's stockholders are its owners, net worth is often listed as **stockholders' equity** on a balance sheet. Using these definitions, we can state the balance sheet equation (also called the basic accounting equation) as follows:

$$\text{Assets} - \text{Liabilities} = \text{Stockholders' Equity,}$$

or:

$$\text{Assets} = \text{Liabilities} + \text{Stockholders' Equity.}$$

Stockholders' equity The difference between the value of a corporation's assets and the value of its liabilities; also known as *net worth*.

This equation tells us that the value of a firm's assets must equal the value of its liabilities plus the value of stockholders' equity. An important accounting convention dating back to the beginning of modern bookkeeping in fifteenth-century Italy holds that balance sheets should list assets on the left side and liabilities and net worth, or stockholders' equity, on the right side. Notice that this means that *the value of the left side of the balance sheet must always equal the value of the right side*. Figure 6A.2 shows Twitter's balance sheet as of December 31, 2014.

A couple of the entries on the asset side of the balance sheet may be unfamiliar: *Current assets* are assets that the firm could convert into cash quickly, such as the balance in its checking account or its accounts receivable, which is money currently owed to the firm for products that have been delivered but not yet paid for. *Goodwill* represents the difference between the purchase price of a company and the market value of its assets. It represents the ability of a business to earn an economic profit from its assets. For example, if you buy a restaurant that is located on a busy intersection and you employ a chef with a reputation for preparing delicious food, you may pay more than the market value of the tables, chairs, ovens, and other assets. This additional amount you pay will be entered on the asset side of your balance sheet as goodwill.

Current liabilities are short-term debts such as accounts payable, which is money owed to suppliers for goods received but not yet paid for, or bank loans that will be paid back in less than one year. Long-term bank loans, the value of outstanding corporate bonds, and other long-term debts are *long-term liabilities*.

MyEconLab Study Plan

Assets		Liabilities and Stockholders' Equity	
Current assets	$4,256	Current liabilities	$ 394
Property and equipment	557	Long-term liabilities	1,563
Goodwill	623	Total liabilities	1,957
Other assets	147	Stockholders' equity	3,626
Total assets	$5,583	Total liabilities and stockholders' equity	$5,583

Note: All values are in millions of dollars.

Figure 6A.2

Twitter's Balance Sheet as of December 31, 2014

Corporations list their assets on the left of their balance sheets and their liabilities on the right. The difference between the value of a firm's assets and the value of its liabilities equals the net worth of the firm, or stockholders' equity. Stockholders' equity is listed on the right side of the balance sheet. Therefore, the value of the left side of the balance sheet must always equal the value of the right side. **Source:** Twitter, *Annual Report, 2014.*

Key Terms

Present value, p. 235   Stockholders' equity, p. 241

6A   **Tools to Analyze Firms' Financial Information, pages 235–243**

LEARNING OBJECTIVE: Understand the concept of present value and the information contained on a firm's income statement and balance sheet.

MyEconLab   Visit **www.myeconlab.com** to complete these exercises online and get instant feedback.

Review Questions

6A.1 Why is money you receive at some future date worth less to you than money you receive today? If the interest rate rises, what effect does this have on the present value of payments you receive in the future?

6A.2 Give the formula for calculating the present value of a bond that will pay a coupon of $100 per year for 10 years and that has a face value of $1,000.

6A.3 Compare the formula for calculating the present value of the payments you will receive from owning a bond to the formula for calculating the present value of the payments you will receive from owning a stock. What are the key similarities? What are the key differences?

6A.4 How is operating income calculated? How does operating income differ from net income? How does net income differ from accounting profit?

6A.5 What is the key difference between a firm's income statement and its balance sheet? What is listed on the left side of a balance sheet? What is listed on the right side?

Problems and Applications

6A.6 **(Related to** Solved Problem 6A.1 **on page 237)** If the interest rate is 10 percent, what is the present value of a bond that matures in two years, pays $85 one year from now, and pays $1,085 two years from now?

6A.7 **(Related to** Solved Problem 6A.1 **on page 237)** Before the 2013 season, the Los Angeles Angels signed outfielder Josh Hamilton to a contract that would pay him an immediate $10 million signing bonus and the following amounts: $15 million for the 2013 season, $15 million for the 2014 season, $23 million for the 2015 season, $30 million for the 2016 season, and $30 million for the 2017 season. The contract also specified that $2 million would be given to a charity. Assume that Hamilton receives each of his five seasonal salaries as a lump-sum payment at the end of the season.

a. Some newspaper reports described Hamilton as having signed a $125 million contract with the Angels. Do you agree that $125 million was the value of this contract? Briefly explain.

b. What was the present value of Hamilton's contract at the time he signed it (assuming an interest rate of 10 percent)? For simplicity, you can ignore the $2 million given to charity.

c. If you use an interest rate of 5 percent, what was the present value of Hamilton's contract?

Source: Drew Silva, "Breaking Down Josh Hamilton's Five-Year, $125M Contract," hardballtalk.nbcsports.com, December 15, 2012.

6A.8 **(Related to** Solved Problem 6A.1 **on page 237)** A winner of the Pennsylvania Lottery was given the choice of receiving $18 million at once or $1,440,000 per year for 25 years.

a. If the winner had opted for the 25 annual payments, how much in total would she have received?

b. At an interest rate of 10 percent, what would be the present value of the 25 payments?

c. At an interest rate of 5 percent, what would be the present value of the 25 payments?

d. What interest rate would make the present value of the 25 payments equal to the one payment of $18 million? (This question is difficult and requires the use of a financial calculator or a spreadsheet. *Hint:* If you are familiar with the Excel spreadsheet program, use the RATE function. You can answer parts (b) and (c) by using the Excel PV [Present Value] function.)

6A.9 **(Related to** Solved Problem 6A.1 **on page 237)** Before the start of the 2000 baseball season, the New York Mets decided that they didn't want Bobby Bonilla playing for them any longer. But Bonilla had a contract with the Mets for the 2000 season that would have obliged the Mets to pay him $5.9 million. When the Mets released Bonilla, he agreed to take the following payments in lieu of the $5.9 million the Mets would have paid him in the year 2000: He would receive 25 equal payments of $1,193,248.20 each July 1 from 2011 to 2035. If you were Bobby Bonilla, which would you rather have had, the lump-sum $5.9 million in 2000 or the 25 payments beginning in 2011? Explain the basis for your decision.

Source: Mike Sielski, "There's No Accounting for This," *Wall Street Journal*, July 1, 2010.

6A.10 Suppose that eLake, an online auction site, is paying a dividend of $2 per share. You expect this dividend to grow 2 percent per year, and the interest rate is 10 percent. What is the most you would be willing to pay for a share of stock in eLake? If the interest rate is 5 percent, what is the most you would be willing to pay? When interest rates in the economy decline, would you expect stock prices in general to rise or fall? Briefly explain.

6A.11 Suppose you buy the bond of a large corporation at a time when the inflation rate is very low. If the inflation rate increases during the time you hold the bond, what is likely to happen to the price of the bond?

6A.12 Use the information in the following table for calendar year 2014 to prepare an income statement for McDonald's Corporation. Be sure to include entries for operating income and net income.

Revenue from company restaurants	$18,169 million
Revenue from franchised restaurants	9,272 million
Cost of operating company-owned restaurants	15,288 million
Income taxes	2,614 million
Interest expense	577 million
General and administrative cost	2,507 million
Cost of restaurant leases	1,697 million

Source: McDonalds Corp., *Annual Report, 2014.*

6A.13 Use the information in the following table on the financial situation of Starbucks Corporation as of September 28, 2014 (the end of the firm's financial year), to prepare a balance sheet for the firm. Be sure to include an entry for stockholders' equity.

Current assets	$4,169 million
Current liabilities	3,039 million
Property and equipment	3,519 million
Long-term liabilities	2,441 million
Goodwill	856 million
Other assets	2,209 million

Source: Starbucks Corp., *Annual Report, 2014.*

6A.14 The *current ratio* is equal to a firm's current assets divided by its current liabilities. Use the information in Figure 6A.2 on page 241 to calculate Twitter's current ratio on December 31, 2014. Investors generally prefer that a firm's current ratio be greater than 1.5. What problems might a firm encounter if the value of its current assets is low relative to the value of its current liabilities?

Key Terms

Bond, p. 219

Coupon payment, p. 219

Crowding out, p. 231

Direct finance, p. 218

Dividends, p. 221

Financial intermediaries, p. 226

Financial markets, p. 226

Indirect finance, p. 218

Interest rate, p. 219

Market for loanable funds, p. 229

Stock, p. 220

6.1 How Firms Raise Funds, pages 218–225

LEARNING OBJECTIVE: Explain how firms raise the funds they need to operate and expand.

Summary

Firms rely on retained earnings—which are profits kept by the firm and not paid out to the firm's owners—or on using the savings of households for the funds they need to operate and expand. With **direct finance**, the savings of households flow directly to businesses when investors buy **stocks** and **bonds** in financial markets. With **indirect finance**, savings flow indirectly to businesses when households deposit money in savings and checking accounts in banks and the banks lend these funds to businesses. Federal, state, and local governments also sell bonds in financial markets, and households also borrow funds from banks. When a firm sells a bond, it is borrowing money from the buyer of the bond. Firms make **coupon payments** to buyers of bonds. The **interest rate** is the cost of borrowing funds, usually expressed as a percentage of the amount borrowed. When a firm sells stock, it is selling part ownership of the firm to the buyer of the stock. **Dividends** are payments by a corporation to its shareholders. The original purchasers of stocks and bonds may resell them in stock and bond markets, such as the New York Stock Exchange. The performance of the U.S. stock market is often measured using stock market indexes. The three most widely followed stock indexes are the Dow Jones Industrial Average, the S&P 500, and the NASDAQ Composite Index.

MyEconLab   Visit **www.myeconlab.com** to complete these exercises online and get instant feedback.

Review Questions

1.1 What is the difference between direct finance and indirect finance? If you borrow money from a bank to buy a new car, are you using direct finance or indirect finance?

1.2 Why is a bond considered to be a loan but a share of stock is not? Why do corporations issue both bonds and shares of stock?

1.3 How do the stock and bond markets provide information to businesses? Why do stock and bond prices change over time?

Problems and Applications

1.4 Suppose that a firm in which you have invested is losing money. Would you rather own the firm's stock or the firm's bonds? Briefly explain.

1.5 Suppose you originally invested in a firm when it was small and unprofitable. Now the firm has grown to be large and profitable. Would you be better off if you had bought the firm's stock or the firm's bonds? Briefly explain.

1.6 If you deposit $20,000 in a savings account at a bank, you might earn 1 percent interest per year. Someone who borrows $20,000 from a bank to buy a new car might have to pay an interest rate of 6 percent per year on the loan. Knowing this, why don't you just lend your money directly to the car buyer and cut out the bank?

1.7 **(Related to the** Module Opener **on page 217)** Were the shares of stock issued as a result of Twitter's initial public offering (IPO) sold in a primary market or a secondary market? Was the IPO an example of direct finance or indirect finance?

1.8 **(Related to the** Making the Connection **on page 219)** According to an article in the *Wall Street Journal*, in May 2015, Moody's Investors Service cut its rating on McDonald's bonds from A3 to A2.
   a. What is Moody's top bond rating? Under what circumstances would Moody's, or the other bond rating agencies, be likely to cut the rating on a firm's bonds?
   b. What will be the likely result of this rating's cut for the interest rate McDonald's will have to pay when it sells new bonds? Briefly explain.

   Source: Chelsey Dulaney, "Moody's Downgrades McDonald's, Following S&P and Fitch," *Wall Street Journal*, May 15, 2015.

1.9 **(Related to the** Making the Connection **on page 219)** Investors use the bond ratings from Moody's, S&P, and Fitch to determine which bonds they will buy and the prices they are willing to pay for them. The rating services charge the firms and governments that issue bonds, rather than investors, for their services. Critics argue that the rating agencies may give higher ratings than are justified in order to continue to sell their services to bond issuing firms. To avoid this impression, why don't Moody's, S&P, and Fitch sell their services directly to investors?

1.10 What effect would the following events be likely to have on the price of Google's stock?
  a. A competitor launches a search engine that is better than Google's.
  b. The corporate income tax is abolished.
  c. Google's board of directors becomes dominated by close friends and relatives of its top management.
  d. The price of wireless Internet connections in developing countries unexpectedly drops, so more and more people worldwide use the Internet.
  e. Google announces a profit of $10 billion, but investors anticipated that Google would earn a profit of $11 billion.

1.11 (Related to the Don't Let This Happen to You **on page 222)** Briefly explain whether you agree with the following statement: "The total value of the shares of Microsoft stock traded on the NASDAQ last week was $250 million, so the firm actually received more revenue from stock sales than from selling software."

1.12 (Related to the Making the Connection **on page 223)** A column in the *Wall Street Journal* listed "trying to forecast what stocks will do next" as one of the three mistakes investors make repeatedly. Briefly explain why trying to forecast stock prices would be a mistake for the average investor.
Source: Morgan Housel, "Three Mistakes Investors Keep Making Again and Again," *Wall Street Journal*, September 12, 2014.

1.13 (Related to Solved Problem 6.1 **on page 224)** In a letter to his company's stockholders, Warren Buffett offered the following opinion: "Most investors, of course, have not made the study of business prospects a priority in their lives. . . . I have good news for these non-professionals: The typical investor doesn't need this skill." Briefly explain Buffett's reasoning.
Source: Warren Buffett, *Letter to Berkshire Shareholders*, March 1, 2014, p. 20.

6.2 Saving, Investment, and the Financial System, pages 225–234
LEARNING OBJECTIVE: Discuss the role of the financial system in facilitating long-run economic growth.

Summary

Financial markets and financial intermediaries together comprise the **financial system**. A well-functioning financial system is an important determinant of economic growth. Firms acquire funds from households, either directly through financial markets—such as the stock and bond markets—or indirectly through financial intermediaries—such as banks. The funds available to firms come from *saving*. There are two categories of saving in the economy: *private saving* by households and *public saving* by the government. The value of total saving in the economy is always equal to the value of total investment spending. In the model of the **market for loanable funds**, the interaction of borrowers and lenders determines the market interest rate and the quantity of loanable funds exchanged.

MyEconLab   Visit www.myeconlab.com to complete these exercises online and get instant feedback.

Review Questions

2.1 Why is a country's financial system important for long-run economic growth?
2.2 How does the financial system—both financial markets and financial intermediaries—provide risk sharing, liquidity, and information to savers and borrowers?
2.3 Briefly explain why the total value of saving in the economy must equal the total value of investment.
2.4 What are loanable funds? Why do businesses demand loanable funds? Why do households supply loanable funds?

Problems and Applications

2.5 Suppose you can receive an interest rate of 3 percent on a certificate of deposit at a bank that is charging borrowers 7 percent on new car loans. Why might you be unwilling to loan money directly to someone who wants to borrow from you to buy a new car, even if that person offers to pay you an interest rate higher than 3 percent?

2.6 An International Monetary Fund Factsheet makes the following observation regarding sound financial systems: "A country's financial system ... provide[s] a framework ... [for] supporting economic growth." Do you agree with this observation? Briefly explain.
Source: "Financial System Soundness," *International Monetary Fund Factsheet*, September 21, 2015.

2.7 Consider the following data for a closed economy:

$Y = \$11$ trillion
$C = \$8$ trillion
$I = \$2$ trillion
$TR = \$1$ trillion
$T = \$3$ trillion

Use these data to calculate the following:
a. Private saving
b. Public saving
c. Government purchases
d. The government budget deficit or budget surplus

2.8 Consider the following data for a closed economy:

$$Y = \$12 \text{ trillion}$$
$$C = \$8 \text{ trillion}$$
$$G = \$2 \text{ trillion}$$
$$S_{\text{Public}} = \$-0.5 \text{ trillion}$$
$$T = \$2 \text{ trillion}$$

Use these data to calculate the following:
a. Private saving
b. Investment spending
c. Transfer payments
d. The government budget deficit or budget surplus

2.9 In problem 2.8, suppose that government purchases increase from $2 trillion to $2.5 trillion. If the values for Y and C are unchanged, what must happen to the values of S and I? Briefly explain.

2.10 Match each of the following scenarios with the appropriate graph of the market for loanable funds.

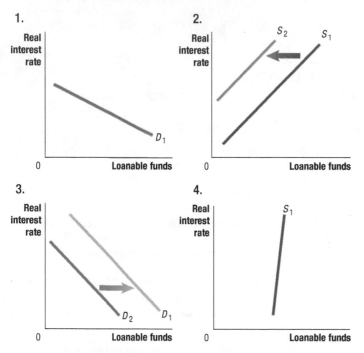

1.

2.

3.

4.

a. An increase in the real interest rate results in only a small increase in private saving by households.
b. A decrease in the real interest rate results in a substantial increase in spending on investment projects by businesses.
c. The federal government eliminates 401(k) retirement accounts.
d. The federal government reduces the tax on corporate profits. (Assume no change in the federal budget deficit or budget surplus.)

2.11 Use the following graph to answer the questions.

a. Does the shift from S_1 to S_2 represent an increase or a decrease in the supply of loanable funds?
b. With the shift in supply, what happens to the equilibrium quantity of loanable funds?
c. With the change in the equilibrium quantity of loanable funds, what happens to the quantity of saving? What happens to the quantity of investment?

2.12 Use the following graph to answer the questions.

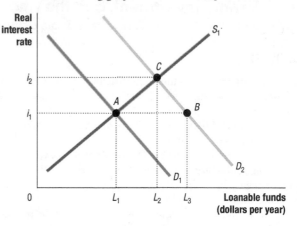

a. With the shift in the demand curve for loanable funds, what happens to the equilibrium real interest rate and the equilibrium quantity of loanable funds?
b. How can the equilibrium quantity of loanable funds increase when the real interest rate increases? Doesn't the quantity of loanable funds demanded decrease when the interest rate increases?
c. How much would the quantity of loanable funds demanded have increased if the interest rate had remained at i_1?
d. How much does the quantity of loanable funds supplied increase with the increase in the interest rate from i_1 to i_2?

2.13 Firms care about their after-tax rate of return on investment projects. In the market for loanable funds, draw a graph and explain the effect of an increase in taxes on business profits. (For simplicity, assume no change in the federal budget deficit or budget surplus.) What happens to the equilibrium real interest rate and the quantity of loanable funds? What will be the effect on the level of investment by firms and the economy's capital stock in the future?

2.14 **(Related to the** Making the Connection **on page 230)** A writer for the *Wall Street Journal* wrote a whimsical "Letter to Stingy American Consumers":

> Dear American Consumer:
>
> This is The *Wall Street Journal*. …The sun shined in April and you didn't spend much money. … You've been saving more too. … This saving is not like you. … Do you know the American economy is counting on you?

Economist Steven Landsburg praised Ebenezer Scrooge for choosing to save rather than spend his money, arguing that saving—not consumption—fuels economic growth. The *Wall Street Journal* letter pretends to chide the American consumer for saving rather than spending income, arguing that spending—not saving—fuels economic growth. Which argument is correct?

Source: John Hilsenrath, "Grand Central: A Letter to Stingy American Consumers," *Wall Street Journal*, June 2, 2015.

2.15 **(Related to the** Making the Connection **on page 230)** The *Making the Connection* claims that Ebenezer Scrooge promoted economic growth more when he was a miser and saved most of his income than when he reformed and began spending freely. Suppose, though, that after he reformed he spent most of his income buying food for the Cratchits and other poor families. Many economists believe that there is a close connection between how much very poor people eat and how much they are able to work and how productive they are while working. Does this fact affect the conclusion about whether the pre-reform or post-reform Scrooge had a more positive impact on economic growth? Briefly explain.

2.16 **(Related to** Solved Problem 10.2 **on page 232)** The federal government in the United States has been running large budget deficits. Suppose that Congress and the president take actions that turn the budget deficits into budget surpluses.
   a. Use a market for loanable funds graph to illustrate the effect of the federal budget surpluses. What happens to the equilibrium real interest rate and the quantity of loanable funds? What happens to the level of saving and investment?
   b. Now suppose that households believe that surpluses will result in Congress and the president cutting taxes in the near future in order to move from budget surpluses to balanced budgets. As a result, households increase their consumption spending in anticipation of paying lower taxes. Briefly explain how your analysis in part (a) will be affected.

2.17 Savers are taxed on the nominal interest payments they receive rather than the real interest payments. Suppose the federal government shifts from taxing nominal interest payments to taxing only real interest payments. (That is, savers will be allowed to subtract the inflation rate from the nominal interest rate they receive and only pay taxes on the resulting real interest rate.) Use a market for loanable funds graph to analyze the effects of this change in tax policy. What happens to the equilibrium real interest rate and the equilibrium quantity of loanable funds? What happens to the level of saving and investment?

Fiscal Policy: Government Spending and Taxes

Module Outline and Learning Objectives

Does Government Spending Create Jobs?

The Golden Gate Bridge is an international symbol of San Francisco. The bridge spans the entrance to San Francisco Bay from the Pacific Ocean. Construction of the bridge began in 1933, and the bridge was open to traffic in 1937. Doyle Drive is a 1.6-mile stretch of U.S. Highway 101 and the main approach to the bridge from the San Francisco side. Doyle Drive was in desperate need of reconstruction, but for many years the city of San Francisco and the state of California had failed to provide the funding. In early 2009, President Barack Obama and Congress enacted the American Recovery and Reinvestment Act (ARRA, often referred to as the "stimulus bill") in an attempt to increase aggregate demand during the recession of 2007–2009. The ARRA is an example of *discretionary fiscal policy* aimed at increasing real GDP and employment. Some of the funds from the act were allocated to the Doyle Drive project. San Francisco Mayor Gavin Newsom welcomed the news: "This project is shovel ready and a signature example of how the federal stimulus can close the funding gap, stimulate the economy, improve transportation, and create jobs in San Francisco."

The Doyle Drive project was designed by the Flatiron Corporation, and construction was carried out by Kiewit Construction, headquartered in Omaha, Nebraska. Kiewit hired hundreds of workers for the project, which was completed in July 2015. The project to rebuild Doyle Drive is an example of increased government spending resulting in increased employment. Or is it? A majority of economists agree that a temporary increase in government spending can lead to increased employment during a recession. But some economists argue that fiscal policy actions like ARRA shift employment from one group of workers to another but do not increase total employment. The argument over the effect of government spending on employment continued years after the end of the recession of 2007–2009.

When the federal government spends more than it collects in taxes, the result is a federal budget deficit. Following the recession, the federal government ran the largest peacetime deficits in history. During 2011 and 2012, Congress and President Obama enacted cuts in federal spending, increases in taxes, and limits on future spending increases to try to reduce the budget deficit. In 2015, Congress and the president somewhat loosened the limits on federal spending while continuing to debate whether additional spending was necessary to help the economy finally make it back to potential GDP.

In this module, we will examine discretionary fiscal policy, the federal budget deficit, and the debate over their effects.

Sources: David R. Baker, "Presidio Parkway, the New Doyle Drive, Is Now Open," sfgate.com, July 13, 2015; Metropolitan Transit Commission, "Speaker Pelosi and Mayor Newsom Announce Doyle Drive Project Is Shovel Ready," February 28, 2009; Jonathan Weisman, "Republicans Aim to Hamper Obama's Policies with Spending Bills," *New York Times*, July 7, 2015; and http://goldengatebridge.org.

Economics in Your Life

What Would You Do with an Extra $500?

Suppose that the federal government announces that it will immediately mail you, and everyone else in the economy, a $500 tax rebate. In addition, you expect that in future years, your taxes will also decrease by $500. How will you respond to this increase in your disposable income? What effect will this tax rebate likely have on equilibrium real GDP in the short run? As you read this module, try to answer these questions. You can check your answers against those we provide on **page 292** at the end of this Module.

I n Module 8A, we will discuss how the Federal Reserve uses monetary policy to pursue macroeconomic policy goals, including price stability and high employment. In this module, we will explore how the government uses *fiscal policy*, which involves changes in taxes and government purchases, to achieve similar policy goals. As we have seen, in the short run, the price level and the levels of real GDP and total employment in the economy depend on aggregate demand and short-run aggregate supply. In the long run, the levels of real GDP and employment depend on long-run aggregate supply. The government can affect the levels of both aggregate demand and aggregate supply through fiscal policy. We will discuss how Congress and the president decide which fiscal policy actions to take to achieve their goals. We will also discuss the debates among economists and policymakers over the effectiveness of fiscal policy.

 7.1

What Is Fiscal Policy?

LEARNING OBJECTIVE: Define fiscal policy.

Fiscal policy Changes in federal taxes and purchases that are intended to achieve macroeconomic policy goals.

Since the end of World War II, the federal government has been committed under the Employment Act of 1946 to intervening in the economy "to promote maximum employment, production, and purchasing power." As we will see in Module 8A, the Federal Reserve's Federal Open Market Committee meets eight times per year to decide whether to change monetary policy. Less frequently, Congress and the president also make changes in taxes and government purchases to achieve macroeconomic policy goals, such as high employment, price stability, and high rates of economic growth. Changes in federal taxes and purchases that are intended to achieve macroeconomic policy goals are called **fiscal policy**.

What Fiscal Policy Is and What It Isn't

In the United States, federal, state, and local governments all have responsibility for taxing and spending. Economists typically use the term *fiscal policy* to refer only to the actions of the federal government. State and local governments sometimes change their taxing and spending policies to aid their local economies, but these are not fiscal policy actions because they are not intended to affect the national economy. The federal government makes many decisions about taxes and spending, but not all of these decisions are fiscal policy actions because they are not intended to achieve macroeconomic policy goals. For example, a decision to cut the taxes of people who buy hybrid cars is an environmental policy action, not a fiscal policy action. Similarly, the spending increases to fund the war on terrorism and the wars in Iraq and Afghanistan were part of defense and homeland security policy, not fiscal policy.   MyEconLab Concept Check

Automatic Stabilizers versus Discretionary Fiscal Policy

Automatic stabilizers Government spending and taxes that automatically increase or decrease along with the business cycle.

There is an important distinction between *automatic stabilizers* and *discretionary fiscal policy*. Government spending and taxes that automatically increase or decrease along with the business cycle are called **automatic stabilizers**. The word *automatic* in this case refers to the fact that changes in these types of spending and taxes happen without actions by the government. For example, when the economy is expanding and employment is increasing, government spending on unemployment insurance payments to workers who have lost their jobs will automatically decrease. During a recession, as employment declines, this type of spending will automatically increase. Similarly, when the economy is expanding and incomes are rising, the amount the government collects in taxes will increase as people pay additional taxes on their higher incomes. When the economy is in a recession, the amount the government collects in taxes will fall.

With discretionary fiscal policy, the government takes actions to change spending or taxes. The tax cuts and spending increases in the American Recovery and Reinvestment Act (ARRA) that Congress and the president enacted in 2009, as mentioned in the module opener, are examples of discretionary fiscal policy actions.   MyEconLab Concept Check

Figure 7.1   The Federal Government's Share of Total Government Expenditures, 1929–2014

Until the Great Depression of the 1930s, the majority of government spending in the United States occurred at the state and local levels.

Since World War II, the federal government's share of total government expenditures has been between two-thirds and three-quarters.

Source: U.S. Bureau of Economic Analysis.

An Overview of Government Spending and Taxes

To provide a context for discussing fiscal policy, it is important to understand the big picture of government taxing and spending. Before the Great Depression of the 1930s, the majority of government spending in the United States took place at the state and local levels. As Figure 7.1 shows, the size of the federal government expanded significantly during the crisis of the Great Depression. Since World War II, the federal government's share of total government expenditures has been between two-thirds and three-quarters.

Economists often measure government spending relative to the size of the economy by calculating government spending as a percentage of GDP. Remember that there is a difference between federal government *purchases* and federal government *expenditures*. When the federal government purchases an aircraft carrier or the services of an FBI agent, it receives a good or service in return. Federal government expenditures include purchases plus federal government spending—such as Social Security payments—that does not involve purchases. As Figure 7.2 shows, federal government *purchases* as a percentage

Figure 7.2

Federal Purchases and Federal Expenditures as a Percentage of GDP, 1950–2014

As a fraction of GDP, the federal government's *purchases* of goods and services have been declining since the Korean War in the early 1950s. Total *expenditures* by the federal government—including transfer payments—as a fraction of GDP slowly rose from 1950 through the early 1990s and fell from 1992 to 2001, before rising again. The recession of 2007–2009 and the slow recovery that followed led to a surge in federal government expenditures, causing them to rise to their highest level as a percentage of GDP since the end of World War II in 1945.

Source: U.S. Bureau of Economic Analysis.

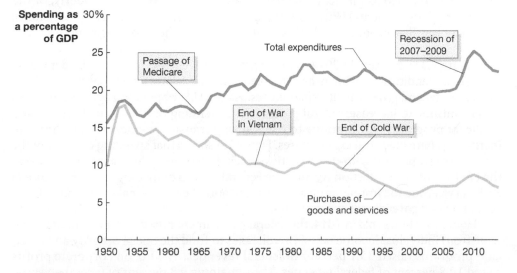

Figure 7.3

Federal Government Expenditures, 2014

Federal government *purchases* can be divided into defense spending—which makes up 19.2 percent of the federal budget—and spending on everything else the federal government does—from paying the salaries of FBI agents, to operating the national parks, to supporting scientific research—which makes up 8.1 percent of the budget. In addition to purchases, there are three other categories of federal government *expenditures*: interest on the national debt, grants to state and local governments, and transfer payments. Transfer payments rose from 25 percent of federal government expenditures in the 1960s to 48.7 percent in 2014.

Source: U.S. Bureau of Economic Analysis.

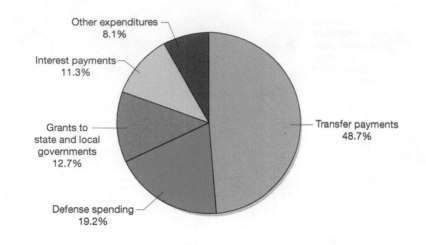

of GDP have actually been falling most of the time since the end of the Korean War in the early 1950s. Total federal *expenditures* as a percentage of GDP rose from 1950 to the early 1990s and then fell from 1992 to 2000, before rising again. The decline in expenditures between 1992 and 2001 was partly the result of the end of the Cold War between the Soviet Union and the United States, which allowed for a substantial reduction in defense spending. Real federal government spending on national defense declined by almost 25 percent between 1990 and 1998, before rising by more than 60 percent between 1998 and 2010 in response to the war on terrorism and the wars in Iraq and Afghanistan and then declining more than 15 percent by 2014 as those wars wound down. The recession of 2007–2009 and the slow recovery that followed led to a surge in federal government expenditures, which in 2011 rose to their highest level as a percentage of GDP since the end of World War II in 1945 before declining again in the following years as a result of limits on spending enacted by Congress and the president.

In addition to purchases, there are three other categories of federal government expenditures: *interest on the national debt, grants to state and local governments,* and *transfer payments.* Interest on the national debt represents payments to holders of the bonds the federal government has issued to borrow money. Grants to state and local governments are payments made by the federal government to support government activity at the state and local levels. For example, to help reduce crime, Congress implemented a program of grants to local governments to hire more police officers. The largest and fastest-growing category of federal expenditures is transfer payments. Some of these programs, such as Social Security and unemployment insurance, began in the 1930s. Others, such as Medicare, which finances health care for the elderly, or the food stamp (Supplemental Nutrition Assistance Program) and Temporary Assistance for Needy Families programs, which are intended to aid the poor, began in the 1960s or later.

Figure 7.3 shows that in 2014, transfer payments were 48.7 percent of federal government expenditures, having nearly doubled since the 1960s, when they were only 25 percent of federal government expenditures. As the U.S. population ages and medical costs continue to increase, federal government spending on the Social Security and Medicare programs will continue to rise, causing transfer payments to consume an increasing share of federal expenditures. Figure 7.3 shows that spending on most of the federal government's day-to-day activities—including running federal agencies such as the Environmental Protection Agency, the Federal Bureau of Investigation, the National Park Service, and the Immigration and Naturalization Service—makes up only 8.1 percent of federal government expenditures.

Figure 7.4 shows that in 2014, the federal government raised 42.8 percent of its revenue from individual income taxes. Payroll taxes to fund the Social Security and Medicare programs raised 35.1 percent of federal revenues. The tax on corporate profits raised 12.8 percent of federal revenues. The remaining 9.3 percent of federal revenues were raised from excise taxes on certain products, such as cigarettes and gasoline, from

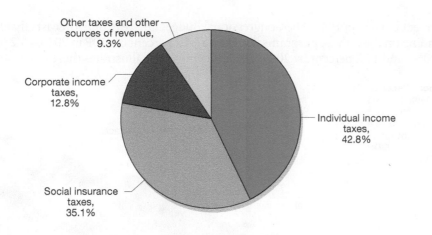

Other taxes and other sources of revenue, 9.3%

Corporate income taxes, 12.8%

Individual income taxes, 42.8%

Social insurance taxes, 35.1%

MyEconLab Real-time data

Figure 7.4

Federal Government Revenue, 2014

In 2014, individual income taxes raised 42.8 percent of the federal government's revenues. Corporate income taxes raised 12.8 percent of revenue. Payroll taxes to fund the Social Security and Medicare programs raised 35.1 percent of revenue. The remaining 9.3 percent of revenues were raised from excise taxes, tariffs on imports, and other sources.

Source: U.S. Bureau of Economic Analysis.

tariffs on goods imported from other countries, from payments by the Federal Reserve from its profits on its security holdings, and from other sources, such as payments by companies that cut timber on federal lands.　　　　　　　　　MyEconLab Concept Check

Making the Connection

MyEconLab Video

Is Spending on Social Security and Medicare a Fiscal Time Bomb?

The federal government established Social Security in 1935 to provide payments to retired workers. The program began as a "pay-as-you-go" system, meaning that payments to current retirees were made with taxes collected from current workers. In the early years of the program, many workers were paying into the system, and there were relatively few retirees. For example, in 1940, more than 35 million workers were paying into the system, and only 222,000 people were receiving benefits—a ratio of more than 150 workers to each retiree. In those early years, most retirees received far more in benefits than they had paid in taxes. The first beneficiary was a legal secretary named Ida May Fuller. She worked for three years after the program began and paid total taxes of only $24.75. During her retirement, she collected $22,888.92 in benefits.

The Social Security and Medicare programs have been very successful in reducing poverty among older Americans, but in recent years, the ability of the federal government to finance current promises has been called into doubt. After World War II, the United States experienced a "baby boom," as birthrates rose and remained high through the early 1960s. Falling birthrates after 1965 have caused long-run problems for the Social Security system because the number of workers per retiree has continually declined. Currently, there are only 2.8 workers per retiree, and that ratio could decline to 2 workers per retiree by 2035. Congress has attempted to deal with this problem by gradually raising the age to receive full benefits from 65 to 67 and by increasing payroll taxes. Social Security and Medicare are financed from a payroll tax on individuals' wages and self-employment income. Workers and firms are each liable for half the tax. In 1940, the payroll tax rate was 2 percent; in 2015, it was 15.3 percent. Beginning in 2013, individuals earning more than $200,000 in either wages or self-employment income have paid two additional Medicare taxes: an additional 0.9 percent tax on their wages and an additional 3.8 percent tax on their investment income.

The federal government established the Medicare program in 1965 to provide health care coverage to people age 65 and over. The long-term financial situation for Medicare is an even greater cause for concern than is Social Security. As Americans live longer and as new—and expensive—medical procedures are developed, the projected expenditures under the Medicare program will eventually far outstrip projected tax revenues. The federal government also faces increasing expenditures under the Medicaid program, which is administered by state governments and provides health care coverage to low-income people. In 2015, federal spending on Social Security, Medicare, and Medicaid equaled 10.1 percent of GDP. Spending on these three programs was less than

3 percent of GDP in 1962. The Congressional Budget Office (CBO) forecasts that federal spending on these three programs will rise to 14.2 percent of GDP in 2040, 16.2 percent by 2060, and 19.8 percent by 2090. The following graph illustrates these forecasts.

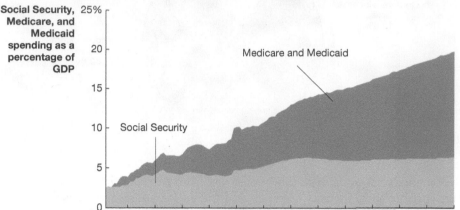

Note: The area labeled "Medicare and Medicaid" also includes federal spending on the Children's Health Insurance Program (CHIP) and federal subsidies to health care exchanges.

Over the past 40 years, the federal government has spent an average of about 21.5 percent of GDP on *all programs* combined—from buying aircraft carriers to paying the salaries of FBI agents to making Social Security and Medicare payments. So, if current trends continue, the federal government will eventually be spending, as a fraction of GDP, nearly as much on these three programs as it currently does on all programs combined.

The Board of Trustees of the Social Security Administration forecasts that through 2090, the gap between the benefits projected to be paid under the Social Security and Medicare programs and projected tax revenues is a staggering $49 *trillion,* or more than two and half times the value of GDP in 2015. If current projections are accurate, policymakers are faced with the choice of significantly restraining spending on these programs, greatly increasing taxes on households and firms, or implementing some combination of spending restraints and tax increases. The alternatives are all unpleasant. A report from the CBO concluded: "Even if taxation reached levels that were unprecedented in the United States, current spending policies could become financially unsustainable."

A lively political debate has taken place over the future of the Social Security and Medicare programs. Some policymakers have proposed increasing taxes to fund future benefit payments. The tax increases needed, however, could be as much as 50 percent higher than current rates, and tax increases of that magnitude could discourage work effort, entrepreneurship, and investment, thereby slowing economic growth. There have also been proposals to slow the rate of growth of future benefits, while guaranteeing benefits to current recipients. While this strategy would avoid the need to raise taxes significantly, it would also require younger workers to save more for their retirements. Some economists and policymakers have argued for slower benefit growth for higher-income workers while leaving future benefits unchanged for lower-income workers. Whatever changes are ultimately made in the Medicare and Social Security programs, the outcome of this policy debate will have important effects on the futures of today's college students.

Sources: Congressional Budget Office, "Supplemental Data for CBO's 2015 Long-Term Budget Outlook," June 2015; Congressional Budget Office, "Baseline Projections of Mandatory Outlays," January 2015; Board of Trustees, Federal Old-Age and Survivors Insurance and Federal Disability Insurance Trust Funds, "The 2015 Annual Report of the Board of Trustees of the Federal Old-Age and Survivors Insurance and Disability Insurance Trust Funds," July 22, 2015; and the Social Security Administration Web site (www.ssa.gov).

MyEconLab Study Plan   **Your Turn:** Test your understanding by doing related problem 1.7 on page 269 at the end of this module.

The Effects of Fiscal Policy on Real GDP and the Price Level

LEARNING OBJECTIVE: Explain how fiscal policy affects aggregate demand and how the government can use fiscal policy to stabilize the economy.

The federal government uses macroeconomic policies to offset the effects of the business cycle on the economy. We will see in Module 8A that the Federal Reserve carries out monetary policy through changes in interest rates and the money supply. Congress and the president carry out fiscal policy through changes in government purchases and taxes. Because changes in government purchases and taxes lead to changes in aggregate demand, they can affect the level of real GDP, employment, and the price level. When the economy is in a recession, *increases* in government purchases or *decreases* in taxes will increase aggregate demand. As we saw in Modules 4 and 4A, the inflation rate may increase when real GDP is beyond potential GDP. Decreases in government purchases or increase in taxes can slow the growth of aggregate demand and reduce the inflation rate.

Expansionary and Contractionary Fiscal Policy

Expansionary fiscal policy involves increasing government purchases or decreasing taxes. An increase in government purchases will increase aggregate demand directly because government purchases are a component of aggregate demand. A cut in taxes has an indirect effect on aggregate demand. Remember that the income households have available to spend after they have paid their taxes is called *disposable income* (see Module 3). Cutting the individual income tax will increase household disposable income and consumption spending. Cutting taxes on business income can increase aggregate demand by increasing investment spending.

Figure 7.5 shows the results of an expansionary fiscal policy, using the basic aggregate demand and aggregate supply model. In this model, there is no economic growth,

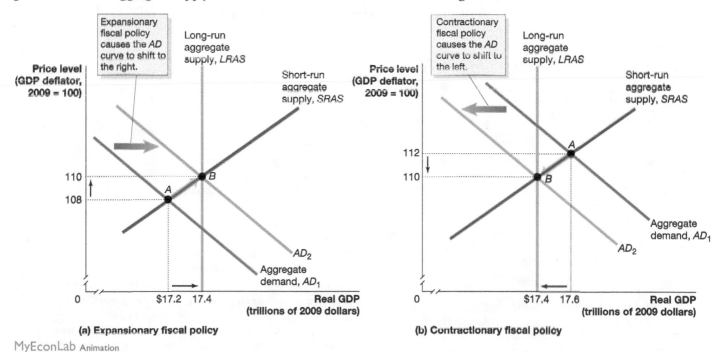

(a) Expansionary fiscal policy

(b) Contractionary fiscal policy

MyEconLab Animation

Figure 7.5   Fiscal Policy

In panel (a), short-run equilibrium is at point A, with real GDP of $17.2 trillion and a price level of 108. Real GDP is below potential GDP, so the economy is in a recession. An expansionary fiscal policy will cause aggregate demand to shift to the right, from AD_1 to AD_2, increasing real GDP from $17.2 trillion to $17.4 trillion and the price level from 108 to 110 (point B).

In panel (b), the economy begins at point A, with real GDP at $17.6 trillion and the price level at 112. Because real GDP is greater than potential GDP, the economy will experience rising wages and prices. A contractionary fiscal policy will cause aggregate demand to shift to the left, from AD_1 to AD_2, decreasing real GDP from $17.6 trillion to $17.4 trillion and the price level from 112 to 110 (point B).

so the long-run aggregate supply (*LRAS*) curve does not shift. Notice that this figure is very similar to Figure 8A.7 on page 523, which shows the effects of an expansionary monetary policy. The goal of both expansionary monetary policy and expansionary fiscal policy is to increase aggregate demand relative to what it would have been without the policy.

In panel (a) of Figure 7.5, we assume that short-run equilibrium occurs at point *A*, where the aggregate demand (AD_1) curve intersects the short-run aggregate supply (*SRAS*) curve. Real GDP is below potential GDP, so the economy is in a recession, with some firms operating below normal capacity and some workers having been laid off. To bring real GDP back to potential GDP, Congress and the president increase government purchases or cut taxes, which will shift the aggregate demand curve to the right, from AD_1 to AD_2. Real GDP increases from $17.2 trillion to potential GDP of $17.4 trillion, and the price level rises from 108 to 110 (point *B*). The policy has successfully returned real GDP to its potential level. Rising production will lead to increasing employment, reducing the unemployment rate.

Contractionary fiscal policy involves decreasing government purchases or increasing taxes. Policymakers use contractionary fiscal policy to reduce increases in aggregate demand that seem likely to lead to inflation. In panel (b) of Figure 7.5, short-run equilibrium occurs at point *A*, with real GDP of $17.6 trillion, which is above potential GDP of $17.4 trillion. With some firms producing beyond their normal capacity and the unemployment rate very low, wages and prices will be increasing. To bring real GDP back to potential GDP, Congress and the president decrease government purchases or increase taxes, which will shift the aggregate demand curve to the left, from AD_1 to AD_2. Real GDP falls from $17.6 trillion to $17.4 trillion, and the price level falls from 112 to 110 (point *B*).

We can conclude that Congress and the president can attempt to stabilize the economy by using fiscal policy to affect the price level and the level of real GDP. Of course, in practice it is extremely difficult for Congress and the president to use fiscal policy to eliminate the effects of the business cycle and keep real GDP always equal to potential GDP.

MyEconLab Concept Check

Don't Let This Happen to You

Don't Confuse Fiscal Policy and Monetary Policy

If you keep in mind the definitions of *money*, *income*, and *spending*, the difference between monetary policy and fiscal policy will be clearer. Students often make these two related mistakes: (1) They think of monetary policy as the Federal Reserve fighting recessions by increasing the money supply so people will have more money to spend; and (2) they think of fiscal policy as Congress and the president fighting recessions by spending more money. In this view, the only difference between fiscal policy and monetary policy is the source of the money.

To understand what's wrong with the descriptions of fiscal policy and monetary policy just given, first remember that the problem during a recession is not that there is too little *money*—currency plus checking account deposits—but too little *spending*. There may be too little spending for a number of reasons. For example, households may cut back on their spending on cars and houses because they are pessimistic about the future. Firms may reduce their spending because they have lowered their estimates of the future profitability of new machinery and factories. Or major trading partners of the United States—such as Japan and Canada—may be suffering from recessions,

which cause households and firms in those countries to reduce their spending on U.S. products.

The purpose of expansionary monetary policy is to lower interest rates, which in turn increases aggregate demand. When interest rates fall, households and firms are willing to borrow more to buy cars, houses, and factories. The purpose of expansionary fiscal policy is to increase aggregate demand by:

1. Having the government directly increase its own purchases, or
2. Cutting income taxes to increase household disposable income and, therefore, consumption spending, or
3. Cutting business taxes to increase investment spending

Just as increasing or decreasing the money supply does not have a direct effect on government spending or taxes, increasing or decreasing government spending or taxes does not have a direct effect on the money supply. Fiscal policy and monetary policy have the same goals, but they attempt to reach those goals in different ways.

MyEconLab Study Plan

Your Turn: Test your understanding by doing related problem 2.6 on page 270 at the end of this module.

Problem	Type of Policy Required	Actions by Congress and the President	Result
Recession	Expansionary	Increase government purchases or cut taxes	Real GDP and the price level rise.
Rising inflation	Contractionary	Decrease government purchases or raise taxes	Real GDP and the price level fall.

Table 7.1

Countercyclical Fiscal Policy

A Summary of How Fiscal Policy Affects Aggregate Demand

Table 7.1 summarizes how fiscal policy affects aggregate demand. Just as we did with monetary policy, we must add a very important qualification to this summary of fiscal policy: The table isolates the effect of fiscal policy *by holding constant monetary policy and all other factors affecting the variables involved.* In other words, we are again invoking the *ceteris paribus* condition we discussed in Module 3. This point is important because, for example, in the actual economy, a contractionary fiscal policy does not cause the price level to fall. A contractionary fiscal policy causes the price level *to rise by less than it would have without the policy.*   MyEconLab Concept Check   MyEconLab Study Plan

7.3 Fiscal Policy in the Dynamic Aggregate Demand and Aggregate Supply Model*

LEARNING OBJECTIVE: Use the dynamic aggregate demand and aggregate supply model to analyze fiscal policy.

The overview of fiscal policy we just finished contains a key idea: Congress and the president can use fiscal policy to affect aggregate demand, thereby changing the price level and the level of real GDP. The discussion of expansionary and contractionary fiscal policy illustrated by Figure 7.5 on page 255 is simplified, however, because it ignores two important facts about the economy: (1) The economy experiences continuing inflation, with the price level rising every year, and (2) the economy experiences long-run growth, with the *LRAS* curve shifting to the right every year. In Module 4 & 4A, we developed a *dynamic aggregate demand and aggregate supply model* that took these two facts into account. In this section, we use the dynamic model to gain a more complete understanding of fiscal policy.

To briefly review the dynamic model, recall that over time, potential GDP increases, which we show by shifting the *LRAS* curve to the right. The factors that cause the *LRAS* curve to shift also cause firms to supply more goods and services at any given price level in the short run, which we show by shifting the *SRAS* curve to the right. Finally, during most years, the aggregate demand curve also shifts to the right, indicating that aggregate expenditure is higher at every price level.

Figure 7.6 shows the results of an expansionary fiscal policy using the dynamic aggregate demand and aggregate supply model. Notice that this figure is very similar to Figure 8A.9 on page 355, which showed the effects of an expansionary monetary policy. The goal of both expansionary monetary policy and expansionary fiscal policy is to increase aggregate demand relative to what it would have been without the policy.

In the hypothetical situation shown in Figure 7.6, equilibrium is initially at point A, with real GDP equal to potential GDP of $17.0 trillion and the price level equal to 110. In the second year, *LRAS* increases to $17.4 trillion, but aggregate demand increases only from AD_1 to $AD_{2(\text{without policy})}$, which is not enough to keep real GDP equal to potential GDP. Let's assume that the Fed does not react to the situation with an expansionary monetary policy. In that case, short-run equilibrium will occur at point B, with real GDP of $17.3 trillion and a price level of 113. The $100 billion gap between real GDP and potential GDP means that some firms are operating at less than their full capacity. Incomes and profits will be falling, firms will begin to lay off workers, and the unemployment rate will increase.

*This section may be omitted without loss of continuity.

Figure 7.6

An Expansionary Fiscal Policy in the Dynamic Model

Equilibrium is initially at point A, with real GDP equal to potential GDP of $17.0 trillion and the price level equal to 110. Without an expansionary policy, aggregate demand will shift from AD_1 to $AD_{2(without\ policy)}$, which is not enough to keep real GDP equal to potential GDP because long-run aggregate supply has shifted from $LRAS_1$ to $LRAS_2$. The new short-run equilibrium is at point B, with real GDP of $17.3 trillion and a price level of 113. Increasing government purchases or cutting taxes will shift aggregate demand to $AD_{2(with\ policy)}$. Equilibrium will be at point C, with real GDP of $17.4 trillion, which is its potential level, and a price level of 115. The price level is higher than it would have been without an expansionary fiscal policy.

Increasing government purchases or cutting taxes can shift aggregate demand to $AD_{2(with\ policy)}$. Equilibrium will be at point C, with real GDP of $17.4 trillion, which is its potential level, and a price level of 115. The price level is higher than it would have been without an expansionary fiscal policy.

Contractionary fiscal policy involves decreasing government purchases or increasing taxes. Policymakers use contractionary fiscal policy to reduce increases in aggregate demand that seem likely to lead to inflation. In Figure 7.7, equilibrium is initially at point A, with real GDP equal to potential GDP of $17.0 trillion and the price level equal to 110. Once again, *LRAS* increases to $17.4 trillion in the second year. In this scenario, the shift in aggregate demand to $AD_{2(without\ policy)}$ results in a short-run macroeconomic equilibrium at point B, with real GDP of $17.5 trillion, which is greater than potential GDP. If we assume that the Fed does not respond to the situation with a contractionary monetary policy, the economy will experience a rising inflation rate. Decreasing government purchases or increasing taxes can keep real GDP from moving beyond its potential level. The result, shown in Figure 7.7, is that in the new equilibrium at point C, the inflation rate is 2.7 percent rather than 4.5 percent.

Figure 7.7

A Contractionary Fiscal Policy in the Dynamic Model

Equilibrium is initially at point A, with real GDP equal to potential GDP of $17.0 trillion and the price level equal to 110. Without a contractionary policy, aggregate demand will shift from AD_1 to $AD_{2(without\ policy)}$, which results in a short-run equilibrium at point B, with real GDP of $17.5 trillion, which is greater than potential GDP, and a price level of 115. Decreasing government purchases or increasing taxes can shift aggregate demand to $AD_{2(with\ policy)}$. Equilibrium will be at point C, with real GDP of $17.4 trillion, which is its potential level, and a price level of 113. The inflation rate will be 2.7 percent, as opposed to the 4.5 percent it would have been without the contractionary fiscal policy.

7.4 The Government Purchases and Tax Multipliers

LEARNING OBJECTIVE: Explain how the government purchases and tax multipliers work.

We saw in the module opener that Congress and the president authorized spending to rebuild Doyle Drive in San Francisco in order to increase aggregate demand during the recession of 2007–2009. Suppose that Congress and the president decide to spend $100 billion on rebuilding Doyle Drive and similar projects. (The total increase in federal spending under the American Recovery and Reinvestment Act (ARRA) of 2009 was actually about $500 *billion*, including the $83 million in ARRA funds contributed to the project to reconstruct Doyle Drive.) How much will equilibrium real GDP increase as a result of this increase in government purchases? We might expect real GDP to increase by more than $100 billion because the initial increase in aggregate demand should lead to additional increases in income and spending. For example, to reconstruct Doyle Drive, the California Department of Transportation hired Kiewit, a private construction firm. Kiewit and its subcontractors, in turn, hired workers for the project. The firms that carried out the many other projects authorized under the ARRA also hired new workers. Workers who were formerly unemployed are likely to increase their spending on cars, furniture, appliances, and other products. Sellers of these products will increase their production and hire more workers, and so on. At each step, real GDP and income will rise, thereby increasing consumption spending and aggregate demand.

Economists refer to the initial increase in government purchases as *autonomous* because it is a result of a decision by the government and is not directly caused by changes in the level of real GDP. The increases in consumption spending that result from the initial autonomous increase in government purchases are *induced* because they are caused by the initial increase in autonomous spending. Economists call the series of induced increases in consumption spending that results from an initial increase in autonomous expenditures the **multiplier effect**.

Figure 7.8 illustrates how an increase in government purchases affects the aggregate demand curve. The initial increase causes the aggregate demand curve to shift to the right because total spending in the economy is now higher at every price level. The shift to the right from AD_1 to the dashed AD curve represents the effect of the initial increase of $100 billion in government purchases. Because this initial increase in government purchases raises incomes and leads to further increases in consumption spending, the aggregate demand curve will ultimately shift from AD_1 all the way to AD_2.

To better understand the multiplier effect, let's start with a simplified analysis in which we assume that the price level is constant. In other words, initially we will ignore

Multiplier effect The series of induced increases in consumption spending that results from an initial increase in autonomous expenditures.

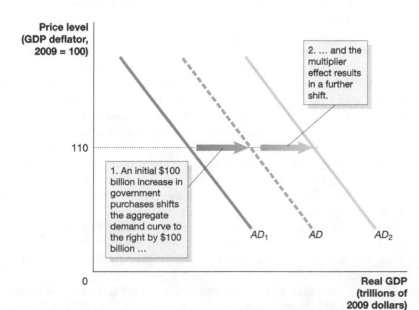

MyEconLab Animation

Figure 7.8

The Multiplier Effect and Aggregate Demand

An initial increase in government purchases of $100 billion causes the aggregate demand curve to shift to the right, from AD_1 to the dashed AD curve, and represents the effect of the initial increase of $100 billion in government purchases. Because this initial increase raises incomes and leads to further increases in consumption spending, the aggregate demand curve will ultimately shift further to the right, to AD_2.

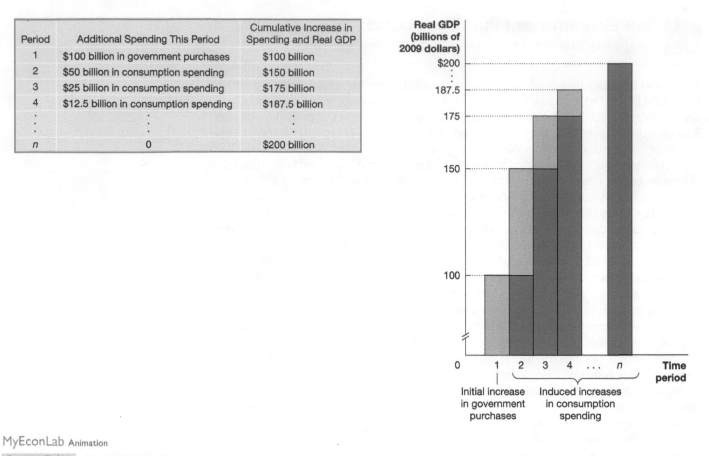

Period	Additional Spending This Period	Cumulative Increase in Spending and Real GDP
1	$100 billion in government purchases	$100 billion
2	$50 billion in consumption spending	$150 billion
3	$25 billion in consumption spending	$175 billion
4	$12.5 billion in consumption spending	$187.5 billion
⋮	⋮	⋮
n	0	$200 billion

MyEconLab Animation

Figure 7.9 **The Multiplier Effect of an Increase in Government Purchases**

Following an initial increase in government purchases, spending and real GDP increase over a number of periods due to the multiplier effect. The new spending and increased real GDP in each period is shown in orange, and the level of spending from the previous period is shown in blue. The sum of the blue and orange areas represents the cumulative increase in spending and real GDP. In total, equilibrium real GDP will increase by $200 billion as a result of an initial increase of $100 billion in government purchases.

the effect of an upward-sloping *SRAS* curve. Figure 7.9 shows how spending and real GDP increase over a number of periods, beginning with the initial increase in government purchases in the first period, which raises real GDP and total income in the economy by $100 billion. How much additional consumption spending will result from $100 billion in additional income? We know that in addition to increasing their consumption spending on domestically produced goods, households will save some of the increase in income, use some to pay income taxes, and use some to purchase imported goods, which will have no direct effect on spending and production in the U.S. economy. In Figure 7.9, we assume that in the second period, households increase their consumption spending by half the increase in income from the first period—or by $50 billion. This spending in the second period will, in turn, increase real GDP and income by an additional $50 billion. In the third period, consumption spending will increase by $25 billion, or half the $50 billion increase in income from the second period.

The multiplier effect will continue through a number of periods, with the additional consumption spending in each period being half of the income increase from the previous period. Eventually, the process will be complete, although we cannot say precisely how many periods it will take, so we simply label the final period *n* rather than give it a specific number. In Figure 7.9, the new spending and increased real GDP in each period is shown in orange, and the level of spending from the previous period is shown in blue. The sum of the blue and orange areas represents the cumulative increase in spending and real GDP.

How large will the total increase in equilibrium real GDP be as a result of the initial increase of $100 billion in government purchases? The ratio of the change in equilibrium real GDP to the initial change in government purchases is called the *government purchases multiplier*:

$$\text{Government purchases multiplier} = \frac{\text{Change in equilibrium real GDP}}{\text{Change in government purchases}}.$$

If, for example, the government purchases multiplier has a value of 2, an increase in government purchases of $100 billion should increase equilibrium real GDP by $2 \times \$100$ billion $= \$200$ billion. We show this result in Figure 7.9 by having the cumulative increase in real GDP equal $200 billion.

Tax cuts also have a multiplier effect because they increase the disposable income of households. When household disposable income rises, so will consumption spending. These increases in consumption spending will set off further increases in real GDP and income, just as increases in government purchases do. Suppose we consider a change in taxes of a specific amount—say, a tax cut of $100 billion—with the tax *rate* remaining unchanged. The expression for this tax multiplier is:

$$\text{Tax multiplier} = \frac{\text{Change in equilibrium real GDP}}{\text{Change in taxes}}.$$

The tax multiplier is a negative number because changes in taxes and changes in real GDP move in opposite directions: An increase in taxes reduces disposable income, consumption, and real GDP, and a decrease in taxes raises disposable income, consumption, and real GDP. For example, if the tax multiplier is -1.6, a $100 billion *cut* in taxes will increase real GDP by $-1.6 \times (-\$100$ billion$) = \$160$ billion. We would expect the tax multiplier to be smaller in absolute value than the government purchases multiplier. To see why, think about the difference between a $100 billion increase in government purchases and a $100 billion decrease in taxes. The whole of the $100 billion in government purchases results in an increase in aggregate demand. But households will save rather than spend some portion of a $100 billion decrease in taxes, and they will spend some portion on imported goods. The fraction of the tax cut that households save or spend on imports will not increase aggregate demand. Therefore, the first period of the multiplier process will involve a smaller increase in aggregate demand than occurs when there is an increase in government purchases, and the total increase in equilibrium real GDP will be smaller.

The Effect of Changes in the Tax Rate

A change in the tax *rate* has a more complicated effect on equilibrium real GDP than does a tax cut of a fixed amount. To begin with, the value of the tax rate affects the size of the multiplier effect. The higher the tax rate, the smaller the multiplier effect. To see why, think about the size of the additional spending increases that take place in each period following an increase in government purchases. The higher the tax rate, the smaller the amount of any increase in income that households have available to spend, which reduces the size of the multiplier effect. So, a cut in the tax rate affects equilibrium real GDP through two channels: (1) A cut in the tax rate increases the disposable income of households, which leads them to increase their consumption spending, and (2) a cut in the tax rate increases the size of the multiplier effect.   MyEconLab Concept Check

Taking into Account the Effects of Aggregate Supply

To this point, as we discussed the multiplier effect, we assumed that the price level was constant. We know, though, that because the SRAS curve is upward sloping, when the AD curve shifts to the right, the price level will rise. As a result of the rise in the price level, equilibrium real GDP will not increase by the full amount that the multiplier effect indicates. Figure 7.10 illustrates how an upward-sloping SRAS curve affects the size of the multiplier. To keep the graph relatively simple, we assume that the SRAS and LRAS curves do not shift. Short-run equilibrium is initially at point A, with real GDP

Figure 7.10

The Multiplier Effect and Aggregate Supply

Short-run equilibrium is initially at point A. An increase in government purchases causes the aggregate demand curve to shift to the right, from AD_1 to the dashed AD curve. The multiplier effect results in the aggregate demand curve shifting further to the right, to AD_2 (point B). Because of the upward-sloping supply curve, the shift in aggregate demand results in a higher price level. In the new equilibrium at point C, both real GDP and the price level have increased. The increase in real GDP is less than that indicated by the multiplier effect with a constant price level.

below its potential level. An increase in government purchases shifts the aggregate demand curve from AD_1 to the dashed AD curve. Just as in Figure 7.8, the multiplier effect causes a further shift in the aggregate demand curve to AD_2. If the price level remained constant, real GDP would increase from $16.0 trillion at point A to $17.2 trillion at point B. However, because the SRAS curve is upward sloping, the price level rises from 110 to 113, reducing the total quantity of goods and services demanded in the economy. The new equilibrium occurs at point C, with real GDP having risen to $17.0 trillion, or by $200 billion less than if the price level had remained unchanged. We can conclude that the actual change in real GDP resulting from an increase in government purchases or a cut in taxes will be less than that indicated by the simple multiplier effect with a constant price level.   MyEconLab Concept Check

The Multipliers Work in Both Directions

Increases in government purchases and cuts in taxes have a positive multiplier effect on equilibrium real GDP. Decreases in government purchases and increases in taxes also have a multiplier effect on equilibrium real GDP, but in this case, the effect is negative. An increase in taxes will reduce household disposable income and consumption. As households buy fewer cars, furniture, refrigerators, and other goods, the firms that sell these goods will cut back their production and begin laying off workers. Falling incomes will lead to further reductions in consumption. A reduction in government spending on defense would set off a similar process of decreases in real GDP and income. The reduction would affect defense contractors first because they sell directly to the government, and then it would spread to other firms.

   We look more closely at the government purchases multiplier and the tax multiplier in the appendix to this module.   MyEconLab Concept Check

Solved Problem 7.4   MyEconLab Interactive Animation

Fiscal Policy Multipliers

Briefly explain whether you agree with the following statement: "Real GDP is currently $17.2 trillion, and potential GDP is $17.4 trillion. If Congress and the president would increase government purchases by $200 billion or cut taxes by $200 billion, the economy could be brought to equilibrium at potential GDP."

Solving the Problem

Step 1: **Review the module material.** This problem is about the multiplier process, so you may want to review the section "The Government Purchases and Tax Multipliers," which begins on page 259.

Step 2: **Explain how the necessary increase in purchases or cut in taxes is less than $200 billion because of the multiplier effect.** The statement is incorrect because it does not consider the multiplier effect. Because of the multiplier effect, an increase in government purchases or a decrease in taxes of less than $200 billion is necessary to increase equilibrium real GDP by $200 billion. For instance, assume that the government purchases multiplier is 2 and the tax multiplier is −1.6. We can then calculate the necessary increase in government purchases as follows:

$$\text{Government puchases multipiler} = \frac{\text{Change in equilibrium real GDP}}{\text{Change in government purchases}}$$

$$2 = \frac{\$200\,\text{billon}}{\text{Change in government purchases}}$$

$$\text{Change in government purchases} = \frac{\$200\,\text{billon}}{2} = \$100\,\text{billon.}$$

And the necessary change in taxes:

$$\text{Tax multipler} = \frac{\text{Change in equilibrium real GDP}}{\text{Change in taxes}}$$

$$-1.6 = \frac{\$200\,\text{billon}}{\text{Change in taxes}}$$

$$\text{Change in taxes} = \frac{\$200\,\text{billion}}{-1.6} = -\$125\,\text{billion.}$$

Your Turn: For more practice, do related problems 4.6 and 4.7 on page 272 at the end of this module.   MyEconLab Study Plan

Appendix

A Closer Look at the Multiplier

LEARNING OBJECTIVE: Apply the multiplier formula.

In this module, we saw that changes in government purchases and changes in taxes have a multiplied effect on equilibrium real GDP. In this appendix, we will build a simple economic model of the multiplier effect. When economists forecast the effect of a change in spending or taxes, they often rely on *econometric models*. These are economic models written in the form of equations, where each equation has been statistically estimated, using methods similar to those used in estimating demand curves.

An Expression for Equilibrium Real GDP

We can write a set of equations that includes the key macroeconomic relationships we have studied in this and previous modules. It is important to note that in this model, we will be assuming that the price level is constant. We know that this assumption is unrealistic because an upward-sloping *SRAS* curve means that when the aggregate demand curve shifts, the price level will change. Nevertheless, our model will be approximately correct when changes in the price level are small. It also serves as an introduction to more complicated models that take into account changes in the price level. For simplicity, we start with three assumptions: (1) Taxes, T, do not depend on the level of real GDP, Y; (2) there are no government transfer payments to households; and (3) we have a closed economy, with no imports or exports. The numbers (with the exception of the *MPC*) represent billions of dollars:

(1) $C = 1{,}000 + 0.75(Y - T)$	Consumption function
(2) $I = 1{,}500$	Planned investment function
(3) $G = 1{,}500$	Government purchases function
(4) $T = 1{,}000$	Tax function
(5) $Y = C + I + G$	Equilibrium condition

The first equation is the consumption function. The marginal propensity to consume, or *MPC*, is 0.75, and 1,000 is the level of autonomous consumption, which is the level of consumption that does not depend on income. We assume that consumption depends on disposable income, which is $Y - T$. The functions for planned investment spending, government spending, and taxes are very simple because we have assumed that these variables are not affected by GDP and, therefore, are constant. Economists who use this type of model to forecast GDP would, of course, use more realistic planned investment, government purchases, and tax functions.

Equation (5)—the equilibrium condition—states that equilibrium GDP equals the sum of consumption, planned investment spending, and government purchases. To calculate a value for equilibrium real GDP, we need to substitute equations (1) through (4) into equation (5). This substitution gives us the following:

$$Y = 1{,}000 + 0.75(Y - 1{,}000) + 1{,}500 + 1{,}500$$

$$= 1{,}000 + 0.75Y - 750 + 1{,}500 + 1{,}500.$$

We need to solve this equation for Y to find equilibrium GDP. The first step is to subtract 0.75Y from both sides of the equation:

$$Y - 0.75Y = 1{,}000 - 750 + 1{,}500 + 1{,}500.$$

Then, we solve for Y:

$$0.25Y = 3,250,$$

or:

$$Y = \frac{3,250}{0.25} = 13,000.$$

To make this result more general, we can replace particular values with general values represented by letters:

$C = \overline{C} + MPC(Y - T)$	Consumption function
$I = \overline{I}$	Planned investment function
$G = \overline{G}$	Government purchases function
$T = \overline{T}$	Tax function
$Y = C + T + G$	Equilibrium condition

The letters with bars above them represent fixed, or *autonomous*, values that do not depend on the values of other variables. So, $\overline{C}$ represents autonomous consumption, which had a value of 1,000 in our original example. Now, solving for equilibrium, we get:

$$Y = \overline{C} + MPC(Y - \overline{T}) + \overline{I} + \overline{G}$$

or:

$$Y - MPC(Y) = \overline{C} - (MPC \times \overline{T}) + \overline{I} + \overline{G}$$

or:

$$Y(1 - MPC) = \overline{C} - (MPC \times \overline{T}) + \overline{I} + \overline{G}$$

or:

$$Y = \frac{\overline{C} - (MPC \times \overline{T}) + \overline{I} + \overline{G}}{1 - MPC}.$$

MyEconLab Concept Check

A Formula for the Government Purchases Multiplier

To find a formula for the government purchases multiplier, we need to rewrite the last equation for changes in each variable rather than levels. Letting Δ stand for the change in a variable, we have:

$$\Delta Y = \frac{\Delta \overline{C} - (MPC \times \Delta \overline{T}) + \Delta \overline{I} + \Delta \overline{G}}{1 - MPC}.$$

We can find a formula for the government purchases multiplier, which is the ratio of the change in equilibrium real GDP to the change in government purchases. If we hold constant changes in autonomous consumption spending, planned investment spending, and taxes, then from the previous equation we have the following:

$$\Delta Y = \frac{\Delta G}{1 - MPC}.$$

So, we have:

$$\text{Government purchases multiplier} = \frac{\Delta Y}{\Delta G} = \frac{1}{1 - MPC}.$$

For an *MPC* of 0.75, the government purchases multiplier will be:

$$\frac{1}{1 - 0.75} = 4.$$

A government purchases multiplier of 4 means that an increase in government spending of \$10 billion will increase equilibrium real GDP by $4 \times \$10$ billion = \$40 billion.

MyEconLab Concept Check

A Formula for the Tax Multiplier

We can also find a formula for the tax multiplier. We start again with this equation:

$$\Delta Y = \frac{\Delta \overline{C} - (MPC \times \Delta \overline{T}) + \Delta \overline{I} + \Delta \overline{G}}{1 - MPC}.$$

Now we hold constant the values of autonomous consumption spending, planned investment spending, and government purchases, but we allow the value of taxes to change:

$$\Delta Y = \frac{-MPC \times \Delta T}{1 - MPC}.$$

So, we have:

$$\text{The tax multiplier} = \frac{\Delta Y}{\Delta T} = \frac{-MPC}{1 - MPC}.$$

For an MPC of 0.75, the tax multiplier will be:

$$\frac{-0.75}{1 - 0.75} = -3.$$

The tax multiplier is a negative number because an increase in taxes causes a decrease in equilibrium real GDP, and a decrease in taxes causes an increase in equilibrium real GDP. A tax multiplier of -3 means that a decrease in taxes of \$10 billion will increase equilibrium real GDP by $-3 \times -\$10$ billion = \$30 billion. Earlier in this module, we discussed the economic reasons for the tax multiplier being smaller than the government spending multiplier.

MyEconLab Concept Check

The "Balanced Budget" Multiplier

What will be the effect of equal increases (or decreases) in government purchases and taxes on equilibrium real GDP? At first, it might appear that the tax increase would exactly offset the government purchases increase, leaving real GDP unchanged. But we have just seen that the government purchases multiplier is larger (in absolute value) than the tax multiplier. We can use our formulas for the government purchases multiplier and the tax multiplier to calculate the net effect of increasing government purchases by \$10 billion at the same time that taxes are increased by \$10 billion:

Increase in real GDP from the increase in government purchases

$$= \$10 \text{ billion} \times \frac{1}{1 - MPC}.$$

$$\text{Decrease in real GDP from the increase in taxes} = \$10 \text{ billion} \times \frac{-MPC}{1 - MPC}.$$

So, the combined effect equals:

$$\$10 \text{ billion} \times \left[\left(\frac{1}{1 - MPC} \right) + \left(\frac{-MPC}{1 - MPC} \right) \right],$$

or:

$$\$10 \text{ billion} \times \left(\frac{1 - MPC}{1 - MPC} \right) = \$10 \text{ billion}.$$

The balanced budget multiplier is, therefore, equal to $(1 - MPC)/(1 - MPC)$, or 1. Equal dollar increases and decreases in government purchases and in taxes lead to the same dollar increase in real GDP in the short run.

MyEconLab Concept Check

The Effects of Changes in Tax Rates on the Multiplier

We now consider the effect of a change in the tax *rate*, as opposed to a change in a fixed amount of taxes. Changing the tax rate actually changes the value of the multiplier. To see this, suppose that the tax rate is 20 percent, or 0.2. In that case, an increase in household income of $10 billion will increase *disposable income* by only $8 billion [or 10 billion $\times$ (1 − 0.2) In general, an increase in income can be multiplied by (1 − *t*) to find the increase in disposable income, where *t* is the tax rate. So, we can rewrite the consumption function as:

$$C = \bar{C} + MPC(1 - t)Y.$$

We can use this expression for the consumption function to find an expression for the government purchases multiplier, using the same method we used previously:

$$\text{Government purchases multiplier} = \frac{\Delta Y}{\Delta G} = \frac{1}{1 - MPC(1 - t)}.$$

We can see the effect of changing the tax rate on the size of the multiplier by trying some values. First, assume that $MPC = 0.75$ and $t = 0.2$. Then:

$$\text{Government purchases multiplier} = \frac{\Delta Y}{\Delta G} = \frac{1}{1 - 0.75(1 - 0.2)} = \frac{1}{1 - 0.6} = 2.5$$

This value is smaller than the multiplier of 4 that we calculated by assuming that there was only a fixed amount of taxes (which is the same as assuming that the marginal tax *rate* was zero). This multiplier is smaller because spending in each period is now reduced by the amount of taxes households must pay on any additional income they earn. We can calculate the multiplier for an MPC of 0.75 and a lower tax rate of 0.1:

$$\text{Government purchases multiplier} = \frac{\Delta Y}{\Delta G} = \frac{1}{1 - 0.75(1 - 0.1)} = \frac{1}{1 - 0.675} = 3.1.$$

Cutting the tax rate from 20 percent to 10 percent increased the value of the multiplier from 2.5 to 3.1.   MyEconLab Concept Check

The Multiplier in an Open Economy

Up to now, we have assumed that the economy is closed, with no imports or exports. We can consider the case of an open economy by including net exports in our analysis. Recall that net exports equal exports minus imports. Exports are determined primarily by factors—such as the exchange value of the dollar and the levels of real GDP in other countries—that we do not include in our model. So, we will assume that exports are fixed, or autonomous:

$$\text{Exports} = \overline{\text{Exports}}.$$

Imports will increase as real GDP increases because households will spend some portion of an increase in income on imports. We can define the *marginal propensity to import* (*MPI*) as the fraction of an increase in income that is spent on imports. So, our expression for imports is:

$$\text{Imports} = MPI \times Y.$$

We can substitute our expressions for exports and imports into the expression we derived earlier for equilibrium real GDP:

$$Y = \bar{C} + MPC(1 - t)Y + \bar{I} + \bar{G} + [\overline{\text{Exports}} - (MPI \times Y)],$$

where the expression $[\overline{\text{Exports}} - (MPI \times Y)]$ represents net exports. We can now find an expression for the government purchases multiplier by using the same method we used previously:

$$\text{Government purchases multiplier} = \frac{\Delta Y}{\Delta G} = \frac{1}{1 - [MPC(1 - t) - MPI]}.$$

We can see the effect of changing the value of the marginal propensity to import on the size of the multiplier by trying some values of key variables. First, assume that $MPC = 0.75$, $t = 0.2$, and $MPI = 0.1$. Then:

$$\text{Government purchases multiplier} = \frac{\Delta Y}{\Delta G} = \frac{1}{1 - (0.75(1 - 0.2) - 0.1)} = \frac{1}{1 - 0.5}$$

$$= 2.$$

This value is smaller than the multiplier of 2.5 that we calculated by assuming that there were no exports or imports (which is the same as assuming that the marginal propensity to import is zero). This multiplier is smaller because spending in each period is now reduced by the amount of imports households buy with any additional income they earn. We can calculate the multiplier with $MPC = 0.75$, $t = 0.2$, and a higher MPI of 0.2:

$$\text{Government purchases multiplier} = \frac{\Delta Y}{\Delta G} = \frac{1}{1 - (0.75(1 - 0.2) - 0.2)} = \frac{1}{1 - 0.4}$$

$$= 1.7.$$

Increasing the marginal propensity to import from 0.1 to 0.2 decreases the value of the multiplier from 2 to 1.7. We can conclude that countries with a higher marginal propensity to import will have smaller multipliers than countries with a lower marginal propensity to import.

Bear in mind that the multiplier is a short-run effect that assumes that real GDP is less than potential GDP. In the long run, real GDP equals potential GDP, so an increase in government purchases causes a decline in the nongovernment components of real GDP but leaves the level of real GDP unchanged.

The analysis in this appendix is simplified compared to what would be carried out by an economist forecasting the effects of changes in government purchases or changes in taxes on equilibrium real GDP in the short run. In particular, our assumption that the price level is constant is unrealistic. However, looking more closely at the determinants of the multiplier has helped us see some important macroeconomic relationships more clearly.   MyEconLab Concept Check

---

7A   A Closer Look at the Multiplier, pages 264–268

LEARNING OBJECTIVE: Apply the multiplier formula.

MyEconLab   Visit www.myeconlab.com to complete these exercises online and get instant feedback.

Problem and Applications

7A.1 Assuming a fixed amount of taxes and a closed economy, calculate the value of the government purchases multiplier, the tax multiplier, and the balanced budget multiplier if the marginal propensity to consume equals 0.6.

7A.2 Calculate the value of the government purchases multiplier if the marginal propensity to consume equals 0.8, the tax rate equals 0.25, and the marginal propensity to import equals 0.2.

7A.3 Use a graph to show the change in the aggregate demand curve resulting from an increase in government

purchases if the government purchases multiplier equals 2. On the same graph, show the change in the aggregate demand curve resulting from an increase in government purchases if the government purchases multiplier equals 4.

7A.4 Using your understanding of multipliers, explain why an increase in the tax rate would decrease the size of the government purchases multiplier. Similarly, explain why a decrease in the marginal propensity to import would increase the size of the government purchases multiplier.

7A.5 In 2012, the ratio of imports to GDP was 14 percent in Japan and 83 percent in Belgium. On the basis of this information, can you draw any conclusions about the relative sizes of the government purchases multiplier in each country?

MODULE SUMMARY AND PROBLEMS

Key Terms

Automatic stabilizers, p. 250   Fiscal policy, p. 250   Multiplier effect, p. 259

 7.1 **What Is Fiscal Policy? pages 250–254**
LEARNING OBJECTIVE: Define fiscal policy.

Summary

Fiscal policy involves changes in federal taxes and purchases that are intended to achieve macroeconomic policy goals. **Automatic stabilizers** are government spending and taxes that automatically increase or decrease along with the business cycle. Since World War II, the federal government's share of total government expenditures has been between two-thirds and three-quarters. Federal government *expenditures* as a percentage of GDP rose from 1950 to the early 1990s, fell between 1992 and 2001, and then rose once again. Federal government *purchases* have declined as a percentage of GDP since the end of the Korean War in the early 1950s. The largest component of federal expenditures is transfer payments. The largest sources of federal government revenue are individual income taxes, followed by social insurance taxes, which are used to fund the Social Security and Medicare systems.

MyEconLab   Visit **www.myeconlab.com** to complete these exercises online and get instant feedback.

Review Questions

1.1 What is fiscal policy? Who is responsible for fiscal policy?

1.2 Economist Mark Thoma wrote, "One of the difficulties in using fiscal policy to combat recessions is getting Congress to agree on what measures to implement. ... Automatic stabilizers bypass this difficulty by doing exactly what their name implies." What are automatic stabilizers? Name two examples of automatic stabilizers and explain how they can reduce the severity of a recession.
Source: Mark Thoma, "The Importance of Automatic Stabilizers to the Economy," cbsnews.com, January 25, 2010.

1.3 What is the difference between federal purchases and federal expenditures? Are federal purchases higher today as a percentage of GDP than they were in 1960? Are federal expenditures as a percentage of GDP higher?

Problems and Applications

1.4 In 2009, Congress and the president enacted "cash for clunkers" legislation that paid up to $4,500 to people buying new cars if they traded in an older, low-gas-mileage car. Was this legislation an example of fiscal policy? Does your answer depend on what goals Congress and the president had in mind when they enacted the legislation?
Source: Justin Lahart, "Trade-in Program Tunes Up Economic Engine," *Wall Street Journal*, August 4, 2009.

1.5 Briefly explain whether each of the following is (1) an example of a discretionary fiscal policy, (2) an example of an automatic stabilizer, or (3) not an example of fiscal policy.
  a. The federal government increases spending on rebuilding the New Jersey shore following a hurricane.
  b. The Federal Reserve sells Treasury securities.
  c. The total amount the federal government spends on unemployment insurance decreases during an expansion.
  d. The revenue the federal government collects from the individual income tax declines during a recession.
  e. The federal government changes the required fuel efficiency for new cars.
  f. Congress and the president enact a temporary cut in payroll taxes.
  g. During a recession, California voters approve additional spending on a statewide high-speed rail system.

1.6 The federal government collected less in total individual income taxes in 1983 than in 1982. Can we conclude that Congress and the president cut individual income tax rates in 1983? Briefly explain.

1.7 **(Related to the** Making the Connection **on page 253)** According to a Congressional Budget Office (CBO) report:

> During the next decade alone, the number of people age 65 or older is expected to rise by more than one-third, and the share of the population age 65 or older is projected to grow from the current 15 percent to 21 percent in 2040.

Why is the over-65 population increasing so rapidly? What are the implications of this increase for future federal spending on Social Security and Medicare as a percentage of GDP? What choices do policymakers face in dealing with this issue?
Source: Congressional Budget Office, "The 2015 Long-Term Budget Outlook," June 2015, p. 21.

7.2   The Effects of Fiscal Policy on Real GDP and the Price Level, pages 255–257

LEARNING OBJECTIVE: Explain how fiscal policy affects aggregate demand and how the government can use fiscal policy to stabilize the economy.

Summary

To fight recessions, Congress and the president can increase government purchases or cut taxes. This expansionary policy increases aggregate demand, raising the level of real GDP and the price level. To fight rising inflation, Congress and the president can decrease government purchases or raise taxes. This contractionary policy reduces aggregate demand relative to what it would otherwise be, thereby reducing the inflation rate.

MyEconLab   Visit www.myeconlab.com to complete these exercises online and get instant feedback.

Review Questions

2.1 What is an expansionary fiscal policy? What is a contractionary fiscal policy?

2.2 If Congress and the president decide that an expansionary fiscal policy is necessary, what changes should they make in government spending or taxes? What changes should they make if they decide that a contractionary fiscal policy is necessary?

Problems and Applications

2.3 Briefly explain whether you agree with the following statements: "An expansionary fiscal policy involves an increase in government purchases or an increase in taxes. A contractionary fiscal policy involves a decrease in government purchases or a decrease in taxes."

2.4 Identify each of the following as (1) part of an expansionary fiscal policy, (2) part of a contractionary fiscal policy, or (3) not part of fiscal policy.
  a. The corporate income tax rate is increased.
  b. Defense spending is increased.

c. The Federal Reserve lowers the target for the federal funds rate.
  d. Families are allowed to deduct all their expenses for day care from their federal income taxes.
  e. The individual income tax rate is decreased.

2.5 Use an aggregate demand and aggregate supply graph to illustrate the situation where equilibrium initially occurs with real GDP equal to potential GDP and then the aggregate demand curve shifts to the left. What actions can Congress and the president take to move real GDP back to potential GDP? Show the results of these actions on your graph. Assume that the *LRAS* curve doesn't shift.

2.6 (Related to the Don't Let This Happen to You **on page 256)** Is it possible for Congress and the president to carry out an expansionary fiscal policy if the money supply does not increase? Briefly explain.

2.7 A political commentator argues: "Congress and the president are more likely to enact an expansionary fiscal policy than a contractionary fiscal policy because expansionary policies are popular and contractionary policies are unpopular." Briefly explain whether you agree.

2.8 (Related to the Module Opener **on page 249)** In 2015, in proposing a $478 billion increase in federal spending on infrastructure, President Obama argued that the spending would increase total employment in the United States.
  a. Will increases in federal spending always increase real GDP and employment in the short run? Briefly explain.
  b. Are there circumstances in which the federal government would not want to increase its spending even if the result was to increase real GDP and employment in the short run? What was President Obama assuming about the state of the economy in 2015?

Source: Michael D. Shear, "Obama Proposes Tax for Upgrade of Infrastructure," *New York Times*, February 2, 2015.

7.3   Fiscal Policy in the Dynamic Aggregate Demand and Aggregate Supply Model, pages 257–258

LEARNING OBJECTIVE: Use the dynamic aggregate demand and aggregate supply model to analyze fiscal policy.

Summary

We can use the *dynamic aggregate demand and aggregate supply model* to look more closely at expansionary and contractionary fiscal policies. This model takes into account that (1) the economy experiences continuing inflation, with the price level rising every year, and (2) the economy experiences long-run growth, with the *LRAS* curve shifting to the right every year. In the dynamic model, an expansionary fiscal policy tries to ensure that the aggregate demand curve will shift far enough to the right to bring about macroeconomic equilibrium with real GDP equal to potential GDP. A contractionary fiscal policy attempts to offset movements in aggregate demand that would cause macroeconomic

equilibrium to occur at a level of real GDP that is greater than potential GDP.

MyEconLab   Visit www.myeconlab.com to complete these exercises online and get instant feedback.

Review Questions

3.1 What are the key differences between how we illustrate an expansionary fiscal policy in the basic aggregate demand and aggregate supply model and in the dynamic aggregate demand and aggregate supply model?

3.2 What are the key differences between how we illustrate a contractionary fiscal policy in the basic aggregate demand and aggregate supply model and in the dynamic aggregate demand and aggregate supply model?

Problems and Applications

3.3 A report from the Congressional Budget Office (CBO) notes, "Potential GDP is CBO's estimate of the maximum sustainable output of the economy." In early 2015, the CBO estimated that the gap between real GDP and potential GDP would fall from 2.9 percent in 2014 to zero in 2017. In 2014, real GDP was $16.3 trillion, and the CBO's estimate of potential GDP was $16.8 trillion. The CBO forecast that potential GDP would increase to $17.5 trillion.

    a. Why does the CBO include the word "sustainable" in its definition of potential GDP?

    b. Draw an aggregate demand and aggregate supply graph to illustrate the macroeconomic situation in 2014 and in 2017 (you do not have to show on your graph the situation in 2015 or 2016). Be sure that your graph contains *LRAS* curves for 2014 and 2017, *SRAS* curves for 2014 and 2017, and *AD* curves for 2014 and 2017, and that it shows equilibrium real GDP and the price levels for both years.

    Sources: Congressional Budget Office, "The 2015 Long-Term Budget Outlook," June 2015, p. 36; and Congressional Budget Office, "The Budget and Economic Outlook: 2015 to 2025," January 2015.

3.4 Use the graph to answer the following questions.

a. If the government takes no policy actions, what will be the values of real GDP and the price level in 2019?

b. What actions can the government take to bring real GDP to its potential level in 2019?

c. If the government takes no policy actions, what will the inflation rate be in 2019? If the government uses fiscal policy to keep real GDP at its potential level, what will the inflation rate be in 2019?

3.5 The hypothetical information in the following table shows what the situation will be in 2019 if Congress and the president do *not* use fiscal policy:

Year	Potential GDP	Real GDP	Price Level
2018	$17.9 trillion	$17.9 trillion	113.7
2019	$18.3 trillion	$17.9 trillion	115.9

a. If Congress and the president want to keep real GDP at its potential level in 2019, should they use an expansionary policy or a contractionary policy? In your answer, be sure to explain whether Congress and the president should increase or decrease government purchases and taxes.

b. If Congress and the president are successful in keeping real GDP at its potential level in 2019, state whether each of the following will be higher, lower, or the same as it would have been if they had taken no action:

    i. Real GDP

    ii. Potential GDP

    iii. The inflation rate

    iv. The unemployment rate

c. Draw an aggregate demand and aggregate supply graph to illustrate your answer. Be sure that your graph contains *LRAS* curves for 2018 and 2019; *SRAS* curves for 2018 and 2019; *AD* curves for 2018 and 2019, with and without fiscal policy action; and equilibrium real GDP and the price level in 2019, with and without fiscal policy.

3.6 Use a dynamic aggregate demand and aggregate supply graph to illustrate the change in macroeconomic equilibrium from 2019 to 2020, assuming that the economy experiences deflation during 2020. In order for deflation to take place in 2020, does the economy also have to be experiencing a recession? Briefly explain.

7.4 The Government Purchases and Tax Multipliers, pages 259–263

LEARNING OBJECTIVE: Explain how the government purchases and tax multipliers work.

Summary

Because of the **multiplier effect**, an increase in government purchases or a cut in taxes will have a multiplied effect on equilibrium real GDP. The *government purchases multiplier* is equal to the change in equilibrium real GDP divided by the change in government purchases. The *tax multiplier* is equal to the change in equilibrium real GDP divided by the change in taxes. Increases in government purchases and cuts in taxes have a positive multiplier effect on equilibrium real GDP. Decreases in government purchases and increases in taxes have a negative multiplier effect on equilibrium real GDP.

MyEconLab   Visit **www.myeconlab.com** to complete these exercises online and get instant feedback.

Review Questions

4.1 Why can a $1 increase in government purchases lead to more than a $1 increase in income and spending?

4.2 Define *government purchases multiplier* and *tax multiplier*.

4.3 Why does a higher income tax rate reduce the multiplier effect?

Problems and Applications

4.4 **(Related to the** Module Opener **on page 249)** Another infrastructure project in northern California funded in part by ARRA funds involved expanding the Caldecott Tunnel between the cities of Oakland and Orinda. A spokesperson for the California state agency in charge of the project mentioned that the Caldecott Tunnel project would have a "ripple effect" on employment. What did the spokesperson mean by a ripple effect?

Source: Zusha Elinson, "Caldecott Tunnel Edges Forward, Tribute to Stimulus Bill," *New York Times*, September 10, 2011.

4.5 In *The General Theory of Employment, Interest, and Money*, John Maynard Keynes wrote:

> If the Treasury were to fill old bottles with banknotes, bury them at suitable depths in disused coal mines which are then filled up to the surface with town rubbish, and leave it to private enterprise ... to dig the notes up again ... there need be no more unemployment and, with the help of the repercussions, the real income of the community ... would probably become a good deal greater than it is.

Which important macroeconomic effect is Keynes discussing here? What does he mean by "repercussions"? Why does he appear unconcerned about whether government spending is wasteful?

Source: John Maynard Keynes, *The General Theory of Employment, Interest and Money*, New York: Harcourt Brace, 1936, p. 128.

4.6 **(Related to** Solved Problem 7.4 **on page 262)** Suppose that real GDP is currently $17.1 trillion, potential GDP is $17.4 trillion, the government purchases multiplier is 2, and the tax multiplier is −1.6.

a. Holding other factors constant, by how much will government purchases need to be increased to bring the economy to equilibrium at potential GDP?

b. Holding other factors constant, by how much will taxes have to be cut to bring the economy to equilibrium at potential GDP?

c. Construct an example of a *combination* of increased government spending and tax cuts that will bring the economy to equilibrium at potential GDP.

4.7 **(Related to** Solved Problem 7.4 **on page 262)** Briefly explain whether you agree with the following statement:

> Real GDP is currently $17.7 trillion, and potential GDP is $17.4 trillion. If Congress and the president would decrease government purchases by $300 billion or increase taxes by $300 billion, the economy could be brought to equilibrium at potential GDP.

4.8 A Federal Reserve publication argues that the size of the multiplier "depends on the type of fiscal policy changes in question and the environment in which they are implemented."

a. What does the author mean by "the type of fiscal policy changes in question"? Why does the type of policy matter for the size of the multiplier?

b. What does the author mean by "the environment in which they are implemented"? Would the size of the multiplier be affected by how close real GDP is to potential GDP? Briefly explain.

Source: Daniel J. Wilson, "Government Spending: An Economic Boost?" *Federal Reserve Bank of San Francisco Economic Letter*, February 6, 2012.

4.9 If the short-run aggregate supply (*SRAS*) curve were a horizontal line at the current price level, what would be the effect on the size of the government purchases and tax multipliers? Briefly explain.

Fiscal Policy: Deficits and Debt

Module Outline and Learning Objectives

7A.1 The Limits to Using Fiscal Policy to Stabilize the Economy

LEARNING OBJECTIVE: Discuss the difficulties that can arise in implementing fiscal policy.

Poorly timed fiscal policy, like poorly timed monetary policy, can do more harm than good. As we will discuss in Module 8A, it takes time for policymakers to collect statistics and identify changes in the economy. If the government decides to increase spending or cut taxes to fight a recession that is about to end, the effect may be to increase the inflation rate. Similarly, cutting spending or raising taxes to slow down an economy that has actually already moved into a recession can increase the length and depth of the recession.

Getting the timing right can be more difficult with fiscal policy than with monetary policy for two main reasons. Control over monetary policy is concentrated in the hands of the Federal Open Market Committee, which can change monetary policy at any of its meetings. By contrast, the president and a majority of the 535 members of Congress have to agree on changes in fiscal policy. The delays caused by the legislative process can be very long. For example, in 1962, President John F. Kennedy concluded that the U.S. economy was operating below potential GDP and proposed a tax cut to stimulate aggregate demand. Congress eventually agreed to the tax cut—but not until 1964. The events of 2001 and 2009 show, though, that it is sometimes possible to authorize changes in fiscal policy relatively quickly. When George W. Bush came into office in January 2001, the economy was on the verge of a recession, and he immediately proposed a tax cut. Congress passed the tax cut, and the president signed it into law in early June 2001. Similarly, Barack Obama proposed a stimulus package as soon as he came into office in January 2009, and Congress had passed the proposal by February.

Even after a change in fiscal policy has been approved, it takes time to implement it. Suppose Congress and the president agree to increase aggregate demand by spending $30 billion more on constructing subway systems in several cities. It will probably take at least several months to prepare detailed plans for the construction. Local governments will then ask for bids from private construction companies. Once the winning bidders have been selected, they will usually need several months to begin the project. Only then will significant amounts of spending actually take place. This delay may push the spending beyond the end of the recession that the spending was intended to fight. Delays of this type are less of a concern during long and severe recessions, such as that of 2007–2009.

Making the Connection
MyEconLab Video

Why Was the Recession of 2007–2009 So Severe?

Even some economists who are normally skeptical of fiscal policy believed that the severity of the 2007–2009 recession required Congress and the president to increase spending and cut taxes to increase aggregate demand. As we will see in Modules 8 and 8A, the recession was accompanied by a financial crisis. The U.S. economy had not experienced a significant financial crisis since the Great Depression of the 1930s. Both the Great Depression and the recession of 2007–2009 were severe. Do recessions accompanied by financial crises tend to be more severe than recessions that do not involve financial crises?

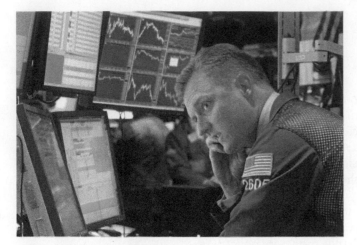

As this stock trader knows, the financial crisis made the recession of 2007–2009 more severe and long-lasting than many other recessions.

In an attempt to answer this question, Carmen Reinhart and Kenneth Rogoff of Harvard University have gathered data on recessions and financial crises in a number of countries. The table at the top of the next page shows the average change in key economic variables during the period following a financial crisis for a number of countries, including the United States during the Great Depression and European and Asian countries in the post–World War II era. The table shows that for these countries, on average, the recessions following financial crises were quite severe:

- Unemployment rates increased by 7 percentage points—for example, from 5 percent to 12 percent—and continued increasing for nearly five years after a crisis had begun.

- Real GDP per capita also declined sharply, and the average length of a recession following a financial crisis has been nearly two years.

- Adjusted for inflation, stock prices declined by more than half, and housing prices declined by more than one-third.

- Government debt soared by 86 percent. The increased government debt was partly the result of increased government spending, including spending to bail out failed financial institutions. But most of the increased debt was due to government budget deficits resulting from sharp declines in tax revenues as wages and profits fell during the recession. (We discuss government budget deficits and government debt in Section 16.6.)

Economic Variable	Average Change	Average Duration of Change	Number of Countries
Unemployment rate	+7 percentage points	4.8 years	14
Real GDP per capita	−9.3%	1.9 years	14
Real stock prices	−55.9%	3.4 years	22
Real house prices	−35.5%	6 years	21
Real government debt	+86%	3 years	13

The following table shows some key indicators for the 2007–2009 U.S. recession compared with other U.S. recessions of the post–World War II period:

	Duration	Decline in Real GDP	Peak Unemployment Rate
Average for postwar recessions	10.4 months	−1.7%	7.6%
Recession of 2007–2009	18 months	−4.2%	10.0%

Consistent with Reinhart and Rogoff's findings that recessions following financial panics tend to be unusually severe, the 2007–2009 recession was the worst in the United States since the Great Depression of the 1930s. The recession lasted nearly twice as long as the average of earlier postwar recessions, GDP declined by more than twice the average, and the peak unemployment rate was about one-third higher than the average.

While some economists argue that better monetary or fiscal policies might have shortened the recession and made it less severe, most economists agree that the financial panic plays a key role in explaining the severity of the 2007–2009 recession.

Note: In the second table, the duration of recessions is based on National Bureau of Economic Research business cycle dates, the decline in real GDP is measured as the simple percentage change from the quarter of the cyclical peak to the quarter of the cyclical trough, and the peak unemployment rate is the highest unemployment rate in any month following the cyclical peak.

Sources: The first table is adapted from data in Carmen M. Reinhart and Kenneth S. Rogoff, *This Time Is Different: Eight Centuries of Financial Folly,* Princeton, NJ: Princeton University Press, 2009, Figures 8.1–8.5; and the second table uses data from the U.S. Bureau of Economic Analysis and National Bureau of Economic Research.

Your Turn: Test your understanding by doing related problem 1.6 on page 294 at the end of this module.

MyEconLab Study Plan

Does Government Spending Reduce Private Spending?

In addition to the timing issue, using increases in government purchases to increase aggregate demand presents another potential problem. We have been assuming that when the federal government increases its purchases by $30 billion, the multiplier effect will cause the increase in aggregate demand to be greater than $30 billion. However, the size of the multiplier effect may be limited if the increase in government purchases causes one of the nongovernment, or private, components of aggregate expenditures—consumption, investment, or net exports—to fall. A decline in private expenditures as a result of an increase in government purchases is called **crowding out**.

MyEconLab Concept Check

Crowding out A decline in private expenditures as a result of an increase in government purchases.

Crowding Out in the Short Run

Consider the case of a temporary increase in government purchases. Suppose the federal government decides to fight a recession by spending $30 billion more this year on subway construction. When the $30 billion has been spent, the program will end, and government purchases will drop back to their previous level. As the spending takes place, income and real GDP will increase. These increases in income and real GDP will cause households and firms to increase their demand for currency and checking account balances to accommodate the increased buying and selling. Figure 7A.1 shows the result, using the money market graph introduced in Module 8A.

At higher levels of real GDP and income, households and firms demand more money at every interest rate. When the demand for money increases, the equilibrium

MyEconLab Animation

Figure 7A.1

An Expansionary Fiscal Policy Increases Interest Rates

An increase in government purchases will increase the demand for money from Money demand$_1$ to Money demand$_2$ as real GDP and income rise. With the supply of money constant, at $950 billion, the result is an increase in the equilibrium interest rate from 3 percent to 5 percent, which crowds out some consumption, investment, and net exports.

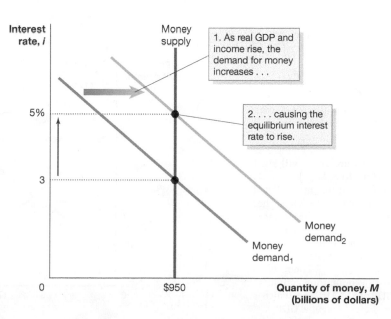

interest rate will rise. Higher interest rates will result in a decline in each component of private expenditures. Consumption spending and investment spending will decline because households will borrow less to buy houses, cars, furniture, and appliances, and firms will borrow less to buy factories, warehouses, and machine tools. Net exports will also decline because higher interest rates in the United States will attract foreign investors. German, Japanese, and Canadian investors will want to exchange the currencies of their countries for U.S. dollars to invest in U.S. Treasury bills and other U.S. financial assets. This increased demand for U.S. dollars will cause an increase in the exchange rate between the dollar and other currencies. When the dollar increases in value, the prices of U.S. products in foreign countries rise—causing a reduction in U.S. exports—and the prices of foreign products in the United States fall—causing an increase in U.S. imports. Falling exports and rising imports mean that net exports are falling.

The greater the sensitivity of consumption, investment, and net exports to changes in interest rates, the more crowding out will occur. In a deep recession, many firms may be pessimistic about the future and have so much excess capacity that investment spending will fall to very low levels and will be unlikely to fall much further, even if interest rates rise. In this case, crowding out is unlikely to be a problem. If the economy is close to potential GDP, however, and firms are optimistic about the future, an increase in interest rates may result in a significant decline in investment spending.

Figure 7A.2 shows that crowding out may reduce the effectiveness of an expansionary fiscal policy. Short-run equilibrium is initially at point A, with real GDP at $17.2 trillion. Real GDP is below potential GDP, so the economy is in a recession. Suppose that Congress and the president decide to increase government purchases to increase real GDP to potential GDP. In the absence of crowding out, the increase in government purchases will shift the aggregate demand curve to $AD_{2(no\ crowding\ out)}$, and equilibrium will be at point B, with real GDP equal to potential GDP of $17.4 trillion. But the higher interest rate resulting from the increased government purchases will reduce consumption, investment, and net exports, causing the aggregate demand curve to shift back to $AD_{2(crowding\ out)}$. The result is a new short-run equilibrium at point C, with real GDP of $17.3 trillion, which is $100 billion short of potential GDP. (Note that the price level increase also contributes to reducing the effect of an increase in government purchases on equilibrium real GDP.)

MyEconLab Concept Check

Figure 7A.2

The Effect of Crowding Out in the Short Run

Equilibrium is initially at point A, with real GDP of $17.2 trillion below potential GDP, so the economy is in a recession. In the absence of crowding out, an increase in government purchases will shift aggregate demand to $AD_{2(no\ crowding\ out)}$, and equilibrium is at potential GDP of $17.4 trillion (point B). But the higher interest rate resulting from the increased government purchases will reduce consumption, investment, and net exports, causing aggregate demand to shift to $AD_{2(no\ crowding\ out)}$. The result is a new short-run equilibrium at point C, with real GDP of $17.3 trillion, which is $100 billion short of potential GDP.

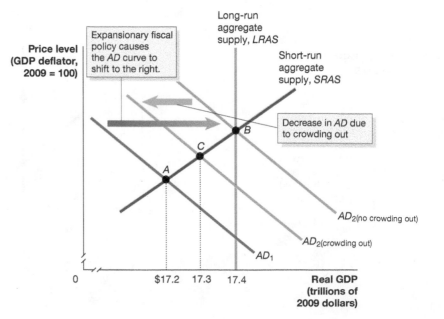

Crowding Out in the Long Run

Most economists agree that in the short run, an increase in government purchases results in partial, but not complete, crowding out. What is the long-run effect of a *permanent* increase in government spending? In this case, most economists agree that the result is complete crowding out. In the long run, the decline in investment, consumption, and net exports exactly offsets the increase in government purchases, and aggregate demand remains unchanged. Recall that *in the long run, real GDP returns to potential GDP* (see Module 4 & 4A). Suppose that real GDP currently equals potential GDP and that government spending is 35 percent of GDP. In that case, private expenditures—the sum of consumption, investment, and net exports—will make up the other 65 percent of GDP. If government spending is increased permanently to 37 percent of GDP, in the long run, private expenditures must fall to 63 percent of GDP. There has been complete crowding out: Private expenditures have fallen by the same amount that government spending has increased. If government spending is taking a larger share of GDP, then private spending must take a smaller share.

An expansionary fiscal policy does not have to cause complete crowding out in the short run. If real GDP is below potential GDP, it is possible for both government purchases and private expenditures to increase. But in the long run, any permanent increase in government spending must come at the expense of private expenditures. Keep in mind, however, that it may take several—possibly many—years to arrive at this long-run outcome. **MyEconLab** Concept Check

Fiscal Policy in Action: Did the Stimulus Package of 2009 Succeed?

As we have seen, Congress and the president can increase government purchases and cut taxes to increase aggregate demand either to avoid a recession or to shorten the length or severity of a recession that is already under way. The recession of 2007–2009 occurred during the end of the presidency of George W. Bush and the beginning of the presidency of Barack Obama. Both presidents used fiscal policy to fight the recession.

In 2008, economists advising President Bush believed that the housing crisis, the resulting credit crunch, and rising oil prices were pushing the economy into a recession. (As we now know, a recession had actually already begun in December 2007.) These economists proposed cutting taxes to increase household disposable income, which would increase consumption spending and aggregate demand. Congress enacted a tax cut that took the form of *rebates* of taxes that households had already paid. Rebate checks totaling $95 billion were sent to taxpayers between April and July 2008.

How effective were the rebates in increasing consumption spending? While economists are still studying the issue, economic analysis can give us some insight. Many economists believe that consumers base their spending on their *permanent income* rather than just on their *current income*. A consumer's permanent income reflects the consumer's expected future income. By basing spending on permanent income, a consumer can smooth out consumption over a period of years. For example, a medical student may have very low current income but a high expected future income. The student may borrow against this high expected future income rather than having to consume at a very low level in the present. Some people, however, have difficulty borrowing against their future income because banks or other lenders may not be convinced that a borrower's future income will be significantly higher than his or her current income. One-time tax rebates, such as the one in 2008, increase consumers' current income but not their permanent income. Only a permanent decrease in taxes increases consumers' permanent income. Therefore, a tax rebate is likely to increase consumption spending less than would a permanent tax cut.

Some estimates of the effect of the 2008 tax rebate, including studies by Christian Broda of the University of Chicago and Jonathan Parker of Northwestern University, and by economists at the Congressional Budget Office, indicate that taxpayers spent between 33 and 40 percent of the rebates they received. Taxpayers who have difficulty borrowing against their future income increased their consumption the most. The 2008 tax rebates totaled $95 billion, so consumers may have increased their spending by about $35 billion.

American Recovery and Reinvestment Act of 2009　Although the tax rebates helped to increase aggregate demand, we will see in Module 8A that the recession worsened in September 2008, following the bankruptcy of the Lehman Brothers investment bank and the deepening of the financial crisis. President Obama took office in January 2009, pledging to pursue an expansionary fiscal policy. Congress responded in February by passing the American Recovery and Reinvestment Act of 2009, an $840 billion package of spending increases and tax cuts that was by far the largest fiscal policy action in U.S. history. The "stimulus package," as it came to be known, is difficult to summarize, but Figure 7A.3 provides some highlights.

About two-thirds of the stimulus package took the form of increases in government expenditures, and one-third took the form of tax cuts. Panel (a) shows the major categories of spending increases. The largest category—health care, social services, and education—included funds for biomedical research and grants to state governments to help fund Medicare spending, as well as funds for many other programs. The energy category included funds for research into alternative energy sources as well as modernization of the electric grid. Transportation and housing included substantial spending on infrastructure projects, such as repairing and expanding highways, bridges, and airports. The spending to reconstruct Doyle Drive in San Francisco, as mentioned in the module opener, is an example of the infrastructure spending included in the act. Individual aid included spending on extended unemployment insurance payments. Panel (b) shows the major categories of tax cuts. The largest category was individual tax cuts, which included a $400 reduction in payroll taxes for workers earning up to $75,000 per year and a tax credit of up to $2,500 for tuition and other college expenses.

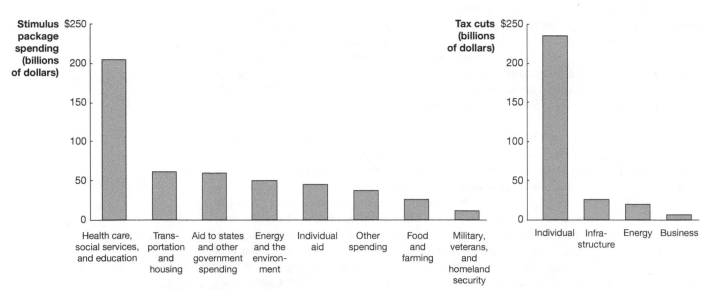

(a) Spending increases in the 2009 stimulus package

(b) Tax cuts in the 2009 stimulus package

MyEconLab Animation

Figure 7A.3　The 2009 Stimulus Package

Congress and President Obama intended the spending increases and tax cuts in the stimulus package to increase aggregate demand and help pull the economy out of the 2007–2009 recession. Panel (a) shows how the increases in spending were distributed, and panel (b) shows how the tax cuts were distributed.

Source: Congressional Budget Office.

Congress and the president intended the changes to federal expenditures and taxes from the stimulus package to be temporary. Figure 7A.4 shows the effect of the stimulus package on federal government expenditures and revenue over time. Panel (a) shows that the effect on federal government expenditures was greatest during 2010 and declined sharply during 2011. Panel (b) shows that the effect on federal government revenue was greatest during 2010 and had declined to almost zero by early 2011.

How Can We Measure the Effectiveness of the Stimulus Package? At the time the stimulus package was passed, economists working for the Obama administration estimated that the increase in aggregate demand resulting from the package would increase real GDP by 3.5 percent by the end of 2010 and increase employment by 3.5 million. In fact, between the beginning of 2009 and the end of 2010, real GDP increased by 4.0 percent, while employment declined by 3.3 million. Do these results indicate that the stimulus package was successful in increasing GDP but not employment? We have to be careful in drawing that conclusion. To judge the effectiveness of the stimulus package, we have to measure its effects on real GDP and employment, *holding constant all other factors affecting real GDP and employment*. In other words, the actual movements in real GDP and employment are a mixture of the effects of the stimulus package and the effects of other factors, such as the Federal Reserve's monetary policy and the typical changes in real GDP and employment during a business cycle that occur independently of government policy. Isolating the effects of the stimulus package from the effects of these other factors is very difficult and explains why economists differ in their views on the effectiveness of the stimulus package.

Table 7A.1 shows estimates from economists at the CBO of the effectiveness of the stimulus package. The CBO is a nonpartisan organization, and many economists believe its estimates are reasonable. But because the estimates depend on particular assumptions about the size of the government purchases and tax multipliers, some

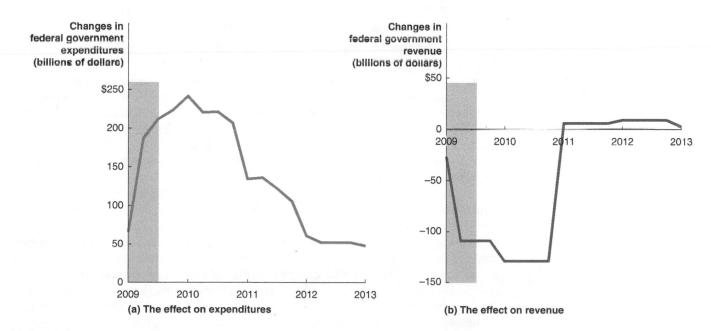

(a) The effect on expenditures   **(b) The effect on revenue**

MyEconLab Animation

Figure 7A.4   **The Effect of the Stimulus Package on Federal Expenditures and Revenue**

Congress and President Obama intended the spending increases and tax cuts in the stimulus package to be temporary. Panel (a) shows that the effect of the stimulus package on federal expenditures was greatest during 2010 and declined in the following years. Panel (b) shows that the effect on federal government revenue was greatest during 2010 and had declined to almost zero by early 2011. **Source:** Federal Reserve Bank of St. Louis.

Year	Change in Real GDP	Change in the Unemployment Rate	Change in Employment (millions of people)
2009	0.4% to 1.8%	−0.1% to −0.5%	0.3 to 1.3
2010	0.7% to 4.1%	−0.4% to −1.8%	0.9 to 4.7
2011	0.4% to 2.3%	−0.2% to −1.4%	0.6 to 3.6
2012	0.1% to 0.8%	−0.1% to −0.6%	0.2 to 1.3
2013	0.1% to 0.4%	0% to −0.3%	0.1 to 0.5
2014	0% to 0.2%	0% to −0.2%	0.1 to 0.3

Source: Congressional Budget Office, "Estimated Impact of the American Recovery and Reinvestment Act on Employment and Economic Output in 2014," February 20, 2015.

economists believe that the CBO estimates are too high, while other economists believe the estimates are too low. To reflect the uncertainty in its calculation, the CBO provides a range of estimates. For example, in the absence of the stimulus package, the CBO estimates that in 2010 between 0.9 million and 4.7 million *fewer* people would have been employed than actually were, and the unemployment rate would have been between 0.4 percent and 1.8 percentage points *higher* than it actually was. By 2014, the effects of the stimulus package were small because several years had passed since most of the temporary spending increases and tax cuts had ended and because the economy had gradually moved back toward potential GDP.

If the CBO's estimates of the effects of the stimulus package are accurate, then this fiscal policy action reduced the severity of the recession of 2007–2009 and its aftermath. However, relative to the severity of the recession, the effect of the package was comparatively small. For example, in 2010, the unemployment rate was 9.6 percent, which was far above the unemployment rate of 4.6 percent in 2007. According to the CBO, without the stimulus package, the unemployment rate would have been somewhere between 10.0 percent and 11.4 percent. So, the stimulus package reduced the increase in the unemployment rate that might otherwise have occurred, but it did not come close to bringing the economy back to full employment.

The Size of the Multiplier: A Key to Estimating the Effects of Fiscal Policy In preparing the values shown in Table 7A.1, the CBO relied on estimates of the government purchases and tax multipliers. Economists have been debating the size of these multipliers for many years. When British economist John Maynard Keynes and his followers first developed the idea of spending and tax multipliers in the 1930s, they argued that the government purchases multiplier might be as large as 10. In that case, a $1 billion increase in government purchases would increase real GDP by $10 billion. Later research by economists indicated that the government purchases multiplier was much smaller, perhaps less than 2.

Estimating an exact number for the multiplier is difficult because over time, several factors can cause the aggregate demand and short-run aggregate supply curves to shift, leading to a change in equilibrium real GDP. It can be challenging to isolate the effect of an increase in government purchases on equilibrium GDP. Before the stimulus package was proposed to Congress in 2009, economists in the Obama administration estimated the package's effect on GDP by using an average of multiplier estimates from the Federal Reserve and from a private macroeconomic forecasting firm. Their estimate that the government purchases multiplier was 1.57 means that a $1 billion increase in government purchases would increase equilibrium real GDP by $1.57 billion.

Because of the difficulty of estimating the size of the multiplier, some economists argue that the value economists in the Obama administration used was too high, while others argue that it was too low. Robert Barro of Harvard University maintains that increases in government spending during wartime are so large relative to other changes in aggregate demand that data from periods of war are best suited to estimating the size of the multiplier. Using such data, Barro estimated that the government purchases multiplier is only 0.8. Lawrence Christiano, Martin Eichenbaum, and Sergio Rebelo of Northwestern University argue, on the other hand, that the multiplier is likely to be larger when, as during 2009, short-term interest rates are near zero. They estimate that for these periods, the government purchases multiplier could be as large as 3.7.

As Table 7A.2 shows, economists' estimates of the size of the multiplier vary widely. The uncertainty about the size of the multiplier indicates the difficulty that economists have in arriving at a firm estimate of the effects of fiscal policy.   MyEconLab Concept Check

Making the Connection

MyEconLab Video

Do We Depend Too Much on the Fed?

We have seen that the recovery from the Great Recession of 2007–2009 was slower than many economists had expected. As Fed Chair Janet Yellen noted in a speech in 2014, "Five years after the end of the recession, the labor market has yet to fully recover." The $840 billion American Recovery and Reinvestment Act (ARRA) of 2009 was by far the largest

Economist Making the Estimate	Type of Multiplier	Size of Multiplier
Congressional Budget Office	Government purchases	0.5–2.5
Lawrence Christiano, Martin Eichenbaum, and Sergio Rebelo, Northwestern University	Government purchases	1.05 when short-term interest rates are not zero; 3.7 when short-term interest rates are expected to be zero for at least five quarters
Tommaso Monacelli, Roberto Perotti, and Antonella Trigari, Universita Bocconi	Government purchases	1.2 after one year; 1.5 after two years
Ethan Ilzetzki, London School of Economics, Enrique G. Mendoza, University of Pennsylvania, and Carlos A. Vegh, University of Maryland	Government purchases	0.8
Valerie Ramey, University of California, San Diego	Military expenditure	0.6–1.1
Robert J. Barro, Harvard University, and Charles J. Redlick, Bain Capital, LLC	Military expenditure	0.4–0.5 after one year; 0.6–0.7 after two years
John Cogan and John Taylor, Stanford University, and Tobias Cwik and Volker Wieland, Goethe University	A permanent increase in government expenditures	0.4
Christina Romer, University of California, Berkeley, and Jared Bernstein, chief economist and economic policy adviser to Vice President Joseph Biden	A permanent increase in government expenditures	1.6
Christina Romer (prior to serving as chair of the Council of Economic Advisers) and David Romer, University of California, Berkeley	Tax	2–3
Congressional Budget Office	Tax	0.3–1.5 for a two-year tax cut for lower- and middle-income people; 0.1–0.6 for a one-year tax cut for higher-income people
Robert J. Barro, Harvard University, and Charles J. Redlick, Bain Capital, LLC	Tax	1.1

Table 7A.2

Estimates of the Size of the Multiplier

Note: The sources of these estimates are given on the Credits page in the back of the book.

fiscal policy action in U.S. history. However, the figure below shows that in 2015, real GDP had not yet returned to potential GDP. The gap between potential GDP and real GDP, which had been as large as 7 percent during the worst of the recession, was still nearly 3 percent—unusually high so far into an economic recovery. The U.S. economy was still operating well below capacity, producing fewer goods and services and creating fewer jobs than it would have at potential GDP.

Should macroeconomic policy rely less on Fed Chair Yellen and her colleagues?

As Table 7A.1 on page 282 showed, by 2011, most of the effects of ARRA on real GDP and employment had already occurred. If macroeconomic policy were to help bring the economy back to potential GDP, it appeared that it would therefore be up to the Federal Reserve. As we saw in Module 15, the Fed used innovative policies, including multiple rounds of quantitative easing (QE), in an attempt to increase aggregate demand. With the Fed having ended the last round of QE in October 2014, some economists and policymakers argued that fiscal policy actions were necessary to expand production and employment. Reports of crumbling bridges and railroad accidents led some policymakers to argue that increased infrastructure spending on highways, bridges, and railroad lines would provide both a short-term boost to aggregate demand and longer-term gains to productivity and economic growth. In 2015, President Obama proposed $478 billion in additional infrastructure spending to be paid for by a new tax on the foreign earnings of U.S. corporations. However, not all economists are convinced of the effectiveness of infrastructure spending, particularly if members of Congress direct the spending to projects in their states or districts that might not produce large benefits relative to their costs.

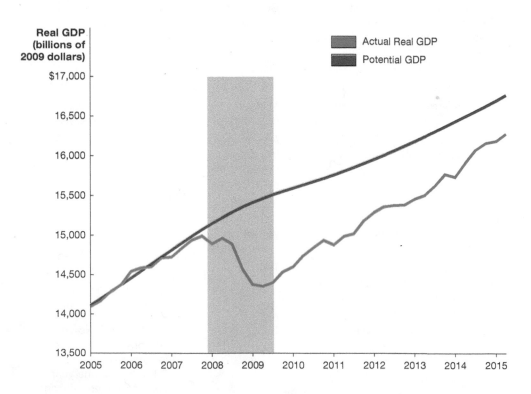

Supporters of infrastructure projects argue that long-term spending might convince businesses that aggregate demand increases would be maintained over a period of years, providing them with the confidence to expand production and employment. Supporters of tax reform to increase economic growth propose lowering tax rates on businesses to spur investment in new innovations and shifting toward consumption-based taxes to spur saving. Some economists argue that trade policy, although not traditionally fiscal policy, could be used to increase the efficiency of the economy and spur exports, while immigration policy could attract high-skilled immigrants, which would increase long-run growth.

The slow recovery from the Great Recession inspired a wide-ranging debate over the use of monetary and fiscal policies to manage the economy.

Sources: Michael D. Shear, "Obama Proposes Tax for Upgrade of Infrastructure," *New York Times*, February 2, 2015; R. Glenn Hubbard, "Stop Depending on the Fed," politico.com, August 20, 2014; Martin S. Feldstein, "Saving the Fed from Itself," *New York Times*, December 8, 2013; Mark Magnier, "Benefits of Infrastructure Spending Not So Clear-Cut, Economists Say," *Wall Street Journal*, February 1, 2015; and Janet L. Yellen, "Labor Market Dynamics and Monetary Policy," Talk delivered at the Federal Reserve Bank of Kansas City Economic Symposium, Jackson Hole, Wyoming, August 22, 2014.

Your Turn: Test your understanding by doing related problem 1.8 on page 294 at the end of this module.

MyEconLab Study Plan

7A.2 Deficits, Surpluses, and Federal Government Debt

LEARNING OBJECTIVE: Define federal budget deficit and federal government debt and explain how the federal budget can serve as an automatic stabilizer.

The federal government's budget shows the relationship between its expenditures and its tax revenue. If the federal government's expenditures are greater than its tax revenue, a **budget deficit** results. If the federal government's expenditures are less than its tax revenue, a **budget surplus** results. As with many other macroeconomic variables, it is useful to consider the size of the surplus or deficit relative to the size of the overall economy. Figure 7A.5 shows that, as a percentage of GDP, the largest deficits of the twentieth century came during World Wars I and II. During major wars, higher taxes only partially offset massive increases in government expenditures, leaving large budget deficits. Figure 7A.5 also shows that during recessions, government spending increases and tax revenues fall, increasing the budget deficit. In 1970, the federal government entered a long period of continuous budget deficits. From 1970 through 1997, the federal government's budget was in deficit every year. From 1998 through 2001, there were four years of budget surpluses. The recessions of 2001 and 2007–2009, tax cuts, and increased government spending on homeland security and the wars in Iraq and Afghanistan helped keep the budget in deficit in the years after 2001.

Figure 7A.5 also shows the effects on the federal budget deficit of the Obama administration's $840 billion stimulus package and the severity of the 2007–2009 recession.

Budget deficit The situation in which the government's expenditures are greater than its tax revenue.

Budget surplus The situation in which the government's expenditures are less than its tax revenue.

MyEconLab Real-time data

Figure 7A.5

The Federal Budget Deficit, 1901–2015

During wars, government spending increases far more than tax revenues, increasing the budget deficit. The budget deficit also increases during recessions, as government spending increases and tax revenues fall.

Note: The value for 2015 is an estimate prepared by the Congressional Budget Office in March 2015.

Sources: *Budget of the United States Government, Fiscal Year 2003, Historical Tables,* Washington, DC: U.S. Government Printing Office, 2002; U.S. Bureau of Economic Analysis; and Congressional Budget Office.

From 2009 through 2011, the federal budget deficit was greater than 8 percent of GDP, which was the first time in the history of the country that the deficit had been this large except during major wars. The economic recovery combined with tax increases and reductions in federal spending lowered the deficit to less than 3 percent of GDP in 2015.

How the Federal Budget Can Serve as an Automatic Stabilizer

Discretionary fiscal policy can increase the federal budget deficit during recessions by increasing spending or cutting taxes to increase aggregate demand. For example, as we have just seen, the Obama administration's spending increases and tax cuts significantly increased the federal budget deficit during 2009 and 2010. In many milder recessions, though, no significant fiscal policy actions are taken. In fact, most of the increase in the federal budget deficit during a typical recession takes place without Congress and the president taking any action but is instead due to the effects of the *automatic stabilizers* we mentioned earlier in this module.

Deficits occur automatically during recessions for two reasons: First, during a recession, wages and profits fall, causing government tax revenues to fall. Second, the government automatically increases its spending on transfer payments when the economy moves into a recession. The federal government's contributions to the unemployment insurance program will increase as unemployment rises. Spending will also increase on programs to aid low-income people, such as the food stamp, Temporary Assistance for Needy Families, and Medicaid programs. These spending increases take place without Congress and the president taking any action. Existing laws already specify who is eligible for unemployment insurance and these other programs. As the number of eligible persons increases during a recession, so does government spending on these programs.

Because budget deficits automatically increase during recessions and decrease during expansions, economists often look at the *cyclically adjusted budget deficit or surplus*, which can provide a more accurate measure of the effects on the economy of the government's spending and tax policies than can the actual budget deficit or surplus. The **cyclically adjusted budget deficit or surplus** measures what the deficit or surplus would be if real GDP were at potential GDP. For example, the federal budget deficit in 2014 was 2.7 percent of GDP. The CBO estimates that if real GDP had been at its potential level, the deficit would have been about 1.6 percent of GDP, with the remaining 1.1 percent representing the increase in the deficit due to the effects of automatic stabilizers. When the federal government runs an expansionary fiscal policy, the result is a cyclically adjusted budget deficit. When the federal government runs a contractionary fiscal policy, the result is a cyclically adjusted budget surplus.

Automatic budget surpluses and deficits can help to stabilize the economy. When the economy moves into a recession, wages and profits fall, reducing the taxes that households and firms owe the government. In effect, households and firms have received an automatic tax cut that keeps their spending higher than it otherwise would have been. In a recession, workers who have been laid off receive unemployment insurance payments, and households whose incomes have fallen below a certain level become eligible for food stamps and other government transfer programs. By receiving this extra income, households are able to spend more than they otherwise would have spent. The extra spending helps reduce the length and severity of the recession. Many economists argue that the lack of an unemployment insurance system and other government transfer programs contributed to the severity of the Great Depression. During the Great Depression, workers who lost their jobs saw their wage income fall to zero and had to rely on their savings, what they could borrow, or what they received from private charities. As a result, many unemployed workers cut back drastically on their spending, which made the downturn worse.

When GDP increases above its potential level, households and firms have to pay more taxes to the federal government, and the federal government makes fewer transfer payments. Higher taxes and lower transfer payments cause total spending to rise by less than it otherwise would have, which helps reduce the chance that the economy will experience higher inflation.

MyEconLab Concept Check

Cyclically adjusted budget deficit or surplus The deficit or surplus in the federal government's budget if the economy were at potential GDP.

Making the Connection

MyEconLab Video

Did Fiscal Policy Fail during the Great Depression?

Modern macroeconomic analysis began during the 1930s, with the publication of *The General Theory of Employment, Interest, and Money* by John Maynard Keynes. One conclusion many economists drew from Keynes's book was that an expansionary fiscal policy would be necessary to pull the United States out of the Great Depression. When Franklin D. Roosevelt became president in 1933, federal government expenditures increased as part of his New Deal program, and there was a federal budget deficit during each remaining year of the decade, except for 1937. The U.S. economy recovered very slowly, however, and did not reach potential GDP again until the outbreak of World War II in 1941.

Some economists and policymakers at the time argued that because the economy recovered slowly despite increases in government spending, fiscal policy had been ineffective. During the debate over President Obama's stimulus package, the argument that fiscal policy had failed during the New Deal was raised again. Economic historians have noted, however, that despite the increases in government spending, Congress and the president had not, in fact, implemented an expansionary fiscal policy during the 1930s. In separate studies, economists E. Cary Brown of MIT and Larry Peppers of Washington and Lee University argued that there was a cyclically adjusted budget deficit during only one year of the 1930s, and that one deficit was small. The following table provides data supporting their arguments. (All variables in the table are nominal rather than real.) The second column shows federal government expenditures increasing from 1933 to 1936, falling in 1937, and then increasing in 1938 and 1939. The third column shows a similar pattern, with the federal budget being in deficit each year after 1933 except for 1937. The fourth column, however, shows that in each year after 1933, the federal government ran a cyclically adjusted budget *surplus*. Because the level of income was so low and the unemployment rate was so high during these years, tax collections were far below what they would have been if the economy had been at potential GDP. As the fifth column shows, in 1933 and again from 1937 to 1939, the cyclically adjusted surpluses were large relative to GDP.

Although government spending increased during the Great Depression, the cyclically adjusted budget was in surplus most years.

Year	Federal Government Expenditures (billions of dollars)	Actual Federal Budget Deficit or Surplus (billions of dollars)	Cyclically Adjusted Budget Deficit or Surplus (billions of dollars)	Cyclically Adjusted Budget Deficit or Surplus as a Percentage of GDP
1929	$2.6	$1.0	$1.24	1.20%
1930	2.7	0.2	0.81	0.89
1931	4.0	−2.1	−0.41	−0.54
1932	3.0	−1.3	0.50	0.85
1933	3.4	−0.9	1.06	1.88
1934	5.5	−2.2	0.09	0.14
1935	5.6	−1.9	0.54	0.74
1936	7.8	−3.2	0.47	0.56
1937	6.4	0.2	2.55	2.77
1938	7.3	−1.3	2.47	2.87
1939	8.4	−2.1	2.00	2.17

Although President Roosevelt proposed many new government spending programs, he had also promised during the 1932 presidential election campaign to balance the federal budget. He achieved a balanced budget only in 1937, but his reluctance to allow the actual budget deficit to grow too large helps explain why the cyclically adjusted budget remained in surplus. Many economists today would agree with

E. Cary Brown's conclusion: "Fiscal policy, then, seems to have been an unsuccessful recovery device in the 'thirties—not because it did not work, but because it was not tried."

Sources: E. Cary Brown, "Fiscal Policy in the 'Thirties: A Reappraisal," *American Economic Review*, Vol. 46, No. 5, December 1956, pp. 475–497; Larry Peppers, "Full Employment Surplus Analysis and Structural Changes," *Explorations in Economic History*, Vol. 10, Winter 1973, pp. 197–210; and U.S. Bureau of Economic Analysis.

MyEconLab Study Plan   **Your Turn:** Test your understanding by doing related problem 2.7 on page 295 at the end of this module.

Should the Federal Budget Always Be Balanced?

Although many economists believe that it is a good idea for the federal government to have a balanced budget when real GDP is at potential GDP, few economists believe that the federal government should attempt to balance its budget every year. To see why economists take this view, consider what the federal government would have to do to keep the budget balanced during a recession, when the budget automatically moves into deficit. To bring the budget back into balance, the government would have to raise taxes or cut spending, but these actions would reduce aggregate demand, thereby making the recession worse. Similarly, when GDP increases above its potential level, the budget automatically moves into surplus. To eliminate this surplus, the government would have to cut taxes or increase government spending. But these actions would increase aggregate demand, thereby pushing GDP further beyond potential GDP and increasing the risk of higher inflation. To balance the budget every year, the government might have to take actions that would destabilize the economy.

Solved Problem 7A.2

MyEconLab Interactive Animation

The Greek Government Confronts a Budget Deficit

According to an article in the *Wall Street Journal*, in 2015, some economists believed that the Greek economy might be about to enter a recession. The article noted, "Renewed recession in Greece … could force the government to impose further spending cuts and tax hikes to avoid a renewed budget deficit."

a. Why would the Greek economy entering a recession lead to the Greek government having a budget deficit?

b. If the Greek government, in reaction to the budget deficit, takes the steps the article indicates, what would be the likely effect on the Greek economy?

Solving the Problem

Step 1: Review the module material. This problem is about the effects of a government attempting to balance its budget during a recession, so you may want to review the sections "How the Federal Budget Can Serve as an Automatic Stabilizer" and "Should the Federal Budget Always Be Balanced?" which are on pages 286 and 288.

Step 2: Answer part (a) by explaining why a government's budget will automatically run a deficit during a recession. Deficits occur automatically during recessions because falling wages and profits cause government tax revenues to fall and because government spending on transfer payments, such as unemployment insurance payments, increases.

Step 3: Answer part (b) by explaining the likely effect on the Greek economy if the Greek government were to cut spending and increase taxes. We have seen that reductions in government spending and increases in taxes will reduce aggregate demand. A reduction in aggregate demand will likely reduce real GDP and employment, making the recession in Greece worse.

Source: Nektaria Stamouli and Stelios Bouras, "Greek Economy Risks Slipping Back Into Recession, Say Analysts," *Wall Street Journal*, April 6, 2015.

MyEconLab Study Plan   **Your Turn:** For more practice, do related problem 2.9 on page 295 at the end of this module.

Some economists argue that the federal government should normally run a deficit, even at potential GDP. When the federal budget is in deficit, the U.S. Treasury sells bonds to investors to raise the funds necessary to pay the government's bills. Borrowing to pay the bills is a bad policy for a household, a firm, or the government when the bills are for current expenses, but it is not a bad policy if the bills are for long-lived capital goods. For instance, most families pay for a new home by taking out a 15- to 30-year mortgage. Because houses last many years, it makes sense to pay for a house out of the income the family makes over a long period of time rather than out of the income they receive in the year they bought the house. Businesses often borrow the funds to buy machinery, equipment, and factories by selling 30-year corporate bonds. Because these capital goods generate profits for the businesses over many years, it makes sense to pay for them over a period of years as well. By similar reasoning, when the federal government contributes to the building of a new highway, bridge, or subway, it may want to borrow funds by selling Treasury bonds. The alternative is to pay for these long-lived capital goods out of the tax revenues received in the year the goods were purchased. But that means that the taxpayers in that year have to bear the whole burden of paying for the projects, even though taxpayers for many years in the future will be enjoying the benefits.   MyEconLab Concept Check

The Federal Government Debt

Every time the federal government runs a budget deficit, the Treasury must borrow funds from investors by selling Treasury securities. For simplicity, we will refer to all Treasury securities as "bonds." When the federal government runs a budget surplus, the Treasury pays off some existing bonds. Figure 7A.5 on page 285 shows that there are many more years of federal budget deficits than years of federal budget surpluses. As a result, the total number of Treasury bonds outstanding has grown over the years. The total value of U.S. Treasury bonds outstanding is called the *federal government debt* or, sometimes, the *national debt*. Each year the federal budget is in deficit, the federal government debt grows. Each year the federal budget is in surplus, the debt shrinks.

Figure 7A.6 shows federal government debt as a percentage of GDP in the years from 1901 to 2015. The ratio of debt to GDP increased during World Wars I and II and the Great Depression, reflecting the large government budget deficits of those years. After the end of World War II, GDP grew faster than the debt until the early 1980s, which caused the ratio of debt to GDP to fall. The large budget deficits of the 1980s and early 1990s sent the debt-to-GDP ratio climbing. The budget surpluses of 1998 to 2001 caused the debt-to-GDP ratio to fall, but it rose again with the return of deficits beginning in 2002. The large deficits beginning in 2008 caused the ratio to rise above 100 percent of GDP for the first time since 1947.   MyEconLab Concept Check

Is Government Debt a Problem?

Debt can be a problem for a government for the same reasons it can be a problem for a household or a business. If a family has difficulty making the monthly mortgage payment, it will have to cut back spending on other goods and services. If the family is unable to make the payments, it will have to *default* on the loan and will probably lose its house. The federal government is not in danger of defaulting on its debt. Ultimately, the government can raise the funds it needs through taxes to make the interest payments on the debt. If the debt becomes very large relative to the economy, however, the government may have to raise taxes to high levels or cut back on other types of spending to make the interest payments on the debt. Interest payments are currently about 11 percent of total federal expenditures. At this level, tax increases or significant cutbacks in other types of federal spending are not required.

In the long run, a debt that increases in size relative to GDP, as happened after 2008, can pose a problem. As we discussed previously, crowding out of investment spending may occur if increasing debt drives up interest rates. Lower investment spending means a lower capital stock in the long run and a reduced capacity of the economy to produce goods and services. This effect is somewhat offset if some of the government debt was incurred to finance improvements in *infrastructure*, such as bridges, highways, and ports; to finance education; or to finance research and development. Improvements in infrastructure, a better-educated labor force, and additional research and development can add to the productive capacity of the economy.   MyEconLab Concept Check   MyEconLab Study Plan

MyEconLab Real-time data

Figure 7A.6

The Federal Government Debt, 1901–2015

The federal government debt increases whenever the federal government runs a budget deficit. The large deficits incurred during World Wars I and II, the Great Depression, and the 1980s and early 1990s increased the ratio of debt to GDP. The large deficits after 2008 caused the ratio to spike up to its highest level since 1947.

Note: The value for 2015 is an estimate prepared by the Congressional Budget Office in March 2015.

Sources: U.S. Bureau of the Census, *Historical Statistics of the United States, Colonial Times to 1970*, Washington, DC: U.S. Government Printing Office, 1975; *Budget of the United States Government, Fiscal Year 2003*, Historical Printing Office, 2002; Federal Reserve Bank of St. Louis; and Congressional Budget Office.

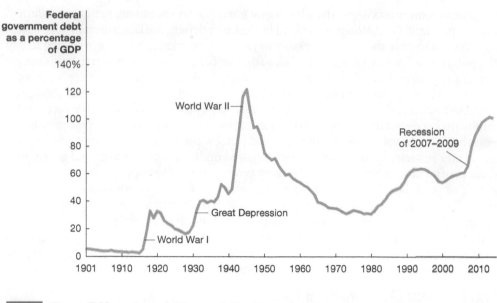

7A.3 The Effects of Fiscal Policy in the Long Run

LEARNING OBJECTIVE: Discuss the effects of fiscal policy in the long run.

Some fiscal policy actions are intended to meet the short-run goal of stabilizing the economy. Other fiscal policy actions are intended to have long-run effects by expanding the productive capacity of the economy and increasing the rate of economic growth. Because these policy actions primarily affect aggregate supply rather than aggregate demand, they are sometimes called *supply-side economics*. Most fiscal policy actions that attempt to increase aggregate supply do so by changing taxes to increase the incentives to work, save, invest, and start a business.

The Long-Run Effects of Tax Policy

Tax wedge The difference between the pretax and posttax return to an economic activity.

The difference between the pretax and posttax return to an economic activity is called the **tax wedge**. It is determined by the *marginal tax rate*, which is the fraction of each additional dollar of income that must be paid in taxes. For example, the U.S. federal income tax has several tax brackets, which are the income ranges within which a tax rate applies. In 2015, for a single taxpayer, the tax rate was 10 percent on the first $9,225 earned during a year. The tax rate rose for higher income brackets, until it reached 39.6 percent on income earned above $413,200. Suppose you are paid a wage of $20 per hour. If your marginal income tax rate is 25 percent, then your posttax wage is $15, and the tax wedge is $5. When discussing the model of demand and supply in Module 3, we saw that increasing the price of a good or service increases the quantity supplied. So, we would expect that reducing the tax wedge by cutting the marginal tax rate on income would result in a larger quantity of labor supplied because the posttax wage would be higher. Similarly, we saw in Module 3 & 3A that a reduction in the income tax rate would increase the posttax return to saving, causing an increase in the supply of loanable funds, a lower equilibrium interest rate, and an increase in investment spending. In general, economists believe that the smaller the tax wedge for any economic activity—such as working, saving, investing, or starting a business—the more of that economic activity that will occur. When workers, savers, investors, or entrepreneurs change their actions as a result of a tax change, economists say that there has been a *behavioral response* to the tax change.

We can look briefly at the effects on aggregate supply of cutting each of the following taxes:

- **Individual income tax.** As we have seen, reducing the marginal tax rates on individual income will reduce the tax wedge workers face, thereby increasing the quantity of labor supplied. Many small businesses are *sole proprietorships*, whose profits are taxed at the individual income tax rates. Therefore, cutting the individual income tax rates also raises the return to entrepreneurship, encouraging the opening of new businesses. Most households are taxed on their returns from saving at the individual income tax rates. Reducing marginal income tax rates, therefore, also increases the return to saving.

- **Corporate income tax.** The federal government taxes the profits corporations earn under the corporate income tax. In 2015, most corporations faced a marginal corporate tax rate of 35 percent. Cutting the marginal corporate income tax rate would encourage investment spending by increasing the return corporations receive from new investments in equipment, factories, and office buildings. Because innovations are often embodied in new investment goods, cutting the corporate income tax can potentially increase the pace of technological change.

- **Taxes on dividends and capital gains.** Corporations distribute some of their profits to shareholders in the form of payments known as *dividends*. Shareholders also may benefit from higher corporate profits by receiving *capital gains*. A capital gain is the increase in the price of an asset, such as a share of stock. Rising profits usually result in rising stock prices and capital gains to shareholders. Individuals pay taxes on both dividends and capital gains (although the tax on capital gains can be postponed if the stock is not sold). As a result, the same earnings are, in effect, taxed twice: once when a corporation pays the corporate income tax on its profits and a second time when individual investors receive the profits in the form of dividends or capital gains. Economists debate the costs and benefits of a separate tax on corporate profits. With the corporate income tax remaining in place, one way to reduce the "double taxation" problem is to reduce the tax rates on dividends and capital gains. These rates were reduced in 2003 before being increased in 2013. Generally, the marginal tax rates on dividends and capital gains are still below the top marginal tax rate on individual income. Lowering the tax rates on dividends and capital gains increases the supply of loanable funds from households to firms, increasing saving and investment and lowering the equilibrium real interest rate.

Tax Simplification

In addition to the potential gains from cutting individual taxes, there are also gains from tax simplification. The complexity of the tax code, which is 3,000 pages long, has created a whole industry of tax preparation services, such as H&R Block. The Internal Revenue Service estimates that taxpayers spend more than 6.4 billion hours each year filling out their tax forms, or about 45 hours per tax return. Households and firms have to deal with more than 480 tax forms to file their federal taxes and spend more than $10 billion per year to hire accountants to help fill out the forms. It is not surprising that there are more H&R Block offices around the country than Starbucks coffeehouses.

If the tax code were greatly simplified, the economic resources currently used by the tax preparation industry would be available to produce other goods and services. In addition to wasting resources, the complexity of the tax code may also distort the decisions households and firms make. For example, the tax rate on dividends has clearly affected whether corporations pay dividends. When Congress passed a reduction in the tax on dividends in 2003, many firms—including Microsoft—began paying dividends for the first time. A simplified tax code would increase economic efficiency by reducing the number of decisions households and firms make solely to reduce their tax payments.   MyEconLab Concept Check

The Economic Effect of Tax Reform

We can analyze the economic effects of tax reduction and simplification by using the aggregate demand and aggregate supply model. Figure 7A.7 shows that without tax changes, the long-run aggregate supply curve will shift from $LRAS_1$ to $LRAS_2$. This shift represents the increases in the labor force and the capital stock and the technological change that would occur even without tax reduction and simplification. To focus on the effect of tax changes on aggregate supply, we will ignore any shifts in the short-run aggregate supply curve, and we will assume that the aggregate demand curve remains unchanged, at AD_1. In this case, equilibrium moves from point A to point B, with real GDP increasing from Y_1 to Y_2 and the price level decreasing from P_1 to P_2.

Figure 7A.7

The Supply-Side Effects of a Tax Change

The initial equilibrium is at point A. With no tax change, the long-run aggregate supply curve shifts to the right, from $LRAS_1$ to $LRAS_2$. Equilibrium moves to point B, with the price level falling from P_1 to P_2 and real GDP increasing from Y_1 to Y_2. With tax reductions and simplifications, the long-run aggregate supply curve shifts further to the right, to $LRAS_3$, and equilibrium moves to point C, with the price level falling to P_3 and real GDP increasing to Y_3.

If tax reduction and simplification are effective, the economy will experience increases in labor supply, saving, investment, and the formation of new firms. Economic efficiency will also be improved. Together these factors will result in an increase in the quantity of real GDP supplied at every price level. We show the effects of the tax changes in Figure 7A.7 by a shift in the long-run aggregate supply curve to $LRAS_3$. With aggregate demand remaining unchanged, equilibrium moves from point A to point C (rather than to point B, which is the equilibrium without tax changes), with real GDP increasing from Y_1 to Y_3 and the price level decreasing from P_1 to P_3. Notice that compared with the equilibrium without tax changes (point B), the equilibrium with tax changes (point C) occurs at a lower price level and a higher level of real GDP. We can conclude that the tax changes have benefited the economy by increasing output and employment while at the same time reducing the price level.

Clearly, our analysis is unrealistic because we have ignored the changes that will occur in aggregate demand and short-run aggregate supply. How would a more realistic analysis differ from the simplified one in Figure 7A.7? The change in real GDP would be the same because in the long run, real GDP is equal to its potential level, which is represented by the *long-run aggregate supply* curve. The outcome for the price level would be different, however, because we would expect both the aggregate demand curve and the short-run aggregate supply curve to shift to the right. The most likely outcome is that the price level would end up higher in the new equilibrium than in the original equilibrium. However, because the position of the long-run aggregate supply curve is further to the right as a result of the tax changes, the increase in the price level will be smaller; that is, the price level at point C is likely to be lower than P_2, even if it is higher than P_3, although—as we will discuss in the next section—not all economists would agree. We can conclude that a successful policy of tax reductions and simplifications will benefit the economy by increasing output and employment and, at the same time, may result in smaller increases in the price level.

How Large Are Supply-Side Effects?

Most economists would agree that there are supply-side effects to reducing taxes: Decreasing marginal income tax rates will increase the quantity of labor supplied, cutting the corporate income tax will increase investment spending, and so on. The magnitude of the effects is the subject of considerable debate, however. For example, some economists argue that the increase in the quantity of labor supplied following a tax cut will be limited because many people work a number of hours set by their employers and lack the opportunity to work additional hours. Similarly, some economists believe that tax changes have only a small effect on saving and investment. In this view, saving and investment are affected much more by changes in income or changes in expectations of the future profitability of new investment due to technological change or improving macroeconomic conditions than they are by changes in taxes.

Economists who are skeptical of the magnitude of supply-side effects believe that tax cuts have their greatest effect on aggregate demand rather than on aggregate supply. In their view, focusing on the effect of tax cuts on aggregate demand, while ignoring any effect on aggregate supply, yields accurate forecasts of future movements in real GDP and the price level, which indicates that the supply-side effects must be small. If tax changes have only small effects on aggregate supply, they are unlikely to reduce the size of price increases to the extent shown in Figure 7A.7.

Ultimately, the debate over the size of the supply-side effects of tax policy can be resolved only through careful study of the effects of differences in tax rates on labor supply and on saving and investment decisions. Some recent studies have arrived at conflicting conclusions, however. For example, a study by Nobel Laureate Edward Prescott of Arizona State University concludes that the differences between the United States and Europe with respect to the average number of hours worked per week and the average number of weeks worked per year are due to differences in tax rates. The lower marginal tax rates in the United States compared with Europe increase the return to working for U.S. workers and result in a larger quantity of labor supplied. But another study by Alberto Alesina and Edward Glaeser of Harvard University and Bruce Sacerdote of Dartmouth College argues that the more restrictive labor market regulations in Europe explain the shorter work weeks and longer vacations of European workers and that differences in tax rates have only a small effect.

As in other areas of economics, differences among economists in their estimates of the supply-side effects of tax changes may narrow over time as they conduct more studies.   MyEconLab Concept Check   MyEconLab Study Plan

Economics in Your Life

What Would You Do with an Extra $500?

How you would respond to a $500 tax rebate and what effect this tax rebate would likely have on equilibrium real GDP in the short run? This module has shown that tax cuts increase disposable income and, therefore, consumption spending. So, you will likely respond to a permanent $500 increase in your disposable income by increasing your spending. How much your spending increases depends in part on your overall financial situation. As mentioned in the module, people who are able to borrow usually try to smooth out their spending over time and don't increase spending much in response to a one-time increase in their income. But if you are a student struggling to get by on a low income and you are unable to borrow against the higher income you expect to earn in the future, you may well spend most of the rebate. This module has also shown that tax cuts have a multiplier effect on the economy. That is, an increase in consumption spending sets off further increases in real GDP and income. So, if the economy is not already at potential GDP, this tax rebate will likely increase equilibrium real GDP in the short run.

Conclusion

In this module, we have seen how the federal government uses changes in government purchases and taxes to achieve its economic policy goals. We have seen that economists debate the effectiveness of discretionary fiscal policy actions intended to stabilize the economy. Congress and the president share responsibility for economic policy with the Federal Reserve. In the next module, we will discuss further some of the challenges that the Federal Reserve faces as it carries out monetary policy. In the following modules, we will look more closely at the international economy, including how monetary and fiscal policy are affected by the linkages between economies.

Visit MyEconLab for a news article and analysis related to the concepts in this module.

Key Terms

Budget deficit, p. 285

Budget surplus, p. 285

Crowding out, p. 277

Cyclically adjusted budget deficit or surplus, p. 286

Tax wedge, p. 290

7A.1 **The Limits to Using Fiscal Policy to Stabilize the Economy, pages 275–285**
LEARNING OBJECTIVE: Discuss the difficulties that can arise in implementing fiscal policy.

Summary

Poorly timed fiscal policy can do more harm than good. Getting the timing right with fiscal policy can be difficult because a president obtaining approval from Congress for a new fiscal policy can be a very long process, and it can take months for an increase in authorized spending to actually take place. Because an increase in government purchases may lead to a higher interest rate, it may result in a decline in consumption, investment, and net exports. A decline in private expenditures as a result of an increase in government purchases is called **crowding out**. Crowding out may cause an expansionary fiscal policy to fail to meet its goal of keeping real GDP at potential GDP.

MyEconLab Visit **www.myeconlab.com** to complete these exercises online and get instant feedback.

Review Questions

1.1 Which can be changed more quickly: monetary policy or fiscal policy? Briefly explain.

1.2 What is meant by "crowding out"? Explain the difference between crowding out in the short run and in the long run.

Problems and Applications

1.3 Some economists argue that because increases in government spending crowd out private spending, increased government spending will reduce the long-run growth rate of real GDP.
   a. Is this outcome most likely to occur if the private spending being crowded out is consumption spending, investment spending, or net exports? Briefly explain.
   b. In terms of its effect on the long-run growth rate of real GDP, would it matter if the additional government spending involves (i) increased spending on highways and bridges or (ii) increased spending on national parks? Briefly explain.

1.4 According to a study by Kanishka Misra of the University of Michigan and Paolo Surico of the London Business School, "Almost half of American families did not adjust their consumption following receipt of the … 2008 tax rebate." Don't we expect that people will increase their consumption if their disposable income increases? Was there anything about the form of the 2008 tax cut that made it more likely that people would not respond by increasing their consumption spending? Briefly explain.

Source: Kanishka Misra and Paolo Surico, "Consumption, Income Changes, and Heterogeneity: Evidence from Two Fiscal Stimulus Programs," *American Economic Journal: Macroeconomics*, Vol. 6, No. 4, October 2014, pp. 84–106.

1.5 We saw that in calculating the stimulus package's effect on real GDP, economists in the Obama administration estimated that the government purchases multiplier has a value of 1.57. John F. Cogan, Tobias Cwik, John B. Taylor, and Volker Wieland argue that the value is only 0.4.
   a. Briefly explain how the government purchases multiplier can have a value of less than 1.
   b. Why does an estimate of the size of the multiplier matter in evaluating the effects of an expansionary fiscal policy?

Source: John Cogan, Tobias Cwik, John Taylor, and Volker Wieland, "New Keynesian versus Old Keynesian Government Spending Multipliers," *Journal of Economic Dynamics and Control*, Vol. 34, No. 3, March 2010, pp. 281–295.

1.6 **(Related to the** Making the Connection **on page 276)** Why would a recession accompanied by a financial crisis be more severe than a recession that did not involve a financial crisis? Were the large budget deficits in 2009 and 2010 primarily the result of the stimulus package of 2009? Briefly explain.

1.7 Suppose that at the same time Congress and the president pursue an expansionary fiscal policy, the Federal Reserve pursues an expansionary monetary policy. How might an expansionary monetary policy affect the extent of crowding out in the short run?

1.8 **(Related to the** Making the Connection **on page 285)** A report from the International Monetary Fund in late 2014 contained the following observations: "Five years after the global financial crisis, the economic recovery continues but remains weak. … Given … the current environment of low government borrowing costs … might this be a good time to increase public infrastructure investment?"
   a. What does the report mean by "low government borrowing costs"? Why would low government borrowing costs be relevant to whether a government increases infrastructure investment?
   b. The report also notes, "In advanced economies an increase in infrastructure investment … is one of the few remaining policy levers available to support growth." What does the report mean by a "policy lever"? Why would the authors of the report consider infrastructure one of the few remaining policy levers?

Source: International Monetary Fund, "World Economic Outlook: Legacies, Clouds, Uncertainties," October 2014, pp. 75–76.

7A.2 Deficits, Surpluses, and Federal Government Debt, pages 285–290

LEARNING OBJECTIVE: Define federal budget deficit and federal government debt and explain how the federal budget can serve as an automatic stabilizer.

Summary

A **budget deficit** occurs when the federal government's expenditures are greater than its tax revenues. A **budget surplus** occurs when the federal government's expenditures are less than its tax revenues. A budget deficit automatically increases during recessions and decreases during expansions. The automatic movements in the federal budget help to stabilize the economy by cushioning the fall in spending during recessions and restraining the increase in spending during expansions. The **cyclically adjusted budget deficit or surplus** measures what the deficit or surplus would be if the economy were at potential GDP. The federal government debt (or national debt) is the value of outstanding bonds issued by the U.S. Treasury. The national debt is a problem if interest payments on it require taxes to be raised substantially or require other federal expenditures to be cut.

MyEconLab   Visit **www.myeconlab.com** to complete these exercises online and get instant feedback.

Review Questions

2.1 In what ways does the federal budget serve as an automatic stabilizer for the economy?

2.2 What is the cyclically adjusted budget deficit or surplus? Suppose that real GDP is currently at potential GDP, and the federal budget is balanced. If the economy moves into a recession, what will happen to the federal budget?

2.3 Why do few economists believe it would be a good idea to balance the federal budget every year?

2.4 What is the difference between the federal budget deficit and federal government debt?

Problems and Applications

2.5 *Wall Street Journal* writers Josh Zumbrun and Nick Timiraos published answers to several of their readers' questions regarding the federal government's debt. Two of the questions were:
 a. Why is government debt different from mine?
 b. How important is it to pay off this debt?

Write a brief response to each of these questions.

Source: Josh Zumbrun and Nick Timiraos, "Q&A: What the $18 Trillion National Debt Means for the U.S. Economy," *Wall Street Journal*, February 1, 2015.

2.6 In a column in the *Financial Times*, the prime minister and the finance minister of the Netherlands argue that the European Union, an organization of 28 countries in Europe, should appoint "a commissioner for budgetary discipline." They believe that "the new commissioner should be given clear powers to set requirements for the budgetary policy of countries that run excessive deficits." What is an "excessive" budget deficit? Does judging whether a deficit is excessive depend in part on whether

the country is in a recession? How can budgetary policies be used to reduce a budget deficit?

Source: Mark Rutte and Jan Kees de Jager, "Expulsion from the Eurozone Has to Be the Final Penalty," *Financial Times*, September 7, 2011.

2.7 (Related to the Making the Connection **on page 287)** The following is from a message by President Herbert Hoover to Congress, dated May 5, 1932:

> I need not recount that the revenues of the Government as estimated for the next fiscal year show a decrease of about $1,700,000,000 below the fiscal year 1929, and inexorably require a broader basis of taxation and a drastic reduction of expenditures in order to balance the Budget. Nothing is more necessary at this time than balancing the Budget.

Do you think President Hoover was correct in saying that, in 1932, nothing was more necessary than balancing the federal government's budget? Explain.

Source: Herbert Hoover, "Special Message to the Congress on Budgetary Legislation," in *Public Papers of the Presidents of the United States: Herbert Hoover, 1932–1933*, 1977, p. 194.

2.8 In February 2013, the Congressional Budget Office (CBO) forecast that the federal budget deficit for fiscal year 2013 would be approximately $850 billion. In May 2013, the CBO revised down its forecast of the budget deficit to $642 billion. The CBO stated that a major reason for the downward revision was "factors related mainly to the strengthening economy."
 a. Why would a "strengthening economy" lead to a downward revision of the projected budget deficit?
 b. Suppose that Congress and the president were committed to balancing the budget each year. Does what happened during 2013 provide any insight into difficulties they might run into in trying to balance the budget every year?

Source: Susan Davis, "CBO Drops 2013 Deficit Estimate to $642 Billion," usatoday.com, May 15, 2013.

2.9 (Related to Solved Problem 7A.2 **on page 288)** An article in the *Wall Street Journal* in 2015 noted that an official of the European Union was forecasting that "Greece faces two years of recession amid sharp budget cuts." What typically happens to a government's budget deficit during a recession? Do governments typical respond with budget cuts as the Greek government did? Briefly explain.

Source: Gabriele Steinhauser and Andrea Thomas, "Greece Faces Two-Year Recession amid Bailout Cuts," *Wall Street Journal*, August 12, 2015.

2.10 In 2015, an article in the *Wall Street Journal* noted that "Prime Minister Shinzo Abe is expected to unveil a plan to balance Japan's budget in five years ... as a step toward reducing the country's debt burden, according to government officials." What is the connection between the government's budget deficit and its debt? If the debt is a "burden," briefly explain what it is a burden on.

Source: Tatsuo Ito, "Japan Government Takes On Its Deficit-Ridden Finances," *Wall Street Journal*, June 17, 2015.

2.11 A political columnist wrote the following:

> Today ... the main purpose [of governments issuing bonds] is to let craven politicians launch projects they know the public, at the moment, would rather not fully finance. The

tab for these projects will not come due, probably, until after the politicians have long since departed for greener (excuse the expression) pastures.

Do you agree with this commentator's explanation for why some government spending is financed through tax receipts and other government spending is financed through borrowing, by issuing bonds? Briefly explain.

Source: Paul Carpenter, "The Bond Issue Won't Be Repaid by Park Tolls," (Allentown, PA) *Morning Call*, May 26, 2002.

7A.3	**The Effects of Fiscal Policy in the Long Run, pages 290–293**

LEARNING OBJECTIVE: Discuss the effects of fiscal policy in the long run.

Summary

Some fiscal policy actions are intended to have long-run effects by expanding the productive capacity of the economy and increasing the rate of economic growth. Because these policy actions primarily affect aggregate supply rather than aggregate demand, they are sometimes called *supply-side economics*. The difference between the pretax and posttax return to an economic activity is called the **tax wedge**. Economists believe that the smaller the tax wedge for any economic activity—such as working, saving, investing, or starting a business—the more of that economic activity will occur. Economists debate the size of the supply-side effects of tax changes.

MyEconLab   Visit **www.myeconlab.com** to complete these exercises online and get instant feedback.

Review Questions

3.1 What is meant by "supply-side economics"?

3.2 What is the "tax wedge"?

Problems and Applications

3.3 It seems that both households and businesses would benefit if the federal income tax were simpler and tax forms were easier to fill out. Why then have the tax laws become increasingly complicated?

3.4 Some economists and policymakers have argued in favor of a "flat tax." A flat tax would replace the current individual income tax system, with its many tax brackets, exemptions, and deductions, with a new system containing a single tax rate and few, or perhaps no, deductions and exemptions. Suppose a political candidate hired you to develop two arguments in favor of a flat tax. What two arguments would you advance? Alternatively, if you were hired to develop two arguments against a flat tax, what two arguments would you advance?

3.5 Suppose that an increase in marginal tax rates on individual income affects both aggregate demand and aggregate supply. Briefly describe the effect of the tax increase on equilibrium real GDP and the equilibrium price level. Will the changes in equilibrium real GDP and the price level

be larger or smaller than they would be if the tax increase affected only aggregate demand? Briefly explain.

3.6 Writing in the *Wall Street Journal*, Martin Feldstein, an economist at Harvard University, argues that "behavioral responses" of taxpayers to the cuts in marginal tax rates enacted in 1986 resulted in "an enormous rise in the taxes paid, particularly by those who experienced the greatest reductions in marginal tax rates." How is it possible for cuts in marginal tax rates to result in an increase in total taxes collected? What does Feldstein mean by a "behavioral response" to tax cuts?

Source: Martin Feldstein, "The Tax Reform Evidence from 1986," *Wall Street Journal*, October 24, 2011.

Real-Time Data Exercises

D7A.1 (Comparing macroeconomic conditions in different countries) The International Monetary Fund (IMF) publishes *The World Economic Outlook*. Go to www.imf.org and look at the most recent version available. The IMF measures the output gap as the difference between real GDP and potential GDP as a percentage of potential GDP. A negative value for the output gap means that real GDP is below potential GDP. Look at the data on the output gap for Japan, the United Kingdom, and the United States for 2013 to 2018 (the values for the later years will be forecasts).

    a. Which country had the largest output gap (in absolute value) in 2013? Which country had the smallest output gap?

    b. Discuss what fiscal policies the governments of these countries could use to bring the output gaps to zero.

    c. Describe at least two problems that these countries would have in implementing your suggested policies.

D7A.2 (Comparing the actual and cyclically adjusted budget deficits in the United States) The Congressional Budget Office (CBO) provides data on the actual and cyclically adjusted budget deficits. You can find data for the years 1965–2014 at https://www.cbo.gov/sites/default/files/114th-congress-2015-2016/reports/49892/49892-breakout-AppendixD.pdf.

    a. The CBO calls the budget deficit or surplus "Deficit or Surplus with Automatic Stabilizers," and calls the cyclically adjusted deficit or surplus the "Deficit or Surplus without Automatic Stabilizers." Briefly explain why the CBO uses these labels.

b. For the years 2000-2014, enter the data from the columns "Deficit or Surplus with Automatic Stabilizers," and "Deficit or Surplus without Automatic Stabilizers" into an Excel spreadsheet. Use the data to graph the budget deficit or surplus and the cyclically adjusted deficit or surplus for these years.

c. Calculate the average surplus or deficit and the average cyclically adjusted surplus or deficit for these years. Which was larger? Briefly explain your result.

D7A.3 (Comparing budget deficits in different countries) The International Monetary Fund (IMF) publishes *The World Economic Outlook*. Go to www.imf.org and find the IMF data for the cyclically adjusted budget deficit as a percentage of potential GDP (which the IMF calls "General Government Structural Balance") for Brazil, China, France, and Germany from 2000 to 2018 (the values for the later years will be forecasts). Use the series for the cyclically adjusted budget deficit that is measured as a percentage of potential GDP.

a. Download the data and plot them in a graph. Which country relied the most on discretionary fiscal policy in response to the financial crisis of 2008 and 2009? Briefly explain how you are able to tell.

b. From 2013 to 2018, which of these four countries is expected to have the most expansionary fiscal policy? Briefly explain.

Money, Banks, and the Federal Reserve System

Module Outline and Learning Objectives

Can Greece Function without Banks?

How often do you use a bank? If you are like most people, you withdraw cash from an ATM a couple of times per week and occasionally deposit checks. You may have visited a bank to apply for a student loan or a car loan. If you own your own business, you will have had many more interactions with banks. For example, you may have taken out a long-term loan to finance expanding your business.

Individuals and businesses in most countries would consider it difficult to function without banks. But that's the situation people in Greece faced in 2015. In 2001, Greece and most other European countries abandoned their individual currencies in favor of the euro. (Greece's currency had been the drachma.) Following the 2007–2009 financial crisis, the Greek government had trouble paying interest on the bonds it had issued. Many people feared that Greece might leave the euro and resume using the drachma. If that happened, the drachma might be worth less than the euro, which gave people in Greece an incentive to hold as many euros as they could. In 2015, Greece appeared to be in danger of defaulting on its debts. People responded by withdrawing large amounts of euros from Greek banks. To keep the banks from losing all their funds, the Greek government decided to close the banks for three weeks and limit withdrawals from ATM machines to 60 euros (about $66) per day.

Closing the banks dealt a heavy blow to the Greek economy. With the banks closed, many businesses insisted on being paid in cash. Consumers had trouble finding cash, though, because many ATMs had been emptied of currency. Some stores began accepting promises to pay later from customers who had no cash. Nikos Manisoitis & Son is a Greek firm that imports spices, pasta, and other products. The owner complained: "We feel like hostages. We can't move our money from the banks, and we fear that we are about to lose everything." Some importers loaded suitcases with euros and flew to other countries to pay their suppliers.

As we saw in Module 3 & 3A, a country needs a well-functioning financial system if its economy is to prosper and grow. Greece's situation in the summer of 2015 shows what can happen when a country's banking system breaks down. In this module, we will study the role banks play in the financial system. We will also discuss the link between changes in the money supply and the inflation rate, as well as provide an overview of the operations of the Federal Reserve, which is the central bank of the United States.

Sources: Suzanne Daley, "Greeks Spend in Droves, Afraid of Losing Savings to a Bailout," *New York Times*, July 8, 2015; Liz Alderman, "Greek Economy under Siege, with Fears That the Worst Is Coming," *New York Times*, July 9, 2015; and "When Banks Die," *Economist*, July 5, 2015.

Economics in Your Life

What if Money Became Increasingly Valuable?

Most people are used to the fact that as prices rise each year, the purchasing power of money falls. You will be able to buy fewer goods and services with $1,000 one year from now, and you will be able to buy even fewer goods and services the year after that. In fact, with an inflation rate of just 3 percent, in 25 years, $1,000 will buy only what $475 can buy today. Suppose that you could live in an economy where the purchasing power of money *rose* each year? What would be the advantages and disadvantages of living in such an economy? As you read this module, try to answer these questions. You can check your answers against those we provide **on page 327** at the end of this module.

I n this module, we will explore the role of money in the economy. We will see how the banking system creates money and what policy tools the Federal Reserve uses to manage the quantity of money in the United States. We will also examine the crisis in the banking system during and after the 2007–2009 recession. At the end of this module, we will explore the link between changes in the quantity of money and changes in the price level. What you learn in this module will serve as an important foundation for understanding monetary policy and fiscal policy, which we study in Modules 7A and 8A.

8.1 What Is Money, and Why Do We Need It?

LEARNING OBJECTIVE: Define money and discuss the four functions of money.

Money Assets that people are generally willing to accept in exchange for goods and services or for payment of debts.

Asset Anything of value owned by a person or a firm.

Could an economy function without money? There are historical examples of economies in which people traded goods for other goods rather than use money. For example, on the American frontier during colonial times, very little money was available, so a farmer might have traded a plow for a cow. Most economies, though, use money. The economic definition of **money** is any asset that people are generally willing to accept in exchange for goods and services or for payment of debts. Recall that an **asset** is anything of value owned by a person or a firm (see Module 6). There are many possible kinds of money: In West Africa, at one time, cowrie shells served as money. During World War II, prisoners of war used cigarettes as money.

Barter and the Invention of Money

To understand the importance of money, let's consider further the situation in economies that do not use money. Economies where goods and services are traded directly for other goods and services are called *barter economies*. Barter economies have a major shortcoming. To illustrate this shortcoming, consider a farmer on the American frontier in colonial days. Suppose the farmer needed a cow and proposed trading a spare plow to a neighbor for one of the neighbor's cows. If the neighbor did not want the plow, the trade would not happen. For a barter trade to take place between two people, each person must want what the other one has. Economists refer to this requirement as a *double coincidence of wants*. The farmer who wants the cow might eventually be able to obtain one if he first trades with some other neighbor for something the neighbor with the cow wants. However, it may take several trades before the farmer is ultimately able to trade for what the neighbor with the cow wants. Locating several trading partners and making several intermediate trades can take considerable time and energy.

To avoid the problems with barter, societies have an incentive to identify a product that most people will accept in exchange for what they have to trade. For example, in colonial times, animal skins were very useful in making clothing. The first governor of Tennessee actually received a salary of 1,000 deerskins per year, and the state's secretary of the Treasury received 450 otter skins per year. A good used as money that also has value independent of its use as money is called a **commodity money**. Historically, once a good became widely accepted as money, even people who did not have an immediate use for it would be willing to accept it. A colonial farmer—or the governor of Tennessee—might not want a deerskin, but as long as he knew he could use the deerskin to buy other goods and services, he would be willing to accept it in exchange for what he had to sell.

Commodity money A good used as money that also has value independent of its use as money.

Trading goods and services is much easier when money becomes available. People only need to sell what they have for money and then use the money to buy what they want. If the colonial family could find someone to buy their plow, they could use the money to buy the cow they wanted. The family with the cow would accept the money because they knew they could use it to buy what they wanted. When money is available, families are more likely to specialize and less likely to produce everything or nearly everything they need themselves.

Most people in modern economies are highly specialized. They do only one thing—work as a nurse, an accountant, or an engineer—and use the money they earn to buy everything else they need. People become much more productive by specializing because they can pursue their *comparative advantage*. The high income levels in modern economies are based on the specialization that money makes possible. We can now answer the question, "Why do we need money?" *By making exchange easier, money allows people to specialize and become more productive.*   MyEconLab Concept Check

The Functions of Money

Anything used as money—whether a deerskin, a cowrie seashell, cigarettes, or a dollar bill—must serve four key functions in the economy:

1. It must act as a medium of exchange.
2. It must serve as a unit of account.
3. It must serve as a store of value.
4. It must offer a standard of deferred payment.

Medium of Exchange Money serves as a medium of exchange when sellers are willing to accept it in exchange for goods or services. When the local supermarket accepts your $5 bill in exchange for bread and milk, the $5 bill is serving as a medium of exchange. With a medium of exchange, people can sell goods and services for money and use the money to buy what they want. An economy is more efficient when people accept a single good as a medium of exchange.

Unit of Account In a barter system, each good has many prices. A cow may be worth 2 plows, 20 bushels of wheat, or 6 axes. Once a single good is used as money, each good has a single price rather than many prices. This function of money gives buyers and sellers a *unit of account*, a way of measuring value in the economy in terms of money. Because the U.S. economy uses dollars as money, each good has a price in terms of dollars.

Store of Value Money allows people to easily store value: If you do not use all your dollars to buy goods and services today, you can hold the rest to use in the future. Money is not the only store of value, however. Any asset—shares of Facebook stock, Treasury bonds, real estate, or Renoir paintings, for example—represents a store of value. Financial assets, such as stocks and bonds, offer an important benefit relative to holding money because they pay a higher rate of interest or may increase in value in the future. Other assets also have advantages relative to money because they provide services. A house, for example, offers you a place to sleep.

Why, then, do people hold any money? The answer has to do with *liquidity*, or the ease with which people can convert an asset into the medium of exchange. Because money is the medium of exchange, it is the most liquid asset. If you want to buy something and you need to sell an asset to do so, you are likely to incur a cost. For example, if you want to buy a car and need to sell bonds or stocks to do so, you will need to pay a commission to your broker. To avoid such costs, people are willing to hold some of their wealth in the form of money, even though other assets offer a greater return as stores of value.

Standard of Deferred Payment Money is useful because it can serve as a standard of deferred payment in borrowing and lending. It can facilitate exchange at a *given point in time* by providing a medium of exchange and unit of account. Money can facilitate exchange *over time* by providing a store of value and a standard of deferred payment. For example, a computer manufacturer may buy hard drives from another firm in exchange for the promise of making payment in 60 days.

How important is it that money be a reliable store of value and standard of deferred payment? People care about how much food, clothing, and other goods and services their dollars will buy. The value of money depends on its *purchasing power*, which refers to its ability to buy goods and services. Inflation causes a decline in purchasing power because with rising prices, a given amount of money can purchase fewer goods and services. When inflation reaches very high levels, money is no longer a reliable store of value or standard of deferred payment.   MyEconLab Concept Check

What Can Serve as Money?

Having a medium of exchange helps to make transactions easier, which allows the economy to work more efficiently. The next question to consider is: What can serve as money? That is, which assets can be used as the medium of exchange? We saw earlier that an asset must, at a minimum, be generally accepted as payment to serve as money. In practical terms, however, it must be even more.

These five criteria make an asset suitable for use as a medium of exchange:

1. The asset must be *acceptable* to (that is, usable by) most people.
2. It should be of *standardized quality* so that any two units are identical.
3. It should be *durable* so that value is not lost by its quickly wearing out.
4. It should be *valuable* relative to its weight so that amounts large enough to be useful in trade can be easily transported.
5. It should be *divisible* so that it can be used in purchases of both low-priced and high-priced goods.

Dollar bills meet all these criteria. What determines the acceptability of dollar bills as a medium of exchange? Basically, it is through self-fulfilling expectations: You value something as money only if you believe that others will accept it from you as payment. A society's willingness to use paper dollars as money is what makes them an acceptable medium of exchange.

Commodity Money Commodity money has value independent of its use as money. Gold, for example, was a common form of money in the nineteenth and early twentieth centuries because it was a medium of exchange, a unit of account, a store of value, and a standard of deferred payment. But commodity money has a significant problem: Its value depends on its purity. Therefore, someone who wanted to cheat could mix a low-value metal, like iron, with a precious metal, like gold or silver. Another problem with using gold as money was that the money supply was difficult to control because it depended partly on unpredictable discoveries of new gold fields.

Federal Reserve The central bank of the United States.

Fiat money Money, such as paper currency, that is authorized by a central bank or governmental body and that does not have to be exchanged by the central bank for gold or some other commodity money.

Fiat Money It can be inefficient for an economy to rely on only gold or other precious metals for its money supply. What if you had to transport bars of gold to settle your transactions? Not only would doing so be difficult and costly, but you would run the risk of being robbed. To get around this problem, private institutions or governments began to store gold and issue paper certificates that could be redeemed for gold. In modern economies, paper currency is generally issued by a *central bank*, which is an agency of the government that regulates the money supply. The **Federal Reserve** is the central bank of the United States. Today, no government in the world issues paper currency that can be redeemed for gold. Paper currency has no value unless it is used as money, and it is therefore not a commodity money. Instead, paper currency is a **fiat money**, which has no value except as money. If paper currency has no value except as money, why do consumers and firms use it?

If you look at the top of a U.S. dollar bill, you will see the words "Federal Reserve Note" because it is issued by the Federal Reserve. Because U.S. dollars are fiat money, the Federal Reserve is not required to give you gold or silver for your dollar bills. Federal Reserve currency is *legal tender* in the United States, which means the federal government requires that it be accepted in payment of debts and requires that cash or checks denominated in dollars be used in payment of taxes. Despite being legal tender, dollar bills would not be a good medium of exchange and could not serve as money if people didn't usually accept them. The key to this acceptance is that *households and firms have confidence that if they accept paper dollars in exchange for goods and services, the dollars will not lose much value during the time they hold them.* Without this confidence, dollar bills would not serve as a medium of exchange.   MyEconLab Concept Check

Making the Connection
MyEconLab Video

Apple Didn't Want My Cash!

If Federal Reserve Notes are legal tender, doesn't that mean that everyone in the United States, including every business, has to accept paper money? The answer to this question is "no," as a woman in California found out when she went to an Apple store in Palo Alto and tried to buy an iPad using $600 in currency. The store refused to sell her the iPad for cash. At that time, the iPad had just been released, and Apple did not want to sell large numbers to people who were buying them to resell on eBay, Craigslist, or elsewhere. So, a customer wanting to buy an iPad had to pay with either a credit card or a debit card, which would make it easier for Apple to keep track of anyone attempting to buy more than the limit of two per customer.

The law doesn't stop Apple from requiring customers to use a credit card rather than cash, but the company decided to lift its ban on paying for iPads with cash after bad publicity.

Because Federal Reserve Notes are legal tender, creditors must accept them in payment of debts, and the government will accept them in payment of taxes. However, as this incident demonstrates, firms do not have to accept cash as payment for goods and services. As the U.S. Treasury Department explains on its Web site:

> There is … no Federal statute mandating that a private business, a person or an organization must accept currency or coins as payment for goods and/or services. … For example, a bus line may prohibit payment of fares in pennies or dollar bills. In addition, movie theaters, convenience stores and gas stations may refuse to accept large denomination currency (usually notes above $20) as a matter of policy.

The woman who tried to buy an iPad for cash was disabled and on a limited income, so the incident led to negative publicity for Apple. As a result, Apple decided to lift its ban on paying for iPads with cash, provided that the customer was willing to set up an Apple account at the time of purchase. In addition, Apple presented a free iPad to the customer who was originally turned down when she tried to pay with cash.

Sources: Michael Winter, "Apple Ends No-Cash Policy and California Woman Gets Free iPad," www.usatoday.com, May 20, 2010; and U.S. Treasury, "FAQs: Currency," www.treasury.gov/resource-center/faqs/Currency/Pages/edu_faq_currency_index2.aspx.

Your Turn: Test your understanding by doing related problem 1.9 on page 329 at the end of this module.

MyEconLab Study Plan

8.2 How Is Money Measured in the United States Today?

LEARNING OBJECTIVE: Discuss the definitions of the money supply used in the United States today.

People are interested in the money supply because, as we will see, changes in the money supply can affect other economic variables, including employment, gross domestic product (GDP), and inflation. If the only function of money was to serve as a medium of exchange, then a narrow definition of the money supply should include only currency, checking account deposits, and traveler's checks because households and firms can easily use these assets to buy goods and services. A broader definition of the money supply would include other assets that can be used as a medium of exchange even though they are not as liquid as currency or checking account deposits. For example, you can't directly buy goods or services with funds in a bank savings account, but it is easy to withdraw funds from your savings account and then use these funds to buy goods and services.

Congress gave the Federal Reserve the responsibility of regulating the money supply and the task of determining how to measure it. The Federal Reserve's measures of the money supply have changed several times over the decades. Currently, the Federal Reserve publishes data on two measures of the money supply: M1 and M2. These measures, sometimes called *monetary aggregates*, are important to understand, so we devote the following sections to discussing them.

M1 The narrow definition of the money supply: the sum of currency in circulation, checking account deposits in banks, and holdings of traveler's checks.

M1: A Narrow Definition of the Money Supply

Figure 8.1 illustrates the definitions of the money supply. The narrow definition of the money supply, **M1**, includes the following:

1. *Currency*, which is all the paper money and coins held by households and firms (not including currency held by banks)
2. The value of all checking account deposits in banks
3. The value of traveler's checks (Because this last category is so small—typically less than $4 billion—relative to the other two categories, we will ignore it in our discussion of the money supply.)

Although currency has almost as large a value as checking account deposits, checking account deposits are used much more often than currency to make payments. More than 80 percent of all expenditures on goods and services are made with checks rather than with currency. In fact, the total amount of currency in circulation—$1.3 trillion in July 2015—is a misleading number. This amount is more than $4,000 per person—adult or child—in the United States. If this sounds like an unrealistically large amount of currency to be held per person, it is. Economists estimate that more than 60 percent of U.S. currency is actually outside the borders of the United States. More than three-quarters of U.S. paper currency is in denominations of $100 or larger—too large to be used for routine buying and selling within the United States.

Who holds these dollars outside the United States? Foreign banks and foreign governments hold some U.S. currency, but most is held by households and firms in countries where there is not much confidence in the local currency or where the underground economy is large. When inflation rates are very high, many households and firms do not want to hold their domestic currency because it is losing its value too rapidly. The value of the U.S. dollar will be much more stable than their domestic currency. If enough people are willing to accept dollars as well as—or instead of—domestic currency, dollars become a second currency for the country. When inflation soared in the African country of Zimbabwe to the point where it took 15 *billion* Zimbabwean dollars

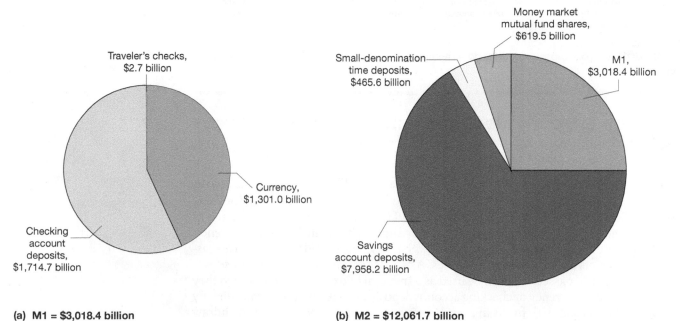

(a) **M1 = $3,018.4 billion**

(b) **M2 = $12,061.7 billion**

MyEconLab Real-time data

Figure 8.1 **Measuring the Money Supply**

The Federal Reserve uses two different measures of the money supply: M1 and M2. Panel (a) shows the assets in M1. Panel (b) shows M2, which includes the assets in M1, as well as money market mutual fund shares, small-denomination time deposits, and savings account deposits.

Source: Board of Governors of the Federal Reserve System, "Federal Reserve Statistical Release, H.6," July 30, 2015.

to buy a can of Coca-Cola, the government went so far as to adopt the U.S. dollar as the country's official currency.   MyEconLab Concept Check

M2: A Broad Definition of Money

Before 1980, U.S. law prohibited banks from paying interest on checking account deposits. Households and firms held checking account deposits primarily to buy goods and services. M1 was, therefore, very close to the function of money as a medium of exchange. Almost all currency, checking account deposits, and traveler's checks were held with the intention of buying and selling, not with the intention of storing value. In 1980, the law was changed to allow banks to pay interest on certain types of checking accounts. This change reduced the difference between checking accounts and savings accounts, although people are still not allowed to write checks against their savings account balances.

After 1980, economists began to pay closer attention to a broader definition of the money supply, **M2**. As panel (b) of Figure 8.1 shows, M2 includes everything that is in M1, plus savings account deposits, small-denomination time deposits—such as certificates of deposit (CDs)—balances in money market deposit accounts in banks, and noninstitutional money market fund shares. Small-denomination time deposits are similar to savings accounts, but the deposits are for a fixed period of time—usually from six months to several years—and withdrawals before that time are subject to a penalty. Mutual fund companies sell shares to investors and use the funds raised to buy financial assets such as stocks and bonds. Some of these mutual funds, such as Vanguard's Treasury Money Market Fund or Fidelity's Cash Reserves Fund, are called *money market mutual funds* because they invest in very short-term bonds, such as U.S. Treasury bills. The balances individual investors hold in these funds are included in M2. Each week, the Federal Reserve publishes statistics on M1 and M2. In the discussion that follows, we will use the M1 definition of the money supply because it corresponds most closely to money as a medium of exchange.

There are two key points to keep in mind about the money supply:

1. The narrowest definition of the money supply consists of *both* currency and checking account deposits.

2. Because balances in checking account deposits are included in the money supply, banks play an important role in the way the money supply increases and decreases. We will discuss this second point further in the next section.   MyEconLab Concept Check

M2 A broader definition of the money supply: It includes M1 plus savings account deposits, small-denomination time deposits, balances in money market deposit accounts in banks, and noninstitutional money market fund shares.

Don't Let This Happen to You

Don't Confuse Money with Income or Wealth

According to *Forbes*, in 2015, Bill Gates's wealth of $79 billion made him the richest person in the world. He also has a very large income, but how much money does he have? Your *wealth* is equal to the value of your assets minus the value of any debts you have. Your *income* is equal to your earnings during the year. Bill Gates's earnings as chairman of Microsoft and from his investments are very large. But his *money* is just equal to what he has in currency and checking accounts. Only a small proportion of Gates's $79 billion in wealth is likely to be in currency or checking accounts. Most of his wealth is invested in stocks and bonds and other financial assets that are not included in the definition of money.

In everyday conversation, we often describe someone who is wealthy or who has a high income as "having a lot of money." But when economists use the word *money*, they are usually referring to currency plus checking account deposits. It is important to keep straight the differences between wealth, income, and money.

Just as money and income are not the same for a person, they are not the same for the whole economy. National income in the United States was equal to $15.1 trillion in 2014. The money supply in 2014 was $2.8 trillion (using the M1 measure). There is no reason why national income in a country should be equal to the country's money supply, nor will an increase in a country's money supply necessarily increase the country's national income.

Source: "The World's Billionaires," *Forbes*, March 2, 2015.

MyEconLab Study Plan

Your Turn: Test your understanding by doing related problems 2.5 and 2.6 on page 329 at the end of this module.

Solved Problem 8.2

MyEconLab Interactive Animation

The Definitions of M1 and M2

Suppose you decide to withdraw $2,000 from your checking account and put the money into a bank certification of deposit (CD). Briefly explain how this action will affect M1 and M2.

Solving the Problem

Step 1: **Review the module material.** This problem is about the definitions of the money supply, so you may want to review the section "How Is Money Measured in the United States Today?" which begins on page 303.

Step 2: **Use the definitions of M1 and M2 to answer the problem.** Funds in checking accounts are included in both M1 and M2. Funds in CDs are included only in M2. It is tempting to answer this problem by saying that shifting $2,000 from a checking account to a CD reduces M1 by $2,000 and increases M2 by $2,000, but the $2,000 in your checking account was already counted in M2. So, the correct answer is that your action reduces M1 by $2,000 but leaves M2 unchanged.

MyEconLab Study Plan

Your Turn: For more practice, do related problems 2.7 and 2.8 on page 329 at the end of this module.

What about Credit Cards and Debit Cards?

Many people buy goods and services with credit cards, yet credit cards are not included in either definition of the money supply. The reason is that when you buy something with a credit card, you are in effect taking out a loan from the bank that issued the credit card. The transaction is complete only when you pay your credit card bill at the end of the month—often with a check or an electronic transfer from your checking account. In contrast, with a debit card, the funds to make the purchase are taken directly from your checking account. In either case, the cards themselves do not represent money. MyEconLab Concept Check

Making the Connection MyEconLab Video

Are Bitcoins Money?

Typically, when we think of "money," we think of currency issued by a government. But we have just seen that currency represents only a small part of the money supply of the United States, whether measured as M1 or M2. The non-currency components of M1 or M2, although not issued by the government, are familiar financial assets such as checking or savings accounts. Some households and firms have shifted away from M1 or M2 to finance their buying and selling of goods and services and are instead using e-money, or digital funds. The best-known form of e-money is PayPal, which until 2015 was owned by eBay, the online auction site. An individual or a firm can set up a PayPal account by transferring funds from a checking account or credit card. As long as a seller is willing to accept funds from a buyer's PayPal (or other e-money) account, e-money functions like conventional government-issued money.

Bitcoins are created by computer calculations, not by central banks.

Recently, journalists, economists, and policymakers have been debating the merits of bitcoin, a new form of e-money. Unlike PayPal and other similar services for transferring money electronically, bitcoin is not owned by a firm but is instead the product of a decentralized system of linked computers. Bitcoin was founded in 2009 by "Satoshi Nakamoto," which is likely an assumed name taken by bitcoin's founder or founders. Bitcoins are produced by people performing the complicated calculations necessary to ensure that online purchases made with bitcoins are legitimate—that is, that someone doesn't try to spend the same bitcoin multiple times. People who successfully complete these calculations are awarded a fixed amount of bitcoins—typically 14. This process of bitcoin "mining" will continue until a maximum of 21 million bitcoins has been produced—a total expected to be reached in 2030.

Because people can buy and sell bitcoins in exchange for dollars and other currencies on Web sites, some people refer to it as a "cryptocurrency." You can buy bitcoins and store them in a "digital wallet" on a smartphone. You can then buy something in a store that accepts bitcoins by scanning a bar code with your phone. A number of Web sites, such as BitPay, which is based in Atlanta, allow merchants to process purchases made with bitcoins in a manner similar to the way they process credit card payments.

Why would buyers and sellers prefer to use bitcoins rather than cash or a credit card? The popularity of bitcoins with some buyers may be due to its being a new and fashionable way to make purchases, and because of the convenience of using a smartphone to make a purchase. In addition, some people are afraid that because central banks in most countries greatly increased the money supply during and after the recession of 2007–2009, the result will eventually be high rates of inflation. These people hope that because the total amount of bitcoins is limited, inflation will not undermine their value. Finally, when you buy something with a credit card, the credit card company has a permanent record of your transaction. Bitcoin transactions are more private because no such record of your transaction exists.

Some retailers prefer bitcoins to credit card purchases because the retailers pay only about 1 percent of the sale in processing costs, as opposed to about 3 percent for a credit card purchase. In addition, a bitcoin sale is final, just as if the purchase were made with cash, unlike credit card sales, where the buyer can dispute the purchase even months after it was made.

Despite these possible benefits to using bitcoin, by 2015, it had not yet been widely adopted. The introduction of Apple Pay and Google Wallet provided consumers with a way to use their smartphones linked to a credit card to make payments, which undercut one of bitcoin's advantages. Some firms also questioned whether the software underlying bitcoin was capable of dealing with a large number of transactions, which would be a barrier to the cryptocurrency being widely used. The most popular online bitcoin exchange, Japan-based Mt. Gox, collapsed, further reducing confidence in the cryptocurrency. At the time of the firm's collapse, the CEO said that software problems had allowed hackers to withdraw more than $500 million worth of bitcoins investors had stored on the exchange. The Japanese police later arrested the CEO.

Some policymakers are concerned that investors on exchanges might manipulate the prices of bitcoins and other virtual currencies. The value of bitcoins in exchange for dollars rose from $5 per bitcoin in June 2012 to $266 per bitcoin in April 2013, before falling to $94 per bitcoin in July 2013 and then rising to $287 in July 2015. Whether these swings in value represented underlying movements in demand and supply for bitcoins or manipulation of their values was not clear.

Should the Federal Reserve include bitcoins and other virtual or cryptocurrencies in its measures of the money supply? So far, the volume of transactions in these currencies has been small, which makes the question of little practical importance. At this point, the Federal Reserve treats virtual currencies as being the equivalent of credit or debit cards, rather than currency or checking account balances, and does not include them in M1 or M2.

Sources: Paul Vigna, "Bitcoiners Decamp to Bretton Woods, Assess the Future of Bitcoin," *Wall Street Journal*, July 30, 2015; Takashi Mochizuki, "Japanese Police Arrest Mark Karpelès of Collapsed Bitcoin Exchange Mt. Gox," *Wall Street Journal*, August 1, 2015; Lingling Wei, "Fed Studying Risks at Online Payment Providers," *Wall Street Journal*, June 3, 2013; and "How Does Bitcoin Work?" *Economist*, April 11, 2013.

Your Turn: Test your understanding by doing related problem 2.11 on page 330 at the end of this module.

MyEconLab Study Plan

8.3 How Do Banks Create Money?

LEARNING OBJECTIVE: Explain how banks create money.

We have seen that the most important component of the money supply is checking accounts in banks. To understand the role money plays in the economy, we need to look more closely at how banks operate. Banks are profit-making private businesses, just like department stores and supermarkets. Some banks are quite small, with just a few branches, and do business in a limited area. Others are among the largest corporations in the United States, with thousands of branches spread across many states. Banks play an important role in the economy by accepting deposits and making loans. By taking these actions, banks fulfill a key function in the *money supply process* by which central banks control the money supply.

Bank Balance Sheets

To understand how banks create money, we need to briefly examine a typical bank balance sheet. On a balance sheet, a firm's assets are listed on the left, and its liabilities and stockholders' equity are listed on the right (see Module 6). Assets are the value of anything owned by the firm, liabilities are the value of anything the firm owes, and stockholders' equity is the difference between the total value of assets and the total value of liabilities. Stockholders' equity represents the value of the firm if it were closed, all its assets were sold, and all its liabilities were paid off. A corporation's stockholders' equity is also called its *net worth*. A bank's stockholders' equity or net worth is also called its *capital*.

Figure 8.2 shows a typical balance sheet for a large bank. The key assets on a bank's balance sheet are its *reserves*, loans, and holdings of securities, such as U.S. Treasury bills. **Reserves** are deposits that a bank has retained rather than loaned out or invested. Banks keep reserves either physically within the bank, as *vault cash*, or on deposit with the Federal Reserve. Banks are required by law to keep as reserves 10 percent of their checking account deposits above a threshold level, which in 2015 was $103.6 million. These reserves are called **required reserves**. The minimum fraction of deposits that banks are required to keep as reserves is called the **required reserve ratio**. We can abbreviate the required reserve ratio as *RR*. Any reserves that banks hold above the legal requirement are called **excess reserves**. The balance sheet in Figure 8.2 shows that loans are a typical bank's largest asset.

Banks make *consumer loans* to households and *commercial loans* to firms. A loan is an asset to a bank because it represents a promise by the person taking out the loan to make certain specified payments to the bank. A bank's reserves and its holdings of securities are also assets because they are things of value the bank owns.

Reserves Deposits that a bank keeps as cash in its vault or on deposit with the Federal Reserve.

Required reserves Reserves that a bank is legally required to hold, based on its checking account deposits.

Required reserve ratio The minimum fraction of deposits banks are required by law to keep as reserves.

Excess reserves Reserves that banks hold over the legal requirement.

Figure 8.2

The Balance Sheet of a Typical Large Bank

The entries on a bank's balance sheet of greatest economic importance are its reserves, loans, and deposits. Notice that the difference between the value of this bank's total assets and its total liabilities is equal to its stockholders' equity. As a consequence, the left side of the balance sheet always equals the right side.
Note: Some entries have been combined to simplify the balance sheet.

Assets (in billions)		Liabilities and Stockholders' Equity (in billions)	
Reserves	$135	Deposits	$1,000
Loans	900	Short-term borrowing	400
Securities	700	Long-term debt	360
Buildings and equipment	15	Other liabilities	275
Other assets	550	Total liabilities	$2,035
		Stockholders' equity	265
Total assets	$2,300	Total liabilities and stockholders' equity	$2,300

Making the Connection
MyEconLab Video

Would You Borrow from an Online Peer-to-Peer Lender?

The basic business of banks is taking in deposits from savers and using those funds to make loans to households and firms. Banks often require *collateral* before making a loan, which means that if the borrower stops making payments on the loan, the bank can seize the asset the borrower pledged as collateral. For example, if you take out a loan to buy a car and stop making payments on the loan, the bank can repossess your car and sell it to get its money back.

In addition to collateral, banks rely on a borrower's *credit score* in deciding whether to make a loan. The best-known credit score is compiled by the FICO company, which rates borrowers on a scale of 350 to 850, with higher scores meaning the borrower is less likely to default. Credit scores are determined by a variety of factors, including whether the borrower has been on time with payments on other loans and on credit cards; how long the borrower has lived at his current residence; how long the borrower has held her current job; and how much other debt the borrower has. Borrowers with high scores are called *prime borrowers*, and borrowers with low scores are called *subprime borrowers*. A bank will typically charge a prime borrower a lower interest rate than it will charge a subprime borrower. The higher interest rate on a *subprime loan* compensates the bank for the greater risk that the borrower will default. Lenders differ in the minimum score they use to consider someone a prime borrower, but it is typically around 650.

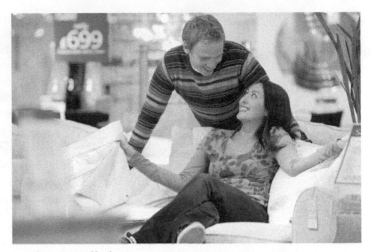

Some people with low credit scores who can't get a bank loan turn to peer-to-peer lending to borrow the funds to meet needs such as buying furniture.

During the housing bubble of the early 2000s, many banks and other lenders made mortgage loans to subprime borrowers buying houses. High default rates on these mortgages following the bursting of the housing bubble in 2006 contributed to the 2007–2009 financial crisis and led policymakers to tighten regulations on banks granting subprime loans. Some consumer advocates also criticize these loans because they believe that the high interest rates exploit borrowers. To avoid both the new regulations and the criticism, many banks have cut back on subprime loans, particularly subprime *personal loans*, which are made to individuals who do not provide collateral for the loan. In past years, after getting a job, many new college graduates would take out a personal loan from a bank to buy the furniture or small appliances needed to set up an apartment. You may have a low credit score if you were late with a couple of credit card payments, have only a short work history, and have just moved into a new apartment. A bank may then consider you a subprime borrower and be unwilling to lend you money.

You could borrow on your credit card by taking a cash advance, but the interest rate is likely to be high—typically more than 20 percent. When banks cut back on subprime personal loans, it left a hole in the financial system. In the past few years, some new businesses have developed to fill that hole. For example, Lending Club and FreedomPlus facilitate peer-to-peer lending on the Internet. These businesses gather information about a borrower, determine the interest rate on the loan, and then post the loan online. Individual investors can then choose to fund the loan. Some loans are funded by a single investor, while others are funded by several investors. The loans can be as short as a few weeks or as long as several years and can have interest rates from 7 percent to more than 20 percent, with the typical interest rate being around 14 percent. Peer-to-peer lending firms are part of the "sharing economy," which also includes the car ride firm Uber and short-term apartment rental firm Airbnb. In the case of peer-to-peer lending, it's money that is being shared.

By 2015, peer-to-peer lending sites were making $10 billion worth of loans. While this amount has been growing rapidly, it still far less than the trillions of dollars in loans of all types made by banks. It remains to be seen whether the peer-to-peer lending sites will end up becoming a major source of credit to households and firms.

Sources: Ianthe Jeanne Dugan and Telis Demos, "New Lenders Spring Up to Cater to Subprime Sector," *Wall Street Journal*, March 5, 2014; and "From the People, for the People," *Economist*, May 9, 2015.

Your Turn: Test your understanding by doing related problems 3.7 and 3.8 on pages 330–331 at the end of this module.

Deposits are a typical bank's largest liability. Deposits include checking accounts, savings accounts, and CDs. Deposits are liabilities to banks because they are owed to the households or firms that have deposited the funds. If you deposit $100 in your checking account, the bank owes you the $100, and you can ask for it back at any time. So, your checking account is an asset to you, and it is a liability to the bank. Banks also borrow short term from other banks and from the Federal Reserve and borrow long term by selling bonds to investors. These *borrowings* are also liabilities.   MyEconLab Concept Check

Using T-Accounts to Show How a Bank Can Create Money

It is easier to show how banks create money by using a T-account than by using a balance sheet. A T-account is a stripped-down version of a balance sheet that shows only how a transaction *changes* a bank's balance sheet. Suppose you deposit $1,000 in currency into an account at Bank of America. This transaction raises the total deposits at Bank of America by $1,000 and also raises its reserves by $1,000. We show this result on the following T-account:

Remember that because the total value of all the entries on the right side of a balance sheet must always be equal to the total value of all the entries on the left side of a balance sheet, any transaction that increases (or decreases) one side of the balance sheet must also increase (or decrease) the other side of the balance sheet. In this case, the T-account shows that we increased both sides of the balance sheet by $1,000.

Initially, this transaction does not increase the money supply. The currency component of the money supply declines by $1,000 because the $1,000 you deposited is no longer in circulation and, therefore, is not counted in the money supply. But the decrease in currency is offset by a $1,000 increase in the checking account deposit component of the money supply.

This initial change is not the end of the story, however. Banks are required to keep 10 percent of deposits as reserves. Because the Federal Reserve pays banks only a low rate of interest on their reserves, banks have an incentive to loan out or buy securities with the other 90 percent. Suppose, for simplicity, that initially Bank of America holds no excess reserves. In that case, Bank of America can keep $100 of your deposit as required reserves and loan out the other $900, which represents its excess reserves. Assume that Bank of America loans out the $900 to someone to buy a very inexpensive used car. Bank of America could give the $900 to the borrower in currency, but usually banks make loans by increasing the borrower's checking account. We can show this transaction with another T-account:

Notice that *by making this $900 loan, Bank of America has increased the money supply by $900.* The initial $1,000 in currency you deposited into your checking account has been turned into $1,900 in checking account deposits—a net increase in the money supply of $900.

But the story does not end here. The person who took out the $900 loan did so to buy a used car. To keep things simple, let's suppose he buys the car for exactly $900 and pays by writing a check on his account at Bank of America. The seller of the used car will now deposit the check in her bank. That bank may also be a branch of Bank of America, but in most cities, there are many banks, so let's assume that the seller of the car has her account at a branch of PNC Bank. Once she deposits the check, PNC Bank will send it to Bank of America to *clear* the check and collect the $900. We show the result in the following T-accounts:

Bank of America

Assets		Liabilities	
Reserves	+$100	Deposits	+$1,000
Loans	+$900		

1. When the $900 check that was deposited in a PNC account arrives to be cleared, the increase in Bank of America's reserves (shown in the previous T-account) falls by $900 to $100 . . .

2. . . . and the increase in Bank of America's deposits falls by $900 to $1,000.

PNC Bank

Assets		Liabilities	
Reserves	+$900	Deposits	+$900

After the check drawn on the account at Bank of America clears, PNC's reserves and deposits both increase by $900.

After the car buyer's check clears, Bank of America has lost $900 in deposits—the amount loaned to the car buyer—and $900 in reserves—the amount it had to pay PNC when PNC sent Bank of America the car buyer's check. PNC has an increase in checking account deposits of $900—the deposit of the car seller—and an increase in reserves of $900—the amount it received from Bank of America.

PNC has 100 percent reserves against this new $900 deposit, but it needs only 10 percent reserves. The bank has an incentive to keep $90 as reserves and to loan out the other $810, which are excess reserves. If PNC does this, we can show the change in its balance sheet by using another T-account:

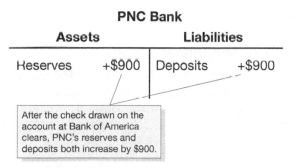

PNC Bank

Assets		Liabilities	
Reserves	+$900	Deposits	+$900
Loans	+$810	Deposits	+$810

By making an $810 loan, PNC has increased both its loans and its deposits by $810.

In loaning out the $810 in excess reserves, PNC creates a new checking account deposit of $810. The initial deposit of $1,000 in currency into Bank of America has now resulted in the creation of $1,000 + $900 + $810 = $2,710 in checking account deposits. The money supply has increased by $2,710 − $1,000 = $1,710.

The process is still not finished. The person who borrows the $810 will spend it by writing a check against his account. Whoever receives the $810 will deposit it in her bank, which could be a Bank of America branch or a PNC branch or a branch of some other bank. That new bank—if it's not PNC—will send the check to PNC and will receive $810 in new reserves. That new bank will have an incentive to loan out 90 percent of these reserves—keeping 10 percent to meet the legal requirement—and the process will go on. At each stage, the additional loans being made and the additional deposits being created are shrinking by 10 percent, because each bank has to keep that amount as required reserves. We can use a table to show the total increase in checking account deposits started by your initial deposit of $1,000. The dots in the table represent additional rounds in the money supply process: MyEconLab Concept Check

Bank	Increase in Checking Account Deposits
Bank of America	$1,000
PNC	+900 ($= 0.9 \times \$1,000$)
Third Bank	+810 ($= 0.9 \times \$900$)
Fourth Bank	+729 ($= 0.9 \times \$810$)
.	+.
.	+.
.	+.
Total change in checking account deposits	$= \$10,000$

The Simple Deposit Multiplier

Your initial deposit of $1,000 increased the reserves of the banking system by $1,000 and led to a total increase in checking account deposits of $10,000. The ratio of the amount of deposits created by banks to the amount of new reserves is called the **simple deposit multiplier**. In this case, the simple deposit multiplier is equal to $10,000/$1,000 = 10. Why 10? How do we know that your initial $1,000 deposit ultimately leads to a total increase in deposits of $10,000?

Simple deposit multiplier The ratio of the amount of deposits created by banks to the amount of new reserves.

There are two ways to answer this question. First, each bank in the money supply process is keeping reserves equal to 10 percent of its deposits. For the banking system as a whole, the total increase in reserves is $1,000—the amount of your original currency deposit. Therefore, the system as a whole will end up with $10,000 in deposits because $1,000 is 10 percent of $10,000.

A second way to answer the question is by deriving an expression for the simple deposit multiplier. The total increase in deposits equals:

$$\$1,000 + [0.9 \times \$1,000] + [(0.9 \times 0.9) \times \$1,000] + [(0.9 \times 0.9 \times 0.9) \times \$1,000] + \ldots$$

or:

$$\$1,000 + [0.9 \times \$1,000] + [0.9^2 \times \$1,000] + [0.9^3 \times \$1,000] + \ldots$$

or:

$$\$1,000 \times (1 + 0.9 + 0.9^2 + 0.9^3 + \ldots).$$

The rules of algebra tell us that an expression like the one in the parentheses sums to:

$$\frac{1}{1 - 0.9}.$$

Simplifying further, we have:

$$\frac{1}{0.10} = 10.$$

So:

$$\text{Total increase in deposits} = \$1,000 \times 10 = \$10,000.$$

Don't Let This Happen to You

Don't Confuse Assets and Liabilities

Consider the following reasoning: "How can checking account deposits be a liability to a bank? After all, they are something of value that is in the bank. Therefore, checking account deposits should be counted as a bank *asset* rather than as a bank liability."

This statement is incorrect. The balance in a checking account represents something the bank *owes* to the owner of the account. Therefore, it is a liability to the bank, although it is an asset to the owner of the account. Similarly, your car loan is a liability to you—because it is a debt you owe to the bank—but it is an asset to the bank.

MyEconLab Study Plan

Your Turn: Test your understanding by doing related problem 3.11 on page 331 at the end of this module.

Note that 10 is equal to 1 divided by the required reserve ratio, *RR*, which in this case is 10 percent, or 0.10. So, we have another way of expressing the simple deposit multiplier:

$$\text{Simple deposit multiplier} = \frac{1}{RR}.$$

This formula makes it clear that the higher the required reserve ratio, the smaller the simple deposit multiplier. With a required reserve ratio of 10 percent, the simple deposit multiplier is 10. If the required reserve ratio were 20 percent, the simple deposit multiplier would fall to 1/0.20, or 5.

We can use this formula to calculate the total increase in checking account deposits from an increase in bank reserves due to, for instance, currency being deposited in a bank:

$$\text{Change in checking account deposits} = \text{Change in bank reserves} \times \frac{1}{RR}.$$

For example, if $100,000 in currency is deposited in a bank and the required reserve ratio is 10 percent, then:

$$\text{Change in checking account deposits} = \$100,000 \times \frac{1}{0.10}$$

$$= \$100,000 \times 10 = \$1,000,000.$$

MyEconLab Concept Check

Solved Problem 8.3

MyEconLab Interactive Animation

Showing How Banks Create Money

Suppose you deposit $5,000 in currency into your checking account at a branch of PNC Bank, which we will assume has no excess reserves at the time you make your deposit. Also assume that the required reserve ratio is 0.10.

a. Use a T-account to show the initial effect of this transaction on PNC's balance sheet.

b. Suppose that PNC makes the maximum loan it can from the funds you deposited. Use a T-account to show the initial effect on PNC's balance sheet from granting the loan. Also include in this T-account the transaction from part (a).

c. Now suppose that whoever took out the loan in part (b) writes a check for this amount and that the person receiving the check deposits it in Bank of America. Show the effect of these transactions on the balance sheets of PNC Bank and Bank of America *after the check has cleared*. On the T-account for PNC Bank, include the transactions from parts (a) and (b).

d. What is the maximum increase in checking account deposits that can result from your $5,000 deposit? What is the maximum increase in the money supply that can result from your deposit? Explain.

Solving the Problem

Step 1:   Review the module material. This problem is about how banks create checking account deposits, so you may want to review the section "Using T-Accounts to Show How a Bank Can Create Money," which begins on page 310.

Step 2:   Answer part (a) by using a T-account to show the effect of the deposit. Keeping in mind that T-accounts show only the changes in a balance sheet that result from the relevant transaction and that assets are on the left side of the account and liabilities are on the right side, we have:

PNC Bank

Assets		Liabilities	
Reserves	+$5,000	Deposits	+$5,000

Because the bank now has your $5,000 in currency in its vault, its reserves (and, therefore, its assets) have risen by $5,000. This transaction also increases your checking account balance by $5,000. Because the bank owes you this money, the bank's liabilities have also risen by $5,000.

Step 3:   Answer part (b) by using a T-account to show the effect of the loan. The problem tells you to assume that PNC Bank currently has no excess reserves and that the required reserve ratio is 10 percent. This requirement means that if the bank's checking account deposits go up by $5,000, the bank must keep $500 as reserves and can loan out the remaining $4,500. Remembering that new loans usually take the form of setting up or increasing a checking account for the borrower, we have:

PNC Bank

Assets		Liabilities	
Reserves	+$5,000	Deposits	+$5,000
Loans	+$4,500	Deposits	+$4,500

The first line of the T-account shows the transaction from part (a). The second line shows that PNC has loaned out $4,500 by increasing the checking account of the borrower by $4,500. The loan is an asset to PNC because it represents the borrower's promise to make certain payments spelled out in the loan agreement.

Step 4:   Answer part (c) by using T-accounts for PNC and Bank of America to show the effect of the check clearing. We now show the effect of the borrower having spent the $4,500 he received as a loan from PNC. The person who received the $4,500 check deposits it in her account at Bank of America. We need two T-accounts to show this activity:

PNC Bank

Assets		Liabilities	
Reserves	+$500	Deposits	+$5,000
Loans	+$4,500		

Bank of America

Assets		Liabilities	
Reserves	+$4,500	Deposits	+$4,500

Look first at the T-account for PNC. Once Bank of America sends the check written by the borrower to PNC, PNC loses $4,500 in reserves, and Bank of America gains $4,500 in reserves. The $4,500 is also deducted from the account of the borrower. PNC is now satisfied with the result. It received a $5,000 deposit in currency from you. When that money was sitting in the bank vault, it wasn't earning any interest for PNC. Now $4,500 of the $5,000 has been loaned out and is earning interest. These interest payments allow PNC to cover its costs, which it has to do to remain in business.

Bank of America now has an increase in deposits of $4,500, resulting from the check being deposited, and an increase in reserves of $4,500. Bank of America is in the same situation as PNC was in part (a): It has excess reserves as a result of this transaction and a strong incentive to lend them out.

Step 5: **Answer part (d) by using the simple deposit multiplier formula to calculate the maximum increase in checking account deposits and the maximum increase in the money supply.** The simple deposit multiplier expression is (remember that RR is the required reserve ratio):

$$\text{Change in checking account deposits} = \text{Change in bank reserves} \times \frac{1}{RR}.$$

In this case, bank reserves rose by $5,000 as a result of your initial deposit, and the required reserve ratio is 0.10, so:

$$\text{Change in checking account deposits} = \$5,000 \times \frac{1}{0.10}$$
$$= \$5,000 \times 10 = \$50,000.$$

Because checking account deposits are part of the money supply, it is tempting to say that the money supply has also increased by $50,000. Remember, though, that your $5,000 in currency was counted as part of the money supply while you had it, but it is not counted when it is sitting in a bank vault. Therefore:

Increase in checking account deposits − Decline in currency in

circulation = Change in the money supply.

Or,

$$\$50,000 - \$5,000 = \$45,000.$$

Your Turn: For more practice, do related problem 3.12 on page 331 at the end of the module.   MyEconLab Study Plan

The Simple Deposit Multiplier versus the Real-World Deposit Multiplier

The story we have just told of the money supply process has been simplified in two ways. First, we assumed that banks do not keep any excess reserves. That is, we assumed that when you deposited $1,000 in currency into your checking account at Bank of America, it loaned out $900, keeping only the $100 in required reserves. In fact, banks often keep some excess reserves to guard against the possibility that many depositors may simultaneously make withdrawals from their accounts. Since the financial crisis that began in 2007, banks have kept substantial excess reserves. The more excess reserves banks keep, the smaller the deposit multiplier. Imagine an extreme case in which Bank of America kept your entire $1,000 as reserves, loaning out none of it. In this case, the process we described earlier—loans leading to the creation of new deposits, leading to the making of additional loans, and so on—will not take place. The $1,000 increase in reserves will lead to just a $1,000 increase in deposits, and the deposit multiplier will be $1,000/$1,000 = 1, not 10.

Second, we assumed that the whole amount of every check is deposited in a bank; no one takes any of it out as currency. In reality, households and firms keep roughly constant the amount of currency they hold relative to the value of their checking account balances. So, we would expect to see people increasing the amount of currency they hold as the balances in their checking accounts rise. Once again, think of the extreme case. Suppose that when Bank of America makes the initial $900 loan to the borrower who wants to buy a used car, the seller of the car cashes the check instead of depositing it. In that case, PNC does not receive any new reserves and does not make any new loans. Once again, the $1,000 increase in your checking account at Bank of America is the only increase in deposits, and the deposit multiplier is 1.

The effect of these two simplifications is to reduce the real-world deposit multiplier to about 1.6 during normal times. So, a $1 increase in the reserves of the banking system typically results in about a $1.60 increase in deposits. Following the financial crisis of 2007–2009, the surge in bank holdings of excess reserves reduced the multiplier to less than 1.

Although the story of the deposit multiplier can be complicated, the key point to bear in mind is that the most important part of the money supply is the checking account balance component. When banks make loans, they increase checking account balances, and the money supply expands. Banks make new loans whenever they gain reserves. The whole process can also work in reverse: If banks lose reserves, they reduce their outstanding loans and deposits, and the money supply contracts.

We can summarize these important conclusions:

1. When banks gain reserves, they make new loans, and the money supply expands.
2. When banks lose reserves, they reduce their loans, and the money supply contracts.

MyEconLab Study Plan

MyEconLab Concept Check

8.4 The Federal Reserve System

LEARNING OBJECTIVE: Compare the three policy tools the Federal Reserve uses to manage the money supply.

Many people are surprised to learn that banks do not keep locked away in their vaults all the funds that are deposited in checking accounts. The United States, like nearly all other countries, has a **fractional reserve banking system**, which means that banks keep less than 100 percent of deposits as reserves. When people deposit money in a bank, the bank loans most of the money to someone else. What happens if depositors want their money back? Depositors withdrawing money would seem to be a problem because banks have loaned out most of the money and can't easily get it back.

In practice, withdrawals are usually not a problem for banks. On a typical day, about as much money is deposited as is withdrawn. If a small amount more is withdrawn than deposited, banks can cover the difference from their excess reserves or by borrowing from other banks. Sometimes depositors lose confidence in a bank when they question the value of the bank's underlying assets, particularly its loans. Often, the reason for a loss of confidence is bad news about the loans the bank has made, whether the news is accurate or not. When many depositors simultaneously decide to withdraw their money from a bank, there is a **bank run**. If many banks experience runs at the same time, the result is a **bank panic**. It is possible for one bank to handle a run by borrowing from other banks, but if many banks simultaneously experience runs, the banking system may be in trouble.

A central bank, like the Federal Reserve in the United States, can help stop a bank panic by acting as a *lender of last resort*. In acting as a lender of last resort, a central bank makes loans to banks that cannot borrow funds elsewhere. The banks can use these loans to pay off depositors. When the panic ends and the depositors put their money back in their accounts, the banks can repay the loans to the central bank.

The Establishment of the Federal Reserve System

Bank panics lead to severe disruptions in business activity because households and firms have trouble gaining access to their accounts and may be unable to borrow money. As we saw in the module opener, in 2015, bank runs in Greece prompted the

Fractional reserve banking system A banking system in which banks keep less than 100 percent of deposits as reserves.

Bank run A situation in which many depositors simultaneously decide to withdraw money from a bank.

Bank panic A situation in which many banks experience runs at the same time.

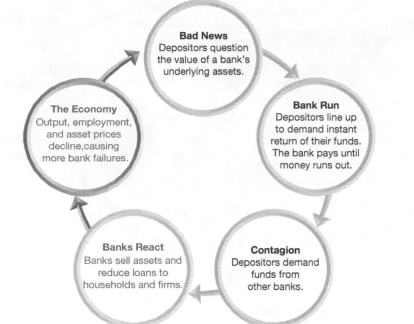

MyEconLab Animation

Figure 8.3

The Feedback Loop during a Bank Panic

Bank runs can cause good banks, as well as bad banks, to fail. Bank failures are costly because they reduce the ability of households and firms to get loans. Once a panic starts, falling incomes, employment, and asset prices can cause more bank failures. This feedback loop means that a panic can continue unless the government intervenes.

government to order banks closed for three weeks, which led to disruptions in the Greek economy, with declines in output and employment. In the United States, each bank panic in the late nineteenth and early twentieth centuries was accompanied by a recession. Figure 8.3 shows how a feedback loop during a bank run can lead to a recession. With the intention of putting an end to bank panics, in 1913, Congress passed the Federal Reserve Act, which set up the Federal Reserve System—often referred to as "the Fed." The system began operation in 1914, with the authority to make loans to banks. The loans the Fed makes to banks are called **discount loans**, and the interest rate it charges on the loans is called the **discount rate**. When a bank receives a loan from the Fed, its reserves increase by the amount of the loan.

The Fed's first test as a lender of last resort came in the early years of the Great Depression of the 1930s, when many banks were hit by bank runs as depositors pulled funds out of checking and savings accounts. Although the Fed had been established to act as a lender of last resort, Fed officials declined to make loans to many banks because the officials were worried that banks experiencing runs had made bad loans and other investments. The Fed believed that making loans to banks that were in financial trouble because of bad investments might reduce the incentive bank managers had to be careful in their investment decisions. Partly due to the Fed's unwillingness to act as a lender of last resort, more than 5,000 banks failed during the early 1930s. Today, many economists are critical of the Fed's decisions in the early 1930s because they believe these decisions increased the severity of the Great Depression. In 1934, Congress established the Federal Deposit Insurance Corporation (FDIC) to insure deposits in most banks up to a limit, which is currently $250,000 per deposit. If the bank you have your checking account in goes out of business, the FDIC will refund your money after a wait of at most two days. Deposit insurance has greatly reduced bank runs because it has reassured all but the largest depositors that their deposits are safe, even if their bank goes out of business. During the financial crisis of 2007–2009, some banks experienced runs when depositors with funds exceeding the deposit insurance limit feared that they would suffer losses if their banks failed.

In setting up the Federal Reserve System, Congress divided the country into 12 Federal Reserve districts, as shown in Figure 8.4. Each district has its own Federal Reserve Bank, which provides services to banks in that district. The real power of the Fed, however, lies in Washington, DC, with the Board of Governors. The seven members of the Board of Governors are appointed by the president of the United States to 14-year,

Discount loans Loans the Federal Reserve makes to banks.

Discount rate The interest rate the Federal Reserve charges on discount loans.

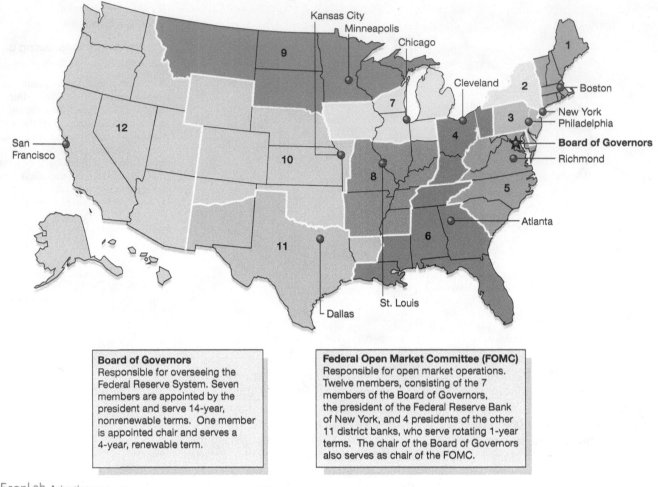

Board of Governors
Responsible for overseeing the Federal Reserve System. Seven members are appointed by the president and serve 14-year, nonrenewable terms. One member is appointed chair and serves a 4-year, renewable term.

Federal Open Market Committee (FOMC)
Responsible for open market operations. Twelve members, consisting of the 7 members of the Board of Governors, the president of the Federal Reserve Bank of New York, and 4 presidents of the other 11 district banks, who serve rotating 1-year terms. The chair of the Board of Governors also serves as chair of the FOMC.

MyEconLab Animation

Figure 8.4 **The Federal Reserve System**

The United States is divided into 12 Federal Reserve districts, each of which has a Federal Reserve Bank. The real power within the Federal Reserve System, however, lies in Washington, DC, with the Board of Governors, which consists of 7 members appointed by the president.

The 12-member Federal Open Market Committee carries out monetary policy.

Source: Board of Governors of the Federal Reserve System.

nonrenewable terms. One member of the Board of Governors is appointed chair and serves a 4-year, renewable term. In addition to acting as a lender of last resort to banks, the Fed acts as a bankers' bank, providing services such as check clearing to banks, and has the responsibility of managing the U.S. money supply. MyEconLab Concept Check

How the Federal Reserve Manages the Money Supply

Although Congress established the Fed primarily to stop bank panics by acting as a lender of last resort, today the Fed is also responsible for managing the money supply. As we will discuss in more detail in Module 8A, managing the money supply is part of **monetary policy**, which the Fed undertakes to pursue macroeconomic policy objectives. To manage the money supply, the Fed uses three *monetary policy tools:*

Monetary policy The actions the Federal Reserve takes to manage the money supply and interest rates to pursue macroeconomic policy objectives.

1. Open market operations

2. Discount policy

3. Reserve requirements

Remember that the most important component of the money supply is checking account deposits. Not surprisingly, all three of the Fed's policy tools are aimed at affecting the reserves of banks as a means of changing the volume of checking account deposits.

Open Market Operations Eight times per year, the **Federal Open Market Committee (FOMC)** meets in Washington, DC, to discuss monetary policy. The committee has 12 voting members:

- The 7 members of the Federal Reserve's Board of Governors.
- The president of the Federal Reserve Bank of New York.
- The presidents of 4 of the other 11 Federal Reserve Banks. These 4 presidents serve one-year rotating terms as voting members of the FOMC.

All 12 Federal Reserve Bank presidents attend meetings and participate in discussions. The chair of the Board of Governors also serves as the chair of the FOMC.

The U.S. Treasury borrows money by selling bills, notes, and bonds. Remember that the *maturity* of a financial asset is the period of time until the purchaser receives payment of the face value or principal. Usually, bonds have face values of $1,000. Treasury bills have maturities of 1 year or less, Treasury notes have maturities of 2 years to 10 years, and Treasury bonds have maturities of 30 years. To control the size of the money supply, the Fed buys and sells Treasury securities in a process called **open market operations.**

To increase the money supply, the FOMC directs the *trading desk*, located at the Federal Reserve Bank of New York, to carry out an *open market purchase* by buying U.S. Treasury securities—most frequently bills, but sometimes notes or bonds—from banks. The Fed pays for the Treasury bills by depositing the funds in the reserve accounts banks maintain with the Fed.

Suppose that the Fed engages in an open market purchase of $10 million. We can illustrate the results with two T-accounts: one for the Fed and one for the banking system. The banking system's T-account is based on the banking system's balance sheet, which simply adds together all the assets and liabilities of all the commercial banks in the United States. As a result of the open market purchase, the banking system's holdings of Treasury bills fall by $10 million and its reserves increase by $10 million:

Banking System

Assets		Liabilities
Treasury bills	–$10 million	
Reserves	+$10 million	

The Fed's holdings of Treasury bills increase by $10 million, and the value of the banking system's reserve balances—which are a liability to the Fed—also increase by $10 million:

Federal Reserve

Assets		Liabilities	
Treasury bills	+$10 million	Reserves	+$10 million

This increase in reserves starts the process of expanding loans and checking account deposits that increases the money supply.

To decrease the money supply, the FOMC directs the trading desk to carry out an *open market sale* by selling Treasury securities. When the buyers of the Treasury securities pay for them with checks, the banking system's reserves fall. This decrease in reserves starts a contraction of loans and checking account deposits that reduces the money supply.

There are three reasons the Fed conducts monetary policy principally through open market operations:

1. Because the Fed initiates open market operations, it completely controls their volume, which means the Fed can carry out both large and small open market operations.

Federal Open Market Committee (FOMC) The Federal Reserve committee responsible for open market operations and managing the money supply in the United States.

Open market operations The buying and selling of Treasury securities by the Federal Reserve in order to control the money supply.

2. Open market operations are easily reversible. For example, if the Fed believes that previous open market purchases have caused the money supply to increase too rapidly, it can engage in open market sales.

3. The Fed can implement its open market operations quickly, with no administrative delay or required changes in regulations.

Many other central banks, including the European Central Bank and the Bank of Japan, also use open market operations to conduct monetary policy.

The Federal Reserve is responsible for putting the paper currency of the United States into circulation. (The currency is actually printed by the U.S. Treasury.) Recall that if you look at the top of a dollar bill, you see the words "Federal Reserve Note." When the Fed takes actions to increase the money supply, commentators sometimes say that it is "printing more money." The main way the Fed increases the money supply, however, is not by printing more currency but by buying Treasury securities. Similarly, to reduce the money supply, the Fed doesn't set fire to stacks of paper currency. Instead, it sells Treasury securities. We will spend more time discussing the Fed's management of the money supply in Module 8A when we discuss monetary policy.

Discount Policy As we have seen, when a bank borrows money from the Fed by taking out a discount loan, the interest rate the bank pays is called the discount rate. By lowering the discount rate, the Fed can encourage banks to take additional loans and thereby increase their reserves. With more reserves, banks will make more loans to households and firms, which will increase checking account deposits and the money supply. Raising the discount rate will have the reverse effect.

Reserve Requirements When the Fed reduces the required reserve ratio, it converts required reserves into excess reserves. For example, suppose a bank has $100 million in checking account deposits, and the required reserve ratio is 10 percent. The bank will be required to hold $10 million as reserves. If the Fed reduces the required reserve ratio to 8 percent, the bank will need to hold only $8 million as reserves. The Fed can thereby convert $2 million worth of reserves from required reserves to excess reserves. This $2 million is then available for the bank to lend out. If the Fed *raises* the required reserve ratio from 10 percent to 12 percent, it will have the reverse effect.

The Fed rarely changes reserve requirements because doing so can disrupt banks' operations by forcing them to significantly change their holdings of loans, bonds, and other securities. Also, because the Fed pays banks only a low interest rate on reserves, the use of reserve requirements to manage the money supply effectively places a tax on banks' deposit-taking and lending activities, which can be costly for the economy. The Fed relies instead on open market operations as its main tool for managing the money supply.   MyEconLab Concept Check

The "Shadow Banking System" and the Financial Crisis of 2007–2009

The banks we have been discussing in this module are *commercial banks*, whose most important economic role is to accept funds from depositors and lend those funds to borrowers. Large firms can sell stocks and bonds on financial markets, but investors are typically unwilling to buy stocks and bonds from small and medium-sized firms because they lack sufficient information about the financial health of smaller firms (see Module 6). So, smaller firms—and households—have traditionally relied on bank loans for their credit needs. In the past 25 years, however, two important developments have occurred in the financial system: (1) Banks have begun to resell many of their loans rather than keeping them until borrowers pay them off, and (2) financial firms other than commercial banks have become important sources of credit to businesses.

Securitization Comes to Banking Traditionally, when a bank made a *residential mortgage loan* to a household to buy a home or made a commercial loan to a business, the bank would keep the loan and collect the payments until the borrower paid off the loan. A financial asset—such as a loan or a stock or a bond—is considered

(a) Securitizing a loan

1. Banks grant loans to households.

2. The loans are bundled into securities.

3. And investors purchase the securities.

(b) The flow of payments on a securitized loan

1. Banks collect loan payments from households.

2. Banks receive a fee for processing the payments.

3. Banks send payments to investors in the securities.

MyEconLab Animation

Figure 8.5   The Process of Securitization

Panel (a) shows how in the securitization process banks grant loans to households and bundle the loans into securities that are then sold to investors.

Panel (b) shows that banks collect payments on the original loans and, after taking a fee, send the payments to the investors who bought the securities.

a **security** if it can be bought and sold in a *financial market*. Shares of stock issued by the Coca-Cola Company are an example of a security because they can be bought and sold on the New York Stock Exchange. When a financial asset is first sold, the sale takes place in the *primary market*. If an investor resells the asset, the sale takes place in the *secondary market*. Prior to 1970, most loans were not securities because they could not be resold—there was no secondary market for them. After 1970, residential mortgages and then other loans, including car loans and commercial loans, began to be *securitized*. The process of **securitization** creates a secondary market in which loans that have been bundled together can be bought and sold in financial markets, just as corporate or government bonds are. Figure 8.5 outlines the securitization process. We will discuss the process of securitization further in Module 8A when we consider monetary policy.

Security A financial asset—such as a stock or a bond—that can be bought and sold in a financial market.

Securitization The process of transforming loans or other financial assets into securities.

The Shadow Banking System   In addition to the changes resulting from securitization, the financial system was transformed in the 1990s and 2000s by the increasing importance of *nonbank financial firms*. Investment banks, such as Goldman Sachs and Morgan Stanley, differ from commercial banks in that they do not accept deposits, and they rarely lend directly to households. Instead, investment banks traditionally concentrated on providing advice to firms issuing stocks and bonds or considering mergers with other firms. In the late 1990s, investment banks expanded their buying of mortgages, bundling large numbers of them together as bonds known as *mortgage-backed securities*, and reselling them to investors. Mortgage-backed securities proved very popular with investors because they often paid higher interest rates than other securities that seemed to have comparable default risk.

Money market mutual funds have also increased their importance in the financial system over time. These funds sell shares to investors and use the money to buy short-term securities such as Treasury bills and commercial paper issued by corporations. Commercial paper represents short-term borrowing corporations use to fund their day-to-day operations. Many corporations that previously met such needs by borrowing from banks began instead to sell commercial paper to money market mutual funds.

Hedge funds raise money from wealthy investors and use sophisticated investment strategies that often involve significant risk. By the mid-2000s, hedge funds had become an important source of demand for securitized loans and an important source of loans to other financial firms.

In 2008, Timothy Geithner, who became Treasury secretary in the Obama administration, used the term the *shadow banking system* to refer to investment banks, money market mutual funds, hedge funds, and other nonbank financial firms engaged in similar activities. By raising money from investors and lending it directly or indirectly to firms and households, these firms were carrying out a function that at one time was almost exclusively carried out by commercial banks.

The Financial Crisis of 2007–2009 The firms in the shadow banking system differed from commercial banks in two important ways: First, the government agencies—including the Federal Reserve—that regulated the commercial banking system did not regulate these firms. Second, these firms were more highly *leveraged*—that is, they relied more heavily on borrowed money to finance their operations—than were commercial banks. If a firm uses a small amount of its own money and a lot of borrowed money to make an investment, both the firm's potential profits and its potential losses are increased. Suppose a firm invests $100 of its own money. If the investment earns a return of $3, the firm has earned 3 percent ($3/$100) on its funds. But if the firm's investment consists of $10 of its own money and $90 it has borrowed, a profit of $3 becomes a return of 30 percent ($3/$10) on the firm's $10 investment. If the investment loses $2, however, the firm's return is −20 percent (−$2/$10). Leveraged investments have a potential for both large gains and large losses.

As mentioned earlier, commercial banks rarely experienced runs after Congress established federal deposit insurance in the 1930s. However, beginning in 2007, some firms in the shadow banking system experienced runs. As we will discuss further in Module 8A, the underlying cause of the financial crisis of 2007–2009 was problems in the U.S. housing market. As housing prices began to fall, a significant number of borrowers defaulted on their mortgages, which caused mortgage-backed securities to lose value. Financial firms that had invested in these securities, including both commercial banks and many firms in the shadow banking system, suffered losses. The more leveraged the firm, the larger the losses. Although deposit insurance helped commercial banks avoid runs, investment banks and other financial firms that had borrowed short term and invested the funds long term were in trouble. As lenders refused to renew their short-term loans, many of these firms had to sell their holdings of securities in an attempt to raise cash. But as the prices of the securities continued to fall, the losses to these firms increased.

In the spring of 2008, the investment bank Bear Stearns was saved from bankruptcy only when the Federal Reserve arranged for it to be acquired by JPMorgan Chase. In the fall of 2008, the Federal Reserve and the U.S. Treasury decided not to take action to save the investment bank Lehman Brothers, which failed. The failure of Lehman Brothers echoed throughout the financial system, setting off a panic. The process of securitization—apart from government-guaranteed residential mortgages—ground to a halt. The well-publicized difficulties of a money market mutual fund that had suffered losses on loans to Lehman Brothers led to a wave of withdrawals from these funds. In turn, the funds were no longer able to fulfill their role as buyers of corporate commercial paper. As banks and other financial firms sold assets and cut back on lending to shore up their financial positions, the flow of funds from savers to borrowers was disrupted. The resulting *credit crunch* significantly worsened the recession that had begun in December 2007.

The Fed's Response The Fed, in combination with the U.S. Treasury, took vigorous action to deal with the financial crisis. We will discuss the Fed's actions further in Module 8A, but for now, we can mention several particularly important policy actions:

- In the fall of 2008, under the Troubled Asset Relief Program (TARP), the Fed and Treasury began attempting to stabilize the commercial banking system by providing funds to banks in exchange for stock. Taking partial ownership of private commercial banks was an unprecedented move by the federal government.

- The Fed also modified its discount policy by setting up several new "lending facilities." These lending facilities made it possible for the Fed to grant discount loans to financial firms—such as investment banks—that had not previously been eligible.

- The Fed addressed problems in the commercial paper market by directly buying commercial paper for the first time since the 1930s.

Although the recession continued into 2009, the extraordinary actions of the Treasury and Fed stabilized the financial system. It took several years, however, for the flow of funds from savers to borrowers to return to normal levels, and economists and policymakers continue to debate the wisdom of some of the Fed's actions. MyEconLab Concept Check

8.5 The Quantity Theory of Money

LEARNING OBJECTIVE: Explain the quantity theory of money and use it to explain how high rates of inflation occur.

People have been aware of the connection between increases in the money supply and inflation for centuries. In the sixteenth century, the Spanish conquered Mexico and Peru and shipped large quantities of gold and silver from those countries back to Spain. The gold and silver were minted into coins and spent across Europe to further the political ambitions of the Spanish kings. Prices in Europe rose steadily during these years, and many observers discussed the relationship between this inflation and the flow of gold and silver into Europe from the Americas.

Connecting Money and Prices: The Quantity Equation

In the early twentieth century, Irving Fisher, an economist at Yale University, formalized the connection between money and prices by using the *quantity equation*:

$$M \times V = P \times Y.$$

The quantity equation states that the money supply (M) multiplied by the *velocity of money* (V) equals the price level (P) multiplied by real output (Y). Fisher defined the **velocity of money**, often called simply "velocity," as the average number of times each dollar of the money supply is used to purchase goods and services included in GDP. Rewriting the original equation by dividing both sides by M, we have the equation for velocity:

$$V = \frac{P \times Y}{M}.$$

Velocity of money The average number of times each dollar in the money supply is used to purchase goods and services included in GDP.

If we use M1 to measure the money supply, the GDP price deflator to measure the price level, and real GDP to measure real output, the value for velocity for 2014 was:

$$V = \frac{1.09 \times \$16.0 \text{ trillion}}{\$2.8 \text{ trillion}} = 6.2.$$

This result tells us that, during 2014, each dollar of M1 was on average spent about six times on goods or services included in GDP.

Because velocity is defined to be equal to $(P \times Y)/M$, we know that the quantity equation must always hold true: The left side of the equation *must* be equal to the right side. A theory is a statement about the world that might possibly be false. Therefore, the quantity equation is not a theory. Irving Fisher turned the quantity equation into the **quantity theory of money** by arguing that velocity was constant. He argued that the average number of times a dollar is spent depends on factors that do not change often, such as how often people get paid, how often they do their grocery shopping, and how often businesses mail bills. Because this assertion may be true or false, the quantity theory of money is, in fact, a theory. MyEconLab Concept Check

Quantity theory of money A theory about the connection between money and prices that assumes that the velocity of money is constant.

The Quantity Theory Explanation of Inflation

The quantity equation gives us a way of showing the relationship between changes in the money supply and changes in the price level, or inflation. To see this relationship more clearly, we can use a handy mathematical rule that states that an equation in which variables are multiplied together is equal to an equation in which the *growth rates* of these variables are *added* together. So, we can transform the quantity equation from:

$$M \times V = P \times Y$$

to:

Growth rate of the money supply + Growth rate of velocity =
Growth rate of the price level (or the inflation rate) + Growth rate of real output.

This way of writing the quantity equation is more useful for investigating the effect of changes in the money supply on the inflation rate. Remember that the growth rate for any variable is the percentage change in the variable from one year to the next. The growth rate of the price level is the inflation rate, so we can rewrite the quantity equation to help understand the factors that determine inflation:

Inflation rate = Growth rate of the money supply +
Growth rate of velocity − Growth rate of real output.

If Irving Fisher was correct that velocity is constant, then the growth rate of velocity will be zero. For example, if velocity is always equal to six, then its percentage change from one year to the next will always be zero. This assumption allows us to rewrite the equation one last time:

Inflation rate = Growth rate of the money supply − Growth rate of real output.

This equation leads to the following predictions:

1. If the money supply grows at a faster rate than real GDP, there will be inflation.
2. If the money supply grows at a slower rate than real GDP, there will be deflation. (Recall that *deflation* is a decline in the price level.)
3. If the money supply grows at the same rate as real GDP, the price level will be stable, and there will be neither inflation nor deflation.

It turns out that Irving Fisher was wrong in asserting that the velocity of money is constant. From year to year, there can be significant fluctuations in velocity. As a result, the predictions of inflation based on the quantity theory of money do not hold every year, but most economists agree that the quantity theory provides useful insight into the long-run relationship between the money supply and inflation: *In the long run, inflation results from the money supply growing at a faster rate than real GDP.*   MyEconLab Concept Check

How Accurate Are Forecasts of Inflation Based on the Quantity Theory?

Note that the accuracy of the quantity theory depends on whether the key assumption that velocity is constant is correct. If velocity is not constant, there may not be a tight link between increases in the money supply and increases in the price level. For example, an increase in the quantity of money might be offset by a decline in velocity, leaving the price level unaffected. Because velocity can move erratically in the short run, we would not expect the quantity equation to provide good forecasts of inflation in the short run. Over the long run, however, there is a strong link between changes in the money supply and inflation. Panel (a) of Figure 8.6 shows by decade the relationship in the United States between the growth of the M2 measure of the money supply and the inflation rate. (We use M2 here because data on M2 are available for a longer period of time than are data for M1.) Because of variations in the rate of growth of real GDP and in velocity, there is not an exact relationship between the growth rate of M2 and the inflation rate. But there is a clear pattern that decades with higher growth rates in the money supply were also decades with higher inflation rates. In other words, most of the variation in inflation rates across decades can be explained by variation in the rates of growth of the money supply.

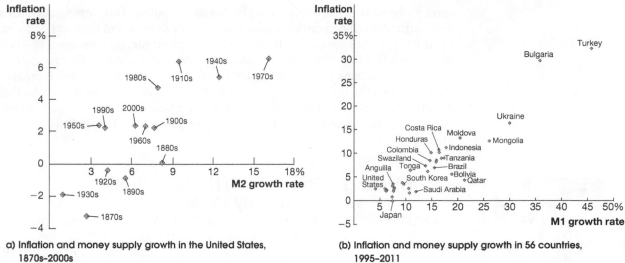

a) Inflation and money supply growth in the United States, 1870s–2000s

(b) Inflation and money supply growth in 56 countries, 1995–2011

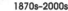MyEconLab Animation

Figure 8.6   The Relationship between Money Growth and Inflation over Time and around the World

Panel (a) shows that, by and large, the rate of inflation in the United States has been highest during the decades in which the money supply has increased most rapidly, and the rate of inflation has been lowest during the decades in which the money supply has increased least rapidly. Panel (b) shows the relationship between money supply growth and inflation for 56 countries between 1995 and 2011. There is not an exact relationship between money supply growth and inflation, but countries such as Bulgaria, Turkey, and Ukraine that had high rates of money supply growth had high inflation rates, and countries such as the United States and Japan had low rates of money supply growth and low inflation rates.

Sources: Panel (a): For the 1870s to the 1960s, Milton Friedman and Anna J. Schwartz, *Monetary Trends in the United States and United Kingdom: Their Relation to Income, Prices, and Interest Rates, 1867–1975*, Chicago: University of Chicago Press, 1982, Table 4.8, and for the 1970s to the 2000s, Federal Reserve Board of Governors and U.S. Bureau of Economic Analysis; Panel (b): International Monetary Fund, *International Monetary Statistics*.

Panel (b) provides further evidence consistent with the quantity theory by looking at rates of growth of the money supply and rates of inflation across 56 countries for the years 1995–2011. Although there is not an exact relationship between rates of growth of the money supply and rates of inflation across countries, panel (b) shows that countries where the money supply grew rapidly tended to have high inflation rates, while countries where the money supply grew more slowly tended to have much lower inflation rates. Not included in panel (b) are data for Zimbabwe, which may be the most extreme case of inflation in recent years. In some years since 1995, the money supply in Zimbabwe grew by more than 7,500 percent. The result was an accelerating rate of inflation that eventually reached 15 billion percent during 2008. Zimbabwe was suffering from *hyperinflation*—that is, a rate of inflation that exceeds 50 percent per month.   MyEconLab Concept Check

High Rates of Inflation

The quantity theory can help us understand the reasons for very high rates of inflation. Hyperinflation is caused by central banks increasing the money supply at a rate far in excess of the growth rate of real GDP. A high rate of inflation causes money to lose its value so rapidly that households and firms avoid holding it. If, as happened in Zimbabwe, the inflation rate becomes high enough, people stop using paper currency, so it no longer serves the important functions of money discussed earlier in this module. Economies suffering from high inflation usually also suffer from very slow growth, if not severe recession.

Given the dire consequences that follow from high inflation, why do governments cause it by expanding the money supply so rapidly? The main reason is that governments often want to spend more than they are able to raise through taxes. Developed countries, such as the United States, can usually bridge gaps between spending and taxes by borrowing through selling bonds to the public. Developing countries often have difficulty selling bonds because investors are skeptical of their ability to pay back the money. If they are unable to sell bonds to the public, governments in developing countries will force their central banks to purchase them. As we discussed previously, when a central bank buys government bonds, the money supply will increase. In the United States, the Federal Reserve always buys Treasury securities from banks, never directly from the U.S. Treasury. This procedure helps ensure that the Treasury only issues bonds in amounts that private investors—rather than the central bank—are willing to buy.

MyEconLab Concept Check

Making the Connection
MyEconLab Video

The German Hyperinflation of the Early 1920s

When Germany lost World War I, a revolution broke out that overthrew Kaiser Wilhelm II and installed a new government known as the Weimar Republic. In the peace treaty of 1919, the Allies—the United States, Great Britain, France, and Italy—imposed payments called *reparations* on the new German government. The reparations were meant as compensation to the Allies for the damage Germany had caused during the war. It was very difficult for the German government to use tax revenue to cover both its normal spending and the reparations.

The German government decided to pay for the difference between its spending and its tax revenues by selling bonds to the central bank, the Reichsbank. After a few years, the German government fell far behind in its reparations payments. In January 1923, the French government sent troops into the German industrial area known as the Ruhr to try to collect the payments directly. German workers in the Ruhr went on strike, and the German government decided to support them by paying their salaries. The government raised the funds by selling additional bonds to the Reichsbank, thereby further increasing the money supply.

The inflationary increase in the money supply was very large: The total number of marks—the German currency—in circulation rose from 115 million in January 1922 to 1.3 billion in January 1923 and then to 497 billion *billion*, or 497,000,000,000,000,000,000, in December 1923. Just as the quantity theory predicts, the result was a staggering high rate of inflation. The German price index that stood at 100 in 1914 and 1,440 in January 1922 had risen to 126,160,000,000,000 in December 1923. The German mark became worthless. The German government ended the hyperinflation by (1) negotiating a new agreement with the Allies that reduced its reparations payments, (2) reducing other government expenditures and raising taxes to balance its budget, and (3) replacing the existing mark with a new mark. Each new mark was worth 1 trillion old marks. The German central bank was also limited to issuing a total of 3.2 billion new marks.

These steps were enough to bring the hyperinflation to an end—but not before the savings of anyone holding the old marks had been wiped out. Most middle-income Germans were extremely resentful of this outcome. Many historians believe that the hyperinflation greatly reduced the allegiance of many Germans to the Weimar Republic and may have helped pave the way for Adolph Hitler and the Nazis to seize power 10 years later.

Sources: Thomas Sargent, "The Ends of Four Big Inflations," *Rational Expectations and Inflation*, 3rd ed., Princeton, NJ: Princeton University Press, 2013; and John Parke Young, *European Currency and Finance*, Washington, DC: Government Printing Office, 1925.

During the German hyperinflation of the 1920s, paper currency became so worthless that people used it to light their stoves.

MyEconLab Study Plan

Your Turn: Test your understanding by doing related problem 5.10 on page 333 at the end of this module.

Continued from page 299

Economics in Your Life

What if Money Became Increasingly Valuable?

At the beginning of this module, we asked you to consider whether you would like to live in an economy in which the purchasing power of money rises every year. The first thing to consider when thinking about the advantages and disadvantages of this situation is that the only way for the purchasing power of money to increase is for the price level to fall; in other words, *deflation* must occur. Because the price level in the United States hasn't fallen for an entire year since the 1930s, most people alive today have experienced only rising price levels—and declining purchasing power of money. Would replacing rising prices with falling prices necessarily be a good thing? It might be tempting to say "yes," because if you have a job, your salary will buy more goods and services each year. But, in fact, just as a rising price level results in most wages and salaries rising each year, a falling price level is likely to mean falling wages and salaries each year. So, it is likely that, on average, people would not see the purchasing power of their incomes increase, even if the purchasing power of any currency they held increased. There can also be a significant downside to deflation, particularly if the transition from inflation to deflation happens suddenly. Recall that the real interest rate is equal to the nominal interest rate minus the inflation rate. If an economy experiences deflation, then the real interest rate will be greater than the nominal interest rate. A rising real interest rate can be bad news for anyone who has borrowed, including homeowners who may have substantial mortgage loans. So, you are probably better off living in an economy experiencing mild inflation than one experiencing deflation.

Conclusion

Money plays a key role in the functioning of an economy by facilitating trade in goods and services and by making specialization possible. Without specialization, no advanced economy can prosper. Households and firms, banks, and the central bank (the Federal Reserve in the United States) are participants in the process of creating the money supply. In Module 8A, we will discuss how the Federal Reserve uses monetary policy to promote its economic objectives.

Visit MyEconLab for a news article and analysis related to the concepts of this module.

MODULE SUMMARY AND PROBLEMS

Key Terms

Asset, p. 300

Bank panic, p. 316

Bank run, p. 316

Commodity money, p. 300

Discount loans, p. 317

Discount rate, p. 317

Excess reserves, p. 308

Federal Open Market Committee (FOMC), p. 319

Federal Reserve, p. 302

Fiat money, p. 302

Fractional reserve banking system, p. 316

M1, p. 304

M2, p. 305

Monetary policy, p. 318

Money, p. 300

Open market operations, p. 319

Quantity theory of money, p. 323

Required reserve ratio, p. 308

Required reserves, p. 308

Reserves, p. 308

Securitization, p. 321

Security, p. 321

Simple deposit multiplier, p. 312

Velocity of money, p. 323

8.1 ## What Is Money, and Why Do We Need It? pages 300–303

LEARNING OBJECTIVE: Define money and discuss the four functions of money.

Summary

A *barter economy* is an economy that does not use money and in which people trade goods and services directly for other goods and services. Barter trade occurs only if there is a *double coincidence of wants*, where both parties to the trade want what the other one has. Because barter is inefficient, there is strong incentive to use **money**, which is any **asset** that people are generally willing to accept in exchange for goods or services or in payment of debts. An *asset* is anything of value owned by a person or a firm. A **commodity money** is a good used as money that also has value independent of its use as money. Money has four functions: It is a medium of exchange, a unit of account, a store of value, and a standard of deferred payment. At one time, governments issued gold coins and paper currency that were convertible into gold. Today, no government in the world issues paper currency that can be redeemed for gold. Instead, paper currency is **fiat money**, which has no value except as money.

MyEconLab   Visit www.myeconlab.com to complete these exercises online and get instant feedback.

Review Questions

1.1 A baseball fan with a Mike Trout baseball card wants to trade it for a Miguel Cabrera baseball card, but everyone the fan knows who has a Cabrera card doesn't want a Trout card. What do economists call the problem this fan is having?

1.2 What is the difference between commodity money and fiat money?

1.3 What are the four functions of money? Can something be considered money if it does not fulfill all four functions?

1.4 Why do businesses accept paper currency when they know that, unlike a gold coin, the paper the currency is printed on is worth very little?

Problems and Applications

1.5 The English economist William Stanley Jevons described a world tour during the 1880s by a French singer, Mademoiselle Zélie. One stop on the tour was a theater in the Society Islands, part of French Polynesia in the South Pacific. She performed for her usual fee, which was one-third of the receipts. This turned out to be 3 pigs, 23 turkeys, 44 chickens, 5,000 coconuts, and "considerable quantities of bananas, lemons, and oranges." She estimated that all of this would have had a value in France of 4,000 francs. According to Jevons, "as Mademoiselle could not consume any considerable portion of the receipts herself, it became necessary in the meantime to feed the pigs and poultry with the fruit." Do the goods Mademoiselle Zélie received as payment fulfill the four functions of money described in this module? Briefly explain.

Source: W. Stanley Jevons, *Money and the Mechanism of Exchange*, New York: D. Appleton and Company, 1889, pp. 1–2.

1.6 (Related to the Module Opener **on page 299)** An article in the *New York Times* in 2015 noted, "A rising number of Greeks in rural areas are swapping goods and services in cashless transactions since the government shut down banks on June 28 for three weeks." If Greeks were able to swap goods and services for other goods and services, did it matter that currency was not available because the banks had been closed? Briefly explain.

Source: Lefteris Karagiannopoulos, "Hay for Cheese? Barter Booms in Cash-Squeezed Rural Greece," *New York Times*, July 29, 2015.

1.7 In the late 1940s, the Communists under Mao Zedong were defeating the government of China in a civil war. The paper currency issued by the Chinese government was losing much of its value, and most businesses refused to accept it. At the same time, there was a paper shortage in Japan. During these years, Japan was still under military occupation by the United States, following its defeat in World War II. Some of the U.S. troops in Japan realized that they could use dollars to buy up vast amounts of paper currency in China, ship it to Japan to be recycled into paper, and make a substantial profit. Under these circumstances, was the Chinese paper currency a commodity money or a fiat money? Briefly explain.

1.8 According to Peter Heather, a historian at King's College London, during the time of the Roman Empire, the German tribes east of the Rhine River (the area the Romans called Germania) produced no coins of their own but used Roman coins instead:

Although no coinage was produced in Germania, Roman coins were in plentiful circulation and could easily have provided a medium of exchange (already in the first century, Tacitus tells us, Germani of the Rhine region were using good-quality Roman silver coins for this purpose).

a. What is a medium of exchange?

b. What does the author mean when he writes that Roman coins could have provided the German tribes with a medium of exchange?

c. Why would any member of a German tribe have been willing to accept a Roman coin from another member of the tribe in exchange for goods or services when the tribes were not part of the Roman Empire and were not governed by Roman law?

Source: Peter Heather, *The Fall of the Roman Empire: A New History of Rome and the Barbarians*, New York: Oxford University Press, 2006, p. 89.

1.9 **(Related to the** Making the Connection **on page 303)** Suppose that Congress passes a new law that requires all firms to accept paper currency in exchange for whatever they are selling. Briefly discuss who would gain and who would lose from this legislation.

1.10 On January 1, 2002, Germany officially adopted the euro as its currency, and the deutsche mark stopped being legal tender. According to an article in the *Wall Street Journal*, even 10 years later many Germans continued using the deutsche mark, and many stores in Germany continued to accept it. Briefly explain how it is possible for people to continue to use a currency when the government that issued it has replaced it with another currency.

Source: Vanessa Fuhrmans, "Who Needs the Euro When You Can Pay with Deutsche Marks?" *Wall Street Journal*, July 18, 2012.

8.2 ## How Is Money Measured in the United States Today? pages 303–307

LEARNING OBJECTIVE: Discuss the definitions of the money supply used in the United States today.

Summary

The narrowest definition of the money supply in the United States today is **M1**, which includes currency, checking account balances, and traveler's checks. A broader definition of the money supply is **M2**, which includes everything that is in M1, plus savings accounts, small-denomination time deposits (such as certificates of deposit [CDs]), money market deposit accounts in banks, and noninstitutional money market fund shares.

MyEconLab   Visit www.myeconlab.com to complete these exercises online and get instant feedback.

Review Questions

2.1 What is the main difference between the M1 and M2 definitions of the money supply?

2.2 Why does the Federal Reserve use two definitions of the money supply rather than one?

2.3 Distinguish among money, income, and wealth. Which one of the three does the central bank of a country control?

Problems and Applications

2.4 Briefly explain whether each of the following is counted in M1.

a. The coins in your pocket

b. The funds in your checking account

c. The funds in your savings account

d. The traveler's checks that you have left over from a trip

e. Your Citibank Platinum MasterCard

2.5 **(Related to the** Don't Let This Happen to You **on page 305)** Briefly explain whether you agree with the following statement: "I recently read that more than half of the money the government prints is actually held by people in foreign countries. If that's true, then the United States is less than half as wealthy as government statistics indicate."

2.6 **(Related to the** Don't Let This Happen to You **on page 305)** An article in the *New York Times* contains the statement: "Income is only one way of measuring wealth." Do you agree that income is a way of measuring wealth?

Source: Sam Roberts, "As the Data Show, There's a Reason the Wall Street Protesters Chose New York," *New York Times*, October 25, 2011.

2.7 **(Related to** Solved Problem 8.2 **on page 306)** Suppose you decide to withdraw $100 in currency from your checking account. What is the effect on M1? Ignore any actions the bank may take as a result of your having withdrawn the $100.

2.8 **(Related to** Solved Problem 8.2 **on page 306)** Suppose you withdraw $1,000 from a money market mutual fund and deposit the funds in your bank checking account. Briefly explain how this action will affect M1 and M2.

2.9 Based on a Survey of Consumer Payment Choice, researchers from the Federal Reserve Bank of Boston estimated that the average consumer, 18 years of age and older, held about $340 in currency. However, as noted in the module, there is actually about $4,000 of currency for every person in the United States.

a. How can the amount of U.S. currency in circulation be so much higher than the amount held by the U.S. population?

b. What does the difference in part (a) imply about the measures of the money supply of the United States?

Source: Kevin Foster, Scott Schuh, and Hanbing Zhang, "The 2010 Survey of Consumer Payment Choice," Federal Reserve Bank of Boston Research Data Report, No. 13-2, November 2013.

2.10 Friedrich Schneider, an economist at the Johannes Kepler University of Linz in Austria, made the following observation about China: "The average Chinese trusts neither the Chinese banks nor the Communist Party."

a. If Schneider is correct, how might businesses and consumers prefer to carry out transactions?

b. The Chinese government has refused to print currency in denominations higher than the 100-renminbi note, which is the equivalent of about $16. The United States prints $100 bills, and all other countries print currency in denominations that are at least that high. Given your answer to part (a), why might the Chinese government be reluctant to print currency in high denominations?

Source: David Barboza, "Chinese Way of Doing Business: In Cash We Trust," *New York Times*, April 30, 2013.

2.11 (Related to the Making the Connection on page 306) In 2015, some business startups were offering the service of transferring money in the form of bitcoins among individuals and businesses in developing countries. At the same time, an article in the *Wall Street Journal* noted that in the United States, "Most ordinary consumers remain wary of using an unproven, six-year-old digital currency that many associate with illicit drugs, extreme price fluctuations and security risks." Why might using bitcoins

be more attractive to individuals and firms in developing countries than to individuals and firms in the United States?

Source: Michael J. Casey and Paul Vigna, "Interest in Bitcoin Grows on Wall Street," *Wall Street Journal*, March 29, 2015.

2.12 The U.S. penny is made primarily of zinc. There have been several times in recent years when zinc prices have been high, and it has cost the U.S. Treasury more than one cent to manufacture a penny. There are currently about 1.4 billion pennies in circulation. Economist François Velde of the Federal Reserve Bank of Chicago has proposed making the current penny worth 5 cents. If the U.S. Treasury adopted Velde's proposal, what would be the effect on the value of M1? Is this change likely to have much effect on the economy? (*Hint:* According to the information given in this module, what is the current value of M1?)

Source: Austan Goolsbee, "Now That a Penny Isn't Worth Much, It's Time to Make It Worth 5 Cents," *New York Times*, February 1, 2007.

8.3 How Do Banks Create Money? pages 307–316

LEARNING OBJECTIVE: Explain how banks create money.

Summary

On a bank's balance sheet, *reserves* and loans are assets, and deposits are liabilities. **Reserves** are deposits that the bank has retained rather than loaned out or invested. **Required reserves** are reserves that banks are legally required to hold. The fraction of deposits that banks are required to keep as reserves is called the **required reserve ratio**. Any reserves banks hold over the legal requirement are called **excess reserves**. When a bank accepts a deposit, it keeps only a fraction of the funds as reserves and loans out the remainder. In making a loan, a bank increases the checking account balance of the borrower. When the borrower uses a check to buy something with the funds the bank has loaned, the seller deposits the check in his or her bank. The seller's bank keeps part of the deposit as reserves and loans out the remainder. This process continues until no banks have excess reserves. In this way, the process of banks making new loans increases the volume of checking account balances and the money supply. This money creation process can be illustrated with T-accounts, which are stripped-down versions of balance sheets that show only how a transaction changes a bank's balance sheet. The **simple deposit multiplier** is the ratio of the change in deposits to the change in reserves. An expression for the simple deposit multiplier is $1/RR$.

MyEconLab   Visit **www.myeconlab.com** to complete these exercises online and get instant feedback.

Review Questions

3.1 What are the largest asset and the largest liability of a typical bank?

3.2 Suppose you decide to withdraw $100 in cash from your checking account. Draw a T-account showing the effect of this transaction on your bank's balance sheet.

3.3 What does it mean to say that banks "create money"?

3.4 Give the formula for the simple deposit multiplier. If the required reserve ratio is 20 percent, what is the maximum increase in checking account deposits that will result from an increase in bank reserves of $20,000? Is this maximum increase likely to occur? Briefly explain.

Problems and Applications

3.5 Following the financial crisis of 2007–2009, Congress passed the Wall Street Reform and Consumer Protection Act, also known as the Dodd-Frank Act. The act increased regulation of the banking system, and from 2010 to 2015 only one new bank opened in the United States. According to an article in the *Wall Street Journal*, "Lawmakers are concerned about the dearth of new banks because small banks make the majority of farm and small-business loans." Why might farms and small-businesses be more likely to rely on banks for funding than would large corporations?

Source: Ryan Tracy, "A Local Bank in Amish Country Flourishes amid Dearth of Small Lenders," *Wall Street Journal*, March 29, 2015.

3.6 The following is from an article on community banks: "Their commercial-lending businesses, funded by their stable deposit bases, make them steady earners." What is commercial lending? In what sense are loans "funded" by deposits?

Source: Karen Richardson, "Clean Books Bolster Traditional Lenders," *Wall Street Journal*, April 30, 2007.

3.7 (Related to the Making the Connection on page 308) In a newspaper column, author Delia Ephron described a conversation with a friend who had a large balance on her credit card with an interest rate of 18 percent per year. The friend was worried about paying off the debt. Ephron was earning only 0.4 percent interest on her bank certificate of deposit (CD). She considered withdrawing the money from her CD and loaning it to her friend so her friend could pay off her credit card balance: "So I was thinking that all of us earning 0.4 percent could instead loan money to our friends at 0.5 percent. … [M]y friend would get out of debt [and] I would earn $5 a month instead of $4." Why don't more people use their savings to make loans rather than keeping the funds in bank accounts that earn very low rates of interest?

Source: Delia Ephron, "Banks Taketh, but Don't Giveth," *New York Times*, January 27, 2012.

3.8 (Related to the Making the Connection **on page 308)** An economist commented on the situation a bank faces when making personal loans to subprime borrowers: "You have to be alert to the trade-off between serving consumers and being viewed as taking advantage of them." If banks charge subprime borrowers a higher interest on loans than they charge prime borrowers, are the banks taking advantage of the subprime borrowers? Briefly explain.

Source: Ianthe Jeanne Dugan and Telis Demos, "New Lenders Spring Up to Cater to Subprime Sector," *Wall Street Journal*, March 5, 2014.

3.9 Suppose that Deja owns a McDonald's franchise. She decides to move her restaurant's checking account to Wells Fargo, which causes the changes shown on the following T-account. If the required reserve ratio is 0.10, or 10 percent, and Wells Fargo currently has no excess reserves, what is the maximum loan Wells Fargo can make as result of this transaction?

Wells Fargo

Assets		Liabilities	
Reserves	+$100,000	Deposits	+$100,000

3.10 Consider the following simplified balance sheet for a bank:

Assets		Liabilities	
Reserves	$10,000	Deposits	$70,000
Loans	$66,000	Stockholders' equity	$6,000

a. If the required reserve ratio is 0.10, or 10 percent, how much in excess reserves does the bank hold?
b. What is the maximum amount by which the bank can expand its loans?
c. If the bank makes the loans in part (b), show the *immediate* effect on the bank's balance sheet.

3.11 (Related to the Don't Let This Happen to You **on page 313)** Briefly explain whether you agree with the following statement: "Assets are things of value that people own. Liabilities are debts. Therefore, a bank will always consider a checking account deposit to be an asset and a car loan to be a liability."

3.12 (Related to Solved Problem 8.3 **on page 313)** Suppose you deposit $2,000 in currency into your checking account at a branch of Bank of America, which we will assume has no excess reserves at the time you make your deposit. Also assume that the required reserve ratio is 0.20, or 20 percent.
a. Use a T-account to show the initial effect of this transaction on Bank of America's balance sheet.
b. Suppose that Bank of America makes the maximum loan it can from the funds you deposited. Using a T-account, show the initial effect of granting the loan on Bank of America's balance sheet. Also include on this T-account the transaction from part (a).
c. Now suppose that whoever took out the loan in part (b) writes a check for this amount and that the person receiving the check deposits it in a branch of Citibank. Show the effect of these transactions on the balance sheets of Bank of America and Citibank after the check has been cleared. (On the T-account for Bank of America, include the transactions from parts (a) and (b).)
d. What is the maximum increase in checking account deposits that can result from your $2,000 deposit? What is the maximum increase in the money supply? Briefly explain.

8.4 The Federal Reserve System, pages 316–323

LEARNING OBJECTIVE: Compare the three policy tools the Federal Reserve uses to manage the money supply.

Summary

The United States has a **fractional reserve banking system** in which banks keep less than 100 percent of deposits as reserves. In a **bank run**, many depositors decide simultaneously to withdraw money from a bank. In a **bank panic**, many banks experience runs at the same time. The **Federal Reserve System** ("the Fed") is the central bank of the United States. It was originally established in 1913 to stop bank panics. The recession of 2007–2009 put renewed emphasis on the Fed's goal of financial market stability. **Monetary policy** refers to the actions the Federal Reserve takes to manage the money supply and interest rates to pursue macroeconomic policy objectives. The Fed's three monetary policy tools are open market operations, discount policy, and reserve requirements. **Open market operations** are the buying and selling of Treasury securities by

the Federal Reserve. The loans the Fed makes to banks are called **discount loans**, and the interest rate the Fed charges on discount loans is the **discount rate**. The **Federal Open Market Committee (FOMC)** meets in Washington, DC, eight times per year to discuss monetary policy. In the past 20 years, a "shadow banking system" has developed. During the financial crisis of 2007–2009, the existence of the shadow banking system complicated the Fed's policy response. A **security** is a financial asset—such as a stock or a bond—that can be bought and sold in a financial market. The process of **securitization** creates a secondary market in which loans that have been bundled together can be bought and sold in financial markets just as corporate or government bonds are.

Review Questions

4.1 Why did Congress decide to establish the Federal Reserve System in 1913?

4.2 What policy tools does the Fed use to control the money supply? Which tool is the most important?

4.3 Why does an open market purchase of Treasury securities by the Federal Reserve increase bank reserves? Why does an open market sale of Treasury securities by the Federal Reserve decrease bank reserves?

4.4 What is the "shadow banking system"? Why were the financial firms of the shadow banking system more vulnerable than commercial banks to bank runs?

Problems and Applications

4.5 In an article in the *Wall Street Journal*, Kevin Brady, a member of Congress from Texas, stated, "To get Congress to pass the Federal Reserve Act [in 1913, President Woodrow] Wilson had to retain the support of … northeastern lawmakers while convincing southern and western Democrats that legislation would not … create a [single] central bank. Wilson's ingenious solution was federalism." Explain what Congressman Brady meant when he stated that Woodrow Wilson used "federalism" to convince Congress to pass the Federal Reserve Act.

Source: Kevin Brady, "How the Fed's East Coast Tilt Warps Monetary Policy," *Wall Street Journal*, June 4, 2015.

4.6 Suppose that the Federal Reserve makes a $10 million discount loan to First National Bank (FNB) by increasing FNB's account at the Fed.

a. Use a T-account to show the effect of this transaction on FNB's balance sheet. Remember that the funds a bank has on deposit at the Fed count as part of its reserves.

b. Assume that before receiving the discount loan, FNB has no excess reserves. What is the maximum amount of this $10 million that FNB can lend out?

c. What is the maximum total increase in the money supply that can result from the Fed's discount loan? Assume that the required reserve ratio is 10 percent.

4.7 An article in the *New York Times* states that "the Bank of Japan, the central bank … is creating money on a vast scale by buying government bonds." How can a central bank "create money" by buying bonds? Doesn't the government create money by printing currency? Briefly explain.

Source: Jonathan Soble, "Japan's Economy Expands, but Less Than Expected," *New York Times*, February 15, 2015.

4.8 Suppose that the Federal Reserve engages in an open market sale of $25 million in U.S. Treasury bills to banks. In the T-accounts for the Fed and for the banking system shown here, fill in the missing information.

Federal Reserve

Assets		Liabilities	
_____	−$25 million	Reserves	−$25 million

Banking System

Assets		Liabilities
Treasury bills	+$25 million	
_____	−$25 million	

4.9 In a speech delivered in June 2008, Timothy Geithner, then president of the Federal Reserve Bank of New York and later U.S. Treasury secretary, said:

> The structure of the financial system changed fundamentally during the boom. … [The] non-bank financial system grew to be very large. … [The] institutions in this parallel financial system [are] vulnerable to a classic type of run, but without the protections such as deposit insurance that the banking system has in place to reduce such risks.

a. What did Geithner mean by the "nonbank financial system"?

b. What is a "classic type of run," and why were institutions in the nonbank financial system vulnerable to such a run?

c. Why would deposit insurance provide the banking system with protection against runs?

Source: Timothy F. Geithner, "Reducing Systemic Risk in a Dynamic Financial System," Remarks at the Economic Club of New York, June 9, 2008.

4.10 An article in the *Wall Street Journal* on the shadow banking system contained the following observation: "If investors rush to the exits en masse, acting as a herd, asset prices could plummet and markets could face funding problems." Why might people who have invested in a money market mutual fund, for example, be more likely to "rush to the exits" if they heard bad news about the fund's investments than would bank depositors if they received bad news about their bank's investments?

Source: Ian Talley, "IMF Warns (Again) of Growing Shadow-Banking Risks," *Wall Street Journal*, April 8, 2015.

4.11 An article in the *Wall Street Journal* reported in 2015 that the People's Bank of China, which is the central bank of China, "is freeing up cash by reducing the amount that banks must keep in reserve." What monetary policy tool was the People's Bank of China using? In what sense did this policy change "free up cash"? What was the People's Bank of China hoping the result of this policy action would be?

Source: Lingling Wei, "China Central Bank Checks Europe Playbook on Credit," *Wall Street Journal*, April 19, 2015.

The Quantity Theory of Money, pages 323–327

8.5

LEARNING OBJECTIVE: Explain the quantity theory of money and use it to explain how high rates of inflation occur.

Summary

The *quantity equation*, which relates the money supply to the price level, is $M \times V = P \times Y$, where M is the money supply, V is the *velocity of money*, P is the price level, and Y is real output. The **velocity of money** is the average number of times each dollar in the money supply is spent during the year. Economist Irving Fisher developed the **quantity theory of money**, which assumes that the velocity of money is constant. If the quantity theory of money is correct, the inflation rate should equal the rate of growth of the money supply minus the rate of growth of real output. Although the quantity theory of money is not literally correct because the velocity of money is not constant, it is true that in the long run, inflation results from the money supply growing faster than real GDP. When governments attempt to raise revenue by selling large quantities of bonds to the central bank, the money supply will increase rapidly, resulting in high rates of inflation.

MyEconLab   Visit **www.myeconlab.com** to complete these exercises online and get instant feedback.

Review Questions

5.1 What is the quantity theory of money? What explanation does the quantity theory provide for inflation?

5.2 Is the quantity theory of money better able to explain the inflation rate in the long run or in the short run? Briefly explain.

5.3 What is hyperinflation? Why do governments sometimes allow it to occur?

Problems and Applications

5.4 If the money supply is growing at a rate of 6 percent per year, real GDP is growing at a rate of 3 percent per year, and velocity is constant, what will the inflation rate be? If velocity is increasing 1 percent per year instead of remaining constant, what will the inflation rate be?

5.5 If velocity does not change when the money supply of a country increases, will nominal GDP definitely increase? Will real GDP definitely increase? Briefly explain.

5.6 During the years from 2010 to 2014, the average annual growth rate of M1 was 12.7 percent, while the inflation rate as measured by the GDP deflator averaged 1.8 percent. Are these values consistent with the quantity equation? If you would need additional information to answer, state what the information is. Are the values consistent with the quantity theory of money? Briefly explain.
Source: Data from the Federal Reserve Bank of St. Louis.

5.7 In an article in the *American Free Press*, Professor Peter Spencer of York University in England is quoted as saying: "This printing of money 'will keep the [deflation] wolf from the door.'" In the same article, Ambrose Evans-Pritchard, a writer for the London-based newspaper *The Telegraph*, is quoted as saying, "Deflation has … insidious traits. It causes shoppers to hold back. Once this psychology gains

a grip, it can gradually set off a self-feeding spiral that is hard to stop."
  a. What is price deflation?
  b. What does Professor Spencer mean by the statement, "This printing of money 'will keep the [deflation] wolf from the door'"?
  c. Why would deflation cause "shoppers to hold back," and what does Evans-Pritchard mean when he says, "Once this psychology gains a grip, it can gradually set off a self-feeding spiral that is hard to stop"?
Source: Doug French, "We Should Celebrate Price Deflation," *American Free Press*, November 17, 2008.

5.8 During the Civil War, the Confederate States of America printed large amounts of its own currency—Confederate dollars—to fund the war. By the end of the war, the Confederate government had printed nearly 1.5 billion paper dollars. How would such a large quantity of Confederate dollars have affected the value of the Confederate currency? With the war drawing to an end, would Southerners have been as willing to use and accept Confederate dollars? How else could they have bought and sold goods?
Source: Federal Reserve Bank of Richmond, "Textual Transcript of Confederate Currency."

5.9 An article in the *Economist* notes that the government of Venezuela running a large budget deficit "caused the money supply almost to quadruple in two years and led to the world's highest inflation rate, of over 60% a year."
  a. Why would running a large budget deficit cause the money supply in Venezuela to increase so rapidly?
  b. If the money supply increased by 150 percent per year (or 300 percent over two years) while the inflation rate was 60 percent, what must have happened to velocity in Venezuela during this period?
Source: "Of Oil and Coconut Water," *Economist*, September 20, 2014.

5.10 **(Related to the** Making the Connection **on page 326)** During the German hyperinflation of the 1920s, many households and firms in Germany were hurt economically. Do you think any groups in Germany benefited from the hyperinflation? Briefly explain.

Real-Time Data Exercises

D8.1 **(The components of M1)** Go to the Web site of the Federal Reserve Bank of St. Louis (FRED) (research.stlouisfed.org/fred2/) and find the most recent values for the following four variables: (1) M1 Money Stock (M1), (2) the Currency Component of M1 (CURRENCY), (3) Total Checkable Deposits (TCD), and (4) Travelers Checks Outstanding (WTCSL). Which of the components of M1 is the largest? Which is the smallest?

D8.2 **(Calculating M1 from data on M2)** Go to the Web site of the Federal Reserve Bank of St. Louis (FRED) (research.stlouisfed.org/fred2/) and find the most recent values for the following four variables: (1) M2 Money Stock (M2), (2) the Total Savings Deposits at all Depository Institutions (SAVINGS), (3) Retail Money Funds (WRMFSL), and (4) Small Time Deposits – Total (WSMTIME).

a. Using these data, calculate the value of M1.
b. What are Retail Money Funds? What percentage of M2 are they?
c. If households were to shift funds from savings accounts to checking accounts, what would happen to the values of M1 and M2?

D8.3 **(The relationship between M1 and M2)** Go to the Web site of the Federal Reserve Bank of St. Louis (FRED) (research. stlouisfed.org/fred2/) and find the most recent monthly values and values from the same month 5 years and 10 years earlier for the M1 Money Stock (M1SL) and the M2 Money Stock (M2SL).
a. Using these data, calculate M1 as a proportion of M2 for each of the years.
b. Explain whether this proportion has increased, decreased, or remained the same over time. Can you think of an explanation for any changes you observe?

D8.4 **(The equation of exchange)** Go to the Web site of the Federal Reserve Bank of St. Louis (FRED) (research.stlouisfed. org/fred2/) and find the most recent values and values for the same quarter in 1985 for the following three variables: (1) Nominal Gross Domestic Product (GDP), (2) the Velocity of M1 Money Stock (M1V), and (3) the Velocity of M2 Money Stock (M2V).
a. Using these data, calculate M1 and M2 for both periods.
b. Describe how M1 velocity and M2 velocity differ in the two quarters.

D8.5 **(Applying the equation of exchange)** Go to the Web site of the Federal Reserve Bank of St. Louis (FRED) (research. stlouisfed.org/fred2/) and find the most recent values and values from the same quarter 10 years earlier for the following three variables: (1) Real Gross Domestic Product (GDPC1), (2) the GDP Price Deflator (GDPDEF), and (3) the M2 Money Stock (M2SL).
a. Using these data, calculate the average annual rate of change in both real GDP and M2 over this 10-year period.
b. If we assume that velocity was constant during this period, what was the average annual inflation rate?
c. Using the GDP Price Deflator data, calculate the average annual inflation rate over this 10-year period.
d. Use your answers to parts (b) and (c) to discuss what must have happened to velocity during this period.

D8.6 **(Applying the equation of exchange)** Go to the Web site of the Federal Reserve Bank of St. Louis (FRED) (research. stlouisfed.org/fred2/) and find the most recent value for Real Gross Domestic Product (GDPC1) and the value from the same quarter eight years in the future for Real Potential Gross Domestic Product (GDPPOT).
a. Using these data, calculate the average annual rate of growth in real GDP over this eight-year period, assuming that real GDP equals potential GDP in the quarter that is eight years in the future.
b. If the velocity of money is constant during this eight-year period, what will the growth rate of M1 have to be if the annual inflation rate averages 2 percent? Briefly explain.
c. Suppose that M1 grows at this rate, but the actual inflation over this period averages more than 2 percent. What can you conclude about velocity during this period?

Module Outline and Learning Objectives

Why Would a Bank Pay a Negative Interest Rate?

In 2015, some banks in Europe were in an unusual—and unwelcome—situation: They were receiving negative nominal interest rates on loans. That is, the banks had to make interest payments to borrowers rather than receive interest payments from borrowers. One borrower in Spain boasted, "I'm going to frame my bank statement, which shows that Bankinter is paying me interest on my mortgage. That's financial history." Why would a bank pay someone to borrow money? The answer is that the interest rates on these loans were not fixed but were instead adjusted based on changes in short-term interest rates that depend on the actions of central banks in Europe. When some of these interest rates became negative, banks had to automatically make the interest rates on some of their mortgage loans negative as well.

Central banks, including the U.S. Federal Reserve, had driven interest rates to historically low levels as they tried to pull their economies out of the severe worldwide recession of 2007–2009. In conducting monetary policy, the Fed often concentrates on the federal funds rate, which is the interest rate that banks charge each other on short-term loans. In December 2008, the Fed reduced its target for the federal funds rate to almost zero, and kept it there for nearly seven years.

In the fall of 2015, many businesspeople, policymakers, and economists were focused on predicting when Fed Chair Janet Yellen would raise the target for the federal funds rate and by how much. Does this focus indicate that the Fed chair is more important to the U.S. economy than the president of the United States? Most economists would answer "yes." The president can take actions that affect the economy, but needs the approval of Congress before enacting most polices. In contrast, the structure of the Fed gives the chair substantial control over monetary policy. As a result, the Fed chair can often have greater influence over the economy than the president.

European banks paying negative interest rates on loans is a striking example of how central bank policy can affect businesses. Homebuilders like Toll Brothers and car dealers like Ford that sell durable goods are also directly affected by changes in interest rates because their customers frequently borrow money to buy these goods. Other businesses will be affected indirectly because changes in interest rates cause changes in aggregate demand. Not surprisingly, many businesses watch the Fed carefully for signs of whether interest rates are likely to rise or fall.

In this module, we will study the Federal Reserve and how monetary policy affects GDP, employment, and inflation.

Sources: Patricia Kowsmann and Jeannette Neumann, "Tumbling Interest Rates in Europe Leave Some Banks Owing Money on Loans to Borrowers," *Wall Street Journal*, April 13, 2015; and Min Zeng, "Government Bond Yields Turn Negative," *Wall Street Journal*, January 14, 2015.

Economics in Your Life

Should You Buy a House during a Recession?

Think ahead a few years to when you might be married and maybe even (gasp!) have children. You decide to leave behind years of renting apartments and buy a house, but then you read a *Wall Street Journal* article that states that a majority of economists predict a recession is likely to begin soon. What should you do? Would it be a good time or a bad time to buy a house? As you read this module, try to answer these questions. You can check your answers against those we provide on **page 371** at the end of this module.

I n Module 8, we saw that banks play an important role in providing credit to households and firms and in creating money in the form of checking account deposits. We
also saw that Congress established the Federal Reserve to stabilize the financial system and that the Fed is responsible for managing the money supply. In this module,
we will discuss the Fed's main policy goals. We will also explore how the Federal Reserve
decides which *monetary policy* actions to take to achieve its goals.

 ## What Is Monetary Policy?

8A.1

LEARNING OBJECTIVE: Define monetary policy and describe the Federal
Reserve's monetary policy goals.

In 1913, Congress passed the Federal Reserve Act, creating the Federal Reserve System (the Fed). The main responsibility of the Fed was to make discount loans to
banks to prevent the bank panics we discussed in Module 8. As a result of the Great
Depression of the 1930s, Congress amended the Federal Reserve Act to give the Federal
Reserve's Board of Governors broader responsibility to act "so as to promote effectively the goals of maximum employment, stable prices, and moderate long-term
interest rates."

Since World War II, the Federal Reserve has carried out an active *monetary policy*.
Monetary policy is the actions the Fed takes to manage the money supply and interest
rates to achieve its macroeconomic policy goals.

> **Monetary policy** The actions the
> Federal Reserve takes to manage the
> money supply and interest rates to
> achieve macroeconomic policy goals.

The Goals of Monetary Policy

The Fed has four main *monetary policy goals* that are intended to promote a well-
functioning economy:

1. Price stability
2. High employment
3. Stability of financial markets and institutions
4. Economic growth

We briefly consider each of these goals.

Price Stability Rising prices reduce the usefulness of money as a medium of
exchange and a store of value. Especially after inflation rose dramatically and unexpectedly during the 1970s, policymakers in most industrial countries have had price
stability as a key policy goal. Figure 8A.1 shows that from the early 1950s until 1968,
the inflation rate in the United States remained below 4 percent per year. Inflation rose
above 10 percent for several years in the late 1970s and early 1980s. After 1992, the
inflation rate has usually been below 4 percent. The 2007–2009 recession caused several months of deflation—a falling price level—during early 2009, and the slowness of
the recovery from the recession resulted in three months of deflation during early 2015.

The inflation rates during the years 1979–1981 were the highest the United States
has ever experienced during peacetime. When Paul Volcker became chairman of the
Federal Reserve's Board of Governors in August 1979, he made fighting inflation his
top policy goal. Later Fed chairs continued to focus on inflation, arguing that if inflation
is low over the long run, the price system will do a better job of efficiently allocating
resources, and the Fed will have the flexibility it needs to increase aggregate demand to
fight recessions. Although the severity of the 2007–2009 recession led the Fed to adopt
extraordinary policy measures that we will discuss later in this module, price stability
remains a key policy goal of the Fed.

High Employment In addition to price stability, high employment (or a low rate
of unemployment) is an important monetary policy goal. Unemployed workers and

MyEconLab Real-time data

Figure 8A.1

The Inflation Rate, January 1952–June 2015

For most of the 1950s and 1960s, the inflation rate in the United States was 4 percent or less. During the 1970s, the inflation rate increased, peaking during 1979–1981, when it averaged more than 10 percent. After 1992, the inflation rate was usually less than 4 percent, until increases in oil prices pushed it above 5 percent during the summer of 2008. The effects of the recession caused several months of deflation—a falling price level—during early 2009, and the slowness of the recovery caused three months of deflation in early 2015.

Note: The inflation rate is measured as the percentage change in the consumer price index from the same month in the previous year.

Source: Federal Reserve Bank of St. Louis.

underused factories and office buildings reduce GDP below its potential level. Unemployment can cause workers who lack jobs to suffer financial distress and lower self-esteem. The goal of high employment extends beyond the Fed to other branches of the federal government. At the end of World War II, Congress passed the Employment Act of 1946, which stated that it was the "responsibility of the Federal Government ... to foster and promote ... conditions under which there will be afforded useful employment, for those able, willing, and seeking to work, and to promote maximum employment, production, and purchasing power." Because price stability and high employment are explicitly mentioned in the Employment Act, it is sometimes said that the Fed has a *dual mandate* to attain these two goals.

Stability of Financial Markets and Institutions   Firms often need to borrow funds as they design, develop, produce, and market their products. Savers look to financial investments to increase the value of their savings as they prepare to buy homes, pay for the educations of their children, and provide for their retirement. The Fed promotes the stability of financial markets and institutions so that an efficient flow of funds from savers to borrowers will occur. As we saw in Module 8, the financial crisis of 2007–2009 brought the issue of stability in financial markets to the forefront.

The financial crisis was similar to the banking crises that led Congress to create the Federal Reserve System in 1913. A key difference is that while earlier banking crises affected commercial banks, the events of 2007–2009 also affected investment banks and other financial firms in the *shadow banking system*. Investment banks, money market mutual funds, and other financial firms can be subject to *liquidity problems* because they often borrow short term—sometimes as short as overnight—and invest the funds in long-term securities. Just as commercial banks can experience a crisis if depositors begin to withdraw funds, investment banks and other financial firms can experience a crisis if investors stop providing them with short-term loans. In 2008, the Fed took several steps to ease the liquidity problems of these financial firms because the Fed believed these problems were increasing the severity of the recession. In Section 8A, we will discuss in more detail the new policies the Fed enacted to help deal with the financial crisis.

Economic Growth   We discussed in Module 3A the importance of economic growth to raising living standards. Policymakers aim to encourage *stable* economic growth, which allows households and firms to plan accurately and encourages firms to engage in the investment that is needed to sustain growth. Policy can spur economic growth by providing incentives for saving to ensure a large pool of investment funds, as well as by providing direct incentives for business investment. Congress and the president, however, may be better able to increase saving and investment than is the Fed. For example, Congress and the president can change the tax laws to increase the return to saving and investing. In fact, some economists question whether the Fed can play a role in promoting economic growth beyond attempting to meet its goals of price stability, high employment, and financial stability.

In the next section, we will look at how the Fed attempts to achieve its monetary policy goals. Although the Fed has multiple monetary policy goals, during most periods, its most important goals have been price stability and high employment. The turmoil in financial markets that began in 2007 led the Fed to put new emphasis on the goal of financial market stability.

MyEconLab Study Plan MyEconLab Concept Check

8A.2 The Money Market and the Fed's Choice of Monetary Policy Targets

LEARNING OBJECTIVE: Describe the Federal Reserve's monetary policy targets and explain how expansionary and contractionary monetary policies affect the interest rate.

The Fed uses its policy tools to achieve its monetary policy goals. Recall that the Fed's policy tools are open market operations, discount policy—making discount loans to banks and changing the discount rate it charges on those loans—and changes in reserve requirements. At times, the Fed encounters conflicts among its policy goals. For example, as we will discuss later in this module, the Fed can raise interest rates to reduce the inflation rate. But higher interest rates typically reduce household and firm spending, which may result in slower growth and higher unemployment. So, a policy that is intended to achieve one monetary policy goal, such as reducing inflation, may make it more difficult to achieve another policy goal, such as high employment.

Monetary Policy Targets

The Fed tries to keep both the unemployment and inflation rates low, but it can't affect either of these economic variables directly. The Fed cannot tell firms how many people to employ or what prices to charge for their products. Instead, the Fed uses variables, called *monetary policy targets*, that it can affect directly and that, in turn, affect variables, such as real GDP, employment, and the price level, that are closely related to the Fed's policy goals. The two main monetary policy targets are the money supply and the interest rate. As we will see, the Fed typically uses the interest rate as its policy target.

Bear in mind that while the Fed has typically used the money supply and the interest rate as its targets, these targets were not central to the Fed's policy decisions during the recession of 2007–2009. As we will discuss in Section 8A.6, because U.S. financial markets suffered a degree of disruption not seen since the Great Depression of the 1930s, the Fed was forced to develop new policy tools. However, it is still important to have a good grasp of how the Fed carries out policy during normal times.

MyEconLab Concept Check

The Demand for Money

The Fed's two monetary policy targets are related. To understand this relationship, we first need to examine the *money market*, which brings together the demand and supply for money. Figure 8A.2 shows the demand curve for money. The interest rate is on the vertical axis, and the quantity of money is on the horizontal axis. Here we are using the M1 definition of money, which equals currency plus checking account deposits. Notice that the demand curve for money is downward sloping.

To understand why the demand curve for money is downward sloping, consider that households and firms have a choice between holding money and holding other

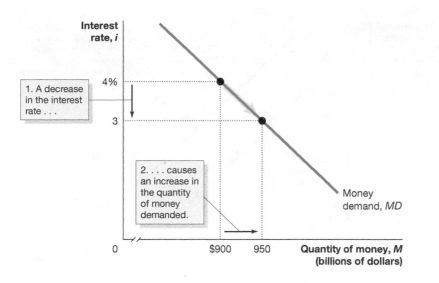

Figure 8A.2

The Demand for Money

The money demand curve slopes downward because a lower interest rate causes households and firms to switch from financial assets such as U.S. Treasury bills to money. All other things being equal, a fall in the interest rate from 4 percent to 3 percent will increase the quantity of money demanded from $900 billion to $950 billion. An increase in the interest rate will decrease the quantity of money demanded.

financial assets, such as U.S. Treasury bills. In making the choice, households and firms take into account that:

- Money has one particularly desirable characteristic: You can use it to buy goods, services, or financial assets.
- Money also has one undesirable characteristic: It earns either a zero interest rate or a very low interest rate.

The currency in your wallet earns no interest, and the money in your checking account earns either no interest or very little interest. Alternatives to money, such as U.S. Treasury bills, pay interest but have to be sold if you want to use the funds to buy something. When interest rates rise on financial assets such as U.S. Treasury bills, the amount of interest that households and firms lose by holding money increases. When interest rates fall, the amount of interest households and firms lose by holding money decreases. Remember that *opportunity cost* is what you have to forgo to engage in an activity. The interest rate is the opportunity cost of holding money.

We now have an explanation for why the demand curve for money slopes downward: When interest rates on Treasury bills and other financial assets are low, the opportunity cost of holding money is low, so the quantity of money demanded by households and firms will be high; when interest rates are high, the opportunity cost of holding money will be high, so the quantity of money demanded will be low. In Figure 8A.2, a decrease in the interest rate from 4 percent to 3 percent causes the quantity of money demanded by households and firms to rise from $900 billion to $950 billion.

Shifts in the Money Demand Curve

The demand curve for a good is drawn holding constant all variables, other than the price, that affect the willingness of consumers to buy the good. Changes in variables other than the price cause the demand curve to shift. Similarly, the demand curve for money is drawn holding constant all variables, other than the interest rate, that affect the willingness of households and firms to hold money. Changes in variables other than the interest rate cause the demand curve to shift. The two most important variables that cause the money demand curve to shift are real GDP and the price level.

Figure 8A.3 illustrates shifts in the money demand curve. An increase in real GDP means that the amount of buying and selling of goods and services will increase. This additional buying and selling increases the demand for money as a medium of exchange, so the quantity of money households and firms want to hold increases at each interest rate, shifting the money demand curve to the right. A decrease in real GDP

Figure 8A.3

Shifts in the Money Demand Curve

Changes in real GDP or the price level cause the money demand curve to shift. An increase in real GDP or an increase in the price level will cause the money demand curve to shift to the right from MD_1 to MD_2. A decrease in real GDP or a decrease in the price level will cause the money demand curve to shift to the left from MD_1 to MD_3.

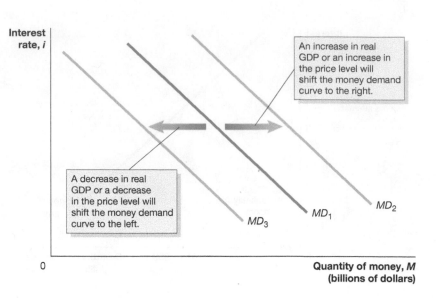

An increase in real GDP or an increase in the price level will shift the money demand curve to the right.

A decrease in real GDP or a decrease in the price level will shift the money demand curve to the left.

decreases the quantity of money demanded at each interest rate, shifting the money demand curve to the left. A higher price level increases the quantity of money required for a given amount of buying and selling. Eighty years ago, for example, when the price level was much lower and someone could purchase a new car for $500 and a salary of $30 per week was typical for someone in the middle class, the quantity of money demanded by households and firms was much lower than today, even adjusting for the effect of the lower real GDP and smaller population of those years. An increase in the price level increases the quantity of money demanded at each interest rate, shifting the money demand curve to the right. A decrease in the price level decreases the quantity of money demanded at each interest rate, shifting the money demand curve to the left.

How the Fed Manages the Money Supply: A Quick Review

Having discussed money demand, we now turn to money supply. In Module 8, we saw how the Federal Reserve manages the money supply. Eight times per year, the Federal Open Market Committee (FOMC) meets in Washington, DC. If the FOMC decides to increase the money supply, it orders the trading desk at the Federal Reserve Bank of New York to purchase U.S. Treasury securities. The sellers of these Treasury securities deposit the funds they receive from the Fed in banks, which increases bank reserves. Typically, banks loan out most of these reserves, which creates new checking account deposits and expands the money supply. If the FOMC decides to decrease the money supply, it orders the trading desk to sell Treasury securities, which decreases bank reserves and contracts the money supply.

Equilibrium in the Money Market

In Figure 8A.4, we include both the money demand and money supply curves. We can use this figure to see how the Fed affects both the money supply and the interest rate. For simplicity, we assume that the Federal Reserve is able to completely control the money supply. With this assumption, the money supply curve is a vertical line, and changes in the interest rate have no effect on the quantity of money supplied. Just as with other markets, equilibrium in the *money market* occurs where the money demand curve crosses the money supply curve. If the Fed increases the money supply, the money supply curve will shift to the right, and the equilibrium interest rate will fall. In Figure 8A.4, when the Fed increases the money supply from $900 billion to $950 billion, the money supply curve shifts to the right from MS_1 to MS_2, and the equilibrium interest rate falls from 4 percent to 3 percent.

In the money market, the adjustment from one equilibrium to another equilibrium is different from the adjustment in the market for a good. In Figure 8A.4, the money

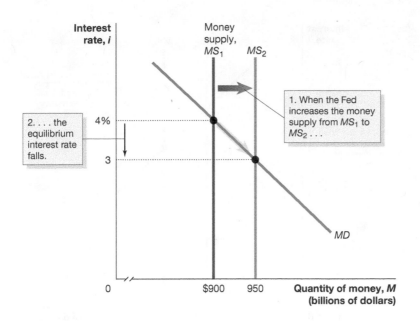

Figure 8A.4

The Effect on the Interest Rate When the Fed Increases the Money Supply

When the Fed increases the money supply, households and firms will initially hold more money than they want, relative to other financial assets. Households and firms use the money they don't want to hold to buy Treasury bills and make deposits in interest-paying bank accounts. This increase in demand allows banks and sellers of Treasury bills and similar securities to offer lower interest rates. Eventually, interest rates will fall enough that households and firms will be willing to hold the additional money the Fed has created. In the figure, an increase in the money supply from $900 billion to $950 billion causes the money supply curve to shift to the right, from MS_1 to MS_2, and causes the equilibrium interest rate to fall from 4 percent to 3 percent.

market is initially in equilibrium, with an interest rate of 4 percent and a money supply of $900 billion. When the Fed increases the money supply by $50 billion, households and firms have more money than they want to hold at an interest rate of 4 percent. What do households and firms do with the extra $50 billion? They are most likely to use the money to buy short-term financial assets, such as Treasury bills, or to deposit the money in interest-paying bank accounts, such as certificates of deposit. This increase in demand for interest-paying bank accounts and short-term financial assets allows banks to offer lower interest rates on certificates of deposit, and it allows sellers of Treasury bills and similar assets to also offer lower interest rates. As the interest rates on certificates of deposit, Treasury bills, and other short-term assets fall, the opportunity cost of holding money also falls. The result is a movement down the money demand curve. Eventually the interest rate falls enough that households and firms are willing to hold the additional $50 billion worth of money the Fed has created, and the money market will be back in equilibrium. To summarize: *When the Fed increases the money supply, the short-term interest rate must fall until it reaches a level at which households and firms are willing to hold the additional money.*

Figure 8A.5 shows what happens when the Fed decreases the money supply. The money market is initially in equilibrium, at an interest rate of 4 percent and a money supply of $900 billion. If the Fed decreases the money supply to $850 billion, households and firms will be holding less money than they would like, relative to other financial assets, at an interest rate of 4 percent. To increase their money holdings, they will sell Treasury bills and other short-term financial assets and withdraw funds from certificates of deposit and other interest-paying bank accounts. Banks will have to offer higher interest rates to retain depositors, and sellers of Treasury bills and similar securities will have to offer higher interest rates to find buyers. Rising short-term interest rates increase the opportunity cost of holding money, causing a movement up the money demand curve. Equilibrium is restored at an interest rate of 5 percent.

A Tale of Two Interest Rates

We have discussed the loanable funds model of the interest rate. In that model, the equilibrium interest rate is determined by the demand and supply for loanable funds. So, we have two models of the interest rate:

1. The loanable funds model is concerned with the *long-term real rate of interest*, which is the interest rate that is most relevant when savers consider purchasing a long-term financial security such as a corporate bond. It is also the rate of interest that is most

Figure 8A.5

The Effect on the Interest Rate When the Fed Decreases the Money Supply

When the Fed decreases the money supply, households and firms will initially hold less money than they want, relative to other financial assets. Households and firms will sell Treasury bills and other financial assets and withdraw money from interest-paying bank accounts. These actions will increase interest rates. Interest rates will rise to the point at which households and firms will be willing to hold the smaller amount of money that results from the Fed's actions. In the figure, a reduction in the money supply from $900 billion to $850 billion causes the money supply curve to shift to the left, from MS_1 to MS_2, and causes the equilibrium interest rate to rise from 4 percent to 5 percent.

relevant to firms that are borrowing to finance long-term investment projects such as new factories or office buildings, or to households that are taking out mortgage loans to buy new homes.

2. The money market model is concerned with the *short-term nominal rate of interest*. When analyzing monetary policy, economists focus on the short-term nominal interest rate because it is the interest rate most affected by increases and decreases in the money supply.

Often—but not always—there is a close connection between movements in the short-term nominal interest rate and movements in the long-term real interest rate. So, when the Fed takes actions to increase the short-term nominal interest rate, usually the long-term real interest rate also increases. In other words, as we will discuss in the next section, when the interest rate on Treasury bills rises, the real interest rate on mortgage loans usually also rises, although sometimes only after a delay. MyEconLab Concept Check

Choosing a Monetary Policy Target

As we have seen, the Fed uses monetary policy targets to affect economic variables, such as real GDP or the price level, that are closely related to the Fed's policy goals. The Fed can use either the money supply or the interest rate as its monetary policy target. As Figure 8A.5 shows, the Fed is capable of affecting both. The Fed has generally focused on the interest rate rather than on the money supply. In 1980, Congress began allowing banks to pay interest on checking accounts. At the same time, money market mutual funds were becoming more popular with small savers as a way to earn higher interest rates than banks offered. As a result of these developments, some economists argued that the Fed should focus less on M1 than on M2. They argued that the relationship between M2 and inflation and changes in GDP was more stable than the relationship between M1 and these variables. But even the relationship between M2 and other key economic variables broke down in the early 1990s. In July 1993, then Fed Chairman Alan Greenspan informed the U.S. Congress that the Fed would cease using M1 or M2 targets to guide the conduct of monetary policy. The Fed has correspondingly increased its reliance on interest rate targets.

There are many different interest rates in the economy. For purposes of monetary policy, the Fed has targeted the interest rate known as the *federal funds rate*. In the next section, we will discuss the federal funds rate before examining how targeting the interest rate can help the Fed achieve its monetary policy goals. MyEconLab Concept Check

The Importance of the Federal Funds Rate

Recall that every bank must keep 10 percent of its checking account deposits above a certain threshold amount as reserves, either as currency held in the bank or as deposits with the Fed (see Module 8). The Fed pays banks only a low interest rate on their reserve deposits, so banks normally have an incentive to invest reserves above the 10 percent minimum rather than leave these funds with the Fed. During the financial crisis, bank reserves soared as banks attempted to meet an increase in deposit withdrawals and as they became reluctant to lend to any borrowers except those with flawless credit histories. Banks continued to hold large reserve deposits for several years following the end of the financial crisis. These conditions were very unusual, however. In normal times, banks keep few excess reserves, and when they need additional reserves, they borrow in the *federal funds market* from banks that have reserves available. The **federal funds rate** is the interest rate banks charge each other on loans in the federal funds market. The loans are usually very short term, often just overnight.

Federal funds rate The interest rate banks charge each other for overnight loans.

Despite the name, the Fed does not actually set the federal funds rate. Instead, the rate is determined by the demand for and supply of reserves. Because the Fed can increase and decrease the supply of bank reserves through open market operations, it can set a *target* for the federal funds rate and usually come very close to hitting it. The FOMC announces a target for the federal funds rate after each meeting. In Figure 8A.6, the orange line shows the Fed's targets for the federal funds rate since 2000. The jagged green line represents the actual federal funds rate on a weekly basis. The figure shows the rapid declines in the target for the federal funds rate beginning in September 2007, as the Fed responded to the start of the financial crisis. In December 2008, the Fed announced a range of 0 to 0.25 percent as its target. The actual federal funds rate fluctuated between 0.06 and 0.23 percent. These very low federal funds rates reflect the severity of the financial crisis.

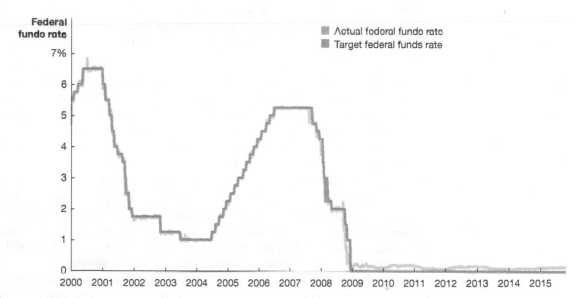

Figure 8A.6   Federal Funds Rate Targeting, January 2000–October 2015

The Fed does not set the federal funds rate. However, the Fed's ability to increase or decrease bank reserves quickly through open market operations keeps the actual federal funds rate close to the Fed's target rate. The orange line is the Fed's target for the federal funds rate, and the jagged green line represents the actual value for the federal funds rate on a weekly basis.

Note: The federal funds target for the period after December 2008 was 0 to 0.25 percent through October 2015.

Source: Board of Governors of the Federal Reserve System.

Because only banks can borrow or lend in the federal funds market, the federal funds rate is not directly relevant for households and firms. However, changes in the federal funds rate usually result in changes in interest rates on both short-term financial assets, such as Treasury bills, and long-term financial assets, such as corporate bonds and mortgages. A change in the federal funds rate has a greater effect on short-term interest rates than on long-term interest rates, and its effect on long-term interest rates may occur only after a lag in time. Although a majority of economists support the Fed's choice of the interest rate as its monetary policy target, some economists believe the Fed should concentrate on the money supply instead. We will discuss these views in Section 8A.5.

MyEconLab Study Plan   MyEconLab Concept Check

 ## 8A.3 Monetary Policy and Economic Activity

LEARNING OBJECTIVE: Use aggregate demand and aggregate supply graphs to show the effects of monetary policy on real GDP and the price level.

The Fed uses the federal funds rate as a monetary policy target because it controls this interest rate through open market operations and because it believes that changes in the federal funds rate will ultimately affect economic variables that are related to its monetary policy goals. It is important to consider again the distinction between the nominal interest rate and the real interest rate. Recall that we calculate the real interest rate by subtracting the inflation rate from the nominal interest rate. Ultimately, the ability of the Fed to use monetary policy to affect economic variables such as real GDP depends on its ability to affect long-term real interest rates, such as the real interest rates on mortgages and corporate bonds. Because the federal funds rate is a short-term nominal interest rate, the Fed sometimes has difficulty affecting long-term real interest rates. Nevertheless, for purposes of the following discussion, we will assume that the Fed is able to use open market operations to affect long-term real interest rates.

How Interest Rates Affect Aggregate Demand

Changes in interest rates affect *aggregate demand*, which is the total level of spending in the economy. Recall that aggregate demand has four components: consumption, investment, government purchases, and net exports. Changes in interest rates will not affect government purchases, but they will affect the other three components of aggregate demand in the following ways:

- **Consumption.**   Many households finance purchases of consumer durables, such as automobiles and furniture, by borrowing. Lower interest payments on loans increase household spending on consumer durables. Higher interest rates reduce household spending on consumer durables. Lower interest rates also reduce the return to saving, leading households to save less and spend more. Higher interest rates increase the return to saving, leading households to save more and spend less.

- **Investment.**   Firms finance most of their spending on machinery, equipment, and factories out of their profits or by borrowing. Firms borrow either in financial markets by issuing corporate bonds or by obtaining loans from banks. Higher interest rates on corporate bonds or on bank loans make it more expensive for firms to borrow, so they will undertake fewer investment projects. Lower interest rates make it less expensive for firms to borrow, so they will undertake more investment projects. Lower interest rates can also have an effect on stock prices, which can increase firms' investment spending. As interest rates decline, stocks become a more attractive investment relative to bonds. The increase in demand for stocks raises their prices. By issuing additional shares of stock, firms can acquire the funds they need to buy new factories and equipment, so investment increases.

  Spending by households on new homes is also part of investment. When interest rates on mortgage loans rise, the cost of buying new homes rises, and fewer new homes will be purchased. When interest rates on mortgage loans fall, more new homes will be purchased.

- **Net exports.** Recall that net exports is equal to spending by foreign households and firms on goods and services produced in the United States minus spending by U.S. households and firms on goods and services produced in other countries. The value of net exports depends partly on the exchange rate between the U.S. dollar and foreign currencies. When the value of the dollar rises, households and firms in other countries will pay more for goods and services produced in the United States, but U.S. households and firms will pay less for goods and services produced in other countries. As a result, the United States will export less and import more, so net exports will fall. When the value of the dollar falls, net exports will rise. If interest rates in the United States rise relative to interest rates in other countries, investing in U.S. financial assets will become more desirable, causing foreign investors to increase their demand for dollars, which will increase the value of the dollar. As the value of the dollar increases, net exports will fall. If interest rates in the United States decline relative to interest rates in other countries, the value of the dollar will fall, and net exports will rise. MyEconLab Concept Check

The Effects of Monetary Policy on Real GDP and the Price Level

In Modules 4 and 4A, we developed the *aggregate demand and aggregate supply model* to explain fluctuations in real GDP and the price level. In the basic version of the model, we assume that there is no economic growth, so the long-run aggregate supply curve does not shift. In panel (a) of Figure 8A.7, we assume that short-run equilibrium is at point A, where the aggregate demand (AD_1) curve intersects the short-run aggregate supply (SRAS) curve. Real GDP is below potential GDP, as shown by the LRAS curve, so the economy is in a recession, with some firms operating below normal capacity and some workers having been laid off. To reach its goal of high employment, the Fed

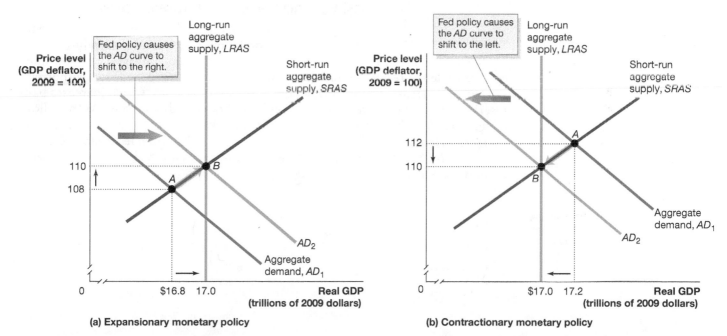

(a) Expansionary monetary policy   (b) Contractionary monetary policy

Figure 8A.7 **Monetary Policy**

In panel (a), short-run equilibrium is at point A, with real GDP of $16.8 trillion and a price level of 108. An expansionary monetary policy causes aggregate demand to shift to the right, from AD_1 to AD_2, increasing real GDP from $16.8 trillion to $17.0 trillion and the price level from 108 to 110 (point B). With real GDP back at its potential level, the Fed can meet its goal of high employment. In panel (b), short-run equilibrium is at point A, with real GDP at $17.2 trillion and the price level at 112. Because real GDP is greater than potential GDP, the economy experiences rising wages and prices. A contractionary monetary policy causes aggregate demand to shift to the left, from AD_1 to AD_2, causing real GDP to decrease from $17.2 trillion to $17.0 trillion and the price level to decrease from 112 to 110 (point B). With real GDP back at its potential level, the Fed can meet its goal of price stability.

Expansionary monetary policy The Federal Reserve's policy of decreasing interest rates to increase real GDP.

carries out an **expansionary monetary policy** by increasing the money supply and decreasing interest rates. Lower interest rates cause an increase in consumption, investment, and net exports, which shifts the aggregate demand curve to the right, from AD_1 to AD_2. Real GDP increases from \$16.8 trillion to potential GDP of \$17.0 trillion, and the price level rises from 108 to 110 (point B). The policy successfully returns real GDP to its potential level. Rising production leads to increasing employment, allowing the Fed to achieve its goal of high employment.

In panel (b) of Figure 8A.7, short-run equilibrium is at point A, with real GDP of \$17.2 trillion, which is above potential GDP of \$17.0 trillion. With some firms producing beyond their normal capacity and the unemployment rate being very low, wages and prices are increasing. To reach its goal of price stability, the Fed needs to carry out a **contractionary monetary policy** by decreasing the money supply and increasing interest rates. Higher interest rates cause a decrease in consumption, investment, and net exports, which shifts the aggregate demand curve from AD_1 to AD_2. Real GDP decreases from \$17.2 trillion to \$17.0 trillion, and the price level falls from 112 to 110 (point B). Why would the Fed want to intentionally cause real GDP to decline? Because in the long run, real GDP cannot continue to remain above potential GDP. Attempting to keep real GDP above potential GDP would result in rising inflation. As aggregate demand declines and real GDP returns to its potential level, upward pressure on wages and prices will be reduced, allowing the Fed to achieve its goal of price stability.

Contractionary monetary policy The Federal Reserve's policy of increasing interest rates to reduce inflation.

We can conclude that the Fed can use monetary policy to affect the price level and, in the short run, the level of real GDP, allowing it to attain its policy goals of high employment and price stability.   MyEconLab Concept Check

---

Making the Connection
MyEconLab Video

Too Low for Zero: Central Banks, Quantitative Easing, and Negative Interest Rates

The Fed and central banks around the world responded to the 2007–2009 recession by pushing overnight lending rates—the federal funds rate in the United States—to nearly zero. But these very low interest rates failed to result in rapid economic recovery. To lower the federal funds rate, the Fed buys Treasury bills through open market purchases, which increases bank reserves. Banks then lend out these reserves to households and firm. As the following graph shows, however, in late 2008, many banks began piling up excess reserves rather than lending out the funds. Total bank reserves had been less than \$50 billion in August 2008, but as the financial crisis became more severe, total reserves soared to more than \$900 billion by May 2009.

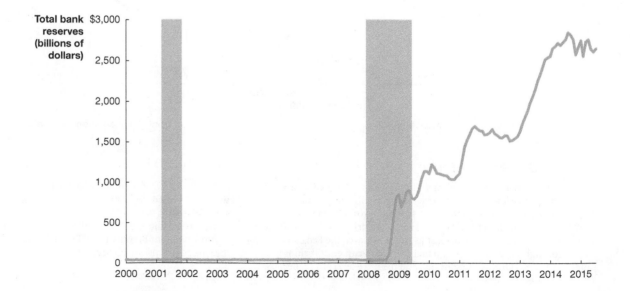

The increase in bank reserves was partly due to the Fed having received authorization from Congress in October 2008 to start paying interest of 0.25 percent on bank reserves held as deposits at the Fed. Primarily, though, the increase in reserves occurred because banks were reluctant to make loans at low interest rates to households and firms whose financial positions had been damaged by the recession. Some economists argued that the Fed was facing a situation known as a *liquidity trap*, in which short-term interest rates are pushed to zero, leaving the central bank unable to lower them further. Liquidity traps may also have occurred in the United States during the 1930s and in Japan during the 1990s.

To try to spur economic recovery, the Fed, the European Central Bank, the Bank of Japan, and other central banks turned to a policy of *quantitative easing* (QE), which involves buying securities beyond the short-term government securities that are usually involved in open market operations. The Fed began purchasing 10-year U.S. Treasury notes to push their interest rates lower. Interest rates on home mortgage loans typically move closely with interest rates on 10-year Treasury notes. The Fed also purchased certain *mortgage-backed securities*. The Fed's objective was to keep interest rates on mortgages low and to keep funds flowing into the mortgage market to help stimulate demand for housing.

The Fed's first round of QE began in November 2008. Because the U.S. economy recovered more slowly than expected, the Fed engaged in two additional rounds of QE before ending the program in October 2014. The use of QE by the Fed and other central banks, combined with very low inflation rates and the slow recovery from the 2007–2009 recession, led to historically low interest rates in most countries. The graph below shows interest rates on 10-year U.S. Treasury notes and on the corresponding German government bonds.

Nominal interest rates on government bonds were so low that real interest rates were nearly zero or even negative. For example, in April 2015, the nominal interest rate on 10-year German government bonds was 0.12%, while the inflation rate in Germany was 0.5%. Even more remarkable, in early 2015, the German government sold 5-year bonds with a *nominal* interest rate of −0.08%. This negative interest rate meant that investors were willing to pay the German government to keep their money for five years. Why would an investor accept a negative interest rate? With interest rates on many corporate bonds and on bank deposits being at very low levels, investors did not believe that the interest rates were sufficiently high to compensate for the default risk on those bonds and deposits. So, investors were willing to receive a negative nominal interest rate from the German government because they believed there was no chance that the government would default. As we saw in the module opener, some banks tie the interest rates they charge on loans to the interest rates on government bonds. The result of determining loan interest rates in this way was that banks like the Spanish bank Bankinter had to make interest payments *to* borrowers.

Economists remain divided over whether central banks had succeeded in using QE to expand the growth of employment and output. Economists who were skeptical of QE pointed to negative nominal interest rates as an example of the distortions in the financial system that had resulted from these policies. Later in this module, we will consider other new programs the Fed put in place to deal with the recession of 2007–2009 and the slow recovery that followed, as its traditional focus on lowering the federal funds rate to stimulate the economy proved ineffective.

Sources: Emese Bartha and Ben Edwards, "Germany Sells Five-Year Debt at Negative Yield for First Time on Record," *Wall Street Journal*, February 25, 2015; and data from the Federal Reserve Bank of St. Louis and the Organization for Economic Co-operation and Development.

MyEconLab Study Plan   **Your Turn:** Test your understanding by doing related problems 3.9 and 3.10 on page 374 at the end of this module.

Can the Fed Eliminate Recessions?

Panel (a) of Figure 8A.7 on page 347 shows a completely successful expansionary monetary policy that shifts the *AD* curve to bring real GDP back to potential GDP. In practice, this ideal is very difficult for the Fed to achieve, as the length and severity of the 2007–2009 recession illustrates. In practice, the best the Fed can do is keep recessions shorter and milder than they would otherwise be.

If the Fed is to succeed in offsetting the effects of the business cycle, it needs to quickly recognize the need for a change in monetary policy. If the Fed is late in recognizing that a recession has begun or that the inflation rate is increasing, it may not be able to implement a new policy quickly enough to do much good. There is typically a *lag*, or delay, between a policy change and its effect on real GDP, employment, inflation, and other economic variables. Nobel Laureate Milton Friedman famously described the lags for monetary policy as "long and variable," which means that it can take months or years for changes in monetary policy to affect real GDP and inflation and that the lags vary based on economic circumstances. Once the Fed reduces the target federal funds rate, it takes time for the interest rates that affect firm and household behavior to also decline. Then it takes time for firms to identify newly profitable investment projects, obtain loans from banks or arrange to sell bonds, and start spending the borrowed funds. Similarly, it takes time for families to respond to lower mortgage interest rates by buying houses and for homebuilders to begin building the houses. As a result, the full effect of a change in monetary policy is typically spread out over several years.

Implementing a policy too late may actually destabilize the economy. To see why, consider Figure 8A.8. The straight line represents the long-run growth trend in real GDP in the United States. On average, real GDP grows about 3 percent per year. The actual path of real GDP differs from the underlying trend because of the business cycle, which is shown by the red curved line. As we saw in Module 3 & 3A, the actual business cycle is more irregular than the stylized cycle shown here.

Suppose that a recession begins in August 2018. Because it takes months for economic statistics to be gathered by the Commerce Department, the Census Bureau, the Bureau of Labor Statistics, and the Fed itself, there is a lag before the Fed recognizes that a recession has begun. Finally, in June 2019, the FOMC concludes that the economy is in recession and begins an expansionary monetary policy. As it turns out, June 2019 is actually the trough of the recession, meaning that the recession has already ended, and an expansion has begun. In these circumstances, the Fed's expansionary policy is not needed to end the recession. The increase in aggregate demand caused by the Fed's lowering interest rates is likely to push the economy beyond potential GDP and cause

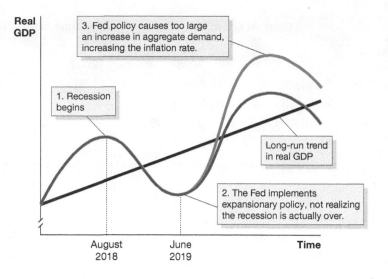

MyEconLab Animation

Figure 8A.8

The Effect of a Poorly Timed Monetary Policy on the Economy

The upward-sloping straight line represents the long-run growth trend in real GDP. The curved red line represents the path real GDP takes because of the business cycle. If the Fed is too late in implementing a change in monetary policy, real GDP will follow the curved blue line. The Fed's expansionary monetary policy results in too great an increase in aggregate demand during the next expansion, which causes an increase in the inflation rate.

a significant acceleration in inflation. Real GDP ends up following the path indicated by the blue curved line. The Fed has inadvertently engaged in a *procyclical policy*, which increases the severity of the business cycle, as opposed to a *countercyclical policy*, which is meant to reduce the severity of the business cycle and which is what the Fed intends to use. As we saw in Module 3 & 3A, the typical recession since 1950 has lasted less than one year, which increases the likelihood that the Fed may accidentally engage in a procyclical policy. Making this mistake is, of course, less likely in a long and severe recession such as the recession of 2007–2009.   MyEconLab Concept Check

Fed Forecasts

Because it can take a long time for a change in monetary policy to affect real GDP, the Fed tries to set policy according to what it forecasts the state of the economy will be in the future, when the policy change actually affects the economy. For example, when the Fed considered raising its target for the federal funds rate in 2015, the lag associated with monetary policy meant that the full effect of the rate increase on the economy would be spread out over several years. In making that increase, the Fed was thinking about the economy's future performance.

For the Fed to succeed in reducing the severity of business cycles, it must often act before a recession or an acceleration of inflation shows up in the economic data. So, good policy requires good economic forecasts based on models that describe accurately how the economy functions. Unfortunately, economic forecasts and models can be unreliable because changes in aggregate demand and short-run aggregate supply can be unpredictable. For example, the forecasts of most economists at the end of 2006 and the beginning of 2007 did not anticipate the severity of the recession that began in December 2007. Only after financial market conditions began to deteriorate rapidly did economists significantly reduce their forecasts of GDP growth in 2008 and 2009.

Table 8A.1 summarizes the Fed's estimates for the growth rate of real GDP for 2007 and 2008 given in its *Monetary Policy Report to Congress*. To keep a recession from starting in 2007, the Fed would have had to change policy before 2007. However, in February 2006, the Fed expected the economy to grow by 3 percent to 4 percent in 2007, so it had little reason to change policy. Similarly, the Fed could have changed policy in an attempt to keep the economy growing in 2008, but it would have had to change policy before 2008, and as late as July 2007, the Fed still expected the economy to grow by 2.5 percent to 3.0 percent in 2008. In fact, real GDP increased by only 1.8 percent in 2007, and it declined by 0.3 percent in 2008. We can conclude that,

Table 8A.1

Fed Forecasts of Real GDP
Growth during 2007 and 2008

Date forecast was made	Forecast Growth Rate		Actual Growth Rate	
	For 2007	For 2008	2007	2008
February 2006	3% to 4%	No forecast	1.8%	−0.3%
May 2006	2.5% to 3.25%	No forecast		
February 2007	2.25% to 3.25%	2.5% to 3.25%		
July 2007	No forecast	2.5% to 3.0%		

Sources: Board of Governors of the Federal Reserve System, *Monetary Policy Report to the Congress*, various dates; and U.S. Bureau of Economic Analysis.

although the Fed could have taken actions that would have at least reduced the severity of the 2007–2009 recession, it could not prevent the recession because it did not see the recession coming.   MyEconLab Concept Check

Making the Connection
MyEconLab Video

Trying to Hit a Moving Target: Making Policy with "Real-Time Data"

The Fed relies on macroeconomic data to formulate monetary policy. One key piece of economic data is GDP, which is calculated quarterly by the Bureau of Economic Analysis (BEA). Unfortunately for Fed policymakers, the GDP data the BEA provides are frequently revised, and the revisions can be large enough that the actual state of the economy can be different from what it at first appeared to be.

The BEA's *advance estimate* of a quarter's GDP is not released until about a month after the quarter has ended. This delay can be a problem for policymakers because it means that they will not receive an estimate of GDP for the period from January through March, for instance, until the end of April. Presenting even more difficulty is the fact that the advance estimate will be subject to a number of revisions. The second estimate of a quarter's GDP is released about two months after the end of the quarter. The third estimate is released about three months after the end of the quarter. Although the BEA used to refer to the third estimate as the "final estimate," in fact, it continues to revise its estimates through the years. The BEA releases its first annual, second annual, and third annual estimates one, two, and three years after the third estimate. And that is not the end: Benchmark revisions occur in later years.

Why are there so many estimates? Because GDP is such a comprehensive measure of output in the economy, it is very time-consuming to collect the necessary data. To provide the advance estimate, the BEA relies on surveys conducted by the Commerce Department of retail sales and manufacturing shipments, as well as data from trade organizations, estimates of government spending, and so on. As time passes, these organizations gather additional data, and the BEA is able to refine its estimates.

Do these revisions to the GDP estimates matter? Sometimes they do, as the following example indicates. At the beginning of 2008, some economists believed that the U.S. economy might be in a recession. The effects of the continuing decline in housing prices were being felt in the financial system, and the unemployment rate was increasing. Members of the Fed's Open Market Committee remained cautiously optimistic, however, forecasting that real GDP would increase about 1.7 percent during the year. The BEA's advance estimate of the first quarter's GDP seemed to confirm that this forecast of slow growth might be accurate by showing an increase in real GDP of 0.6 percent at an annual rate. As the following graph shows, though, that estimate of real GDP growth was revised a number of times over the years, mostly downward.

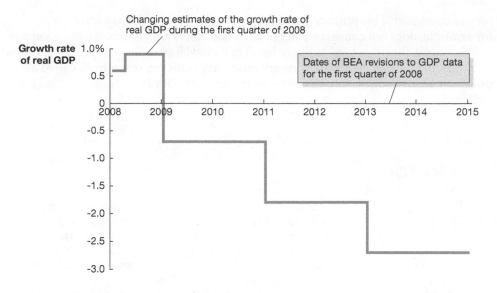

Currently, BEA data indicate that real GDP actually declined by 2.7 percent at an annual rate during the first quarter of 2008. This swing of more than 3 percentage points is a large difference, which changes the picture of what happened during the first quarter of 2008 from one of an economy experiencing slow growth to one of an economy suffering a sharp downturn as it fell into the worst recession since the Great Depression of the 1930s. The National Bureau of Economic Research has since determined that December 2007 was the beginning of the recession of 2007–2009.

This example shows that in addition to the other problems the Federal Reserve encounters in successfully conducting monetary policy, it must make decisions using data that may be subject to substantial revisions.

Sources: Federal Reserve Bank of Philadelphia, "Historical Data Files for the Real-Time Data Set," August 7, 2015; Board of Governors of the Federal Reserve System, "Minutes of the Federal Open Market Committee January 29–30, 2008," February 20, 2008; and Bruce T. Grimm and Teresa Weadock, "Gross Domestic Product: Revisions and Source Data," *Survey of Current Business*, Vol. 86, No. 2, February 2006, pp. 11–15.

Your Turn: Test your understanding by doing related problems 3.11 and 3.12 on page 374 at the end of this module.   MyEconLab Study Plan

A Summary of How Monetary Policy Works

Table 8A.2 compares the steps involved in expansionary and contractionary monetary policies. We need to note an important qualification to this summary. At every point, we should add the phrase "relative to what would have happened without the policy." The table isolates the effect of monetary policy, *holding constant all other factors affecting the variables involved*. In other words, we are invoking the *ceteris*

Table 8A.2   **Expansionary and Contractionary Monetary Policies**

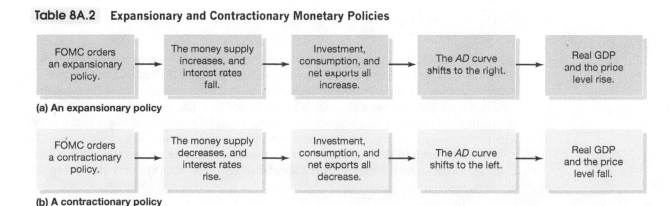

(a) An expansionary policy

(b) A contractionary policy

paribus condition. This point is important because a contractionary monetary policy, for example, does not cause the price level to fall; instead, a contractionary monetary policy causes the price level *to rise by less than it would have without the policy*. One final note on terminology: An expansionary monetary policy is sometimes called a *loose* policy, or an *easy* policy. A contractionary monetary policy is sometimes called a *tight* policy.

MyEconLab Concept Check

Don't Let This Happen to You

Remember That with Monetary Policy, It's the Interest Rates—Not the Money—That Counts

It is tempting to think of monetary policy as working like this: If the Fed wants more spending in the economy, it increases the money supply, and people spend more because they now have more money. If the Fed wants less spending in the economy, it decreases the money supply, and people spend less because they now have less money. In fact, that is *not* how monetary policy works. Remember the important difference between money and income: The Fed increases the money supply by buying Treasury bills. The sellers of the Treasury bills have just exchanged one asset—Treasury bills—for another asset—a check from the Fed; the sellers have *not* increased their income. Even though the money supply is now larger, no one's income has increased, so no one's spending should be affected.

It is only when this increase in the money supply results in lower interest rates that spending is affected. When interest rates are lower, households are more likely to buy new homes and automobiles, and businesses are more likely to buy new factories and warehouses. Lower interest rates also lead to a lower value of the dollar, which lowers the prices of exports and raises the prices of imports, thereby increasing net exports. It isn't the increase in the money supply that has brought about this additional spending, *it's the lower interest rates*. To understand how monetary policy works, and to interpret news reports about the Fed's actions, remember that it is the change in interest rates, not the change in the money supply, that is most important.

MyEconLab Study Plan

Your Turn: Test your understanding by doing related problem 3.13 on page 375 at the end of this module.

MyEconLab Study Plan

8A.4 Monetary Policy in the Dynamic Aggregate Demand and Aggregate Supply Model*

LEARNING OBJECTIVE: Use the dynamic aggregate demand and aggregate supply model to analyze monetary policy.

The overview of monetary policy we just finished contains a key idea: The Fed can use monetary policy to affect aggregate demand, thereby changing the price level and the level of real GDP. The discussion of monetary policy illustrated by Figure 8A.7 on page 347 is simplified, however, because it ignores two important facts about the economy:

1. The economy experiences continuing inflation, with the price level rising every year.
2. The economy experiences long-run growth, with the *LRAS* curve shifting to the right every year.

In Module 4 & 4A, we developed a *dynamic aggregate demand and aggregate supply model* that takes into account these two facts. In this section, we use the dynamic model to gain a more complete understanding of monetary policy. Let's briefly review the dynamic model. Recall that over time, the U.S. labor force and the U.S. capital stock will increase. Technological change will also occur. The result will be an increase in potential GDP, which we show by the long-run aggregate supply curve shifting to the right. These factors will also result in firms supplying more goods and services at any given price level in the short run, which we show by the short-run aggregate supply curve shifting to the

*This section may be omitted without loss of continuity.

right. During most years, the aggregate demand curve will also shift to the right, indicating that aggregate expenditure will be higher at every price level. Aggregate expenditure usually increases for these key reasons:

• As population grows and incomes rise, consumption will increase over time.

• As the economy grows, firms expand capacity, and new firms are established, increasing investment spending.

• An expanding population and an expanding economy require increased government services, such as more police officers and teachers, so government purchases will expand.

The Effects of Monetary Policy on Real GDP and the Price Level: A More Complete Account

During certain periods, *AD* does not increase enough during the year to keep real GDP at potential GDP. This slow growth in aggregate demand may be due to households and firms becoming pessimistic about the future state of the economy, leading them to cut back their spending on consumer durables, houses, and factories. As we have seen, the collapse of the housing bubble and the resulting financial crisis had a negative effect on aggregate demand during the 2007–2009 recession. There are other reasons why aggregate demand might grow slowly: The federal government could decide to balance the budget by cutting back its purchases and raising taxes, or recessions in other countries might cause a decline in U.S. exports. In the hypothetical situation shown in Figure 8A.9, in the first year, equilibrium is at point A, with potential GDP of $17.0 trillion and a price level of 110. In the second year, *LRAS* increases to $17.4 trillion, but *AD* increases only to $AD_{2(\text{without policy})}$, which is not enough to keep real GDP at potential GDP. If the Fed does not intervene, the new short-run equilibrium will occur at $17.3 trillion (point B). The $100 billion gap between this level of real GDP and potential GDP at $LRAS_2$ means that some firms are operating at less than their normal capacity. Incomes and profits will fall, firms will begin to lay off workers, and the unemployment rate will rise.

MyEconLab Animation

Figure 8A.9

An Expansionary Monetary Policy

Initially, equilibrium is at point A, with real GDP of $17.0 trillion and a price level of 110. Without monetary policy, aggregate demand will shift from AD_1 to $AD_{2(\text{without policy})}$, which is not enough to keep the economy at full employment because long-run aggregate supply has shifted from $LRAS_1$ to $LRAS_2$. Short-run equilibrium is at point B, with real GDP of $17.3 trillion and a price level of 112. By lowering interest rates, the Fed increases investment, consumption, and net exports sufficiently to shift aggregate demand to $AD_{2(\text{with policy})}$. Equilibrium will be at point C, with real GDP of $17.4 trillion, which is its full employment level, and a price level of 113. The price level is higher than it would have been if the Fed had not acted to increase spending in the economy.

Economists at the Federal Reserve closely monitor the economy and continually update forecasts of future levels of real GDP and prices. When these economists anticipate that aggregate demand is not growing fast enough to allow the economy to remain at full employment, they present their findings to the FOMC, which decides whether circumstances require a change in monetary policy. For example, suppose that the FOMC meets and considers a forecast from the staff indicating that during the following year, a gap of $100 billion will open between equilibrium real GDP and potential GDP. In other words, the macroeconomic equilibrium illustrated by point B in Figure 8A.9 will occur. The FOMC may then decide to carry out an expansionary monetary policy to lower interest rates to stimulate aggregate demand. The figure shows the results of a successful attempt to do this: AD has shifted to the right, and equilibrium occurs at potential GDP (point C). The Fed will have successfully headed off the falling incomes and rising unemployment that otherwise would have occurred. Bear in mind that we are illustrating a perfectly executed monetary policy that keeps the economy at potential GDP, which is difficult to achieve in practice for reasons discussed in the previous section.

Notice in Figure 8A.9 that the expansionary monetary policy caused the inflation rate to be higher than it would have been. Without the expansionary policy, the price level would have risen from 110 to 112, so the inflation rate for the year would have been 1.8 percent. By shifting the aggregate demand curve, the expansionary policy caused the price level to increase from 112 to 113, raising the inflation rate from 1.8 percent to 2.7 percent.   MyEconLab Concept Check

Using Monetary Policy to Fight Inflation

In addition to using an expansionary monetary policy to reduce the severity of recessions, the Fed can use a contractionary monetary policy to keep aggregate demand from expanding so rapidly that the inflation rate begins to increase. Figure 8A.10 shows the situation during 2005 and 2006, when the Fed faced this possibility. During 2005,

Figure 8A.10

A Contractionary Monetary Policy in 2006

In 2005, equilibrium is at point A, with real GDP equal to potential GDP of $14.2 trillion and a price level of 92.0. From 2005 to 2006, potential GDP increased from $14.2 trillion to $14.6 trillion, as long-run aggregate supply increased from $LRAS_{2005}$ to $LRAS_{2006}$. The Fed raised interest rates because it believed the housing boom was causing aggregate demand to increase too rapidly. Without the increase in interest rates, aggregate demand would have shifted from AD_{2005} to $AD_{2006(without policy)}$, and the new short-run equilibrium would have occurred at point B. Real GDP would have been $14.8 trillion—$200 billion greater than potential GDP—and the price level would have been 96.1. The increase in interest rates resulted in aggregate demand increasing only to $AD_{2006(with policy)}$. Equilibrium occurred at point C, with real GDP of $14.6 trillion, which was equal to potential GDP, and the price level rose only to 94.8.

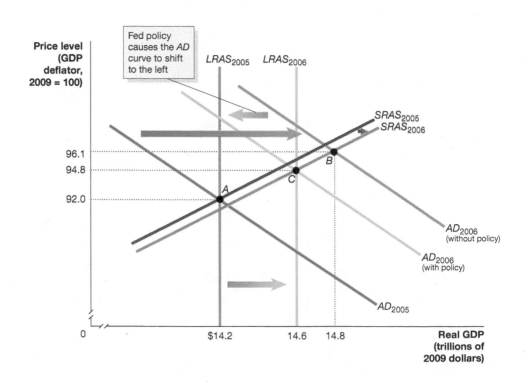

real GDP was equal to potential GDP, but Fed Chair Alan Greenspan and other members of the FOMC were concerned that the continuing boom in the housing market might lead aggregate demand to increase so rapidly that the inflation rate would begin to accelerate. The Fed had been gradually increasing the target for the federal funds rate since mid-2004.

When Ben Bernanke was appointed Fed chair in early 2006, he advocated continued increases in the target for the federal funds rate to slow the growth in aggregate demand. By June 2006, the target for the federal funds rate had been raised to 5.25 percent, from the low target rate of 1 percent that had prevailed from June 2003 to May 2004. The FOMC issues a statement after each meeting that summarizes the committee's views on the current state of the economy and gives some indication of how monetary policy might change in the near future. After its meeting on June 29, 2006, the FOMC included the following remarks in its statement:

> The Federal Open Market Committee decided today to raise its target for the federal funds rate ... to 5-1/4 percent. Recent indicators suggest that economic growth is moderating from its quite strong pace earlier this year, partly reflecting a gradual cooling of the housing market and the lagged effects of increases in ... interest rates. ... Although the moderation in the growth of aggregate demand should help to limit inflation pressures over time, the Committee judges that some inflation risks remain.

The committee kept the target for the federal funds rate constant at 5.25 percent until September 2007, when concern about problems in financial markets led it to cut the target to 4.75 percent. Although it is impossible to know exactly what would have happened during 2006 without the Fed's policy change, Figure 8A.10 presents a plausible scenario. The figure shows that without the Fed's actions to increase interest rates, aggregate demand would have shifted farther to the right, and equilibrium would have occurred at a level of real GDP that was beyond the potential level. The price level would have risen from 92.0 in 2005 to 96.1 in 2006, meaning that the inflation rate would have been 4.5 percent. Because the Fed kept aggregate demand from increasing as much as it otherwise would have, short-run equilibrium occurred at potential GDP, and the price level in 2006 rose to only 94.8, keeping the inflation rate at 3.0 percent.

MyEconLab Concept Check

Solved Problem 8A.4

MyEconLab Interactive Animation

The Effects of Monetary Policy

The hypothetical information in the following table shows what the values for real GDP and the price level will be in 2019 if the Fed does *not* use monetary policy:

Year	Potential GDP	Real GDP	Price Level
2018	$17.9 trillion	$17.9 trillion	114
2019	18.3 trillion	18.1 trillion	116

a. If the Fed wants to keep real GDP at its potential level in 2019, should it use an expansionary policy or a contractionary policy? Should the trading desk buy Treasury bills or sell them?

b. Suppose the Fed's policy is successful in keeping real GDP at its potential level in 2019. State whether each of the following will be higher or lower than if the Fed had taken no action:

   i. Real GDP

   ii. Potential GDP

   iii. The inflation rate

   iv. The unemployment rate

c. Draw an aggregate demand and aggregate supply graph to illustrate your answer. Be sure that your graph contains LRAS curves for 2018 and 2019; SRAS curves for 2018 and 2019; AD curves for 2018 and for 2019, with and without monetary policy action; and equilibrium real GDP and the price level in 2019, with and without policy.

Solving the Problem

Step 1: **Review the module material.** This problem is about the effects of monetary policy on real GDP and the price level, so you may want to review the section "The Effects of Monetary Policy on Real GDP and the Price Level: A More Complete Account," which begins on page 355.

Step 2: **Answer the questions in part (a) by explaining how the Fed can keep real GDP at its potential level.** The information in the table tells us that without monetary policy, the economy will be below potential GDP in 2019. To keep real GDP at its potential level, the Fed must undertake an expansionary policy. To carry out an expansionary policy, the trading desk needs to buy Treasury bills. Buying Treasury bills will increase reserves in the banking system. Banks will increase their loans, which will increase the money supply and lower the interest rate.

Step 3: **Answer part (b) by explaining the effect of the Fed's policy.** If the Fed's policy is successful, real GDP in 2019 will increase from $18.1 trillion, as given in the table, to its potential level of $18.3 trillion. Potential GDP is not affected by monetary policy, so its value will not change. Because the level of real GDP will be higher, the unemployment rate will be lower than it would have been without policy. The expansionary monetary policy shifts the AD curve to the right, so short-run equilibrium will move up the short-run aggregate supply ($SRAS$) curve, and the price level will be higher.

Step 4: **Answer part (c) by drawing the graph.** Your graph should look similar to Figure 8A.9.

Equilibrium in 2018 is at point A, with the AD and $SRAS$ curves intersecting along the $LRAS$ curve. Real GDP is at its potential level of $17.9 trillion, and the price level is 114. Without monetary policy, the AD curve shifts to $AD_{2019(\text{without policy})}$, and short-run equilibrium is at point B. Because potential GDP has increased from $17.9 trillion to $18.3 trillion, real GDP of $18.1 trillion is below the potential level. The price level has increased from 114 to 116. With policy, the AD curve shifts to $AD_{2019(\text{with policy})}$, and equilibrium is at point C. Real GDP is at its potential level of $18.3 trillion. We don't have enough information to be sure of the new equilibrium price level. We do know that it will be higher than 116. The graph shows the price level rising to 118. Therefore, without the Fed's expansionary policy, the inflation rate in 2019 would have been about 1.8 percent. With policy, it will be about 3.5 percent.

Extra Credit: Bear in mind that, in reality, the Fed is unable to use monetary policy to keep real GDP exactly at its potential level, as this problem suggests.

Your Turn: For more practice, do related problems 4.4 and 4.5 on pages 375–376 at the end of this module.

MyEconLab Study Plan

8A.5 A Closer Look at the Fed's Setting of Monetary Policy Targets

LEARNING OBJECTIVE: Describe the Fed's setting of monetary policy targets.

We have seen that in carrying out monetary policy, the Fed changes its target for the federal funds rate depending on the state of the economy. Is the Fed's approach correct? During times when the economy is not experiencing a financial crisis, is using the federal funds rate as a target the best way to conduct monetary policy? If the Fed targets the federal funds rate, how should it decide what the target level should be? In this section, we consider these important issues concerning the Fed's targeting policy.

Should the Fed Target the Money Supply?

Some economists have argued that rather than use an interest rate as its monetary policy target, the Fed should use the money supply. Many of the economists who make this argument belong to a school of thought known as *monetarism*. The leader of the monetarist school was Milton Friedman, who was skeptical that the Fed would be able to correctly time changes in monetary policy.

Friedman and his followers favored replacing *monetary policy* with a *monetary growth rule*. Ordinarily, we expect monetary policy to respond to changing economic conditions: When the economy is in recession, the Fed reduces interest rates, and when inflation is increasing, the Fed raises interest rates. A monetary growth rule, in contrast, is a plan for increasing the money supply at a constant rate that does not change in response to economic conditions. Friedman and his followers proposed a monetary growth rule of increasing the money supply every year at a rate equal to the long-run annual growth rate of real GDP, which has been about 3 percent since 1950. If the Fed adopted this monetary growth rule, it would stick to it through changing economic conditions.

But what happens under a monetary growth rule if the economy moves into recession? Shouldn't the Fed abandon the rule to drive down interest rates? Friedman argued that the Fed should stick to the rule even during recessions because he believed that active monetary policy destabilizes the economy by increasing the number of recessions and their severity. By keeping the money supply growing at a constant rate, Friedman argued, the Fed would greatly increase economic stability.

During the 1970s, some economists and politicians pressured the Federal Reserve to adopt a monetary growth rule. Most of that pressure has disappeared in recent years because the fairly close relationship between movements in the money supply and movements in real GDP and the price level that existed before 1980 has become much weaker. Since 1980, the growth rate of M1 has been unstable. In some years, M1 has grown more than 10 percent, while in other years, it has actually fallen. Yet despite these wide fluctuations in the growth of M1, growth in real GDP has been fairly stable, and inflation has remained low during most years. MyEconLab Concept Check

Why Doesn't the Fed Target Both the Money Supply and the Interest Rate?

Most economists believe that the interest rate is the best monetary policy target. But as we have just seen, other economists believe the Fed should target the money supply. Why doesn't the Fed satisfy both groups by targeting both the money supply and the interest rate? The simple answer is that the Fed can't target both at the same time. To see why, look at Figure 8A.11, which shows the money market.

Figure 8A.11

The Fed Can't Target Both the Money Supply and the Interest Rate

The Fed is forced to choose between using either the interest rate or the money supply as its monetary policy target. In this figure, the Fed can set a target of $900 billion for the money supply or a target of 5 percent for the interest rate, but the Fed can't hit both targets because it can achieve only combinations of the interest rate and the money supply that represent equilibrium in the money market.

Source: Federal Reserve Bank of St. Louis.

Taylor rule A rule developed by John Taylor that links the Fed's target for the federal funds rate to economic variables.

Remember that the Fed controls the money supply, but it does not control money demand. Money demand is determined by decisions of households and firms as they weigh the trade-off between the convenience of money and its low interest rate compared with other financial assets. Suppose the Fed is targeting the interest rate and decides, given conditions in the economy, that the interest rate should be 5 percent. Or, suppose the Fed is targeting the money supply and decides that the money supply should be $900 billion. Figure 8A.11 shows that the Fed can bring about an interest rate of 5 percent or a money supply of $900 billion, but it can't bring about both. The point representing an interest rate of 5 percent and a money supply of $900 billion is not on the money demand curve, so it can't represent an equilibrium in the money market. The Fed can only attain combinations of the interest rate and the money supply that represent equilibrium. Therefore, the Fed has to choose between targeting an interest rate and targeting the money supply. For most of the period since World War II, the Fed has chosen the federal funds rate as its target.   MyEconLab Concept Check

The Taylor Rule

How does the Fed choose a target for the federal funds rate? The discussions at the meetings of the FOMC can be complex, and they take into account many economic variables. John Taylor of Stanford University has analyzed Fed decision making and developed the **Taylor rule** to explain federal funds rate targeting. The Taylor rule begins with an estimate of the value of the equilibrium real federal funds rate, which is the federal funds rate—adjusted for inflation—that would be consistent with real GDP being equal to potential GDP in the long run. Taylor believes this rate to be 2 percent. According to the Taylor rule, the Fed should set the target for the federal funds rate so that it is equal to the sum of the inflation rate, the equilibrium real federal funds rate, and two additional terms. The first of these additional terms is the *inflation gap*—the difference between current inflation and a target rate; the second is the *output gap*—the percentage difference between real GDP and potential GDP. The inflation gap and output gap are each given "weights" that reflect their influence on the federal funds target rate. With weights of 1/2 for both gaps, we have the following Taylor rule:

Federal funds target rate = Current inflation rate + Equilibrium real federal funds rate
+ [(1/2) × Inflation gap] + [(1/2) × Output gap].

The Taylor rule includes expressions for the inflation gap and the output gap because the Fed is concerned about both inflation and fluctuations in real GDP. Taylor demonstrated that if the equilibrium real federal funds rate is 2 percent and the target rate of inflation is 2 percent, the preceding equation does a good job of explaining changes in the Fed's target for the federal funds rate during most years. Consider an example in which the current inflation rate is 1 percent, and real GDP is 1 percent below potential GDP. In that case, the inflation gap equals 1 percent − 2 percent = −1 percent, and the output gap is also −1 percent. Inserting these values in the Taylor rule, we can calculate the predicted value for the federal funds target rate:

Federal funds target rate $= 1\% + 2\% + [(1/2) \times -1\%] + [(1/2) \times -1\%] = 2\%$

The Taylor rule accurately predicted changes in the federal funds target during the period of Alan Greenspan's leadership of the Federal Reserve from 1987 to 2006. For the period of the late 1970s and early 1980s, when Paul Volcker was chairman of the Federal Reserve, the Taylor rule predicts a federal funds rate target *lower* than the actual target the Fed used. In other words, Chairman Volcker kept the federal funds rate at an unusually high level to bring down the very high inflation rates of the late 1970s and early 1980s. In contrast, using data from the chairmanship of Arthur Burns from 1970 to 1978, the Taylor rule predicts a federal funds rate target *higher* than the actual target. Chairman Burns kept the federal funds rate at an unusually low level during these years, which helps to explain why the inflation rate grew worse. During the mid-2000s, the actual federal funds rate was also lower than the predicted federal funds rate. Some economists, including Taylor, argue that these low targets for the federal funds rate contributed to the excessive increase in spending on housing that we will discuss in the next section.

Taylor has proposed that the Fed adopt an explicit rule to guide its monetary policy actions. The Fed would not be constrained to mechanically following the exact Taylor rule given earlier, but whatever rule the Fed adopted, it would have to publically justify deviating from the rule, if a majority of the FOMC came to believe that was necessary. Representative Kevin Brady, Chairman of the Congressional Joint Economic Committee, has introduced the Sound Dollar Act, one provision of which incorporates Taylor's proposal. Former Fed Chair Ben Bernanke and most current members of the FOMC are against the proposal because they believe it might limit the Fed's ability to pursue innovative policies in a financial crisis. They also note that the Taylor rule does not account for changes over time in the equilibrium real interest rate, or for changes the FOMC might want to make in the target inflation rate. MyEconLab Concept Check

Solved Problem 8A.5

MyEconLab Interactive Animation

Applying the Taylor Rule

An article in the *Wall Street Journal* discussed the views of John Williams, the president of the Federal Reserve Bank of San Francisco, about the Taylor rule. According to the article, Williams argued that if the Fed had attempted to follow the Taylor rule during the recession of 2007–2009, it would have had to do "something not easily done, and that would have been for the Fed to have pushed short-term rates deeply into negative territory."

a. What does it mean for an interest rate to be negative?
b. Use the equation for the Taylor rule to show how the federal funds rate target might be negative. Assume that the equilibrium real federal funds rate and the target rate of inflation are both 2 percent and the current inflation rate is 0 percent.

Solving the Problem

Step 1: **Review the module material.** This problem is about using the Taylor rule to evaluate monetary policy, so you may want to review the section "The Taylor Rule," which begins on page 360.

Step 2: **Answer part (a) by explaining what it means for an interest rate to be negative.** We expect interest rates to be positive, which results in the borrower paying the lender back more than the amount of the funds borrowed. As we saw in the module opener and discussed further in the *Making the*

Connection on page 348, with a negative interest rate, the borrower would pay the lender back less than the amount of the funds borrowed. Note that Williams is referring to a negative *nominal* interest rate, which is very rare. A negative *real* interest rate that results from the inflation rate being higher than the nominal interest rate occurs more frequently.

Step 3: **Answer part (b) by constructing an example where the target federal funds rate might be negative.** This is the equation for the Taylor rule:

Federal funds target rate = Current inflation rate
+ Equilibrium real federal funds rate
+ [(1/2) × Inflation gap]
+ [(1/2) × Output gap].

If we substitute the values given in the problem, we have:

Federal funds rate target = 0% + 2% + [(1/2) × (0% − 2)]
+ [(1/2) × output gap],

or:

Federal funds taget rate target = 1% + [(1/2) × output gap].

So, for the federal funds rate target to be negative, the output gap will have to be larger (in absolute value) than −2%. For example, if the output gap is −4%, then:

Federal funds rate target = 1% + [(1/2) × (−4)] = −1%

In fact, the output gap rose above −6 percent during the recession. So, Williams is correct that following the Taylor rule exactly would have required the federal funds rate to be negative, which means that banks would have to have been willing to pay interest when lending to other banks in the federal funds market rather than receive interest. This outcome is very unlikely.

Extra Credit: The inability of the Fed to push the federal funds rate to negative values is sometimes called the *zero lower bound* to monetary policy.

Source: Michael S. Derby and Benjamin Fritz, "Fed's Williams Says Summer Rate Rise Possible if Data Supports Action," *Wall Street Journal*, May 1, 2015.

Your Turn: For more practice, do related problems 5.5, 5.6, and 5.7 on pages 376–377 at the end of this module.

Inflation Targeting

Inflation targeting A framework for conducting monetary policy that involves the central bank announcing its target level of inflation.

Many economists and central bankers believe that *inflation targeting* provides a useful framework for carrying out monetary policy. With **inflation targeting**, a central bank publicly sets an explicit target for the inflation rate over a period of time, and the government and the public then judge the performance of the central bank on the basis of its success in hitting the target.

Beginning in the 1980s, inflation targeting was adopted by a number of central banks around the world, including the Bank of England and, after its founding in the late 1990s, the European Central Bank. After many years of not having an explicit inflation target, the Fed announced in 2012 that it would attempt to maintain an average inflation rate of 2 percent per year.

With inflation targeting, the Fed can still respond to periods of recession or other economic problems without following an inflexible rule. An inflation target allows monetary policy to focus on inflation and inflation forecasts except during times of severe recession. Arguments supporting the Fed's use of an explicit inflation target focus on the following points. First, announcing explicit targets for inflation draws the public's attention to what the Fed can actually achieve in practice. Most economists believe that over the long run, monetary policy has a greater effect on inflation than on the growth of real GDP. Second, announcing an inflation target provides an anchor for inflationary expectations. If households, firms, and participants in financial markets believe that the Fed will hit an annual inflation target of 2 percent, then they will expect that if inflation is temporarily lower or higher, it will eventually return to the target rate. Third, inflation targets promote accountability for the Fed by providing a yardstick against which its performance can be measured.

Some economists and policymakers were critical of the Fed's decision to adopt an explicit inflation target. Opponents make several arguments. First, rigid numerical targets for inflation diminish the flexibility of monetary policy to address other policy goals. Second, because monetary policy affects inflation with a lag, inflation targeting requires that the Fed use forecasts of future inflation, which may turn out to be inaccurate. Third, holding the Fed accountable only for a goal of low inflation may make it more difficult for elected officials to monitor the Fed's support for good economic policy overall. Finally, inflation targets may increase uncertainty over whether the Fed will take prompt action to return the economy to full employment following a recession.

Economists and policymakers continue to debate whether inflation targets improve economic policy.

MyEconLab Concept Check

Making the Connection	**Should the Fed Worry about the Prices of Food and Gasoline?**

MyEconLab Video

Surveys show that many people in the United States are skeptical about whether changes in the consumer price index (CPI) are a good measure of inflation. The CPI measures the price level based on a market basket that contains 211 goods and services, including shirts, refrigerators, textbooks, and doctor visits. But many people think of inflation in terms of increases in the prices of the goods they buy most frequently—particularly food and gasoline.

Not only does the Fed not concentrate on changes in the prices of food and gasoline, it actually prefers to *exclude* food and gasoline prices when measuring inflation. Fed policymakers refer to these adjusted measures of inflation as "core" inflation. Why does the Fed ignore the prices that many people think are the most important? The key reason is that monetary policy affects the economy with a lag of many months. As a result, Fed policymakers don't want to react to every movement—up or down—in prices. The green line in the graph shows the CPI calculated using prices for all 211 goods and services in the consumer market basket. The red line shows the CPI calculated by leaving out the prices of food and energy, such as gasoline and natural gas used in heating homes.

As the graph shows, food and energy prices are much more volatile than are the prices of all the goods in the CPI. For instance, during the recession of 2007–2009, the inflation rate measured by the CPI was negative—deflation occurred—during nine months. When changes in food and energy prices are excluded, by contrast, the inflation rate is positive in every month. This pattern repeated in early 2015, when falling energy prices caused the CPI to decline for several months.

Why are food and energy prices so volatile? Food prices can be volatile because weather-related problems such as too little or too much rain can lead to large fluctuations in supply. Energy prices can fluctuate when political unrest in the Middle East or other energy-producing regions disrupts supply or when the Organization of the Petroleum Exporting Countries (OPEC) oil cartel attempts to increase prices. Because the factors that cause volatility in food and energy prices tend not to persist for more than a few months, they don't have a long-lasting effect on the overall rate of inflation. As Fed Chair Janet Yellen has put it, Fed policymakers "pay attention to core inflation and similar measures because, in light of the volatility of food and energy prices, core inflation has been a better forecaster of overall inflation." In other words, to reach its goal of price stability, the Fed has to concentrate on the underlying inflation rate and avoid being distracted by temporary increases in food or energy prices—however painful the typical consumer may find those increases to be.

The Fed's preferred measure of inflation is the core *personal consumption expenditures (PCE) price index*, which excludes food and energy prices. The PCE price index is a measure of the price level that is similar to the GDP deflator, except it includes only the prices of goods from the consumption category of GDP. The PCE price index includes the prices of more goods and services than the CPI, so it is a broader measure of inflation.

The following graph shows movements in the CPI, the PCE price index, and the core PCE price index from January 2000 through July 2015. Although the three measures of inflation move roughly together, the core PCE price index has been more stable than the other two. Note in particular that in early 2009, when the CPI and the PCE price index were indicating that the economy was experiencing deflation, the core PCE price index was still showing inflation rates above 1 percent. The core PCE price index also showed more stability in late 2014 and early 2015, a period of rapid declines in oil prices.

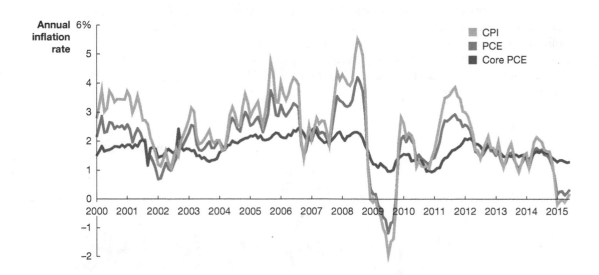

If you want to know what the Fed thinks the current inflation rate is, look at data on the core PCE price index. The Bureau of Economic Analysis publishes these data monthly.   MyEconLab Real-time data

Your Turn: Test your understanding by doing related problem 5.9 on page 377 at the end of this module.

8A.6   Fed Policies during the 2007–2009 Recession

LEARNING OBJECTIVE: Describe the policies the Federal Reserve used during the 2007–2009 recession.

As we have seen, the Fed's traditional response to a recession is to lower the target for the federal funds rate. The severity of the recession of 2007–2009, particularly the problems in financial markets during those years, complicated the Fed's job. By December 2008, the Fed had effectively lowered the target for the federal funds rate to zero, but the zero interest rate alone did not result in a sufficient increase in aggregate demand to end the recession. In this section, we will discuss some of the additional policy measures the Fed took during the 2007–2009 recession. Some of these measures were used for the first time in the Fed's history.

The Inflation and Deflation of the Housing Market Bubble

To understand the 2007–2009 recession and the financial crisis that accompanied it, we need to start by considering the housing market. The Fed lowered the target for the federal funds rate during the 2001 recession to stimulate demand for housing. The policy was successful, and most builders, such as Toll Brothers, experienced several years of high demand. By 2005, however, many economists argued that a "bubble" had formed in the housing market. As we discussed in Module 6, the price of any asset reflects the returns the owner of the asset expects to receive. For example, the price of a share of stock reflects the profitability of the firm issuing the stock because the owner of a share of stock has a claim on the firm's profits.

Many economists believe, however, that sometimes a *stock market bubble* can form when the prices of stocks rise above levels that can be justified by the profitability of the firms issuing the stocks. Stock market bubbles end when enough investors decide stocks are overvalued and begin to sell. Why would an investor be willing to pay more for stocks than would be justified by their underlying value? There are two main explanations:

1. The investor may be caught up in the enthusiasm of the moment and, by failing to gather sufficient information, may overestimate the true value of the stocks.

2. The investor may expect to profit from buying stocks at inflated prices if the investor can sell them at even higher prices before the bubble bursts.

The price of a house should reflect the value of the housing services it provides. We can use the rents charged for comparable houses in an area to measure the value of housing services. We would expect, then, that housing prices and rents would increase at roughly the same rate. If prices of single-family homes rise significantly relative to rents for single-family homes, it is likely that the housing market is experiencing a bubble. As Figure 8A.12 shows, housing prices and housing rents generally

Housing prices and rents (1987:I = 100)

350
300
250
200
150
100
50
0

1987 1989 1991 1993 1995 1997 1999 2001 2003 2005 2007 2009 2011 2013 2015

Housing prices

Rents

MyEconLab Real-time data

Figure 8A.12

Housing Prices and Housing Rents, 1987–2015

Typically, housing prices increase at about the same rate as housing rents. But during the housing bubble, housing prices increased far more than did rents.

Note: For both series, the values for the first quarter of 1987 (1987:I) are set equal to 100.
Source: Federal Reserve Bank of St. Louis.

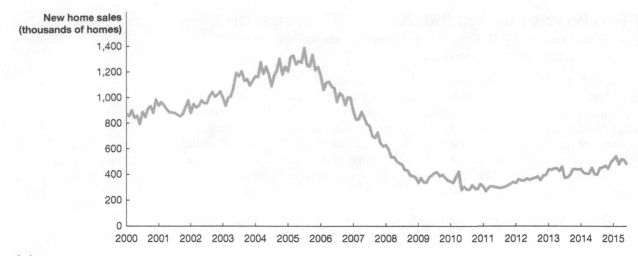

Figure 8A.13   The Housing Bubble

Sales of new homes in the United States went on a roller-coaster ride, rising by 60 percent between January 2000 and July 2005 before falling by 80 percent between July 2005 and May 2010.

Note: The data are seasonally adjusted at an annual rate.
Source: U.S. Bureau of the Census.

increase at about the same rate, but between January 2000 and May 2006, housing prices nearly doubled, while rents increased by less than 25 percent. This large divergence between housing prices and rents is evidence of a bubble. In addition, in some cities, there was an increase in the number of buyers who did not intend to live in the houses they purchased but were using them as investments. Like stock investors during a stock market bubble, these housing investors were expecting to make a profit by selling houses at higher prices than they had paid for them, and they were not concerned about whether the prices of the houses were above the value of the housing services provided.

During 2006 and 2007, the air was rapidly escaping from the housing bubble. Figure 8A.13 shows new home sales for each month from January 2000 through June 2015. New home sales rose by 60 percent between January 2000 and July 2005 and then fell by 80 percent between July 2005 and May 2010. Sales then began to gradually increase but were still at low levels well into 2015. Sales of existing homes followed a similar pattern. Prices of new and existing homes in most markets also began to decline beginning in 2006, and the inventory of unsold homes offered for sale soared. Some homebuyers began having trouble making their loan payments. When lenders foreclosed on some of these loans, the lenders sold the homes, causing housing prices to decline further. *Subprime loans* are loans granted to borrowers with flawed credit histories. Some mortgage lenders that had concentrated on making subprime loans suffered heavy losses and went out of business, and most banks and other lenders tightened the requirements for borrowers. This *credit crunch* made it more difficult for potential homebuyers to obtain mortgages, further depressing the market.

The decline in the housing market affected other markets as well. For example, with home prices falling, consumption spending on furniture, appliances, and home improvements declined because many households found it more difficult to borrow against the value of their homes.

Was the housing bubble the result of overly optimistic expectations by homebuyers and builders that new residential construction and housing prices would indefinitely continue to rise at rapid rates? While overly optimistic expectations may have played some role in the housing bubble, many economists believe that changes in the market for mortgages may have played a bigger role.   MyEconLab Concept Check

The Changing Mortgage Market

Until the 1970s, the commercial banks and savings and loans that granted mortgages kept the loans until the borrowers paid them off. As we saw in Module 8, a financial asset such as a mortgage is a security only if it can be resold in a secondary market. Many members of Congress believed that home ownership could be increased by creating a secondary market in mortgages. If banks and savings and loans could resell mortgages, then individual investors would in effect be able to provide funds for mortgages. The process would work like this: If a bank or savings and loan granted a mortgage and then resold the mortgage to an investor, the bank could use the funds received from the investor to grant another mortgage. In this way, banks and savings and loans could grant more mortgage loans because they would no longer depend only on deposits for the funds needed to make the loans. One barrier to creating a secondary market in mortgages was that most investors were unwilling to buy mortgages because they were afraid of losing money if the borrower stopped making payments, or *defaulted*, on the loan.

To reassure investors, Congress used two *government-sponsored enterprises (GSEs)*: the Federal National Mortgage Association ("Fannie Mae") and the Federal Home Loan Mortgage Corporation ("Freddie Mac"). These two institutions stand between investors and banks that grant mortgages. Fannie Mae and Freddie Mac sell bonds to investors and use the funds to purchase mortgages from banks. By the 1990s, a large secondary market existed in mortgages, with funds flowing from investors through Fannie Mae and Freddie Mac to banks and, ultimately, to individuals and families borrowing money to buy houses.   MyEconLab Concept Check

The Role of Investment Banks

By the 2000s, further changes had taken place in the mortgage market. First, investment banks became significant participants in the secondary market for mortgages. As we have seen, investment banks, such as Goldman Sachs and Morgan Stanley, differ from commercial banks in that they do not take in deposits and rarely lend directly to households. Instead, investment banks concentrate on providing advice to firms issuing stocks and bonds or considering mergers with other firms. Investment banks began buying mortgages, bundling large numbers of them together as bonds called *mortgage-backed securities*, and reselling them to investors. Mortgage-backed securities proved very popular with investors because they often paid higher interest rates than other securities that investors believed had comparable default risk.

Second, by the height of the housing bubble in 2005 and early 2006, lenders had greatly loosened the standards for obtaining a mortgage loan. Traditionally, only borrowers with good credit histories and who were willing to make a down payment equal to at least 20 percent of the value of the house they were buying would be able to receive a mortgage. By 2005, however, lenders were issuing many mortgages to subprime borrowers with flawed credit histories. In addition, "Alt-A" borrowers—who stated but did not document their incomes—and borrowers who made very small down payments found it easier to get loans. Lenders also created new types of *adjustable-rate mortgages* that allowed borrowers to pay a very low interest rate for the first few years of the mortgage and then pay a higher rate in later years. The chance that the borrowers using these nontraditional mortgages would default was higher than for borrowers using traditional mortgages. Why would borrowers take out mortgages if it might be difficult for them to make the payments, and why would lenders grant these mortgages? Both borrowers and lenders were anticipating that housing prices would continue to rise, which would reduce the chance that borrowers would default on the mortgages and would also make it easier for borrowers to convert to more traditional mortgages in the future.

Unfortunately, the decline in housing prices led to rising defaults among subprime and Alt-A borrowers, borrowers with adjustable-rate mortgages, and borrowers who had made only small down payments. When borrowers began defaulting on mortgages, the values of many mortgage-backed securities declined sharply. Investors feared that if they purchased these securities, they would not receive the promised payments because the payments on the securities depended on borrowers making their mortgage payments, which an increasing number of borrowers were failing to do. Many commercial and investment banks owned these mortgage-backed securities, so the decline in the value of the securities caused these banks to suffer heavy losses. By mid-2007, the decline in the value of mortgage-backed securities and the large losses suffered by commercial and investment banks began to concern investors and policymakers. Many investors refused to buy mortgage-backed securities, and some investors would buy only bonds issued by the U.S. Treasury.   MyEconLab Concept Check

Making the Connection
MyEconLab Video

The Wonderful World of Leverage

Traditionally, most people taking out a mortgage made a down payment equal to 20 percent of the price of the house and borrowed the remaining 80 percent. During the housing boom, however, many people purchased houses with down payments of 5 percent or less. These borrowers were highly *leveraged*, which means that their investment in their house was made mostly with borrowed money.

To see how leverage works in the housing market, consider the following example: Suppose you buy a $200,000 house on January 1, 2018. On January 1, 2019, the price of the house—if you decide to sell it—has risen to $220,000. What return have you earned on your investment in the house? The answer depends on how much you invested when you bought the house. For example, if you paid $200,000 in cash for the house, your return on that $200,000 investment is the $20,000 increase in the price of the house divided by your $200,000 investment, or 10 percent. Suppose that rather than paying cash, you made a down payment of 20 percent, or $40,000, and borrowed the rest by taking out a mortgage loan of $160,000. Now the return on your investment in the house is the $20,000 increase in the price of the house divided

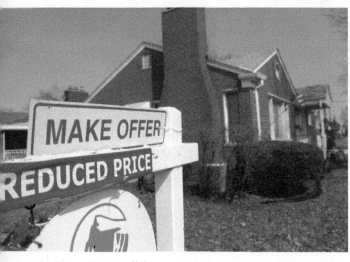

Making a very small down payment on a home mortgage leaves a buyer vulnerable to falling house prices.

by your $40,000 investment, or 50 percent. If the down payment is less than 20 percent, your return on investment will be higher. The second column in the following table shows how the return on your investment increases as your down payment decreases:

| Down Payment | Return on your investment as a result of . . . | |
	a 10 percent increase in the price of your house.	a 10 percent decrease in the price of your house.
100%	10%	−10%
20	50	−50
10	100	−100
5	200	−200

An investment financed at least partly by borrowing is called a *leveraged investment*. As this example shows, the larger the fraction of an investment financed by borrowing, the greater the degree of leverage in the investment, and the greater the potential return. But as the third column in the table shows, the reverse is also true: The greater the leverage, the greater the potential loss. To see why, suppose once again that you buy a house for $200,000, except that in this case, after one year, the price of the house falls to $180,000. If you paid $200,000 in cash for the house—so your leverage was zero—the $20,000 decline in the price of the house represents a loss of 10 percent of your investment. But if you made a down payment of only $10,000 and borrowed the remaining $190,000, then the $20,000 decline in the price of the house represents a loss of 200 percent of your investment. In fact, the house is now worth $10,000 less than the amount of your mortgage loan. The *equity* in your house is the difference between the market price of the house and the amount you owe on a loan. If the amount you owe is greater than the price of the house, you have *negative equity*. A homeowner who has negative equity is also said to be "upside down" or "underwater" on his or her mortgage.

When the housing bubble burst and housing prices started to fall, many people found that they had negative equity. In that situation, some people defaulted on their loans, sometimes by simply moving out and abandoning their homes. Leverage had contributed to the housing boom and bust and the severity of the 2007–2009 recession.

Your Turn: Test your understanding by doing related problem 6.9 on page 378 at the end of this module.

MyEconLab Study Plan

The Fed and the Treasury Department Respond

Because the problems in financial markets resulting from the bursting of the housing bubble were so severe, the Fed entered into an unusual partnership with the U.S. Treasury Department to develop suitable policies. Fed Chairman Ben Bernanke and U.S. Treasury Secretaries Henry Paulson (in the Bush administration) and Timothy Geithner (in the Obama administration) responded to the crisis by intervening in financial markets in unprecedented ways.

Initial Fed and Treasury Actions The financial crisis significantly worsened following the bankruptcy of the investment bank Lehman Brothers on September 15, 2008. So it is useful to look at the actions taken by the Fed and the Treasury before and after that date. Table 8A.3 shows four key actions the Fed and Treasury took to deal with problems in the financial system before the bankruptcy of Lehman Brothers.

Date	Action	Goal
March 2008	Although the Fed traditionally made discount loans only to commercial banks, the Fed announced it would temporarily make discount loans to *primary dealers*—firms that participate in regular open market transactions with the Fed.	Provide short-term funds to these dealers, some of which are investment banks, so they would not have to raise funds by selling securities, which might further reduce the prices of these securities.
March 2008	The Fed announced that it would loan up to $200 billion of Treasury securities in exchange for mortgage-backed securities.	Make it possible for primary dealers that owned mortgage-backed securities that were difficult or impossible to sell to have access to Treasury securities that they could use as collateral for short-term loans.
March 2008	The Fed and the Treasury helped JPMorgan Chase acquire the investment bank Bear Stearns, which was close to failing.	Avoid a financial panic that the Fed and the Treasury believed would result from Bear Stearns's failure. Its failure might have caused many investors and financial firms to stop making loans to other investment banks.
September 2008	The Treasury moved to have the federal government take control of Fannie Mae and Freddie Mac. Although the federal government sponsored Fannie Mae and Freddie Mac, they were actually private businesses. The firms were placed under the supervision of the Federal Housing Finance Agency.	Avoid further devastating a weak housing market. The Treasury believed that the bankruptcy of Fannie Mae and Freddie Mac would have caused a collapse in confidence in mortgage-backed securities.

Table 8A.3

Treasury and Fed Actions at the Beginning of the Financial Crisis

Responses to the Failure of Lehman Brothers Some economists and policymakers criticized the decision by the Fed and the Treasury to help arrange the sale of Bear Stearns to JPMorgan Chase. Their main concern was with the *moral hazard problem*, which is the possibility that managers of financial firms such as Bear Stearns might make riskier investments if they believe that the federal government will save them from bankruptcy. The Treasury and the Fed acted to save Bear Stearns because they believed that the failure of a large financial firm could have wider economic repercussions. As we discussed in Module 8, when a financial firm sells off its holdings of bonds and other assets, it causes their prices to fall, which in turn can undermine the financial position of other firms that also own these assets. In September 2008, when the investment bank Lehman Brothers was near bankruptcy, the Fed and the Treasury had to weigh the moral hazard problem against the possibility that the failure of Lehman Brothers would lead to further declines in asset prices and endanger the financial positions of other firms. Chairman Ben Bernanke and other Fed officials were also concerned that they lacked the legal authority to make loans to Lehman Brothers. They believed that the Federal Reserve Act prohibited making loans to a firm that was insolvent, meaning that the value of the firm's assets—such as its holdings of mortgage securities—was less than the value of its liabilities—such as the loans it had received from other financial firms.

The Fed and the Treasury decided to allow Lehman Brothers to go bankrupt, which it did on September 15. The adverse reaction in financial markets was stronger than the Fed and the Treasury had expected, and just two days later, the Fed agreed to provide an $85 billion loan to the American International Group (AIG)—the largest insurance company in the United States—in exchange for the federal government receiving an 80 percent ownership stake, effectively giving the government control of the company.

One important result of the failure of Lehman Brothers was the heavy losses suffered by Reserve Primary Fund, a money market mutual fund that had made short-term loans to Lehman Brothers. The problems at Reserve led many investors to withdraw their funds from it and other money market funds. These withdrawals reduced the ability of the money market funds to purchase commercial paper from corporations. Because in recent years corporations had become dependent on selling commercial paper to finance their operations, the Treasury and the Fed moved to stabilize this market and ensure that the flow of funds from investors to corporations continued. The Treasury announced a plan to temporarily provide insurance for deposits in money market mutual funds, similar to the existing insurance on bank deposits. The Fed announced that for a limited time, it would lend directly to corporations by purchasing three-month commercial paper issued by nonfinancial corporations.

Finally, in October 2008, Congress passed the *Troubled Asset Relief Program* (*TARP*), under which the Treasury attempted to stabilize the commercial banking system by providing funds to banks in exchange for stock. Taking partial ownership positions in private commercial banks was an unprecedented action for the federal government.

Many of the Treasury's and the Fed's new approaches to policy were controversial because they involved partial government ownership of financial firms, implicit guarantees to large financial firms that they would not be allowed to go bankrupt, and unprecedented intervention in financial markets. Although the approaches were new, they were intended to achieve the traditional macroeconomic policy goals of high employment, price stability, and stability of financial markets. What remains to be seen is whether these new approaches represent a permanent increase in federal government involvement in U.S. financial markets or whether policy will eventually return to more traditional approaches.

Continued from page 337

Economics in Your Life

Should You Buy a House during a Recession?

At the beginning of this module, we asked whether it is a good idea to buy a house during a recession. Buying a house is the largest purchase you are likely to make in your lifetime, so you need to carefully consider a number of factors, including the price of the house relative to comparable houses in the neighborhood; whether house prices in the neighborhood have been rising or falling; and the location of the house relative to stores, work, and good schools. Also important is the interest rate you will have to pay on the mortgage loan you would need in order to buy the house. As we have seen in this module, during a recession, the Fed often takes actions to lower interest rates. So, mortgage rates are typically lower during a recession than at other times. You may want to take advantage of low interest rates to buy a house during a recession. But recessions are also times of rising unemployment, and you would not want to make a commitment to borrow a lot of money for 15 or more years if you were in danger of losing your job. We can conclude that if your job seems secure, buying a house during a recession may be a good idea.

Conclusion

Monetary policy is one way governments pursue goals for inflation, employment, and financial stability. The chair of the Federal Reserve may have a greater ability than the president of the United States to affect the U.S. economy. Congress and the president, however, also use their power over spending and taxes to try to stabilize the economy. In Module 7 and 7A, we discussed how *fiscal policy*—changes in government spending and taxes—affect the economy.

Visit MyEconLab for a news article and analysis related to the concepts of this module.

MODULE SUMMARY AND PROBLEMS

Key Terms

Contractionary monetary policy, p. 348

Expansionary monetary policy, p. 348

Federal funds rate, p. 345

Inflation targeting, p. 362

Monetary policy, p. 338

Taylor rule, p. 360

8A.1 **What Is Monetary Policy? pages 338–340**
LEARNING OBJECTIVE: Define monetary policy and describe the Federal Reserve's monetary policy goals.

Summary

Monetary policy is the actions the Fed takes to manage the money supply and interest rates to achieve its macroeconomic policy goals. The Fed has four *monetary policy goals* that are intended to promote a well-functioning economy: price stability, high employment, stability of financial markets and institutions, and economic growth.

 Visit **www.myeconlab.com** to complete these exercises online and get instant feedback.

Review Questions

1.1 When Congress established the Federal Reserve in 1913, what was its main responsibility? When did Congress broaden the Fed's responsibilities?

1.2 What are the Fed's four monetary policy goals?

1.3 In what sense does the Fed have a "dual mandate"?

1.4 How can investment banks be subject to liquidity problems?

Problems and Applications

1.5 What is a bank panic? Why are policymakers more concerned about bank failures than failures of restaurants or clothing stores?

1.6 An article in the *Wall Street Journal* quoted a Federal Reserve economist as referring to "the Fed's existing dual mandate

to achieve maximum sustainable employment in the context of price stability."
a. Does "maximum sustainable employment" mean a zero percent unemployment rate? Briefly explain.
b. Does "price stability" mean a zero percent inflation rate? Briefly explain.
Source: Pedro Nicolaci Da Costa, "Fed Should Make Bond Buys a Regular Policy Tool, a Boston Fed Paper Finds," *Wall Street Journal*, April 23, 2015.

1.7 A former Federal Reserve official argued that at the Fed, "the objectives of price stability and low long-term interest rates are essentially the same objective." Briefly explain his reasoning.
Source: William Poole, "Understanding the Fed," *Federal Reserve Bank of St. Louis Review*, Vol. 89, No. 1, January/February 2007, p. 4.

1.8 In the summer of 2015, many economists and policymakers expected that the Federal Reserve would increase its target for the federal funds rate by the end of the year. Some economists argued, though, that it would be better for the Fed to leave its target unchanged. At the time, the unemployment rate was 5.3 percent, close to full employment, but the inflation rate was below the Fed's target of 2 percent. What policy goal would the Fed promote if it did *not* increase its target for the federal funds rate? Briefly explain.
Source: Min Zeng, "Inflation Expectations Fall, Making Rate Hike 'More Difficult to Justify,'" *Wall Street Journal*, August 6, 2015.

8A.2 **The Money Market and the Fed's Choice of Monetary Policy Targets, pages 340–346**
LEARNING OBJECTIVE: Describe the Federal Reserve's monetary policy targets and explain how expansionary and contractionary monetary policies affect the interest rate.

Summary

The Fed's *monetary policy targets* are economic variables that it can affect directly and that in turn affect variables such as real GDP and the price level that are closely related to the Fed's policy goals. The two main monetary policy targets are the money supply and the interest rate. The Fed has most often chosen to use the interest rate as its monetary policy target. The Federal Open Market Committee announces a target for the **federal funds rate** after each meeting. The federal funds rate is the interest rate banks charge each other for overnight loans. To

lower the interest rate, the Fed increases the money supply. To raise the interest rate, the Fed decreases the money supply. In a graphical analysis of the money market, when the money supply curve shifts to the right, the result is a movement down the money demand curve and a new equilibrium at a lower interest rate. When the money supply curve shifts to the left, the result is a movement up the money demand curve and a new equilibrium at a higher interest rate.

MyEconLab Visit **www.myeconlab.com** to complete these exercises online and get instant feedback.

Review Questions

2.1 What is a monetary policy target? Why does the Fed use policy targets?

2.2 What do economists mean by the *demand for money*? What is the advantage of holding money? What is the disadvantage? Why does an increase in the interest rate decrease the quantity of money demanded?

2.3 Draw a demand and supply graph showing equilibrium in the money market. Suppose the Fed wants to lower the equilibrium interest rate. Show on the graph how the Fed would accomplish this objective.

2.4 What is the federal funds rate? What role does it play in monetary policy?

Problems and Applications

2.5 In the following graph of the money market, what could cause the money supply curve to shift from MS_1 to MS_2? What could cause the money demand curve to shift from MD_1 to MD_2?

2.6 In 2015, one article in the *Wall Street Journal* discussed the possibility of "a September quarter-point increase in the Fed's range for overnight target rates," while another article noted, "the U.S. central bank's discount rate ... has been set at 0.75% since February 2010."
  a. What is the name of the Fed's "target rate"?
  b. Briefly explain who borrows money and who lends money at this "target rate."
  c. What is the discount rate, and how is it different from the "target rate"?

Sources: Justin Lahart, "Jobs Give Fed Green Light; Inflation Sets Speed Limit," *Wall Street Journal*, August 7, 2015; and Ben Leubsdorf, "Five Regional Fed Banks Asked to Raise Discount Rate," *Wall Street Journal*, July 14, 2015.

2.7 In response to problems in financial markets and a slowing economy, the Federal Open Market Committee (FOMC) began lowering its target for the federal funds rate from 5.25 percent in September 2007. Over the next year, the FOMC cut its federal funds rate target in a series of steps. Economist Price Fishback of the University of Arizona observed, "The Fed has been pouring more money into the banking system by cutting the target federal funds rate to 0 to 0.25 percent in December 2008." What is the relationship between the federal funds rate falling and the money supply increasing? How does lowering the target for the federal funds rate "pour money" into the banking system?

Source: Price Fishback, "The Financial Meltdown Now and Then," freakonomics.com, May 12, 2009.

2.8 An article in the *New York Times* in 1993 stated the following about Fed Chairman Alan Greenspan's decision to no longer announce targets for the money supply: "Since the late 1970's, the Federal Reserve has made many of its most important decisions by setting a specific target for growth in the money supply ... and often adjusted interest rates to meet them." If the Fed would no longer have a specific target for the money supply, what was it targeting? Why did the Fed give up targeting the money supply?

Source: Steven Greenhouse, "Fed Abandons Policy Tied to Money Supply," *New York Times*, July 23, 1993.

8A.3 | ## Monetary Policy and Economic Activity, pages 346–354

LEARNING OBJECTIVE: Use aggregate demand and aggregate supply graphs to show the effects of monetary policy on real GDP and the price level.

Summary

An **expansionary monetary policy** lowers interest rates to increase consumption, investment, and net exports. This increase in aggregate demand increases real GDP and the price level. An expansionary monetary policy can help the Fed achieve its goal of high employment. A **contractionary monetary policy** raises interest rates to decrease consumption, investment, and net exports. This decrease in aggregate demand reduces both real GDP and the inflation rate below what they would be in the absence of policy. A contractionary monetary policy can help the Fed achieve its goal of price stability.

Review Questions

3.1 Briefly discuss how an increase in interest rates affects each component of aggregate demand.

3.2 If the Fed believes the economy is headed for a recession, what actions should it take? If the Fed believes the inflation rate is about to sharply increase, what actions should it take?

3.3 What is quantitative easing? Why have central banks used this policy?

Problems and Applications

3.4 A student says the following: "I understand why the Fed uses expansionary policy, but I don't understand why it would ever use contractionary policy. Why would the government ever want the economy to contract?" Briefly answer the student's question.

3.5 In explaining why monetary policy did not pull Japan out of a recession in the early 2000s, an official at the Bank of Japan was quoted as saying that despite "major increases in the money supply," the money "stay[ed] in banks." Explain what the official meant by saying that the money stayed in banks. Why would that be a problem? Where does the money go if an expansionary monetary policy is successful?

Source: James Brooke, "Critics Say Koizumi's Economic Medicine Is a Weak Tea," *New York Times*, February 27, 2002.

3.6 An article in the *Wall Street Journal* discussing the Federal Reserve's monetary policy included the following observation: "Fed officials have been signaling since last year that they expected to raise rates in 2015 … pushing up the value of the currency and contributing to the economic slowdown officials now confront."
   a. What does "pushing up the value of the currency" mean?
   b. Why would the Fed's increasing U.S. interest rates cause the value of the currency to increase?
   c. Why would an increase in the value of the currency contribute to a slowdown in the growth of the U.S. economy?

Source: Jon Hilsenrath, "Fed's Rate Decisions Hang on Dollar, Growth Concerns," *Wall Street Journal*, April 22, 2015.

3.7 According to an article in the *Wall Street Journal*, "Brazil's economy grew just 2.3% in 2013, compared with 7.5% in 2010. The country also has struggled with persistently high inflation, which has forced its central bank to raise interest rates."
   a. Why would the Brazilian central bank have been "forced" to raise interest rates because of rising inflation?
   b. Could the increase in interest rates be connected to the slowing rate of economic growth? Briefly explain.

Source: Emily Glazer and Luciana Magalhaes, "Brazil's Debt-Laden Firms Try to Stay Afloat," *Wall Street Journal*, March 18, 2014.

3.8 William McChesney Martin, who was Federal Reserve chairman from 1951 to 1970, was once quoted as saying, "The role of the Federal Reserve is to remove the punchbowl just as the party gets going." What did he mean?

3.9 **(Related to the** Making the Connection **on page 350)** An article in the *Wall Street Journal* in 2015 reported that the interest rate on five-year German government bonds had become negative: "The negative yield means investors are effectively paying the German state for holding its debt." The article quoted an investment analyst as saying: "The negative yield is not scaring investors away."
   a. What caused the interest rate on German government bonds to become negative?
   b. Why are investors willing to buy bonds with a negative interest rate?

Source: Emese Bartha and Ben Edwards, "Germany Sells Five-Year Debt at Negative Yield for First Time on Record," *Wall Street Journal*, February 25, 2015.

3.10 **(Related to the** Making the Connection **on page 350)** An article in the *Wall Street Journal* notes that before the financial crisis of 2007–2009, the Fed "managed just one short-term interest rate and expected that to be enough to meet its goals for inflation and unemployment."
   a. What short-term interest rate is the article referring to? How would the Fed expect controlling that one interest rate would allow it to meet its goals for inflation and unemployment?
   b. The article also notes that after the financial crisis, "the Fed is working through a broader spectrum of interest rates." What does "a broader spectrum of interest rates" mean? How is the Fed able to affect a broader spectrum of interest rates?

Source: Jon Hilsenrath, "Easy-Money Era a Long Game for Fed," *Wall Street Journal*, March 17, 2013.

3.11 **(Related to the** Making the Connection **on page 352)** Each year, the president's Council of Economic Advisers prepares and sends to Congress *The Economic Report of the President*. The report published in February 2008 contained the following summary of the economic situation: "Economic growth is expected to continue in 2008. Most market forecasts suggest a slower pace in the first half of 2008, followed by strengthened growth in the second half of the year."
   a. What in fact happened to economic growth during 2008?
   b. What conclusion can you draw from your answer to part (a) with respect to economic forecasting and the formulation of economic policy?

Source: Executive Office of the President, *Economic Report of the President*, 2008, Washington, DC: USGPO, 2008, p. 17.

3.12 **(Related to the** Making the Connection **on page 352)** The following is from a Federal Reserve publication:

> In practice, monetary policymakers do not have up-to-the-minute, reliable information about the state of the economy and prices. Information is limited because of lags in the publication of data. Also, policymakers have less-than-perfect understanding of the way the economy works, including the knowledge of when and to what extent policy actions will affect aggregate demand. The operation of the economy changes over time, and with it the response of the economy to policy measures. These limitations add to uncertainties in the policy process and make determining the appropriate setting of monetary policy … more difficult.

If the Fed itself admits that there are many obstacles in the way of effective monetary policy, why does it still engage in active monetary policy rather than use a monetary growth rule, as suggested by Milton Friedman and his followers?

Source: Board of Governors of the Federal Reserve System, *The Federal Reserve System: Purposes and Functions*, Washington, DC, 1994.

3.13 (Related to the Don't Let This Happen to You **on page 354)** Briefly explain whether you agree with the following statement: "The Fed has an easy job. Say it wants to increase real GDP by $200 billion. All it has to do is increase the money supply by that amount."

3.14 (Related to the Module Opener **on page 337)** An investment blog said about Fed Chair Janet Yellen, "She is arguably the world's most powerful woman, and perhaps the most powerful person in the world. Can you name anybody with more might?" Do you agree with this assessment? Briefly explain.

Source: Barbara Friedberg, "Fed Chief Janet Yellen: The Most Powerful Woman in the World," blog.personalcapital.com, September 17, 2014.

8A.4 Monetary Policy in the Dynamic Aggregate Demand and Aggregate Supply Model, pages 354–359

LEARNING OBJECTIVE: Use the dynamic aggregate demand and aggregate supply model to analyze monetary policy.

Summary

We can use the *dynamic aggregate demand and aggregate supply model* introduced in Modules 4 and 4A to look more closely at expansionary and contractionary monetary policies. The dynamic aggregate demand and aggregate supply model takes into account that (1) the economy experiences continuing inflation, with the price level rising every year, and (2) the economy experiences long-run growth, with the *LRAS* curve shifting to the right every year. In the dynamic model, an expansionary monetary policy tries to ensure that the aggregate demand curve will shift far enough to the right to bring about macroeconomic equilibrium with real GDP equal to potential GDP. A contractionary monetary policy attempts to offset movements in aggregate demand that would cause macroeconomic equilibrium to occur at a level of real GDP that is greater than potential GDP.

MyEconLab   Visit www.myeconlab.com to complete those exercises online and get instant feedback.

Review Questions

4.1 What are the key differences between how we illustrate an expansionary monetary policy in the basic aggregate demand and aggregate supply model and in the dynamic aggregate demand and aggregate supply model?

4.2 What are the key differences between how we illustrate a contractionary monetary policy in the basic aggregate demand and aggregate supply model and in the dynamic aggregate demand and aggregate supply model?

Problems and Applications

4.3 Explain whether you agree with this argument:

If the Fed actually ever carried out a contractionary monetary policy, the price level would fall. Because the price level has not fallen in the United States over an entire year since the 1930s, we can conclude that the Fed has not carried out a contractionary policy since the 1930s.

4.4 (Related to Solved Problem 8A.4 **on page 357)** Use the graph to answer the following questions.

a. If the Fed does not take any policy action, what will be the level of real GDP and the price level in 2019?

b. If the Fed wants to keep real GDP at its potential level in 2019, should it use an expansionary policy or a contractionary policy? Should the trading desk be buying Treasury bills or selling them?

c. If the Fed takes no policy action, what will be the inflation rate in 2019? If the Fed uses monetary policy to keep real GDP at its potential level, what will be the inflation rate in 2019?

4.5 (Related to Solved Problem 8A.4 **on page 357)** The hypothetical information in the following table shows what the situation will be in 2019 if the Fed does *not* use monetary policy.

Year	Potential GDP	Real GDP	Price Level
2018	$17.9 trillion	$17.9 trillion	110.0
2019	18.3 trillion	18.2 trillion	112.0

a. If the Fed wants to keep real GDP at its potential level in 2019, should it use an expansionary policy or a contractionary policy? Should the trading desk be buying T-bills or selling them?

b. If the Fed's policy is successful in keeping real GDP at its potential level in 2019, state whether each of the following will be higher, lower, or the same as it would have been if the Fed had taken no action:
   i. Real GDP
   ii. Potential GDP
   iii. The inflation rate
   iv. The unemployment rate

c. Draw an aggregate demand and aggregate supply graph to illustrate the effects of the Fed's policy. Be sure that your graph contains *LRAS* curves for 2018 and 2019; *SRAS* curves for 2018 and 2019; *AD* curves for 2018 and 2019, with and without monetary policy action; and equilibrium real GDP and the price level in 2019, with and without policy.

4.6 According to an article in the *Wall Street Journal*, the Reserve Bank of India lowered its key policy interest rate in 2015, "citing weakness in parts of the economy as well as favorable inflation figures." The article notes that the central bank lists constraints to further interest rate cuts, including the "risk that inflation could flare again."

a. Use the dynamic aggregate demand and aggregate supply model to show where the Reserve Bank of India expected real GDP to be in 2015 without the interest rate cut, and indicate what the central bank is trying to achieve with the interest rate cut. Assume, for simplicity, that real GDP in India in 2014 equaled potential GDP.

b. Is there a connection between India experiencing slow growth in output at the same time that it experienced a lower inflation rate? Briefly explain.

Source: Gabriele Parussini, "India Cuts Key Interest Rate for Second Time This Year," *Wall Street Journal*, March 4, 2015.

8A.5 | ## A Closer Look at the Fed's Setting of Monetary Policy Targets, pages 359–364

LEARNING OBJECTIVE: Describe the Fed's setting of monetary policy targets.

Summary

Some economists have argued that the Fed should use the money supply, rather than an interest rate, as its monetary policy target. Milton Friedman and other monetarists argued that the Fed should adopt a monetary growth rule of increasing the money supply every year at a fixed rate. Support for this proposal declined after 1980 because the relationship between movements in the money supply and movements in real GDP and the price level weakened. John Taylor analyzed the factors involved in Fed decision making and developed the **Taylor rule** for federal funds targeting. The Taylor rule links the Fed's target for the federal funds rate to economic variables. Over the past decade, many economists and central bankers have expressed significant interest in using **inflation targeting**, under which monetary policy is conducted to commit the central bank to achieving a publicly announced inflation target. In 2012, the Fed joined a number of foreign central banks in adopting inflation targeting. The Fed's performance in the 1980s, 1990s, and early 2000s generally received high marks from economists.

MyEconLab   Visit www.myeconlab.com to complete these exercises online and get instant feedback.

Review Questions

5.1 What is a *monetary rule*, as opposed to a *monetary policy*? What monetary rule would Milton Friedman have liked the Fed to follow? Why has support for a monetary rule of the kind Friedman advocated declined since 1980?

5.2 For more than 20 years, the Fed has used the federal funds rate as its monetary policy target. Why doesn't the Fed target the money supply at the same time?

5.3 What is the Taylor rule? What is its purpose?

Problems and Applications

5.4 In an interview, Paul Volcker, chairman of the Federal Reserve's Board of Governors from 1979 to 1987, was asked about the Fed's use of monetary policy to reduce the rate of inflation. Volcker replied:

> The Federal Reserve had been attempting to deal with ... inflation for some time. ... By the time I became chairman ... we adopted an approach of ... saying, We'll take the emphasis off of interest rates and put the emphasis on the growth in the money supply, which is at the root cause of inflation ... we will stop the money supply from increasing as rapidly as it was ... and interest rates went up a lot. ... We said ... we'll take whatever consequences that means for the interest rate because that will enable us to get inflation under control.

Explain why the Fed, while Paul Volcker was chairman, did not target both the growth of the money supply and interest rates.

Source: "Paul Volcker Interview," http://www.pbs.org/fmc/interviews/volcker.htm.

5.5 **(Related to** Solved Problem 8A.5 **on page 361)** Suppose that the equilibrium real federal funds rate is 2 percent and the target rate of inflation is 2 percent. Use the following information and the Taylor rule to calculate the federal funds rate target:

> Current inflation rate = 4 percent
> Potential GDP = 17.0 trillion
> Real GDP = 17.17 trillion

5.6 **(Related to** Solved Problem 8A.5 **on page 361)** In discussing the Taylor rule, John Taylor wrote, "I realize that there are differences of opinion about what is the best rule to guide policy and that some at the Fed (including Janet Yellen) now prefer a rule with a higher coefficient [on the output gap]."

   a. If Fed policy were guided by a Taylor rule with a coefficient of 1, rather than 0.5, on the output gap, would the federal funds rate be higher or lower during a recession? Briefly explain.

   b. Why might economists and policymakers disagree over the best rule to guide monetary policy?

   Source: John Taylor, "Cross-Checking 'Checking in on the Taylor Rule,'" www.economicsone.com, July 16, 2013.

5.7 (Related to Solved Problem 8A.5 **on page 361)** Two economists at the Federal Reserve Bank of Cleveland note that "estimates of potential GDP are very fluid, [which] suggests there is considerable error in our current measure." They conclude that "this lack of precision should be recognized when policy recommendations are made using a Taylor-type rule." Briefly explain their reasoning.

   Source: Charles Carlstrom and Timothy Stehulak, "Mutable Economic Laws and Calculating Unemployment and Output Gaps—An Application to Taylor Rules," Federal Reserve Bank of Cleveland, June 6, 2015.

5.8 While serving as the president of the Federal Reserve Bank of St. Louis, William Poole stated, "Although my own preference is for zero inflation properly managed, I believe that a central bank consensus on some other numerical goal of reasonably low inflation is more important than the exact number." Briefly explain why the economy might benefit from an explicit inflation target even if the target chosen is not a zero rate of inflation.

   Source: William Poole, "Understanding the Fed," *Federal Reserve Bank of St. Louis Review*, Vol. 89, No. 1, January/February 2007, p. 4.

5.9 (Related to the Making the Connection **on page 363)** October 2015 was the forty-second consecutive month that the rate of inflation as measured by the personal consumption expenditures (PCE) price index was below the Federal Reserve's target of 2 percent.

   a. Briefly explain why using the consumer price index (CPI) might yield a rate of inflation different from that found using the PCE price index.

   b. Explain how the choice of the price index the Federal Reserve uses to measure inflation can affect monetary policy.

   Source: Zeppo Mitchell, "Inflation Misses Fed 2% Target for 38th Straight Month," *Wall Street Journal*, August 3, 2015.

8A.6 ## Fed Policies during the 2007–2009 Recession, pages 365–370

LEARNING OBJECTIVE: Describe the policies the Federal Reserve used during the 2007–2009 recession.

Summary

A housing bubble that began to deflate in 2006 helped cause the recession of 2007–2009 and an accompanying financial crisis. In response, the Federal Reserve instituted a variety of policy actions. In a series of steps, it cut the target for the federal funds rate from 5.25 percent in September 2007 to effectively zero in December 2008. The decline in the housing market caused wider problems in the financial system, as defaults on home mortgages rose and the value of mortgage-backed securities declined. The Fed and the U.S. Treasury Department implemented a series of new policies to provide liquidity and restore confidence. The Fed expanded the types of firms eligible for discount loans and began lending directly to corporations by purchasing commercial paper. Under the *Troubled Asset Relief Program*, the Treasury provided financial support to banks and other financial firms in exchange for part ownership. The Treasury also moved to have the federal government take control of Fannie Mae and Freddie Mac, government-sponsored firms that play a key role in the mortgage market. The failure of the investment bank Lehman Brothers in September 2008 led to a deepening of the financial crisis and provided the motivation for some of the new policies. Ultimately, the new policies stabilized the financial system, but their long-term effects remain the subject of debate.

MyEconLab   Visit **www.myeconlab.com** to complete these exercises online and get instant feedback.

Review Questions

6.1 What is a mortgage? What were the important developments in the mortgage market during the years after 1970?

6.2 Beginning in 2008, the Federal Reserve and the U.S. Treasury Department responded to the financial crisis by intervening in financial markets in unprecedented ways. Briefly summarize the actions of the Fed and the Treasury.

Problems and Applications

6.3 A newspaper article in the fall of 2007 stated, "The luxury-home builder Hovnanian Enterprises reported its fourth consecutive quarterly loss on Thursday, citing continuing problems of credit availability and high inventory." Why was Hovnanian suffering losses? What does the article mean by "credit availability"? How would problems of credit availability affect a homebuilder such as Hovnanian Enterprises?

   Source: "New Loss for Home Builder," Associated Press, September 7, 2007.

6.4 An article in a Federal Reserve publication observes that "20 or 30 years ago, local financial institutions were the only option for some borrowers. Today, borrowers have access to national (and even international) sources of mortgage finance." What caused this change in the sources of mortgage finance? What would be the likely consequence of this change for the interest rates borrowers have to pay on mortgages? Briefly explain.

Source: Daniel J. McDonald and Daniel L. Thornton, "A Primer on the Mortgage Market and Mortgage Finance," *Federal Reserve Bank of St. Louis Review,* January/February 2008, pp. 31–45.

6.5 The Federal Reserve releases transcripts of its Federal Open Market Committee (FOMC) meetings only after a five-year lag in order to preserve the confidentiality of the discussions. When the transcripts of the FOMC's 2008 meetings were released, one member of the Board of Governors was quoted as saying in an April 2008 meeting, "I think it is very possible that we will look back and say, particularly after the Bear Stearns episode, that we have turned the corner in terms of the financial disruption." Did this member's analysis turn out to be correct? Briefly explain why his prediction may have seemed reasonable at the time.

Source: Jon Hilsenrath, "New View into Fed's Response to Crisis," *Wall Street Journal,* February 21, 2014.

6.6 In late 2012, the U.S. Treasury sold the last of the stock it had purchased in the insurance company AIG. The Treasury earned a profit on the $22.7 billion it had invested in AIG in 2008. An article in *Wall Street Journal* noted, "This step in AIG's turnaround, which essentially closes the book on one of the most controversial bailouts of the financial crisis, seemed nearly unattainable in 2008, when the insurer's imminent collapse sent shockwaves through the global economy."
a. Why did the federal government bail out AIG?
b. Why was the government bailout controversial?
c. Does the fact the federal government earned a profit on its investment in AIG mean that economists and policymakers who opposed the bailout were necessarily wrong? Briefly explain.

Source: Jeffrey Sparshott and Erik Holm, "End of a Bailout: U.S. Sells Last AIG Shares," *Wall Street Journal,* December 11, 2012.

6.7 Recall that *securitization* is the process of turning a loan, such as a mortgage, into a bond that can be bought and sold in secondary markets. An article in the *Economist* notes:

> That securitization caused more subprime mortgages to be written is not in doubt. By offering access to a much deeper pool of capital, securitization helped to bring down the cost of mortgages and made home-ownership more affordable for borrowers with poor credit histories.

What is a "subprime mortgage"? What is a "deeper pool of capital"? Why would securitization give mortgage borrowers access to a deeper pool of capital? Would a subprime borrower be likely to pay a higher or a lower interest rate than a borrower with a better credit history? Under what circumstances might a lender prefer to loan money to a borrower with a poor credit history rather than to a borrower with a good credit history? Briefly explain.

Source: "Ruptured Credit," *Economist,* May 15, 2008.

6.8 In 2015, Richard Fuld, the last CEO of Lehman Brothers, gave a talk in which, according to an article in the *Wall Street Journal,* "He outlined what he called the 'perfect storm' of events that led to the financial crisis, saying 'it all started with the government' and policies that subsidized cheap loans for people to buy homes in order to help them chase the American dream."
a. Briefly outline the events that led to the financial crisis. Do you agree with Fuld that the events constitute a "perfect storm"—that is, a series of unfortunate events happening at the same time in a way that would have been difficult to anticipate?
b. Which government policies mentioned in the module could be said to be subsidizing cheap loans? What does Fuld mean by saying that these policies were intended to help people "chase the American dream"?

Source: Maureen Farrell, "Lehman's Fuld Says It Wasn't His Fault," *Wall Street Journal,* May 28, 2015.

6.9 **(Related to the** Making the Connection **on page 368)** Suppose you buy a house for $150,000. One year later, the market price of the house has risen to $165,000. What is the return on your investment in the house if you made a down payment of 20 percent and took out a mortgage loan for the other 80 percent? What if you made a down payment of 5 percent and borrowed the other 95 percent? Be sure to show your calculations in your answer.

Real-Time Data Exercises

D8A.1(Following news of FOMC meetings) Go to www.federalreserve.gov, the Web site for the Federal Reserve Board of Governors, and read the most recent Federal Open Market Committee (FOMC) press release. At the Web site, select "Monetary Policy" at the top of the screen and then select "Federal Open Market Committee" on the far left of the screen. Select "Meeting calendars and information." Finally, scroll down and select Statement for the date of the most recent FOMC meeting. Answer the following questions on the basis of the FOMC press release.
a. Did the FOMC change the target for the federal funds rate? If so, what was the change?
b. On balance, in its statement, does the FOMC appear to be more concerned about slow economic growth or high inflation?
c. Did the FOMC change the interest rate paid on bank reserves?
d. Did the Fed announce any other monetary policy actions?

D8A.2(Movements in the federal funds rate relative to the target) Go to the Web site of the Federal Reserve Bank of St. Louis (FRED) (research.stlouisfed.org/fred2) and download and graph the data series for the effective federal funds rate (DFF), the upper limit of the target range for the federal funds rate (DFEDTARU), and the lower limit for the target range (DFEDTARL). Plot on the same graph values for all three data series from December 16, 2008, to the most recent day available. Over this period, has the Fed been able to keep the effective federal funds rate within the target range? Briefly explain.

D8A.3   **(Comparing different measures of the inflation rate)** Go to the Web site of the Federal Reserve Bank of St. Louis (FRED) (research.stlouisfed.org/fred2/) and find the most recent values and values from the same month one year before for the following three measures of the price level: (1) the Consumer Price Index for All Urban Consumers: All Items (CPIAUCSL), (2) the Personal Consumption Expenditures: Chain-type Price Index (PCEPI), and (3) the Personal Consumption Expenditures excluding food and energy (chain-type price index) (DPCCRG3A086NBEA).

a. Using these data, calculate the inflation rate over this year as measured by each of the three price indexes.

b. Which of the three measures of inflation was highest during this year? Which measure was lowest? Why do the measures of inflation differ?

IBM Sings the Dollar Blues

The company that became the International Business Machines Corporation (IBM) was founded in New York City in 1911. For decades, under the leadership of CEOs Tom Watson, Sr., and his son Tom Watson, Jr., IBM was best known for manufacturing large computer systems used by corporations. As business computing made the transition from mainframes to desktop computers, IBM established a new standard with its personal computers powered by Intel chips and using an operating system developed by Microsoft. In 2015, IBM was well into another transition, away from manufacturing hardware and toward selling cloud-based computing software services. As CEO Virginia Rometty put it, "We've reinvented this company one more time." Today, IBM has more than 375,000 employees, $90 billion in revenue, and $20 billion in profits.

Most people think of IBM as a giant of U.S. business. However, as the company name indicates, IBM is an international company with offices throughout Europe, Latin America, Africa, and Asia. In 2014, more than two-thirds of IBM's revenue was earned outside the United States. As a result, the company's profits are affected by fluctuations in the value of the dollar in exchange for other currencies. In some years, converting revenue from foreign currencies yields fewer dollars than in other years. For example, in 2014, IBM's global revenue was nearly $2 billion lower when measured in terms of dollars than when measured in local currencies—pounds in Great Britain, euros in Germany, yen in Japan. Why the discrepancy? The value of the dollar had increased relative to most other currencies. So, converting pounds, euros, and yen into dollars yielded fewer dollars for IBM. As an article in the *Wall Street Journal* put it, "The company . . . has run into a stiff headwind from the rising value of the dollar."

As we saw in Module 8A, one reason for the increasing value of the U.S. dollar in 2015 was rising U.S. interest rates. Higher interest rates made financial investments in the United States more attractive to foreign investors, which increased the demand for U.S. dollars and the exchange rate between the dollar and other currencies. In this module and the next, we will look more closely at how exchange rates are determined and at other important issues involving the international financial system.

Sources: Don Clark, "IBM Pumps $4 Billion into Cloud and Mobile Initiatives," *Wall Street Journal*, February 26, 2015; Steve Lohr, "IBM Revenue Falls 13% Despite Big Gains in New Fields," *New York Times*, July 20, 2015; and International Business Machines Corporation, *2014 IBM Annual Report*, February 24, 2015.

Economics in Your Life

The South Korean Central Bank and Your Car Loan

Suppose that you are shopping for a new car, which you plan to finance with a loan from a local bank. While reading an article in the *Wall Street Journal* on your smartphone one morning, you see this headline: "The Bank of Korea, South Korea's central bank, announces it will sell its large holdings of U.S. Treasury bonds." Will the Bank of Korea's decision to sell its U.S. Treasury bonds affect the interest rate you pay on your car loan? As you read this module, try to answer this question. You can check your answer against the one we provide on **page 401** at the end of this module.

I n this module, we look closely at the linkages among countries at the macroeconomic level. Countries are linked by trade in goods and services and by flows of financial investment. We will see how policymakers in all countries take these linkages into account when conducting monetary policy and fiscal policy.

9.1 The Balance of Payments: Linking the United States to the International Economy

LEARNING OBJECTIVE: Explain how the balance of payments is calculated.

Today, consumers, firms, and investors routinely interact with consumers, firms, and investors in other economies. A consumer in France may use computer software produced in the United States, watch a television manufactured in South Korea, and wear a sweater made in Italy. A U.S. firm like IBM may sell its products in dozens of countries around the world. An investor in London may sell a U.S. Treasury bill to an investor in Mexico City. Nearly all economies are **open economies** and have extensive interactions in trade or finance with other countries. Open economies interact by trading goods and services and by making investments in each other's economies. A **closed economy** has no interactions in trade or finance with other countries. No economy today is completely closed, although a few countries, such as North Korea, have very limited economic interactions with other countries.

A good way to understand the interactions between one economy and other economies is through the **balance of payments**, which is a record of a country's trade with other countries in goods, services, and assets. Just as the U.S. Bureau of Economic Analysis is responsible for collecting data on the gross domestic product (GDP), it is also responsible for collecting data on the balance of payments. Table 9.1 shows the balance of payments for the United States in 2014. Notice that the table contains three "accounts": the *current account*, the *financial account*, and the *capital account*.

The Current Account

The **current account** records *current*, or short-term, flows of funds into and out of a country. The current account for the United States includes: (1) exports and imports of goods and services (recall that the difference between exports and imports of goods and services is called *net exports*); (2) income received by U.S. residents from investments in other countries and income paid on investments in the United States owned by residents of other countries (the difference between investment income received and investment income paid is called *net income on investments*); and (3) the difference between transfers made to residents of other countries and transfers received by U.S. residents from other countries (called *net transfers*). If you make a donation to a charity caring for orphans in Afghanistan, it will be included in net transfers. Any payments received by U.S. residents are positive numbers in the current account, and any payments made by U.S. residents are negative numbers in the current account.

The Balance of Trade Part of the current account is the **balance of trade**, which is the difference between the value of the goods a country exports and the value of the goods the country imports. The balance of trade is the largest item in the current account and is a topic that politicians and the media often discuss. If a country exports more goods than it imports, it has a *trade surplus*. If a country exports less than it imports, it has a *trade deficit*. In 2014, the United States had a trade deficit of $741 billion. In the same year, Japan had a trade deficit of $121 billion, and China had a trade surplus of $369 billion. Figure 9.1 on page 384 shows imports and exports of goods between the United States and its trading partners and between Japan and its trading partners. The data show that the United States ran a trade deficit in 2014 with all its major trading partners and with every region of the world apart from Latin America (except Mexico) and Africa. Japan ran trade surpluses with the United States, Asia (except China), and Latin America, and it ran trade deficits with the other regions. (Note that exports from

Open economy An economy that has interactions in trade or finance with other countries.

Closed economy An economy that has no interactions in trade or finance with other countries.

Balance of payments The record of a country's trade with other countries in goods, services, and assets.

Current account The part of the balance of payments that records a country's net exports, net income on investments, and net transfers.

Balance of trade The difference between the value of the goods a country exports and the value of the goods a country imports.

Current Account

Exports of goods	$1,633	
Imports of goods	−2,374	
Balance of trade		−741
Exports of services	711	
Imports of services	−477	
Balance of services		234
Income received on investments	823	
Income payments on investments	−585	
Net income on investments		238
Net transfers		−120
Balance on current account		**−389**

Financial Account

Increase in foreign holdings of assets in the United States	1,031	
Increase in U.S. holdings of assets in foreign countries	−792	
Balance on financial account		239

Balance on Capital Account

	0
Statistical discrepancy	150
Balance of payments	0

Note: Subtotals may not sum to totals because of rounding.

Source: U.S. Bureau of Economic Analysis, "U.S. International Transactions," June 18, 2015.

MyEconLab Real-time data

Table 9.1

The U.S. Balance of Payments, 2014 (billions of dollars)

> The sum of the balance of trade and the balance of services equals net exports.

the United States to Japan in panel (a) of Figure 9.1 should equal imports by Japan from the United States in panel (b). These two numbers are different because international trade statistics are not measured exactly.)

Net Exports Equals the Sum of the Balance of Trade and the Balance of Services   Recall that *net exports* is a component of aggregate expenditure. Net exports is not explicitly shown in Table 9.1, but we can calculate it by adding the balance of trade and the balance of services. The *balance of services* is the difference between the value of the services a country exports and the value of the services the country imports. Notice that, technically, net exports is *not* equal to the current account balance because this account also includes net income on investments and net transfers. Because these other two items are relatively small, though, it is often a convenient simplification to think of net exports as being equal to the current account balance.   MyEconLab Concept Check

The Financial Account

The **financial account** records purchases of assets a country has made abroad and foreign purchases of assets in the country. The financial account records long-term flows of funds into and out of a country. There is a *capital outflow* from the United States when an investor in the United States buys a bond issued by a foreign company or government or when a U.S. firm builds a factory in another country. There is a *capital inflow* into the United States when a foreign investor buys a bond issued by a U.S. firm or by the government or when a foreign firm builds a factory in the United States. Notice that we are using the word *capital* here to apply not just to physical assets, such as factories, but also to financial assets, such as shares of stock. When firms build or buy facilities in

Financial account The part of the balance of payments that records purchases of assets a country has made abroad and foreign purchases of assets in the country.

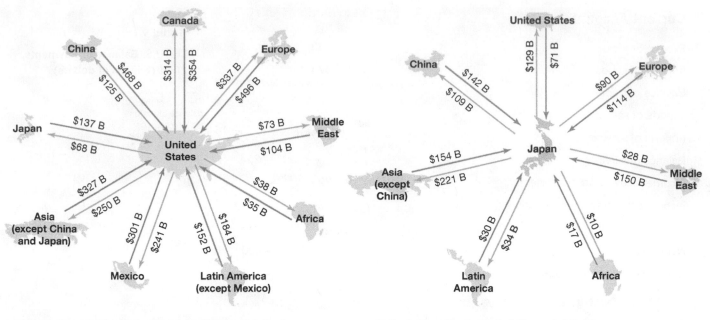

(a) Trade flows for the United States (in billions of dollars)

(b) Trade flows for Japan (in billions of dollars)

MyEconLab Animation

Figure 9.1   **Trade Flows for the United States and Japan, 2014**

Panel (a) shows that in 2014, the United States ran a trade deficit with all its major trading partners and with every region of the world except for Latin America and Africa. Panel (b) shows that Japan ran trade deficits with China, Latin America, Europe, Africa, and the Middle East, and it ran trade surpluses with the United States and Asia. In each panel, the green arrows represent exports from the United States or Japan, and the red arrows represent imports.

Note: Japanese data are converted from yen to dollars at the average 2014 exchange rate of 105.7 yen per dollar.
Sources: U.S. Bureau of Economic Analysis, "U.S. International Transactions," June 18, 2015; and Japanese Ministry of Finance, *Trade Statistics of Japan.*

---

foreign countries, they are engaging in *foreign direct investment*. When investors buy stock or bonds issued in another country, they are engaging in *foreign portfolio investment*.

Another way of thinking of the balance on the financial account is as a measure of *net capital flows*, or the difference between capital inflows and capital outflows. (Here we are omitting a few transactions included in the capital account, as discussed in the next section.) A concept closely related to net capital flows is **net foreign investment**, which is equal to capital outflows minus capital inflows. Net capital flows and net foreign investment are always equal but have opposite signs: When net capital flows are positive, net foreign investment is negative, and when net capital flows are negative, net foreign investment is positive. Net foreign investment is also equal to net foreign direct investment plus net foreign portfolio investment. In Section 9.3, we will use the relationship between the balance on the financial account and net foreign investment to understand an important aspect of the international economic system.   MyEconLab Concept Check

Net foreign investment The difference between capital outflows from a country and capital inflows, also equal to net foreign direct investment plus net foreign portfolio investment.

The Capital Account

A third, less important, part of the balance of payments is called the *capital account*. The **capital account** records relatively minor transactions, such as migrants' transfers—which consist of goods and financial assets people take with them when they leave or enter a country—and sales and purchases of nonproduced, nonfinancial assets. A nonproduced, nonfinancial asset is a copyright, patent, trademark, or right to natural resources. The definitions of the financial account and the capital account are often misunderstood because the capital account prior to 1999 recorded all the transactions now included in both the financial account and the capital account. In other words, capital account transactions went from being a very important part of the balance of payments to being a relatively unimportant part. Because the balance on what is now called the capital account is so small—only $45 million in 2014,

Capital account The part of the balance of payments that records relatively minor transactions, such as migrants' transfers and sales and purchases of nonproduced, nonfinancial assets.

which we rounded to zero in Table 9.1—for simplicity we will ignore it in the remainder of this module.   MyEconLab Concept Check

Why Is the Balance of Payments Always Zero?

The sum of the current account balance, the financial account balance, and the capital account balance equals the balance of payments. Table 9.1 on page 383 shows that the balance of payments for the United States in 2014 was zero. It's not just by chance that this balance was zero; *the balance of payments is always zero*. Notice that the current account balance in 2014 was –$389 billion. The balance on the financial account (which has the opposite sign to the balance on the current account) was $239 billion. To make the balance on the current account equal to the balance on the financial account, the balance of payments includes an entry called the *statistical discrepancy*. (Remember that we are ignoring the balance on the capital account. If we included it, we would say that the statistical discrepancy takes on a value equal to the difference between the current account balance and the sum of the balance on the financial account and the balance on the capital account.)

Why does the U.S. Department of Commerce include the statistical discrepancy entry to force the balance of payments to equal zero? If the sum of the current account balance and the financial account balance does not equal zero, some imports or exports of goods and services or some capital inflows or capital outflows were not measured accurately.

To better understand why the balance of payments must equal zero every year, consider the following: In 2014, the United States spent $389 billion more on goods, services, and other items in the current account than it received. What happened to that $389 billion? We know that every dollar of that $389 billion was used by foreign individuals or firms to invest in the United States or was added to foreign holdings of dollars. We know this because logically there is nowhere else for the dollars to go: If the dollars weren't spent on U.S. goods and services—and we know they weren't because if they had been, they would have shown up in the current account—they must have been spent on investments in the United States or not spent at all. Dollars that aren't spent are added to foreign holdings of dollars. Changes in foreign holdings of dollars are called *official reserve transactions*. Foreign investment in the United States and additions to foreign holdings of dollars both show up as positive entries in the U.S. financial

Don't Let This Happen to You

Don't Confuse the Balance of Trade, the Current Account Balance, and the Balance of Payments

The terminology of international economics can be tricky. Remember that the *balance of trade* includes only trade in goods; it does not include services. This observation is important because the United States, for example, usually imports more *goods* than it exports, but it usually exports more *services* than it imports. As a result, the U.S. trade deficit is almost always larger than the current account deficit. The *current account balance* includes the balance of trade, the balance of services, net investment income, and net transfers. Net investment income and net transfers are much smaller than the balance of trade and the balance of services.

Even though the *balance of payments* is equal to the sum of the current account balance and the financial account balance—and must equal zero—you may sometimes see references to a balance of payments "surplus" or "deficit."

These references have two explanations. The first is that the person making the reference has confused the balance of payments with either the balance of trade or the current account balance. This mistake is very common. The second explanation is that the person is not including official reserve transactions in the financial account. If we separate changes in U.S. holdings of foreign currencies and changes in foreign holdings of U.S. dollars from other financial account entries, the current account balance and the financial account balance do not have to sum to zero, and there can be a balance of payments surplus or deficit. These distinctions may sound complicated—and they are! But don't worry. Knowing how official reserve transactions are accounted for is not crucial to understanding the basic ideas behind the balance of payments.

MyEconLab Study Plan

Your Turn: Test your understanding by doing related problem 1.6 on pages 419–420 at the end of this module.

account. Therefore, a current account deficit must be exactly offset by a financial account surplus, leaving the balance of payments equal to zero. Similarly, a country that runs a current account surplus, such as China, must run a financial account deficit of exactly the same size. If a country's current account surplus is not exactly equal to its financial account deficit, or if a country's current account deficit is not exactly equal to its financial account surplus, some transactions must not have been accounted for. The statistical discrepancy is included in the balance of payments to compensate for these uncounted transactions.   MyEconLab Concept Check

---

Solved Problem 9.1   MyEconLab Interactive Animation

Understanding the Arithmetic of the Balance of Payments

Test your understanding of the relationship between the current account and the financial account by evaluating the following assertion by a political commentator:

The industrial countries are committing economic suicide. Every year, they invest more and more in emerging countries, such as South Korea. Every year, more U.S., Japanese, and European manufacturing firms move their factories to emerging countries. With extensive new factories and low wages, emerging countries now export far more to the industrial countries than they import.

Solving the Problem

Step 1: **Review the module material.** This problem is about the relationship between the current account and the financial account, so you may want to review the section "Why Is the Balance of Payments Always Zero?" which begins on page 385.

Step 2: **Explain the errors in the commentator's argument.** The argument sounds plausible. It would be easy to find statements similar to this one in recent books and articles by well-known political commentators. But the argument contains an important error: The commentator has failed to understand the relationship between the current account and the financial account. The commentator asserts that emerging countries are receiving large capital inflows from industrial countries. In other words, emerging countries are running financial account surpluses. The commentator also asserts that emerging countries are exporting more than they are importing. In other words, they are running current account surpluses. As we have seen in this section, it is impossible to run a current account surplus *and* a financial account surplus simultaneously. A country that runs a current account surplus *must* run a financial account deficit and vice versa.

Extra Credit: Most emerging economies that have received large inflows of foreign investment during the past two decades, such as South Korea, Thailand, and Malaysia, have run current account deficits: They import more goods and services than they export. Emerging economies that run current account surpluses, such as Singapore, also run financial account deficits: They invest more abroad than other countries invest in them.

The point here is not obvious; if it was, it wouldn't confuse so many intelligent politicians, journalists, and political commentators. Unless you understand the relationship between the current account and the financial account, you won't be able to understand a key aspect of the international economy.

MyEconLab Study Plan   **Your Turn:** For more practice, do related problems 1.7, 1.8, and 1.9 on page 420 at the end of this module.

9.2 The Foreign Exchange Market and Exchange Rates

LEARNING OBJECTIVE: Explain how exchange rates are determined and how changes in exchange rates affect the prices of imports and exports.

A firm that operates entirely within the United States will price its products in dollars and will use dollars to pay its suppliers' bills, wages and salaries to its workers, interest to its bondholders, and dividends to its shareholders. A multinational corporation such as IBM, in contrast, may sell its products in many different countries and receive payments in many different currencies. Its suppliers and workers may also be spread around the world and may have to be paid in local currencies. In addition to exchanging currencies, corporations may also use the international financial system to borrow in a foreign currency. For example, during a period of rapid expansion in East Asian countries such as Thailand and South Korea during the late 1990s, many large firms received dollar loans from foreign banks. When firms make extensive use of foreign currencies, they must deal with fluctuations in the exchange rate.

The **nominal exchange rate** is the value of one country's currency in terms of another country's currency. Economists also calculate the *real exchange rate*, which corrects the nominal exchange rate for changes in prices of goods and services. We discuss the real exchange rate later in this section. The nominal exchange rate determines how many units of a foreign currency you can purchase with $1. For example, the exchange rate between the U.S. dollar and the Japanese yen can be expressed as ¥100 = $1. (This exchange rate can also be expressed as how many U.S. dollars are required to buy 1 Japanese yen: $0.01 = ¥1.) The market for foreign exchange is very active, with the equivalent of more than $4 trillion worth of currency being traded each day. The exchange rates that result from this trading are reported on a number of online sites devoted to economic news and in the business or financial sections of most newspapers.

Banks and other financial institutions around the world employ currency traders, who are linked together by computer. Rather than exchange large amounts of paper currency, they buy and sell deposits in banks. For example, a bank buying or selling dollars will actually be buying or selling dollar bank deposits. Dollar bank deposits exist not just in banks in the United States but also in banks around the world. Suppose that the Crédit Agricole bank in France wants to sell U.S. dollars and buy Japanese yen. The bank may exchange U.S. dollar deposits that it owns for Japanese yen deposits owned by the Deutsche Bank in Germany. Businesses and individuals usually obtain foreign currency from banks in their own country.

Nominal exchange rate The value of one country's currency in terms of another country's currency.

Making the Connection
MyEconLab Video

Exchange Rate Listings

You can find the exchange rates between the dollar and other major currencies on many online sites, such as wsj.com, Bloomberg.com, or finance.yahoo.com, as well as in the financial pages of most newspapers. The exchange rates in the following table are for August 14, 2015. The euro is the common currency used by 19 European countries, including France, Germany, and Italy, but not the United Kingdom.

Exchange Rate between the U.S. Dollar and the Indicated Currency		
Currency	Units of Foreign Currency per U.S. Dollar	U.S. Dollars per Unit of Foreign Currency
Canadian dollar	1.31	0.763
Japanese yen	124.32	0.008
Mexican peso	16.37	0.061
British pound	0.64	1.56
Euro	0.90	1.11

Notice that the expression for the exchange rate stated as units of foreign currency per U.S. dollar is the *reciprocal* of the exchange rate stated as U.S. dollars per unit of foreign currency. So, the exchange rate between the U.S. dollar and the British pound can be stated as either 0.64 British pounds per U.S. dollar or 1/0.64 = 1.56 U.S. dollars per British pound.

Banks are the most active participants in the market for foreign exchange. Typically, banks buy currency for slightly less than the amount for which they sell it. This spread between the buying and selling prices allows banks to cover their costs from currency trading. Therefore, when most businesses and individuals buy foreign currency from a bank, they receive fewer units of foreign currency per dollar than would be indicated by the exchange rate shown on online business sites or printed in the newspaper.

Source: *Wall Street Journal*, August 14, 2015.

MyEconLab Study Plan

Your Turn: Test your understanding by doing related problem 2.5 on pages 420–421 at the end of this module.

The market exchange rate is determined by the interaction of demand and supply, just as other prices are. There are three sources of foreign currency demand for the U.S. dollar:

1. Foreign firms and households that want to buy goods and services produced in the United States.

2. Foreign firms and households that want to invest in the United States either through foreign direct investment—buying or building factories or other facilities in the United States—or through foreign portfolio investment—buying stocks and bonds issued in the United States.

3. Currency traders who believe that the value of the dollar in the future will be greater than its value today.

Equilibrium in the Market for Foreign Exchange

Figure 9.2 shows the demand and supply of U.S. dollars for Japanese yen. Notice that as we move up the vertical axis, the value of the dollar increases relative to the value of the yen. When the exchange rate is ¥150 = $1, the dollar is worth 1.5 times as much relative to the yen as when the exchange rate is ¥100 = $1. Consider, first, the demand curve for dollars in exchange for yen. The demand curve has the normal downward slope. When the value of the dollar is high, the quantity of dollars demanded will be low. A Japanese investor will be more likely to buy a $1,000 bond issued by the U.S.

MyEconLab Animation

Figure 9.2

Equilibrium in the Foreign Exchange Market

When the exchange rate is ¥150 to the dollar, the exchange rate is above its equilibrium level, and there will be a surplus of dollars. When the exchange rate is ¥100 to the dollar, it is below its equilibrium level, and there will be a shortage of dollars. At an exchange rate of ¥120 to the dollar, the foreign exchange market is in equilibrium.

Treasury when the exchange rate is ¥100 = $1 and the investor pays only ¥100,000 to buy $1,000 than when the exchange rate is ¥150 = $1 and the investor must pay ¥150,000. Similarly, a Japanese firm is more likely to buy $150 million worth of microchips from Intel Corporation when the exchange rate is ¥100 = $1 and the microchips can be purchased for ¥15 billion than when the exchange rate is ¥150 = $1 and the microchips cost ¥22.5 billion.

Now consider the supply curve for dollars in exchange for yen. The supply curve has the normal upward slope. When the value of the dollar is high, the quantity of dollars supplied in exchange for yen will be high. A U.S. investor will be more likely to buy a ¥200,000 bond issued by the Japanese government when the exchange rate is ¥200 = $1 and he needs to pay only $1,000 to buy ¥200,000 than when the exchange rate is ¥100 = $1 and he must pay $2,000. The owner of a U.S. electronics store is more likely to buy ¥20 million worth of television sets from the Sony Corporation when the exchange rate is ¥200 = $1 and she needs to pay only $100,000 to purchase the televisions than when the exchange rate is ¥100 = $1 and she must pay $200,000.

As in any other market, equilibrium occurs in the foreign exchange market where the quantity supplied equals the quantity demanded. In Figure 9.2, ¥120 = $1 is the equilibrium exchange rate. At exchange rates above ¥120 = $1, there will be a surplus of dollars and downward pressure on the exchange rate. The surplus and the downward pressure will not be eliminated until the exchange rate falls to ¥120 = $1. If the exchange rate is below ¥120 = $1, there will be a shortage of dollars and upward pressure on the exchange rate. The shortage and the upward pressure will not be eliminated until the exchange rate rises to ¥120 = $1. Surpluses and shortages in the foreign exchange market are eliminated very quickly because the volume of trading in major currencies such as the dollar and the yen is large, and currency traders are linked together by computer.

Currency appreciation occurs when the market value of a country's currency increases relative to the value of another country's currency. **Currency depreciation** occurs when the market value of a country's currency decreases relative to the value of another country's currency.   MyEconLab Concept Check

Currency appreciation An increase in the market value of one currency relative to another currency.

Currency depreciation A decrease in the market value of one currency relative to another currency.

How Do Shifts in Demand and Supply Affect the Exchange Rate?

Shifts in the demand and supply curves cause the equilibrium exchange rate to change. Three main factors cause the demand and supply curves in the foreign exchange market to shift:

1. Changes in the demand for U.S.-produced goods and services and changes in the demand for foreign-produced goods and services
2. Changes in the desire to invest in the United States and changes in the desire to invest in foreign countries
3. Changes in the expectations of currency traders about the likely future value of the dollar and the likely future value of foreign currencies

Shifts in the Demand for Foreign Exchange Consider how the three factors just listed will affect the demand for U.S. dollars in exchange for Japanese yen. During an economic expansion in Japan, the incomes of Japanese households will rise, and the demand by Japanese consumers and firms for U.S. goods will increase. At any given exchange rate, the demand for U.S. dollars will increase, and the demand curve will shift to the right. Similarly, if interest rates in the United States rise, the desirability of investing in U.S. financial assets will increase, and the demand curve for dollars will also shift to the right. **Speculators** are currency traders who buy and sell foreign exchange in an attempt to profit from changes in exchange rates. If a speculator becomes convinced that the value of the dollar is going to rise relative to the value of the yen, the speculator will sell yen and buy dollars. If the current exchange rate is ¥120 = $1, and the speculator is convinced that it will soon rise to ¥140 = $1, the speculator could sell

Speculators Currency traders who buy and sell foreign exchange in an attempt to profit from changes in exchange rates.

¥600,000,000 and receive $5,000,000 (= ¥600,000,000/¥120) in return. If the speculator is correct and the value of the dollar rises against the yen to ¥140 = $1, the speculator will be able to exchange $5,000,000 for ¥700,000,000 (= $5,000,000 × ¥140) for a profit of ¥100,000,000.

To summarize, the demand curve for dollars shifts to the right when incomes in Japan rise, when interest rates in the United States rise, or when speculators decide that the value of the dollar will rise relative to the value of the yen.

During a recession in Japan, Japanese incomes will fall, reducing the demand for U.S.-produced goods and services and shifting the demand curve for dollars to the left. Similarly, if interest rates in the United States fall, the desirability of investing in U.S. financial assets will decrease, and the demand curve for dollars will shift to the left. Finally, if speculators become convinced that the future value of the dollar will be lower than its current value, the demand for dollars will fall, and the demand curve will shift to the left.

Shifts in the Supply of Foreign Exchange The factors that affect the supply curve for dollars are similar to those that affect the demand curve for dollars. An economic expansion in the United States increases the incomes of Americans and increases their demand for goods and services, including goods and services made in Japan. As U.S. consumers and firms increase their spending on Japanese products, they must supply dollars in exchange for yen, which causes the supply curve for dollars to shift to the right. Similarly, an increase in interest rates in Japan will make financial investments in Japan more attractive to U.S. investors. These higher Japanese interest rates will cause the supply curve for dollars to shift to the right, as U.S. investors exchange dollars for yen. Finally, if speculators become convinced that the future value of the yen will be higher relative to the dollar than it is today, the supply curve for dollars will shift to the right as traders attempt to exchange dollars for yen.

A recession in the United States will decrease the demand for Japanese products and cause the supply curve for dollars to shift to the left. Similarly, a decrease in interest rates in Japan will make financial investments in Japan less attractive and cause the supply curve for dollars to shift to the left. If traders become convinced that the future value of the yen will be lower relative to the dollar, the supply curve will also shift to the left.

Adjustment to a New Equilibrium The factors that affect the demand and supply for currencies are constantly changing. Whether the exchange rate increases or decreases depends on the direction and size of the shifts in the demand curve and supply curve. For example, as Figure 9.3 shows, if the demand curve for dollars in exchange

Figure 9.3

Shifts in the Demand and Supply Curve Resulting in a Higher Exchange Rate

Holding other factors constant, an increase in the supply of dollars will decrease the equilibrium exchange rate. An increase in the demand for dollars will increase the equilibrium exchange rate. In the case shown in this figure, both the demand curve and the supply curve have shifted to the right. Because the demand curve has shifted to the right by more than the supply curve, the equilibrium exchange rate has increased from ¥120 to $1 at point A to ¥130 to $1 at point B.

for Japanese yen shifts to the right by more than the supply curve shifts, the equilibrium exchange rate will increase. MyEconLab Concept Check

Some Exchange Rates Are Not Determined by the Market

To this point, we have assumed that exchange rates are determined by the market. This assumption is a good one for many currencies, including the U.S. dollar, the euro, the Japanese yen, and the British pound. Some currencies, however, have *fixed exchange rates* that do not change over long periods. For example, for more than 10 years, the value of the Chinese yuan was fixed against the U.S. dollar at a rate of 8.28 yuan to the dollar. As we will discuss in more detail in Module 9, a country's central bank has to intervene in the foreign exchange market to buy and sell its currency if it wishes to keep the exchange rate fixed. MyEconLab Concept Check

How Movements in the Exchange Rate Affect Exports and Imports

When the market value of the dollar increases, the foreign currency price of U.S. exports rises, and the dollar price of foreign imports falls. Suppose that initially the market exchange rate between the U.S. dollar and the euro is $1 = €1. In that case, a Blu-ray disc that has a price of $20 in the United States will have a price of €20 in France. A bottle of French wine that has a price of €50 in France will have a price of $50 in the United States. Now suppose the market exchange rate between the U.S. dollar and the euro changes to $1.20 = €1. Because it now takes more dollars to buy a euro, the dollar has *depreciated* against the euro, and the euro has *appreciated* against the dollar. The depreciation of the dollar has decreased the euro price of the Blu-ray disc from €20 to $20/(1.20 dollars/euro) = €16.67. The dollar price of the French wine has risen from $50 to €50 ×1.20 dollars/euro = $60. As a result, we would expect more Blu-ray discs to be sold in France and less French wine to be sold in the United States.

To generalize, we can conclude:

1. A depreciation in the domestic currency will increase exports and decrease imports, thereby increasing net exports. If real GDP is currently below potential GDP, then, holding all other factors constant, a depreciation in the domestic currency should increase net exports, aggregate demand, and real GDP.

2. An appreciation in the domestic currency should have the opposite effect: Exports should fall, and imports should rise, which will reduce net exports, aggregate demand, and real GDP. MyEconLab Concept Check

---

Making the Connection
MyEconLab Video

Is a Strong Currency Good for a Country?

News stories often refer to a country as having a "strong" currency when the currency's value has been rising relative to other countries' currencies. Should a country want a strong currency? "Strong" certainly seems better than "weak," so most people would answer "yes" to that question. During late 2014 and 2015, as investors anticipated that the Federal Reserve would take action to increase U.S. interest rates, the value of the dollar increased, as shown in the graph on the next page. The graph shows the *trade-weighted exchange rate* for the U.S. dollar, which is an index number similar to the consumer price index (CPI). Just as the CPI weights individual prices by the share the product takes up in a household's budget, the trade-weighted exchange rate for the U.S. dollar weights each individual exchange rate by the share of that country's trade with the United States.

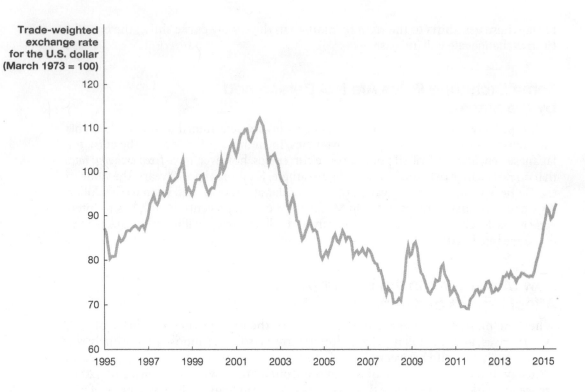

Trade-weighted exchange rate for the U.S. dollar (March 1973 = 100)

In June 2015, President Barack Obama attended a meeting of the Group of 7, an organization of high-income countries. He was initially quoted as saying at that meeting that a strong dollar was a problem for the United States. There was a public outcry, and the president later denied he had made the statement. But clearly, not everyone in a country benefits from a strong currency. Firms that are exporters generally don't benefit. As one headline in the *Wall Street Journal* put it, "Strong Dollar Squeezes U.S. Firms." The CEO of Caterpillar, the U.S.-based heavy equipment manufacturer, was quoted as saying, "The rising dollar will not be good for U.S. manufacturing and the U.S. economy." A strong dollar increases the foreign currency price of U.S. exports, so to buy U.S.-produced goods, European consumers have to pay more euros, Canadian consumers have to pay more Canadian dollars, and Japanese consumers have to pay more yen. The result is a decline in profits for U.S. exporters. As we saw in the module opener, IBM experienced a lower profit in 2014 due to the strong dollar. U.S. firms facing competition from foreign imports can also be hurt by a strong dollar as the dollar prices of foreign imports are reduced.

Although a strong dollar can be bad news for U.S. exporters like Caterpillar and IBM, it can actually be *good* news for U.S. consumers. Between the beginning of 2014 and the middle of 2015, the average price of goods imported into the United States dropped by over 9 percent. U.S. consumers benefited from lower prices of imported goods from cars to clothing to electronics.

If many U.S. firms were hurt by the strong value of the dollar in 2014 and 2015, while U.S. consumers were helped, the reverse was true in Japan, where the value of the yen was falling. The Bank of Japan was pursuing an expansionary monetary policy that had driven Japanese interest rates to low levels. Investors reacted by selling yen and buying U.S. dollars and other currencies, driving down the value of the yen. The value of the yen declined by more than 30 percent in exchange for the U.S. dollar. Five Japanese automobile companies were able to report record profits as the prices of the cars they were exporting fell in terms of dollars and other foreign currencies. But because Japan relies heavily on imports of food, oil, and other important goods, consumers suffered as yen prices of foreign imports soared. As one Japanese politician put it, the Japanese government, by allowing the value of the yen to decline, had shown "little concern for . . . ordinary households."

We can conclude that neither a "strong" currency nor a "weak" currency is all good or all bad for a country's businesses and households. Swings in exchange rates create both winners and losers.

Sources: James Ramage, "Dollar Retreats as Investors Cash in on Jobs-Report Gains," *Wall Street Journal*, June 8, 2015; Paul Ziobro, Josh Mitchell, and Theo Francis, "Strong Dollar Squeezes U.S. Firms," *Wall Street Journal*, January 27, 2015; Mitsuru Obe, "Falling Yen Stirs Debate in Japan," *Wall Street Journal*, December 7, 2014; and data from the Federal Reserve Bank of St. Louis and the U.S. Bureau of Economic Analysis.

Your Turn: Test your understanding by doing related problem 2.6 on page 421 at the end of this module.

MyEconLab Study Plan

Don't Let This Happen to You

Don't Confuse What Happens When a Currency Appreciates with What Happens When It Depreciates

One of the most confusing aspects of exchange rates is that they can be expressed in two ways. We can express the exchange rate between the dollar and the yen either as how many yen can be purchased with $1 or as how many dollars can be purchased with ¥1. That is, we can express the exchange rate as ¥100 = $1 or as $0.01 = ¥1.

When a currency appreciates, it increases in value relative to another currency. When it depreciates, it decreases in value relative to another currency. If the exchange rate changes from ¥100 = $1 to ¥120 = $1, the dollar has appreciated and the yen has depreciated because it now takes more yen to buy $1. If the exchange rate changes from $0.010 = ¥1 to $0.015 = ¥1, however, the dollar has

depreciated and the yen has appreciated because it now takes more dollars to buy ¥1. This situation can appear somewhat confusing because the exchange rate seems to have "increased" in both cases. To determine which currency has appreciated and which has depreciated, it is important to remember that an appreciation of the domestic currency means that it now takes *more* units of the foreign currency to buy one unit of the domestic currency. A depreciation of the domestic currency means it takes *fewer* units of the foreign currency to buy one unit of the domestic currency. This observation holds no matter which way we express the exchange rate.

MyEconLab Study Plan

Your Turn: Test your understanding by doing related problem 2.7 on page 421 at the end of the module.

Solved Problem 9.2

MyEconLab Interactive Animation

Subaru Benefits from a Weak Yen

Today, most Japanese automobile companies have manufacturing plants in the United States. Honda, for example, exports from Japan only 21 percent of the cars it sells in the United States. Fuji Heavy Industries, whose main car brand is Subaru, is an exception in still producing most of its cars in Japan. An article in the *Wall Street Journal* observed that for Fuji Heavy Industries, "the plunging yen has turned a

problem—a shortage of production in the U.S.—into an unexpected boon."

a. What does the article mean by a "plunging yen"?
b. Why would a plunging yen be a boon for Fuji Heavy Industries?
c. Briefly explain whether a plunging yen would help or hurt Honda.

Solving the Problem

Step 1: **Review the module material.** This problem is about changes in the value of a currency, so you may want to review the section "How Movements in the Exchange Rate Affect Exports and Imports" on page 391.

Step 2: **Answer part (a) by explaining what the article means by a "plunging yen."** In this case, a plunging yen means a yen that is worth less in exchange for the U.S. dollar. With a plunging yen, a larger number of yen would be needed to exchange for one U.S. dollar.

Step 3: **Answer part (b) by explaining how a plunging yen will affect Fuji Heavy Industries.** When Fuji Heavy Industries manufactures cars in Japan, it pays its production costs—including the salaries of its assembly-line workers and payments to its suppliers—with yen. With a falling value of the yen, the dollar price of cars Fuji sells in the United States decreases. As a result,

Fuji will gain sales from other companies, particularly those that produce their cars in the United States. If Fuji produced its cars in the United States, it would *not* have gained this advantage.

Step 4: **Answer part (c) by explaining whether a plunging yen will help or hurt Honda.** Because most of the cars Honda sells in the United States are also produced here, most of the company's production costs and also most of the revenue it earns are in dollars. So, Honda will not be directly affected by fluctuations in the yen–dollar exchange rate. Honda will, though, likely lose some sales to Fuji as the dollar prices of Subarus declines.

Extra Credit: Managers at Honda, Toyota, and Nissan are aware that when the value of the yen declines against the dollar, they would be better off producing in Japan the cars they planned to sell in the United States. But, unlike the managers of Fuji, the managers of these firms decided that moving production to the United States would allow them to plan better and to stabilize their profits because their sales would no longer be affected as much by fluctuations in the exchange rate.

Source: Yoko Kubota, "Subaru Rides a Weaker Yen into the U.S.," *Wall Street Journal*, November 15, 2014.

MyEconLab Study Plan   **Your Turn:** For more practice, do related problem 2.10 on page 421 at the end of this module.

The Real Exchange Rate

Real exchange rate The price of domestic goods in terms of foreign goods.

We have seen that an important factor in determining the level of a country's exports to and imports from another country is the relative prices of each country's goods. The relative prices of two countries' goods are determined by two factors: the relative price levels in the two countries and the nominal exchange rate between the two countries' currencies. Economists combine these two factors in the **real exchange rate**, which is the price of domestic goods in terms of foreign goods. Recall that the price level is a measure of the average prices of goods and services in an economy. We can calculate the real exchange rate between two currencies as:

$$\text{Real exchange rate} = \text{Norminal exchange rate} \times \left(\frac{\text{Domestic price level}}{\text{Foreign price level}}\right).$$

Notice that both changes in the nominal exchange rate and changes in the relative price levels cause movements in the real exchange rate. Suppose that the exchange rate between the U.S. dollar and the British pound is \$1 = £1, the price level in the United States is 100, and the price level in the United Kingdom is also 100. Then the real exchange rate between the dollar and the pound is:

$$\text{Real exchange rate} = 1 \text{ pound/dollar} \times \left(\frac{100}{100}\right) = 1.00.$$

Now suppose that the nominal exchange rate increases to 1.1 pounds per dollar, while the price level in the United States rises to 105 and the price level in the United Kingdom remains 100. In this case, the real exchange rate will be:

$$\text{Real exchange rate} = 1.1 \text{ pound/dollar} \times \left(\frac{105}{100}\right) = 1.15.$$

The increase in the real exchange rate from 1.00 to 1.15 tells us that the prices of U.S. goods and services are now 15 percent higher relative to British goods and services.

Real exchange rates are reported as index numbers, with one year chosen as the base year. As with the consumer price index, the main value of the real exchange rate is in tracking changes over time—in this case, changes in the relative prices of domestic goods in terms of foreign goods.

MyEconLab Study Plan   MyEconLab Concept Check

9.3 The International Sector and National Saving and Investment

LEARNING OBJECTIVE: Define and apply the saving and investment equation.

Having studied what determines the exchange rate, we are now ready to explore further the linkages between the U.S. economy and foreign economies. Until 1970, U.S. imports and exports were usually 4 percent to 5 percent of GDP. Imports and exports are now three times as large a fraction of U.S. GDP. Imports have also consistently been larger than exports, meaning that net exports have been negative.

Net Exports Equal Net Foreign Investment

If your spending is greater than your income, what can you do? You can sell some assets—maybe those 20 shares of stock in IBM your grandparents gave you—or you can borrow money. A firm can be in the same situation: If a firm's costs are greater than its revenues, it has to make up the difference by selling assets or by borrowing. A country is in the same situation when it imports more than it exports: The country must finance the difference by selling assets—such as land, office buildings, or factories—to foreigners or by borrowing from foreigners.

In other words, for any country, a current account deficit must be exactly offset by a financial account surplus. When a country sells more assets to foreigners than it buys from foreigners, or when it borrows more from foreigners than it lends to foreigners—as it must if it is running a current account deficit—the country experiences a net capital inflow and a financial account surplus. Remember that net exports is roughly equal to the current account balance. Remember also that the financial account balance is roughly equal to net capital flows, which are in turn equal to net foreign investment but with the opposite sign. To review these two points, look again at Table 9.1 on page 383, which shows that the current account balance is determined mainly by the balance of trade and the balance of services, and the financial account is equal to net capital flows. Also, remember the definition of net foreign investment.

When imports are greater than exports, net exports are negative, and there will be a net capital inflow as people in the United States sell assets and borrow to pay for the surplus of imports over exports. Therefore, net capital flows will be equal to net exports (but with the opposite sign), and net foreign investment will also be equal to net exports (with the same sign). Because net exports are usually negative for the United States, in most years, the United States must be a net borrower from abroad, and U.S. net foreign investment will be negative.

We can summarize this discussion with the following equations:

$$\text{Current account balance} + \text{Financial account balance} = 0$$

or:

$$\text{Current account balance} = -\text{Financial account balance}$$

or:

$$\text{Net exports} = \text{Net foreign investment.}$$

The last equation tells us, once again, that countries such as the United States that import more than they export must borrow more from abroad than they lend abroad: If net exports are negative, net foreign investment will also be negative by the same amount. Countries such as China that export more than they import must lend abroad more than they borrow from abroad: If net exports are positive, net foreign investment will also be positive by the same amount.   MyEconLab Concept Check

Domestic Saving, Domestic Investment, and Net Foreign Investment

We can think of the total saving in any economy as equal to saving by the private sector plus saving by the government sector, which we call *public saving* (see Module 6, Section 6.2). When the government runs a budget surplus by spending less than it receives in taxes, public saving is positive. When the government runs a budget deficit, public saving is negative. Negative saving is also known as *dissaving*. We can write the following expression for the level of saving in the economy:

$$\text{National saving} = \text{Private saving} + \text{Public saving}$$

or:

$$S = S_{\text{private}} + S_{\text{public}}.$$

Private saving is equal to what households have left of their income after spending on consumption goods and paying taxes (for simplicity, we assume that transfer payments are zero):

$$\text{Private saving} = \text{National income} - \text{Consumption} - \text{Taxes}$$

or:

$$S_{\text{private}} = Y - C - T.$$

Public saving is equal to the difference between government spending and taxes:

$$\text{Government saving} = \text{Taxes} - \text{Government spending}$$

or:

$$S_{\text{public}} = T - G.$$

Finally, remember the basic macroeconomic equation for GDP or national income:

$$Y = C + I + G + NX.$$

We can use this last equation, our definitions of private and public saving, and the fact that net exports equal net foreign investment to arrive at an important relationship, called the **saving and investment equation**:

Saving and investment equation An equation that shows that national saving is equal to domestic investment plus net foreign investment.

$$\text{National saving} = \text{Domestic investment} + \text{Net foreign investment}$$

or:

$$S = I + NFI.$$

This equation is an *identity* because it must always be true, given the definitions we have used.

The saving and investment equation tells us that a country's saving will be invested either domestically or overseas. If you save $1,000 and use the funds to buy a bond issued by IBM, IBM may use the $1,000 to partially pay for a cloud computing facility in the United States (I) or for a software consulting office in China (NFI).

Solved Problem 9.3

MyEconLab Interactive Animation

Arriving at the Saving and Investment Equation

Use the definitions of private and public saving, the equation for GDP or national income, and the fact that net exports (NX) must equal net foreign investment (NFI) to arrive at the saving and investment equation.

Solving the Problem

Step 1: **Review the module material.** This problem is about the saving and investment equation, so you may want to review the section "Domestic Saving, Domestic Investment, and Net Foreign Investment," which begins on page 395.

Step 2: **Derive an expression for national saving (S) in terms of national income (Y), consumption (C), and government purchases (G).** We can bring together the four equations we need:

1. $S_{\text{private}} = Y - C - T$
2. $S_{\text{public}} = T - G$

3. $Y = C + I + G + NX$

4. $NX = NFI$

Because national saving (S) appears in the saving and investment equation, we need to find an equation for it in terms of the other variables. Adding equation (1) plus equation (2) yields national saving:

$$S = S_{private} + S_{public} = (Y - C - T) + (T - G) = Y - C - G.$$

Step 3: **Use the result from step 2 to derive an expression for national saving in terms of investment (I) and net exports (NX).** Because GDP (Y) does not appear in the saving and investment equation, we need to substitute the expression for it given in equation (3):

$$S = (C + I + G + NX) - C - G$$

and simplify:

$$S = I + NX.$$

Step 4: **Use the results of steps 2 and 3 to derive the saving and investment equation.** Finally, substitute net foreign investment for net exports:

$$S = I + NFI.$$

Your Turn: For more practice, do related problem 3.8 on page 422 at the end of this module.   MyEconLab Study Plan

---

A country such as the United States that has negative net foreign investment must be saving less than it is investing domestically. To understand why, rewrite the saving and investment equation by moving domestic investment to the left side:

$$S - I = NFI.$$

If net foreign investment is negative—as it is for the United States nearly every year—domestic investment (I) must be greater than national saving (S).

In most years, the level of saving in Japan has been well above domestic investment. The result has been high levels of Japanese net foreign investment. For example, Japanese automobile companies Toyota, Honda, and Nissan have all constructed factories in the United States. Sony purchased the Columbia Pictures film studio. Japan has made many similar investments in countries around the world, which has sometimes caused resentment in those countries. There were some protests in the United States in the 1980s, for example, when Japanese investors purchased the Pebble Beach golf course in California and the Rockefeller Center complex in New York City. (Both were eventually purchased by U.S. investors.)

Japan typically needs a high level of net exports to help offset a low level of domestic investment. When exports of a product begin to decline and imports begin to increase, governments are often tempted to impose tariffs or quotas to reduce imports. In fact, some Japanese firms have been urging the Japanese government to impose trade restrictions on imports from China.   MyEconLab Concept Check   MyEconLab Study Plan

9.4 The Effect of a Government Budget Deficit on Investment

LEARNING OBJECTIVE: Explain the effect of a government budget deficit on investment in an open economy.

The link we have just developed among saving, investment, and net foreign investment can help us understand some of the effects of changes in a government's budget deficit. When the government runs a budget deficit, national saving will decline unless private saving increases by the amount of the budget deficit, which is unlikely. As the saving and investment equation ($S = I + NFI$) shows, the result of a decline in national saving must be a decline in either domestic investment or net foreign investment. The algebra is clear, but why, economically, does an increase in the government budget deficit cause a fall in domestic investment or net foreign investment?

To understand the answer to this question, remember that if the federal government runs a budget deficit, the U.S. Treasury must raise an amount equal to the deficit by selling bonds. To attract investors, the Treasury may have to raise the interest rates on its bonds. As interest rates on Treasury bonds rise, other interest rates, including those on corporate bonds and bank loans, will also rise. Higher interest rates will discourage some firms from borrowing funds to build new factories or to buy new equipment or computers. Higher interest rates on financial assets in the United States will attract foreign investors. Investors in Canada, Japan, or China will have to buy U.S. dollars to be able to purchase bonds in the United States. This greater demand for dollars will increase their value relative to foreign currencies. As the value of the dollar rises, exports from the United States will fall, and imports to the United States will rise. Net exports and, therefore, net foreign investment will fall.

When a government budget deficit leads to a decline in net exports, the result is sometimes called the *twin deficits*, which refers to the possibility that a government budget deficit will also lead to a current account deficit. The twin deficits idea first became widely discussed in the United States during the early 1980s, when the federal government ran a large budget deficit that resulted in high interest rates, a high exchange value of the dollar, and a large current account deficit.

Figure 9.4 shows that in the early 1980s, the United States had large federal budget deficits and large current account deficits. The figure also shows, however, that the twin deficits idea does not consistently match the experience of the United States after 1990. The large federal budget deficits of the early 1990s occurred at a time of relatively small current account deficits, and the budget surpluses of the late 1990s occurred at a time of then-record current account deficits. Both the current account deficit and the federal budget deficit increased in the early 2000s, but the federal budget deficit declined in the mid-2000s much more than did the current account deficit. Beginning in 2008, the federal budget deficit soared and then sharply declined, while the current account deficit declined.

The experience of other countries also shows only mixed support for the twin deficits idea. Germany ran large budget deficits and large current account deficits during the early 1990s, but both Canada and Italy ran large budget deficits during the 1980s

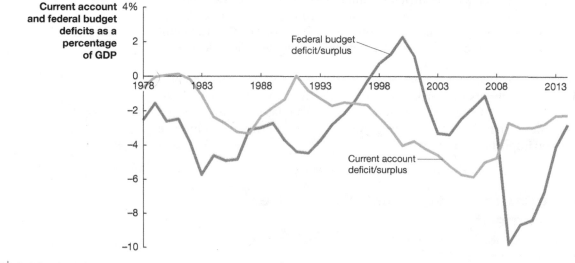

MyEconLab Real-time data

Figure 9.4 The Twin Deficits, 1978–2014

During the early 1980s, large federal budget deficits occurred at the same time as large current account deficits, but twin deficits did not occur in most other periods during these years.
Source: U.S. Bureau of Economic Analysis.

without running current account deficits. The saving and investment equation shows that an increase in the government budget deficit will not lead to an increase in the current account deficit, provided that either private saving increases or domestic investment declines. According to the twin deficits idea, when the federal government ran budget surpluses in the late 1990s, the current account should also have been in surplus, or at least the current account deficit should have been small. In fact, the increase in national saving due to the budget surpluses was more than offset by a sharp decline in private saving, and the United States ran very large current account deficits. MyEconLab Concept Check

Making the Connection	Why Is the United States Called the "World's Largest Debtor"?

MyEconLab Video

The following graph shows the current account balance as a percentage of GDP for the United States for the period 1960–2014. The United States has had a current account deficit every year since 1982, with the exception of 1991. Between 1960 and 1975, the United States ran a current account deficit in only five years. Many economists believe that the current account deficits of the 1980s were closely related to the federal budget deficits of those years. High interest rates attracted foreign investors to U.S. bonds, which raised the exchange rate between the dollar and foreign currencies. The high exchange rate reduced U.S. exports and increased imports, leading to current account deficits.

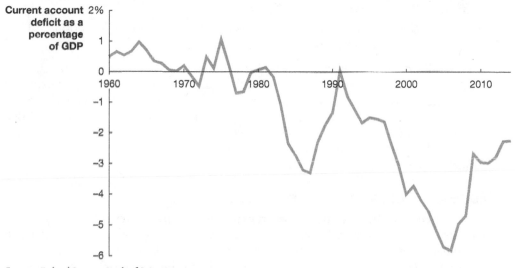

MyEconLab Real-time data

Source: Federal Reserve Bank of St Louis.

As the federal budget deficit narrowed in the mid-1990s and disappeared in the late 1990s, the foreign exchange value of the dollar remained high—and large current account deficits continued—because foreign investors persisted in investing in the United States, despite low interest rates. In the late 1990s, a number of countries around the world, such as South Korea, Indonesia, Brazil, and Russia, suffered severe economic problems. In a process known as a *flight to quality*, many investors sold their investments in those countries and bought investments in the United States. In addition, the strong performance of the U.S. stock market through the spring of 2000 attracted many investors. Finally, the sharp decline in private saving in the United States that began during the late 1990s also contributed to the U.S. current account deficit. The fall in the value of the dollar after 2008 helped reduce the size of the current account deficit. In late 2014 and 2015, though, the deficit was increasing along with the value of the dollar.

Are persistent current account deficits a problem for the United States? Current account deficits result in U.S. net foreign investment being negative. Each year, foreign investors accumulate many more U.S. assets—such as stocks, bonds, and factories—than U.S. investors accumulate foreign assets. In 1986, for the first time since the nineteenth century, the value of foreign-owned assets in the United States became larger than the value of U.S.-owned assets abroad. At the end of 2014, foreign investors owned about $7 trillion more of U.S. assets than U.S. investors owned of foreign assets, which is why the United States is sometimes called "the world's largest debtor." But the continued willingness of foreign investors to buy U.S. stocks and bonds and of foreign companies to build factories in the United States can be seen as a vote of confidence in the strength of the U.S. economy and the buying power of U.S. consumers. When private saving rates declined in the United States to historically low levels in the mid-2000s, only the continued flow of funds from foreign investors made it possible for the United States to maintain the high levels of domestic investment required for economic growth. Beginning in 2009, private saving rates increased, but public saving turned sharply negative between 2009 and 2012 as the federal budget deficit soared. Even though public saving has been less negative in the past few years, domestic investment in the United States remains reliant on funds from foreign investors.

Source: Elena L. Nguyen, "The U.S. Net International Investment Position at the End of the First Quarter of 2015, Year 2014, and Annual Revisions," *Survey of Current Business*, July 2015, pp. 1–10.

MyEconLab Study Plan

Your Turn: Test your understanding by doing related problem 4.7 on page 423 at the end of this module.

 ## 9.5 Monetary Policy and Fiscal Policy in an Open Economy

LEARNING OBJECTIVE: Compare the effectiveness of monetary policy and fiscal policy in an open economy and in a closed economy.

When we discussed monetary policy and fiscal policy, we did not emphasize that the United States is an open economy (see Modules 7 and 7A). Now that we have explored some of the links among economies, we can look at the difference between how monetary policy and fiscal policy work in an open economy and how they work in a closed economy. Economists refer to the ways in which monetary policy and fiscal policy affect the domestic economy as *policy channels*. An open economy has more policy channels than does a closed economy.

Monetary Policy in an Open Economy

When the Federal Reserve engages in an expansionary monetary policy, it typically buys Treasury securities to lower interest rates and stimulate aggregate demand. In a closed economy, the main effect of lower interest rates is on domestic investment spending and purchases of consumer durables. In an open economy, lower interest rates will also affect the exchange rate between the dollar and foreign currencies. Lower interest rates will cause some investors in the United States and abroad to switch from investing in U.S. financial assets to investing in foreign financial assets. The result is a lower demand for the dollar relative to foreign currencies and a decline in the dollar's value. A lower exchange rate will decrease the prices of U.S. products in foreign markets and increase the prices of foreign products in the United States. As a result, net exports will increase. This additional policy channel will increase the ability of an expansionary monetary policy to affect aggregate demand.

When the Fed wants to reduce aggregate demand to reduce inflation, it engages in a contractionary monetary policy. The Fed sells Treasury securities to increase interest rates and reduce aggregate demand. In a closed economy, the main effect is once again on domestic investment spending and purchases of consumer durables. In an open economy, higher interest rates will lead to a higher foreign exchange value of the dollar. The prices of U.S. products in foreign markets will increase, and the prices of foreign products in the United States will fall. As a result, net exports will fall. The contractionary policy will have a larger effect on aggregate demand, and therefore it will be more effective in slowing the growth in economic activity. To summarize: *Monetary policy has a greater effect on aggregate demand in an open economy than in a closed economy.* MyEconLab Concept Check

Fiscal Policy in an Open Economy

To engage in an expansionary fiscal policy, the federal government increases its purchases or cuts taxes. Increases in government purchases directly increase aggregate demand. Tax cuts increase aggregate demand by increasing household disposable income and business income, which results in increased consumption spending and investment spending. An expansionary fiscal policy may result in higher interest rates. In a closed economy, the main effect of higher interest rates is to reduce domestic investment spending and purchases of consumer durables. In an open economy, higher interest rates will also lead to an increase in the foreign exchange value of the dollar and a decrease in net exports. Therefore, in an open economy, an expansionary fiscal policy may be less effective because the *crowding out effect* may be larger. In a closed economy, only consumption and investment are crowded out by an expansionary fiscal policy. In an open economy, net exports may also be crowded out.

The government can fight inflation by using a contractionary fiscal policy to slow the growth of aggregate demand. A contractionary fiscal policy cuts government purchases or raises taxes to reduce household disposable income and consumption spending. It also reduces the federal budget deficit (or increases the budget surplus), which may lower interest rates. Lower interest rates will increase domestic investment and purchases of consumer durables, thereby offsetting some of the reduction in government spending and increases in taxes. In an open economy, lower interest rates will also reduce the foreign exchange value of the dollar and increase net exports. Therefore, in an open economy, a contractionary fiscal policy will have a smaller effect on aggregate demand and therefore will be less effective in slowing an economy. In summary: *Fiscal policy has a smaller effect on aggregate demand in an open economy than in a closed economy.*   MyEconLab Concept Check   MyEconLab Study Plan

Continued from page 381

Economics in Your Life

The South Korean Central Bank and Your Car Loan

At the beginning of this module, we posed this question: Will the Bank of Korea's decision to sell its U.S. Treasury bonds affect the interest rate you pay on your car loan? To sell its holdings of Treasury bonds, South Korea's central bank may have to offer them at a lower price. When the prices of bonds fall, the interest rates on them rise. As the interest rates on U.S. Treasury bonds increase, the interest rates on corporate bonds and bank loans, including car loans, may also increase. So, the decision of the Bank of Korea has the potential to increase the interest rate you pay on your car loan. In practice, the interest rate on your car loan is likely to be affected only if the Bank of Korea sells a very large number of bonds and if investors consider it likely that other foreign central banks may soon do the same thing. The basic point is important, however: Economies are interdependent, and interest rates in the United States are not determined entirely by the actions of people in the United States.

Conclusion

At one time, U.S. policymakers—and economics textbooks—ignored the linkages between the United States and other economies. In the modern world, these linkages have become increasingly important, and economists and policymakers must take them into account when analyzing the economy. In Module 9, we will discuss further how the international financial system operates.

Visit MyEconLab for a news article and analysis related to the concepts in this module.

Bayer Uses a Weak Euro to Increase Sales

Most people in the United States know the German firm Bayer mainly from its aspirin, which is sold in bottles with labels that display the firm's name in a distinctive cross. Although the chemical formula for aspirin had been known for decades, it was only in 1899 that Bayer began marketing aspirin as a pain reliever. Because no other effective over-the-counter pain relievers were available until the 1950s, Bayer aspirin was probably the most profitable medication ever sold.

Today, Bayer sells a variety of products, including prescription and over-the-counter pharmaceuticals and agricultural products. Bayer's acquisition of Merck & Company's over-the-counter unit in 2014 added brand names such as Coppertone, Dr. Scholl's, and Claritin to its product line. In addition to exports, Bayer has affiliates in North America, Latin and South America, Europe and Asia that manufacture and sell its products. As a result, it receives revenue in many different currencies. As the exchange rate of each of the currencies changes relative to the euro, the value of Bayer's sales and profits change.

German manufacturers benefited from the introduction of the euro, the common currency of 19 members of the European Union. Because of the euro, Bayer and other German firms don't have to worry about fluctuations in exchange rates within most of Europe. Before the adoption of the euro, countries such as France, Italy, and Spain were able to bring about declines in the exchange values of their currencies, which made the output of their companies' products more competitive with those of Germany. These countries can no longer pursue this strategy in competing with Germany. When Bayer and other German companies export outside Europe, they still must deal with fluctuations in the value of the euro. When the value of the euro increases, as it did during 2012 and 2013, the prices of goods exported from Germany increase, and Bayer's sales can be hurt. But when the value of the euro falls, as it did during 2014 and 2015, it's good news for Bayer and other German exporters. For example, in the second quarter of 2015, Bayer's profits rose nearly 20 percent as a result of the lower value of the euro.

In this module, we will look more closely at the international financial system and at what determines fluctuations in exchange rates.

Sources: Bryce Hoffman, "Bayer CEO Focuses On Company's Strengths," *Forbes*, April 4, 2015; Christopher Alessi, "Bayer Profit Rises on Healthy Currency Effects," *Wall Street Journal*, July 29, 2015; Peter Loftus, "Bayer Bulks Up Its Medicine Chest With Merck Brands," *Wall Street Journal*, May 7, 2014; and American Chemical Society, "Molecule of the Week: Aspirin," June 4, 2012.

Economics in Your Life

Exchange Rate Risk Can Affect Your Savings

Suppose that you decide to accept a job in Japan. You plan to work there for the next 10 years, build up some savings, and then return to the United States. As you prepare for your move, you read that economists expect the average productivity of Japanese firms to grow faster than the average productivity of U.S. firms over the next 10 years. If economists are correct, all else being equal, will the savings that you accumulate (in yen) be worth more or less in U.S. dollars than it would have been worth without the relative gains in Japanese productivity? As you read this module, try to answer this question. You can check your answer against the one we provide on **page 418** at the end of this module.

A key fact about the international economy is that exchange rates among the major currencies fluctuate. These fluctuations have important consequences for firms, consumers, and governments. In Module 9, we discussed the basics of how exchange rates are determined. We also looked at the relationship between a country's imports and exports, and at capital flows into and out of a country. In this module, we will look further at the international financial system and at the role central banks play in the system.

9.6 Exchange Rate Systems

LEARNING OBJECTIVE: Describe how different exchange rate systems operate.

A country's exchange rate can be determined in several ways. Some countries simply allow the exchange rate to be determined by demand and supply, just as other prices are. A country that allows demand and supply to determine the value of its currency is said to have a **floating currency**. Some countries attempt to keep the exchange rate between their currency and another currency constant. For example, China kept the exchange rate constant between its currency, the yuan, and the U.S. dollar, from 1994 until 2005, when it began allowing greater exchange rate flexibility. When countries can agree on how exchange rates should be determined, economists say that there is an **exchange rate system**. Currently, many countries, including the United States, allow their currencies to float most of the time, although they occasionally intervene to buy and sell their currency or other currencies to affect exchange rates. In other words, many countries attempt to *manage* the float of their currencies. As a result, the current exchange rate system is a **managed float exchange rate system**.

Historically, the two most important alternatives to the managed float exchange rate system were the *gold standard* and the *Bretton Woods system*. These were both **fixed exchange rate systems**, in which exchange rates remained constant for long periods. Under the gold standard, a country's currency consisted of gold coins and paper currency that the government was committed to redeem for gold. The gold standard was a fixed exchange rate system that lasted from the nineteenth century until the 1930s.

Under the gold standard, exchange rates were determined by the relative amounts of gold in each country's currency, and the size of a country's money supply was determined by the amount of gold available. To rapidly expand its money supply during a war or an economic depression, a country would need to leave the gold standard. By the mid-1930s, in response to the Great Depression, the United States and most other countries had abandoned the gold standard. Although during the following decades there were occasional discussions about restoring the gold standard, there was no serious attempt to do so.

A conference held in Bretton Woods, New Hampshire, in 1944 set up an exchange rate system in which the United States pledged to buy or sell gold at a fixed price of $35 per ounce. The central banks of all other members of the new Bretton Woods system pledged to buy and sell their currencies at a fixed rate against the dollar. By fixing their exchange rates against the dollar, these countries were fixing the exchange rates among their currencies as well. Unlike under the gold standard, neither the United States nor any other country was willing to redeem its paper currency for gold domestically. The United States would redeem dollars for gold only if they were presented by a foreign central bank. Fixed exchange rate regimes can run into difficulties because exchange rates are not free to adjust quickly to changes in demand and supply for currencies. As we will see in the next section, central banks often encounter problems if they are required to keep an exchange rate fixed over a period of years. By the early 1970s, the difficulty of keeping exchange rates fixed led to the end of the Bretton Woods system. The appendix to this module contains additional discussion of the gold standard and the Bretton Woods system.

Floating currency The outcome of a country allowing its currency's exchange rate to be determined by demand and supply.

Exchange rate system An agreement among countries about how exchange rates should be determined.

Managed float exchange rate system The current exchange rate system, under which the value of most currencies is determined by demand and supply, with occasional government intervention.

Fixed exchange rate system A system under which countries agree to keep the exchange rates among their currencies fixed for long periods.

MyEconLab Concept Check   MyEconLab Study Plan

Don't Let This Happen to You

Remember That Modern Currencies Are Fiat Money

Although the United States has not been on the gold standard since 1933, many people still believe that somehow gold continues to "back" U.S. currency. The U.S. Department of the Treasury still owns billions of dollars' worth of gold bars, most of which are stored at the Fort Knox Bullion Depository in Kentucky. (Even more gold is stored in a basement of the Federal Reserve Bank of New York, which holds about one-quarter of the world's monetary gold supply—almost 10 percent of all the gold ever mined.

This gold, however, is entirely owned by foreign governments and international agencies.) The gold in Fort Knox no longer has any connection to the amount of paper money issued by the Federal Reserve. U.S. currency—like the currencies of other countries—is *fiat money*, which means it has no value except as money (see Module 8). The link between gold and money that existed for centuries has been broken in modern economies.

MyEconLab Study Plan

Your Turn: Test your understanding by doing related problem 1.3 on page 425 at the end of this module.

9.7

The Current Exchange Rate System

LEARNING OBJECTIVE: Discuss the three key features of the current exchange rate system.

The current exchange rate system has three important features:

1. The United States allows the dollar to float against other major currencies.
2. Nineteen countries in Europe have adopted a single currency, the **euro**.
3. Some developing countries have attempted to keep their currencies' exchange rates fixed against the dollar or another major currency.

Euro The common currency of many European countries.

We begin our discussion of the current exchange rate system by looking at the changing value of the dollar over time. In discussing the value of the dollar, we can look further at what determines exchange rates in the short run and in the long run.

The Floating Dollar

Since 1973, the value of the U.S. dollar has fluctuated widely against other major currencies. Panel (a) of Figure 9.5 shows the exchange rate between the U.S. dollar and

(a) The U.S. dollar and the Canadian dollar

(b) The U.S. dollar and the Japanese yen

MyEconLab Real-time data

Figure 9.5 **Canadian Dollar–U.S. Dollar and Yen–U.S. Dollar Exchange Rates, 1973–2015**

Panel (a) shows that from the end of the Bretton Woods system in 1973 through August 2015, the U.S. dollar gained more than 30 percent in value against the Canadian dollar. Panel (b) shows that during the same period, the U.S. dollar lost almost 60 percent of its value against the Japanese yen.
Source: Federal Reserve Bank of St Louis.

the Canadian dollar between January 1973 and August 2015, and panel (b) shows the exchange rate between the U.S. dollar and the Japanese yen for the same period. Remember that the dollar increases in value when it takes more units of foreign currency to buy $1, and it falls in value when it takes fewer units of foreign currency to buy $1. From January 1973 to August 2015, the U.S. dollar lost nearly 60 percent in value against the yen, while it gained more than 30 percent in value against the Canadian dollar. Both exchange rates fluctuated substantially during those years.   MyEconLab Concept Check

What Determines Exchange Rates in the Long Run?

Over the past 40 years, why has the value of the U.S. dollar fallen substantially against the Japanese yen but risen against the Canadian dollar? In the short run, the two most important causes of exchange rate movements are changes in interest rates—which cause investors to change their views of which countries' financial investments will yield the highest returns—and changes in investors' expectations about the future values of currencies. Over the long run, other factors are also important in explaining movements in exchange rates.

The Theory of Purchasing Power Parity   It seems reasonable that, in the long run, exchange rates should be at a level that makes it possible to buy the same amount of goods and services with the equivalent amount of any country's currency. In other words, the purchasing power of every country's currency should be the same. The idea that in the long run exchange rates move to equalize the purchasing power of different currencies is called the theory of **purchasing power parity**.

> **Purchasing power parity** The theory that in the long run exchange rates move to equalize the purchasing powers of different currencies.

Consider a simple example: Suppose that a Hershey candy bar has a price of $1 in the United States and £1 in the United Kingdom and that the exchange rate is £1 = $1. In that case, at least with respect to candy bars, the dollar and the pound have equivalent purchasing power. If the price of a Hershey bar increases to £2 in the United Kingdom but stays at $1 in the United States, the exchange rate will have to change to £2 per $1 in order for the pound to maintain its relative purchasing power. As long as the exchange rate adjusts to reflect purchasing power, it will be possible to buy a Hershey bar for $1 in the United States or to exchange $1 for £2 and buy the candy bar in the United Kingdom.

If exchange rates are not at the values indicated by purchasing power parity, it appears that there are opportunities to make a profit. Suppose a Hershey candy bar sells for £2 in the United Kingdom and $1 in the United States, and the exchange rate between the dollar and the pound is £1 = $1. In this case, it would be possible to exchange £1 million for $1 million and use the dollars to buy 1 million Hershey bars in the United States. The Hershey bars could then be shipped to the United Kingdom, where they could be sold for £2 million. The result of these transactions would be a profit of £1 million (minus any shipping costs). In fact, if the dollar–pound exchange rate fails to reflect the purchasing power for many products—not just Hershey bars—this process could be repeated until an extremely large profit was made. In practice, though, as people attempted to make this profit by exchanging pounds for dollars, they would bid up the value of the dollar until it reached the purchasing power parity exchange rate of £2 = $1. Once the exchange rate reflected the purchasing power of the two currencies, there would be no further opportunities for profit. This mechanism appears to guarantee that exchange rates will be at the levels determined by purchasing power parity.

Three real-world complications keep purchasing power parity from being a complete explanation of exchange rates, even in the long run:

1. **Not all products can be traded internationally.**   Where goods are traded internationally, profits can be made whenever exchange rates do not reflect their purchasing power parity values. However, more than half of all goods and services produced in the United States and most other countries are not traded internationally. When goods are not traded internationally, their prices will not be the same in

every country. Suppose that the exchange rate is £1 for $1, but the price for having a cavity filled by a dentist is twice as high in the United States as it is in the United Kingdom. In this case, there is no way to buy up the low-priced British service and resell it in the United States. Because many goods and services are not traded internationally, exchange rates will not reflect exactly the relative purchasing powers of currencies.

2. **Products and consumer preferences are different across countries.** We expect the same product to sell for the same price around the world, but if a product is similar but not identical to another product, their prices might be different. For example, a 3-ounce Hershey candy bar may sell for a different price in the United States than does a 3-ounce Cadbury candy bar in the United Kingdom. Prices of the same product may also differ across countries if consumer preferences differ. If consumers in the United Kingdom like candy bars more than do consumers in the United States, a Hershey candy bar may sell for more in the United Kingdom than in the United States.

3. **Countries impose barriers to trade.** Most countries, including the United States, impose *tariffs* and *quotas* on imported goods. A **tariff** is a tax imposed by a government on imports. A **quota** is a government-imposed numerical limit on the quantity of a good that can be imported. For example, the United States has a quota on imports of sugar. As a result, the price of sugar in the United States is much higher than the price of sugar in other countries. Because of the quota, there is no legal way to buy up the cheap foreign sugar and resell it in the United States.

Tariff A tax imposed by a government on imports.

Quota A numerical limit that a government imposes on the quantity of a good that can be imported into the country.

Making the Connection
MyEconLab Video

The Big Mac Theory of Exchange Rates

In a lighthearted attempt to test the accuracy of the theory of purchasing power parity, the *Economist* regularly compares the prices of Big Macs in different countries. If purchasing power parity holds, you should be able to take the dollars required to buy a Big Mac in the United States and exchange it for the amount of foreign currency needed to buy a Big Mac in any other country. The following table is from July 2015, when Big Macs were selling for an average price of $4.79 in the United States. The "implied exchange rate" shows what the exchange rate would be if purchasing power parity held for Big Macs. For example, a Big Mac sold for 49 pesos in Mexico and $4.79 in the United States, so for purchasing power parity to hold, the exchange rate should have been 49 pesos/$4.79, or 10.23 pesos = $1. The actual exchange rate in July 2015 was 15.74 pesos = $1. So, on Big Mac purchasing power parity grounds, the Mexican peso was *undervalued* against the dollar by 35 percent: ([10.23 − 15.74]/15.74) × 100 = −35%). That is, if Big Mac purchasing power parity held, it would have taken 35 percent fewer Mexican pesos to buy a dollar than it actually did.

Is the price of a Big Mac in Mexico City the same as the price of a Big Mac in New York?

Could you take advantage of this difference between the purchasing power parity exchange rate and the actual exchange rate to become fabulously wealthy by buying up low-priced Big Macs in Mexico City and reselling them at a higher price in New York? Unfortunately, the low-priced Mexican Big Macs would be a soggy mess by the time you got them to New York. The fact that Big Mac prices are not the same around the world illustrates one reason purchasing power parity does not hold exactly: Many goods are not traded internationally.

Country	Big Mac Price	Implied Exchange Rate	Actual Exchange Rate
Mexico	49 pesos	10.23 pesos per dollar	15.74 pesos per dollar
Japan	370 yen	77.24 yen per dollar	123.94 yen per dollar
United Kingdom	2.89 pounds	0.60 pound per dollar	0.64 pound per dollar
Switzerland	6.5 Swiss francs	1.36 Swiss francs per dollar	0.95 Swiss francs per dollar
Indonesia	30,500 rupiahs	6,367 rupiahs per dollar	13,345 rupiahs per dollar
Canada	5.85 Canadian dollars	1.22 Canadian dollars per U.S. dollar	1.29 Canadian dollars per U.S. dollar
China	17 yuan	3.55 yuan per dollar	6.21 yuan per dollar

Source: "The Big Mac Index," *Economist*, July 16, 2015.

Your Turn: Test your understanding by doing related problem 7.10 on page 426 at the end of this module.

MyEconLab Study Plan

Solved Problem 9.7

MyEconLab Interactive Animation

Calculating Purchasing Power Parity Exchange Rates Using Big Macs

Fill in the missing cells in the following table. Remember that the implied exchange rate shows what the exchange rate would be if purchasing power parity held for Big Macs. Assume that the Big Mac is selling for $4.79 in the United States. Explain whether the U.S. dollar is overvalued or undervalued relative to each currency and predict what will happen in the future to each exchange rate if the actual exchange rate moves toward the purchasing power parity exchange rate. Finally, calculate the implied exchange rate between the Polish zloty and the Brazilian real (the plural of *real* is *reais*) and explain which currency is undervalued in terms of Big Mac purchasing power parity.

Country	Big Mac Price	Implied Exchange Rate	Actual Exchange Rate
Brazil	13.5 reais		3.15 reais per dollar
Poland	9.6 zlotys		3.77 zlotys per dollar
South Korea	4,300 won		1,143.5 won per dollar
Sweden	43.7 kronor		8.52 kronor per dollar

Solving the Problem

Step 1: **Review the module material. This problem is about the theory of purchasing power parity as illustrated by prices of Big Macs, so you may want to review the section "The Theory of Purchasing Power Parity,"** which begins on page 405, and the *Making the Connection,* **"The Big Mac Theory of Exchange Rates" on page 406.**

Step 2: **Fill in the table. To calculate the purchasing power parity exchange rate, divide the foreign currency price of a Big Mac by the U.S. price. For example, the implied exchange rate between the Brazilian real and the U.S. dollar is 13.5 reais/$4.79, or 2.82 reais per dollar.**

Country	Big Mac Price	Implied Exchange Rate	Actual Exchange Rate
Brazil	13.5 reais	2.82 reais per dollar	3.15 reais per dollar
Poland	9.6 zlotys	2.00 zlotys per dollar	3.77 zlotys per dollar
South Korea	4,300 won	897.7 won per dollar	1,143.5 won per dollar
Sweden	43.7 kronor	9.12 kronor per dollar	8.52 kronor per dollar

Step 3: Explain whether the U.S. dollar is overvalued or undervalued against the other currencies. The dollar is overvalued if the actual exchange rate is greater than the implied exchange rate, and it is undervalued if the actual exchange rate is less than the implied exchange rate. In this case, the dollar is overvalued against the real, the zloty, and the won, but it is undervalued against the krona. So, we would predict that in the future the value of the dollar should rise against the krona but fall against the real, the zloty, and the won.

Step 4: Calculate the implied exchange rate between the zloty and the real. The implied exchange rate between the zloty and the real is 9.6 zlotys/13.5 reais, or 0.71 zlotys per real. We can calculate the actual exchange rate by taking the ratio of zlotys per dollar to reais per dollar: 3.77 zlotys/3.15 reais, or 1.20 zlotys per real. Therefore, the zloty is undervalued relative to the real because our Big Mac purchasing power parity calculation tells us that it should take fewer zlotys to buy a real than it actually does.

Source: "The Big Mac Index," *Economist*, July 16, 2015.

Your Turn: For more practice, do related problem 7.11 on page 426 at the end of this module.

The Four Determinants of Exchange Rates in the Long Run We can take into account the shortcomings of the theory of purchasing power parity to develop a more complete explanation of how exchange rates are determined in the long run. There are four main determinants of exchange rates in the long run:

1. **Relative price levels.** The purchasing power parity theory is correct in arguing that, in the long run, the most important determinant of exchange rates between two countries' currencies is their relative price levels. If prices of goods and services rise faster in Canada than in the United States, the value of the Canadian dollar has to decline to maintain demand for Canadian products. Over the past 40 years, the price level in Canada has risen somewhat faster than the price level in the United States, while the price level in Japan has risen more slowly. These facts help explain why the U.S. dollar has increased in value against the Canadian dollar while losing value against the Japanese yen.

2. **Relative rates of productivity growth.** When the productivity of a firm increases, the firm is able to produce more goods and services using fewer workers, machines, or other inputs. The firm's costs of production fall, and usually so do the prices of its products. If the average productivity of Japanese firms increases faster than the average productivity of U.S. firms, Japanese products will have relatively lower prices than U.S. products, which increases the quantity demanded of Japanese products relative to U.S. products. As a result, the value of the yen should rise against the dollar. For most of the period from the early 1970s to the early 1990s, Japanese productivity increased faster than U.S. productivity, which contributed to the fall in the value of the dollar versus the yen. However, between 1992 and 2015, U.S. productivity increased faster than Japanese productivity, which explains why the value of the dollar stopped its rapid decline against the yen in the early 1990s.

3. **Preferences for domestic and foreign goods.** If consumers in Canada increase their preferences for U.S. products, the demand for U.S. dollars will increase relative to the demand for Canadian dollars, and the U.S. dollar will increase in value relative to the Canadian dollar. During the 1970s and 1980s, many U.S. consumers increased their preferences for Japanese products, particularly automobiles and consumer electronics. This greater preference for Japanese products helped to increase the value of the yen relative to the dollar.

4. **Tariffs and quotas.** The U.S. sugar quota forces firms such as Hershey Foods Corporation to buy expensive U.S. sugar rather than less expensive foreign sugar. The quota increases the demand for dollars relative to the currencies of foreign sugar

producers and, therefore, leads to a higher exchange rate. Changes in tariffs and quotas have not been a significant factor, though, in explaining trends in the U.S. dollar–Canadian dollar or U.S. dollar–yen exchange rates.

Because these four factors change over time, the value of one country's currency can increase or decrease by substantial amounts in the long run. These changes in exchange rates can create uncertainty for firms. A decline in the value of a country's currency lowers the foreign currency prices of the country's exports and increases the prices of imports. An increase in the value of a country's currency has the reverse effect. Firms can be both helped and hurt by exchange rate fluctuations. MyEconLab Concept Check

The Euro

A second key aspect of the current exchange rate system is that most countries in Western Europe have adopted a single currency. After World War II, many of these countries wanted to more closely integrate their economies. In 1957, Belgium, France, West Germany, Italy, Luxembourg, and the Netherlands signed the Treaty of Rome, which established the European Economic Community, often called the European Common Market. Tariffs and quotas on products being shipped within the European Common Market were greatly reduced. Over the years, Britain, Sweden, Denmark, Finland, Austria, Greece, Ireland, Spain, and Portugal joined the European Economic Community, which was renamed the European Union (EU) in 1991. By 2015, 28 countries were members of the EU.

EU members decided to move to a common currency beginning in 1999. Three of the 15 countries that were then members of the EU—the United Kingdom, Denmark, and Sweden—decided to retain their domestic currencies. The move to a common currency took place in several stages. On January 1, 1999, the exchange rates of the 12 participating countries were permanently fixed against each other and against the common currency, the *euro*. At first, the euro was a pure *unit of account*. No euro currency was actually in circulation, although firms began quoting prices in both domestic currency

MyEconLab Animation

Figure 9.6

Countries Adopting the Euro

The 19 member countries of the European Union (EU) that have adopted the euro as their common currency as of the end of 2015 are shaded with red hash marks. The members of the EU that have not adopted the euro are colored tan. Countries in white are not members of the EU.

and in euros. On January 1, 2002, euro coins and paper currency were introduced, and on June 1, 2002, the old domestic currencies were withdrawn from circulation. Figure 9.6 shows the 19 countries in the EU that had adopted the euro as of the end of 2015. These countries are sometimes called the *eurozone.*

A new European Central Bank (ECB) was also established. Although the central banks of the member countries continue to exist, the ECB has assumed responsibility for monetary policy and for issuing currency. The ECB is run by a governing council that consists of a six-member executive board—appointed by the participating governments—and the governors of the central banks of the 19 member countries that have adopted the euro. The ECB represents a unique experiment in allowing a multinational organization to control the domestic monetary policies of independent countries. MyEconLab Concept Check

Making the Connection
MyEconLab Video

Greece and Germany: Diverse Economies, Common Currency

Most of Europe experienced relative economic stability from the introduction of the euro in 2002 to the beginning of the global economic downturn in 2007. With low interest rates, low inflation rates, and expanding employment and production, the advantages of having a common currency seemed obvious. Firms no longer had to worry about exchange rate instability when selling within Europe, and the cost of doing business was reduced because, for example, it was no longer necessary for a French firm to exchange francs for marks to do business in Germany.

By 2008, however, some economists and policymakers questioned whether the euro was making the effects of the global recession worse. The countries using the euro cannot pursue independent monetary policies because the ECB determines those policies from its headquarters in Frankfurt, Germany. Countries that were particularly hard hit by the recession—for example, Spain, where the unemployment rate had more than doubled to 18 percent by 2009 and was 22 percent in mid-2015—were unable to pursue a more expansionary policy than the ECB was willing to implement for the eurozone as a whole. Similarly, countries could not attempt to revive their exports by allowing their currencies to depreciate because (1) many of their exports were to other eurozone countries, and (2) the value of the euro was determined by factors affecting the eurozone as a whole.

In 2010, a *sovereign debt* crisis developed when investors began to believe that a number of European governments, particularly those of Greece, Ireland, Spain, Portugal, and Italy, would have difficulty making interest payments on their bonds—or sovereign debt. The International Monetary Fund and the European Union put together aid packages to keep the countries from defaulting. In exchange for the aid, these countries were required to adopt *austerity programs*—cutting government spending and raising taxes—even though doing so sparked protests from unions, students, and other groups. The controversy was greatest over Greece, which had large debts and a high unemployment rate, and where political resistance to multiple rounds of austerity made it uncertain whether the country would remain in the eurozone.

Did the euro contribute to the slow recovery from the 2007–2009 financial crisis? The figure below shows the average unemployment rate for the eurozone countries for the period 2007–2014 compared with the unemployment rates for the United States, the United Kingdom, and Iceland. The eurozone was still suffering from high unemployment rates more than seven years after the beginning of the financial crisis. The German economy, however, performed very well during and after the financial crisis, with its unemployment rate in 2014 being below what it had been in 2007. In fact, German firms, including Bayer, benefited from the euro because if the country had retained the deutsche mark as its currency, the deutsche mark would likely have increased in value during 2014 and 2015. The euro decreased in value during that period, thereby increasing German exports more than would have happened without the common currency. As the blue line shows, the unemployment rate in the eurozone looks significantly worse if Germany is left out.

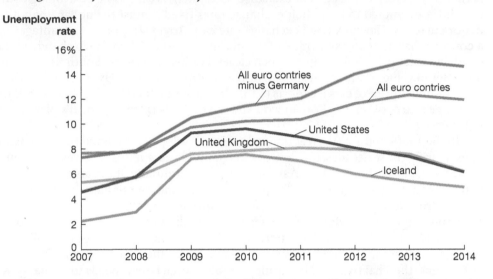

The United Kingdom, Iceland, and the United States all use their own currencies and all recovered more quickly from the financial crisis and recession than did most of the countries using the euro. The United Kingdom is a member of the European Union but continues to use the pound as its currency. Iceland is not a member of the European Union and does not use the euro. The situation in Iceland is particularly interesting because no country was more severely affected by the global financial crisis. Although it is a small country, its banks aggressively made loans around the world in the years leading up to the crisis. By 2007, Icelandic banks had made loans equal to nine times the country's GDP. When many borrowers defaulted on those loans, the government of Iceland took over the banks and assumed their debt of about $100 billion—or more than $300,000 for each citizen of Iceland. Iceland's krona, the British pound, and the U.S. dollar all depreciated against the euro in the period immediately following the financial crisis, which was good news for these countries because it helped them increase exports, but it was bad news for countries using the euro, many of which faced declining exports outside Europe.

The crisis over Greece highlighted another key problem facing the euro: the lack of coordinated government spending policies. The eurozone is a *monetary union*—the member countries all use the same currency and follow a joint monetary policy—but not a *fiscal union*—the member countries pursue independent fiscal policies. Although we don't usually think of countries in these terms, the states of the United States, the provinces of Canada, and the prefectures of Japan represent both monetary unions and fiscal unions. If during a recession Nevada suffers a particularly sharp decline in production and employment, the federal government provides support to the economy of Nevada through unemployment insurance and other transfer programs. Greece, by contrast, must fund such payments largely from its own revenues. The resulting large government budget deficits contributed to the sovereign debt crisis discussed earlier.

Some economists and policymakers wonder whether a monetary union of such diverse economies can survive in the absence of further fiscal integration. However, the political support for further fiscal integration of the eurozone countries seemed lacking. In 2015, the ultimate fate of Europe's great economic experiment of having independent countries use a single currency was very much in doubt.

Note: Data for the figure are from the International Monetary Fund. The unemployment rate for the euro countries is for all members of the eurozone as of 2008, weighted by their shares in total employment in 2007.

Sources: Nektaria Stamouli, "Greece Wants European Parliament Involved in Overseeing Bailout," *Wall Street Journal*, August 19, 2015; "A Third Bail-out Gets the Green Light," *Economist*, August 15, 2015; and Terence Roth, "Everything You Need to Know about European Political Union," *Economist*, July 27, 2015.

Your Turn: Test your understanding by doing related problems 7.12 and 7.13 on page 427 at the end of this module.

MyEconLab Study Plan

Pegging against the Dollar

A final key feature of the current exchange rate system is that some developing countries have attempted to keep their exchange rates fixed against the dollar or another major currency. Having a fixed exchange rate can provide important advantages for a country that has extensive trade with another country. When the exchange rate is fixed, business planning becomes much easier. For instance, if the South Korean won increases in value relative to the dollar, Korean car manufacturer Hyundai may have to raise the dollar price of cars it exports to the United States, thereby reducing sales. If the exchange rate between the Korean won and the dollar is fixed, Hyundai's planning is much easier.

In the 1980s and 1990s, an additional reason developed for having fixed exchange rates. During those decades, the flow of foreign investment funds to developing countries, particularly those in East Asia, increased substantially. It became possible for firms in countries such as Korea, Thailand, Malaysia, and Indonesia to borrow dollars directly from foreign investors or indirectly from foreign banks. For example, a Thai firm might borrow U.S. dollars from a Japanese bank. If the Thai firm wants to build a new factory in Thailand with the borrowed dollars, it has to exchange the dollars for the equivalent amount of Thai currency, the baht. When the factory opens and production begins, the Thai firm will be earning the additional baht it needs to exchange for dollars to make the interest payments on the loan. A problem arises if the value of the baht falls against the dollar. Suppose that the exchange rate is 25 baht per dollar when the firm takes out the loan. A Thai firm making an interest payment of $100,000 per month on a dollar loan could buy the necessary dollars for 2.5 million baht. But if the value of the baht declines to 50 baht to the dollar, it would take 5 million baht to buy the dollars necessary to make the interest payment. These increased payments might be a crushing burden for the Thai firm. The government of Thailand would have a strong incentive to avoid this problem by keeping the exchange rate between the baht and the dollar fixed.

Finally, in the 1980s and 1990s, some countries feared the inflationary consequences of a floating exchange rate. When the value of a currency falls, the prices of imports rise. If imports are a significant fraction of the goods consumers buy, a fall in the value of the currency may significantly increase the inflation rate. During the 1990s, an important part of Brazil's and Argentina's anti-inflation policies was a fixed exchange rate against the dollar. (As we will see, there are difficulties with following a fixed exchange rate policy, and ultimately, both Brazil and Argentina abandoned fixed exchange rates.)

The East Asian Exchange Rate Crisis of the Late 1990s

When a country keeps its currency's exchange rate fixed against another country's currency, it is **pegging** its currency. It is not necessary for both countries involved in a peg to agree to it. When a developing country has pegged the value of its currency against the dollar, the responsibility for maintaining the peg has been entirely with the developing country.

Countries attempting to maintain a peg can run into problems, however. When the government fixes the price of a good or service, the result can be persistent surpluses or shortages. Figure 9.7 shows the exchange rate between the dollar and the Thai baht. The figure is drawn from the Thai point of view, so we measure the exchange rate on the vertical axis as dollars per baht. The figure represents the situation in the 1990s, when the government of Thailand pegged the exchange rate between the dollar and the baht above the equilibrium exchange rate, as determined by demand and supply. A currency pegged at a value above the market equilibrium exchange rate is said to be *overvalued*. A currency pegged at a value below the market equilibrium exchange rate is said to be *undervalued*.

Pegging both made it easier for Thai firms to export products to the United States and protected Thai firms that had taken out dollar loans. The pegged exchange rate was 25.19 baht to the dollar, or about $0.04 to the baht. By 1997, this exchange rate was well above the market equilibrium exchange rate of 35 baht to the dollar, or about $0.03

Pegging A policy by which a country keeps fixed the exchange rate between its currency and another country's currency.

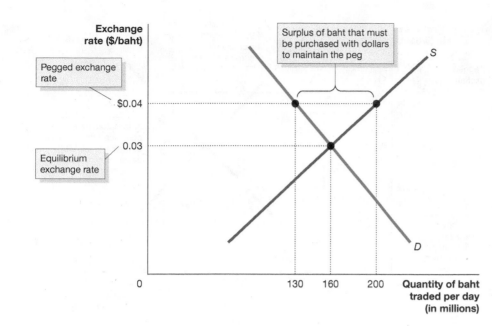

Exchange rate ($/baht)

Surplus of baht that must be purchased with dollars to maintain the peg

S

Pegged exchange rate

$0.04

0.03

Equilibrium exchange rate

D

0   130 160   200   **Quantity of baht traded per day (in millions)**

Figure 9.7

By 1997, the Thai Baht Was Overvalued against the Dollar

The government of Thailand pegged the value of the baht against the dollar to make it easier for Thai firms to export to the United States and to protect Thai firms that had taken out dollar loans. The pegged exchange rate of $0.04 per baht was well above the equilibrium exchange rate of $0.03 per baht. In the example in this figure, the overvalued exchange rate created a surplus of 70 million baht, which the Thai central bank had to purchase with dollars.

to the baht. The result was a surplus of baht on the foreign exchange market. To keep the exchange rate at the pegged level, the Thai central bank, the Bank of Thailand, had to buy these baht with dollars. In doing so, the Bank gradually used up its holdings of dollars, or its *dollar reserves*. To continue supporting the pegged exchange rate, the Bank borrowed additional dollar reserves from the International Monetary Fund (IMF). The Bank of Thailand also raised interest rates to attract more foreign investors to investments in Thailand, thereby increasing the demand for the baht. The Bank of Thailand took these actions even though allowing the value of the baht to decline against the dollar would have helped Thai firms exporting to the United States by reducing the dollar prices of their goods. The Thai government was afraid of the negative consequences of abandoning the peg even though the peg had led to the baht being overvalued.

Although higher domestic interest rates helped attract foreign investors, they made it more difficult for Thai firms and households to borrow the funds they needed to finance their spending. As a consequence, domestic investment and consumption declined, pushing the Thai economy into recession. International investors realized that there were limits to how high the Bank of Thailand would be willing to push interest rates and how many dollar loans the IMF would be willing to extend to Thailand. These investors began to speculate against the baht by exchanging baht for dollars at the official, pegged exchange rate. If, as they expected, Thailand were forced to abandon the peg, they would be able to buy back the baht at a much lower exchange rate, making a substantial profit. Because these actions by investors make it more difficult to maintain a fixed exchange rate, they are called *destabilizing speculation*. Figure 9.8 shows the results of this destabilizing speculation. The decreased demand for baht shifted the demand curve for baht from D_1 to D_2, increasing the quantity of baht the Bank of Thailand needed to buy in exchange for dollars.

Foreign investors also began to sell off their investments in Thailand and exchange their holdings of baht for dollars. This *capital flight* forced the Bank of Thailand to run through its dollar reserves. Dollar loans from the IMF temporarily allowed Thailand to defend the pegged exchange rate. Finally, on July 2, 1997, Thailand abandoned its pegged exchange rate against the dollar and allowed the baht to float. Thai firms that had borrowed dollars were now faced with interest payments that were much higher than they had planned. Many firms were forced into bankruptcy, and the Thai economy plunged into a deep recession.

Many currency traders became convinced that other East Asian countries, such as South Korea, Indonesia, and Malaysia, would have to follow Thailand and abandon their pegged exchange rates. The result was a wave of speculative selling of these countries'

MyEconLab Animation

Figure 9.8

Destabilizing Speculation against the Thai Baht

In 1997, the pegged exchange rate of $0.04 = 1 baht was above the equilibrium exchange rate of $0.03 = 1 baht. As investors became convinced that Thailand would have to abandon its pegged exchange rate against the dollar and allow the value of the baht to fall, they decreased their demand for baht, causing the demand curve to shift from D_1 to D_2. The new equilibrium exchange rate became $0.02 = 1 baht. To defend the pegged exchange rate, the Bank of Thailand had to increase the quantity of baht it purchased in exchange for dollars from 70 million to 140 million per day. The *destabilizing speculation* by investors caused Thailand to abandon its pegged exchange rate in July 1997.

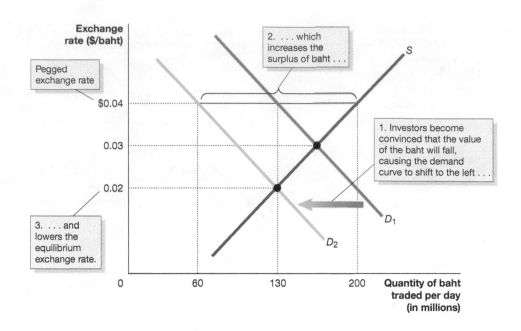

currencies. These waves of selling—sometimes called *speculative attacks*—were difficult for countries to fight off. Even if a country's currency was not initially overvalued at the pegged exchange rate, the speculative attacks would cause a large reduction in the demand for the country's currency. The demand curve for the currency would shift to the left, which would force the country's central bank to quickly exhaust its dollar reserves. Within a few months, South Korea, Indonesia, the Philippines, and Malaysia abandoned their pegged currencies. All these countries also plunged into recession.

The Decline in Pegging Following the disastrous events experienced by the East Asian countries, the number of countries with pegged exchange rates declined sharply. Most countries that continue to use pegged exchange rates are small and trade primarily with a single, much larger, country. For instance, several Caribbean countries continue to peg against the dollar, and several former French colonies in Africa that formerly pegged against the French franc now peg against the euro. Overall, the trend has been toward replacing pegged exchange rates with managed floating exchange rates.   MyEconLab Concept Check

Making the Connection
MyEconLab Video

The Chinese Yuan: The World's Most Controversial Currency

In 1978, China began to move away from central planning and toward a market system. The result was a sharp acceleration in economic growth. Real GDP per capita grew at a rate of 6.5 percent per year between 1979 and 1995 and at the even more rapid rate of 8.8 percent per year between 1996 and 2014. An important part of Chinese economic policy was the decision in 1994 to peg the value of the Chinese currency, the yuan, to the dollar at a fixed rate of 8.28 yuan to the dollar. Pegging against the dollar ensured that Chinese exporters would face stable dollar prices for the goods they sold in the United States. By the early 2000s, many economists and policymakers argued that the yuan was undervalued against the dollar—possibly significantly undervalued. Some policymakers claimed that the undervaluation of the yuan gave Chinese firms an unfair advantage in competing with U.S. firms.

To support the undervalued exchange rate, the Chinese central bank had to buy large amounts of dollars with yuan. By 2005, the Chinese government had accumulated more than $700 billion, a good portion of which it had used to buy U.S. Treasury bonds. By this time, China was coming under pressure from its trading partners to allow the yuan to increase in value. Chinese exports of textile products were driving some textile producers out of business in Japan, the United States, and Europe. China had also begun to export more sophisticated products, including televisions, personal computers, and cellphones. Politicians in other countries were anxious to protect their domestic industries from Chinese competition, even if the result was higher prices for their consumers. In the United States and other countries, accusations that the Chinese government was intentionally undervaluing the yuan became a heated political issue. The Chinese government was reluctant to allow the market to determine the value of the yuan, however, because it believed high levels of exports were needed to maintain rapid economic growth.

In July 2005, the Chinese government announced that it would switch from pegging the yuan against the dollar to linking the value of the yuan to the average value of a basket of currencies—the dollar, the Japanese yen, the euro, the Korean won, and several other currencies. Although the Chinese central bank did not explain the details of how this linking of the yuan to other currencies would work, it declared that it had switched from a peg to a managed floating exchange rate. As the figure below shows, the value of the yuan gradually increased versus the dollar for most of the period from 2005 to 2015. The exception is the period from July 2008 to May 2010, when the exchange rate stabilized at about 6.83 yuan to the dollar, indicating that China had apparently returned to a "hard peg." This change in policy led to renewed criticism from policymakers in the United States. In mid-2010, President Barack Obama argued that "market-determined exchange rates are essential to global economic activity." In the face of this criticism, the Chinese central bank allowed the yuan to resume its slow increase in value versus the dollar. (Note that the figure shows the number of yuan per dollar, so an increase represents a *depreciation* of the yuan relative to the dollar and a decrease represents an *appreciation* of the yuan relative to the dollar.)

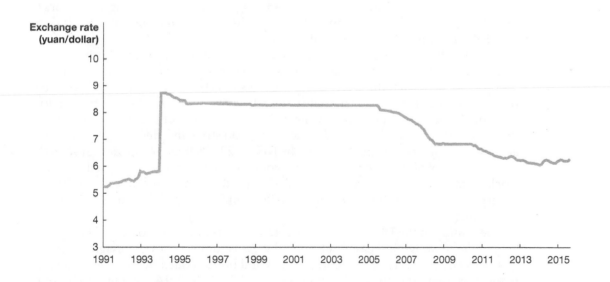

In 2015, the Chinese government was concerned that the growth rate of real GDP had slowed to about 7 percent, the lowest rate in more than 6 years. On August 11 of that year, the yuan was once again in the news when the Chinese central bank made a surprise announcement that it would buy dollars with yuan in order to reduce its value by about 3 percent, the largest one-day decline in the currency since 1994. The Chinese central bank again stated that it would allow the market to play a greater role in determining the value of the yuan. Many policymakers and economists were skeptical that the central bank truly intended to relax its control over the currency. And once again, politicians in the United States and elsewhere were critical of what they considered to be an attempt by the Chinese government to manipulate the value of yuan to gain an unfair advantage over its trading partners.

As long as the Chinese central bank continues to override the market to control the value of the yuan, controversy over Chinese exchange rate policies is likely to continue.

Sources: "Yuan Thing after Another," *Economist*, August 15, 2015; Lingling Wei, "China Moves to Devalue Yuan," *Wall Street Journal*, August 11, 2015; Greg Ip, "Why China's Yuan 'Reform' Merits Skepticism," *Wall Street Journal*, August 19, 2015; and Federal Reserve Bank of St. Louis.

MyEconLab Study Plan

Your Turn: Test your understanding by doing related problems 7.19 and 7.20 on page 427 at the end of this module.

9.8 International Capital Markets

LEARNING OBJECTIVE: Discuss the growth of international capital markets.

One important reason exchange rates fluctuate is that investors seek out the best investments they can find anywhere in the world. For instance, if Chinese investors increase their demand for U.S. Treasury bills, the demand for dollars will increase, and the value of the dollar will rise. But if interest rates in the United States decline, foreign investors may sell U.S. investments, and the value of the dollar will fall.

Shares of stock and long-term debt, including corporate and government bonds and bank loans, are bought and sold on *capital markets*. Before 1980, most U.S. corporations raised funds only in U.S. stock and bond markets or from U.S. banks. And U.S. investors rarely invested in foreign capital markets. In the 1980s and 1990s, European governments removed many restrictions on foreign investments in their financial markets. It became possible for U.S. and other foreign investors to freely invest in Europe and for European investors to freely invest in foreign markets. Improvements in communications and computer technology made it possible for U.S. investors to receive better and more timely information about foreign firms and for foreign investors to receive better information about U.S. firms. The growth in economies around the world also increased the savings available to be invested.

Although at one time the U.S. capital market was larger than all other capital markets combined, that is no longer the case. Today, there are large capital markets in Europe and Japan, and there are smaller markets in Latin America and East Asia. The three most important international financial centers today are New York, London, and Tokyo. Each day, the *Wall Street Journal* provides data not just on the Dow Jones Industrial Average and the Standard & Poor's 500 stock indexes of U.S. stocks, but also on foreign stock indexes such as the Nikkei 225 average of Japanese stocks, the FTSE 100 index of stocks on the London Stock Exchange, and the Hang Seng Index of stocks traded on the Hong Kong stock exchange. By 2015, corporations, banks, and governments were raising more than $1 trillion in funds on global financial markets each year.

Beginning in the 1990s, the flow of foreign funds into U.S. stocks and bonds—or *portfolio investments*—increased substantially. As Figure 9.9 shows, foreign purchases of stocks and bonds issued by corporations and bonds issued by the federal government increased dramatically between 1995 and 2007. In 2014, foreign purchases of U.S. corporate stocks and bonds, while still substantial, had declined, partly because of low interest rates in the United States. Growth in China, India, and some European countries also attracted both U.S. and foreign investors to securities issued in those countries. The fact that the United States continued to run large current account deficits resulted in a continuing foreign demand for U.S. government bonds. The current account deficits led to an accumulation of dollars by foreign central banks and foreign investors who used the dollars to purchase U.S. government bonds.

Figure 9.10 shows the distribution in June 2015 of foreign holdings of U.S. stocks and bonds by country. Japan and China together hold almost one-quarter of foreign-owned U.S. securities. The large holdings in the Cayman Islands and Luxembourg are the result of investors taking advantage of the favorable tax treatment of investment income available in those countries.

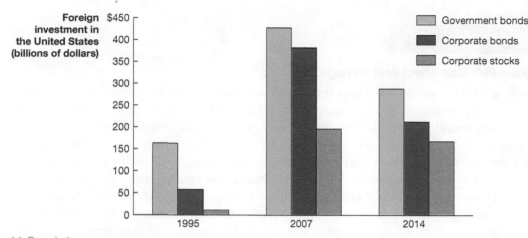

MyEconLab Animation

Figure 9.9   **Growth of Foreign Portfolio Investment in the United States**

Between 1995 and 2007, there was a large increase in foreign purchases of stocks and bonds issued by U.S. corporations and of bonds issued by the federal government. In 2014, partly because of low interest rates in the United States, foreign purchases of U.S. corporate stocks and bonds had declined. Foreign purchases of U.S. government bonds remained high.

Sources: International Monetary Fund, *International Capital Markets*, August 2001; and Board of Governors of the Federal Reserve System.

The globalization of financial markets has helped increase growth and efficiency in the world economy. It is now possible for the savings of households around the world to be channeled to the best investments available. It is also possible for firms in nearly every country to tap the savings of foreign households to gain the funds needed for expansion. No longer are firms forced to rely only on the savings of domestic households to finance investment.

But the globalization of financial markets also has a downside, as the events of 2007–2009 showed. Because financial securities issued in one country are held by investors and firms in many other countries, if those securities decline in value, the financial pain will be widely distributed. For example, the sharp decline in the value of mortgage-backed securities issued in the United States hurt not only U.S. investors and financial firms but investors and financial firms in many other countries as well.   MyEconLab Concept Check   MyEconLab Study Plan

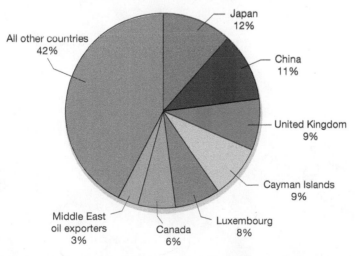

MyEconLab Animation

Figure 9.10   **The Distribution of Foreign Holdings of U.S. Stocks and Bonds by Country, June 2015**

Investors in China and Japan own almost one-quarter of foreign-owned U.S. stocks and bonds.

Source: U.S. Department of the Treasury.

Continued from page 402

Economics in Your Life

Exchange Rate Risk Can Affect Your Savings

At the beginning of this module, we posed this question: If economists are correct about the relative rates of average productivity growth between Japan and the United States in the next decade, then, all else being equal, will the savings that you accumulate (in yen) be worth more or less in U.S. dollars than the savings would have been worth without the relative gains in Japanese productivity? We saw in this module that when the average productivity of firms in one country increases faster than the average productivity of firms in another country, the value of the faster-growing country's currency should—all else being equal—rise against the slower-growing country's currency. But the savings that you accumulate in yen while you are in Japan are likely to be worth more in U.S. dollars than they would have been worth without the gains in Japanese productivity.

Conclusion

Fluctuations in exchange rates continue to cause difficulties for firms and governments. From the gold standard to the Bretton Woods system to currency pegging, governments have attempted to find a workable system of fixed exchange rates. Fixing exchange rates runs into the same problems as fixing any other price: As demand and supply shift, surpluses and shortages will occur unless the price adjusts. Nineteen countries in Europe are attempting to avoid this problem by using a single currency. Economists are looking closely at the results of that experiment.

Visit MyEconLab for a news article and analysis related to the concepts in this module.

MODULE SUMMARY AND PROBLEMS

Key Terms

Balance of payments, p. 382

Balance of trade, p. 382

Capital account, p. 384

Closed economy, p. 382

Currency appreciation, p. 389

Currency depreciation, p. 389

Current account, p. 382

Euro, p. 404

Exchange rate system, p. 403

Financial account, p. 383

Fixed exchange rate system, p. 403

Floating currency, p. 403

Net foreign investment, p. 384

Nominal exchange rate, p. 387

Managed float exchange rate system, p. 403

Open economy, p. 382

Pegging, p. 412

Purchasing power parity, p. 405

Quota, p. 406

Real exchange rate, p. 394

Tariff, p. 406

Saving and investment equation, p. 396

Speculators, p. 389

9.1 | **The Balance of Payments: Linking the United States to the International Economy, pages 382–386**

LEARNING OBJECTIVE: Explain how the balance of payments is calculated.

Summary

Nearly all economies are **open economies** that trade with and invest in other economies. A **closed economy** has no transactions in trade or finance with other economies. The **balance of payments** is the record of a country's trade with other countries in goods, services, and assets. The **current account** records a country's net exports, net investment income, and net transfers. The **financial account** shows investments a country has made abroad and foreign investments received by the country. The **balance of trade** is the difference between the value of the goods a country exports and the value of the goods a country imports. **Net foreign investment** is the difference between capital outflows from a country and capital inflows. The **capital account** is a part of the balance of payments that records relatively minor transactions. Apart from measurement errors, the sum of the current account and the financial account must equal zero. Therefore, the balance of payments must also equal zero.

 MyEconLab   Visit www.myeconlab.com to complete these exercises online and get instant feedback.

Review Questions

1.1 What is the relationship among the current account, the financial account, and the balance of payments?

1.2 What is the difference between net exports and the current account balance?

1.3 The late economist Herbert Stein described the accounts that comprise a country's balance of payments:

> A country is more likely to have a deficit in its current account the higher its price level, the higher its gross [domestic] product, the higher its interest rates, the lower its barriers to imports, and the more attractive its investment opportunities—all compared with conditions in other countries—and the higher its exchange rate. The effects of a change in one of these factors on the current account balance cannot be predicted without considering the effect on the other causal factors.

a. Briefly describe the transactions included in a country's current account.

b. Briefly explain why, compared to other countries, a country is more likely to have a deficit in its current account, holding other factors constant, if it has each of the following:

i. A higher price level

ii. An increase in interest rates

iii. Lower barriers to imports

iv. More attractive investment opportunities

Source: Herbert Stein, "Balance of Payments," *Library of Economics and Liberty*, http://www.econlib.org.

Problems and Applications

1.4 In 2014, France had a current account deficit of €19.5 billion (approximately $25.9 billion). Did France experience a net capital outflow or a net capital inflow during 2014? Briefly explain.

Source: Banque de France, "France's Balance of Payments," https://www.banque-france.fr/en/economics-statistics/stats-infos/frances-balance-of-payments.html.

1.5 Use the information in the following table to solve for the value of the statistical discrepancy and prepare a balance of payments account, like the one shown in Table 9.1 on page 383. Assume that the balance on the capital account is zero.

Increase in foreign holdings of assets in the United States	$1,181
Exports of goods	856
Imports of services	−256
Statistical discrepancy	?
Net transfers	−60
Exports of services	325
Income received on investments	392
Imports of goods	−1,108
Increase in U.S. holdings of assets in foreign countries	−1,040
Income payments on investments	−315

1.6 **(Related to the** Don't Let This Happen to You **on page 385)** In 2014, Germany had a balance of trade surplus of €217 billion and a current account surplus of €215 billion. Explain how Germany's current account surplus could be smaller than its trade surplus. In 2014, what would we expect Germany's balance on the financial account to have been? Briefly explain.

Source: Statistisches Bundesamt.

1.7 **(Related to** Solved Problem 9.1 **on page 386)** A news article notes, "China recorded a current-account surplus of $76.6 billion in the second quarter but that was offset by a deficit of the same amount on its capital and financial account." Is this outcome surprising? Briefly explain.

Source: Grace Zhu, "China's Current-Account Surplus at $76.6 bln: SAFE," marketwatch.com, August 7, 2015.

1.8 **(Related to** Solved Problem 9.1 **on page 386)** An article in the *Wall Street Journal* about China's balance of payments contained the following observations: "A country's balance of payments still has to add up to zero. If foreign investors wish to acquire assets denominated in yuan, the necessary implication is that China will have to run a trade deficit."

a. Do you agree that the balance of payments must add up to zero?

b. If China were to have a deficit in its balance of trade of −100 billion yuan, must it have a surplus in its financial account of +100 billion yuan? Briefly explain.

Source: Andrew Colquhoun, "The Yuan Isn't Ready to Be a Global Reserve Currency," *Wall Street Journal*, August 12, 2015.

1.9 **(Related to** Solved Problem 9.1 **on page 386)** An article in the *New York Times* has the headline "U.S. Trade Deficit Widened Over Summer." The first sentence in the article is, "The current-account trade deficit widened slightly in the July–September quarter." The statement that the "trade deficit for goods and services" declined during this period appears later in the article. Is this article's headline consistent with the two statements in the article? Briefly explain.

Source: Associated Press, "U.S. Trade Deficit Widened Over Summer," *New York Times*, December 17, 2014.

1.10 An article in the *Wall Street Journal* refers to "debt-strapped emerging markets already struggling with current-account deficits." Why might we expect that countries running current account deficits might also have substantial foreign debts?

Source: Anjani Trivedi, "Emerging Markets Suffer Largest Outflow in Seven Years," *Wall Street Journal*, June 12, 2015.

9.2 | **The Foreign Exchange Market and Exchange Rates, pages 386–394**

LEARNING OBJECTIVE: Explain how exchange rates are determined and how changes in exchange rates affect the prices of imports and exports.

Summary

The **nominal exchange rate** is the value of one country's currency in terms of another country's currency. The exchange rate is determined in the foreign exchange market by the demand and supply of a country's currency. Changes in the exchange rate are caused by shifts in demand or supply. The three main sets of factors that cause the demand and supply curves in the foreign exchange market to shift are: (1) changes in the demand for U.S.-produced goods and services and changes in the demand for foreign-produced goods and services; (2) changes in the desire to invest in the United States and changes in the desire to invest in foreign countries; and (3) changes in the expectations of currency traders—particularly **speculators**—concerning the likely future value of the dollar and the likely future values of foreign currencies. **Currency appreciation** occurs when a currency's market value increases relative to another currency. **Currency depreciation** occurs when a currency's market value decreases relative to another currency. The **real exchange rate** is the price of domestic goods in terms of foreign goods. The real exchange rate is calculated by multiplying the nominal exchange rate by the ratio of the domestic price level to the foreign price level.

MyEconLab   Visit **www.myeconlab.com** to complete these exercises online and get instant feedback.

Review Questions

2.1 If the exchange rate between the Japanese yen and the U.S. dollar expressed in terms of yen per dollar is ¥125 = $1, what is the exchange rate when expressed in terms of dollars per yen?

2.2 Suppose that the current exchange rate between the dollar and the euro is €0.80 = $1. If the exchange rate changes to €0.85 = $1, has the euro appreciated or depreciated against the dollar? Briefly explain.

2.3 Why do foreign households and foreign firms demand U.S. dollars in exchange for foreign currency? Why do U.S. households and firms supply U.S. dollars in exchange for foreign currency?

2.4 What are the three main sets of factors that cause the supply and demand curves in the foreign exchange market to shift?

Problems and Applications

2.5 **(Related to the** Making the Connection **on page 387)** On January 1, 2002, there were 15 member countries in the European Union. Twelve of those countries eliminated their own individual currencies and began using a new common currency, the euro. For a three-year period from January 1, 1999, through December 31, 2001, these 12 countries priced goods and services in terms of both their own currencies and the euro. During that period, the values of their currencies were fixed against each other and against the euro. So during that time, the dollar had an exchange rate against each of these currencies and against the euro. The following table shows the fixed exchange rates of four European currencies against the euro and their exchange rates against the U.S. dollar on March 2, 2001. Use the information in the table on the next page to calculate the exchange rate between the dollar and the euro (in euros per dollar) on March 2, 2001.

Currency	Units per Euro (fixed)	Units per U.S. Dollar (as of March 2, 2001)
German mark	1.9558	2.0938
French franc	6.5596	7.0223
Italian lira	1,936.2700	2,072.8700
Portuguese escudo	200.4820	214.6300

2.6 **(Related to the** Making the Connection **on page 391)** Paul De Grauwe, an economist at the London School of Economics, wrote in the *Economist* that the quantitative easing policies of the European Central Bank "will contribute to a further weakening of the euro vis-à-vis other currencies such as the dollar, the pound and the yuan, thereby increasing exports and boosting inflation."

 a. What does De Grauwe mean by "a weakening of the euro"?

 b. What is quantitative easing, and why should it lead to a weakening of the euro?

 c. If you ran a business in France that exports to the United States and Japan, would this development help you? If you were a consumer in France, would this development help you? Briefly explain.

 Source: Paul De Grauwe, "The Sad Consequences of the Fear of QE," *Economist*, January 21, 2015.

2.7 **(Related to the** Don't Let This Happen to You **on page 393)** If we know the exchange rate between Country A's currency and Country B's currency and we know the exchange rate between Country B's currency and Country C's currency, then we can compute the exchange rate between Country A's currency and Country C's currency.

 a. Suppose the exchange rate between the Japanese yen and the U.S. dollar is currently ¥95 = $1 and the exchange rate between the British pound and the U.S. dollar is £0.64 = $1. What is the exchange rate between the yen and the pound?

 b. Suppose the exchange rate between the yen and the dollar changes to ¥100 = $1 and the exchange rate between the pound and the dollar changes to £0.55 = $1. Has the dollar appreciated or depreciated against the yen? Has the dollar appreciated or depreciated against the pound? Has the yen appreciated or depreciated against the pound?

2.8 Graph the demand and supply of U.S. dollars for euros and label each axis. Show graphically and explain the effect on the demand and supply of dollars and the resulting change in the exchange rate of euros for U.S. dollars if the European Central Bank takes action to increase interest rates.

 Source: Jon Hilsenrath, "Rising Dollar and Falling Oil Could Be Recipe for a U.S. Asset Boom," *Wall Street Journal*, December 11, 2014.

2.9 Use the graph to answer the following questions.

 a. Briefly explain whether the dollar appreciated or depreciated against the yen.

 b. Which of the following events could have caused the shift in demand shown in the graph?

 i. Interest rates in the United States declined.

 ii. Income rose in Japan.

 iii. Speculators began to believe the value of the dollar would be higher in the future.

2.10 **(Related to** Solved Problem 9.2 **on page 393)** An article in the *Wall Street Journal* notes, "For every one yen rise in the value of the dollar, Fuji Heavy's full-year operating profit increases by ¥9.7 billion, the company says." Would Honda's profits be likely to increase as much as a result of a rise in the value of the dollar versus the yen? Briefly explain.

 Source: Yoko Kubota, "Subaru Rides a Weaker Yen into the U.S.," *Wall Street Journal*, November 15, 2014.

2.11 According to an article in the *Wall Street Journal*, in 2014, "The Australian dollar tumbled after muted inflation data scotched investors' expectations that the central bank would raise interest rates."

 a. Why would the inflation rate being lower than expected make it less likely that the Australian central bank would raise interest rates?

 b. Why would the fact that it was less likely that the Australian central bank was going to raise interest rates cause the value of the Australian dollar to fall?

 Source: James Ramage, "Australian Dollar Tumbles after Data Scotches Rate-Increase Expectations," *Wall Street Journal*, April 23, 2014.

2.12 **(Related to the** Module Opener **on page 381)** In preparing their financial statements, U.S. firms with sales in foreign currencies have to engage in "foreign currency translations"; that is, they have to convert foreign currency values into U.S. dollars. In its *2014 Annual Report*, IBM made the following statement: "As with all companies with a similar global business profile, with the dollar strengthening, the company also expects that currency will have a significant translation impact on its profit growth."

a. What does the report mean by "the dollar strengthening"?

b. As a U.S.-based company, doesn't IBM benefit when the U.S. dollar is stronger? Briefly explain.

Source: International Business Machines Corporation, *2014 IBM Annual Report*, February 24, 2015, p. 64.

2.13 In the summer of 2015, the exchange rate of China's currency, the yuan, declined against other currencies. The lower value for the yuan was expected to have a negative effect on firms such as Apple and Yum Brands (owners of KFC and Pizza Hut) that have stores or restaurants in China. But the lower value of the yuan was expected to benefit Foxconn, a firm based in Taiwan that assembles iPhones in China. Briefly explain how the decline in the value of the yuan would have a negative effect on firms, such as Apple and Yum, but would benefit other firms, such as Foxconn, that also operate in China.

Source: Lorraine Luk and Eva Dou, "Devalued Yuan Set to Take Bite Out of Apple, Give Boost to Chinese Rivals," *Wall Street Journal*, August 11, 2015.

9.3 The International Sector and National Saving and Investment, pages 395–397

LEARNING OBJECTIVE: Define and apply the saving and investment equation.

Summary

A current account deficit must be exactly offset by a financial account surplus. The financial account is equal to net capital flows, which is equal to net foreign investment but with the opposite sign. Because the current account balance is roughly equal to net exports, we can conclude that net exports will equal net foreign investment. National saving is equal to private saving plus government saving. Private saving is equal to national income minus consumption and minus taxes. Government saving is the difference between taxes and government spending. GDP (or national income) is equal to the sum of investment, consumption, government spending, and net exports. We can use this fact, our definitions of private and government saving, and the fact that net exports equal net foreign investment to arrive at an important relationship known as the **saving and investment equation:** $S = I + NFI$.

MyEconLab   Visit **www.myeconlab.com** to complete these exercises online and get instant feedback.

Review Questions

3.1 Explain the relationship between net exports and net foreign investment.

3.2 What is the saving and investment equation? If national saving declines, what will happen to domestic investment and net foreign investment?

3.3 If a country saves more than it invests domestically, what must be true of its net foreign investment?

Problems and Applications

3.4 Writing in the *New York Times*, Simon Johnson, an economist at MIT, makes the argument that people outside the United States may at some point decide to "save less (in which case they may hold onto their existing United States government debt but not want to buy so much of new issues)." What does saving by people outside the United States have to do with sales of U.S. government debt? Does the level of domestic investment occurring in foreign countries matter for your answer? Briefly explain.

Source: Simon Johnson, "The Real Fiscal Risks in the United States," *New York Times*, December 6, 2012.

3.5 In 2014, domestic investment in Japan was 21.7 percent of GDP, and Japanese national saving was 22.4 percent of GDP. What percentage of GDP was Japanese net foreign investment?

3.6 In 2014, France's net foreign investment was negative. Which was larger in France in 2014: national saving or domestic investment? Briefly explain.

3.7 Briefly explain whether you agree with the following statement: "Because in 2014 national saving was a larger percentage of GDP in the United States than in the United Kingdom, domestic investment must also have been a larger percentage of GDP in the United States than in the United Kingdom."

3.8 (**Related to** Solved Problem 9.3 **on page 396**) Look again at Solved Problem 9.3, where the saving and investment equation $S = I + NX$ is derived. In deriving this equation, we assumed that national income was equal to Y. But Y only includes income *earned* by households. In the modern U.S. economy, households receive substantial transfer payments—such as Social Security payments and unemployment insurance payments—from the government. Suppose that we define national income as being equal to $Y + TR$, where TR equals government transfer payments, and we also define government spending as being equal to $G + TR$. Show that after making these adjustments, we end up with the same saving and investment equation.

3.9 Use the saving and investment equation to explain why the United States experienced large current account deficits in the late 1990s.

3.10 Former congressman and presidential candidate Richard Gephardt once proposed that tariffs be imposed on imports from countries with which the United States has a trade deficit. If this proposal were enacted and if it were to succeed in reducing the U.S. current account deficit to zero, what would be the likely effect on domestic investment spending within the United States? Assume that no other federal government economic policy is changed. (*Hint:* Use the saving and investment equation to answer this question.)

9.4 The Effect of a Government Budget Deficit on Investment, pages 397–400

LEARNING OBJECTIVE: Explain the effect of a government budget deficit on investment in an open economy.

Summary

When the government runs a budget deficit, national saving will decline unless private saving increases by the full amount of the budget deficit, which is unlikely. As the saving and investment equation ($S = I + NFI$) shows, the result of a decline in national saving must be a decline in either domestic investment or net foreign investment.

MyEconLab   Visit www.myeconlab.com to complete these exercises online and get instant feedback.

Review Questions

4.1 What happens to national saving when the government runs a budget surplus? What is the twin deficits idea? Did it hold for the United States in the 1990s? Briefly explain.

4.2 Why were the early and mid-1980s particularly difficult times for U.S. exporters?

4.3 Why is the United States sometimes called the "world's largest debtor"?

Problems and Applications

4.4 An investment analyst recommended that investors "gravitate toward the stronger currencies and countries that are running current-account and fiscal surpluses," such as South Korea and Taiwan.
  a. Holding all other factors constant, would we expect a country that is running a government budget surplus to have a currency that is increasing in value or decreasing in value? Briefly explain.
  b. Holding all other factors constant, would we expect a country that has a currency that is increasing in value to have an increasing or decreasing current account surplus? Briefly explain.
  c. Is the combination of economic characteristics this analyst has identified likely to be commonly found among countries? Briefly explain.

Source: Paul J. Lim, "Suddenly, BRIC Markets Are on a Shakier Foundation," *New York Times*, January 9, 2015.

4.5 According to an article in the *Economist*, "countries with persistent current-account deficits tend to have higher real interest rates than surplus countries." What do high interest rates have to do with current account deficits?
Source: "Carry on Trading," *Economist*, August 10, 2013.

4.6 Section 9.4 states: "The budget surpluses of the late 1990s occurred at a time of then-record current account deficits." Holding everything else constant, what would the likely effect have been on domestic investment in the United States during those years if the current account had been balanced instead of being in deficit?

4.7 **(Related to the** Making the Connection **on page 399)** Why might "the continued willingness of foreign investors to buy U.S. stocks and bonds and foreign companies to build factories in the United States" result in the United States running a current account deficit?

4.8 An article in GulfNews.com noted that in September 2012, the Indian government of Prime Minister Manmohan Singh made "urgently needed reforms to reduce the fiscal deficit and attract foreign investment to help the current account deficit and growth."
  a. Could there be a connection between India's fiscal (budget) deficit and its current account deficit? Briefly explain.
  b. How would attracting foreign investment help the current account deficit and (economic) growth?
  c. The article further notes that the Reserve Bank of India (the central bank) stated, "Financing the CAD [current account deficit] with increasingly risky and volatile flows increases the economy's vulnerability to sudden shifts in risk appetite and liquidity preference, potentially threatening macroeconomic and exchange rate stability." What does India's central bank mean by "risky and volatile flows" that finance the current account deficit? How could those flows threaten India's macroeconomic stability?

Source: "India's Central Bank Lowers Interest Rate," gulfnews.com, January 29, 2013.

9.5 Monetary Policy and Fiscal Policy in an Open Economy, pages 400–401

LEARNING OBJECTIVE: Compare the effectiveness of monetary policy and fiscal policy in an open economy and in a closed economy.

Summary

When the Federal Reserve engages in an expansionary monetary policy, it buys government bonds to lower interest rates and increase aggregate demand. In a closed economy, the main effect of lower interest rates is on domestic investment spending and purchases of consumer durables. In an open economy, lower interest rates will also cause an increase in net exports. When the Fed wants to slow the rate of economic growth to reduce inflation, it engages in a contractionary monetary policy by selling government bonds to increase interest rates and reduce aggregate demand. In a closed economy, the main effect is once again on domestic investment and purchases of consumer durables. In an open economy, higher interest rates will also reduce net exports. We can conclude that monetary policy has a greater impact on aggregate demand in an open economy than in a closed economy. To engage in an expansionary fiscal policy, the government increases government spending or cuts taxes. An expansionary fiscal policy can lead to higher interest rates. In a closed economy, the main effect of higher interest rates is on domestic investment spending and spending on consumer durables. In an open economy, higher interest rates will also reduce net exports. A contractionary fiscal policy will reduce the budget deficit and may lower interest rates. In a closed economy, lower interest rates increase domestic investment and spending on consumer durables. In an open economy, lower interest rates also increase net exports. We can conclude that fiscal policy has a smaller effect on aggregate demand in an open economy than in a closed economy.

MyEconLab   Visit www.myeconlab.com to complete these exercises online and get instant feedback.

Review Questions

5.1 What is meant by a *policy channel*?

5.2 Why does monetary policy have a greater effect on aggregate demand in an open economy than in a closed economy?

5.3 Why does fiscal policy have a smaller effect on aggregate demand in an open economy than in a closed economy?

Problems and Applications

5.4 An article in the *Economist* quotes the finance minister of Peru as saying, "We are one of the most open economies of Latin America." What did he mean by Peru being an "open economy"? Is fiscal policy in Peru likely to be more or less effective than it would be in a less open economy? Briefly explain.
Source: "Hold on Tight," *Economist*, February 2, 2013.

5.5 Suppose that Federal Reserve policy leads to higher interest rates in the United States.
  a. How will this policy affect real GDP in the short run if the United States is a closed economy?
  b. How will this policy affect real GDP in the short run if the United States is an open economy?
  c. How will your answer to part (b) change if interest rates also rise in the countries that are the major trading partners of the United States?

5.6 An economist remarks, "In the 1960s, using fiscal policy would have been a better way to stabilize the economy, but I believe that monetary policy is better today." What has changed about the U.S. economy that might have led the economist to this conclusion?

5.7 Suppose the federal government increases spending without also increasing taxes. In the short run, how will this action affect real GDP and the price level in a closed economy? How will the effects of this action differ in an open economy?

Real-Time Data Exercises

D9.1 **(Exchange rate movements)** Go to the Web site of the Federal Reserve Bank of St. Louis (FRED) (research. stlouisfed.org/fred2/) and download the most recent value and the value from the same month one year earlier from FRED for the U.S./Euro Foreign Exchange Rate (EXUSEU).

  a. Using these values, compute the percentage change in the euro's value.
  b. Explain whether the dollar appreciated or depreciated against the euro.

D9.2 **(Exchange rate movements)** Go to the Web site of the Federal Reserve Bank of St. Louis (FRED) (research. stlouisfed.org/fred2/) and download and plot the U.S. dollar–euro exchange rate (EXUSEU), the U.S. dollar–yen exchange rate (EXJPUS), and the U.S. dollar–Canadian dollar exchange rate (EXCAUS) for the period from 2001 to the present. Answer the following questions on the basis of your graphs.
  a. In what year did the euro reach its highest value?
  b. During the financial crisis of 2007–2009, did the yen appreciate or depreciate against the dollar? Briefly explain.
  c. Against which currency did the U.S. dollar depreciate the most during this period?

D9.3 **(Exchange rate movements)** One way to gauge the general value of one currency relative to other currencies is to calculate the *trade-weighted exchange rate*, which is an index number similar to the consumer price index. The trade-weighted exchange rate for the U.S. dollar weights each individual exchange rate by the share of that country's trade with the United States. Go to the Web site of the Federal Reserve Bank of St. Louis (FRED) (research. stlouisfed.org/fred2/) and download monthly data on the trade-weighted exchange rate for the U.S. dollar against major currencies (TWEXMMTH) from 1973 to the present.
  a. What has been the long-term trend in the exchange value of the dollar? What effect should changes in the exchange rate during this period have had on U.S. net exports? Briefly explain.
  b. What has been the trend in the exchange value of the dollar over the past year? What effect should changes in the exchange rate during the past year have had on U.S. net exports? Briefly explain.

D9.4 **(Exchange rates and exports)** Go to the Web site of the Federal Reserve Bank of St. Louis (FRED) (research.stlouisfed.org/fred2/) and find the most recent values for the Japan/U.S. Foreign Exchange Rate (DEXJPUS) and the U.S. Exports of Goods to Japan (EXPJP) and the values for one year earlier. Given the change in the exchange rate between the two periods, is the change in U.S. exports to Japan consistent with what the analysis in this module would predict? Briefly explain.

D9.5 **(Exchange rates and imports)** Go to the Web site of the Federal Reserve Bank of St. Louis (FRED) (research. stlouisfed.org/fred2/) and find the most recent values from FRED for the Japan/U.S. Foreign Exchange Rate (DEXJPUS) and the U.S. Imports of Goods from Japan (IMPJP) and the values for one year earlier. Given the change in the exchange rate between the two periods, is the change in U.S. imports from Japan consistent with what the analysis in this module would predict? Briefly explain.

9.6 Exchange Rate Systems, pages 403–404

LEARNING OBJECTIVE: Describe how different exchange rate systems operate.

Summary

When countries agree on how exchange rates should be determined, economists say that there is an **exchange rate system**. A **floating currency** is the outcome of a country allowing its currency's exchange rate to be determined by demand and supply. The current exchange rate system is a **managed float exchange rate system**, under which the value of most currencies is determined by demand and supply, with occasional government intervention. A **fixed exchange rate system** is a system under which countries agree to keep the exchange rates among their currencies fixed. Under the gold standard, the exchange rate between two currencies was automatically determined by the quantity of gold in each currency. By the end of the Great Depression of the 1930s, every country had abandoned the gold standard. Under the Bretton Woods system, which was in place between 1944 and the early 1970s, the United States agreed to exchange dollars for gold at a price of $35 per ounce. The central banks of all other members of the system pledged to buy and sell their currencies at a fixed rate against the dollar.

MyEconLab   Visit **www.myeconlab.com** to complete these exercises online and get instant feedback.

Review Questions

6.1 What is an exchange rate system? What is the difference between a fixed exchange rate system and a managed float exchange rate system?

6.2 How were exchange rates determined under the gold standard? How did the Bretton Woods system differ from the gold standard?

Problems and Applications

6.3 **(Related to the** Don't Let This Happen to You **on page 404)** Briefly explain whether you agree with the following statement: "The Federal Reserve is limited in its ability to issue paper currency by the amount of gold the federal government has in Fort Knox. To issue more paper currency, the government first has to buy more gold."

6.4 An article in the *Atlantic* referred to a poll of economists that found no support for the United States to readopt the gold standard:

> It prevents the central bank from fighting recessions by outsourcing monetary policy decisions to how much gold we have—which, in turn, depends on our trade balance and on how much of the shiny rock we can dig up. When we peg the dollar to gold we have to raise interest rates when gold is scarce, regardless of the state of the economy.

Why does the writer state that a gold standard would prevent "the central bank from fighting recessions"?

Source: Matthew O'Brien, "Why the Gold Standard Is the World's Worst Economic Idea, in 2 Charts," *Atlantic*, August 26, 2012.

6.5 The United States and most other countries abandoned the gold standard during the 1930s. Why would the 1930s have been a particularly difficult time for countries to have remained on the gold standard? (*Hint:* Think about the macroeconomic events of the 1930s and about the possible problems with carrying out an expansionary monetary policy while remaining on the gold standard.)

6.6 After World War II, why might countries have preferred the Bretton Woods system to reestablishing the gold standard? In your answer, be sure to note the important ways in which the Bretton Woods system differed from the gold standard.

9.7 The Current Exchange Rate System, pages 404–406

LEARNING OBJECTIVE: Discuss the three key features of the current exchange rate system.

Summary

The current exchange rate system has three key features: (1) The U.S. dollar floats against other major currencies, (2) most countries in Western Europe have adopted a common currency, and (3) some developing countries have fixed their currencies' exchange rates against the dollar or against another major currency. Since 1973, the value of the U.S. dollar has fluctuated widely against other major currencies. The theory of **purchasing power parity** states that in the long run, exchange rates move to equalize the purchasing power of different currencies. This theory helps to explain some of the long-run movements in the value of the U.S. dollar relative to other currencies. Purchasing power parity does not provide a complete explanation of movements in exchange rates for several reasons, including the existence of *tariffs* and *quotas*. A **tariff** is a tax imposed by a government on imports. A **quota** is a government-imposed limit on the quantity of a good that can be imported. Currently, 19 European Union member countries use a common currency known as the **euro**. The experience of the countries using the euro will provide economists with information about the costs and benefits to countries of using the same currency.

When a country keeps its currency's exchange rate fixed against another country's currency, it is **pegging** its currency. Pegging can result in problems similar to the difficulties countries encountered with fixed exchange rates under the Bretton Woods system. If investors become convinced that a country pegging its exchange rate will eventually allow the exchange rate to decline to a lower level, the demand curve for the currency will shift to the left. This destabilizing speculation makes it difficult for a central bank to maintain a fixed exchange rate.

MyEconLab   Visit www.myeconlab.com to complete these exercises online and get instant feedback.

Review Questions

7.1 What is the theory of purchasing power parity? Does the theory give a complete explanation for movements in exchange rates in the long run? Briefly explain.

7.2 Briefly describe the four determinants of exchange rates in the long run.

7.3 Which European countries currently use the euro as their currency? Why did these countries agree to replace their previous currencies with the euro?

7.4 What does it mean when one currency is "pegged" against another currency? Why do countries peg their currencies? What problems can result from pegging?

Problems and Applications

7.5 An article in the *Toronto Star* discussed the Canadian teams that play in the National Hockey League, the National Basketball Association, Major League Baseball, and Major League Soccer. The article noted, "Under their collective agreements players get paid in U.S. dollars. The majority of [team] revenue, however, is in Canadian currency." Are Canadian professional sports teams better off when the Canadian dollar increases in value relative to the U.S. dollar or when it decreases in value? Briefly explain.
Source: Josh Rubin, "MLSE, Blue Jays Deal with Dollar Dive," thestar.com, January 25, 2015.

7.6 An article in the *Economist* discussed the situation facing the U.S. economy in mid-2015: "The combination of weaker-than-expected CPI inflation and some dovish comments in the minutes of the Federal Reserve's July meeting have caused the dollar … to fall. Inflation continues to languish close to zero due to cheap oil and the effect of a strengthening dollar." By "dovish comments," the article meant that some members of the Fed's Federal Open Market Committee did not believe that the target for the federal funds rate should be raised in the coming months.
  a. If investors come to believe that the Fed might not be increasing interest rates, why would the value of the dollar decline?
  b. What does "the strengthening of the dollar" mean? Why would a strengthening of the dollar reduce the inflation rate in the United States?

Source: "Fed Leaders Begin to Recognise that September Is Too Soon to Hike Rates," *Economist*, August 20, 2015.

7.7 Consider this statement:

> It takes more than 120 yen to buy 1 U.S. dollar and more than 1.5 dollars to buy 1 British pound. These values show that the United States must be a much wealthier country than Japan and that the United Kingdom must be wealthier than the United States.

Do you agree with this reasoning? Briefly explain.

7.8 According to the theory of purchasing power parity, if the inflation rate in Australia is higher than the inflation rate in New Zealand, what should happen to the exchange rate between the Australian dollar and the New Zealand dollar? Briefly explain.

7.9 In December 2014, you needed 30 percent more pesos to buy one U.S. dollar than you had needed in December 2004. Over the same time period, the consumer price index in Mexico increased 49.5 percent, and the consumer price index in the United States increased 23.3 percent. Are these data consistent with the theory of purchasing power parity? Briefly explain.

7.10 (Related to the Making the Connection **on page 406**) Look again at the table on page 668 that shows the prices of Big Macs and the implied and actual exchange rates. Indicate whether the U.S. dollar is overvalued or undervalued against each currency.

7.11 (Related to Solved Problem 9.7 **on page 407**) Fill in the missing values in the following table. Assume that the Big Mac is selling for $4.79 in the United States. Explain whether the U.S. dollar is overvalued or undervalued relative to each of the other currencies and predict what will happen in the future to each exchange rate if the actual exchange rate moves toward the purchasing power parity exchange rate. Finally, calculate the implied exchange rate between the Russian ruble and the New Zealand dollar and explain which currency is overvalued in terms of Big Mac purchasing power parity.

Country	Big Mac Price	Implied Exchange Rate	Actual Exchange Rate
Chile	2,100 pesos		642.45 pesos per dollar
Israel	17.5 shekels		3.78 shekels per dollar
Russia	107 rubles		56.82 rubles per dollar
New Zealand	5.9 New Zealand dollars		1.51 New Zealand dollars per U.S. dollar

Source: "The Big Mac Index," *Economist*, July 16, 2015.

7.12 (Related to the Making the Connection **on page 410**) Britain decided not to join other European Union countries in using the euro as its currency. One British opponent of adopting the euro argued, "It comes down to economics. We just don't believe that it's possible to manage the entire economy of Europe with just one interest rate policy. How do you alleviate recession in Germany and curb inflation in Ireland?"

a. What interest rate policy would be used to alleviate recession in Germany?

b. What interest rate policy would be used to curb inflation in Ireland?

c. What does adopting the euro have to do with interest rate policy?

Source: Alan Cowell, "Nuanced Conflict over Euro in Britain," *New York Times*, June 22, 2001.

7.13 **(Related to the** Making the Connection **on page 410)** An article in *USA Today* argues, "Ironically, the euro's fall—and the benefit for German exports—is largely the result of eurozone policies that Germany has taken the lead in opposing . . . [including] easier money policies by the European Central Bank."

a. How does the "euro's fall" benefit German exports?

b. How is the euro's fall related to policies of the European Central Bank?

Source: Mihret Yohannes, "Germany Benefits from Weak Euro Policies It Deplores," usatoday.com, March 4, 2015.

7.14 In January 2007, before the financial crisis, the exchange rate was $1.30 per euro. In July 2008, during the financial crisis, the exchange rate was $1.58 per euro. Was this change in the dollar–euro exchange rate good news or bad news for U.S. firms exporting goods and services to Europe? Was it good news or bad news for European consumers buying goods and services imported from the United States? Briefly explain.

7.15 Although it is a member of the European Community, Denmark is not part of the eurozone; it has its own currency, the krone. Because the krone is pegged to the euro, Denmark's central bank is obliged to maintain the value of the krone within 2.25 percent either above or below the value of the euro. To maintain the peg with the euro, in 2015 the Danish central bank was forced to offer negative interest rates on deposits of krone that it held. Was the Danish central bank's action in response to an increase or a decrease in the value of the euro? Briefly explain.

Source: Charles Duxbury and Josie Cox, "Denmark Cuts Rates Again to Protect Currency Peg," *Wall Street Journal*, February 5, 2015.

7.16 **(Related to the** Module Opener **on page 402)** The German firm Bayer reported that its pharmaceutical group experienced a 21 percent increase in profit for the second quarter of 2015. The firm stated that the increase was partly the result of "favorable currency effects."

a. Briefly explain what the firm means by "favorable currency effects."

b. How would favorable currency effects increase Bayer's profit?

c. Would these effects still have raised Bayer's profit if all of the firm's production and all of its sales were within Europe? Briefly explain.

Source: Christopher Alessi, "Bayer Profit Rises on Healthy Currency Effects," *Wall Street Journal*, July 29, 2015.

7.17 Use the graph to answer the following questions.

a. According to the graph, is there a surplus or a shortage of baht in exchange for U.S. dollars? Briefly explain.

b. To maintain the pegged exchange rate, will the Thai central bank need to buy baht in exchange for dollars or sell baht in exchange for dollars? How many baht will the Thai central bank need to buy or sell?

7.18 The *Economist* observed, "In Argentina, many loans were taken out in dollars: this had catastrophic consequences for borrowers once the peg collapsed." What does the article mean when it says that Argentina's "peg collapsed"? Why was this collapse catastrophic for borrowers in Argentina who had taken out dollar loans?

Source: "Spoilt for Choice," *Economist*, June 3, 2002.

7.19 **(Related to the** Making the Connection **on page 414)** Graph the demand and supply of Chinese yuan for U.S. dollars and label each axis. To maintain a pegged exchange rate, the Chinese central bank can use yuan to buy U.S. dollars. Indicate whether the Chinese central bank would typically be interested in pegging the exchange rate above or below the market equilibrium exchange rate, and show on the graph the quantity of yuan the Chinese central bank would have to supply each trading period.

7.20 **(Related to the** Making the Connection **on page 414)** In August 2015, after the Chinese central bank moved to decrease the value of the yuan in exchange for the dollar, a column in the *Wall Street Journal* offered this opinion: "China's trading partners are right to suspect that the real purpose of the so-called reform is a competitive devaluation that boosts exports and growth at the rest of the world's expense."

a. What does the writer mean by a "competitive devaluation"?

b. How would such a devaluation boost Chinese exports and growth?

c. Why would a boost in Chinese exports and growth come at the rest of the world's expense?

Source: Greg Ip, "Why China's Yuan 'Reform' Merits Skepticism," *Wall Street Journal*, August 19, 2015.

9.8 International Capital Markets, pages 416–417

LEARNING OBJECTIVE: Discuss the growth of international capital markets.

Summary

A key reason exchange rates fluctuate is that investors seek out the best investments they can find anywhere in the world. Since 1980, the markets for stocks and bonds have become global. Foreign purchases of U.S. corporate bonds and stocks and U.S. government bonds have increased greatly in the period since 1995. As a result of the globalization of capital markets, firms around the world are no longer forced to rely only on the savings of domestic households for funds.

MyEconLab   Visit **www.myeconlab.com** to complete these exercises online and get instant feedback.

Review Questions

8.1 What were the main factors behind the globalization of capital markets in the 1980s and 1990s?

8.2 Briefly describe the pattern of foreign investments in U.S. securities between 1995 and 2014.

Problems and Applications

8.3 Why are foreign investors more likely to invest in U.S. government bonds than in U.S. corporate stocks and bonds?

8.4 The text states that "the globalization of financial markets has helped increase growth and efficiency in the world economy." Briefly explain which aspects of globalization help to increase growth in the world economy.

8.5 The global financial crisis of 2007–2009 led some economists and policymakers to suggest the reinstitution of capital controls—or limits on the flow of foreign exchange and financial investments across countries—which existed in many European countries prior to the 1960s. Why would a financial crisis lead policymakers to reconsider using capital controls? What problems might result from reinstituting capital controls?

Real-Time Data Exercises

D9.1 (Big Mac prices and purchasing power parity) Go to the Web site of the Federal Reserve Bank of St. Louis Federal Reserve (FRED) (research.stlouisfed.org/fred2/) and find the most recent values for the Japan/U.S. Foreign Exchange Rate (DEXJPUS), China/U.S. Foreign Exchange Rate (DEXCHUS), and the Mexico/U.S. Foreign Exchange Rate (DEXMXUS).

a. Explain whether the exchange rates are quoted as U.S. dollars per unit of foreign currency or units of foreign currency per U.S. dollar.

b. Suppose a Big Mac sells for 300 yen in Japan, 14 yuan in China, and 34 pesos in Mexico. What is the price of a Big Mac in each country in terms of U.S. dollars?

c. Are your results from part (b) consistent with the theory of purchasing power parity? Briefly explain.

d. Assuming no transportation costs and a no-cost means of preserving Big Macs while they are being transported, explain in which county you would want to purchase a Big Mac and in which country you would want to sell the same Big Mac in order to make the highest profit possible.

D9.2 (Explaining movements in the yuan-dollar exchange rate) Go to the Web site of the Federal Reserve Bank of St. Louis (FRED) (research.stlouisfed.org/fred2/) and find the values for the China/U.S. Foreign Exchange Rate (DEXCHUS) from 1981 to the most recent date available.

a. Compared with its value in 1981, has the yuan appreciated or depreciated against the U.S. dollar? Briefly explain.

b. Summarize the movements in the yuan–dollar exchange rate during these years and explain why the pattern occurred.

D9.3 (Analyzing global capital flows) The U.S. Treasury publishes data on capital flows. Treasury International Capital Flows can be found at www.treasury.gov/resource-center/data-chart-center/tic/Pages/index.aspx. Go to "Monthly Transactions in Long-Term Securities."

a. Look at recent net purchases of long-term securities. How has the volume of purchases changed over the past five years?

b. Now look at gross purchases of long-term securities. Which countries hold the most U.S. securities? How have foreign holdings of U.S. securities changed over time?

Appendix

The Gold Standard and the Bretton Woods System

LEARNING OBJECTIVE: Explain the gold standard and the Bretton Woods system.

It is easier to understand the current exchange rate system by considering further two earlier systems—the gold standard and the Bretton Woods system—that together lasted from the early nineteenth century through the early 1970s.

The Gold Standard

As we saw in this module, under the gold standard, the currency of a country consisted of gold coins and paper currency that people could redeem for gold. Great Britain adopted the gold standard in 1816, but as late as 1870, only a few nations had followed. In the late nineteenth century, however, Great Britain's share of world trade had increased, as had its overseas investments. The dominant position of Great Britain in the world economy motivated other countries to adopt the gold standard. By 1913, every country in Europe, except Spain and Bulgaria, and most countries in the Western Hemisphere had adopted the gold standard.

Under the gold standard, the exchange rate between two currencies was automatically determined by the quantity of gold in each currency. If there was 1/5 ounce of gold in a U.S. dollar and 1 ounce of gold in a British pound, the price of gold in the United States would be $5 per ounce, and the price of gold in Britain would be £1 per ounce. The exchange rate would therefore be $5 = £1.   MyEconLab Concept Check

The End of the Gold Standard

From a modern point of view, the greatest drawback to the gold standard was that the central bank lacked control of the money supply. The size of a country's money supply depended on its gold supply, which could be greatly affected by chance discoveries of gold or by technological change in gold mining. For example, the gold discoveries in California in 1849 and Alaska in the 1890s caused rapid increases in the U.S. money supply. Because the central bank cannot determine how much gold will be discovered, it lacks the control of the money supply necessary to pursue an active monetary policy. During wartime, countries usually went off the gold standard to allow their central banks to expand the money supply as rapidly as was necessary to pay for the war. Britain left the gold standard at the beginning of World War I in 1914 and did not resume redeeming its paper currency for gold until 1925.

When the Great Depression began in 1929, governments came under pressure to leave the gold standard to allow their central banks to pursue active monetary policies. In 1931, Great Britain became the first major country to abandon the gold standard. A number of other countries also went off the gold standard that year. The United States remained on the gold standard until 1933, and a few countries, including France, Italy, and Belgium, stayed on even longer. By the late 1930s, the gold standard had collapsed.

The earlier a country abandoned the gold standard, the easier time it had fighting the Depression with expansionary monetary policies. The countries that abandoned the gold standard by 1932 suffered an average decline in production of only 3 percent between 1929 and 1934. The countries that stayed on the gold standard until 1933 or later suffered an average decline of more than 30 percent. The devastating economic performance of the countries that stayed on the gold standard the longest during the 1930s is the key reason no attempt was made to bring back the gold standard in later years.   MyEconLab Concept Check

The Bretton Woods System

In addition to the collapse of the gold standard, the global economy suffered during the 1930s from tariff wars. The United States had started the tariff wars in June 1930 by enacting the Smoot-Hawley Tariff Act, which raised the average U.S. tariff rate to more than 50 percent. Many other countries raised tariffs during the next few years, leading to a collapse in world trade.

As World War II was coming to an end, economists and government officials in the United States and Europe concluded that they needed to restore the international economic system to avoid another depression. In 1947, the United States and most other major countries, apart from the Soviet Union, began participating in the General Agreement on Tariffs and Trade (GATT), under which they worked to reduce trade barriers. The GATT was very successful in sponsoring rounds of negotiations among countries, which led to sharp declines in tariffs. U.S. tariffs dropped from an average rate of more than 50 percent in the early 1930s to an average rate of less than 2 percent in 2015. In 1995, the GATT was replaced by the World Trade Organization (WTO), which has similar objectives.

The effort to develop a new exchange rate system to replace the gold standard was more complicated than establishing the GATT. A conference held in Bretton Woods, New Hampshire, in 1944 set up a system in which the United States pledged to buy or sell gold at a fixed price of $35 per ounce. The central banks of all other members of the new **Bretton Woods system** pledged to buy and sell their currencies at a fixed rate against the dollar. By fixing their exchange rates against the dollar, these countries were fixing the exchange rates among their currencies as well. Unlike under the gold standard, neither the United States nor any other country was willing to redeem its paper currency for gold domestically. The United States would redeem dollars for gold only if they were presented by a foreign central bank. The United States continued the prohibition, first enacted in the early 1930s, against private citizens owning gold, except in the form of jewelry or rare coins. The prohibition was not lifted until the 1970s, when it again became possible for Americans to own gold as an investment.

Under the Bretton Woods system, central banks were committed to selling dollars in exchange for their own currencies. This commitment required them to hold *dollar reserves*. If a central bank ran out of dollar reserves, it could borrow them from the newly created **International Monetary Fund (IMF)**. In addition to providing loans to central banks that were short of dollar reserves, the IMF would oversee the operation of the system and approve adjustments to the agreed-on fixed exchange rates.

Under the Bretton Woods system, a fixed exchange rate was called a *par exchange rate*. If the par exchange rate was not the same as the exchange rate that would have been determined in the market, the result would be a surplus or a shortage. For example, Figure 9A.1 shows the exchange rate between the dollar and the British pound. The figure is drawn from the British point of view, so we measure the exchange rate on the vertical axis as dollars per pound. In this case, the par exchange rate between the dollar and the pound is above the equilibrium exchange rate, as determined by demand and supply.

At the par exchange rate of $4 per pound, the quantity of pounds demanded by people who want to buy British goods and services or who want to invest in British assets is smaller than the quantity of pounds supplied by people who would like to exchange them for dollars. As a result, the Bank of England must use dollars to buy the surplus of £1 million per day. Only at an exchange rate of $2.80 per pound would the surplus be eliminated. If the par exchange rate was below the equilibrium exchange rate, there would be a shortage of domestic currency in the foreign exchange market.

A persistent shortage or surplus of a currency under the Bretton Woods system was seen as evidence of a *fundamental disequilibrium* in a country's exchange rate. After consulting with the IMF, countries in this position were allowed to adjust their exchange rates. In the early years of the Bretton Woods system, many countries found that their currencies were *overvalued* versus the dollar, meaning that their par exchange rates were too high. A reduction in a fixed exchange rate is a **devaluation**. An increase in a fixed exchange rate is a **revaluation**. In 1949, there was a devaluation of several currencies,

Bretton Woods system An exchange rate system that lasted from 1944 to 1973, under which countries pledged to buy and sell their currencies at a fixed rate against the dollar.

International Monetary Fund (IMF) An international organization that provides foreign currency loans to central banks and oversees the operation of the international monetary system.

Devaluation A reduction in a fixed exchange rate.

Revaluation An increase in a fixed exchange rate.

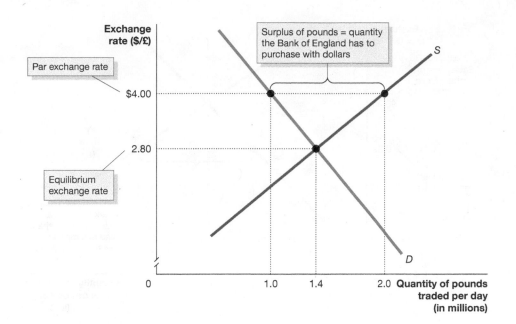

MyEconLab Animation

Figure 9A.1

A Fixed Exchange Rate above Equilibrium Results in a Surplus of Pounds

Under the Bretton Woods system, if the par exchange rate was above equilibrium, the result would be a surplus of domestic currency in the foreign exchange market. If the par exchange rate was below equilibrium, the result would be a shortage of domestic currency. In the figure, the par exchange rate between the pound and the dollar is $4 = £1, while the equilibrium exchange rate is $2.80 = £1. This gap forces the Bank of England to buy £1 million per day in exchange for dollars.

including the British pound, reflecting the fact that those currencies had been overvalued against the dollar.   MyEconLab Concept Check

The Collapse of the Bretton Woods System

By the late 1960s, the Bretton Woods system faced two severe problems. The first was that after 1963, the total number of dollars held by foreign central banks was larger than the gold reserves of the United States. In practice, most central banks—with the Bank of France being the main exception—rarely redeemed dollars for gold. But the basis of the system was a credible promise by the United States to redeem dollars for gold if called upon to do so. By the late 1960s, as the gap between the dollars held by foreign central banks and the gold reserves of the United States grew larger and larger, other countries began to doubt the U.S. promise to redeem dollars for gold.

The second problem the Bretton Woods system faced was that some countries with undervalued currencies, particularly West Germany, were unwilling to revalue their currencies. Governments resisted revaluation because it would have increased the prices of their countries' exports. Many German firms put pressure on the government not to endanger their sales in the U.S. market by raising the exchange rate of the deutsche mark against the dollar. Figure 9A.2 shows the situation the German government faced in 1971. The figure takes the German point of view, so the exchange rate is expressed in terms of dollars per deutsche mark.

Under the Bretton Woods system, the Bundesbank, the German central bank, was required to buy and sell deutsche marks for dollars at a rate of $0.27 per deutsche mark. The equilibrium that would have prevailed in the foreign exchange market if the Bundesbank had not intervened was about $0.35 per deutsche mark. Because the par exchange rate was below the equilibrium exchange rate, the quantity of deutsche marks demanded by people wanting to buy German goods and services or wanting to invest in German assets was greater than the quantity of deutsche marks supplied by people who wanted to exchange them for dollars. To maintain the exchange rate at $0.27 per deutsche mark, the Bundesbank had to buy dollars and sell deutsche marks. The number of deutsche marks supplied by the Bundesbank was equal to the shortage of deutsche marks at the par exchange rate.

By selling deutsche marks and buying dollars to defend the par exchange rate, the Bundesbank was increasing the West German money supply, risking an increase in the inflation rate. Because Germany had suffered a devastating hyperinflation during the 1920s, the fear of inflation was greater in Germany than in any other industrial country. No German government could survive politically if it allowed a significant increase in

Figure 9A.2

West Germany's Undervalued Exchange Rate

The Bundesbank, the German central bank, was committed under the Bretton Woods system to defending a par exchange rate of $0.27 per deutsche mark (DM). Because this exchange rate was lower than what the equilibrium market exchange rate would have been, there was a shortage of DMs in the foreign exchange market. The Bundesbank had to supply DMs equal to the shortage in exchange for dollars. The shortage in the figure is equal to 1 billion DMs per day.

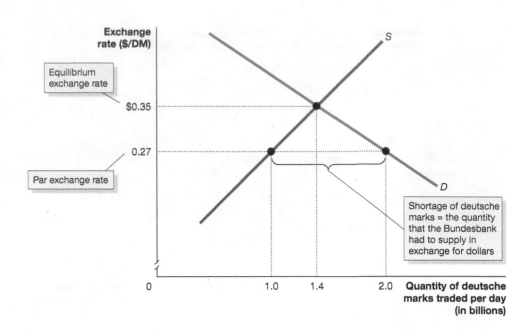

inflation. Knowing this fact, many investors in Germany and elsewhere became convinced that, eventually, the German government would have to allow a revaluation of the mark.

During the 1960s, most European countries, including Germany, relaxed their **capital controls**, which are limits on the flow of foreign exchange and financial investment across countries. The loosening of capital controls made it easier for investors to speculate on changes in exchange rates. For instance, an investor in the United States could sell $1 million and receive about 3.7 million deutsche marks at the par exchange rate of $0.27 per deutsche mark. If the exchange rate rose to $0.35 per deutsche mark, the investor could then exchange deutsche marks for dollars, receiving $1.3 million at the new exchange rate: a return of 30 percent on an initial $1 million investment. The more convinced investors became that Germany would have to allow a revaluation, the more dollars they exchanged for deutsche marks. Figure 9A.3 shows the results.

Capital controls Limits on the flow of foreign exchange and financial investment across countries.

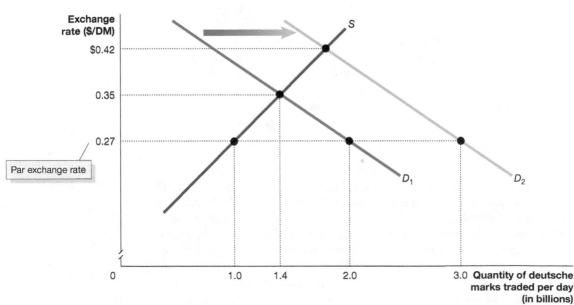

Figure 9A.3 **Destabilizing Speculation against the Deutsche Mark, 1971**

In 1971, the par exchange rate of $0.27 = 1 deutsche mark was below the equilibrium exchange rate of $0.35 = 1 deutsche mark. As investors became convinced that West Germany would have to revalue the deutsche mark, they increased their demand for marks, shifting the demand curve from D_1 to D_2. The new equilibrium exchange rate became $0.42 = 1 deutsche mark. This increase in demand raised the quantity of marks the Bundesbank had to supply in exchange for dollars to defend the par exchange rate from 1 billion deutsche marks to 2 billion deutsche marks per day.

The increased demand for deutsche marks by investors hoping to make a profit from the expected revaluation of the mark shifted the demand curve for marks to the right, from D_1 to D_2. Because of this expectation, the Bundesbank had to increase the marks it supplied in exchange for dollars, raising further the risk of inflation in Germany. As we saw in this module, because these actions by investors make it more difficult to maintain a fixed exchange rate, they are called *destabilizing speculation*. By May 1971, the Bundesbank had to buy more than $250 million per day to support the fixed exchange rate against the dollar. Finally, on May 5, the West German government decided to allow the mark to float. In August, President Richard Nixon elected to abandon the U.S. commitment to redeem dollars for gold. Attempts were made over the next two years to reach a compromise that would restore a fixed exchange rate system, but by 1973, the Bretton Woods system was effectively dead.   MyEconLab Concept Check   MyEconLab Study Plan

Key Terms

Bretton Woods system, p. 430

Capital controls, p. 432

Devaluation, p. 430

International Monetary Fund (IMF), p. 430

Revaluation, p. 430

9.A ## The Gold Standard and the Bretton Woods System, pages 429–434

LEARNING OBJECTIVE: Explain the gold standard and the Bretton Woods system.

MyEconLab   Visit www.myeconlab.com to complete these exercises online and get instant feedback.

Review Questions

9A.1   What determined the exchange rates among currencies under the gold standard? Why did the gold standard collapse?

9A.2   Briefly describe how the Bretton Woods system operated.

9A.3   What is the difference between a devaluation and a revaluation?

9A.4   What are capital controls?

9A.5   What role did the International Monetary Fund play in the Bretton Woods system?

9A.6   What is destabilizing speculation? What role did it play in the collapse of the Bretton Woods system?

Problems and Applications

9A.7   Suppose that under the gold standard, there was 1/5 ounce of gold in a U.S. dollar and 1 ounce of gold in a British pound. Demonstrate that if the exchange rate between the dollar and the pound was $4 = £1 rather than $5 = £1, you could make unlimited profits by buying gold in one country and selling it in the other. If the exchange rate was $6 = £1, how would your strategy change? For simplicity, assume that there was no cost to shipping gold from one country to the other.

9A.8   If a country is using the gold standard, what is likely to happen to its money supply if new gold deposits are discovered in the country, as happened in the United States with the gold discoveries in California in 1849? Is this change in the money supply desirable? Briefly explain.

9A.9   An article in the *Economist* observes, "When the Depression [of the 1930s] struck, this gold standard became a noose around the necks of struggling economies." In

what sense was the gold standard a "noose around the necks of struggling economies" during the 1930s?

Source: "A Brief Post on Competitive Devaluation," *Economist*, October 31, 2011.

9A.10   An article in the *Economist* observed that there were "some perturbing parallels between the gold standard and the euro." What parallels are there between the gold standard and the euro? What would make these parallels perturbing?

Source: "Perturbing Parallels," *Economist*, July 5, 2013.

9A.11   An article in the *New York Times* states, "On Aug. 15, 1971, President Nixon unhitched the value of the dollar from the gold standard." Is the author of this article correct that the United States abandoned the gold standard in 1971? What led President Nixon to take the action described in the article?

Source: "Bretton Woods System" *New York Times*, August 20, 2015.

9A.12   An opinion column in the *New York Times* offers the view that "zealous money printing in the 1960s led to the inevitable collapse of the Bretton Woods system (and complete fiat money was born)."
   a. What does the author mean by "zealous money printing"?
   b. Why would zealous money printing have led to the collapse of the Bretton Woods system?
   c. What does the author mean by saying that the collapse of the Bretton Woods system resulted in "complete fiat money"?

Source: Mark Spitznagel, "The Myth of Black Swan Market Events," *New York Times*, February 13, 2015.

9A.13   One economist has argued that the East Asian exchange rate crisis of the late 1990s was due to "the simple failure of governments to remember the lessons from the breakdown of the Bretton Woods System." What are these lessons? In what sense did the East Asian governments fail to learn these lessons?

Source: Thomas D. Willett, "Crying for Argentina," *Milken Institute Review*, Second Quarter 2002.

9A.14 Economists Michael Bordo of Rutgers University and Angela Redish of the University of British Columbia have argued that the "Bretton Woods system functioned for a number of years but beginning in the late 1960s, in the face of inflationary US monetary policy it became a slow moving train wreck." Why would inflationary U.S. monetary policy cause problems for the Bretton Woods system?

Source: Michael Bordo and Angela Redish, "Putting the 'System' in the International Monetary System," www.voxeu.org, June 20, 2013.

9A.15 An article in the *Economist* notes that after the end of the Bretton Woods system, "the Europeans did not like leaving their currencies to the whims of the markets." What does it mean for a country to leave its currency to the "whims of the markets"? What problems might a country experience as a result? What exchange rate system did most European countries ultimately adopt?

Source: "Forty Years On," *Economist*, August 13, 2011.

Real-Time Data Exercise

D9A.1 **(Gold prices and the gold standard)** Go to the Web site of the Federal Reserve Bank of St. Louis (FRED) (research.stlouisfed.org/fred2/) and find the Gold Fixing Price 10:30 A.M. (London time) in the London Bullion Market in U.S. Dollars (GOLDAMGBD228NLBM) from 1968 to the most recent available date.

a. What explains the relative stability of the price of gold from 1968 to 1971?

b. What implications do the movements in gold prices since 1971 have for an attempt by the United States and other countries to reestablish a gold standard?

GLOSSARY

A

Absolute advantage The ability of an individual, a firm, or a country to produce more of a good or service than competitors, using the same amount of resources.

Accounting profit A firm's net income, measured as revenue minus operating expenses and taxes paid.

Adverse selection The situation in which one party to a transaction takes advantage of knowing more than the other party to the transaction.

Aggregate demand (AD) curve A curve that shows the relationship between the price level and the level of planned aggregate expenditure in the economy, holding constant all other factors that affect aggregate expenditure.

Aggregate demand and aggregate supply model A model that explains short-run fluctuations in real GDP and the price level.

Aggregate expenditure (AE) Total spending in the economy: the sum of consumption, planned investment, government purchases, and net exports.

Aggregate expenditure model A macroeconomic model that focuses on the short-run relationship between total spending and real GDP, assuming that the price level is constant.

Allocative efficiency A state of the economy in which production is in accordance with consumer preferences; in particular, every good or service is produced up to the point where the last unit provides a marginal benefit to society equal to the marginal cost of producing it.

Asset Anything of value owned by a person or a firm.

Asymmetric information A situation in which one party to an economic transaction has less information than the other party.

Autarky A situation in which a country does not trade with other countries.

Automatic stabilizers Government spending and taxes that automatically increase or decrease along with the business cycle.

Autonomous expenditure An expenditure that does not depend on the level of GDP.

B

Balance of payments The record of a country's trade with other countries in goods, services, and assets.

Balance of trade The difference between the value of the goods a country exports and the value of the goods a country imports.

Balance sheet A financial statement that sums up a firm's financial position on a particular day, usually the end of a quarter or year.

Bank panic A situation in which many banks experience runs at the same time.

Bank run A situation in which many depositors simultaneously decide to withdraw money from a bank.

Black market A market in which buying and selling take place at prices that violate government price regulations.

Bond A financial security that represents a promise to repay a fixed amount of funds.

Bretton Woods system An exchange rate system that lasted from 1944 to 1973, under which countries pledged to buy and sell their currencies at a fixed rate against the dollar.

Budget deficit The situation in which the government's expenditures are greater than its tax revenue.

Budget surplus The situation in which the government's expenditures are less than its tax revenue.

Business cycle Alternating periods of economic expansion and economic recession.

C

Capital account The part of the balance of payments that records relatively minor transactions, such as migrants' transfers and sales and purchases of nonproduced, nonfinancial assets.

Capital controls Limits on the flow of foreign exchange and financial investment across countries.

Capital Manufactured goods that are used to produce other goods and services.

Cash flow The difference between the cash revenues received by a firm and the cash spending by the firm.

Catch-up The prediction that the level of GDP per capita (or income per capita) in poor countries will grow faster than in rich countries.

Centrally planned economy An economy in which the government decides how economic resources will be allocated.

Ceteris paribus ("all else equal") condition The requirement that when analyzing the relationship between two variables—such as price and quantity demanded—other variables must be held constant.

Circular-flow diagram A model that illustrates how participants in markets are linked.

Closed economy An economy that has no interactions in trade or finance with other countries.

Commodity money A good used as money that also has value independent of its use as money.

Comparative advantage The ability of an individual, a firm, or a country to produce a good or service at a lower opportunity cost than competitors.

Competitive market equilibrium A market equilibrium with many buyers and sellers.

Complements Goods and services that are used together.

Consumer price index (CPI) A measure of the average change over time in the prices a typical urban family of four pays for the goods and services they purchase.

Consumer surplus The difference between the highest price a consumer is willing to pay for a good or service and the actual price the consumer pays.

Consumption Spending by households on goods and services, not including spending on new houses.

Consumption function The relationship between consumption spending and disposable income.

Contractionary monetary policy The Federal Reserve's policy of increasing interest rates to reduce inflation.

Corporate governance The way in which a corporation is structured and the effect that structure has on the corporation's behavior.

Corporation A legal form of business that provides owners with protection from losing more than their investment should the business fail.

Coupon payment An interest payment on a bond.

Crowding out A decline in private expenditures as a result of an increase in government purchases.

Currency appreciation An increase in the market value of one currency relative to another currency.

Currency depreciation A decrease in the market value of one currency relative to another currency.

Current account The part of the balance of payments that records a country's net exports, net income on investments, and net transfers.

Cyclically adjusted budget deficit or surplus The deficit or surplus in the federal government's budget if the economy were at potential GDP.

Cyclical unemployment Unemployment caused by a business cycle recession.

D

Deadweight loss The reduction in economic surplus resulting from a market not being in competitive equilibrium.

Deflation A decline in the price level.

Demand curve A curve that shows the relationship between the price of a product and the quantity of the product demanded.

Demand schedule A table that shows the relationship between the price of a product and the quantity of the product demanded.

Demographics The characteristics of a population with respect to age, race, and gender.

Devaluation A reduction in a fixed exchange rate.

Direct finance A flow of funds from savers to firms through financial markets, such as the New York Stock Exchange.

Discount loans Loans the Federal Reserve makes to banks.

Discount rate The interest rate the Federal Reserve charges on discount loans.

Discouraged workers People who are available for work but have not looked for a job during the previous four weeks because they believe no jobs are available for them.

Disinflation A significant reduction in the inflation rate.

Dividends Payments by a corporation to its shareholders.

Dumping Selling a product for a price below its cost of production.

E

Economic efficiency A market outcome in which the marginal benefit to consumers of the last unit produced is equal to its marginal cost of production and in which the sum of consumer surplus and producer surplus is at a maximum.

Economic growth model A model that explains growth rates in real GDP per capita over the long run.

Economic growth The ability of an economy to produce increasing quantities of goods and services.

Economic model A simplified version of reality used to analyze real-world economic situations.

Economic profit A firm's revenues minus all of its implicit and explicit costs.

Economics The study of the choices people make to attain their goals, given their scarce resources.

Economic surplus The sum of consumer surplus and producer surplus.

Economic variable Something measurable that can have different values, such as the incomes of doctors.

Efficiency wage An above-market wage that a firm pays to increase workers' productivity.

Employed In government statistics, someone who currently has a job or who is temporarily away from his or her job.

Entrepreneur Someone who operates a business, bringing together the factors of production—labor, capital, and natural resources—to produce goods and services.

Equity The fair distribution of economic benefits.

Euro The common currency of many European countries.

Excess reserves Reserves that banks hold over the legal requirement.

Exchange rate system An agreement among countries about how exchange rates should be determined.

Excludability The situation in which anyone who does not pay for a good cannot consume it.

Expansion The period of a business cycle during which total production and total employment are increasing.

Expansionary monetary policy The Federal Reserve's policy of decreasing interest rates to increase real GDP.

Explicit cost A cost that involves spending money.

Exports Goods and services produced domestically but sold in other countries.

External economies Reductions in a firm's costs that result from an increase in the size of an industry.

F

Factor market A market for the factors of production, such as labor, capital, natural resources, and entrepreneurial ability.

Factors of production Labor, capital, natural resources, and other inputs used to make goods and services.

Federal funds rate The interest rate banks charge each other for overnight loans.

Federal Open Market Committee (FOMC) The Federal Reserve committee responsible for open market operations and managing the money supply in the United States.

Federal Reserve The central bank of the United States.

Fee-for-service A system under which doctors and hospitals receive a payment for each service they provide.

Fiat money Money, such as paper currency, that is authorized by a central bank or governmental body and that does not have to be exchanged by the central bank for gold or some other commodity money.

Final good or service A good or service purchased by a final user.

Financial account The part of the balance of payments that records purchases of assets a country has made abroad and foreign purchases of assets in the country.

Financial intermediaries Firms, such as banks, mutual funds, pension funds, and insurance companies, that borrow funds from savers and lend them to borrowers.

Financial markets Markets where financial securities, such as stocks and bonds, are bought and sold.

Financial system The system of financial markets and financial intermediaries through which firms acquire funds from households.

Fiscal policy Changes in federal taxes and purchases that are intended to achieve macroeconomic policy goals.

Fiscal policy Changes in federal taxes and purchases that are intended to achieve macroeconomic policy objectives.

Fixed exchange rate system A system under which countries agree to keep the exchange rates among their currencies fixed for long periods.

Floating currency The outcome of a country allowing its currency's exchange rate to be determined by demand and supply.

Foreign direct investment (FDI) The purchase or building by a corporation of a facility in a foreign country.

Foreign portfolio investment The purchase by an individual or a firm of stocks or bonds issued in another country.

Fractional reserve banking system A banking system in which banks keep less than

100 percent of deposits as reserves.

Free market A market with few government restrictions on how a good or service can be produced or sold or on how a factor of production can be employed.

Free trade Trade between countries that is without government restrictions.

Frictional unemployment Short-term unemployment that arises from the process of matching workers with jobs.

G

GDP deflator A measure of the price level, calculated by dividing nominal GDP by real GDP and multiplying by 100.

Globalization The process of countries becoming more open to foreign trade and investment.

Government purchases Spending by federal, state, and local governments on goods and services.

Gross domestic product (GDP) The market value of all final goods and services produced in a country during a period of time, typically one year.

H

Health care Goods and services, such as prescription drugs, consultations with a doctor, and surgeries, that are intended to maintain or improve a person's health.

Health insurance A contract under which a buyer agrees to make payments, or *premiums*, in exchange for the provider's agreeing to pay some or all of the buyer's medical bills.

Human capital The accumulated knowledge and skills that workers acquire from formal training and education or from life experiences.

I

Implicit cost A nonmonetary opportunity cost.

Imports Goods and services bought domestically but produced in other countries.

Income effect The change in the quantity demanded of a good that results from the effect of a change in the good's price on consumers' purchasing power.

Income statement A financial statement that shows a firm's revenues, costs, and profit over a period of time.

Indirect finance A flow of funds from savers to borrowers through financial intermediaries such as banks. Intermediaries raise funds from savers to lend to firms (and other borrowers).

Industrial Revolution The application of mechanical power to the production of goods, beginning in England around 1750.

Inferior good A good for which the demand increases as income falls and decreases as income rises.

Inflation rate The percentage increase in the price level from one year to the next.

Inflation targeting A framework for conducting monetary policy that involves the central bank announcing its target level of inflation.

Interest rate The cost of borrowing funds, usually expressed as a percentage of the amount borrowed.

Intermediate good or service A good or service that is an input into another good or service, such as a tire on a truck.

International Monetary Fund (IMF) An international organization that provides foreign currency loans to central banks and oversees the operation of the international monetary system.

Inventories Goods that have been produced but not yet sold.

Investment Spending by firms on new factories, office buildings, machinery, and additions to inventories, plus spending by households and firms on new houses.

Isocost line All the combinations of two inputs, such as capital and labor, that have the same total cost.

K

Keynesian revolution The name given to the widespread acceptance during the 1930s and 1940s of John Maynard Keynes's macroeconomic model.

L

Labor force participation rate The percentage of the working-age population in the labor force.

Labor force The sum of employed and unemployed workers in the economy.

Labor productivity The quantity of goods and services that can be produced by one worker or by one hour of work.

Law of demand A rule that states that, holding everything else constant, when the price of a product falls, the quantity demanded of the product will increase, and when the price of a product rises, the quantity demanded of the product will decrease.

Law of supply A rule that states that, holding everything else constant, increases in price cause increases in the quantity supplied, and decreases in price cause decreases in the quantity supplied.

Liability Anything owed by a person or a firm.

Limited liability A legal provision that shields owners of a corporation from losing more than they have invested in the firm.

Long-run economic growth The process by which rising productivity increases the average standard of living.

M

M1 The narrow definition of the money supply: the sum of currency in circulation, checking account deposits in banks, and holdings of traveler's checks.

M2 A broader definition of the money supply: It includes M1 plus savings account deposits, small-denomination time deposits, balances in money market deposit accounts in banks, and noninstitutional money market fund shares.

Macroeconomics The study of the economy as a whole, including topics such as inflation, unemployment, and economic growth.

Managed float exchange rate system The current exchange rate system, under which the value of most currencies is determined by demand and supply, with occasional government intervention.

Marginal analysis Analysis that involves comparing marginal benefits and marginal costs.

Marginal benefit The additional benefit to a consumer from consuming one more unit of a good or service.

Marginal cost The additional cost to a firm of producing one more unit of a good or service.

Marginal product of labor The additional output a firm produces as a result of hiring one more worker.

Marginal propensity to consume (MPC) The slope of the consumption function: The amount by which consumption spending changes when disposable income changes.

Marginal propensity to save (MPS) The amount by which saving changes when disposable income changes.

Market A group of buyers and sellers of a good or service and the institution or arrangement by which they come together to trade.

Market-based reforms Changes in the market for health care that would make it more like the markets for other goods and services.

Market demand The demand by all the consumers of a given good or service.

Market economy An economy in which the decisions of households and firms interacting in markets allocate economic resources.

Market equilibrium A situation in which quantity demanded equals quantity supplied.

Market for loanable funds The interaction of borrowers and lenders that determines the market interest rate and the quantity of loanable funds exchanged.

Menu costs The costs to firms of changing prices.

Microeconomics The study of how households and firms make choices, how they interact in markets, and how the government attempts to influence their choices.

Mixed economy An economy in which most economic decisions result from the interaction of buyers and sellers in markets but in which the government plays a significant role in the allocation of resources.

Monetarism The macroeconomic theories of Milton Friedman and his followers, particularly the idea that the quantity of money should be increased at a constant rate.

Monetary growth rule A plan for increasing the quantity of money at a fixed rate that does not respond to changes in economic conditions.

Monetary policy The actions the Federal Reserve takes to manage the money supply and interest rates to achieve macroeconomic policy goals.

Money Assets that people are generally willing to accept in exchange for goods and services or for payment of debts.

Moral hazard The actions people take after they have entered into a transaction that make the other party to the transaction worse off.

Multiplier effect The process by which an increase in autonomous expenditure leads to a larger increase in real GDP.

Multiplier The increase in equilibrium real GDP divided

by the increase in autonomous expenditure.

N

Natural rate of unemployment The normal rate of unemployment, consisting of frictional unemployment and structural unemployment.

Net exports Exports minus imports.

Net foreign investment The difference between capital outflows from a country and capital inflows, also equal to net foreign direct investment plus net foreign portfolio investment.

New classical macroeconomics The macroeconomic theories of Robert Lucas and others, particularly the idea that workers and firms have rational expectations.

New growth theory A model of long-run economic growth that emphasizes that technological change is influenced by economic incentives and so is determined by the working of the market system.

Nominal exchange rate The value of one country's currency in terms of another country's currency.

Nominal GDP The value of final goods and services evaluated at current-year prices.

Nominal interest rate The stated interest rate on a loan.

Nonaccelerating inflation rate of unemployment (NAIRU) The unemployment rate at which the inflation rate has no tendency to increase or decrease.

Normal good A good for which the demand increases as income rises and decreases as income falls.

Normative analysis Analysis concerned with what ought to be.

O

Open economy An economy that has interactions in trade or finance with other countries.

Open market operations The buying and selling of Treasury securities by the Federal Reserve in order to control the money supply.

Opportunity cost The highest-valued alternative that must be given up to engage in an activity.

P

Partnership A firm owned jointly by two or more persons and not organized as a corporation.

Patent The exclusive right to produce a product for a period of 20 years from the date the patent is applied for.

Patient Protection and Affordable Care Act (ACA) Health care reform legislation passed by Congress and signed by President Barack Obama in 2010.

Pegging A policy by which a country keeps fixed the exchange rate between its currency and another country's currency.

Per-worker production function The relationship between real GDP per hour worked and capital per hour worked, holding the level of technology constant.

Perfectly competitive market A market that meets the conditions of having (1) many buyers and sellers, (2) all firms selling identical products, and (3) no barriers to new firms entering the market.

Phillips curve A graph showing the short-run relationship between the unemployment rate and the inflation rate.

Positive analysis Analysis concerned with what is.

Potential GDP The level of real GDP attained when all firms are producing at capacity.

Present value The value in today's dollars of funds to be paid or received in the future.

Price ceiling A legally determined maximum price that sellers may charge.

Price floor A legally determined minimum price that sellers may receive.

Price level A measure of the average prices of goods and services in the economy.

Open market operations The buying and selling of Treasury securities by the Federal Reserve in order to control the money supply.

Principal–agent problem A problem caused by agents pursuing their own interests rather than the interests of the principals who hired them.

Producer price index (PPI) An average of the prices received by producers of goods and services at all stages of the production process.

Producer surplus The difference between the lowest price a firm would be willing to accept for a good or service and the price it actually receives.

Production possibilities frontier (PPF) A curve showing the maximum attainable combinations of two goods that can be produced with available resources and current technology.

Product market A market for goods—such as computers—or services—such as medical treatment.

Productive efficiency A situation in which a good or service is produced at the lowest possible cost.

Property rights The rights individuals or firms have to the exclusive use of their property, including the right to buy or sell it.

Protectionism The use of trade barriers to shield domestic firms from foreign competition.

Purchasing power parity The theory that in the long run exchange rates move to equalize the purchasing powers of different currencies.

Q

Quantity demanded The amount of a good or service that a consumer is willing and able to purchase at a given price.

Quantity supplied The amount of a good or service that a firm is willing and able to supply at a given price.

Quantity theory of money A theory about the connection between money and prices that assumes that the velocity of money is constant.

Quota A numerical limit a government imposes on the quantity of a good that can be imported into the country.

R

Rational expectations Expectations formed by using all available information about an economic variable.

Real business cycle model A macroeconomic model that focuses on real, rather than monetary, causes of the business cycle.

Real business cycle models Models that focus on real rather than monetary explanations of fluctuations in real GDP.

Real exchange rate The price of domestic goods in terms of foreign goods.

Real GDP The value of final goods and services evaluated at base-year prices.

Real interest rate The nominal interest rate minus the inflation rate.

Recession The period of a business cycle during which total production and total employment are decreasing.

Required reserve ratio The minimum fraction of deposits banks are required by law to keep as reserves.

Required reserves Reserves that a bank is legally required to hold, based on its checking account deposits.

Reserves Deposits that a bank keeps as cash in its vault or on deposit with the Federal Reserve.

Revaluation An increase in a fixed exchange rate.

Rule of law The ability of a government to enforce the laws of the country, particularly with respect to protecting private property and enforcing contracts.

S

Saving and investment equation An equation that shows that national saving is equal to domestic investment plus net foreign investment.

Scarcity A situation in which unlimited wants exceed the limited resources available to fulfill those wants.

Securitization The process of transforming loans or other financial assets into securities.

Security A financial asset—such as a stock or a bond—that can be bought and sold in a financial market.

Separation of ownership from control A situation in a corporation in which the top management, rather than the shareholders, controls day-to-day operations.

Short-run aggregate supply (SRAS) curve A curve that shows the relationship in the short run between the price level and the quantity of real GDP supplied by firms.

Shortage A situation in which the quantity demanded is greater than the quantity supplied.

Simple deposit multiplier The ratio of the amount of deposits created by banks to the amount of new reserves.

Single-payer health care system A system, such as the one in Canada, in which the government provides health insurance to all of the country's residents.

Socialized medicine A health care system under which the government owns most of the hospitals and employs most of the doctors.

Sole proprietorship A firm owned by a single individual and not organized as a corporation.

Speculators Currency traders who buy and sell foreign exchange in an attempt to profit from changes in exchange rates.

Stagflation A combination of inflation and recession, usually resulting from a supply shock.

Stock A financial security that represents partial ownership of a firm.

Stockholders' equity The difference between the value of a corporation's assets and the value of its liabilities; also known as *net worth*.

Structural relationship A relationship that depends on the basic behavior of consumers and firms and that remains unchanged over long periods.

Structural unemployment Unemployment that arises from a persistent mismatch between the skills or attributes of workers and the requirements of jobs.

Substitutes Goods and services that can be used for the same purpose.

Substitution effect The change in the quantity demanded of a good that results from a change in price, making the good more or less expensive relative to other goods that are substitutes.

Supply curve A curve that shows the relationship between the price of a product and the quantity of the product supplied.

Supply schedule A table that shows the relationship between the price of a product and the quantity of the product supplied.

Supply shock An unexpected event that causes the short-run aggregate supply curve to shift.

Surplus A situation in which the quantity supplied is greater than the quantity demanded.

T

Tariff A tax imposed by a government on imports.

Tax incidence The actual division of the burden of a tax between buyers and sellers in a market.

Tax wedge The difference between the pretax and posttax return to an economic activity.

Taylor rule A rule developed by John Taylor that links the Fed's target for the federal funds rate to economic variables.

Technological change A positive or negative change in the ability of a firm to produce a given level of output with a given quantity of inputs.

Terms of trade The ratio at which a country can trade its exports for imports from other countries.

Too-big-to-fail policy A policy under which the federal government does not allow large financial firms to fail, for fear of damaging the financial system.

Trade The act of buying and selling.

Trade-off The idea that, because of scarcity, producing more of one good or service means producing less of another good or service.

Transfer payments Payments by the government to households for which the government does not receive a new good or service in return.

U

Underground economy Buying and selling of goods and services that is concealed from the government to avoid taxes or regulations or because the goods and services are illegal.

Unemployed In government statistics, someone who is not currently at work but who is available for work and who has actively looked for work during the previous month.

Unemployment rate The percentage of the labor force that is unemployed.

V

Value added The market value a firm adds to a product.

Velocity of money The average number of times each dollar in the money supply is used to purchase goods and services included in GDP.

Voluntary exchange A situation that occurs in markets when both the buyer and the seller of a product are made better off by the transaction.

Voluntary export restraint (VER) An agreement negotiated between two countries that places a numerical limit on the quantity of a good that can be imported by one country from the other country.

W

Wall Street Reform and Consumer Protection Act (Dodd-Frank Act) Legislation passed during 2010 that was intended to reform regulation of the financial system.

World Trade Organization (WTO) An international organization that oversees international trade agreements.

COMPANY
INDEX

Key terms appear in **boldface**.

CREDITS

Photo

Front matter, *page ix(t),* Courtesy of Glenn Hubbard; *page ix(b),* Courtesy of Tony O'Brien

Module 1, *page 2,* Eduardo Munoz/Reuters; *page 15,* Andrew Burton/Reuters/Landov

Module 3, *page 40,* Regina H. Boone/Detroit Free Press/TNS/Tribune Content Agency LLC/Alamy Stock Photo; *page 45B,* Mikael Damkier/Shutterstock; *page 45C,* Yoshio Tomii/SuperStock; *page 45L,* Eric Gevaert/Shutterstock; *page 45R,* Bill Aron/PhotoEdit, Inc.; *page 45T,* JupiterImages/Getty Images; *page 49,* Herve Coste/MAXPPP/Newscom; *page 51,* Nureldin Abdallah Mohamed/Reuters; *page 62,* Bradley C. Bower/Bloomberg/Getty Images

Module 3A, *page 91,* Franck Iren/Author's Image Ltd/Alamy Stock Photo; *page 94,* Grant Neuenburg/Corbis; *page 98,* Peter Turnley/Corbis; *page 115,* Claro Cortes IV/Corbis

Module 4, *page 128,* Steve Allen/Allen Creative/Alamy Stock Photo

Module 4A, *page 150,* Kimberly White/Corbis; *page 170,* Lebrecht Music and Arts Photo Library/Alamy Stock Photo

Module 5, *page 172,* Hon Siu Keung/EyePress/Newscom; *page 190,* Kin Cheung/AP Images; *page 201,* Everett Collection/SuperStock

Module 6, *page 223,* Wang Lei/CHINE NOUVELLE/SIPA/Newscom; *page 230,* Everett Collection

Module 7, *page 248,* Bob Kreisel/Alamy Stock Photo

Module 7A, *page 276,* Richard Drew/AP Images; *page 284,* Bao Dandan/Xinhua/Alamy Stock Photo; *page 287,* AP Images

Module 8, *page 298,* Laurence Geai/SIPA/Newscom; *page 303,* Bloomberg/Getty Images; *page 306,* Bloomberg/Getty Images; *page 309,* Air Images/Shutterstock; *page 321,* Lynne Sladky/AP Images; *page 321,* Ezio Petersen/UPI/Landov; *page 321,* Eightfish/Alamy; *page 321,* Dietmar Plewka/imagebroker/Alamy; *page 326,* Bettmann/Corbis

Module 8A, *page 336,* PHILIPPE DESMAZES/AFP/Getty Images; *page 368,* Rebecca Cook/Reuters/Corbis

Module 9, *page 380,* Du Gang/ZUMA Press/Newscom; *page 406,* Bloomberg/Getty Images

Text

Module 3 *page 42,* Christina Rogers, "Ford Trims Production in China on Select Models to Avoid Price Cuts," *Wall Street Journal,* May 21, 2015.

Module 3A *page 86,* Richard Sylla, "Financial Systems and Economic Modernization," *Journal of Economic History,* Vol. 62. No. 2, June 2002.

pages 101–102, Joseph Schumpeter, *Socialism, and Democracy,* New York: Harper, 1962 (originally published 1942), p. 13.

page 104, Robert J. Gordon, "Is U.S. Economic Growth Over? Innovation Confronts Six Headwinds," NBER Working Paper 18315, August 2012.

page 175, Edward Glaeser and Claudia Goldin, eds., *Corruption and Reform: Lessons from America's History,* Chicago, IL: University of Chicago Press, 2006.